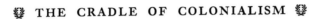 THE CRADLE OF COLONIALISM

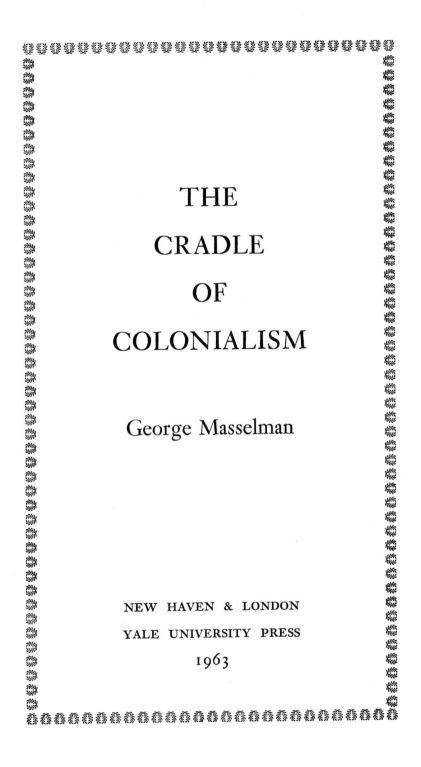

THE
CRADLE
OF
COLONIALISM

George Masselman

NEW HAVEN & LONDON
YALE UNIVERSITY PRESS
1963

Preface

Colonies as fragmentary settlements of a people beyond their hereditary boundaries, must have come into being shortly after the dawn of civilization. Relations with the mother country would have been tenuous, and the resources of the alien land exploited to only a limited extent. Phoenicia and Greece are examples of this phase. With the Roman Empire came a more intensified form of colonialism, to be followed by those of the Mongols and Turks. Spain and Portugal were next, and they were the first to use the oceans as avenues of conquest. Until then, colonies had been administered as feudal domains. The turning point came with the emergence of capitalism in western Europe in the sixteenth century.

Modern colonialism was fostered by the large number of people willing to invest their money in the hope of making a profit. It thus acquired a broader base, which led to an intensified form of exploitation. The East Indies—the Spice Islands—were the lodestone, as they had been during the Age of Discovery. The Dutch were the first to apply the principle of capital investment to overseas ventures, creating in time a Dutch Empire. They drove the Spanish and Portuguese from the East Indies and successfully rebuffed an attempt by the English to gain a foothold there. The English were forced to withdraw from East Asia and to focus their attention instead on India itself. This was a crucial moment in history, and from it flowed the forces that set the pattern of modern colonialism for hundreds of years to come.

During most of the seventeenth century, the Dutch retained supremacy. They tightened their hold over the East Indies and extended it to Ceylon and Formosa. They could have taken possession of Australia and New Zealand by right of discovery, and would have done so, if the prospects of trade had been more promising. They were safely ensconced in South Africa and well established in the American hemisphere, occupying large tracts of land along the Delaware and Hudson rivers and in Brazil. This burgeoning empire helped to create Holland's Golden Age. Prosperity, however, took its toll. When a vigorous merchant class became one of bankers, the old spirit was gone. By the end of the

century the English forged slowly ahead. A contributory factor
was the need for larger vessels in an expanding international trade,
and these the shallow Dutch waters could not accommodate.

Though the American Revolution meant the end of colonialism in the Western Hemisphere in the eighteenth century, the
nineteenth century saw the partition of Africa and the upsurge
of empire building in Asia.

The era of modern colonialism is today drawing to a close,
but the problems left in its wake will make themselves felt for
a long time to come. Not the least of these problems is the fact
that the newly independent countries—the former colonies—have
become the ideological, economic, and political battlegrounds
between the nations of the free world and the communist states.
This book is an account of how the Dutch set in motion the cycle
of colonialism in Southeast Asia.

Redding, Conn.   GEORGE MASSELMAN
September 1963

Contents

Preface   v

List of Illustrations   ix

Book I

1.	The Land and the People	3
2.	The Sea	8
3.	The Sea Lanes Become Longer	16
4.	The Town	23
5.	Independence at Any Price	35
6.	Factors of Trade Expansion	44
7.	From Guilds to Capitalism	53
8.	Three Merchants and a Minister	62
9.	Linschoten and His Itinerary	69
10.	North to the Indies	79
11.	South to the Indies	86
12.	The Second and Third Voyages North	98

Book II

1.	Amsterdam Collects	109
2.	The Rush to the Indies	119
3.	The Prime Mover of the United Company	133
4.	The Formation of the United East India Company	141
5.	By Trial and Error	151
6.	War and Trade Do Not Mix	161
7.	The Seventeen Under Attack	172
8.	1607: The Burgeoning Year	180
9.	Early Asiatic Trade: the Hindu Period	193
10.	Background in Asia	204
11.	The Portuguese Age	215

Book III

1.	Jan Pieterszoon Coen	229
2.	The Bottom of the Ladder	241
3.	Coen's First Contact with the Indies	254
4.	The English versus the Dutch	266

5. The English East India Company   276
6. A Servant of the English Company   285
7. Up the Ladder   296
8. Blueprint for Empire   307
9. The Rendezvous   316
10. The Price of Monopoly   326
11. Second in Command   335
12. The Final Rung   345
13. 1618   355
14. The Crisis   364
15. The Siege   377
16. The Birth of an Empire   390
17. Steps Toward Consolidation   400
18. The Conquest of Banda   415
19. The English Withdrawal   424
20. Monopoly or Free Trade?   433
21. Mission Accomplished   445

Epilogue   454

Afterword: Three Men   471

Bibliography   477

Index   511

Illustrations

Facing Page

1. Harbor of Amsterdam. Topografische Atlas   32
   Gemeente Archiefdienst, Amsterdam.
2. Petrus Plancius delivering a lesson in navigation.   90
   Nederlands Historisch Scheepvaartmuseum,
   Amsterdam.
3. Johan van Oldebarnevelt, age 70. Engraved from a   135
   painting by M. Mierevelt (1617).
4. Reynier Pauw, age 61. Gemeente Archief, Amsterdam. 186
5. Jan Pieterszoon Coen, ca. 1626. Westfriesch Museum, 298
   Hoorn.
6. Laurens Reael, painted ca. 1618 in the East Indies.   336
   Rijksmuseum, Amsterdam.

Maps

1. The Lowlands.   34
2. North to the Indies.   78
3. The Moluccas.   108
4. Indonesia.   118
5. Amboyna group.   160
6. Java.   192
7. Ternate and Tidore.   214
8. India and Arabia.   284
9. Djakarta in 1619.   376
10. Banda Islands.   414
11. Batavia in 1629.   444

BOOK I

I

The
Land
and
the People

The land had started as a barren of sand and clay left behind by
the retreating ice. It was the delta for the melting glaciers, deposit-
ing debris gathered over thousands of years across half of Europe,
from Scandinavia, Germany, and the Alps. Wind and tide created
a fringe of dunes along the edge, stretching from Belgium in the
south to the mouth of the Weser in the north. Behind the dunes
vast swamps were formed, constantly fed by the rivers of western
Europe. These rivers carved their way through the dunes, creating complex flats which eventually became the Lowlands. Prehistoric men scorned this inhospitable place, preferring to live
on higher land towards the east.[1]

   The first mention of this area is found in the *Odyssey*, where it
is vaguely described as "a land of fog and gloom where there is
no sun." The sea beyond is the "Sea of Death, where Hell be-
gins." Pythias, the Greek geographer who traveled there during
the fourth century B.C., is a little more explicit. He calls it "the
end of the world, where the sea rises and falls and where the water
is sucked in and out like a sea-lung." [2] It was around this time that
men first settled in this soggy wilderness. No one knows for certain why or whence they came, but it is assumed because they
were blond and blue-eyed, that they came from Scandinavia. The
first traveler to mention them was a Roman, Pliny the Elder,
who called them Frisii, a name which has persisted to this day.
"They are water and mud workers," he wrote. "During storms

   1. Their burial grounds, marked by dolmen, are now historic monuments
in the eastern part of the Netherlands, mainly in the province of Drente.
   2. Pythias was a citizen of the Greek colony Massalia (Marseilles) and it
is generally assumed that he was sent on his journey to gain valuable information about the sources of tin and amber.

3

they live on their mounds and burn mud." The mud was peat, just about the only natural resource the country had to offer.[3]

The mounds Pliny the Elder mentions were man-made, the first successful attempt to reclaim land from the sea. At low tide when the flats were bare, the men went out, filling willow baskets and hand barrows with clay and piling it laboriously into higher land. The work continued endlessly—day after day, year after year. "Out with the ebb, up with the flood," the old saying went.[4] It was indeed the moon and not the sun which dictated the daily schedule. In one small area some 60 miles by 12, can still be counted 1,260 such mounds, measuring from five to 40 acres each, some as high as 30 feet above normal sea level. They represent the toil of twelve centuries.[5] Fortunately, iron tools had found their way into western Europe at about the time the Frisians began making land. Without the iron spade, the task would have been impossible. Iron spades and iron hands did the job, moved by a stubborn determination.

The men who did this work proudly called themselves free, giving allegiance only to their community. When the Roman legions came down the Rhine, the Frisians refused to pay tribute, claiming that the sea took all the taxes they could afford to pay. Like the Scottish whom they resembled in other respects, the Frisians were never subdued by Rome.

Their oldest set of laws was the Ewa, the law of Divine Right; it was held so sacred that it could not be written down. It taught a man to judge his own mind, to fight evil, to protect innocence, and to prohibit cruelty. "No command can break it!" It preached "right above might" and "freedom above slavery." "Murder must be cooled with murder . . . a murderer's back must be broken . . . a thief must be beheaded." Lesser crimes were fined, the size of the fine depending on the offense. Cutting off a man's nose cost 78 shillings, his ear 38; killing someone's hunting dog cost eight shillings, but a pet dog, 12. Touching a woman's breast against her will was four shillings.[6] The men who pronounced judgment were the Ewa-sayers, also called Asegas, leaders of their people.

There came a time when the mounds could no longer support

3. Pliny the Elder visited this region in 47 A.D.
4. J. Romein, *Geschiedenis van de noord-nederlandsche geschiedschrijving in de middeleeuwen* (Haarlem, Tjeenk Willink, 1932), p. 149.
5. J. van Veen, *Dredge, Drain, Reclaim* (The Hague, Nijhoff, 1948), p. 14.
6. Ibid., pp. 15-19.

the growing population. Fishing was still very primitive, and more land was needed for food and forage. To solve the problem, the mounds were linked together by dikes. Now the struggle against the sea became even more formidable. The mounds had been relatively safe, even at the time of the spring tides or when storms pushed the waters of the Atlantic into the North Sea, but a narrow ribbon of sand and clay was a different matter. Six times in recorded history the sea undid all their labors; but each time the land was reclaimed, and every century ended with an accretion. From the thirteenth to the fifteenth century, some 100,000 acres were added each century, and during the sixteenth almost twice that much.

Old Dutch history can be broken down into three epochs, each characterized by a cardinal issue. Until about 800 A.D. it was the building of the mounds. The next two centuries were the age of the Vikings, the wild Norsemen who came to plunder and rape. The third was the era of the Sea Wall, or Golden Hoop.

In this third epoch, dike-building became part of every man's life and the Asegas of old became dike-masters who ordered the labor. "You shall keep the law of peace against family and neighbors. Clean the sluices . . . heighten the sea dikes and dams . . . repair the roads and make drainings under the roads." [7] They knew too well that if the work were neglected, disaster might strike. Thus, on a December night in the year 1287, the sea once more smashed the dikes and some fifty thousand people were drowned between the Vlie and the River Lauwers.[8] After every great flood there was always the terrible sickness, an epidemic for which there was no cure. *Frisia non cantat* is a term found in the old books. These people had, indeed, little cause for singing.

Diking produced its own code of law. When a break occurred, drums sounded for all men to pick up their spades and rush to the scene. At such times all feuding had to be suspended on pain of death. A man who rebelled was instantly killed or buried alive in the breach, with a pole through his body. It was a matter of dike or die. Important issues were discussed at the *Thing*, a periodic gathering; attendance was compulsory except for those who were needed on the dikes. Everyone was supposed to participate in such

7. Ibid., pp. 20–23.
8. P. H. Witkamp, *Geschiedenis der zeventien Nederlanden, 3* (Arnhem-Nijmegen, 1885), 641. The Vlie was the most northern part of what until then had been a small inland lake. Now it became an outlet to the North Sea, deepened by the constant scouring of the tides.

discussions, especially on matters with which he was familiar. "He who knows better must say so," was the rule.

The constant fight against the sea could not have been successful without some mechanical help. The earliest device, the one that made diking possible, was the automatic sluice gate. It had the appearance of a heavy wooden door with a hinge at the top that allowed it to swing out. The water could run off freely with the ebb, but at high tide the pressure of the water from the outside kept the floodgate tightly shut. This system not only solved the drainage problem but also made land available that had formerly been submerged at high tide. The Dutch soon found, however, that they could not impede the natural flow of water with impunity. One of the problems their system created was silting, which made it necessary to clean the bottoms of waterways at periodic intervals. This was first done by means of a perforated bucket, attached to the end of a long pole, with which brawny men scooped up the mud. It was not a very efficient method and was superseded by the first dredge. The dredge was a "scratcher," a heavy rake dragged along the bottom of a canal or stream by a boat; it loosened the silt, which was then carried out to sea with the ebb. From this developed the Amsterdam mud-mill—wooden buckets, hinged together in an endless chain, which scooped the mud from the bottom in a continuous operation. Motive power was at first supplied by men on a treadmill which set the wooden gears in motion, but the men were later replaced by horses, and the wooden buckets by ones of copper.[9]

The third important invention was the adaptation of the windmill to pump water. This made it possible to pump out lakes whose bottoms were beneath the low-water mark and which had so far defied all attempts at reclamation. No one of these inventions can be singled out as the most important—all three were indispensable in the long battle. However, regardless of the additional acres wrested from the sea, they proved inadequate to provide for the needs of a growing population. It was not only a matter of being deficient in foodstuffs—there were other shortages. Except for willows that were cultivated for their shoots to make baskets and mats, and some stunted oaks on high ground, the Lowlands had no trees to speak of, and the people were dependent on peat for fuel. There were many peat bogs, and each town had its own source of supply. This solution to one

9. Van Veen, pp. 76–78.

problem created another in turn. The continual digging for peat formed lakes, which collected the drainage water from surrounding country. The water eventually found an outlet to the sea, and what had been an inland body of water now became a tidal basin. Over the years the constant scouring of ebb and flood gnawed at the shore lines. Thus, while the Dutch were fighting the sea on one front, the water-wolf, as the erosion was called, attacked them on another, carrying away the same land which at an earlier stage had been created with so much effort. Fighting the sea on two fronts proved impossible. There was no alternative except to curtail the digging of peat. This caused a dwindling in the supply of salt as well as of fuel, for their only source of salt had been peat ash.

It is not surprising that the Dutch, stubborn people that they were, should have looked for other sources of supply for the goods they lacked. They found them beyond their borders: up the rivers which tapped a vast hinterland, but especially across the sea. The sea had been their hereditary enemy. Why not try to make it an ally? It was the beginning of a partnership profitable beyond their wildest hopes.

2

The
Sea

Economic need drove the Dutch to the sea, but favorable geographic location made it possible to reap a living from it. The same rivers which had provided the raw material for their land were also the arteries by which large areas of western Europe could be reached. Their multiple delta also happened to be located half way between Scandinavia and the Baltic in the north and the countries of southwestern Europe. Due west, across the narrow sea, lay England and Scotland. Each of these areas produced something the others needed, water provided the cheapest means of transportation, and the Dutch, with their long heritage of living with the sea, were able to take advantage of the combination of circumstances.

Trade, primitive as it must have been, must have started in very early times, but there is no proof of any appreciable sea trade in western Europe during the first six or seven centuries of the Christian era. Thereafter, trade grew steadily. In the beginning of the eighth century, Frisians went to London for wool and slaves.[1] Somewhat later they appeared in France, at the fair of St. Denis on the Seine below Paris, loading their boats with honey, wine, and red madder for dyeing. St. Denis was the former Catulliacum of Roman Gaul, and the first market place in western Europe where spices and other exotic products from the legendary East Indies could be bought. These rare goods arrived after a long and tortuous journey—by native craft sailing from island to island, and then by ancient caravan routes across the deserts. In the final stages they had to traverse the length of the Mediterranean and up the Rhone into the heart of France. All this involved much changing of hands and the payment of tolls and tributes, with the result that spices were often literally worth their weight in gold. It is not likely that the earliest Dutch

1. H. C. Diferee, *De Geschiedenis van den nederlanschen handel* (Amsterdam, 1905), p. 23. The same toll had to be paid for slaves as for horses.

8

traders were interested in such costly products, unless perhaps they had been especially commissioned by their abbots to buy myrrh and frankincense for religious services.

During the long reign of Charlemagne the Dutch gradually extended their trading area. It was now safe to travel far up the Rhine, hauling the boats upstream and floating down with the current, carrying lumber, grain, and wine. Near the mouth of the Rhine the town of Dorestad, remnant of another Roman settlement, became the first trading center in the Lowlands[2] from which vessels sailed across the North Sea to York and other English towns. By inland waters traders sailed north to the west coast of Denmark. Here they moored their vessels and carried the cargo across Jutland to the shores of the Baltic Sea. This trade might have developed in a more orderly fashion if the Norsemen had stayed home, instead of emerging from their fjords to pillage and burn wherever their long ships could take them. For two centuries the Norse roamed the seas, and the trade of the Lowlands dwindled to almost nothing. Only the Dutch settlements far up the Rhine remained intact, but others, like Dorestad, carried the brunt of the attacks. Several times Dorestad was ransacked and burnt to the ground, never thereafter to regain its former status. Another town, more favorably situated nearer the mouth of the river, inherited its trade and grew to become one of the great seaports of modern times—Rotterdam.

When the Viking raids had subsided and more peaceful conditions prevailed, the Dutch gradually resumed their trading. Progress kept pace with the slow economic development of Europe during the Middle Ages, until a series of disasters struck the Lowlands in the thirteenth century. Prior to this time, the Zuiderzee had been a fresh-water lake, probably not more than one fifth its present size, protected in the north by a continuous bulwark of dunes. In a series of storms the sea broke through this barrier and penetrated deep into the Lowlands. It never retreated, which seems to confirm the theory that the storms alone could not have been responsible, and that the land itself must have sunk, or the sea level had gradually risen. There are no records to give us a clear picture of the calamity, but it is certain that many thousands of people were drowned, and that many others moved away.[3]

2. Dorestad was located at or near the site of modern Wijk bij Duurstede.
3. See above, p. 5.

Friesland was then cut in half, separated by a wide body of water. The western part, long known as West Friesland, became part of Holland, and its towns were later to play an important role in the development of Dutch trade. Not until the present century was the connection restored, when modern engineers threw a dike across the gap as part of a huge reclamation project which will reduce the Zuiderzee to its original size. The dune barrier had been broken up into a number of islands through which the North Sea surged back and forth with every ebb and flood. For seven centuries these *wadden* islands remained a characteristic part of the Netherlands, but the end of their individual existence is now in sight. A master plan calls for linking them together again and restoring the old shoreline as it was before the Zuiderzee was formed.

Great as the calamity had been in loss of land and lives, the creation of the Zuiderzee was a turning point in Dutch history. Until then the emphasis had been on the creation and cultivation of land, but thereafter, with a large and protected sea arm reaching deep within their borders, the Dutch turned to trade more vigorously than ever before. Starting as fishing villages, towns sprang up all along the Zuiderzee and each developed a lively trade, especially with the Baltic. This Eastland trade had, indirectly, also found its origin in the disasters of the thirteenth century. In the year 1272, the Wittewierum abbots Emo and Menko recorded that after a series of floods had ravaged the land, many people left the country to seek a better livelihood elsewhere.[4] Most went to the Baltic shores, where they cleared forests and used their knowledge of draining and diking to reclaim marshes along the coast. The German princes encouraged this immigration, for they were quick to realize that more land meant more tax levies. They granted the Dutch settlers the right to acquire the land they reclaimed on a perpetual leasehold against payment of a yearly rent. This system spread over most of the area and became known as Dutch or Flemish Right.[5] Under such conditions of private ownership, rather than the previous serfdom, the production of grain and forest products increased rapidly.

4. A. C. J. de Vrankrijker, "De Nederlanders in Oostzee en Middellandsche Zee," in C. W. Wormser, ed., *Nederland in de vijf Werelddeelen* (Leiden, Burgersdijk & Niermans, 1947), p. 17.
5. Ibid., pp. 19–20.

The Eastern Baltic, first developed by these refugees from the great floods, eventually produced enough grain to supply the whole of Europe.

There were several important problems to be solved, however, before the Dutch were able to exploit to the full the advantages offered by the Baltic trade. They had to struggle against the powerful Hanseatic League, a federation of free German towns which had a tight grip on Baltic trade, especially in the west. Two member towns of the League, Hamburg and Lübeck, controlled the overland route between the North Sea and the Baltic. Such transport was expensive, and trade between East and West had been largely confined to goods of high value—woolens from Flanders being bartered for pelts from the Eastland. To avoid this route, the Dutch built ships which were both large and seaworthy enough to sail around Jutland, through the treacherous waters which separated it from Norway. This direct route changed the whole aspect of Baltic trade, because goods of comparatively smaller intrinsic value, such as grain and lumber, could now also be shipped profitably.[6] The route was opened in the middle of the thirteenth century, primarily by such towns as Kampen and Deventer on the east coast of the newly created Zuiderzee. The Frisians, dike builders and land reclaimers, were loath to follow their example and as a result went into an economic decline.[7]

Access to such products created an almost complete economic change in the standard of living of the Dutch. Houses could now be built from straight boards instead of gnarled and scarce oak; the building of ships was also promoted. Rye bread became the staff of life, and the beer for which the Eastland towns were famous was now within the means of the common man. Demand for these goods increased and so did the problem of how to pay for them. The Dutch had some excess production of butter and cheese, but it would not begin to pay for the increased demand for imported goods. Once more the sea provided the answer.

The Dutch had fished off their coast for centuries, but the amounts they caught were strictly limited to what they themselves could consume, because fresh herrings were a highly perishable commodity. This problem was solved, providentially, just when

6. Ibid., p. 8. These ships and their crews were called *ommelands vaarders*, literally meaning that they sailed around the land.
7. Romein, *Geschiedschrijving*, p. 59.

the need for an export product had become most acute. In the latter half of the fourteenth century, a certain Willem Beukelsz.[8] of Zealand discovered that a herring could be preserved almost indefinitely if he salted it after removing the guts. The consequences of this humble invention were immense. For the first time in their history the Dutch had access to a surplus commodity that could readily be exchanged for goods they needed from abroad. Perhaps the people of Europe were avid for a change from the monotonous fare of the medieval diet: they took to herring with a will. As much as the Dutch could supply, they sold, and as a result the fishing industry grew rapidly, until it became, in the words of the States General, "one of the Chiefest Mines of the Netherlands." [9] Marliani, the physician of Emperor Charles V, wrote, "the Hollanders fish more gold and silver out of the sea than other countries dig out of the ground." [10]

For the Dutch, the herring fishery became a gold mine, and indispensable for the welfare of the country. It was realized early that in order to maintain this steady source of income, the quality of the herring should be standardized. Control was vested in the College of Great Fishery, a semiprivate organization which, in efficiency, would compare well with any modern enterprise—although it would have run afoul of anti-trust laws. The number of ports where all fish had to be delivered and packed was limited to five.[11] Other important towns, such as Amsterdam and Hoorn, which tried in vain to become members of the College were forced to develop their trade in other directions.

The regulations of the College specified that all herrings were to be carefully graded as to size and quality, and that every barrel must show the mark of the town, the cooper, and the man who had done the packing. Other regulations prescribed the correct method for curing, and the kind of salt that should be used. The fishing boats themselves, their management, crew, and tackle, came under the supervision of the College, and it promoted their

8. 'sz.' as an abreviation of 'szoon' is the customary Dutch spelling, as in Pietersz. (Pieterszoon) and other names throughout this book.

9. *Groot Placaet-boeck van de Staten Generaal* (The Hague, 1658–1797), entry for July 19, 1606.

10. R. Fruin, *Tien jaren uit den tachtigjarigen oorlog, 1588–98* (5th ed., The Hague, 1899), p. 185.

11. H. A. H. Kranenburg, *De Zeevisscherij van Holland in den tijd der Republiek* (Amsterdam, 1946), pp. 74–79. The College was established in 1567, the member towns being Enkhuizen, Schiedam, Delft, Rotterdam, and Briel.

efficiency. To guard against foreign competition, the fishermen were prohibited from selling their catch in foreign ports. During the season, the boats stayed on the fishing grounds for months on end. Their catch was collected at regular intervals by a fleet of fast yachts especially constructed for the purpose.

The best fishing grounds were off the Scottish and English coasts. About the middle of June the fleet would set out for Scotland, where the fishing began, and from there, on specified dates, the boats moved gradually southward until they finally reached the mouth of the Thames during December and January. All fishing stopped on January 31,[12] to allow the herring to propagate and thus ensure a continuous supply. As early as 1295, the Dutch assured themselves of access to the fishing grounds. They had been granted the Right of Free Fishing in English waters by King Edward I, and similar agreements were concluded in the following centuries. The English honored these agreements until James I, envious of the prosperity of the Dutch, tried to repudiate them.[13]

The security of the fishing fleet at sea was provided by armed convoys. Since this was a matter of national protection, the warships were built and fitted out by the States (provincial government) of Holland and Zealand rather than by the College. To meet the cost of maintaining them a tax or convoy duty was levied on the catch of each boat. In due course this tax was levied on all merchant ships and thus provided the Admiralties with the funds to maintain a navy.[14]

It is no exaggeration to say that the Great Fishery provided the experience and the means which later enabled the Dutch Republic to become a maritime power of the first magnitude. By trial and error they learned the art of seamanship and navigation, experimenting with hulls and rigging to build the best vessel for each particular purpose. Above all the enterprise taught them to rely upon the sea.

The Great Fishery was succeeding well, yet it no longer seemed enough. The Baltic Sea trade should be expanded, and there were other seas, beyond the horizon, which they had never seen. In foreign markets, they heard fabulous tales, perhaps exag-

12. G. Edmundson, *Anglo-Dutch Rivalry During the First Half of the Seventeenth Century* (Oxford, Clarendon Press, 1911), pp. 159–60.
13. Ibid., pp. 19–21.
14. Kranenburg, *Zeevisscherij*, pp. 146–47.

gerated—but they had seen the spices and the silk with their own eyes.

It was the herring fishery that led them onward. The curing of fish demanded much salt, which came at first from Bourgneuf on the French coast near Rochelle. Later a better quality was available from San Lucar in Portugal. In the beginning, French and Portuguese ships carried the salt north, but the Dutch soon entered the trade themselves.[15] By about 1500, the towns of Hoorn and Enkhuizen had some sixty vessels employed in the salt trade alone. Before the rough salt could be used, it had to be refined, and salt-boilers set up shop in almost every Dutch port. The refined salt created a demand abroad, and the Dutch set out to satisfy it.[16] All that was needed to obtain more salt was to put more ships into the salt trade. This was far simpler than to try to wrest more land from the sea, in order to produce more of the butter and cheese which had been their earliest export product. The dairy industry was also carefully supervised, although on a scale less elaborate than that of the Great Fishery.

These restrictions and regulations must have been irksome at times to a people whose main trait was hardly submissiveness. Unlike most European countries, theirs had no long history of feudalism. Mound building and diking, to be sure, had been subject to strict laws, because they demanded teamwork and discipline. But once the work had been finished, the new land was divided among the men who had helped make it. Similarly, the Dutch now accepted the restrictions imposed on the various trades as a necessary evil, and there was plenty of opportunity for exercising individualism. Anyone who wanted to go fishing could do so, as long as he abided by the rules, and delivered his catch to one of the five authorized towns. It made no difference whether he owned one boat or ten, or whether or not he was joined by others in his venture. A man could start a salt-refining business with one kettle or a hundred, depending upon his capital and initiative. Nothing stopped him from fitting out a ship to fetch salt from wherever he wanted. The salt once refined, he could take to the Baltic and exchange it for grain and other products. When more grain arrived in Holland than the country could consume, he could load his ship with grain and, on the

15. M. A. Verkade, *De Opkomst van de Zaanstreek* (Utrecht, 1952), pp. 104–05.
16. Fruin, *Tien jaren*, pp. 186–87.

outward voyage, barter it for salt. A man did not have to be a burgher of one of the fishing towns to engage in trade, nor did he have to be a farmer or a salt refiner. After the goods were branded and weighed, he could buy as little or as much as he could afford, and sell it wherever there was a profit to be made.

In that manner—private enterprise regulated by town and College ordinances—Dutch trade expanded by leaps and bounds, especially after the decline of the Hanseatic League.

3

The
Sea Lanes
Become Longer

After the formation of the Zuiderzee, when the Dutch became seriously interested in overseas trade, the Hanseatic League, or Hansa, was already a powerful organization. It reached its peak during the fourteenth century, when more than 70 towns were among its members, including some Dutch towns on the eastern shore of the Zuiderzee.[1] Such membership afforded important privileges, but it also imposed restrictions whose severity is indicated by the refusal of the newer towns on the recently created western shore, such as Amsterdam, Hoorn, and Enkhuizen, to submit to them. They tempered their refusal to join by proclaiming themselves Friends of the Hansa, a phrase which before long proved as meaningless as has, on occasion, "nonaggression pact." The independent towns must have sensed that more was to be gained by open competition than by becoming satellites of the Hansa.

By sailing directly into the Baltic, the Dutch *ommeland* (round-the-land) skippers, proved that they could carry freight more economically than the Hansa. Contemporary historians ascribed this to the fact that the Dutch built ships that could carry more cargo with a smaller crew than the unwieldy bottoms the Hansa was still using. Guicciardini, the Italian historian, described "the courage and ability of the Dutch skippers, who sail straight to their destination and refuse to seek shelter even in the heaviest storm."[2]

1. Stavoren, Kampen, Zwolle, Deventer, Zutphen, and Harderwijk. In addition to these, some other Dutch towns were members of the Hansa, such as Groningen, Leeuwarden, and Dokkum in the north, and Utrecht, Dordrecht, and Middelburg more inland and south. All these towns had joined the league during the thirteenth century, when Amsterdam was still little more than a fishing village.
2. Francesco Guicciardini, *Descrittione di tutti i Paesi Bassi* (Antwerp, 1588), p. 40.

The still powerful Hansa could not have been expected to remain idle while the Dutch nibbled away at their long-established monopoly. The uneasy friendship turned into bitter rivalry and finally led to open warfare. The conflict lasted three years and ended with the Peace of Copenhagen in 1441. Many ships had been lost on both sides and trade through the Baltic had come to a standstill.[3] It was the first important naval warfare in which the Dutch participated, and the result was inconclusive. Nevertheless, from this time on, the decline of the Hansa proceeded rapidly. The aggressive Dutch undoubtedly contributed to it, but there were other important factors which hastened the process. The Hansa had always had its own fishing grounds in the Baltic near the island of Schonen, but during the fifteenth century the herring inexplicably disappeared. The Baltic towns then became entirely dependent on the Dutch for this product, and the Hansa suffered as a result.

Perhaps the most important reason for the decline of the Hansa lay within the organization itself. The Dutch historian Fruin writes:

> Rich and senile, she had all the handicaps of age and wealth. Small profits no longer attracted her while, on the other hand, she recoiled from the risks involved in those unruly times to maintain her former position on the seas. She started to complain about the injustice done to her—she, who formerly knew how to protect her own rights. Attacked by pirates at sea, and by the free-wheeling competition of the Hollanders, she no longer had the resilience to fight back. Whatever trade she lost was quickly picked up by the Dutch and, once lost, she was never to regain it.[4]

Throughout the sixteenth century, the Dutch consolidated their control over the Baltic trade. Previously, a good many Eastland towns had continued to import their own goods. "But," as Velius wrote in his *Kroniek van Hoorn*, "not long afterwards the picture changed . . . our shipping increased steadily, as did the number of our sailors. Accustomed to a sober life, they were able to get along with less than the foreigners. Thus we sailed them out of the water and appropriated the trade for ourselves!"

3. Friedel Vollbehr, *Die Holländer und die deutsche Hanse* (Lübeck, 1930), pp. 44–46.
4. Fruin, *Tien jaren*, p. 192.

A few figures will show how well the Dutch acquitted themselves in this self-appointed task. All vessels sailing into or out of
the Baltic had to pass through the Oresund, where they had to
pay a toll to the King of Denmark. Traffic lists have been preserved dating from the year 1497, when some 400 ships entered
the Baltic, of which some 280 were Dutch. Throughout the
sixteenth century, the total number of entering ships steadily
increased to a peak of about 2,500. On the average, about 55
per cent were Dutch. Dutch ships were larger than their competitors', however, and, taking this factor into consideration, it
can be safely estimated that the Dutch moved at least 75 per
cent of all the goods involved in this trade, which was the backbone of the economy of most of Europe. The remaining quarter
was divided among France, England, Norway, Portugal, and the
towns of the Hansa.[5]

The Baltic trade thus became the foundation on which the
prosperity of the Lowlands was to be based for a long time to
come. But it was based on bulk goods with a relatively low unit
value. Dutch merchants realized that if more valuable merchandise
were carried, their profits would rise in proportion. This kind
of trade had so far eluded them. It was this dilemma perhaps,
which gave rise to the old legend of The Widow of Stavoren.
Having inherited her husband's affairs, she asked one of her skippers to bring back the most valuable goods he could find. He
returned with a full cargo of perfect grain. The widow had expected something entirely different and angrily ordered the cargo
to be dumped into the sea. As a result, a shoal formed at the exact
spot, leading to the decline of the town. Whether the tale be
true or not, the shoal appears on the map to this day as Widow's
Sand.

More expensive cargoes, while not distant, were so firmly
controlled as to seem permanently beyond reach. Their market
was just south of the Lowlands, in Flanders, and they were in
the hands of powerful merchants well able to protect their own
interest. By the sixteenth century, the ancient market of St. Denis
had long since had its day. It had declined when the long trek
from the Mediterranean—up the Rhone and down the Seine—
could no longer compete with a direct route through the Strait

5. See Nina Ellenger Bang and Knud Korst, eds., *Tabeller over skipsfart
og varetransport gennem Oresund, 1497–1600*, 2 vols. (Copenhagen, 1906 and
1933).

of Gibraltar. During the Middle Ages, Bruges, with a direct outlet to the North Sea, had taken the place of St. Denis. For many years, Bruges was the greatest market place in western Europe. It became a center for the English wool merchants and headquarters for the Hansa.

In the long history of European trade, however, Bruges was only an intermediate stage. The center moved slowly north. A prolonged period of unsettled conditions in the vicinity hurt Bruges' overland trade routes and when the Zwin silted up, the town was doomed as a great market place. It then became Antwerp's turn. More favorably situated on the broad Scheldt, Antwerp surpassed Bruges and kept pace with the steadily increasing commerce of western Europe. After a century of steady growth, Antwerp reached its zenith around 1550. Guicciardini, in his *Description of All the Netherlands*, described in detail its manifold activities and great wealth, and Baduro, a Venetian who must have witnessed great commercial activity in his own town, proclaimed that nowhere in the world was there so much business as in Antwerp.[6] Such wealth promoted the arts; Antwerp became the cradle of the Flemish school of painting. It was in these southern provinces, Brabant and Flanders, that the arts of printing and cartography rose to new heights. So great was their fame throughout the world that, when ships from Holland first reached distant shores—whether of northern Russia or the Indies—their crews were hailed as *Flamengos*.[7]

Antwerp became, moreover, what Bruges had never been—a financial stronghold where currency and commercial paper found a ready market. Famous banking houses, such as the Fugger and Welser of Germany, and the Gualterotti and the Buonvisi of Italy maintained branches there.[8] From them the Dutch learned the use of new techniques for trading: bank drafts and Italian bookkeeping. The first made it possible for a merchant to pay for merchandise far from his own counting house, without actual shipment of bullion; the second provided an accurate system for keeping accounts in constant order.

The products upon which this prosperity was based were mainly luxuries—cloth woven from English wool, wine and olive

6. Fruin, *Tien jaren*, p. 183.
7. Ibid., p. 191. Before long, however, the men from the northern Netherlands became known as Hollanders.
8. Ibid., p. 183. See also P. Geyl, *Geschiedenis van de nederlandse stam, 1* (Amsterdam, 1948), 174–75.

oil from France, Spain, and Italy, dried fruit from Greece and Turkey, silks from Persia, and, rarest and most sought after of all, spices from the far Indies. The arduous routes by which such spices had to be transported made the price prohibitive for all but the wealthiest people. The situation changed dramatically when the voyages of Columbus, Magellan, Dias, and Da Gama revealed the route to the Spice Islands, and thereby broke the monopoly the Turks had exercised through their domination over the Near East, the land bridge over which all spices and other Asiatic goods had to pass.

Portugal was the first to benefit from the new route, which led directly from Lisbon to the Indies. Greater quantities of spices became available and at lower prices, which brought them within reach of many people who had never before been able to indulge in such luxury. By present standards, the cost of spices was still exorbitant, but it was apparently justified by their supposedly great therapeutic value. Antwerp, with its wealthy merchants and established connections, became the distribution center for spices for the whole of northwestern Europe. The merchants who controlled Antwerp's trade were not all Flemish: the majority were foreigners, members of firms in Venice, Augsburg, Genoa, and other renowned markets of an earlier period. They had followed the trend, and with the experience and great wealth at their disposal, had been able to gain a solid footing in the trade. But these men were primarily financiers, quite willing to stay in their counting houses and let others bring the goods to them so that they could make a profit. In their prosperity, the Hansa merchants had carried their own goods, but when the decline set in, the Dutch transported them. The Dutch themselves could not provide capital sufficient to finance the purchase of the large quantities of grain and lumber that Antwerp was able to absorb, but there were foreign merchants willing and able to finance them. The Dutch had only to provide the ships and carry the cargo at a stipulated fee. It was a mutually satisfactory arrangement in which each side contributed that for which it was best qualified. In this manner the Dutch became aware of an additional asset they could exploit: their services.

Trade with southern Europe began to follow the pattern of development of the Baltic trade: Spanish and Portuguese vessels had at first carried the goods north, but as the new sea lanes to East and West India proved more and more promising, they gradually abandoned the northern waters, which once more were inherited by the Dutch. The maritime discoveries of the early sixteenth century brought Spain and Portugal their age of greatness—silver and gold from the Americas made Spain the most powerful nation in the world, and Portugal grew rich upon the spice trade. Indirectly, however, they also made possible the growing prosperity of the Dutch. Willem Usselinx, one of the Flemish merchants who emigrated to Zealand after the fall of Antwerp, described the situation thus: "Formerly the Spanish merchants maintained a very large trade with the Netherlands, but as they began to savor the greater profits of the Indies, they gradually allowed this old trade to go to us." [9]

During the first two-thirds of the sixteenth century, the Hollanders gradually increased their control over the carrying trade of western Europe. Under Charles V, the Netherlands, both North and South, had been united and brought under the crown of Spain. Having been born in Ghent, Charles favored the Lowlands, and extended to the Dutch the same privileges in Spanish ports as were enjoyed by Spanish merchants. The Dutch took full advantage of these favors; Amsterdam benefited the most. In a report to the English economist, Sir Thomas Gresham, dated 1560, we read: "The next esterly wyndes at Amsterdam they look for 300 to 400 sayle of gret ships out of Estlands, apparteyning to Holland only, laden with corn and other." [10]

Profit from commerce in herring and salt, and the expanding carrying trade, made it possible for the Dutch to begin to acquire the necessary capital to engage in business transactions independent of foreign financiers.[11] The process might have developed in a gradual and peaceful manner, but for the Reformation. The doctrines of Luther and Calvin were received with enthusiasm in the Lowlands, especially as they applied to economic life. Theoretically, the Church had represented restriction and disapproval of commercial enterprise: it had approved the feudal guild systems, which dictated all the actions of their members, including what profits were to be considered "fair." And the

9. Fruin, *Tien jaren*, p. 188. This is part of a remonstrance in which Usselinx presented his views as to the necessity of the United Netherlands' retaining freedom of trade with the West Indies in their peace negotiations with Spain.

10. J. M. Burgon, *Life and Times of Sir Thomas Gresham*, 1 (2 vols. London, 1839), 294.

11. Geyl, *Geschiedenis*, 1, 176.

guilds were closed corporations, with strict rules for admittance. The Church had also nominally condemned the lending of money at interest.

A rising merchant class, in which initiative and freedom of action were prerequisites for success, which thrived on buying as cheaply as possible and selling to the highest bidder, could see no wrong in charging interest for the use of money which otherwise would lie idle. It is not surprising that a new doctrine, which did not disapprove such activities, had considerable appeal to men who were part of an emerging economic system based on risk of capital. Calvin also taught people to work hard—"idleness is the devil's own pillow"—and preached frugality for everyone, from the highest to the lowest. This too appealed to the rising young merchant: it promoted savings, which provided capital for promising ventures. The Church, with its multitude of apparently idle monks and hoards of unused treasure, had not exemplified such virtues. The new merchant class approved the ethics of reform.

Philip II was as much a religious zealot as his father, but, while Charles V had considered it his mission to defend Europe against the Moslem invaders, Philip made it his life's task to stamp out Protestantism. The Netherlands had to carry the brunt of his wrath. A strong and absolute monarch, Philip used every means at his command to attain his end. In the year 1568 the Spanish moved into the Netherlands and furious war broke out. It struck the Lowlands as the greatest calamity of all time. Little could the Dutch have known that they were to emerge from it the greatest maritime power in the seventeenth century. The merchants of Amsterdam could not have dreamt that this war would prove to be a blessing in disguise, just as the formation of the Zuiderzee had been three hundred years before. By the end of the sixteenth century, Amsterdam had fallen heir to the wealth of Antwerp which it had coveted so long.

4

The
Town

Compared to some other Dutch towns, whose histories go back to Roman times, Amsterdam was a late arrival. It is first mentioned in the thirteenth century, just long enough ago to have acquired a legend as to its origin. The legend tells of a longboat of Norsemen, foundered on the north coast of Friesland, the only survivor a young man. The Frisians had not forgotten the indignities they had suffered at the hands of his countrymen, and demanded his life, but among them there was one who took pity on the young Viking and, accompanied by a dog, took him away in his fishing boat. A storm drove them south until they reached a bit of dry land at the mouth of a river, later known as the Amstel. From this modest beginning, with two men and a dog, Amsterdam, according to the legend, grew.[1] Of the three, only the dog gained a lasting place in history—it became a tradition for all ships to carry a dog on board. Eventually the dog became a symbol of ownership, and no vessel could be considered abandoned so long as the animal was still on board.

The creation of the Zuiderzee, while a boon to a large part of the Lowlands, especially favored the small settlement at the mouth of the Amstel. Safely tucked away in the southwestern corner, it was less exposed to periodic storms than almost any other town. There was also a broad inlet, called the Y, that provided a safe anchorage under almost any conditions.[2] The Amstel itself, a broad stream with almost no current, made a perfect harbor for the flat-bottomed boats that plied the inland waters to nearly every part of the country.

1. Jan Mens, *Amsterdam: paradijs der herinnering* (Amsterdam, 1947), p. 13.
2. The name *Y* is derived from an old Dutch word, *ie*, meaning "water" (A. A. Kok, *De Historische schoonheid van Amsterdam*, Amsterdam, 1947, p. 13). Amsterdam, being situated close to the Zuiderzee, benefited most from the scouring of the tides which provided deep water, in contrast with other towns on the banks of the Y situated further inland.

The Frisians were the first to take advantage of this location. After the great floods of the twelfth century, many of the survivors had left the land. Some went as far as the shores of the Baltic, but others tried their luck nearer home. By means of their skill at diking, they brought the waters around the small village under control. A sea dike on the north side gave protection against the flood waters of the Y, as did the dikes on either bank of the Amstel. At the southern end of the river dikes, a broad dam was thrown across the Amstel over large culverts, provided with sluice gates that kept the water out at high tide. The three dikes became the first streets, and the dam gave the town its name.[3] The dam also made the town a trading center, since all goods had to be trans-shipped at this point.

It was almost inevitable that Amsterdam should have grown when contact among the countries of western Europe developed to greater proportion. Both Holland and Zealand were to benefit from a geographic location that placed them halfway between northern and southern Europe,[4] but Amsterdam was especially favored. From its protected site on the Y and with its access to the Zuiderzee, it provided a less dangerous route to the Baltic than other towns while, at the same time, the inland waters at its back offered easy access to almost every other town in the Lowlands, and to those up the Rhine as well.

The earliest known document concerning Amsterdam dates from the year 1247, when the Lord of Amstel complained to the Hansa town of Lübeck about a vessel which had been detained there. The first mention of the name Amsterdam, then Amstelledamme, does not occur until 1275 when Floris V, Count of Holland, granted it freedom from tolls throughout the whole of his domain. Other towns also shared in such privileges, in accord with Floris' policy of strengthening them as a bulwark against his often recalcitrant liege lords.[5] Amsterdam continued to grow, though it would be several hundred years before it showed signs of becoming one of the major ports of western Europe. Early

3. The oldest recorded name is Amestelledamme, in which 'stelle' is presumed to mean roadstead. See C. G. 'tHooft, "De 'Stelle' of Reede in het Y, als verklaring van den naamsoorsprong van 'Ame Stelle Damme' " *Amstelodamum, 32* (1935), 1–34.

4. Since Dutch ports rarely froze over they also had an advantage over the Hansa towns in the Baltic in this respect.

5. Some twenty years later Amsterdam also acquired the important Staple right, which forced transient merchants to unload their goods and offer them for sale locally.

in the sixteenth century, it ranked among the larger towns in Holland, but even then, according to a tax list of 1514, it was smaller than Leiden, Delft, and Haarlem.

By the middle of the sixteenth century, Amsterdam had grown larger than them all, only Antwerp in Flanders being larger. Amsterdam merchants controlled their own trade, rather than serving as agents for wealthy Italian and German firms. This made a solid foundation on which to build future power. But although this rising merchant class was becoming rich, its members had little to say in the affairs of the town, which was governed by an oligarchy that had been in power long before the merchants had risen to their new affluence. This ruling group was staunchly Catholic, and unswerving in its loyalty to the king of Spain. In earlier times, these men, or their fathers, had been merchants too, but they had long since shifted to investment within the town, far safer than the risks involved in overseas trade. The new merchants were of a different mind, and it is not surprising that their interests should clash.

The result of the struggle between these two factions affected not only the future of Amsterdam but also helped to shape the course of events in Europe and Asia, for it is extremely doubtful whether the Lowlands could have stood successfully against Spain and, as a result, absorb its holdings in Asia, had the young merchants been unable to gain control.

Theoretically, the town was ruled by a Vroedschap,[6] a board of Regents, appointed for life. It consisted of 36 members and had the right of co-optation, which meant that it filled its own vacancies. It is understandable that such a self-perpetuating body should become a closely knit clique, containing only men of like minds and interests. The Vroedschap's most important function was to elect, from among its members, the four or five mayors who held office for one year, but who could be re-elected if they gained enough influence. These mayors exercised the real power, and among them, one invariably managed to gather the reins into his hands. There was no official title for this exalted position, nor were its duties clearly described, but in the popular mind it became known as the Magnificat.

6. *Vroed* literally means "wise," but the word is now used only in connection with childbirth, such as *vroedvrouw* (midwife). The term *Vroedschap* dates from the early part of the fifteenth century, and it was clear from the beginning that only the wealthiest burghers were considered for membership.

So reactionary a group could not have maintained itself indefinitely during an era of violent change, but its demise might not have been quite so complete had it been less stubborn in adhering to Spain and Catholicism, long after the rest of the Lowlands had been in open rebellion against both. Ironically, it had been a Protestant sect that had stiffened its attitude some thirty years before the crises came. In 1535 a group of militant Anabaptists had tried to take possession of the town by force. The teachings of Luther and Calvin had previously made few converts, and these the city fathers had ignored, as long as the services were held in private homes and behind locked doors. The Anabaptists were not content with this dispensation, possessed as they were with burning zeal to save all men by bringing God's Kingdom to Earth. In this Kingdom everyone was to be equal, all possessions were to be shared, and a doctrine of brotherly love would forbid the bearing of arms. The Anabaptists were willing to admit that in the beginning some force might have to be applied to make certain skeptics conform.

In the beginning the Anabaptists were satisfied with giving away or destroying their own valuables. But when this did not draw enough attention, they began to demonstrate in public; some were arrested and put to the rack, but this only increased their fervor. Men and women disrobed themselves in the streets and burned their clothes in bonfires. They ran naked through the streets, crying that doomsday was at hand unless everyone forthwith entered the Kingdom. Then some were executed. As in many such movements, the death of their martyrs raised the Anabaptists' enthusiasm to fever pitch. The climax came when they succeeded in taking possession of the town hall on the Dam and, in the first attempt to dislodge them, one of the mayors was killed. The zealots were too few in number to hold out for more than a day. Those who survived the siege were beheaded and strung up by the feet in groups. Some seven women among them were tied in sacks and drowned.[7]

This broke the movement, but the mayors had been thoroughly alarmed, and took stringent measures to prevent any recurrence. To remind themselves of the consequences of heresy, they had a full account of the events carved on a stout beam in the town church, and commissioned a series of paintings for the town hall

7. F. J. Dubiez, "De Onlusten van de wederdoopers te Amsterdam in 1535," *Ons Amsterdam, 3* (1958), 66–76.

which portrayed the incidents in all their gruesome detail. All who had ever shown the slightest lenience towards Protestants were dismissed from office and their places taken by men of proven loyalty, mostly close friends and relatives. The town government then developed into a narrow-minded coterie of inter-related and inter-dependent families. There was no room for liberals: the whole rising middle-class was excluded.

The merchants, resentful and without influence, were the highest taxpayers. But they had further grounds for complaint: not enough attention was being given the canals and, as a result, they had been fouling up for years. In some cases they had been arbitrarily dammed, which reduced their effectiveness as means of transport. The courts, staffed by favorites who had little or no interest in trade, were slow and inefficient. Processing of civil suits took forever, much to the dismay of litigants anxious for a decision. There was a serious lack of fire protection, especially on the Lastage, the area where the shipyards, sail lofts, and ropewalks were located. There was also reason for the merchants to believe that, in a recent capital levy of ten per cent, their property had been assessed out of all proportion to assessments on property owned by the oligarchy.

At the town hall, their complaints fell on deaf ears, and the merchants finally decided to seek relief at a higher level. In the year 1564 they presented a bill of complaints to Margaret of Parma, who ruled the Netherlands in the name of her brother, Philip II of Spain. They confined themselves almost entirely to economic problems; not a word was mentioned about religious differences. There were some 70 petitioners, none of whom put his name to the document for fear of reprisal. Nevertheless, Margaret was sympathetic, because William of Orange, her stadholder in Holland, had pleaded their cause. The mayors of Amsterdam first learned about the petition when they were ordered to apply remedies. It did not take much guessing on their part to decide who were the instigators, but the time had not yet arrived to move openly against them. Prompted by their loyalty to Philip, the mayors introduced certain reforms which, in turn, might have led to others; but important events were crowding upon the scene and left no room for orderly procedure.[8]

Incensed at the growing Calvinist enthusiasm among his sub-

8. J. Z. Kannegieter, "Amsterdam en de opstand tegen Spanje," *Ons Amsterdam*, 2 (1959), 34–42.

jects, Philip, this "most Catholic king," had launched his Counter Reformation. With it came the Inquisition and its implements: examinations, informers, confiscations, the rack, the auto–da–fé. Resentment among the Lowland Protestants rose to a climax in 1566 when, in a spontaneous and irresistible fury, the rabble stormed the churches and wantonly destroyed everything they could lay their hands on. The wave of vandalism started in the south and soon engulfed all the Lowlands, including Amsterdam.

The mayors had only to look at the paintings on their walls to be reminded of the Anabaptist uprising, but now they were confronted with an even more serious problem. Joost Buyck had fallen heir to the Magnificat: his face, with its eagle beak of a nose and thin, tight mouth, strongly suggests that he was a man who brooked no nonsense. Determined to keep the town within the Catholic fold and loyal to Spain, the First Mayor used all the powers at his command to quell disturbances. Two important bits of news soon reached Amsterdam, and both played into his hands: the Duke of Alva, despised as Philip's executioner, was on his way north, and William of Orange had left the Lowlands. The mayors lost no time in taking advantage of these events to step up their persecutions. The time had come to rid themselves of the troublesome merchants who, in their opinion, had become far too independent. Examinations on the rack quickly elicited the names of the seventy petitioners and of others who had sympathized with them.

The merchants had only to look at the gallows on the Dam or sniff the air on the days of execution to know that any one of them might soon suffer the same fate unless he managed to get away. Many did: a Cant, a Hooft, a Bardesius, a Pauw, and other important burghers. Everything had to be left behind, goods, houses, and all real property frugally acquired during years of capital formation. Merchants with ships at sea were the most fortunate, for they still had their sources of income. Others, with nothing to fall back on, joined the rebel fleet that had started to harass the coast. For them, piracy was the quickest way to revenge. They began calling themselves geuzen, or beggars, after an invective thrown at them by a grandee; they adopted the name as a rallying cry.[9] Most of them were young men, but when they finally managed to return, they proudly called themselves the

9. In an aside to Margaret of Parma, he had referred to a delegation of Dutch dignitaries as "Ils ne sont que des *gueuse*." Professor Geyl has called the Sea Beggars the shock troops of Calvinism. It was this armed force of

Old Beggars. It would be ten long years before this happened, and during that period Amsterdam would be the center of Philip's campaign in the Lowlands.

Though the merchants had been unable to carry into exile anything of great value, their mere absence did much to bring about the downfall of the Catholic regency. Amsterdam had become the granary not only of the Lowlands but for most of western Europe as well. With its most important merchants gone and the approaches across the Zuiderzee blockaded by the rebel fleet, the stocks of grain and other essential goods gradually dwindled away. Alva, after a promising start in which town after town had fallen into his hands, found it increasingly difficult to supply his troops. The town fathers did what they could, but, when they, too, ran out of money, the Spanish legions mutinied and the campaign ground to a halt. Alva had to leave town in the dead of night because he was unable to pay even his personal debts. Even in the face of these adversities, Joost Buyck refused to capitulate. The annals of those years paint a dismal picture:

> The rebels seem to have everything in profusion . . . they trade freely and become rich. This town, on the other hand, is getting poorer and poorer, and seems destined to wither away.

One year later:

> We are in such poverty and desolation that it is necessary to close the treasury and proclaim a moratorium. And all this misery and calamity is caused, because Amsterdam persists in remaining obedient to the Catholic religion and the Royal Majesty.[10]

When the tide began to turn in the north, it was inevitable that Amsterdam could not hold out much longer. Another mutiny of Spanish troops, this time in the south, hastened the process. The mutiny resulted in the sack of Antwerp, which is recorded in history as the Spanish Fury of 1576. It caused all factions, Catholic and Protestant alike, to join hands in a united effort to rid the Netherlands of the hated Spaniard. By the end of the

---

extremists that enabled a vigorous minority to seize power under the name of the Prince of Orange and in time persuade the majority of its ideals. See P. Geyl, *The Netherlands Divided* (*1609–1648*) (London, 1936), p. 16.

10. H. Brugmans, *Opkomst en bloei van Amsterdam* (Amsterdam, Meulenhoff, 1944), pp. 83–84.

year, this unity was formalized in the Pacification of Ghent. It was to have no lasting effect, but the immediate result was that Amsterdam found itself completely isolated.

It must be said to the credit of Joost Buyck and his clique that they refused to relinquish their principles. It is possible that they, too, were now imbued with the spirit of martyrdom, or they may have realized that their fate was sealed whether they stepped down voluntarily or not. The end came on May 26, 1578, the day of the Alteration. Earlier that month the States General had sent a delegation to the mayors for the purpose of putting the municipal guard under the command of the States rather than the town and thus avoid a bloody siege. When the mayors refused to yield, the townsmen rose in protest—"laborers, artisans, shopkeepers . . . people of all sorts." [11] Thousands moved towards the Dam, pressing down the narrow streets which converged there from all directions. It seemed that a riot was inevitable; stones were pried loose from the pavement, and some had already been heaved at the city hall when the sound of trumpets brought the mob to its senses. The people listened docilely while a herald read a proclamation.

At the last moment, the officers of the three companies of the guard had taken a hand in the situation by declaring themselves on the side of the States General. The mayors had no choice. Their friends and relatives, as well as the most prominent clerics and monks of the town, were rounded up. Early in the afternoon the whole lot was herded aboard two ships that carried them away from the town and put them ashore on a dike beyond the walls to find sanctuary as best they could.

The Alteration was a revolution. In religion and in matters of trade and influence, it was a complete victory for the merchants, who returned from exile as soon as they could. They were given important posts, and before long the Old Beggars were in full control. They were of one mind: they wanted to trade with the least amount of restriction, and the town had to be reorganized accordingly. During the ten years of stubborn refusal to join the revolt against Spain, Amsterdam had set the clock back, while other towns on the Zuiderzee, such as Hoorn and Enkhuizen, had prospered. However, the factors which had always favored Amsterdam soon made up for lost time. Towns like Leiden and Haarlem, with their woolens and linens, could boast of a greater industrial development, but the fruits of growing

11. P. C. Hooft, *Nederlandsche historien* (Amsterdam, 1656), p. 537.

European trade were mainly gathered in Amsterdam, although a number of other ports in Holland and Zealand managed to get their share.

Aside from their geographic location and a long affinity with the sea, there was another important factor which favored the Lowlands in the new economic era. Unlike other European countries, such as England and France, neither Holland nor Zealand had an entrenched aristocracy with a vested interest in productive land and hence no need to apply its full energy to the development of trade. In general, this top stratum disdained commerce, with the result that merchants in those countries did not rank high socially. In the Lowlands, the situation was completely reversed, and nowhere was this more pronounced than in Amsterdam, where the merchants actually ruled the town.

During the early years following the Alteration, the merchants were all more or less on the same level, as they all had to start over again from scratch. They had the experience, but most of them were badly in need of capital. To solve this problem, few among them hesitated to use certain short cuts, and thus they rose most quickly to the top. J. E. Elias, in his exhaustive study of the new patriciate of Amsterdam, minces no words: "There is hardly one of its members whose fortune was not based on some illicit activity, such as piracy and counterfeiting." [12] Once a stake had been acquired, most of them preferred to forget the methods of their earlier exploits and concentrate on developing their businesses through legal means. These men became the class of great merchants, and from among them were chosen the men who occupied the pillows at the city hall. "This Holland regent class," according to Geyl, "is not only the most important political factor, but also the most notable social phenomenon in the Netherlands throughout the seventeenth century and beyond. The intermixing of commerce and government, the concentration of political power in middle-class hands, made an unpleasant impression on many foreigners, as indeed did the whole sudden outburst of commercial capitalism in the Northern Netherlands." [13]

The new regime inherited a town that was still confined within its medieval walls. The Catholic hierarchy had repeatedly denied requests to build on the surrounding land, on the pretext that it would endanger the defense of the town. A more cynical view

12. J. E. Elias, *De Vroedschap van Amsterdam, 1573–1795* (Haarlem, 1903), pp. 34–35.
13. Geyl, *Netherlands Divided*, p. 248.

had been that it would lower the value of the houses within the walls, in which the mayors and their associates had a dominant interest. The revival of trade after the Alteration drew many people to Amsterdam not only from the rural areas but also from abroad. By 1585 the town had only about 30,000 inhabitants, but at the turn of the century this figure had risen to 50,000, and was doubled within the next 20 years.[14] It is indicative of the spirit prevailing in Amsterdam that it was felt the town could absorb so many people while other towns, such as Leiden and Haarlem, barred immigrants lest they become a liability.

Around 1585, the old town was bursting at the seams, and the first plan was drawn up for its enlargement through development of a wide strip of land along its periphery. Within less than ten years this addition proved inadequate, and a more ambitious plan was required, and in 1612 a third. The men who fostered this planning were merchants, unabashedly in pursuit of profits, but with great pride in their town. Each successive plan was fitted into the previous one, until they grew into a symmetrical whole. Three concentric half circles of canals embraced the town, with wide pavements on either side, soon to be lined with stately linden trees. Appropriately, the people called their town the Half Moon, and this name was given to the Amsterdam ship that was the first to sail up the Hudson River. The Amstel continued to bisect the town. The eastern half was called the Old Side and the western half became the New Side. The latter was planned as a residential section, and during the seventeenth century many imposing homes were built along its canals.[15]

The Old Side remained the commercial district, as it had been from the very beginning. Here were the merchants' establishments, warehouses, shipyards—everything that was required for the proper maintenance of trading ventures reaching ever further across the seas. Flat-bottomed barges shuttled back and forth between the warehouses along the canals and the seagoing ships that were moored in the Y, just outside a double row of pilings which enclosed the inner harbor. These piles, each as big as a strong mast, had been driven deep into the clay bottom by a pile driver, the power being supplied by a score of brawny men who hoisted the heavy iron monkey into the air and then let it drop.

14. Brugmans, *Opkomst*, p. 98.
15. For the expansion of Amsterdam, see Kok, *Historische schoonheid*, passim.

5

Independence
at Any Price

During the first fifteen years, the Dutch rebellion against Spain was personified by Prince William of Orange, who was to go down in history as William the Silent, the Father of his country.[1] It had been his dream to unite all the seventeen provinces, both north and south, in a solid front against Spain. As a result of the sack of Antwerp, this dream seemed about to be realized. The outrage against people and property helped to smooth over the differences between the Catholic south and the Protestant north, leading to the compact known as the Pacification of Ghent. Its avowed purpose was to drive the Spanish from all of the Netherlands, but it also offered freedom of religion. Protestantism was formally established in the north, while in the Catholic south, Protestants received the assurance that they would not be persecuted. The Inquisition was to be abolished forever.

It soon became apparent, however, that the schism between the two religious factions could not be bridged so easily. Alarmed at the virile growth of Calvinism, a number of southern provinces formed a league for the protection of their faith and at the same time professed their allegiance to King Philip of Spain. This ended William's hope for a United Netherlands. From then on the two factions were to go their own way. The separation was formalized in January of 1579, when the seven northern provinces confederated themselves in the Union of Utrecht.[2] The boundaries were approximately those of the Netherlands in the twentieth

1. His official title was Stadholder (keeper of the towns) of the three provinces: Holland, Zealand, and Utrecht. Originally he had acted on behalf of Philip II of Spain, but after the revolt his allegiance was in fact transferred to the States General.

2. For a detailed account of the events leading to both the Pacification of Ghent and the Union of Utrecht, see P. J. Blok, *History of the People of the Netherlands*, 3 (New York, 1900), 96–139. See also Geyl, *Nederlandse stam*, 1, 245–66.

century. At no time, even at the height of its power, did the
republic have serious ambitions to extend its territory in Europe.
Whatever additional land it acquired was wrested from the sea.
Its conquests were to be overseas, thousands of miles away.

The main task confronting the young federation was to defend
itself against Spain, then the most powerful nation in the world.
As a political entity, the federation was ill prepared for the struggle, consisting as it did of many different factions, each of which
had its own special interests. The five provinces in the east and
north [3] were envious of the prosperity of Holland and Zealand
which, in turn, were rivaling each other in matters of trade. Even
within a single province there was no love lost among certain
towns. Only Prince William was respected by all, and it was his
leadership that enabled the seven provinces to subdue their grievances and present a united front against the enemy. Most people
thought the country should be ruled by a monarch, but William
did not aspire to this role. The governing body was the States
General,[4] in which each province had one vote regardless of the
number of deputies it sent.

The Spanish had in the meantime marshaled a strong force in
the Catholic south for a concentrated attempt to stamp out the
revolt. Town after town in the south, east, and north fell into
their hands, and the rebels' backs were to the sea. Only Holland
and Zealand were still free. The greatest blow fell when Prince
William was assassinated in 1584. His last words were to implore
God: "Have mercy on the people!"

The friction between provinces and towns that had been kept
in check by his leadership now increased. The courage of the
Dutch seemed to leave them completely. In despair, the States
General offered the crown to Henry of France and to Queen
Elizabeth of England, only to be turned down by both. Neither
cared to take on the responsibility of defending the Lowlands
against such a powerful opponent as Spain. Henry, for the time
being a Protestant, had his own troubles, hard pressed as he was
to protect his throne against a powerful league of Catholic nobles.
The war of the Huguenots in 1584 was in so critical a stage that
he could give the Dutch no assistance whatever. They turned
to Elizabeth and sent a delegation to London to plead with the

3. Friesland, Groningen, Overysel, Gelderland, and Utrecht.
4. During the deliberations leading to the Union of Utrecht, Holland had
tried in vain to acquire a more equitable representation, claiming that its
yearly contribution into the treasury was more than that of the six other
provinces put together.

Queen. Among the delegation's members was a young lawyer, Johan van Oldebarnevelt, who was destined to become the driving force behind the formation of the United East India Company.[5]

Elizabeth was no friend to the rebels. That a group of commoners should renounce allegiance to a rightful king was to her unthinkable, and she did not want to precipitate an open war with Philip. She did not, on the other hand, want to see all the Netherlands firmly under Spanish rule and thus become an imminent threat to her own domain. And so she dallied. The talks in London dragged on for months. In the end, the Duke of Parma, Philip's capable governor and soldier, forced her hand. To the towns he had already taken he added the most important of all: Antwerp fell to him in August 1585, and the specter of a Spanish coast across the North Sea suddenly loomed large. Elizabeth refused the crown, but she agreed to help, for a price. She would send the Earl of Leicester with five thousand men if the Dutch would repay her in full. As guarantee, the English were to be allowed to occupy three strategic towns, Flushing, Fort Rammekens, and Briel. It was to take more than thirty years before this pledge could finally be redeemed. In the negotiations, Oldebarnevelt played a major role; it was just about the last important service he was allowed to render his country.

Leicester arrived in December 1585. He stayed only two years and left in disgust, complaining bitterly of "that thankless mob," as he called the Dutch. There were several reasons why his stewardship was not successful. In the field, he was no match for Parma; the troops he had brought had been recruited mainly in the slums of London, and were a sorry lot. Exploiting the envy of the poorer provinces of Holland and Zealand, he had himself proclaimed Governor General, with greater powers than even Prince William had possessed. Above all, he invoked the enmity of Holland, which had ships, commerce, and energy, and which contributed the greatest share of the taxes and imposts needed to finance the war. The merchants of Amsterdam had no qualms about dealing with the enemy to earn profits, and this trade was the life blood that kept the rebellion going. Leicester refused to see the matter that way.[6]

5. A. de Fouw, Jr., *Onbekende raadspensionarissen* (The Hague, Daamen, 1946), p. 26.
6. F. Snapper, *Oorlogsinvloeden op de overzeese handel van Holland, 1551–1719* (Amsterdam, Ellerman Harms, 1959), pp. 34–35.

Almost everything Spain required to maintain her fleet came from the Baltic: lumber, hemp, flax, tar. This trade was now controlled by the Dutch. Philip had tried to enlist the old Hansa League for the purpose, but that decadent organization no longer considered itself strong enough to risk running afoul of its virile competitors. As a result Philip was confronted with a vexing dilemma. He knew that land forces alone might never bring the Dutch rebels to their knees, but it was difficult for him to clear his conscience of the fact that he was dependent upon these same heretics for the fleet he needed to defeat them, and that the silver from his own mines in the Americas stiffened the Dutch in their unholy revolt.

In this trade, the Dutch had gravitated towards Lisbon. At the outbreak of the rebellion, Portugal was an independent country and thus no barrier to Dutch vessels, but after Philip had annexed its crown in 1580, the situation changed. According to the policy he then followed, Dutch ships might suddenly be confiscated and their crews hauled before the Inquisition. There were many instances of Dutch sailors ending their lives at the galley oars, their ships pressed into service to carry Spanish troops. But the lure of profits for Amsterdam and other towns was too great to be denied. If the orange, white, and blue of the Dutch flag was onerous to Philip, perhaps the colors of certain Baltic states would be less so. The notaries in Amsterdam were kept busy counterfeiting papers.[7] At this point, Leicester intervened.

Using his dictatorial powers, he issued an edict prohibiting all trade with Spain, claiming that it aided the enemy. This was undoubtedly true, but Leicester ignored the fact that it was even more beneficial to the Dutch. Nor were his motives entirely altruistic. Foreseeing the probability that the merchants would find a way to circumvent his edict, he made them subject to heavy fines that were intended to bring millions into his depleted treasury. This was more than Holland would take. Oldebarnevelt had recently been appointed Pensionary (Chief Magistrate) of the States of Holland[8] and under his guidance, this body rescinded

---

7. J. H. Kernkamp, *De Handel op den vijand, 1572–1609, 1* (Utrecht, Kemink & Zoon, 1931), 201–02.

8. The word state is derived from the French *état*, but the Dutch word 'Standen' (social strata) is analogous, because the States originally consisted of representatives from the nobility, the clergy, and the towns within the province. In Holland and Zealand the towns became the dominant factor. For the functions of the Pensionary (Advocate), see p. 137 f.

most of the powers previously granted Leicester, leaving the other provinces to do as they liked.

Thwarted in his ambition to rule the Lowlands by decree, Leicester ingratiated himself with certain dissident factions which had their own reasons to feel none too kindly towards the powerful merchant-magistrates of Amsterdam and other towns. These factions were to be found among the lower classes and the expatriates from the south, who shared a blind hatred for everything tinged with Spain and Catholicism. Their leaders were the Calvinist ministers, who thundered from their pulpits against the merchants whom they accused of putting profits before God and country. It did not take much to excite the rank and file among the burghers, and the result was lawlessness, and even mutiny, among the troops. When order was finally restored, Leicester was gone, but he left behind a badly divided country.[9]

With this ominous beginning, the Dutch entered the most important period of their history, the ten or twelve years during which they moved from the brink of disaster to a state of equality with their powerful neighbors. They were years of indomitable spirit and resourcefulness, and of some gross mistakes on the part of the enemy. Both played a part, and it is difficult to judge which weighed heaviest in the balance.[10]

The period had begun with an all-out effort by Spain, both by land and sea, to quell the revolt. Parma's legions had been pressing relentlessly, until the Dutch were left with little more than Holland and Zealand, a water-logged area bounded to the south by the mouth of the Scheldt, which was also threatened by Parma, anxious to take Flushing, the key to the blockade of Antwerp. If he were to succeed, Antwerp would regain its former importance and become once more the rival of Amsterdam. Antwerp might even be made the base for an attack that could result in the complete subjugation of the Lowlands.

Philip was planning an attack by sea as well. It was no secret on either side of the North Sea that he was fitting out a strong fleet, for the purpose of bringing Elizabeth to her knees while at the same time subduing the Dutch once and for all. Late in

9. On Leicester in the Netherlands, see Blok, *History of the Netherlands*, 3, 197-233.

10. Until this time the Union of Utrecht had been a dead letter, but now it became a type of provisional constitution. The federation was established and the province of Holland took the lead. See R. Fruin, *Geschiedenis der staatsinstellingen in Nederland* (The Hague, 1901), p. 175.

1586, the Queen sent Sir Francis Drake to Holland to enlist the support of the States General for a joint expedition to Spanish and Portuguese ports—to "singe the king's beard" by destroying his ships before they were ready to sail.

Drake was an intrepid seafarer who had made a great name for himself in his voyage around the world. On the coast of Chile and Peru he had managed to rob the Spanish of an amazing amount of treasure. After sailing as far north as California, he had followed Magellan's example and set sail for the Moluccas, where he had found a small quantity of cloves. When, shortly afterwards, he ran upon a shoal, he had had to lighten his ship: "Three tons of cloves were thrown out, eight of the guns and a quantity of meal and pulse; but none of the treasure, though that was the heaviest part of the cargo." [11] The episode illustrates the style of the early English adventurers. In contrast to the Dutch, who followed later, they came as freebooters, and not as traders.

The States General agreed to support Drake's venture and ordered every town of importance to contribute one or more vessels to his fleet.[12] The details were to be arranged directly with the owners, and it may be assumed that the wily merchants, who believed in "profits next to God," were able to glean some first-hand information about the legendary Spice Islands. So far, not a single Dutchman had ever set foot there, and none had as yet any serious intention to do so, but advance knowledge could do no harm. Drake's Spanish raid in 1587 was only partially successful and did not prevent the sailing of the Armada in the following year.

The Armada was the largest fleet that had ever put to sea— more than 130 ships, ranging from 300 to 1,200 tons. It carried over 3,000 guns and nearly 20,000 soldiers, in addition to some 8,000 sailors and 2,000 galley slaves. This great force was to be further augmented by Parma's 17,000 seasoned veterans, who were to join Admiral Medina Sidonia as soon as his fleet reached Calais.

The invasion appeared, theoretically, to be as good as accomplished. Parma had not approved of the project; he had cautioned that Flushing should first be taken in order to secure the Scheldt and open the port of Antwerp, but Philip was overconfident, and Parma's advice was rejected. The Dutch effectively blockaded

11. R. Southey, *English Seamen* (London, 1895), p. 280.

12. J. L. Motley, *History of the United Netherlands*, 2 (London, 1875), 97–98.

the coast and prevented Parma's legions from joining the fleet. The English seamen, with smaller and more maneuverable vessels and by an adroit use of fire ships, demoralized the Spaniards. A fierce storm and poor seamanship—the Spanish were unfamiliar with northern waters—drove the Armada into the North Sea. Only half the ships that had set sail so proudly were able to return to the homeland, and their condition was appalling. A scapegoat had to be found, and the grandees picked Parma, whom they accused of deliberately delaying to join the fleet until the storm had made it impossible to do so. They ignored the fact that, if Parma's advice had been heeded, neither the Dutch blockade nor the storm would have presented a problem.[13]

For Spain, the defeat was the beginning of a slow but steady decline. On the sea, at least, the Dutch no longer feared the Spanish, and the idea was planted in some minds that perhaps the time was coming to go to the Indies themselves, to engage the enemy there, and to make some profits. The Armada's defeat was also de facto vindication of the merchants who had traded with the enemy. They had earned millions by enabling Philip to build his navy, half of which was now at the bottom of the ocean.

Spain was by no means finished. The debacle of the Armada had not affected Parma's strength, and, with his forces still fully intact, he planned to invade the Lowlands the following year (1589). It might have turned out badly for the Dutch if Philip's attention had not been diverted by events in France. Henry III, constantly harassed by the league of Catholic nobles led by the pretender to his throne, the Duke of Guise, had decided on a drastic move. Unable to defeat Guise in open warfare, he had him assassinated, as Philip had done with William of Orange. Philip regarded the league as one of his strongest allies against the heretics in France, and he decided to give it his full support. Parma was ordered to refrain from action in the Lowlands and to turn south instead.[14]

For the Dutch, this was welcome respite. It gave them an opportunity to put their own house in order, which had been left in a deplorable condition by Leicester's machinations. His former adherents had been made powerless, but the masses were still restive. The merchant–magistrates were guided by the conviction that the lower classes could best be controlled if they had a hero

13. Ibid., pp. 435–508. See also G. Mattingly, *The Armada* (Boston, 1959).
14. Fruin, *Tien jaren*, pp. 21–22.

of noble lineage to admire. Under the guidance of Oldebarnevelt, young Prince Maurice, the second son of William of Orange, was groomed for the role. (The oldest son, Philip William, was a hostage in Madrid.) Maurice was first given the title of Stadholder of Holland and Zealand and soon afterwards became Captain and Admiral–General of the Union. By enlisting the support of the clergy, Oldebarnevelt gradually succeeded in transferring the people's affection for the departed Leicester to Maurice. For a number of years these two men were to make a formidable team: Oldebarnevelt was among the foremost statesmen of Europe, and Maurice became the most proficient Dutch general in the field.

The Dutch were no warriors; they disliked campaigning. Consequently, the army consisted mainly of foreigners, mercenaries from England, Scotland, and especially, the impoverished German states. These were trained by Maurice and his older cousin William Lodewyk, the Stadholder of Friesland, who had made a thorough study of the art of war as practised by the Greeks and the Romans. In this he may have been inspired by Machiavelli, who earlier in the century had expressed his astonishment that, while jurisprudence, philosophy, medicine, and other arts were widely adopted from the ancients, his contemporaries ignored their writings on statesmanship and the art of war, in both of which they had been equally proficient. William Lodewyk re-enacted ancient battles on a large table, moving lead soldiers around and planning adaptations of his tactics to suit the more advanced weapons of modern times. He also enforced discipline by insisting on regular drills and marching in formation, much to the amusement of his Frisian subjects, who had never seen anything like it. He also made his troops dig their own trenches and earthwork, work formerly left to local farmers. Maurice was his cousin's most diligent pupil, and he soon proved that on the field of battle he had few equals.[15]

During the years 1591 and 1592, the Dutch, though with a great many misgivings in certain quarters, departed from a strategy of defense to attack. The time seemed propitious. Parma's attention was diverted to France, and he was, in addition, a sick man. Town after town, in the east and south, was recaptured, and the Spanish were driven from the seven northern provinces. Much was accomplished by using water as a means of transport. Every body of water became an artery along which troops and equipment

15. Ibid., pp. 89–92.

were moved quickly and in quantity and often to the complete surprise of the enemy.

These local victories by no means ended the war, which was to continue for another 50 years, interrupted only by a twelve-year truce, but they restored self-confidence, and with it came a resurgence of courage and enterprise. Trade was expanded, new sea lanes were opened, and plans were made to go directly to the Indies. The English had proved that it was possible for an enemy of Spain to get to the Indies without much trouble: Drake had done it in 1579 and Cavendish in 1587. If it were seamanship that was required, the voyage was as good as made, for the Dutch considered themselves sailors second to none. But the merchants who had to finance such an undertaking were too practical to rely solely on buccaneering, as the English had done, nor were they interested in embarking upon such an arduous venture for mere adventure. It was trade they wanted, and, to pursue it halfway round the globe demanded knowledge, capital, and organization.

6

Factors of
Trade Expansion

The Dutch had been able to dislodge the Spanish from the north-ern provinces, but they could do no more. The enemy remained solidly entrenched in the south, and the dream of William of Orange was shattered. How did this cleavage of the Dutch-speaking area cut off Flanders and Brabant and leave them asso-ciated with the Walloon provinces? It could not have been a matter of religious preference, since while all of the Netherlands was still under Spanish rule, Calvinism was as strong in those two provinces as in the north. After the uprising in 1576, determined Calvinist minorities managed to gain control in most of the towns in Flanders and Brabant, just as these minorities had done in Hol-land and Zealand after 1572, prodded by the militant action of the Sea Beggars.

It is Geyl's thesis that the cleavage was conditional on the geographical situation.[1] In Holland and Zealand, inland waters and rivers provided both a natural defense and direct outlets to the sea, which fostered spiritual and economic ties with the rest of Protestant Europe. The southern provinces, being cut off from the sea by the fall of Antwerp, had no such advantages. They were, moreover, close to the center of Spanish military power. Thus, Parma managed to re-establish Spanish hegemony in Flan-ders and Brabant not because the people were more inclined towards Catholicism but because they were more exposed to his attack.

It had been Philip's main concern to enforce Catholicism in his realm. Every other consideration was secondary. Parma accom-plished this by following a moderate policy. He restored the privileges of the towns and granted a general amnesty to those who returned to the Catholic fold. Diehard Calvinists were al-lowed to depart with as much of their property as could be con-

1. Geyl, *Netherlands Divided*, pp. 15–18.

verted into cash.[2] Many thousands took advantage of this lenience by going north, mainly to Holland and Zealand. They knew they were welcome there, and this area offered the best chance for starting a new life. Because these men had been forced to leave their homeland and had suffered, or at least witnessed, the horrors of the Inquisition, their hatred for the Spanish was too deep to allow for compromise.

The cleavage brought economic decline to the south, but it proved to be a boon to the north. The Dutch controlled the sea and their blockade of the Scheldt brought Antwerp's trade to a standstill. Amsterdam inherited Antwerp's trade, and the records show that its population increased in direct proportion to Antwerp's decline. It was another step in the movement of the center of European trade northward: from St. Denis, to Bruges, to Antwerp, and now to Amsterdam.

The refugees included men of learning, merchants, and manufacturers, who contributed much to the rise of the Dutch Republic.[3] A Caron and an Aerssens served as ambassadors to London and Paris, a Plancius mapped the route to the Indies, a Moucheron and an Usselinx contributed their fortunes and energy in endeavors to exploit new lands.[4] Many others played their part in the upsurge of commerce and industry that was the prelude to Holland's Golden Age, for it was not Amsterdam alone that benefited from the fall of Antwerp and the general retrogression in the south. With the emigrants came the weaving establishments that had made Flanders famous throughout Europe. The woolen industry moved to Leiden, where it was later to provide a livelihood for the English Puritans before they set sail on the Mayflower. Linen weaving developed in Haarlem, and its products became known as the finest of their kind in the world.

English wool, formerly shipped exclusively to Antwerp, now came to Holland, but no longer entirely in the raw. A number of Flemish refugees had gone to England, where they had set up their weaving frames. England also exported cloth, but since the art of finishing and dyeing had not yet been mastered there, wool

2. P. J. Blok, *Geschiedenis van het nederlandsche volk*, 3, (Groningen, 1896), 298.

3. The term "Dutch Republic" has come into general use but the official name was "United Provinces" or "United Netherlands." See A. Hyma, *A History of the Dutch in the Far East* (Ann Arbor, 1953), p. 34.

4. For the names of some other important emigrants see Fruin, *Tien jaren*, pp. 190–91.

had to be shipped in the gray. The Dutch bought this cloth and processed it in their own establishments, which had sprung up everywhere. Sir Walter Raleigh had good reason to complain of the ineptness of his countrymen in letting this trade slip through their fingers: "Our bayes are sent white to Amsterdam, and there dressed, dyed and shipped for Spain, Portugal, etc. where they are sold by the name of Flemish bayes; so that we lose the very name of our homebred commodities." [5]

Here we have an illustrious contemporary testifing to the continued Spanish dependence on the Dutch for goods it could not obtain elsewhere, just as in Leicester's time. He also identifies one of the main reasons why the English were to be overtaken by the Dutch during this period: they were slower to adjust themselves to the rapid changes that were taking place in the economic world. Their economy was based on husbandry, not trade, and from the relative safety of their island kingdom they felt as yet no great urge to bestir themselves. With the Dutch, the situation was reversed. They were fighting open war against the most powerful nation on earth, and great sums were required to hire mercenaries, to buy armaments, and to build war vessels. To raise the money, the people were heavily taxed: merchants, weavers, farmers, fishermen—everyone. It must have dismayed these profit-minded folk to see their money being spent on a great risk, promising no return but a still elusive independence. But fight they must, and, without outside help, they had to pay for it themselves. It called for ingenuity, greater output, and more trade.[6]

Trade with the Baltic was intensified and the warehouses in Amsterdam soon bulged with grain, available to whoever was willing to pay the price. In 1590, after a number of poor crops, the whole of Italy faced famine. The Dutch were ready to come to the rescue. "What's one man's poison, signor, is another man's meat!" [7] Although that line was not written until some twenty years later, the Dutch behaved as if they had always known it. Ships from the town of Hoorn, laden with grain, were the first

5. Sir Walter Raleigh, "Observations touching trade and commerce with the Hollanders and others, wherein is proved that our sea and land commodities serve to enrich and strengthen other countries than our own," in William Oldys and Thomas Birch, eds., *The Works of Sir Walter Raleigh, 8* (Oxford, 1829), 351–76.

6. The expansion of Dutch trade was greatly enhanced by the lack of interest in this field of other western European nations. See Diferee, *Geschiedenis van den nederlandschen handel,* p. 128.

7. Beaumont and Fletcher, *Love's Cure,* III.2.

Dutch ships to venture into the Mediterranean. They were followed by others, and a whole new trading area was opened.

Activity in the herring fisheries was also stepped up, and this increased demand for salt. The need for salt had been the motivation for some of the earliest Dutch ventures southward, first to the coast of France and then to Portugal. Now the Dutch had to go still farther, because Philip could deny them access to Setubal. On they went to the Cape Verde Islands, known also as the Salt Islands. The quality of the salt was poor, but the problem was remedied by improving the method of refining. From the Cape Verde Islands, it was not difficult to get to Guinea and the fabled coasts of Africa. The names given these lands by the Portuguese were enough to inspire a Dutchman—the Gold Coast, the Pepper Coast, the Ivory Coast, the Slave Coast! Barent Erikszen of Medemblik was the first in Africa, in 1593.

As had happened in the Mediterranean, this first contact was soon followed by others, and before long the Portuguese were no longer lords and masters in their own domain. It was the first time the Dutch had tackled the enemy in his own territory, and the results promised well for similar encroachments in other parts of the world. That the profits did not live up to expectations was due mainly to the fact that the African trade grew too rapidly. Too many merchants were competing against each other for acquiring the goods in the field, thereby raising their costs, and then flooding the market in competition at home, driving prices and profits down.[8] Free trade had been the lodestone which had guided them thus far, but now they were faced with a situation in which it seemed to play them false. It was something to bear in mind for the future.

This expansion in so many directions called for more ships, and in such large numbers that the old method of sawing lumber by hand was no longer satisfactory. There were other problems as well, and, in solving them, the Dutch proved themselves worthy contenders for a preferred position in the new economic era which was about to begin. When we associate the idea of industrial revolution with coal and iron, we ignore the fact that there were earlier industrial revolutions based on other factors. The English had possessed coal for centuries, but used it only for primitive heating and the forging of iron, until they learned how to wed it to iron. In a similar fashion, wind had been blow-

8. G. Brandt, *Historie van Enkhuizen* (Enkhuizen, 1666), p. 195.

ing immemorially across the flat lands of Holland and across the sea, but its energy had been used to only a limited extent. The Dutch proceeded to make more effective use of it by harnessing it to wood on an unprecedented scale.[9]

Then as now, necessity was the mother of invention. It had led Beukelsz. to develop a method for curing fish. Another need arose when the Dutch were faced with the problem of building and operating a large merchant fleet with minimum expenditures in manpower and materials. Pieter Jansz. Liorne from the town of Hoorn accomplished both by designing a new type of vessel in the year 1594. It became known as a flute, the English version of the Dutch *fluit*. This ship was about four times as long as it was wide, much longer in proportion than any ship previously built. It was also of shallow draft. These two factors made it faster and easier to handle, because the mizzen carried only a lateen sail. The flutes were also built lighter, serving the dual purpose of saving on materials and increasing cargo capacity.[10]

For a time, the flute was an object of ridicule. With its bulging sides, curving sharply inwards at the deck, it was unlike anything a self-respecting seaman had ever set sail on. Liorne had a good reason for designing a vessel with the smallest possible deck, without sacrificing any of its cargo capacity. The Oresund tolls were a heavy burden. They were determined by the deck area of a ship, and, by reducing it, the wily shipbuilder from Hoorn was able to achieve a considerable saving on every voyage into the Baltic. It took the Danes almost 70 years before they realized that they were being cleverly cheated. They produced a new formula which took into account the length of a vessel and the width of the hull amidships. This, of course, raised the tolls, but the Dutch, undaunted as ever, built ships in the shape of an hourglass, with as narrow a waist as possible. Although this type of vessel did not prove to be practical, it shows that the Dutch were great innovators, who did not hesitate to do the unexpected if it protected their purse.

The light flute ships represented still another departure from

9. For this industrial development, see M. A. Verkade, *De Opkomst van de Zaanstreek* (Utrecht, 1952), pp. 167–247.

10. The flute was actually an improvement over the earlier *Vlie-boot* of which there were already over 2,000 in use, according to a survey ordered by the States General in 1588. See S. C. van Kampen, *De Rotterdamse particuliere scheepsbouw in de tijd van de Republiek* (Assen, 1953), pp. 53–55.

the accepted principle that ships should serve a dual purpose, for war as well as for peace. This dual-purpose vessel was much heavier and proved unable to compete with the flute in carrying freight quickly and cheaply. Sir Walter Raleigh wrote: "By the structure of roominess of their shipping, holding much merchandise, though sailing with fewer hands than our ships could; thereby carrying their goods much cheaper to and from foreign parts, than England can." [11]

Equally telling is the account of Aitzema, the Dutch historian of the seventeenth century:

> The Hollanders had applied all their diligence and ingenuity to build light and inexpensive ships because in this manner they could sail cheaper than other nations. In Sweden, however, it was a policy that all ships had to be built heavy so that they could be used for war purposes if necessary. The same applied to all the coal ships in England, as well as all Eastland vessels . . . but in Holland they had built since many years flutes and other light vessels which, by charging lesser freight, were able to compete successfully with all other countries.

Velius reported that within eight years some 80 flutes went down the ways in Hoorn alone.[12]

Another invention which greatly enhanced progress in the new age of wind and wood was an improved windmill, especially as it was adapted to the sawing of lumber in the year 1596. The timing was fortunate both because it followed close upon the design of the first flute ship and helped meet the increased demand for lumber caused by the rapid expansion of the towns. Although this invention did for wind and wood what Watson's steam engine was to accomplish for coal and iron, we look in vain for the name of the inventor; the records simply describe him as "a clever fellow from a village in West Friesland." Windmills were quickly adapted to other operations, such as the crushing of oilseeds and the pumping of water, but sawing lumber was their greatest contribution, as long as the Dutch depended on wooden

11. Oldys and Birch, eds., *Raleigh's Works, 8*, 351–76.
12. L. van Aitzema, *Saken van staet en oorlogh in ende omtrent de Vereenigde Nederlanden, 1621–68, 3* (The Hague, 1669–72), 818. See also T. Velius, *Chroniek van Hoorn* (Hoorn, 1648), p. 271. For the importance of the flute in the development of Dutch trade, see also Violet Barbour, *Capitalism in Amsterdam in the Seventeenth Century* (Baltimore, 1950), p. 19.

ships for trade and defense. Because there are now few wooden ships left, it must not be assumed that they were inferior in all respects to the steel hull. In fact, during the age of exploration along uncharted coasts, the wooden hull was preferable in that it is many times stronger and more resilient at point of impact than steel. A steel hull would have been a total loss the first time it struck a reef, whereas a wooden ship suffered little damage, and could be repaired with simple carpenter's tools.

Mechanical sawing brought another innovation which is usually credited to a much later period. It was now possible to cut planks and beams more uniformly, and to more exact specifications. This meant that lumber could be sawn in advance, stored according to size, and the stockpile drawn upon as needed. This reduced the time it had formerly taken to build ships, the more so as their hulls approached standardization. It was one of the earliest forms of mass production. Dutch shipbuilders became famous all over Europe, and many of them were eventually employed by other countries. It is indicative of the advanced techniques in Holland to read these men's complaints about the inordinate amount of manual labor they had to perform abroad.

It is no exaggeration to say that the flute ship played a major role in the phenomenal progress the Dutch made from the end of the sixteenth century on. It is equally true that without the sawmills on the banks of the River Zaan (Peter the Great was to learn about shipbuilding there) they might have been hard pressed to provide the many ships they needed. To keep up with the burgeoning fisheries and trade and to anticipate normal losses from the common perils of the sea were difficult enough, but the Dutch found other dangers that interfered with shipping and that could only be met by building more and more bottoms.

Spain remained a constant threat. She needed many goods which only the Dutch were able to supply in sufficient quantity, and, if Philip had fully realized this, the course of the Spanish empire in the seventeenth century might have been more fortunate, but he was less interested in the economic facts of life than in his avowed mission to save men's souls. For a while, he might tolerate Dutch ships in his ports, but when he became too conscience-stricken, he would suddenly impound them all.

Another source of danger was the pirate's nest at Dunkirk, in the narrowest part of the Channel. Passing ships were an easy mark for these marauders, who called themselves privateers because they operated under letters of marque from the King of Spain. It fell to the admiralties of Holland and Zealand to try to protect the merchant ships, and this was an expensive operation. Buzanval records that as many as sixty warships were needed to blockade this part of the coast. But no matter how closely they were watched, some pirate ships managed to elude their guards from time to time. Harassing the herring fleet became almost a sport with them, since most fishermen were Mennonites who refused to carry arms. In a few hours, pirates could ruin hundreds of fishermen by destroying the nets—just for fun, since they gained nothing by it.

Lone merchantmen were no less vulnerable. Unable to sail their prizes back to Dunkirk through the blockade, the pirates were content with taking the most valuable part of the cargo. A reluctant skipper soon revealed where it was stowed after he had been nailed to the deck, and, if the pirates felt so inclined, they might scuttle the ship to boot. They often took the skipper as hostage, demanding a high ransom once they had returned to their lair. In one case, the Dutch intercepted a pirate vessel which had collected no less than 21 skippers. So great were the losses that the Dutch eventually risked an army to penetrate deep into enemy territory, in a vain effort to eradicate this nest.[13]

There was still another kind of interference, and from a side that professed to be friendly. Although nominally allied with the republic, the English did not approve its flourishing trade while their own was lagging far behind. The Oresund toll figures show that, during the last two decades of the sixteenth century, Dutch ships entering the Baltic outnumbered English ships by about seven to one. Elizabeth was as much concerned to see her country become the greatest seafaring nation in the world as her father had been.

Envy bred resentment, with the result that the Dutch were harassed at every opportunity. Hurault de Maisse, the French ambassador to London, referred to this matter in 1598:

> Without excluding them openly, the government here makes their [the Dutch] competition with the English as difficult as possible. Thus they are prohibited from exporting money and have to take in payment whatever goods the English are willing to dispose of. The admiralty is wont to charge a very

13. Fruin, *Tien jaren*, pp. 199–201. See also Blok, *Geschiedenis, 3,* 475–76.

high fee for safe conduct and if they are unwilling to pay this the skippers are liable to be intercepted by privateers, and from whom they can regain their ship and cargo only after a costly and time-consuming lawsuit at the English courts.[14]

It was not only Elizabeth's government that caused trouble. At the beginning of the rebellion, and even before, certain Dutch towns had been forced to borrow money. Usually they had been able to do so only on condition that all inhabitants assume a personal liability. Because of the war, many of these obligations had fallen greatly and could often be bought at a fraction of their face value. English merchants might have lacked the ability to compete with the Dutch in open trading, but they were clever enough to recognize an opportunity when they saw one. Having bought such obligations cheaply, they bided their time until a vessel from the town on their paper arrived at an English port. They then put a lien on it and demanded payment in full. Whether or not the London merchants could make their claims stick, the best the Dutch could hope for was another costly delay for their ships.[15]

All told, the obstacles were many, but, good merchants, they were willing to pay the price for success. "Trade suffered," Fruin writes, "but the profits still greatly surpassed the losses. For each ship lost twenty arrived safely. And what did it matter if one merchant went bankrupt when twenty others became rich? The misfortune of a few was negligible compared to the prosperity of many." [16]

14. Fruin, *Tien jaren* (9th ed., 1941), p. 208.
15. Ibid., p. 209.
16. Ibid., p. 210.

7

From Guilds to Capitalism

Columbus launched the age of discovery, and the whole world was rapidly becoming known. The new age was dominated by Spain and Portugal, whose navigators explored the Americas, the coasts of Africa and Asia, and the islands of the East Indies. With the pact of Tordesillas in 1494, these two countries had divided the world between themselves, and proceeded to exploit their discoveries. For a hundred years, they had no competition, but by the end of this period there were others who wanted to share in the spoils. Every country in northwestern Europe made its bid, but it was the youngest and smallest among them that was to be the most successful.

There were certain factors that particularly qualified the Dutch for a major role in this development. They were a resourceful people, accustomed to hardship and discipline, who had been forced to go to sea because they had not land enough to feed themselves. Fishing led to trade, which was fostered by a favorable geographical location. Gradually they overtook their competitors, especially the Hansa, and from then on they made rapid strides. The war with Spain created problems which could be met only by a still greater expansion of trade and shipping.[1] The fall of Antwerp to the Spanish infused the young republic with new blood: Flemish merchants and, even, whole industries escaped to the north. With this background, the Dutch were in a favorable position to try to wrest control of the Asiatic trade from the Spanish and Portuguese. But a few questions are still left unanswered. How could Holland and Zealand, with fewer than a million inhabitants, finance such a huge undertaking? And how

---

1. In 1596 the States General declared: "The general welfare of the country depends upon our dominion of the sea, and our conduct of the war in the waters." See Geyl, *Nederlandse stam, 1,* 311.

could their merchants protect themselves against the increased risks that were bound to result? The solution of both problems involved a new concept of business organization, and it is here that modern capitalism, based on private enterprise, found one of its earliest applications.

The circumstances which in the Middle Ages gave rise to the establishment of local guilds of tradesmen and artisans, also applied to merchants who traveled abroad. The main purpose of the guild was to provide mutual protection for a group of people who were engaged in the same type of business. A merchant encountered many dangers as soon as he left his town, and it was safer to travel in the company of others. Arriving at a market, it was equally necessary for merchants to stick together in order to protect themselves against the whims of local magistrates and the local lord of the land. Trade was generally encouraged because it was necessary and profitable, but there was no guarantee that certain privileges, once granted, might not be withdrawn if it so suited the authorities. Strength lay in the numbers and solidarity of association. A prime example was the English brotherhood of merchants which controlled the wool trade with the continent for several centuries.[2]

Among the privileges of the guilds was the right to settle differences among themselves according to the laws of their country and with judges of their own choosing. In matters having to do with the community, they were represented by a body of elders, elected by seniority. Besides safeguarding the lives and goods of its members, the guild kept close watch on the moral conduct of the individual merchants, enforced regulations pertaining to the quality of the goods, and, most significantly, guaranteed a livelihood to every one of its number. This was accomplished through a strict limitation on the quantity each merchant was permitted to sell. Among the English merchant adventurers, this so-called "stint of trade" was the object of constant vigilance. The quantity depended on a member's seniority. The longer he had been a brother, the greater his share became, but never more than that, because it was a firm rule that "the rich should not eat the poor." This spirit of brotherhood was carried so far that, if a merchant had been unable to sell his full allotment, the others

2. Edmundson, *Anglo-Dutch Rivalry*, appendix D. See also W. E. Lingelback, *The Merchant Adventurers of England, Their Laws and Ordinances* (Philadelphia, 1903).

were obliged to include the difference in their next year's quota.

To become a member of the guild, a man had to be highly recommended and serve a long apprenticeship as well. As long as he followed the rules, his progress was assured, and after many years he might become one of the elders, but even then his volume of business was limited. Upon his death, the advantages won during a lifetime could not be bequeathed to someone else. The system guaranteed a comfortable living, but it discouraged personal initiative and risk-taking. It had many of the characteristics of bureaucracy. In a static economic age, the guilds might have lasted even longer than they did, but they were unable to adjust to the rapid expansion of European trade during the sixteenth century. It is indicative that the English, with their veneration for old and tested institutions, adhered to the guilds longer than the Dutch.

With the political and economic configuration changing more rapidly on the continent of Europe, after the Middle Ages, than in England, a different system emerged. The formation of large political entities by absorption and consolidation of many principalities led to more stable conditions that were conducive to trade. This was especially true after the formation of the vast Burgundian–Austrian empire of which the Netherlands was a part. With the increase in commerce, new institutions appeared for the protection and regulation of overseas shipping. They were the admiralties, whose duty it was to enforce maritime law and to protect the shipping of all merchants, irrespective of the commodity they dealt in. The cost of this service was met by levying convoy duties on all vessels. Some of the functions of the earlier merchant guilds were thereby taken over by a central organization. It was a new concept, and it brought about further change.

The guilds had been an association of merchants, dealing in the same product, who lived in different towns. At home, they had practically no contact with each other, and it was not until they congregated at a common market place abroad that their organization became effective. The English merchants had their wool staple for a long time in Bruges, until it moved elsewhere on the continent, but never in England, and all decisions were made abroad. The Hansa had operated in a similar fashion. The new admiralties proved that it was possible to establish a central organization at home. Admiralties appeared in almost every country of western Europe, and Holland's, with that country's predominance in overseas trade, outranked them all. And in Holland another kind of organization was formed, the college, which brought about even greater cohesion in the various fields of commerce.

The College of Fisheries was among the earliest, but in time others were established to regulate trade with Bergen, Muscovy, and the Levant. These were quasi-official bodies operating under a decree from the States General. They prescribed measures for the safety of ship and cargo, such as the size and condition of the vessel, its gear, and the minimum crew required. There were also regulations for sailing in convoy and for carrying a specified number of guns as protection against an enemy or pirates. In time of war, the Colleges were allowed to fit out their own warships if they were headed for waters where the admiralties did not cruise. They also had the right to appoint consuls in foreign ports.[3]

Under these conditions, it was no longer necessary for a merchant to accompany his goods abroad. He could stay in his counting house, knowing that his interests were being safeguarded. This left him free to engage in as many operations as he wished, the more so in that he was not bound by any such restrictions as had been imposed by the earlier guilds. The regulations that did exist were for the protection of all trade, but it was up to the individual merchant to decide how much or how little he was willing to venture. Nor were the colleges concerned with a man's private life—something which had been of concern to the earlier guilds, where it had been important to present a respectable front before strangers. Morality-policing had, moreover, become irrelevant since a merchant no longer accompanied his goods. The colleges were equally indifferent as to a man's background, nor did he have to serve an apprenticeship. All that was required of him was that he pay his share of the levies and that his skipper abide by the rules. The personality of a merchant was no longer important, only the amount of business he did was.

Such a liberal attitude attracted many more people to overseas trade than had the old system. But with these incentives and opportunities, where did a man find funds sufficient to set him up in business? There were very few men in Holland during this period of expansion who were able to finance a costly undertaking that involved fitting out a ship and paying for the cargo as

3. S. van Brakel, *De Hollandsche handelscompagnien der zeventiende eeuw; hun ontstaan, hunne inrichting* (The Hague, 1908).

well. Finding the necessary capital was a primary difficulty, and the manner in which it was solved provided the beginning of the stock companies that were to become the foundation of modern capitalism. The medieval economy had little need for capital, as is exemplified by the merchant guilds, who stifled private initiative and competition. The rising Dutch took a different view: they were avid for as much trade as possible, and they had no fear of competition, because the demand for goods in the new economic age always seemed greater than the supply. The only thing that could hold a merchant back was a lack of capital. He could, of course, associate himself with others and engage in a joint venture; or he could persuade outsiders to put up the money, offering them a corresponding share of the profits. In either case, the participants risked only the amount they invested, and, after the voyage was over, the whole transaction could be liquidated by selling both cargo and vessel.

It is not surprising that, in a country so dependent upon the sea, the origin of the concept of limited liability can be found in shipping. From the earliest times, sea trade had been a risky business: ships were fragile, the seas almost entirely uncharted, and there were dangers of piracy and mutiny. These dangers forced a shipowner to limit his liability to the value of his ship and, if it had to be abandoned, for whatever reason, the crew lost all claim to wages. This principle was first known in Holland as *bodemerij*, and from this was derived the English word bottomry, a term still current in admiralty law. From this developed the concept of voluntary bottomry, which enabled a skipper to borrow money abroad if it were needed for repairs. A letter of bottomry would be executed, actually a mortgage on the vessel and/or the cargo. The money lender considered it a speculative investment because the premium was high, but it was also a means of transferring money, the letter of bottomry serving as a draft.[4]

This method gradually progressed to the point where a shipowner or merchant would accept money before departure from people who were anxious to participate in a promising venture. It was an important step forward because it opened new sources of capital among small merchants and tradesmen, willing to invest part of their savings without running the total risk. What most influenced these small investors was not the venture itself

4. W. M. F. Mansvelt, *Rechtsvorm en geldelijk beheer bij de Oost-Indische compagnie* (Amsterdam, 1922), pp. 42–43.

but the standing of the merchant behind it. If he had a reputation for making money, they would flock to his doorstep as soon as it was known that he was organizing another voyage. Such voyages became known as "ventures on parts." The parts were in varying amounts, some recorded as small as $\frac{1}{192}$, which made it possible for people of modest means to participate. This type of investment was already well established in the fifteenth century, as probate records of Amsterdam show. Of about 1,100 legacies recorded, 147 contained parts in ships.[5]

The system had its drawbacks. By the middle of the sixteenth century, it had developed to such an extent that owners and merchants could borrow on ship and cargo to their full value, even before the voyage had begun. This was considered a dangerous procedure because there was evidence that it led to neglect of hull and gear. In 1549, Charles V prohibited voluntary bottomry completely, though the prohibition proved impossible to enforce. Entrepreneurs and investors had found each other, and the age of modern capitalism was slowly dawning.

The "ventures on parts" were indeed the forerunners of the stock companies. Parts could be bought and sold in the open market, and by the end of the sixteenth century they were being replaced by shares of a fixed denomination. Out of this grew the corporation, the company with limited liability, the "nameless" company. They were nameless because capital took over the function which had previously been exercised by individuals. Management, to be sure, was in the hands of directors who might or might not have a financial interest in the company but as individuals they were no longer crucial. They could be replaced by others if the occasion arose. It was this transition from person to capital that marked the beginning of a new economic era: the impersonal or nameless element of capital now provided the driving force. At the same time it made for continuity, because companies were organized for a number of years rather than for a single voyage. And all the while the capital remained in the company. Stocks could be sold but not withdrawn.

The advantages of this type of financing hardly need elaboration. It is still the mainstay of financial undertakings in free societies, except for those undertakings so large and of such national interest that only governments are able to finance them. For the Dutch, it solved the problem of financing an expanding economy,

5. Van Brakel, *Handelscompagnien.*

enabling them to undertake ventures greater than ever before. A striking example of this is presented by the United East India Company, which was formed in 1602 with a capital of about 6.5 million guilders.

By spreading the cost of a voyage among a number of people, the individual risk was proportionately reduced, but it still left the investors liable if the ship failed to return. Marine insurance was the answer. There is evidence that it was already an established practice in the Middle Ages. Insurance contracts were registered in Bruges as early as the fourteenth century.[6] Since insurance is a refined form of gambling, that might have been its origin. The unpredictable outcome of a voyage offered an opportunity for speculation on its success or failure. For the participants, it was a means of protecting their investment, insuring it, and the underwriters were attracted by the elements of chance and profit. An old Dutch saying aptly describes the procedure: "In case of loss the insurer steps into the shoes of the insured."[7]

The rates were high by modern standards, running from four to five per cent in peacetime and up to 15 per cent during war. The insurance business became so well organized in Holland that English owners often preferred to insure themselves there, even when the rates were higher. The Dutch settled claims more promptly; in England each underwriter had to be sued individually, and proof of loss was likely to be demanded as well. On the other hand, Dutch underwriters were known on occasion to have spread false rumors about pirates, thus driving up the rates.

There remains another factor to be considered in the developments that were pushing the Dutch towards empire. With business widening in scope and becoming more complex, a merchant could no longer rely on his memory and his notebook to tell him where he stood, especially if he was engaged in a number of ventures at the same time. What he needed was a method whereby all his transactions could be reduced to a set of figures. The solution was bookkeeping. With the passing of time, the word has lost much of its original luster; it was once looked upon as a great scientific development. It is indicative of the great need for it that it so soon reached a stage of near-perfection. With the introduction of double entry, or Italian, bookkeeping, the science was firmly established.

6. Diferee, *Nederlandschen handel*, p. 65.
7. Mansvelt, *Rechtsvorm*, pp. 40–42.

As the name implies, it originated in Italy where it had been used long before the first book on the subject was published in Venice by Luca Pacioli in the year 1494. It was appropriately entitled, *Everything about Arithmetic, Geometry, and Proportion*. The first Dutchman to write about it was Gemma Frisius, an astronomer whose name has been perpetuated on the moon. His *Practical Arithmetic* was published in 1540. Three years later the first book on the subject in Dutch appeared. It was from the hand of Master Impyn of Antwerp, who stated that he had learned the art of double-entry bookkeeping in Italy, where he had lived for twelve years.[8]

As far as is known, these two works were the only ones available in their field for some time, but towards the end of the century there were many more. When Elcius Mellema, the son of a mayor of Leeuwarden, published his *Bookkeeping in the Italian Manner*, he gave credit to no less than fifteen previous authors on the subject. This interest kept pace with the upsurge of economic activity, and the art of bookkeeping became an indispensable tool. During the following decades, many more books on the subject appeared, one particularly worthy of note because the name of the author was to become a byword in the Dutch language. It was the *Cyferinghe (Computations)* of Bartjens. When a Dutchman now says that something is "according to Bartjens," he means that it is beyond dispute.

The incentive behind all this activity was of course the profit motive, but there were other inducements. Every aggressive Dutchman aspired to be a merchant, not only to achieve freedom from physical labor, but also to rise to honor and respect. At no other time in history had a merchant class reached so high a social level as that which it occupied in the Lowlands during this period. What the landed gentry, the nobility, and the high clergy were in other European countries, the merchants were in Holland and Zealand. And their position did not depend on the whim of a sovereign. Any man could try to enter this class. Any man might, by careful planning, audacity, and luck, become one of the great merchants to whom the highest magisterial offices of the town were available.

The merchants did not hesitate to elevate their status: their vocation lacked trappings—a counting house is not to be compared with a manor. Sons and grandsons bought land and ap-

8. Ibid., pp. 22 ff.

propriated a title, often adopting a coat of arms based on the sign which had once adorned the façade of the family's place of business. They were no longer interested in risky ventures, preferring to invest their money in bonds and land. Some became eminent lawyers and statesmen, serving their country well on numerous occasions. They were the men who, in Amsterdam, built stately homes along the canals and, as regents, were responsible for the new city hall that was known there as the eighth wonder of the world. They patronized the arts and had their portraits painted, singly and in groups, by Rembrandt, Van der Helst, and others. They presided, in fact, over Holland's Golden Age.

But their fathers and grandfathers, the merchants, had established the foundation for this illustrious period during the few decades they were in power. And it was then that they launched their greatest venture: the beginning of an empire in Asia.

8

Three
Merchants
and a Minister

It was not until 1592 that the Dutch began to consider the possibilities of going directly to the Indies, and even then it took several more years before their plans could be put into effect. Why they waited so long needs to be explained, especially since the English had already been there twice in the persons of Drake and Cavendish. To the English, the seas were primarily a source of loot: the Spanish spoke of the English as *piratas* while they called the Dutch simply *rebeldes*.[1] For booty, the English were willing to go to the ends of the earth, but the Dutch, though they did not scorn a windfall, had learned from long experience that this did not provide a regular source of income. Besides, they had always been guided by the maxim, "cost comes before gain."

To the Dutch the East Indies meant only one thing: spices. But they had always made a profit on spices by going no farther than Portugal, and until 1580, Lisbon had been completely open to them. The Portuguese, in fact, had encouraged the Dutch to trade in their country, by granting them many privileges. They were guaranteed safety of person and property, they had their own judges for settling disputes among themselves, and they were allowed freedom of religion within their own quarter. The Portuguese even went as far as to prohibit the re-export of spices to their own merchants and thus reserved this trade exclusively for the foreigners. There was only one restriction: no foreign ship was allowed to sail to the Indies. The penalty was confiscation of the ship and committal of the crew to a lifetime in the galleys. The Dutch had carefully weighed the issue. By going directly to the source, profits would undoubtedly be greater, but the risks and costs would also increase proportionately. The route itself

1. W. W. Hunter, *A History of British India*, 1 (London, Longmans, Green, 1919), 85–86.

was almost completely unknown. Not a single Dutchman had yet set foot in the Indies.

The Portuguese had guarded their secrets well, and there were severe penalties for any of their sailors who tried to pass information to a foreigner. It had taken them a very long time to get there themselves, and they had no intention of letting others benefit from their endeavors. Under the guidance of Prince Henry the Navigator,[2] they had started to explore the west coast of Africa but by the time of his death in 1460, they had reached no farther than Sierra Leone, thus progressing no more than 18° latitude during some forty years. It took another twenty-six years before Bartolomeu Dias succeeded in rounding the southernmost tip of Africa. He called it the Cape of Storms, but his master John II named it the Cape of Good Hope, because the route to the Indies seemed at long last within reach. It was not until 1498 that Vasco da Gama finally reached the coast of India by continuous sea voyage.

To try to discourage others, the Portuguese painted a gruesome picture of the dangers attending a voyage to the Indies. Many of the reported details were, of course, exaggerated, but Dutch sailors had seen with their own eyes in what deplorable condition both ships and crews often returned to Lisbon. The hulls were encrusted with barnacles and long beards of marine growth sprouted from the sides. Some ships were fairly honeycombed by *teredos* (shipworms) and felt so spongy to the touch that it was a wonder the ships had held together. Of the crews, many died en route, and the survivors were invariably in a sad state from disease and privations such as the Dutch had never had to endure in northern coastal waters.

The financial risk also kept the Dutch from making an early attempt. It took large amounts of money to fit out a few ships which, under the most favorable conditions, would need several years to make the round trip. The merchants were cautious, and most still had only limited means. A combination of merchants could accomplish it, aided by a number of small investors, but the latter were even less inclined than the merchants to put their money into a dubious venture.

2. Ibid., pp. 61–77. Many books have been written about this precursor of the Age of Discovery, and still more can be expected as a result of the prize offered by the Portuguese government for his biography, to commemorate his death in the year 1460.

All these reasons seemed strong enough to deter the Dutch, but events were coming that forced them to appraise the situation anew. Philip had annexed Portugal, creating difficulties for the Dutch at Lisbon. Elizabeth, through Leicester, had tried to make the Dutch abandon all trade with the enemy. English captains, more daring after the defeat of the Armada, proceeded to harass the Spanish wherever they could, and in the absence of enemy vessels they had no qualms about boarding Dutch ships on the pretext that they might be carrying contraband. Important names in English naval history participated in this piracy: Grenfell, Martin Frobisher, Mansfield, and others. The States General protested vehemently against this practice but, though Elizabeth promised relief, redress was extremely slow, and Caron, the Dutch ambassador, was sent from pillar to post.

The Amsterdam merchants suffered most from these adversities, and some of them began to consider the possibilities of going directly to the Spice Islands. Bypassing Lisbon was rapidly becoming a matter of necessity, if they did not want to lose the lucrative spice trade which had fallen to them after the capture of Antwerp. The prospect of such a loss was hard for these profit-minded men to contemplate. With the influx of silver into western Europe from the Spanish Americas, the standard of living was rising everywhere, and with it had come an increased demand for spices and other luxury goods.

The earliest plan was set in motion by three merchants who had been prodded into action by a refugee from the south. The three merchants were Jan Jansz. Carel, Hendrik Hudde, and Reynier Pauw.[3]

Carel had become a burgher of Amsterdam in 1578, after the Alteration, when he established himself as a dealer in dairy products. He was soon important enough to become purveyor to the household of William of Orange. Exporting cheese and butter to Spain and Portugal, he had become interested in the spice trade and wanted to go directly to the source. In time his business expanded considerably, and the records show that he traded throughout the Mediterranean, the Baltic, and, eventually, the West Indies as well. In 1592, he was in his forties.

Hendrik Hudde was about the same age as Carel. His father had been a merchant in grain from the Baltic, and one of the

3. For additional biographical data on Carel, Hudde, and Pauw, see Elias, *Vroedschap.*

wealthiest men in Amsterdam. Having become an ardent Protestant, the elder Hudde had been forced to flee and spend ten years in exile. Hendrik returned with his father after the Alteration and took over the grain business, which was located in a house called The Three Kings.

Reynier Pauw came from a well-to-do family in Gouda. His father, like many others in the provinces, had been attracted by the opportunities a town like Amsterdam offered an ambitious young man. Arriving with a little capital, he soon engaged in a number of activities, but his main business was, like Hudde's, grain. He became factor in Holland for the King of Denmark and was thus a man of considerable importance. Since he was also a leader in the Calvinist movement, he, too, had been forced to flee when the troubles broke out, taking along his whole family, including the four-year-old Reynier.

In the year of action, 1592, Reynier Pauw was twenty-eight years old, the youngest of the three merchants, but judging from later accomplishments, he might well have been the instigator of the original plan. He was well established as a merchant in lumber and salt. He was also active in the town government, having been appointed alderman in 1590 and member of the council the following year. Greater honors were in store for him. In the end, he held the Magnificat of Amsterdam in his hands. He was to become the epitome of the merchant class: energetic, unpretentious, and aggressive to the point of ruthlessness.

Both Hudde and Pauw lived in the Warmoesstraat, which was the name given to the first dike thrown up on the right bank of the Amstel and which indicated that at one time there had been truck gardens on the land side. Carel had his house on the nearby Dam. There must have been a good deal of furtive coming and going when the three merchants laid their plans, which were, at first, little more than secret investigations. They were prodded into taking action by the appearance, earlier that year, of charts that purported to show the route to the East Indies.

The man who had produced the charts was Petrus Plancius, a Protestant theologian and a student of cartography and navigation.[4] He was born in 1552 in Dranoutre, a small village on the French border. His father must have been quite well off, for he was able to send his son abroad to acquire the best education

4. See J. Keuning, *Petrus Plancius, theoloog en geograaf, 1552–1622* (Amsterdam, Van Kampen, 1946).

available. Peter Platevoet, as he was called before he Latinized
his name, studied in Germany and England. His main subjects
were theology, history, and languages, but he also delved into
mathematics, geography, and astronomy. He undoubtedly had a
brilliant mind, but his drive to acquire as much knowledge as
he could and thereby excel his fellow men may well have been
fostered by his affliction: he was a hunchback. A late portrait
shows him in the customary tight-fitting skullcap, with full
beard and moustache. It is not an unkindly face, but the raised
eyebrows and the deep creases across his high forehead give him
a somewhat contemptuous expression, almost an expression of
sardonic pity, as it were, for anyone who might disagree with
him. His many quarrels during a long lifetime prove that he
had this trait to a marked degree, especially when the matter
touched on was theology. He was an uncompromising Calvinist
who preached predestination, and that man must accept as his due
whatever God willed him to be. His God was a wrathful God,
who constantly watched from above and meted out punishment
to whoever deviated from the straight and narrow path. A more
liberal religious belief was gradually finding acceptance in the
Lowlands. It was opposed to the doctrine of predestination, and
preached tolerance for all creeds, even the Catholic. Plancius
would accept none of this, and from his pulpit he denounced the
movement. In the years to come, these religious differences would
increase in intensity until they finally threatened the unity of
the republic itself, and in these bitter feuds Plancius became the
leader of the irreconcilables.[5]

It seems difficult to reconcile such fanaticism with the fact
that Plancius was also a great scientist. Perhaps it can only be
explained by the sufferings he had witnessed as a dedicated disciple
of the new gospel in his homeland. Baudartius, a contemporary
theologian, wrote that Plancius preached night after night in
different towns and villages which were not always close together.
For this work, he never asked a penny, paying all expenses out
of his own pocket. Quite a few members of his congregation had
been burned alive, and he would have suffered the same lot if
he had not managed to elude his persecutors. His library was
confiscated and burned publicly in Ypres. After Brussels had
fallen to Parma, Plancius realized that the cause in the south was
lost, and he fled the country. His name had preceded him, and

5. See Geyl, *Netherlands Divided*, p. 50.

he was soon called to Amsterdam, first to preach a few sermons as a test of his qualifications. By the end of 1585, his appointment was confirmed.

Plancius was then thirty-three years old, and it would be several more years before he was able to prove that he was interested in something else besides the word of God. He was not always able to keep the two sides of his nature in their proper places. In later years, one of his opponents, Cunaeus of Leiden, had something to say about this. "I have been told," he wrote Plancius, "that you frequently climb into the pulpit without having properly prepared your sermon. You switch then to subjects which have nothing to do with religion. You talk as a geographer about the Indies and the New World, or you discuss the stars. And if this no longer suits your fancy you turn upon Leyden and curse our professors." [6]

His first attempt at cartography came in 1590 when he supplied five maps for a Bible. According to the printer, Laurens Jacobszoon, their purpose was "to acquaint the reader with the location of all the countries and places mentioned in the Old and New Testament." But one of the maps supplied by Plancius obviously went beyond this. It was entitled, "A portrayal of the whole world, corrected in many places." Actually, it was little more than a copy of a late Mercator map published a few years earlier by the famous cartographer who had first become interested in this science through Gemma Frisius.

The first important work Plancius did in this field was his large map of the world, which he presented to the States General on April 15, 1592, and for which he received a gratuity of 300 guilders. The printer Cornelis Claesz. of Amsterdam obtained for this map a copyright for twelve years. The map was grandly entitled, "A geographical and hydrographical map of the whole world, showing all countries, towns, places and seas under their respective degrees of longitude and latitude; capes, promontories, headlands, ports, shoals, sandbanks and cliffs are drawn in the most accurate manner." At the bottom appeared 16 columns of text, "a short explanation of the characteristics of the lands and the people." [7]

At the same time Cornelis Claesz. petitioned for a copyright covering no less than 25 additional maps which he had obtained

6. Keuning, *Petrus Plancius*, p. 26.
7. Ibid., p. 77.

"through Dominie Peter Plancius from Bartolomeo de Lasso, cosmographer and master of navigation for the King of Spain." [8] The petition further states that: "He has also obtained a clear description in the Spanish language, showing the secrets of the route to the East and West Indies, Africa, China and similar countries, including the peculiarities of the people, fruits, and other mercantile products."

It would be interesting to know how Plancius had managed to collect all this information at a time when those "secrets" were jealously guarded by the Spanish and Portuguese. Could it be that, even then, a brotherhood of scientists rebelled against political regulation that hampered a free exchange of knowledge?

As a result of this sudden windfall of charts and sailing directions, lack of knowledge could no longer serve as a reason for postponing a direct voyage to the Indies. Though the three merchants realized the need for action lest they be defeated by competitors, they were not yet prepared to take the first step. As appears from subsequent documents, they first wanted to "obtain additional secret information about trade in the East Indies and the Moluccas, by sending a certain person to Lisbon . . . to safeguard his person, a few people provided him with goods so that he be taken for a merchant." [9]

We know now who these "few people" were and that it was Reynier Pauw who provided the agent. The agent was his cousin, Cornelis de Houtman, who was to check the data Plancius had obtained and to try to ferret out anything else he could. The learned dominie had participated in their discussions, and from this time on he was the trusted consultant for the Amsterdam merchants on all matters dealing with navigation.

Houtman left on his mission in the summer of 1592 and returned safely after more than two years. To the extent that he had been able to maintain his disguise, he accomplished his mission, but the information he gleaned added nothing to what the Dutch had already obtained from another source during his absence.

8. Ibid., p. 83.
9. J. K. J. de Jonge, *De Opkomst van het nederlandsch gezag in Oost-Indie*, 1 (The Hague, 1862), 254.

9

Linschoten and His Itinerary

At the time Houtman left for Lisbon, Jan Huyghen van Linschoten was on the last leg of his voyage home after a lengthy stay in Goa. He was in his late twenties, and both his head and his notebooks were crammed with all he had seen and heard. He arrived in September, 1592. It was his massive amount of information that fairly pushed the Dutch into a series of ventures which charted the way to empire.

Linschoten was not the first Hollander to return home with an eyewitness report. A certain Dirck Gerritsz. Pomp had preceded him by a year or two. But it was the information that mattered, not the date. The two men had actually left Goa in 1589 on the same Portuguese ship, but Linschoten had stayed on the Azores to earn some money by assisting a merchant from Antwerp. Pomp, on the other hand, had done quite well for himself and had sailed straight home. As a boy of eleven he had gone to Lisbon, where he had two married aunts. He apparently liked it there well enough to stay, and, at the age of twenty-four he entered Portuguese service in the Indies, serving in minor capacities, such as cannoneer or constable. He managed to do a little trading, and during his twenty years there, did much traveling, twice going as far as to China and Japan. After an absence of thirty-five years, his birthplace, Enkhuizen, received him with open arms and the people listened in awe to all the fabulous stories he had to tell. Soon they began calling him Dirck Gerritsz. China, and this name stuck to him until his death. He was not the kind of man to write a book about his experiences, but he was a great talker, and some of the matter of his stories got into print. But, all told, it was not very important, especially when compared with the wealth of information his former shipmate had collected.[1]

Jan Huyghen van Linschoten was born in 1563 in Haarlem, where his father was an innkeeper. His mother had been married before to a man named Tin by whom she had had two sons. Before Jan was ten years old, the family moved to Enkhuizen, a thriving town which, together with Hoorn, had benefited, at the expense of Amsterdam, from the expansion of trade during the first decade of the rebellion. It is not impossible that Jan's mother was the instigator of the move. Dutch women were strong-minded, and those from Haarlem, in particular, had proved that they could hold ther own with any man. During the long siege later known as the Blood Bath of Haarlem, the women fought shoulder to shoulder with the men. They had their own battalion under Kenau Hasselaar, a respectable widow close to fifty years of age. When the town was half starved out and the Spaniards managed to scale the walls, the women were on the ramparts till the last, pitching burning tar hoops around the heads of the attackers and pouring hot sand and boiling oil down their necks.[2]

Bustling Enkhuizen, with ships arriving almost daily from foreign lands, must have given the boy the wanderlust, as much as his two stepbrothers. Their mother was not one to keep them tied to her apron strings. The two older boys were the first to leave, having set their minds on Spain. When Jan was sixteen he joined them at Seville. He later wrote: "With their help I wanted to get some experience about that country and a knowledge of the language." He arrived just when Philip II had concluded the annexation of Portugal. One of his brothers managed to find a place for him in the retinue of a Spanish grandee who was traveling to Lisbon to gain what advantage he could from the new political situation.

As already noted, the joining of the two countries would soon begin to hamper Dutch trade with Lisbon and, as a result, force the merchants to consider going directly to the Indies. It was this same event that enabled Linschoten to gather the necessary information that was to accelerate the process. One of his two brothers died in an epidemic, but the other, Willem Tin, went

1. J. W. IJzerman, *Dirck Gerritsz. Pomp, alias Dirck Gerritsz. China, 1544–1604* (The Hague, 1915).
2. J. L. Motley, *The Rise of the Dutch Republic,* 2 (London, 1856), 363–88. See also Blok, *Geschiedenis, 3,* 117–20.

along to Lisbon. Willem was apparently a resourceful young man. When he learned that a new archbishop had been appointed to Goa he wangled the job of *escrivao*, or clerk, for himself and succeeded in having his young brother taken along in a minor capacity.

The ships carrying Dom Frei Vincente da Fonseca and his retinue to Goa left Lisbon in April 1583, and more than nine years were to elapse before Jan returned to his native land. Nowhere in his subsequent writings does he show that he had any ulterior motives in collecting the wealth of information that eventually appeared in his *Itinerary*. All he wanted to do was to tell his story and let his countrymen know what strange and wonderful things he had encountered. Others, especially the merchants in Amsterdam, would carefully screen this data, and decide how it could best be used.

When Linschoten at last returned to Enkhuizen in September 1592, he found many changes, but was glad to report that "mother, brother, and sister were in good health." The town surgeon was Berent ten Broecke, better known as Bernardus Paludanus. He, too, had traveled a great deal, in Europe, the eastern Mediterranean, Turkey, Syria, the Holy Land, and Egypt. He had received a degree in medicine in Padua and in 1586 settled in Enkhuizen. He was then already a man of some renown, because of the rarities he had brought back from his travels. One was a lump of flesh-colored earth he had picked up in Damascus, "the very same earth from which Adam had been fashioned." He kept adding to his collection, and in time his chamber of rarities became famous throughout Europe. Nothing was more natural than that Paludanus should have taken Linschoten under his wing, and before long the two were collaborating on the *Itinerary*.[3]

The full title of this work was *Itinerario, Voyage, or Passage by Jan Huyghen van Linschoten to East or Portugal's India*. It was a monumental work, covering just about every aspect of India conceivable in that period, and India was then thought to cover a far larger area than it is now known. With Goa as its focal point (according to the *Itinerary*), India stretched westward as far as Prester John's Land (Ethiopia). It included all of southeast Asia, and it was only grudgingly admitted that China and Japan might have to be excluded. All of the East India

3. W. J. van Balen, *Naar de Indische wonderwereld, met Jan Huyghen van Linschoten* (Amsterdam, 1942), pp. 12–13.

archipelago fell within its boundaries: Sumatra, Java, and the Spice Islands. Linschoten had a great deal to say about all these lands. He himself had never been further than Goa, but every traveler in that vast territory was bound to arrive in Goa sooner or later, and the inquisitive Hollander had been adept at acquiring information. Republished in modern times with annotations by later historians, the *Itinerary* comprises no less than five heavy volumes.[4]

It is impossible to review such a vast amount of material in a few paragraphs, but we should look at certain bits of information that the Dutch merchants considered sufficiently important to warrant plans for direct trade with the Indies. They knew very well, for example, what goods they wanted to buy—spices first and foremost—but what should they send in return? Linschoten provided the answer: Ships leaving Lisbon carry little cargo, only a few casks of oil and wine; the rest is ballast and victuals. The most important item they carry is bullion, chests with "pieces of eight." These coins, which the Spaniards struck from the ever increasing supply of silver from Mexico and Peru, had become legal tender throughout the known world. This was welcome news since the Dutch received a steady flow of *reals* in payment for goods the Spanish could buy only from them. This silver had fed the rebellion, and, ironically enough, it could now also be used to compete with the enemy in the Indies.

From what the Dutch had been able to learn about the route, the first stretch, to the Cape of Good Hope, presented the greatest difficulties, because of the doldrums off the African coast. Ships had been known to drift on a leaden sea for months on end while their crews were decimated by scurvy. Linschoten reported that the Portuguese sailed across the Atlantic as far as the Abrolhos under the coast of Brazil and then altered their course towards the Cape. Experience had proved that this route lessened the chances of becoming becalmed. Scurvy remained the scourge of every long voyage, and the ships "refreshed" wherever they could. The sick were taken ashore to regain their strength, and if possible, fresh water was taken on board, and, if available, vegetables, oranges, and limes. Linschoten knew all the suitable places for refreshing, from the Canary Islands to the Cape and beyond

4. *Itinerario: Voyage ofte schipvaert van Jan Huyghen van Linschoten naer oost ofte Portugaels Indiën, 1579-1592* (The Hague, 1910-39). All quotations from Linschoten in this chapter have been taken from this work.

to Sao Lourenço (Madagascar). He also provided sailing directions for use in the Indian Ocean: what time of the year was best for going between Madagascar and the African Coast, when it was safer to stay east of the island, etc.

He had noticed the lack of discipline on Portuguese vessels and the fact that their seamanship often left much to be desired: "most of the crew are inexperienced people who have never before been to sea." Nor was he impressed by the conditions he found in Goa. Although it was the capital of the Portuguese empire in Asia, seat of the viceroy and the archbishop, the defenses were badly neglected, and he was told that this was true of other settlements. Everyone, from the viceroy down, seemed interested mainly in making his fortune and returning with it to Portugal. For some, apparently, the opportunity to do so was readily at hand, but Linschoten laments the fact that he is unable to do the same. "If only I had a hundred ducats," he wrote, "I could easily make six or seven times that much. But to try it with empty hands is impossible." From these and other observations, Linschoten reached the conclusion that the Portuguese had lost much of their former prowess: "They do not seem to have much stomach for fighting any more, nor do they want to discover and conquer new lands, the way they did in years past. Everyone, including the clergy, is out for himself and little heed is given to the welfare of the country and the King's service."

About Malacca, the Portuguese stronghold on the west coast of the Malay Peninsula, Linschoten had a great deal to say. He had obtained his information from Gerrit van Afhuysen, a former factor of the pepper there who was originally from Antwerp. Afhuysen called it the "crossroads of the farther Indies, where all goods are collected from the whole area before they are shipped to Lisbon via Goa." There were pepper from Sumatra, cloves from the Moluccas, nutmeg and mace from the Banda group. From China and Japan came silk and porcelain, gathered at Macao. Because of Malaya's central location, the Malay language "is useful throughout the whole of the Indies." The three Amsterdam merchants took note of this information and sent word to Houtman in Lisbon to engage a few persons who were "proficient in the Malay language." Houtman, however, was unable to fulfill their request.

Across the Strait of Malacca was the island of Sumatra where pepper grew. The Portuguese had no factors there, one of the reasons being that the King of Achin was "very powerful and their arch-enemy." After they had finally reached the Indies, the Dutch tried for years to cultivate his friendship, but the king had as little use for them as he had had for the Portuguese. Cornelis Houtman was to find this out at the cost of his life.

"The Island is very rich in mines of Gold and Silver. . . . there is a well flowing over with pure balsam." This balsam was highly inflammable and called naphta by the Arab traders. The Portuguese said it was a remedy against rheumatism. Linschoten's commentary goes on: "Cloves are found exclusively in the five islands of the Moluccas. The flowers are at first white, then turn green and finally yellow. At this stage they are picked, dried and smoked, which turns them black." He warned that cloves attract moisture and thus become heavier when placed near water. The Dutch had cause to remember this, because it was a favorite trick of native merchants and it caused spoilage in transit. "The women," he added, "chew cloves to keep their breath clean."

"The nutmeg tree looks like a pear tree, and the islands where they grow are as unhealthy as the Moluccas. Many who trade there die, but regardless of the perils of illness and death, the profits to be made there make them go back just the same." This information about the perils of the Spice Islands had, of course, been circulated by the Portuguese in order to discourage trespassers.

The learned Dr. Paludanus made many contributions to the *Itinerary*, and his style, where Linschoten is simple and straightforward, is wordy and bombastic, and he misses no opportunity to inform the reader that he, too, has traveled far. Furthermore, having a degree from the University of Padua, he considers himself particularly qualified to set down the therapeutic qualities of the various spices. According to the doctor,

> Cinnamon warms, opens, and tones up the intestines. It is good for catarrh, making it move down from the head to the lower parts. It cures dropsy as well as defects and obstructions in the kidneys. Oil of cinnamon strengthens all organs: heart, stomach, liver, etc. . . . [Nutmegs] fortify the brain and sharpen the memory; they warm the stomach and expel winds. They give a clean breath, force the urine, stop diarrhea, and cure upset stomachs.

These, and the many other claims he made, in an age when man's organs and bodily functions were almost entirely unknown, were not lightly dismissed. The doctor of Enkhuizen firmly believed everything he claimed for these spices, and so did his audience. After the *Itinerary* had been translated into several languages, his nostrums became trusted throughout Europe, and, by that time, the Dutch had an effective monopoly in the spice trade. Linschoten reported that no more than five ships a year sailed from Goa to Lisbon, and what they carried in spices had been enough to supply the demand. What would happen if many times that quantity reached the European market? The Dutch were able to solve this problem by eliminating competition among themselves and by stern measures in the producing areas. This would not have prevented a glut on the market, however, if the demand had not also increased many times over, and for this stimulation, some of the credit should go to Dr. Paludanus.

From a historical point of view, perhaps nothing is more important than what Linschoten had to say about Java:

> This Island is abundant in rice and all other victuals. The principal port is Sunda Kalapa which gave the name to Strait Sunda. In this place there is much pepper. It also has cloves, nutmegs and mace. Here one can trade without any interference because the Portuguese do not go there, as the Javanese themselves carry their goods to Malacca.

There was a great deal more, but these were the main points which made the Dutch set their course for this particular spot. When they finally reached it, they liked it well enough to make it the focal point of their activities.

Although the complete *Itinerary* was not published until 1596, the part dealing with the route to the Indies had already been printed in advance. Even before that, the Amsterdam merchants must have known a great deal about its subject matter through Plancius, whom Linschoten met soon after his return in 1592. Considering the fact that more than two years were to elapse before their ships set sail for the Indies, we can assume that the merchants would not be rushed into a major venture merely on the testimony of a young man who had never been farther east than Goa. It was also consistent with their cautious approach to the matter to do nothing until Cornelis Houtman had returned from Lisbon. This delayed the first attempt to reach the Indies via the Cape of Good Hope, but there were other plans afoot to try to get there by a different route.

Linschoten's *Itinerary* soon became a best seller.[5] A second edition followed in short order, and within two years it was translated into English and German. There were also editions in Latin and French. Within a few years, all of western Europe knew as much about the Indies as the Dutch, and it is hardly surprising that the desire was aroused in many countries to profit from this knowledge. This widespread interest was a by-product of the *Itinerary* which confronted the Dutch even before they reached the Indies themselves.

5. The name Linschoten has been perpetuated in the *Linschoten Vereeniging,* a society established in 1908 for the purpose of publishing original accounts of Dutch voyages. It is the Dutch counterpart of the English Hakluyt Society

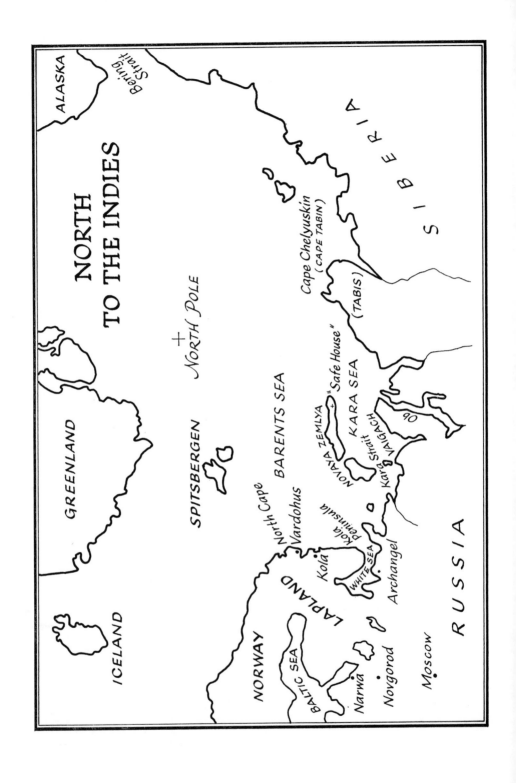

NORTH
TO THE INDIES

NORTH POLE

GREENLAND

ICELAND

SPITSBERGEN

BARENTS SEA

North Cape
Vardøhus

NORWAY

LAPLAND

Kola
Kola Peninsula
WHITE SEA
Archangel

BALTIC SEA

Narwa
Novgorod
Moscow

RUSSIA

NOVAYA ZEMLYA
"Safe House"
KARA SEA
Kara Strait
VAIGACH
OB

Cape Chelyuskin
(CAPE TABIN)

(TABIS)

SIBERIA

ALASKA
Bering Strait

IO

North to
the Indies

Columbus died convinced that he had discovered the sea route to the Indies. Others were not quite so sanguine, and before long a few attempts were made to find a passage further north. The first to try was John Cabot, an Italian in the service of the English. He was followed a few years later by the Cortereal brothers of Portugal. Both attempts were failures, but the Portuguese spread the word that they had reached Japan and China via the northwest and had returned by the same route, all in a single summer.[1] The Dutch were not impressed. They had no evidence that the Portuguese were using this "easy" route in preference to the long voyage around the Cape of Good Hope.

Influential people in Enkhuizen bore these facts in mind after their interest in a northern passage to the Indies had been aroused. Linschoten had spoken about the island of Japan. "It is a cold land with much rain, snow and also ice," he reported. Since this would correspond with the winter climate of Holland, it was reasoned that Japan was located at about the same latitude. Their townsman, Dirck Gerritsz. China, had twice traveled from Goa to Japan without much difficulty. Thus, all of the Indies would lie open once Japan had been reached; all that seemed to be involved was to sail north and then east. At no time had the Dutch seriously considered a northwest passage. Henry Hudson's voyage is not really an exception, because the English navigator had reached the shores of North America only by disobeying orders from his Dutch employers.[2]

The Dutch were not the first to explore the northeastern waters. Around the middle of the century, the English had formed what was called The Mystery, Company, and Fellowship of Merchant Adventurers for Discovery of Unknown Lands. In

1. V. Stefansson, *Great Adventures and Explorations* (New York, 1947), pp. 143–48.
2. W. J. van Balen, *Nederlands voorhoede* (Amsterdam, 1941), pp. 71–73.

79

1553 this company sent out three ships under Sir Hugh Willoughby and Richard Chancellor. Two of the ships foundered on the coast of Lapland with the loss of all hands, including Willoughby. Chancellor managed to enter the White Sea and from there traveled overland to Moscow. To his disappointment, he found the Dutch already thoroughly entrenched there in the fur trade. This was a normal extension of Dutch trade in the Baltic. Narwa had been the most northerly port their ships frequented, and from there it was a simple matter to reach Moscow via Novgorod. Chancellor, however, succeeded in obtaining valuable privileges for trading in the White Sea. As a result, the English formed the Muscovy Company, which soon developed a thriving trade in furs, whale oil, walrus teeth, and crystal.[3] The Dutch merchants disliked nothing so much as to see any kind of business pass them by, and, before long, their ships, too, appeared on the coast of Lapland, much to the displeasure of the English.

In the meantime, another Englishman, Stephen Burrough, had sailed further east, between Novaya Zemlya and the Island of Vaigach. This was the Kara Strait, leading into the Kara Sea, and it was optimistically assumed to be the gateway to the Indies, particularly since Burrough had found open water. The prevailing concept of the polar region was still based on the writings of ancient historians, whose opinions carried considerable weight with the learned men of the sixteenth century. Pliny the Elder had spoken of a circular sea at the top of the world and a land called Tabis that penetrated this sea in the far north. To the east of this land was an opening which connected the Polar Sea with the great ocean where Cipango, Cathay, and the Indies lay.[4] Considering the fact that all this was probably a figment of Pliny's imagination, it is quite remarkable that his assumptions are so close to reality. The Polar Sea is actually there, and it is connected with the Pacific Ocean by the Bering Strait. The land Tabis is the present Cape Chelyuskin, and it became the goal of every navigator who tried to find a northeast passage. To reach Tabis one had only to sail through the Kara Sea, and, once Cape Tabin had been rounded, the journey was as good as accomplished.

3. K. W. L. Bezemer, "Ter zee en te land in het hooge Noorden," in C. W. Wormser, ed., Nederland in de vijf Werelddeelen (Leiden, 1947), pp. 63–69.

4. S. Muller Fzn., De Reizen der Nederlanders naar de Noordpool (Haarlem, 1877), p. 2.

All this had fired the imagination of a resourceful young man from Brussels, Oliver Brunel. Entirely on his own, he managed to reach the Kola Peninsula in 1558 and intended to sail further east on a Russian boat. The English, already incensed by the appearance of Dutch ships on this coast, denounced him to the Russians as a spy. Since by his own admission he had come to these parts for the sole purpose of investigating a possible route, the Russians threw him into prison. The incident is one of the early examples of Dutch–English commercial rivalry that went beyond mere competition.

For twelve years Brunel remained in prison, until he was finally released through the influence of some Russian merchants, the brothers Stroganov. In their service, he traveled throughout the whole of Russia, as far south as Astrakhan and eastward beyond the Ural mountains to the mouth of a broad river that flowed into the Polar Sea, the River Ob. Finally, the Stroganovs sent him on a business trip to the Netherlands.

Here was a man who, like Linschoten at a later date, seemed to know a large area of the world better than anyone else, and before long he met people who were very much interested in what he was able to tell them. One was Gerardus Mercator, the famous cartographer, who never lost an opportunity to add to his map of the world. Another was the Antwerp merchant, Balthasar de Moucheron, who was already doing business with Moscow via Narwa. In trade as well as science, Oliver Brunel's contributions greatly influenced the Dutch in the decision to attempt to find a northeast passage.[5]

The immediate result was that Moucheron and other Dutch merchants extended their activities around the Kola Peninsula into the White Sea which, because of the Gulf Stream, remained free of ice the year round. Much to the chagrin of the English, they received permission from the Czar to establish a factory at Novo Cholmogory, later named Archangel. In 1582 the English tried in vain to enlist outside support against this irksome competition. They pointed out to the King of Denmark that the Dutch, by diverting their Russian trade from Narwa in the Baltic to the White Sea, would eliminate the payment of tolls at Copenhagen and thus reduce his revenue. Why not apply some pressure on the Dutch and make them stick to their accustomed route?

5. S. Muller Fzn., *Geschiedenis der Noordsche Compagnie* (Utrecht, 1874).

But the King had no desire for a quarrel with the Dutch, because their ships were still paying him more tolls than those of all other countries combined.

Fear of the Spaniards and Portuguese was still very great in Holland, especially in those waters halfway around the globe where they had been able to build up strength for almost a century. A voyage by way of the north would largely eliminate this danger. The unhealthy conditions to be expected on the southern route were no less a problem. A loss of ten or 20 per cent of the crew on Portuguese ships was common, and sometimes the figure ran higher. These were men adjusted from birth to a warm climate. How would Dutch sailors fare, accustomed as they were to a far more invigorating climate? A voyage by way of the North seemed almost a lark by comparison.

It was confidently expected that a northern passage would save at least 2,000 miles. On the world map of Mercator, which first appeared in 1569 and whose ingenious projection is still the basis for all nautical charts, this was not so apparent. His projection enabled a navigator to establish the true compass course between two points, but, to accomplish this on a flat surface, Mercator had had to draw all meridians parallel to each other instead of having them converge at the poles. On a globe, however, the polar regions retained their true size, and even a layman could see that it was shorter to go to the Indies via the North Pole than to sail halfway to the South Pole and then back north again. Globes had just become available. The first of which there is any record was made in 1580 by Jacob Florisz. van Langren.[6] One of his globes is still in existence, in the Navigation Museum in Amsterdam, and it is tempting to imagine it is one of those on which Dutch merchants spread their fingers when they deliberated how best to get to the Indies.

After the fall of Antwerp, Balthasar de Moucheron had been forced to move to Zealand, and from there had continued his trade with Archangel, while at the same time collecting as much information as possible about the North. His plan had the support of two important men, Jacob Valck, the treasurer general of Zealand, and Dr. Francois Maelson, formerly of Enkhuizen but now the trusted counselor of Prince Maurice. The first move was made in December 1593, when Moucheron appeared before Prince Maurice to submit his plan. Among those present, besides

6. Keuning, *Petrus Plancius*, pp. 94–96.

Valck and Maelson, were Oldebarnevelt and other members of the States of Holland. Moucheron offered to put up one quarter of the cost, provided he receive in return one quarter of all the tolls levied at the Kara Strait on vessels passing to and from the Indies. He also wanted to be in full charge of the expedition. The committee seemed agreeable to his proposal, subject to the approval of the States of Holland and Zealand. It soon became clear, however, that the governing bodies of these two important provinces had different ideas. Zealand was willing to give Moucheron one eighth of the expected revenue and leadership of the venture, but Holland, that is, Amsterdam, turned him down flat. Oldebarnevelt, already a notable mediator, called the opposing factions together in March 1594. After several futile meetings, it was finally decided that the northern route was of such importance that the matter was one for the States General and should not be a private undertaking. The admiralties of Zealand and West Friesland were ordered to fit out one ship each, at Veere and Enkhuizen. The expected tolls would accrue to the States General, but, in view of his valuable advice, Moucheron was promised a liberal compensation and a yearly pension if the voyage proved a success. Moucheron had to accept disappointment, but he did not do so without complaining bitterly that his treasure had been taken from him. He foresaw nothing but trouble. The King of Denmark, who laid claim to the Kara Strait, would object to another sovereign nation usurping his assumed right and might well retaliate by sequestering Dutch vessels passing through the Oresund. This would not happen, he reasoned, if the enterprise remained in private hands.[7]

The Amsterdam merchants had been dubious about this northern venture while they awaited the return of their agent from Lisbon. It was only after Plancius had pointed out to them that Amsterdam would fish behind the net if the voyage proved a success that they finally agreed to contribute a ship. In accord with the earlier decision that this should not be a private undertaking, the ship was sponsored by the town government, but since the town government was controlled by the merchants it amounted to a private undertaking anyway. Nor did Amsterdam consider itself bound to follow the route prescribed for the two admiralty ships. The latter, following the advice of Moucheron, were to stick

7. J. A. van der Chijs, *Stichting van de Vereenigde O. I. Compagnie* (Leiden, 1856), pp. 19–24.

close to the land, entering the Kara Sea between the Island of
Vaigach and the mainland. The Amsterdam ship, however, was
to follow a more audacious plan of which the learned Dominie
Plancius had been the instigator. It called for staying west of
Novaya Zemlya and sailing as due north as possible, across the
Pole if necessary. Using a globe, he had no trouble convincing
the Amsterdam merchants that this was indeed the shortest route
to the Indies. He had other reasons for wanting to avoid the Kara
Sea and stay away from the coast of Siberia. Everyone knew that
fresh water froze more readily than salt water. It was more than
likely that the rivers emptying into the Polar Sea would cause
enormous ice floes along the coast. He also suggested that Novaya
Zemlya might well be part of the mainland, thus making the Kara
Sea a bay, and a dead end. By going due north, Plancius argued,
both difficulties would be avoided.[8] Theoretically, his deductions
were sound, but it took almost four hundred years and an atomic
submarine to prove that it could be done.

The squadron left on June 5, 1594. To be prepared for any
eventuality, it carried letters patent written in Slavic, Latin, and
Arabic. The admiralty ships were under the command of Cornelis
Nay, a skipper from Enkhuizen who had served Moucheron in
the past. With him went Linschoten, still out to see the world
and now convinced that a northern route offered the best possibility. He was charged with keeping a careful record—"from day
to day, and hour by hour, of all that we encountered during the
voyage."

Willem Barentsz. was in charge of the Amsterdam ship. He
was known as an able mariner, and he had received instruction
from Plancius in the latest developments in the field of celestial
navigation. This was his first attempt at finding a northern passage; two more were to follow. All three were failures, but his
name, nevertheless, was destined to go down in history as one
of the great navigators and polar explorers of all time.

Nay and Barentsz. stayed together until they were well beyond
the North Cape. Each then went his own way, having decided
where to rendezvous later in the season. According to his instructions, Barentsz. set sail for Novaya Zemlya and then north along
the west coast. Everything went smoothly until he reached the
northern part of the island, where he ran into "great store of ice,
as much as they could descry out of the top, that lay like a plain

8. Bezemer, *Nederland*, pp. 85–87.

field of ice." During the next three weeks, Barentsz. tried in vain to find a passage through the ice. He sailed some 1,500 miles and changed course more than 80 times. He was forced to turn back and head for the rendezvous, which both skippers reached on August 15.[9]

Nay had good news. He had sailed through the Strait of Waigach without trouble and into the Kara Sea, which proved to be free of ice. He proceeded eastward until he reached the mouth of a river. Here he ran into a little ice and, because the season was coming to a close, he decided to turn back. There was no doubt in anyone's mind that Nay could have sailed straight on to Cathay if he had only arrived a little earlier. Flushed with success, they wrote new names on the map: the mainland became New Holland, the Kara Sea became the New North Sea, and the Strait of Vaigach became Strait Nassau.

Together they headed south for the Norwegian coast. On August 24, Vardohus was reached, and the curious Danes plied them with questions. Nothing had been accomplished, the Dutch told them. There was ice everywhere, and they had been forced to turn back. "Not for anything in the world would they try it a second time!" [10]

The ships arrived at Texel on September 16, only a month after Nay had left the Kara Sea. Here they separated, each going to his home port, one with good news, the other with bad.

Linschoten was summoned to The Hague to report in person to Prince Maurice and Oldebarnevelt. He convinced them that the Kara Sea was a "ready-made and certain passage." This conviction was shared by almost everyone in the republic and preparations were made at once to prove it the following year.

Amsterdam played no great part in these discussions, primarily because Willem Barentsz., following the course indicated by Dominie Plancius, had accomplished nothing. But the Amsterdam merchants had something else to consider: Cornelis Houtman had returned from Lisbon.

9. Stefansson, *Great Adventures*, pp. 428–30.
10. Bezemer, pp. 89–93.

II

South
to the Indies

There is no record of just what Cornelis Houtman had been able
to accomplish during his sojourn in Lisbon. Most likely his information was no more than a confirmation of what Linschoten
had already supplied, but this was apparently enough to convince
his employers that some action should be taken. They had this
to say about it:

> Which person, after having investigated this matter [East
> Indies trade] for about two years, returned to Amsterdam in
> the beginning of the year 1594. In the presence of the Wor-
> shipful Petrus Plancius and all other members, this matter
> was once more thoroughly examined. After many discussions
> it was finally resolved that, in the Name of the Lord, a
> beginning should be made with the navigation and other
> affairs. To which end we again sent instructions to Lisbon
> to engage several persons who were familiar with the Malay
> language, but in this our agent was not successful.[1]

A whole year was to elapse after Houtman's return before the
plan was put into effect. The voyage could not have got under
way much sooner in any case. It was common knowledge that
the best time for departure was during the early part of the year,
for it offered the most favorable wind conditions in both the
Atlantic and Indian oceans. For the Amsterdam merchants, the
intervening year consisted of waiting, money raising, and prepara-
tion.

The waiting was not just for the Malay interpreters: far more
important was to learn how the northern voyages had turned out.
This took until late September. It was a great disappointment for
all concerned to hear that the Amsterdam ship had been blocked
by ice where Plancius had expected open water, and it was even
more disconcerting to have two small towns, Veere and Enkhui-

1. De Jonge, *Opkomst, 1,* 93–94, 254–56.

zen, gloating over the fact that their ships had found the gateway
to the Indies. There must have been much walking to and fro
between the houses in the Warmoesstraat and the rectory of the
nearby Old Church where Plancius lived.

We know the result of these deliberations but can only guess at
how they arrived at their decision. This much is certain: the
three original promoters[2] belonged to the hard core of the
merchant class that ruled Amsterdam, Amsterdam dictated policy
in the province of Holland, and Holland was the backbone of
the republic. These three men felt their power, especially Reynier
Pauw who would one day be Magnificat of Amsterdam. Rather
than leave the glory and the spoils to others, they decided to
sail around the Cape of Good Hope regardless of how the next
northern attempt would turn out.

For men of their reputation, it was not difficult to find participants to finance the undertaking. Their names were Pieter Hasselaer, Jan Poppen, Hendrik Buick, Dirk van Os, Syvert Sem, and
Arend ten Grootenhuys.[3] These men should be remembered not
only because they backed this venture but also because they were
the vanguard of the age of modern capitalism. Every one of these
men, with one exception, had started with little or nothing. They
had taken advantage of the opportunities offered by a new conception of life.[4]

Pieter Hasselaer had started as a laborer in a brewery, but in
1587 he was able to buy his own, the White Eagle. From then
on, his progress was assured, and he eventually became one of the
leaders in the Russian trade. Dirk van Os was one of the Flemish
refugees who had been able to find a niche for himself in Amsterdam. Jan Poppen, or Jehan Poppe as he was originally known,
was another early Horatio Alger. A few years before the troubles
broke out, he had come to Amsterdam from Germany without
a penny. He found employment with a herring merchant in the
Warmoesstraat. When, in 1568, his employer was forced to flee
together with other prominent Calvinists, Jan Poppen took care
of the business. Undoubtedly he took advantage of being a foreigner, and therefore not involved in local problems. He acquitted
himself well and, after the Alteration, married his employer's

2. Carel, Hudde, and Pauw. See above, Chapter 8.
3. Van der Chijs, *Stichting O. I. Compagnie,* pp. 29–30.
4. The following biographical data about these men is derived from Elias,
Vroedschap.

niece, whose father was also in the herring business. He rose gradually to the top and, at the time of his death in 1616, he had become the richest man in Amsterdam. He left about one million guilders, an enormous amount for those times, when a boss carpenter earned less than one guilder per day, and when half that much was considered a good wage for the average workman.

The composition of Poppen's estate is a striking example of what was happening to the merchant class as a whole: the gradual shift from risky ventures to a safer investment in land and town property. About half of the Poppen estate was represented by farm land which he had acquired by financing the draining of a lake north of Amsterdam. Real estate holdings in the town itself accounted for about 100,000 guilders. Some 300,000 guilders were in debentures of the East India Company, bearing interest of from 4 to 5 per cent and fully secured by the stocks of spices the company had in its warehouses. Against this, there were only 30,000 guilders invested in ordinary shares of the East India Company, which had a paid-in capital of between six and seven million guilders and of which he had been one of the original founders. Eight years after his death, the last remnants of Jan Poppen's former business activities were liquidated, and his granddaughter had married a nobleman.[5]

Arend ten Grootenhuys was the nephew of Hendrik Hudde and only 24 years old. Hudde may have had a foreboding that he would not live much longer (he died less than two years later), and this might well have prompted him to make sure that his family would be represented in the venture he had started with Pauw and Carel.

These nine men raised a capital of 290,000 guilders of which 100,000 were earmarked for trade goods, especially for the silver reals that Linschoten had recommended. The organization was called the Compagnie van Verre, denoting the fact that it intended to trade in faraway places. Four ships were built at Amsterdam, three measuring between 300 and 400 tons each, and the fourth a yacht of 50 tons. Prince Maurice was present at the launching of the *Mauritius*. The two largest vessels were called the *Hollandia* and the *Amsterdam*. The yacht was named *Duifke* (Little Dove), and a gallant little ship she proved to be. After ten years

5. W. van Ravesteyn Jr., *Onderzoekingen over de economische en sociale ontwikkeling van Amsterdam gedurende de 16de en het eerste kwart der 17de eeuw* (Amsterdam, 1906), pp. 331-33.

and several voyages back and forth to the Indies, it was the *Duifke,* with Willem Jansz. as skipper, that discovered Australia.

The ships were fitted out as thoroughly as possible, carrying spare masts, anchors, cables, and triple sets of sails. Cannon were borrowed from various towns, with the States of Holland guaranteeing their return upon completion of the voyage. This was the only contribution made by the government, and not too generous a one at that since the Company had to send an agent to England to buy 30 more cannon, almost half the total number.[6]

The fleet carried a total of 248 officers and men. As was to become the custom on all subsequent voyages, there was no single commander whose word was final. All major decisions had to be taken in a plenary council which consisted of navigators and supercargoes (called "merchants") from all the vessels. Some, however, had a preferred status and could speak first on an issue, and could break a tie. One of these was Jan Meulenaer, skipper of the *Mauritius;* another was Cornelis Houtman, "chief merchant" on the same vessel. He was thirty years old, and had none of the traits that make for sound judgment, but he had done some work for the company in Lisbon and he was, moreover, the cousin of Reynier Pauw. His father was a brewer in Gouda, and his grandfather had been a merchant in lumber and coffins. His younger brother, Frederik, sailed on the *Hollandia* as a "junior merchant."

One of the ablest men in the fleet was Pieter Dircksz. Keyzer, the chief navigator. He had already made several voyages to Brazil and had been trained for this venture by Petrus Plancius, who taught him all that was then known about navigation and astronomy.[7] The ordinary crew consisted of riffraff from the waterfront. Few sailors could be found who were willing to volunteer for so risky an adventure, which would profit them little even if it proved a success and they came out of it alive. As a special inducement, everyone in the fleet was made a shareholder to the amount of two months wages—not much to a sailor who earned about ten guilders a month.[8]

There were 18 officers in the fleet. There was also a group of young men of almost the same number who had been motivated solely by the prospect of adventure. They came from well-to-do families, and it was hoped that they might benefit from an experi-

6. Van der Chijs, pp. 31–33.
7. Keuning, *Petrus Plancius,* pp. 102–03.
8. De Jonge, *Opkomst, 1,* 97.

ence such as this. A few were serious, and in time made names for themselves, but the majority were irresponsible hotheads who rarely missed an opportunity to cause trouble. The company learned from the experience, and, in the future, "young blades of quality" were screened carefully before they were hired.

One man who was absent from the roster was Linschoten, which is remarkable considering that he had twice sailed around the Cape. The reasons for his exclusion were numerous. They were the result of rivalries among personalities, towns, and even provinces. During their early meetings, Plancius must have decided that Linschoten did not have much more to offer than second-hand information and that he was vague on the more specific data the Dominie needed for his charts and navigation studies. For his part, Linschoten came to regard Plancius as a dogmatic preacher who tried to tell everybody what the world was like without ever having left his study. It was the conventional antipathy between a man of practice and a man of theory. That this friction existed at an early stage in the negotiations is illustrated by the manner in which Linschoten expressed himself regarding Plancius' opposition to the Kara Sea venture: "With thousands of spurious reasons, Plancius tries to prove that this route is neither good nor possible." [9]

If the Dominie had been nothing more than an adviser to the Company, this personal animosity might not have prevented certain directors from insisting that Linschoten be offered an important post because of his qualifications. But Plancius was more than a consultant. He had put 5,400 guilders into the company [10] and, judging from the instructions he issued to several members of the fleet and from what is known of his subsequent activities, he was also the final arbiter in deciding which men were qualified to serve as skipper and navigator. From the start of preparations to reach the Indies, Plancius had given a course in navigation and allied subjects. It was a carefully defined curriculum with required attendance, as appears from the following company resolution: "The navigators shall gather at the house of Petrus Plancius five days a week, from Monday till Friday, from nine in the morning until five in the evening." For the year 1600 we find an entry in the books of the Compagnie van Verre which shows that he was well paid for his services: "To Petrus Plancius, by order of the

9. Keuning, *Petrus Plancius*, p. 112.
10. Ibid., p. 99.

2. Petrus Plancius delivering a lesson in navigation.

directors, for instructing the navigators of ten ships: the sum of 500 pounds." [11]

There was still another reason why Linschoten's presence was not essential. The part of the *Itinerary* dealing specifically with the route to the Indies had been printed well in advance of the rest of the work, more than likely at the behest of the Amsterdam merchants. A copy of this book was taken along on the voy-age, and the navigators were thus acquainted with everything Linschoten could have told them in person.

What was Linschoten's attitude in the matter? The possibility that he had actually been invited and had turned down the offer cannot be ruled out. In his home town of Enkhuizen, he was treated as a favorite son, and, under the sponsorship of Doctor Paludanus, his fame was spreading. He had participated in the first northern venture and after finding the Kara Sea free of ice, he may have been convinced that a northeast passage was the answer, rather than a southern route, the hazards of which he knew better than anyone else in Holland. The second northern venture was then being organized, and Linschoten was to go along in the important capacity of "Chief Merchant." What more could he have asked for?

There was also the rivalry between the towns. Plancius was committed to Amsterdam, Linschoten belonged to Enkhuizen. There was no love lost between Amsterdam and the merchants of Zealand. The latter, once again led by Moucheron, joined forces with Enkhuizen in a venture which almost everyone believed was to be crowned with success.

In 1595, the two fleets set sail, both with the same objective—a spot halfway around the globe that no Dutchman had ever seen. The Amsterdam ships were the first to leave. The gap of Texel at the most northern point of Holland was the jumping off place for all vessels from towns around the Zuiderzee, and the fleet sailed from there on April 2. The instructions were short and to the point: to sail to the Indies by way of the Cape of Good Hope and to bring back as many spices as the ships could carry. They were to avoid the enemy and be friendly with the natives. Petrus Plancius had added some instructions of his own. Pieter Keyzer, the chief pilot, had the task of measuring the position of the stars in the southern hemisphere by means of the astrolabe and to chart

11. Ibid., pp. 106–07. The Flemish pound was valued at six Dutch guilders.

them carefully.[12] Frederik Houtman, the younger brother of Cornelis, was to make exact measurements of variations of the compass needle at frequent intervals.[13]

The beginning was auspicious. By April 19 they passed the Canary Islands, and on the 26th, they landed at Isla de Mayo in the Cape Verde group. Then lack of wind slowed them. The equator was not crossed until June 4, and it was June 27 before they sighted the Abrolhos off the coast of Brazil. This was the point at which the Portuguese always altered their course, according to Linschoten, and the Dutch did the same. But they had been 87 days en route, and their problems were mounting. Scurvy was raging among the men, and navigation became difficult since they were losing the familiar constellations of the northern hemisphere. There was great relief when they spotted birds with black and white feathers, which Linschoten had reported were always noticed by the Portuguese in the neighborhood of Tristan d'Acunha. This gave them their bearings, and the ships headed for the south coast of Africa.

The sight of land on August 2 was met with joy, for the number of sick had increased alarmingly. They managed to barter some iron hoops and old bread knives for a few oxen and sheep, but this was not enough to cure the sick who needed fresh fruit and vegetables. It was urgent that a better place for "refreshing" be found, and they hoped that Madagascar might provide it. Head winds and adverse currents near this island pushed them back time and again, and it was not until two months after leaving the Cape that they finally dropped anchor in the Bay of St. Augustin on the southwest coast of Madagascar. By now, seventy-one men had died, and they were buried on a small island in the bay. It was named Holland Cemetery.

Among the dead was Jan Dignumsz., the respected skipper of the *Hollandia*, and his death caused the first of a number of discords that were from then on to plague the voyage. It was started

12. Keyzer located 121 new stars. These constellations of the southern hemisphere appeared for the first time on the celestial globe by Jodocus Hondius in 1600.

13. Establishing even an approximate longitude was one of the most difficult problems navigators confronted in the seventeenth century. Plancius, like others before him, adhered to the belief that there was a direct relationship between the variation of a compass and longitude. Thus by making as many observations as possible it was hoped that the problem could be solved. See Keuning, *Petrus Plancius*, p. 106 and pp. 120–35.

by Gerrit van Beuningen, chief merchant on the *Hollandia* and a rival of Cornelis Houtman. He took it upon himself to open the sealed orders from the directors to the Ships' Council, indicating who should succeed a deceased skipper. Pieter Keyzer was the man designated, but the Council was so incensed at Beuningen's highhanded attitude that they refused to accept Keyzer, claiming he was too sick. Bitter quarrels broke out which Keyzer tried to settle by asking to have his name withdrawn "so that we can continue our voyage in peace and friendship, and to the profit of ourselves and the Company." [14]

It took a long time for the sick to get back on their feet, and in the meantime the others were brawling among themselves. It was February before the fleet could continue the voyage, and by then the period of favorable winds in the Indian Ocean was over. It took another four months before they finally sighted Engano off the west coast of Sumatra. Being so near their goal, the Ships' Council decided that, for the sake of presenting a united front, the interminable bickerings would have to stop. They summoned Beuningen to answer a number of serious accusations, one of which was that he had tried to shoot Cornelis Houtman. The majority wanted to hang him forthwith, but more sober heads prevailed. He was put in irons instead, and stayed there until the fleet returned to Amsterdam. This drastic measure was temporarily effective, but not for long. In subsequent brawls, the crews also became involved, and all semblance of discipline went by the boards.

Under these unhappy conditions, the Dutch ships finally dropped anchor on the roadstead of Bantam, almost fifteen months from the day they had sailed from Texel.[15] But the main purpose of the venture at least had been accomplished. They were received cordially and given a house from which to do their trading. But the relationship deteriorated quickly. Some accounts blame the Portuguese, and accuse them of informing the King of Bantam that the Dutch were nothing but pirates like the English, who had been in those waters earlier. This seemed to be confirmed by the fact that Houtman, expecting to buy spices for a song, refused to pay anywhere near the asking price. The people of Bantam were even more suspicious when the Dutch began to sound the entire stretch of the roadstead. The situation became

14. De Jonge, *Opkomst*, 2, 191.
15. On the importance of Bantam at this time, see M. A. P. Meilink-Roelofsz, *Asian Trade and European Influence*, The Hague, 1962, pp. 239–44.

so strained that even water was refused them, and they had to sail to Sumatra to get it. On this mission, Pieter Keyzer died in the Sunda Strait, "by which the Company suffered a great loss." [16] Indeed it was. His astronomical observations proved to be of great value, and Von Humboldt ranked him among the great men in the history of navigation.

When the ships returned to Bantam, they found the comrades they had left behind in prison, including Cornelis Houtman, and that the king was considering an offer from the Portuguese in Malacca to sell them as slaves for 4,000 pieces of eight. After lengthy palavers and the payment of a substantial ransom, the prisoners were released. This apparently cleared the air, and a pact was concluded which allowed the Dutch to trade on the same basis as the Portuguese and Chinese. It was the high point of Houtman's career. Had he been a man of sober judgment, much might have been gained from the agreement, but he was a braggart, vain, and vindictive. Through deaths and intrigue, he was now practically the leader of the expedition. He refused to buy any but small lots of spices, insisting that the merchants should sail directly to the source, the Moluccas in the eastern part of the archipelago. He would show the people of Bantam that he did not need them, and he would first take revenge for having been imprisoned. Frank van der Does, who kept a careful record, wrote in his journal: "And thus it was decided to do all possible harm to the town." Among other irresponsible deeds, they pilfered two junks arriving from Banda with spices, and another small vessel from Borneo. "And after we had revenged ourselves to the satisfaction of our leaders, we prepared to sail on." [17]

They made their way slowly east along the north coast of Java, everywhere preceded by men from Bantam who warned the natives against the Dutch. At Sidayu, near what is now Surabaya, the ships were boarded by a large number of Javanese. In the melee that followed, twelve men of the *Amsterdam* were slashed to death, including the skipper and a merchant. Off the coast of Madura, a royal *prahu* came out to meet them. The crew of the *Amsterdam*, trigger-happy after the recent onslaught, fired three

16. De Jonge, *Opkomst*, 2, 197.
17. Ibid., 2, 332. There are seven journals in existence about this voyage, that of Frank van der Does being the most informative. All seven, together with other documents, appear in *De Eerste schipvaart*, edited and annotated by G. P. Rouffaer and J. W. IJzerman (3 vols. The Hague, 1915–1929).

salvos at the hapless boat, killing the prince, his priest, and a number of Madurese. Among the survivors were a woman and the prince's son, a boy of eight. After this, it seemed unwise to try to land there, and the ships sailed to Bawean, a small island to the north of Java.

Conditions on the fleet had reached just about their lowest ebb. Of the 248 men who had started on the voyage, only 94 were alive, and even this small number included many who were sick and maimed. Most of their ablest men had died, leaving a motley group of individuals whose tempers were frayed by the many setbacks they had suffered. Worst of all for the company, they still had no cargo to speak of. Dead men could draw no wages, but the directors would not be pleased if their ships returned with empty holds.

A decision had to be made promptly before the ships became unmanned hulks. In the council, the extent of the discord was limited only by the physical condition of its members. The principal opposing factions consisted of Houtman and the merchants on one side and the navigators and boatswains on the other. Houtman was all for returning to Bantam to buy the spices he had previously rejected, but the West Monsoon was blowing through the Java Sea at full force, and the skippers said they could not buck it. Then why not sail east with it, to the Moluccas? This was still Houtman's pet project, because there a full cargo at low cost was almost assured. Again he ran into opposition from the seamen. Led by the oldest remaining skipper, Jan Meulenaer of the *Mauritius*, they flatly refused to penetrate any further into the archipelago, thus to risk forfeiting the last slim chance of ever getting home. The hot sun had raised havoc with the seaworthiness of the ships, and the seams had become gaping furrows as wide as a man's thumb. A heeling ship would be a sieve. The bottoms were thickly encrusted with barnacles, and long festoons of seaweed drifted from the sides. With their decimated crews, the sailors argued, they could not possibly make the necessary repairs even if a protected beach were found.

Neither side would budge. After a particularly bitter argument, Meulenaer suddenly died under suspicious circumstances. Two barbers testified before the council that his face was blue and purple and that his hair came out in bunches: "a child could tell he had been poisoned." [18]

The crew of the *Mauritius* accused Houtman of having insti-

18. Ibid., *2*, 345.

gated the murder to get his opponent out of the way. At the first opportunity, they seized the chief merchant and put him in irons, expecting the council to condemn him to death. Fortunately for Houtman, the council held that no sufficient proof had been presented and he was released. This last event must have had a sobering effect, and all plans to sail either east or west were abandoned. All apparently agreed that it was best to sail south through the Bali Strait and then home as best they could. The *Amsterdam* had earlier struck a bad leak, and it was decided to put the torch to her after some 30 tons of nutmeg and the chests of silver reals were transferred to the other vessels. "A costly fire for the Company," Van der Does wrote in his journal.

They left Bawean and sailed for Bali. It was their final stop in the Indies and, ironically, the friendliest. The island had nothing to offer in the form of trade, but there were other attractions— a carefree way of life and comely women who, according to custom, unblushingly displayed their wares. Two young men found these charms irresistible, and the fleet sailed without them.[19]

The last few days in the Indies pointed up the reasons for the unrewarding outcome of the voyage. Faced with the prospect of having to explain to the directors, each tried to blame the other for the blunders that had been made. "The officers," Van der Does wrote, "upbraided each other with many and loud words for what had occurred at Bantam."

On this sour note, anchors were raised, and the three ships headed for home on February 26, 1597. The return journey presented no special problems. After only five and a half months at sea, they arrived at Texel on August 14.

The voyage had lasted almost two and a half years, much longer than it usually took the Portuguese. Of the original 248 men, only 89 returned, and seven of them died soon afterwards as a result of scurvy and other maladies. The ships had fared better than the men, and after the necessary overhauling, all three eventually returned to service. The silver reals had withstood the journey best of all, as most returned to Amsterdam in mint condition. But this could hardly please directors and stockholders who had expected their money to be put to work. Even so, the cargo consisted of 245 bags of pepper, 45 tons of nutmeg, and 30 bales of mace. There were also a few porcelain plates, originally

19. The first of many who fell under the spell of Bali, their names, Emanuel Roodenburgh and Jacob Claesz., deserve mention.

from China. This was only a fraction of what could have been returned if the leadership had been better.

The Compagnie van Verre let it be known that the venture showed a loss. Others reported that the value of the spices more than covered the original investment.[20] But the issue of profit or loss was overshadowed by the fact that the door to the Indies had been opened.

20. Brugmans, *Opkomst en bloei van Amsterdam,* p. 126. Here a profit of 87,000 guilders is mentioned.

12

The Second
and Third
Voyages North

The enthusiasm which preceded the second voyage north was intense. The States General backed it to the hilt and ordered that seven ships, large and small, be readied in Amsterdam, Hoorn, Enkhuizen, Middelburg, and Rotterdam.[1] The route was based on the results of the previous voyage: through Strait Nassau into the Kara Sea and hence around Cape Tabin. Additional encouragement for this plan had come from across the Channel. Treasurer Valck of Zealand had bought a manuscript from Richard Hakluyt which showed that the famous English geographer also recommended this route.[2]

The main object was still to traverse the passage, but, since the success of this was more or less taken for granted, the prospect of trading in Cipango and Cathay was not overlooked. To foster the participation of private merchants, the government offered to waive the customary convoy duties and tolls and allow the goods to be carried free of charge. The merchants were also allowed to place supercargoes on the vessels to act as their representatives. In anticipation of large profits, a number of companies were quickly formed in most of the major towns, and they provided a great deal of money and merchandise for the project. As an example of the eventualities prepared for, goldsmiths and diamond-cutters were to be taken along so that precious metals and jewels could be worked en route and their value assessed.

In these preliminary activities Moucheron had been very active. The restless refugee merchant considered a northeast passage as good as accomplished, and he was already planning how best to exploit it. In a lengthy report to the States General, he advised

1. Resolution of the States General to the Admiralty Colleges of these towns, dated May 11, 1595.
2. De Jonge, *Opkomst*, *1*, 20.

that the Strait of Vaigach (now Strait Nassau) be fortified to give the Dutch a monopoly on the route. "In case no respectable people can be found to stay in this (inhospitable) region the year round," he said, "then the fort should be manned by condemned criminals." [3] Though optimistic, the cautious gentlemen in The Hague were unwilling to go this far just yet. As with the previous voyage, letters patent were issued in various languages for presentation to foreign potentates to assure them that the Dutch came with honorable intentions.

Another document drawn up for this voyage was a Letter of Articles promulgated by Prince Maurice in his capacity as Admiral-General of the United Netherlands. It contained the sea laws by which everyone in the fleet, from highest to lowest, had to conduct himself during the voyage. This document is dated June 13, 1595 when the Houtman ships were already at sea, but it is on record that "articles" were read on departure to their crews as well, and it seems certain that they were the same. The lack of discipline on the southern voyage can perhaps be best explained by the mediocre caliber of the leadership and the high mortality rate among the skippers and mates.

Codes of law governing maritime affairs had long been known. One of the earliest was the Rhodian Sea, compiled between 600 and 800 A.D. in the Byzantine empire. As traffic by sea increased, others appeared, such as the Sea Laws of Oleron which served as a model for the Black Book of the Admiralty in England. The Hansa was governed by the Visby Sea Laws, and Spain had its Consulato del Mar. Sebastian Cabot had compiled a long list of instructions for the Willoughby-Chancellor expedition of 1553. It contained 33 items, about half of which dealt with the conduct of the crew. The remainder consisted of admonitions on how best to deal with the peoples encountered in foreign lands to the advantage of the company. These included the following: "Do not disclose to any nation the state of our religion, but pass it over in silence. [To obtain information,] allure or take a person aboard your ships . . . and if the person taken may be made drunk with your beer or wine, you shall know the secrets of his heart. . . . Esteem your own commodities above all other, and in countenance show not much to desire the foreign commodities. . . .

3. This report was transmitted by the States of Zealand, to whom Balthasar de Moucheron had presented it on April 8, 1595. See Van der Chijs, *Stichting*, pp. 40–42.

If people appear gathering stones, gold or other like on the sands, you may draw nigh, playing upon the drum or such other instruments as may allure them to harkening." [4]

The Dutch thought of similar ideas for use in their early ventures, but instructions were issued separately, and there was no need to incorporate them in a code of law designed primarily to enforce discipline at sea. The Letter of Articles issued to the second northern venture deserves more than passing mention because it presents a picture of the problems encountered on shipboard in those days.

All hands were admonished to be guided by God Almighty and to listen attentively to His word at prayer and sermon. Those who cursed or used His name in vain would be flogged at the mainmast and pay a fine to the poor. Whoever refused to obey orders from the skipper or his delegate received the death penalty. A court consisting of the highest officers had full jurisdiction, and the sentence was to be executed at once by the provost. Anyone who interfered with the provost or refused to lend assistance was punished as a mutineer. Desertion or the unauthorized use of a boat were punished by a severe flogging. No one was allowed to go ashore without permission or allowed to stay there overnight. Whoever started a fist fight was thrown in irons and put on a diet of bread and water. If a shipmate tried to give the offender food or otherwise ease his lot, he received the same punishment. Pulling a knife, even as a threat only, was more serious. For a first offender, it meant three successive dunkings into the sea from the yardarm. For a second offense, he was to be keelhauled. A kindhearted skipper might give him an oily rag on which to clamp his teeth and furnish a heavy weight to make him sink fast and deep so that his head would not be bashed against the keel. If a fight drew blood, the offending hand was nailed to the mast and the other tied behind the man's back. He would stay there until he

---

4. "Ordinances, instructions, and advertisements of and for the direction of the intended voyage for Cathay, compiled, made, and delivered by the right worshipful M. Sebastian Cabota Esquire, governour of the mysterie and companie of the Marchants adventurers for the discoverie of Regions, Dominions, Islands and places unknowen, the 9. day of May, in the yere of our Lord God 1553. and in the 7. yeere of the reigne of our most dread soveraigne Lord Edward the 6. by the grace of God, king of England, Fraunce and Ireland, defender of the faith, and of the Church of England and Ireland, in earth supreame head," in Richard Hakluyt, *Principal Navigations, Voyages, Traffiques, and Discoveries of the English Nation.* See Stefansson, *Great Adventures,* pp. 389–99.

was desperate enough to tear himself loose; in addition, he forfeited all his wages, one half going to the poor and the other into the common fund. If a man happened to kill his opponent, he was tied back to back with his victim and thrown overboard.

The problem of food and drink was also considered. No one was to cajole the cook or even appear in the galley to try to get additional victuals. The crew had to be content with whatever was put before them, and those who were caught throwing food or drink overboard received corporal punishment. It was conceded that some drinking water or other liquid might be spilled upon the deck, but if the spot was greater than could be covered by a hand or a foot, it was not considered a permissible accident.

There were strict rules against sleeping on watch, entering the powder hold, and unauthorized firing of musket or cannon. To guard against fire, no light of any kind was allowed below decks. Nor was the matter of cleanliness and sanitation overlooked: "To prevent the stench from causing sickness the morning watches shall daily clean and wash the ships. No one shall defecate nor make water except at the head. Wet clothing may not be carried below decks, but first has to be dried."

To protect the merchants, crew members were allowed to bring aboard chests and bales containing only personal gear. It was emphasized that all ships should remain together and come to each other's rescue in case of need. There were 42 articles in all, and they covered just about every phase of misconduct likely to be encountered.[5]

Leadership of the fleet was given to the best men that could be found. Cornelis Nay was again in command, with Willem Barentsz. as his chief navigator. The ships' merchants were Linschoten, Jan Ryp, Jacob van Heemskerck, and two relatives of Moucheron. A successful voyage was generally anticipated when the fleet left Texel on July 2, 1595. This was about a month later than the expedition of the previous year, but the fact was considered to be of minor importance since everyone expected to be off the China coast before winter. After the legendary Cape Tabin had been rounded, two fast yachts were to turn back with the glad tidings for the people at home that the main body of the fleet

5. For a complete list of the Dutch ships' articles see Van der Chijs, *Stichting*, pp. 138–45. For a general discussion of the subject, see J. C. de Jonge, *Geschiedenis van het nederlandsche zeewezen* (6 vols. Haarlem, 1858–62).

would spend the winter in China and return the following season.

Everyone in the fleet, from captain to cabin boy, was in high spirits until Strait Nassau was reached. Here their expectations were shattered against a barrier of ice.[6] The Kara Sea was full of it. After several futile attempts to find an opening, landing parties were sent to the mainland to learn what they could. They met a number of Samoyeds who ran off as soon as they saw the Dutch, leaving ten well laden sleds behind. Two sailors appropriated a few pelts but gained nothing from them. One of the articles forbade stealing from natives on pain of being keelhauled three times in a row. One of the sailors had his head torn off banging into the keel; the other, although he survived the ordeal, was put ashore where he soon froze to death. Several other encounters ashore, with hungry polar bears, and decaying whales that spread a putrid stench all over the camp, did not improve the morale of the men. A small mutiny broke out on one of the ships, and five ringleaders were hanged. After almost six weeks of frustration, the council decided to turn back. The fleet arrived at Texel in the middle of October. In the meantime, the Houtman squadron had managed to get as far as Madagascar.

Disappointment at the failure of this second northern venture was understandably great. The government and the States of Holland and Zealand lost interest and refused to lend their support to any further attempts in that direction. The most the States of Holland were prepared to do was to offer a reward of 25,000 guilders to anyone who succeeded.[7] Almost three centuries later, someone was able to claim the reward: the Swede, Nordenskjold. Unfortunately for him, a closefisted Dutch government turned him down under the pretext that the offer had expired.

Few still believed in the feasibility of a northern route. Linschoten did, and he pointed out that it had taken the Portuguese many years before they finally succeeded in rounding the Cape of Good Hope. Nor was Dominie Plancius discouraged. In fact, he saw the ice barrier in the Kara Sea as a vindication of his theory that

6. For further details about this voyage, as well as the first and third, see S. P. L'Honoré Naber, ed., *Reizen van Jan Huyghen van Linschoten naar het Noorden, 1594–95* (The Hague, 1914), and his *Reizen van Willem Barentsz., Jacob van Heemskerck, Jan Cornelisz. Rijp en anderen naar het Noorden, 1594–97*, Told by Gerrit de Veer (2 vols. The Hague, 1917). An interesting account by an anonymous participant of the second voyage, "Meer oder Seehanen Buch," is mentioned by C. P. Burger in *De Poolzee-Reizen van 1595–96* (The Hague, 1921).

7. Resolution of February 19, 1596.

it was impossible to sail along the coast and that open water would be found in a more northerly direction. Willem Barentsz., having already made two voyages, was also of the opinion that a third attempt should be made before abandoning the northern route entirely.[8]

Only Amsterdam lent a willing ear, especially since the matter would this time be entirely in the hands of its own merchants, the government and other towns having eliminated themselves. By the end of March, it was decided to fit out two ships. Houtman had been gone for over a year, and there was no way of knowing how he had fared. This time the merchants were not going to wait until he returned.

On May 18, 1596, the ships sailed into the North Sea. Barentsz. was in command of one ship, and with him sailed Jacob van Heemskerck, who was highly regarded in Amsterdam and had been given the title of captain. Though this move might have been expected to cause friction, the two men got on well together. Jan Ryp was skipper of the other vessel. Plancius had been the spearhead of the operation, and it is understandable that Linschoten was not invited.

After reaching the west coast of Novaya Zemlya, Barentsz. and Ryp got into a dispute as to the interpretation of their instructions. Barentsz. held that they should turn east afer reaching the northernmost point of this land. Ryp, on the other hand, insisted on continuing due north, thus exactly following Plancius' earlier suggestion to "cross the North Pole if necessary." Barentsz. was persuaded to accompany Ryp for a while longer, and in doing so they discovered Spitsbergen, but he refused to go any further in this direction. Ryp was equally persistent. It was now July, and the time for experimentation was rapidly drawing to a close. Each went his own way. After some aimless cruising around Spitsbergen, always surrounded by ice, Ryp turned back to rejoin the other ship. But Barentsz. had disappeared. Ryp turned his ship towards home.

Barentsz. had returned to Novaya Zemlya and then sailed north along the coast. Reaching its northernmost point, which they called the Hook of Desire, they found that the coast turned east and then south. A stretch of open water promised a passage, and for a while they actually believed that the voyage had been won. But it proved to be a delusion. Before long the ship was crowded

8. Keuning, *Petrus Plancius*, pp. 113–17.

by ice and, almost overnight, it was locked in solid. It was now September, and they realized that they were marooned for the winter. Only a solid shelter could safely see them through, and they fortunately found a quantity of logs and driftwood along the shore, so that they did not have to tear down the ship with which they hoped to escape as soon as the ice had melted.

It was a long winter and a hard one. A careful journal was kept by Gerrit de Veer, son of a well-known burgher of Amsterdam, who had also been on the previous voyage. By mid-October they moved into the Safe House they had built from logs, "according the Norwegian manner." It was about 30 by 18 feet, and sixteen men lived in it for eight months. The hardships were great, and there were times when they almost froze or suffocated to death. But morale was good because, as Gerrit de Veer wrote, "As much as possible only single men had been mustered, so that they would not be distracted by a longing for wife and children."

On Three Kings' Day in early January, they had a party, each man supplying a two-day ration of flour and wine. The constable was crowned King of Novaya Zemlya. February 12 was a happy day because they shot a polar bear "that gave us a hundred pounds of fat." By May, the ordeal was beginning to tell on the men, the firewood was giving out, and they had to make preparations for getting under way. The ship had been crushed by the ice and proved unfit to continue the journey. They put their ebbing strength into building and repairing two open boats. The skipper himself was ill and failing fast, but he kept after the men, sometimes with a dry sense of humor. "Our lives depend on it, boys. If we cannot get the boats ready we shall have to die here as burghers of Novaya Zemlya." [9]

On June 14 they sailed away in the open boats, hugging the shore and dodging ice constantly. A few days out, Willem Barentsz. knew that he was almost finished, and he asked de Veer, "Lift me up, Gerrit. I want to see that land once more." Three days later he died. Led by Heemskerck, the men reached the Kola Peninsula by the end of August, after more than two months of sailing under the most difficult conditions. At Kola occurred one of those coin-

9. The site of the Safe House was visited first by Captain Elling Carlsen, a Norwegian whaler in 1871, and in 1876 by the Englishman Charles Gardiner. The house was only partly caved in after a period of almost three hundred years. Both men brought back a quantity of clothes, tools, and other utensils which are now in the collection of the Rijksmuseum at Amsterdam.

cidences that enliven history: they encountered the same Jan Ryp who had been with them the previous year, and who had returned on a trading mission. Heemskerck and his small group of survivors sailed home on Ryp's vessel, and they appeared before the Amsterdam merchants in the clothes they had worn in Novaya Zemlya "with fur caps made of white foxes."

Before long all of Europe knew about their experiences. Gerrit de Veer's journal was promptly published, and within a few years it was translated into several foreign languages. The book became an epic in the annals of navigation. The world was opening up and nothing stirred men's imaginations so much as stories about unknown regions. Spitsbergen had been discovered. They had gone further north than anyone before, to 81° latitude. They had been the first to survive a long winter in the Arctic, which was a great feat in itself. In the waters around Spitsbergen and Novaya Zemlya, they had seen large numbers of whales, and this proved to be the only economic advantage gained from the venture. It did not take the Dutch long to exploit this information, and a thriving whaling industry developed as a result.

In the attempt to find a northern passage to the Indies, the third attempt had been another failure, but it did not matter: Houtman had returned, with his southern mission accomplished.

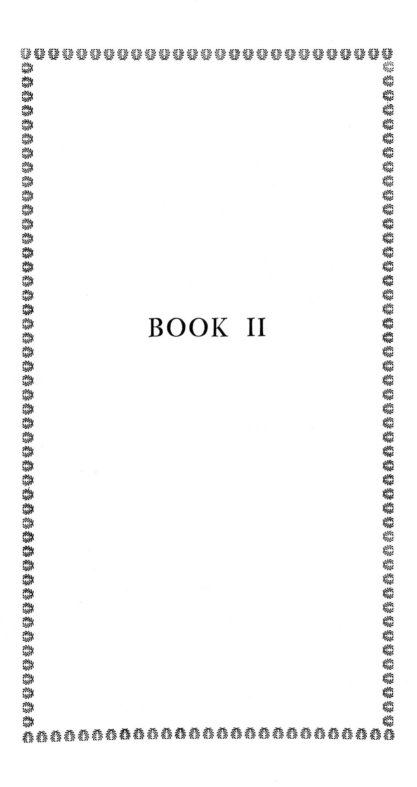

BOOK II

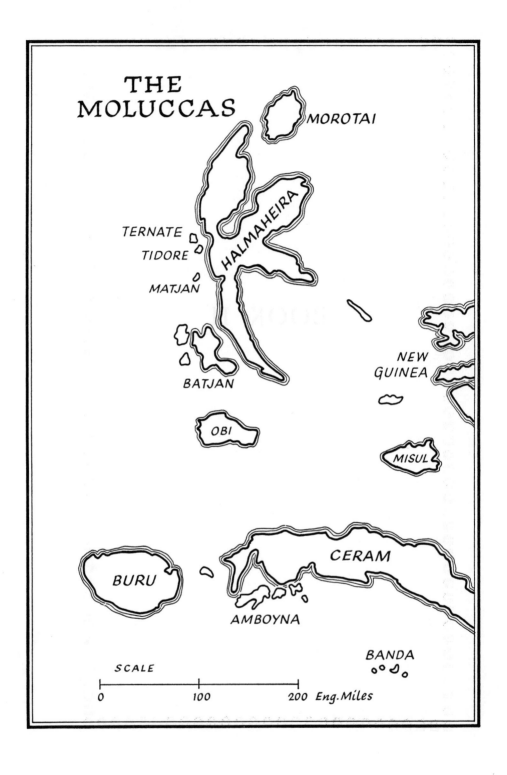

THE
MOLUCCAS

MOROTAI

HALMAHEIRA

TERNATE
TIDORE

MATJAN

BATJAN

NEW
GUINEA

OBI

MISUL

CERAM

BURU

AMBOYNA

BANDA

SCALE

0   100   200   Eng. Miles

I

Amsterdam Collects

It did not take the Amsterdam group long to realize that the first voyage south, regardless of its meager results, offered great possibilities. How vast these possibilities were no one could have anticipated. Within three weeks of Houtman's return, the Amsterdam merchants, with Oldebarnevelt as their spokesman, petitioned the States General for freedom of convoy duties and contributions of powder and shot for several successive voyages to the Indies. After this request had been granted, the Compagnie van Verre wasted no time in organizing a second voyage. The old ships were repaired and the keels laid of new ones for the fleet that was to sail in the spring of the following year.

The news spread through the Lowlands like wildfire, much the same as when the United States learned some 250 years later that gold had been found at Sutter's creek. Rumors invaded every town in the land, and Dutchmen everywhere came forward to invest in the venture. But a man had to know a wealthy merchant, one of the promoters, who was willing to accept his money. Those who had participated in the first venture did not have any trouble buying themselves a part, but others were not so fortunate. The fabulous Indies proved to be a magnet which attracted more capital than was needed at this early stage.

Another group of Amsterdam merchants entered the field before the year was out. They called themselves The New Company for Voyages to East India. This company requested and received the same privileges as the Compagnie van Verre: the States General played no favorites. But this was only the beginning: Zealand was not going to be left behind, nor was the town of Rotterdam. Zealand organized two companies, one headed by the mayor of Middelburg and the other by Moucheron, who now had the full backing of the town of Veere. Like many others, Moucheron had become discouraged about the possibility of finding a northern passage to the Indies. Rotterdam also accounted for two separate companies.[1] Altogether these companies sent out 22 vessels in 1598. The rush to the Indies was on.

In this year began the period of the so-called "preliminary" or "fore-companies." It was a short period—only four years—in which each company struck out on its own. To some it brought enormous profits, while others suffered great losses. Free enterprise held sway, and caused a state of economic chaos which threatened to ruin the East Indies trade even before it had been properly launched. It became obvious that competition among themselves would not yield the results the Dutch expected.

The experienced merchants of Amsterdam realized from the start that something of this sort was bound to happen, and they decided to form the strongest company in the country in order to compete effectively with the other towns. When their two fleets were about to sail, the Compagnie van Verre and the New Company joined forces to create "a solid foundation for trade." This consolidation became known as the Old Company because it was the first among others springing up like mushrooms in almost every important town. The board of directors was enlarged to seventeen, all belonging to the elite of the Amsterdam merchant class. Gerrit Bicker headed the list. He was a member of one of the oldest families of the town and, at 54, a man of considerable experience.[2] Reynier Pauw, though only in his early thirties, ranked second.

These men raised a capital of nearly 800,000 guilders, the largest amount that had ever been brought together in the Lowlands for a private venture. Dominie Plancius was again heavily interested, and only his vocation kept him from being a director.[3] The meager results of the first voyage had by no means deterred him from investing more money. He knew that mistakes had been made, especially in navigation. He had carefully studied the journal covering the day by day progress of the journey, and, by comparing it with the journals of more expeditious voyages, he was able to point out the pitfalls to be avoided.[4] A wrong course in

1. Van der Chijs, *Stichting O. I. Compagnie*, pp. 55–69.
2. Gerrit Bicker died in 1604, the year after he had become one of the mayors of Amsterdam. He left four sons, who were so successful in business that it was said that they divided the world between them.
3. Plancius was actively engaged in raising money for the United Company. See J. G. van Dillen, *Het oudste aandeelhoudersregister van de Kamer Amsterdam der Oost-Indische Compagnie* (The Hague, 1958), pp. 24–26.
4. See "Instructions presented by Petrus Plancius for the East Indian navigation," De Jonge, *Opkomst, 1*, 184–94.

the Atlantic Ocean had delayed arrival at the Cape of Good Hope, which should have been rounded rather than touched. After leaving the Cape, the Houtman ships had stayed too near the African coast, which forced them into the Mozambique Channel where they lost several months bucking adverse winds and currents. If they had sailed in a more easterly direction, the ships could easily have made the east coast of Madagascar, where the Portuguese usually landed before crossing over to Goa. Each delay had brought on another, with the result that the Indian Ocean had to be crossed during the wrong season, when the winds blew from the east. On all these matters, Plancius had written an elaborate report, and it became part of the instructions for the second southern voyage.

The matter of leadership was also scrutinized more closely. The command was vested in a few key men whose reputation would enforce respect. The admiral was Jacob van Neck, a man of an entirely different caliber from Cornelis Houtman. He came from a solid Amsterdam family and had received a good education. Being more of a merchant than a sailor, he had prepared himself for the important post by taking special lessons in navigation. Second in command was Vice-Admiral Wybrand van Warwyck. Next came Jacob van Heemskerck, who had made a name for himself on two attempts to find a northeast passage. A survivor of the terrible winter on Novaya Zemlya, he started out as ship's merchant, but during the voyage was promoted to vice admiral. Among the instructions Van Neck received from the directors was the usual one, that complete secrecy should be maintained about everything they encountered: "So that no one shall be able to use such knowledge to the detriment of our company."

The fleet sailed from Texel on May 1, 1598. It consisted of eight vessels, of which two were small yachts, also called pinnaces.[5] Following Plancius' sailing directions, they made good progress through the Atlantic, and within three months rounded the Cape of Good Hope. They then ran into heavy storms, and the fleet was split in two. Van Neck with three vessels refreshed

5. Yachts were never a distinct type of vessel as far as shape or rigging was concerned. The *Duifke* which accompanied the first voyage was in fact a miniature three-master of only 50 tons. The larger vessels, called "ships," measuring roughly between 400 and 600 tons, were of the type called *Spiegel* (mirror) ships because of their flat sterns, known to the English as transoms. They were built as warships and it was not until the danger from the Portuguese and Spanish had waned that the more economical flute ships were used in the East India traffic.

on the east coast of Madagascar before continuing the voyage without the rest of the fleet. His ships arrived at Bantam on November 25, having completed the outward voyage in less than seven months.

Considering the unsavory reputation the Dutch had earned for themselves on the previous expedition, it came as a surprise that they were now quite cordially received. For this they had to thank the Portuguese. When the Portuguese viceroy at Goa, Francesco da Gama, learned that the Dutch had been brazen enough to invade his domain, he had sent a fleet to hunt them down, but it arrived at Bantam after Houtman had sailed. Chagrined, the Portuguese decided to take revenge on the town for having allowed the Dutch to land there. The Bantamese resisted as best they could and by a stroke of good fortune actually succeeded in boarding three Portuguese vessels, and by sheer numbers overpowered the crews. After taking everything they could lay their hands on, the Bantamese set fire to the ships, which burned to the waterline. This took the fight out of the Portuguese, and the remainder of the squadron sailed back to Goa.

The Bantamese were justifiably elated with their victory and loot, but the wiser among them realized that the Portuguese were bound to return some day and demand retribution. As was to happen in other parts of the Indies, the Dutch were considered the lesser of two evils, primarily because the Portuguese had a long list of cruelties to their discredit, whereas the Dutch, being newcomers, had no such record. Though the Dutch were now more or less welcome, this did not prevent the King of Bantam from demanding a high toll before he allowed them to start buying. Instead of quibbling, Van Neck offered to pay an even higher tribute than had been asked. "Some may think," he wrote in his journal, "that we are a bit too liberal with the money of our Masters. But if they will look at it soberly they will have to agree that, at places where our nation previously left as an enemy, a certain amount of goodwill is not misplaced." [6]

After this magnanimous gesture, buying proceeded at a rapid pace, and within one month Van Neck had gathered enough spices to fill the holds of his three ships. He also came in contact with a renegade Portuguese, from whom he obtained valuable information about the Moluccas, the island group in the far east-

6. See J. Keuning, ed., *De tweede schipvaart der Nederlanders naar Oost-Indie onder Jacob Cornelisz. van Neck en Wybrant Warwijck, 1598–1600* (5 vols. The Hague, 1938–47).

ern corner of the archipelago where all the cloves came from.

It was the last day of the year. The ships were full and would soon be leaving for home. What further reason was needed for a real Dutch new year's eve celebration, loud and wet? There was yet further joy, for on that day their missing friends hove into sight. The journal reads that "they were joyously received and made welcome." It was a far cry from the new year's eve two years before, when the ships of the first voyage were at Bawean, their holds empty, Houtman just released from irons, the men snarling at each other, and a leaking ship to be burned the following day. Heemskerck, too, may have been reminiscing while quaffing his spiced wine and stuffing his belly. Two years earlier, he had been cooped up in a smoky cabin in the frozen wasteland of Novaya Zemlya, wondering if he would ever come out alive. But here he was, half a world away and very much alive.

Van Neck soon learned what had happened to Warwyck's squadron. After their separation near the southern tip of Africa, another storm had prevented Warwyck's ships from landing on the east coast of Madagascar as planned. They sighted the island Do Cerne (occasionally visited by the Portuguese), found a sheltered anchorage, and promptly renamed the island Mauritius. It proved to be a perfect refreshing place. Birds and fish were abundant, and there was "plenty of water to fill the men's bellies," Heemskerck recorded. They put a rooster and seven hens ashore and planted all kinds of seeds, including orange and lemon, "Invoking the Allmighty God's blessing that He may lend His power to make them multiply and grow for the benefit of those who will visit this island after us." [7]

Van Neck obtained a full cargo for a fourth ship and set sail for home. Before his departure, it was agreed that Warwyck and Heemskerck would head east with four ships and visit the Spice Islands.[8] Because of their singular wealth, these small islands had been coveted throughout the ages by the Javanese, the Malays,

7. De Jonge, *Opkomst*, 2, 392.
8. The Spice Islands, referred to by the Dutch as the Moluccas or the Great East, comprise the area in the eastern part of the Indies archipelago where cloves, nutmegs, and mace are produced. Cloves came from the Amboyna group of islands and neighboring Ceram, as well as Ternate. This clove-producing area was supposed to be under the sovereignty of the ruler of Ternate. Nutmegs and mace were produced only in the small Banda group. The name Spice Islands appeared on a map for the first time in the fifteenth century. Prior to that, Europe knew only that spices came from somewhere in the East. See H. J. de Graaf, *Geschiedenis van Indonesië* (The Hague, Van Hoeve, 1949), pp, 129–30,

the Moors and lately, by the Portuguese. They were now about
to receive a new set of masters.

The four ships under Van Neck reached Amsterdam in July
1599, after a speedy and uneventful voyage. The whole round
trip had been made in 14½ months, just about half the time it
had taken Houtman. They were received with great fanfare when
it became known that the ships carried in their holds 600,000
pounds of pepper, 250,000 pounds of cloves, and smaller quantities of nutmegs and mace. A treasure indeed! "For as long as
Holland has been Holland," the record states, "there have never
arrived ships as richly laden as these." [9] Led by eight trumpeters,
all the men marched triumphantly to the Dam, while every church
bell in town was ringing loudly. The town fathers willingly dug
into their pockets, regaled them with as much wine as they could
hold, and presented Van Neck with a gold plated silver cup.
The enthusiasm was fully justified. The proceeds of the cargo
of the four ships not only paid for the whole venture of eight
ships, but netted an additional profit of 100 per cent. And the four
other vessels were still to be heard from. Petrus Plancius' inspired
investment was paying off very well indeed.

Warwyck's squadron had, in the meantime, reached its destination in the far corner of the archipelago. They had run into no
trouble, except on the coast of Madura where the king of Arissabaya took revenge for the onslaught he and his people had suffered at the hands of the Dutch a few years earlier. He succeeded
in capturing a number of sailors who had ventured ashore, and did
not release them until a large ransom had been paid. After this
interlude, the ships continued their journey with dispatch for
the west monsoon, without which it was impossible to sail east
in those waters, was nearly spent.

In March 1599 they reached Amboyna. Because this island was
the main staple for cloves and because, from it, control could be
exercised over the Banda Islands, it could be called the key to the
Spice Islands. There was a Javanese colony at Hitu whence the
Moslems had been able to gain a great deal of ground in the
Moluccas, even before the arrival of the Portuguese in the Indies
in 1497.[10] The capitan Hitu received the Dutch well,[11] and they

9. De Jonge, *Opkomst*, 2, 206.
10. B. Schrieke, *Indonesian Sociological Studies*, 1 (The Hague, Van
Hoeve, 1955), 33.
11. The capitan Hitu was the most influential headman of Hitu, the

were given a house in which to display their wares and start buying, but there were not enough cloves available to fill even a single ship. It was decided that Warwyck should sail north to Ternate and Heemskerck to Banda. Each was to find his own way home.

Jacob van Heemskerck had been born in Amsterdam in 1567. He was the son of a sail maker, but it was said that he had the manner of a grandee. He could at times be haughty, an uncommon trait among the republican Dutch, but whatever the men thought of his manner and the rigid discipline he maintained, they fully appreciated his capabilities and courage. They even coined a phrase about them. Boarding an enemy ship with a saber in hand and a knife between the teeth was called "fighting a la Heemskerck." He resembled the English gentleman adventurers, more interested in action than in trade. When, on the coast of Madura, one of the chief merchants rebuked him for risking the company's property, he retorted, "When we risk our lives, the Lords of the Company may damn well risk their ships!" [12]

The Banda group toward which Heemskerck was heading consisted of only a few very small islands, but it was the only place in the whole world that produced nutmegs and mace, both coming from the same fruit. The islands had been visited since time immemorial by traders seeking these priceless goods. As a result the people had completely lost its original identity, and there was no islander whose antecedents had not been infused with alien genes, mostly from Javanese traders who had monopolized the spice trade for many centuries. Heemskerck found the inhabitants untrustworthy and complained that they repeatedly reneged on promises to deliver goods at an agreed price. They were also adept at juggling weights, substituting lighter ones for those used at earlier weighings. Bales of mace, the most valued of all the spices, were often loaded with the much cheaper nutmegs. To a Dutchman, whose word was his bond, such sharp practice was indeed distasteful. Only by threatening to hoist anchor if dishonesty continued did he finally succeed in buying a reasonable amount. "A man needs seven eyes," Heemskerck wrote

northern peninsula of Amboyna; he represented the 'king' of Ternate. The man who held this office at this time retained his function until his death in 1633. See W. P. Coolhaas, ed., *Generale missiven van de Gouverneurs-Generaal en raden aan de heren XVII der Verenigde Oostindische Compagnie* (The Hague, 1960), p. 74, n. 5.

12. De Jonge, *Opkomst*, 2, 209–10.

in his journal, "if he does not want to be cheated. These people are so crooked and brazen that it is almost unbelievable." [13]

Heemskerck returned to Amsterdam in May 1600, and again the church bells were ringing and the men were given a chance to drink their fill. It is recorded that when the spices were finally stored in the warehouse of the Old Company, "the air of the whole neighborhood was sweetened by their savory smell." Some may well have observed that the air also smelled like money.

Warwyck came home in September of the same year. At Ternate he had been received with open arms because the 'king' [14] was at war with neighboring Tidore, supported by the Portuguese, as well as with the Spanish, who had an important base in the Philippine Islands. He left one of his merchants and a few assistants behind to continue buying cloves in order to have a cargo ready when the next company ships would arrive. The man in charge was Frank van der Does, who had been on the first voyage in a minor capacity, but who had acquitted himself well by keeping a detailed journal of all that had happened. On the return trip, Warwyck succeeded in buying some more pepper at Bantam although the Zealand Company, whose ships had now also arrived on the spot, had bought heavily and at greatly increased prices. The evils of unbridled competition were beginning to make themselves felt.

Jacob van Neck made one more voyage to the Indies. On this occasion he lost three fingers in a sea battle with a Spanish-Portuguese fleet near Ternate. This made him decide that he had stretched his luck far enough and that he had better stay home. It turned out that he was one of the few early Indies men who lived to enjoy the fruits of his endeavors. He became an alderman and later a mayor of Amsterdam, and he was also a member of two admiralty colleges as well as some other important bodies. He died in 1638 at the age of seventy.

In every respect this second venture launched by merchants of Amsterdam had been a phenomenal success. Aside from the fabu-

13. This was one of the first complaints the Dutch had expressed against the people of Banda. In the end it led to the complete subjugation of these islands by the Dutch.

14. The Dutch called every local potentate a 'king,' whether he was the chief of some small coastal town or of a somewhat larger domain. Having proclaimed themselves a republic, the Dutch did not consider it irreverent to use the title 'king' indiscriminately. The English, on the other hand, with their ancient heritage of kingship, rarely used this term in their communications because it would have offended their own sovereign.

lous profits, all ships had returned safely, although the loss of life from sickness had again been great. But this was something that had to be accepted as God's will. In addition, the Dutch had learned much, and they intended to put this knowledge to good advantage. Factors had been left behind at Ternate and Banda, and with this a certain continuity of trade had been established. It is not surprising that these glowing reports made other merchants all the more anxious to share in the spoils.

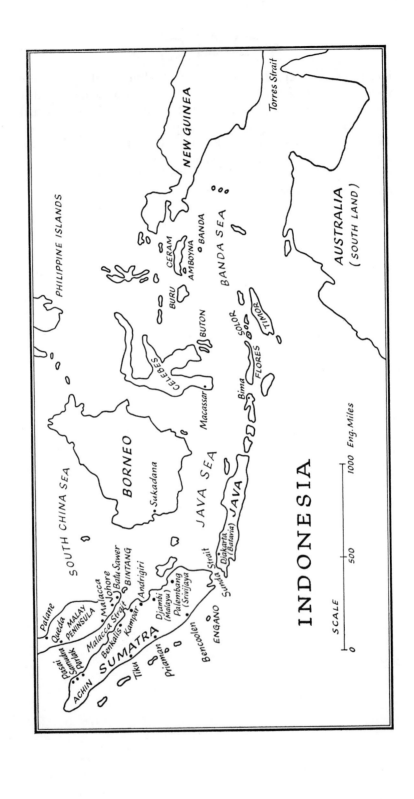

TORRES STRAIT

NEW GUINEA

PHILIPPINE ISLANDS

BANDA

AMBOYNA

CERAM

BANDA SEA

BURU

AUSTRALIA
(SOUTH LAND)

BUTON

SOLOR

TIMOR

CELEBES

FLORES

Macassar

Bima

SOUTH CHINA SEA

BORNEO

JAVA SEA

Sukadana

JAVA

Djakarta
(Batavia)

Patane

Queda

MALAY
PENINSULA

Malacca

Johore

Batu Sawer

Malacca Strait

Bintang

Benkalis

Andrigiri

Kampar

Djambi
(Malayu)

Sunda Strait

Pasai
Samudra
Perlak

ACHIN

SUMATRA

Tiku

Priaman

Bencoolen

ENGANO

Palembang
(Srivijaya)

INDONESIA

SCALE

0   500   1000 Eng. Miles

2

The
Rush
to the Indies

Even before the results of the Van Neck voyage were known, the Old Company had decided to send out a few more ships. In this they were prodded by Zealand and Rotterdam who had sent no less than 14 ships to the Indies during 1598. To be outnumbered almost two to one was not to the liking of the Amsterdam merchants, especially since they looked upon themselves as having prior rights, as pioneers in this field.

The *Sun,* the *Moon,* and the *Morningstar* left at the end of April 1599, with Steven van der Hagen in command. He was specifically instructed "to bear constantly in mind that the Zealanders are our enemies in trade, and therefore not to be trusted." [1] When he arrived at Bantam, there was little pepper available, and the price had skyrocketed as well, all because of the Zealanders who had bought everything in sight. There was nothing left to do but sail east towards the Spice Islands. Van der Hagen sailed for Ambon, and the other two ships headed for Banda. The latter arrived at a propitious moment because the small Dutch contingent that had been left there under Adriaan Veen was having a difficult time.

Native merchants from East Java had for many years maintained a lively trade with Banda, bartering for its spices which they sold in turn at Bantam or Malacca. The Portuguese, for the main part, had been satisfied with this arrangement and had done little to disrupt it. The Dutch, of course, were of a different mind. Their code demanded that they buy as cheaply as possible, and this meant cutting out the middlemen. When the Javanese merchants realized that they were being eliminated, they massed a fleet of thirteen large *prahus* at Tuban, each carrying over a hundred men. They sailed for Banda, determined to dislodge the

1. De Jonge, *Opkomst, 2,* 225–26.

Dutch by fair means or foul. The attack was imminent when the *Moon* and *Morningstar* arrived on the scene and saved the day. Against their cannons and muskets the Javanese felt helpless, and they returned to Tuban with the east monsoon. Adriaan Veen and his few companions had enough pluck to stay on at Banda after the Dutch ships departed for Amboyna to join Van der Hagen. There was little doubt that the Javanese would return the following season.[2]

At Banda arose a situation which no one had yet anticipated, and it pointed to one of the weaknesses in the manner in which the Indies trade was being conducted during the period of the "fore-companies." Each voyage was a separate financial undertaking which had to be liquidated in full as soon as it was completed. Not only were the profits disbursed but the ships were also sold as well, each participant receiving his pro rata share. Although the ships now at Banda had sailed under the auspices of the Old Company, the capital for this venture had in large measure been supplied by a different group of participants, each of whom expected to collect his full share of the profits. When Adriaan Veen wanted to load the spices he had so diligently collected, the skipper of the *Moon* was naturally perplexed. Who was to get the profits on this cargo, the participants of the first voyage, or those of the second? There were heated arguments, but it was obviously a matter which no simple sailor and sub-merchant could settle between themselves. In the end they agreed to load the spices and to let the directors of the Old Company fight it out in Amsterdam.

Van der Hagen, in the meantime, had done very well at Ambon. Not only had he obtained a full cargo of cloves but he had also received permission from the king, capitan Hitu, to build a fort in exchange for the promise that the Dutch would protect the Amboinese against the Portuguese who were bound to appear sooner or later. It was named Kasteel van Verre after the original company, and it was the first of a number of Dutch strongholds that would dot the Indies before long. Leaving a small garrison, Van der Hagen returned to Bantam and from there sailed for home in the company of certain other Dutch vessels which were now appearing in the Indies in growing numbers. The Old Company had scored another success.

2. See De Jonge, *2*, 226–29, and the original documents quoted on pp. 456–67.

It was apparent from the beginning that the Amsterdam merchants could not count on having the field to themselves. Of the two Zealand companies that had been formed soon after Houtman's return, the one headed by Moucheron was the first to leave, actually some six weeks ahead of the Amsterdam fleet under Van Neck. But being first did not necessarily mean that the venture was going to be more successful. It did prove, however, that the energetic refugee from Spanish oppression was not going to be left behind when it came to opening new areas of trade. Even before coming to Zealand he had approached William of Orange with a plan to find a northeast passage, and he had played an important role in the first futile attempts. He had also been among the first to send his ships to the west coast of Africa and to the West Indies.

As a personality, Balthasar de Moucheron had little in common with the staid merchants of his adopted country. His father had been a French nobleman, a Huguenot who had been forced to flee from his native land. Balthasar was proud of this noble lineage, and all his ships carried the Moucheron colors—a Burgundy cross on a green field. When he moved to Zealand after the fall of Antwerp, the town fathers of Middelburg had welcomed him with open arms, expecting to profit from his wealth and extensive business activities. He was a restless entrepreneur for whom no venture was too great or too risky. The failure of the northern voyages, in which the Middelburg magistrates had backed Moucheron, made them wonder if perhaps he was not a little too rich for their blood. The relationship cooled and without regret they saw him move to nearby Veere. This town had been an important wool staple during the Middle Ages but it was now well past its prime. But the memory of a glorious past had lingered, and the burghers were daily reminded of it by the sight of their huge cathedral, which had never been finished. Moucheron seemed just the man to bring the town back to prosperity. The magistrates offered him certain privileges and a large house if he agreed to send out 18 ships yearly from Veere and conduct all his business there. Moucheron readily accepted these conditions, fully expecting that everything he turned his hand to was bound to prosper.[3]

3. De Jonge, *Opkomst*, *1*, 108–16. See also J. H. de Stoppelaar, *Balthasar de Moucheron: Een bladzijde uit de Nederlandsche handelsgeschiedenis tijdens den tachtigjarigen oorlog* (The Hague, 1901).

It is difficult to understand why Moucheron selected Cornelis Houtman to head his expedition to the Indies as it was commonly known that this blusterer had lost the good graces of the Amsterdam company because of his irresponsible behavior on the first voyage. Besides Cornelis, Moucheron also hired his brother Frederik as well as some others who had been along on that journey. It was typical of Moucheron that he should engage an Englishman as pilot. His name was John Davis, and he had already made three voyages in an attempt to find a northwest passage to the Indies. He had indeed discovered the entrance, now called Davis Strait, but it would take several hundred years, as it did with the northeast passage, before this was finally proved. Since he had not succeeded in actually completing his journey, the English refused to support him in any further attempts. He made much of this slight when he offered his services to Moucheron, complaining that his own people were turning their backs to him. It made a convincing story, but it became evident in time that John Davis had a more substantial reason for wanting to join a Dutch expedition to the Indies.[4]

This time Cornelis Houtman was even more unfortunate than he had been on his previous voyage. Once more he got stuck on the southwest coast of Madagascar, where he was so well remembered from his earlier visit that the natives fled into the interior. Rather than go to Bantam, where he had established an even worse reputation, Houtman decided to sail to Sumatra. But so slow was his progress that, when he finally reached Achin on the north coast of the island, Van Neck was practically home again, although he had left six weeks later than Houtman.

They were well received in Sumatra, and it seemed that Houtman's luck was finally changing for the better; he was able to buy a few hundred tons of pepper. But the amicable relationship soon deteriorated after four Portuguese vessels from Malacca appeared on the scene. In exchange for giving the Dutch his moral support, the Sultan of Achin wanted Houtman to assist him in his war

4. See De Jonge, *Opkomst*, 2, 211–16. Because of the scanty material available from Dutch sources, De Jonge obtained his data about this voyage from Davis' journal, first reproduced in *Purchas, his Pilgrimes, contayning a history of the World in Sea-Voyages and Lande Travels by Englishmen and others* (Glasgow, 1905–07), (a reproduction of the original 1625 publication). More specific information about this phase of John Davis' life and adventures is to be found in A. H. Markham, ed., *The Voyages and Works of John Davis, the Navigator* (London, 1880).

against the Sultan of Johore. But Houtman had only two ships at his disposal, the *Lion* and the *Lioness,* and he was unwilling to commit them to this extent, especially since one had already a full cargo of pepper. The Achinese, a proud and aggressive people, were infuriated at what they took to be an insult. At an opportune moment they overran one of the ships and slaughtered a good many of the crew. Cornelis Houtman was one of them. It is ironic that he should have lost his life when, for once in his career, he had been sensible rather than foolhardy.

The attack had come as a complete surprise, but once the Dutch had recovered from it they gave no quarter. They managed to clear the decks, killing most of the attackers and throwing the others overboard. A number of Dutchmen who were ashore at the time had to suffer the Sultan's wrath; all but eight were summarily decapitated. The eight men who were spared this ordeal were put into prison. One of them was Frederik Houtman, who was soon able to prove that he was cut of different cloth from his elder brother. During his imprisonment, which lasted more than two years, he compiled the first Dutch-Malay dictionary, "In the Malay and Madagascar languages with many Arabic and Turkish words, for the special benefit of those who visit the lands of the East Indies." [5] He was the first to note the similarity between these two languages, which eventually established the fact that a lively intercourse had been maintained between Madagascar and the East Indies over many centuries, although they were situated on opposite shores of the Indian Ocean. He also managed to add and correct much astronomical data about the constellations in the southern hemisphere, thus proving himself a worthy pupil of Skipper Pieter Keyzer, who had died in the crow's nest during the first voyage while engaged with similar observations.

The *Lion* and the *Lioness* never reached Java. After a desultory peregrination in the Strait of Malacca and a futile attempt to liberate the prisoners in Achin, they tried to reach Ceylon, but adverse winds drove them off. After many additional hardships and with a crew that was practically decimated, they arrived in Zealand at the end of July with barely enough pepper for one ship. It was a full year after Van Neck had returned with his

5. This dictionary was first published in Amsterdam by Jan Evertsz. Kloppenburgh in 1603, and included the additional observations Frederik Houtman had made about the constellations in the southern hemisphere. De Jonge states that a copy of this rare book is in the Royal Library at The Hague.

fabulous cargo. Balthasar de Moucheron and his stockholders could hardly look upon this venture as having been very productive.

The ones who perhaps profited most from it, at least indirectly, were the English. Three days after his safe return, the English pilot, John Davis, wrote a letter to Robert, the Earl of Essex, "According to those directions which your Lordship gave me in charge at my departure; when it please You to employ me in this voyage for the Discovering of these Eastern Ports of the World, to the service of Her Majesty and the good of our Country." This missive accompanied the meticulous journal John Davis had kept on the voyage, and it reveals why he had been so anxious to join this venture. Before the year was out the English had organized their own East India Company under a charter from Elizabeth.

The other Zealand venture was organized by Ten Haeff, the mayor of Middelburg.[6] It set out to sea only a week after Moucheron's two vessels, thus putting both Zealand ventures into the water well ahead of the fleet fitted out by the Old Company of Amsterdam. Their squadron started with three ships, but one capsized in the Channel when it fired a broadside in a salute to the English before Dover. In the hurry to get under way the ship had been improperly ballasted. The remaining two ships did not reach Bantam until almost a year later, six months after Van Neck, who had in the meantime been able to obtain enough cargo for four ships. Whatever spices were left at Bantam after this wholesale buying had been acquired by the merchants of five Chinese junks and a vessel from Gujerat. When the Middelburg ships arrived there was not a bag of pepper to be had. They had to wait for the new crop to arrive on the market, and it took eight months before they were able to obtain a full cargo for both ships. The shrewd Bantamese merchants took advantage of their predicament by making them pay an exorbitant price.

Both Zealand ventures had not come up to expectations, but the one from Veere had been the least rewarding. The stockholders put the blame on Moucheron, because he had organized the voyage almost singlehanded. They joined forces with the

6. For the Ten Haeff venture, see De Jonge, *Opkomst*, 2, 216–17. See also W. S. Unger, ed., *De Oudste reizen van de Zeeuwen naar Oost-Indie, 1598–1604* (The Hague, 1948).

Middelburg group in 1600, forming the United Zealand Company. Moucheron lost all his backers and had to shift for himself, but he was still a man to be reckoned with. He proved this the following year when the States General initiated deliberations to unite all East India companies into one. From then on, however, it became apparent that he was behind the times. It was his ambition to be a great merchant whose word was law, like the men of Venice and Augsburg in the past. But a new economic era had dawned, one which demanded large amounts of capital provided by many participants in order to reduce the risks, and a sizable board of directors that reached decisions jointly. In such a heterogeneous body, Moucheron did not feel at home, and he preferred to remain an independent operator.[7] He began losing money, and before long he was unable to meet his obligations to the town of Veere. Its magistrates took back their house and rescinded the other privileges they had granted him. Within six years he was bankrupt, and the States of Zealand banished him from their province. Bitter at the Dutch, he tried to gain support from King Henry IV for the establishment of a French East India Company, only to be thwarted by the Dutch Ambassador in Paris. Balthasar de Moucheron died a poor and embittered man.

If the Zealand ventures had been far from prosperous, the two which left Rotterdam the same year (1598) were outright failures. Instead of sailing around the Cape of Good Hope, both squadrons went west through the Strait of Magellan, expecting to reach the Indies by crossing the Pacific Ocean. This longer and almost unknown route contributed to their miseries. But this was the way the Rotterdammers wanted to go, because spices in the Indies were not their prime interest. They were more concerned with trying to emulate Francis Drake and take as much booty as he had with the *Golden Hind* on the west coast of South America. But the secret leaked out, and the Spaniards were waiting for them.

One of these two ventures was organized by Pieter van der Hagen and Johan van der Veken. Both were expatriates from the Southern Netherlands who had transferred their business to Rotterdam. Their fierce hatred for the Spanish may in part explain this deviation from the normal route. They had to give their personal bond for the cannon and munition borrowed from various towns. Their fleet consisted of five ships, under Jacques

7. De Jonge, *Opkomst, 1,* 118.

Mahu and Simon de Cordes.[8] Counting on the Lord's blessing, the ships were named *Hope, Faith, Love, Trust,* and *Revelation.* Dirck Pomp China was skipper of the *Revelation,* a yacht, and he must have relished the opportunity to revisit the lands where no Dutchman except himself had yet set foot.

The *Faith* could not make it through the Strait of Magellan and returned to Rotterdam, the only ship of the fleet to be saved for the owners. The other four were able to enter the Pacific Ocean, but only after fighting both the elements and the natives for several months, and a loss of two hundred men. The Pacific Ocean belied its name, and heavy storms scattered the fleet. Dirck Pomp China sailed north along the coast of Chile, but at Valparaiso he fell into the hands of the Spanish. For many years it was presumed that he had surreptitiously sold his ship to the enemy and lived handsomely off the proceeds. This fable was so widely accepted than an eminent Dutch historian of the present century wrote "With this stench, Dirck Pomp departs from the pages of history." But documents in the Spanish archives, subsequently unearthed, leave no doubt that this first Dutchman to reach China and Japan, had been grossly maligned. The Spanish had taken the *Revelation,* and Dirck China was put in prison.[9] After three or four years he was finally released in an exchange of prisoners and returned to his home land. There is no record as to what happened to him after this, but it is more than likely that he spent his last years telling all who would listen about his latest adventures.

The *Trust* came closest to reaching its destination. After crossing the Pacific it reached the Island of Tidore in the Moluccas, only to be captured by a Spanish-Portuguese force. The other two ships, the *Hope* and the *Love,* had in the meantime headed for Japan, of which Dirck China had told such wonders. On this journey the *Hope* wandered off course and was never heard from again. Only the *Love* reached Japan with the crew in a deplorable condition, only eight or nine of whom were able to stand on their feet. The Shogun treated them well but he was fascinated with the ship and appropriated it for himself. He did

8. For further details about this voyage see F. C. Wieder, ed., *De Reis van Mahu en de Cordes door de Straat van Magalhaes naar Zuid-Amerika en Japan, 1598–1600* (3 vols. The Hague, 1923–25).

9. See J. W. IJzerman, ed., *Dirck Gerritsz. Pomp, His Voyage and Sojourn in South America* (The Hague, 1915).

not enjoy this product of the western world very long—the *Love* soon ran aground and became a total loss.

What was left of the crew stayed in Japan, and, of these, two names stand out. One was the English mate, William Adams, who managed to ingratiate himself with the Shogun and who was later able to assist his countrymen when the English East India Company established a factory in Japan. The other was the merchant Melchior van Santvoort who served the Dutch equally well when the time came. For the backers, of course, the whole venture had been a total loss. Van der Hagen went bankrupt and Van der Veken only barely managed to keep his head above water by having the States of Holland intercede for him against the towns who demanded payment for the cannon they had lent on his personal bond.

The fifth and final voyage of the year had been organized by Oliver van Noort, a Rotterdam tavern keeper who was known as a devil-may-care individual. His appetite for adventure had been whetted by the tales of many seafaring men who passed the time in his establishment, The Double White Key. Among these there must have been Simon de Danser, who inspired Longfellow to write a poem which appeared in one of the earliest issues of the *Atlantic Monthly* magazine.

> In his house by the Meuse, with its roof of tiles
> and weathercocks flying aloft in the air,
> there are silver tankards of antique styles;
> plunder of convents and castles, and piles
> of carpets, rich and rare.
>
> But when the winter rains begin,
> he sits and smokes by the blazing brands.
> And old sea-faring men come in,
> goat-bearded, gray, and with double chin,
> and rings upon their hands.
>
> And they talk of ventures lost or won,
> and their talk is ever and ever the same,
> while they drink the red wine of Tarragon,
> from the cellars of some Spanish Don,
> or convents set aflame.
>
> Restless at times, with heavy strides
> he paces his parlor to and fro.

He is like a ship that at anchor rides,
and swings with the rising and falling tides,
and tugs at her anchor tow.

Voices mysterious far and near,
sound of the wind and sound of the sea,
are calling and whispering in his ear:
"Simon Danz, why stayest thou here?
Come forth and follow me!"

This was the spirit in which Oliver van Noort embarked on his venture. It is easy to picture him, leaning across his bar and with a stubby finger enticing his customers to put up their savings. In this way he raised enough money to fit out two ships. He also made it clear that he was not going to stay home like other aloof merchants and wait for the profits to come into the till; he was going to take command himself. And he made no bones about the fact that he intended "to singe the beard of the King of Spain" whenever the opportunity presented itself. The word spread from Rotterdam to Antwerp and Brussels by stealthy couriers and thence to Lisbon and Madrid, and then across the Atlantic to Brazil, Peru, and Chile. The Spanish were alerted. There were quite a few people of means to whom such a forthright action appealed. They were the ones who did not subscribe to the admonition of the cautious Amsterdam merchants who had instructed their skippers, "Never engage the enemy in combat unless you have to defend yourself." Such people were to be found even in Amsterdam—a group there supplied enough money to add two more vessels to Van Noort's expedition which left in July.[10]

It was apparent from the start that the tavern keeper turned buccaneer was not on a peaceful mission. At the first stop, the Cape Verde Islands, there was trouble with the natives, and Oliver's brother, Cornelis, was killed. At Rio de Janeiro the ships were shelled by Portuguese shore batteries and had to make a hasty retreat. Proceeding slowly down the coast, one of the four ships sprung a bad leak and had to be abandoned. It took fourteen months before they finally reached the Strait of Magellan, and five different attempts before they managed to get through. Of the 250 men with which the voyage had started, 100 were dead. Not

10. De Jonge, *Opkomst, 1,* 124–29, *2,* 222–25. See also J. W. IJzerman, ed., *De Reis om de wereld door Olivier van Noort, 1598–1601* (2 vols. The Hague, 1926).

everyone had agreed that the passage through the Strait should be negotiated at any cost. After having been driven back a few times to the Atlantic side, the Vice Admiral, Pieter Claesz., argued loudly against such foolhardiness. As a result, the Council condemned him to be put ashore for his insubordination, "With some bread and wine," the journal reads, "but there was no place for him to go on that wild coast. He would either starve to death or be eaten by the natives. After this was done the General [Van Noort] ordered a prayer to be said in the whole fleet, and every one was warned to take this example to heart."

Now at last, Van Noort was in the waters where Sir Francis Drake had once been so lucky, but for him they proved less fortunate. One ship was lost soon after they headed up the coast, leaving only two. The Spaniards were waiting for them. "At Lima," the journal states, "they knew for over a year that we were coming, even the name of the Admiral. The whole country was up in arms, and their ships of war were ready to take care of us." [11] After several engagements, the two ships became separated. One sailed across the Pacific and safely reached the Moluccas, but this luck became disaster when it foundered on the coast of Ternate.

Van Noort kept cruising northward along the coast, taking his booty where he could. He captured a small Spanish ship, and the two sailed as far north as California before they, too, started across the Pacific. The prize became unseaworthy and had to be abandoned. With only one ship left, Van Noort reached the Philippine Islands, two years and four months after he had left the Meuse. Among these islands he impartially looted everything that came his way, thus building up a reputation for the Dutch as being nothing but pirates. He tried to reach Bantam for a load of pepper, but the west monsoon pushed him eastward through the Java Sea, and he had to go home via the Bali Strait, as Houtman had done on the first voyage.

He reached Rotterdam on August 12, 1601, after a voyage of more than three years. He was the first Dutchman to sail clear around the globe, but the loot he brought back did not begin to pay for the venture. Van Noort's voyage was also unique in another respect. He was the only one who had handled the whole operation from beginning to end: he had raised the money, represented his company in its dealings with the States General, and

11. Van Balen, *Nederlands Voorhoede*, pp. 126–27.

he had also taken command of the expedition. The merchant-promotors of all the other companies invariably stayed at home. He had of course many backers, but since the government frowned on privateering which could easily become piracy, they had wisely refrained from having their names openly associated with a venture of this kind.

In England, until the end of the sixteenth century, such caution was completely lacking. The great captains of the Elizabethan era—Hawkins, Drake, Cavendish, and others—were all avowed buccaneers, with the Queen herself often an interested party. Not until the formation of the English East India Company did the English begin to realize that there was more to be gained from trade than from booty in that part of the world. This did not necessarily mean that the Dutch were adverse to taking prizes when the opportunity beckoned—it was a matter of degree rather than of substance. The second voyage of Jacob van Heemskerck in the service of the Amsterdam merchants is a case in point.[12]

He sailed on April 23, 1601, in command of a fleet consisting of eight vessels. In the middle of the Atlantic, just north of the equator, Heemskerck ran into Oliver van Noort who told him that he had just sailed around the world. After arriving at Bantam, Heemskerck found that competition from other Dutch companies had driven up the price of pepper far beyond what he had paid on his previous voyage. He left five ships at Bantam to fill their holds as best they could while he went to look elsewhere for a cargo. On the north coast of Java, Heemskerck captured a small Portuguese vessel which carried documents to show that the Spanish and Portuguese had regained power in most of the Moluccas. This decided him to turn west instead, to Patane in the Gulf of Siam. He also found that the Portuguese had hung seventeen Dutchmen at Macao, all of them shipmates on his previous journey. Patane, next to Bantam and Malacca, was an important source of pepper, and when Heemskerck reached it there were already four other Dutch vessels on the roadstead, all vying for a cargo of pepper. Buying proceeded slowly, and Heemskerck was beginning to feel that he was dragging his heels when the news came that two Portuguese caracks were on their annual journey from Macao to Malacca. At this point Heemskerck turned privateer.

One carack escaped, but the other, the *Catharina*, fell into his

12. De Jonge, *Opkomst*, 2, 259-72.

hands after a day long battle. For its time, the *Catharina* was an enormous ship of 1,400 tons. The wealth it carried was in keeping with its size: copper from Japan, silk from China, and some bullion from the mines of Mexico and Peru. When this booty arrived at Amsterdam it was valued at over three million guilders. By far the greatest part of this were 1,200 bales of raw Chinese silk which was sold at auction in Amsterdam for 2¼ million guilders.[13] This marked the beginning of a thriving silk trade which, before the century was out, would prove to be more important than the spices that had been the original Dutch goal. The booty also included a quantity of Chinese porcelain, and this brought a new word into the Dutch vocabulary. From then until the present, the finest Chinese porcelain became known as *kraak* (carack) porcelain.

In accordance with established practice, fifteen per cent of the total went to the States General, five per cent to the crew, and Heemskerck, as admiral, received one per cent for himself. The balance was distributed to the stockholders. Small wonder that Holland was jubilant, and there were quite a few who asked themselves if this was not a better way to make quick profits than by pursuing an ordinary spice trade which was gradually destroying itself in internecine rivalry. Even Hugo Grotius, the jurist and future author of *De jure belli et pacis* (Paris, 1625) which made him the Father of International Law, could not restrain himself, and called this feat, "the most beautiful and worthiest fruit of Voyaging to the Indies." Grotius made this statement in connection with a commission he had received from the Lords Seventeen of the recently established United East India Company to prove that the capture of the Portuguese carack was legally justified. The right of a private company to take prizes was hotly contested in the Netherlands at that time and even denied by the Mennonites. *De Jure Praedae* was written by Grotius in 1604, when he was 21 years old, and it was the first of his works on international law. *De Jure Praedae* was not then published in its entirety and the manuscript was not recovered until 1868.[14]

The sober merchants of Holland, especially those of Amsterdam, were unwilling to share this enthusiasm. It was true that

13. K. Glamann, *Dutch Asiatic Trade, 1620–1740* (The Hague, 1958) p. 112.
14. J. and A. Romein, *Erflaters van onze beschaving* (Amsterdam, 1938), pp. 44–49.

profits from the Indies trade were already diminishing because competition was driving up the cost of spices, and the unprecedented quantities that arrived in Europe were depressing the market. But it was commerce that had made Holland great and they believed it was best to stick to something that had proved itself. An occasional windfall, as Heemskerck had brought home, was of course gratefully received, but such were few and far between. On the other hand, trade itself had never failed the Dutch, and if it now created problems because of unbridled competition, then there was only one thing to do: eliminate this evil by operating under a monopoly.

3

The
Prime Mover
of the
United Company

It was obvious to most men that something drastic had to be done if the fruits of these early voyages were not to be dissipated. In the few years since Houtman's return, some ten companies had been organized and between them they had sent out 14 fleets, totaling 65 ships. A few of these ventures had been extremely profitable, but most had only broken even or worse. The Amsterdam companies had been the most fortunate so far, but even here it was admitted that the profits from the spice trade were diminishing because "They sail each other the shoes off their feet, and the money out of their pockets." [1]

At first the Old Company of Amsterdam tried to meet competition by sheer force, because, considering itself the strongest, it expected to be victorious. When it was learned that a Zealand fleet was about to set sail, the directors instructed their skippers in language that was plain enough. "You know as well as we do," they wrote, "what losses it would cause us if the Zealand ships were to arrive before ours are fully loaded. Therefore, buy! Buy everything you can lay your hands on, and load it as quickly as possible. Even if you have no room for it, keep on buying and bind it to yourselves for future delivery. You must see to it that

1. De Jonge, *Opkomst*, *1*, 136; for a thorough analysis of the difficulties encountered by the fore-companies, see his app. 18, "Memorandum submitted to the States General about the need for a unification of the East-India Companies." It is not recorded by whom this well-reasoned remonstrance was submitted. Checking the spelling of certain words, De Jonge deduces that it must have been written by a refugee from the southern Netherlands and he wonders, not without reason, whether it may not have been Willem Usselinx. For the latter see Limburg, *Cultuurdragers*, pp. 285–313.

we shall not suffer in the least at the hands of the Zealanders. With them we have no agreement or understanding of any kind." [2]

The Amsterdam merchants were keen enough to realize that this policy alone would not save the day. Something that went to the root of the problem was needed and, with this in mind, they petitioned the States of Holland for a monopoly on all trade east of the Cape of Good Hope for a period of 25 years. It was a model writ and logically argued but so brazen that only a group of Amsterdam merchants cognizant of their power would have dared to present it.

Aside from the fact that this document shows Amsterdam's attitude, it is important because it set into motion the discussions which led to the formation of the United East India Company. The document is undated, but it must have been presented around August or September of the year 1601. In part it is a recapitulation of how the Indies trade began and how it had developed. It reminded the States of Holland that certain merchants of Amsterdam had sent Houtman to Lisbon and, after his return, financed the first voyage to the Indies. All this had cost a great deal of money, and the returns from this first venture had been far below expectations. Had they given up? No! For the glory of the country, they had fitted out eight ships in 1598, three in 1599, ten in 1600, and thirteen in the early part of the year 1601. Altogether, their ships amounted to more than half of all those that had sailed for the Indies during these four years, and it was an established fact that the Old Company of Amsterdam had been more successful, by far, than any of the other Dutch companies. "For many and various reasons," the petition concluded, "it is advisable that this commerce must be conducted by one administration, because if it is left in the hands of a number of companies, then this promising trade will come to naught." [3]

Lucid as it was, the argument failed: the opposition was too strong. When this matter was discussed in the States of Holland during October, the majority held that Amsterdam's request was too one-sided.

The opposition was led by Johan van Oldebarnevelt who, as advocate (chancellor or attorney general), was the dominant fig-

2. Instructions by the directors of the Amsterdam Company to the Admirals and Councils of "our fleets in East India," 1601.

3. Remonstrance submitted to the States of Holland and West-Friesland by the directors of the East India Company within the town of Amstelredam. See De Jonge, *Opkomst*, 1, 254–56.

3. Johan van Oldebarnevelt, age 70.

ure in this assembly. As a statesman he realized that the East Indies trade was something in which the whole country should participate, rather than a single town, no matter how important Amsterdam was in both the polity and the economy of the republic. In their resolution, the States of Holland agreed that "good order, supervision, and a single administration was essential to develop this trade to the best advantage and honor of these lands," but they wished to accomplish this in such a manner that the whole country should benefit. Accordingly they instructed their delegates in the States General that "not only the directors of the Amsterdam company should be called into consultation, but also those of Middelburg, the Meuse and the Northern Quarter . . . so that these men can discuss ways and means whereby this aforementioned navigation and trade shall be secured for many years to come." [4]

Thus the matter was transferred to the highest political body in the country where Oldebarnevelt, as head of the delegation from Holland, also played a leading role. It was not the first time that he had been forced to oppose certain powerful individuals or groups because their partisan interest, as he saw it, was inimical to the common good.

A portrait of him painted at some later date by Mierevelt shows a strong and somewhat forbidding face with a high, creased forehead and heavy eyebrows. His icy blue eyes are stern and piercing above high cheekbones; he has a full moustache and a long, forked beard. It is a face that El Greco would have liked to paint.

Johan van Oldebarnevelt was born in 1547 at Amersfoort, a town some twenty miles east of Amsterdam. His father was a landowner of modest means and there is nothing in the records to indicate that he was of that noble lineage Johan occasionally mentioned, in rather vague terms. After attending the Latin school in his birthplace, he studied at The Hague and then at the university at Louvain.[5] Having absorbed all they could teach him there, he went to Bourges in France, where Calvin had studied. His main interest was reading law which then as now provided a solid foundation for a political career. The persecution of the Huguenots forced him to leave France, and he pursued his studies at Cologne and later at Heidelberg, which was a hotbed of Cal-

4. Resolutions of the States of Holland, October 22–31, 1601.
5. Oldebarnevelt studied on a scholarship, a further indication that he came from a modest background.

vinism. In this environment he became converted, but not without reservations. Calvin preached that all men were equal before God. As long as this was restricted to the religious sphere, Oldebarnevelt had no objections, but he resented it when the Calvinists tried to extend this principle to political theory.

Early in life he had reached the conclusion that the masses were not qualified to govern themselves; instead, they should be guided by a select number of men who had the background and the ability to do so. Oldebarnevelt had become the leader of the oligarchy in the province of Holland, and the consolidation of the Republic as a burgher aristocracy and a loose confederation, in which the preponderance of Holland was the unifying factor, had been largely his work.[6]

After the revolt against Spain broke out, Oldebarnevelt returned to his homeland and began practicing law in The Hague. Like many a young lawyer, he found it difficult and had to take on all sorts of odd jobs to maintain himself. At a time when many believed that the revolt was doomed, he threw in his lot with the Prince of Orange, and volunteered for military service in attempts to relieve the sieges of Haarlem and Leiden. After this, the young jurist moved to Delft where the Prince kept his headquarters. It was not long before he was picked for small missions, and his name acquired some luster when in 1573 he succeeded in settling disturbances among the English mercenaries.

From then on he slowly moved up; his opportunity came when Rotterdam invited him in 1576 to become the town's advocate. In this capacity he attended sessions in the States of Holland, where he soon acquired a reputation for being able to solve complex problems. During the negotiations leading to the treaty of Ghent, Oldebarnevelt was much in the foreground. This noble attempt to join north and south in the fight against Spain proved to be short-lived, but it had given him ample opportunity to prove his ability as a mediator.[7]

When the north realized that it would have to stand on its own, the States of Holland turned to Oldebarnevelt to prepare for the Union of Utrecht, which marked the establishment of the Dutch Republic. It meant pulling together many contentious factions

6. Geyl, *Netherlands Divided*, p. 14.

7. Much has been written about Oldebarnevelt. In English, a standard work is J. L. Motley, *The Life and Death of John of Barneveld, with View of the Primary Causes and Movements of the 30 Years' War* (2 vols. The Hague and London, 1874).

in the provinces and towns and among landowners and merchants. There was also the important question of who should head this new polity. The cry was for William of Orange, but Oldebarnevelt refused to agree with the prevailing belief that the country needed a monarch. He was in great favor with Prince William; nevertheless, he used all possible means to curb the influence of the stadholder. He wanted the real power to be wielded by the States General, in which each of the seven provinces would be represented on the basis of what it contributed yearly to the exchequer. Since Holland provided more than half, it should therefore have a corresponding number of votes. The smaller provinces refused to accept his idea of proportional representation based on wealth, and as a result Holland was allotted no more votes than any of the others. But Holland was not to be sidetracked so easily. Because of its great wealth and the personality of Oldebarnevelt, the province nevertheless became the dominant factor in the government.

The advocate fought hard for his proposal that religious freedom should be extended to all creeds, including the Catholic. He saw no benefit in having the commonwealth renounce a Catholic theocracy only to adopt an equally oppressive one which the Calvinist clergy demanded. His resolution was carried, but it marked the beginning of a bitter struggle. While Oldebarnevelt was gaining power he was also making enemies. The Calvinists began calling him "Pope John."

Soon after his father's assassination, Prince Maurice had been named stadholder, and for this Oldebarnevelt had been largely responsible.[8] In the beginning, the relationship between the two was cordial enough. The young prince relied on the older statesman for guidance, and he also realized that he needed the support of Holland to finance his military operations. But when these exploits became more and more successful and he had acquired a name as a military genius, his ambition grew in proportion. He was, after all, commander in chief of the armed forces, the son of William of Orange and, as stadholder, the titular head of the country. Considering all this, he found it more and more difficult to have to acknowledge the fact that a mere commoner was the real leader instead of himself.

There is no simple parallel in history with which to compare the office held by Oldebarnevelt. As Advocate-General, he was

8. See Geyl, *Nederlandse stam, 1,* 298.

actually the servant of the sovereign States, a functionary who made the necessary arrangements and prepared the agenda for their sessions. In this capacity he was the only person in a position to lend continuity to whatever decisions were made, because he was also charged with the responsibility of seeing them carried out. A man of less energy might well have been content to look upon this job as being purely administrative, but not Oldebarnevelt.[9]

Being in a position to oversee the whole complex picture, he managed to gather all the executive power in his own hands. It was to his office that the Dutch envoys reported from all the capitals of Europe, and he also had his own agents who reported to him directly. Thus he became the one man in the republic who knew better than anyone else what was going on, and he had no doubt about his ability to cope with all the implications. The power it gave him had not been implicit in the office to which he had been appointed; it was only through his own efforts that he made it into a vehicle which enabled him to meet the many problems that confronted the young republic.[10]

It was inevitable that a man who wielded so much power and saw fit to use it "for the good of the commonwealth as a whole," could not count on being accepted with equal equanimity by all the different factions in the republic. In the principles which Oldebarnevelt himself laid down as being the prerequisites for a viable state, some of the reasons can be found for the fact that, in the years to come, opposition to him mounted steadily.

"If we do not create a government with sufficient authority to rule these lands," he said, "to hold the provinces and towns to their duty of contribution and orderly unity, to oppose the un-

9. For the functions of the *landsadvocaat*, see R. Fruin, *Staatsinstellingen in Nederland*, pp. 231–33. Oldebarnevelt's salary amounted to only 1,200 guilders per year, and out of this he had to defray his own office expenses. The salary, however, was of minor consideration because it was greatly augmented by gifts ('for services rendered') by private persons, towns, provinces, and foreign potentates. As a result Oldebarnevelt managed to amass great wealth. This practice of accepting gratuities on the part of the highest dignitary in the republic was discouraged and as a result the salary was gradually increased. By 1668 it was raised to 6,000 guilders and the Advocate-General was prohibited from accepting gifts.

10. In matters of great urgency and importance, such as secret negotiations with foreign powers, the States General appointed a special committee, consisting of one delegate from each of the seven provinces. In this committee Oldebarnevelt, by virtue of his office as Advocate of Holland, was always the eighth member.

willing and obstructionists, to counteract the enemy's machinations, to defend these lands against all injuries and perils, without having to wait for reports and consultations of the individual provinces and towns—then we shall be lost! Because no republic can exist without a good order in a central government." [11]

The first significant break between Oldebarnevelt and Prince Maurice occurred in the year 1600. The Dunkirk pirates had become increasingly brazen during the past few years and now, with the richly laden East India ships all having to pass through the narrow Channel, the problem was becoming more urgent than ever. The merchants requested armed support from the government to eradicate this pirate's nest once and for all. It would be a calamity, they argued, if such wealth were to be lost to the country on its very doorstep and to fall into enemy hands instead. Oldebarnevelt pleaded their case in the States General, fully aware that it was the revenue from overseas trade which had to finance the war effort. Maurice objected strenuously. He reasoned that, from a military standpoint, such an expedition was too ambitious. After much hard fighting, the republic had been able to secure its borders by a ring of fortified towns, and was now relatively safe within this bastion. He considered it foolhardy to attack the enemy on its own terrain. But the Advocate-General persisted and the States General ordered Maurice to the attack.

At Newport, the Dutch forces were met by a strong Spanish army. Thanks to Maurice's generalship, the battle was won, but the losses he suffered were so great that he preferred not to proceed to Dunkirk, which was heavily fortified. The States General allowed Maurice to withdraw his troops. Dunkirk, the object, had not been reached and nothing had been gained. At The Hague there were recriminations, and the rift between Prince Maurice and his mentor began to widen. [12]

The year following the futile Dunkirk expedition, Oldebarne-

11. Limburg, *Cultuurdragers*, pp. 184–85. For a more elaborate account of Oldebarnevelt's political creed see M. L. van Deventer, ed., *Gedenkstukken van Johan van Oldenbarnevelt en zijn tijd (1577–1609)*, 3 (The Hague, 1860–65), 142.

12. J. L. Motley, *History of the United Netherlands*, 4 (London, 1876), 1–51. This chapter gives a full account of the Dunkirk campaign. The capture of Dunkirk would have been the last chance to weld Brabant and Flanders to the North. It is Professor Geyl's opinion that Maurice did not make a great enough effort toward this important goal. See Geyl, *Nederlandse stam*, 1, 318–19.

velt ran foul of the Amsterdam merchants, who did not take it lightly when he opposed their request for a monopoly of the East India trade.

When these powerful factions—the Calvinists, the House of Orange, and Amsterdam—finally joined forces, Oldebarnevelt's fate was sealed. But this was still in the future, and in the meantime he continued his efforts to weld the young republic into a solid entity. Not the least of his many accomplishments was the formation of the United East India Company.

4

The
Formation
of the
United East India Company

It speaks for the farsightedness of the States General that it tried to arrange an orderly development of the East India trade even before the first fleets sailed in 1598. Early in January of that year all companies were instructed to send delegates to The Hague for a discussion of this matter. The delegations from Holland arrived on the stipulated date, and it turned out that they were in principle inclined to accept certain restrictive measures. The Zealand delegation had been delayed by ice and did not arrive until after the Holland delegates had already returned to their counting-houses. Its members proved far less amenable than those of Holland. "The companies of Zealand," they said, "cannot agree to put themselves under one company and one admiralty." The States General, as yet not too sure of its powers, did not try to force the issue. However, it did pass a resolution admonishing all companies "to conduct themselves wisely and treat each other as friends," and if they should reach a port where another company was engaged in buying, then they should move on and buy else-where.[1]

It was sound advice, but no one paid any attention to it. For one thing, it ran counter to the spirit of unfettered competition which until then had dominated all aspects of Dutch trade. Every merchant was more or less convinced that he knew more and was better qualified than any of his competitors, and that it served his interest best if he kept his own counsel. This was even more true of the individual companies. There was another reason why competition could not be reduced by trying to avoid contact in the Indies. The paternal advice of the States General assumed that

1. Resolution of the States General, dated January 19, 1598.

it was possible to buy spices almost anywhere, but there were actually only three or four places where sufficient quantities could be obtained.[2]

For a few years the government did nothing further about the matter except to advise restraint whenever a new company applied for a charter. It also showed its interest in the trade as a whole by granting patents, copyrights, and cash rewards to anyone who made a worthwhile contribution to the arts of navigation and geography. When, in 1599, still another company was organized in Amsterdam, the States General tried to keep its ships out of the Spice Islands, and issued a charter that was only good for the China trade. It was called the New Brabant Company, because most of the participants were refugee merchants from the south who had been brought together by Isaac Lemaire, as rugged an individualist as Moucheron. In December they sent out four ships under Pieter Both and Paulus van Caerden, to be followed a few months later by two more. But this company paid as little attention to the government's caution as any of the others.[3]

The rivalry among the companies at home foreshadowed what was to happen after their ships had arrived in the Indies, where they would soon be cutting each other's throats. They tried to hire crews away from each other, and their skippers and pilots were bound by contract never to enter the service of another company or to divulge anything they might learn in the course of a voyage.

Towards the end of 1601, when it was evident that some companies were headed for bankruptcy, the States General felt the time had come to try to bring about a consolidation. Oldebarnevelt had been concerned about this matter from the beginning, and his patience was apparently wearing thin. Shortly after the States of Holland had turned down the request of the Amsterdam Company for a monopoly, this body asked the States General to call a meeting of all interested parties.[4]

The meeting was held at The Hague in the beginning of December at the Inn of Brille where the Zealand delegation was staying. The only inference to be drawn from this is that it seemed

2. Achin and Bantam for pepper, and the Moluccas for cloves, mace, and nutmegs.
3. This relatively late arrival in the field provided the first two governors general of the United East India Company: Pieter Both and Gerard Reynst.
4. Resolution of the States of Holland, dated October 31, 1601.

a sound diplomatic move not to antagonize the obstreperous Zealanders right from the start. The first point of discussion was the share each geographical area was to contribute. Without much quibbling, it was agreed that Amsterdam should supply half the capital, Zealand one quarter and The Meuse and Northern Quarter each one eighth. The next item was the composition of the board of directors and the site of its headquarters. The majority voted for Amsterdam, but the Zealanders insisted that alternate meetings of the board should be held at Middelburg. The main stumbling block was the manner of voting.

The deputies from Zealand proposed that the board should cast no more than four votes: one each for Amsterdam, Zealand, the Meuse, and the Northern Quarter. Amsterdam, already committed to provide half the capital, flatly rejected this. The Zealanders stuck to their guns, although the other companies were willing to allot Amsterdam a more equitable number of votes. According to the minutes, the delegates became embroiled and they broke up without having settled the issue. Two days later the Zealanders informed the States General that they had taken leave of the delegations from Holland because they were not authorized to offer better terms.

The States General, not satisfied with the way the negotiations were developing, ordered every town involved to have its representatives return to The Hague for further deliberations. They reconvened on January 15, 1602. Oldebarnevelt acted as moderator, and he wasted no time before warning all those present that they were impairing the national interest by failing to reach an agreement. "It is well-known," he said, "that the King of Spain is relishing this discord, because it would be difficult for him to combat a strong and united company. It is therefore to the interest of the commonwealth that all parties get together and place themselves under one organization." [5]

Oldebarnevelt's exhortation contained the veiled threat that if the Zealand companies refused to be amenable, they might well be bypassed completely, as the States General had the power to withhold the charter which was a prerequisite for any India voyage. The need for action was not solely a domestic problem. The English had in the meantime established their own East India

5. For these and subsequent negotiations preceding the granting of the charter, see De Jonge, *Opkomst*, *1*, 140–47, and 261–71. Also Van der Chijs, *Stichting*, pp. 82–88.

Company with an exclusive monopoly. The realization that England might reap the fruits of the spadework done by the Dutch contributed to a more conciliatory atmosphere among the disputants.

Amsterdam made the important concession of not insisting on a veto power to which it should have been entitled by providing 57.4 per cent of the capital. The number of directors was set at 17: eight from Amsterdam, four from Zealand, and two each from the Chambers of the Meuse and the Northern Quarter. The seventeenth member was to be appointed in rotation by one of the three smaller chambers, thus assuring them that the powerful metropolis should never have a majority. Appropriately enough, the board was invariably called *De Heeren Zeventien*, or just *Zeventien*. Amsterdam also agreed to have the Lords Seventeen hold their meetings in Zealand during certain years.

With these and other less important issues finally agreed upon, only the consent of the States of Holland and Zealand were needed to make a United Company official and to submit a charter to the States General for its approval. It was now the end of January 1602, and only a few months remained before ships of the new company would have to sail, if they were to take advantage of a favorable monsoon in the Indian Ocean. If everything were not settled by then, a whole year would inevitably be lost.

Oldebarnevelt expedited matters in Holland, and its delegates at The Hague were instructed to take appropriate action. Zealand, however, was hesitant, and for a while it seemed as if the whole enterprise would come to naught. The men in power in Middelburg were wondering why Amsterdam had been so willing to make concessions. What else could it mean than that those "grasping" northerners felt they had got the best of the bargain? And there was yet another stumbling block—Balthasar de Moucheron. He was still a powerful merchant, and, with the town of Veere behind him, he could not easily be ignored.

Moucheron professed his willingness to participate in a United Company, but only under certain stringent conditions. He reasoned as follows: at present he had six ships at sea, all engaged in the India trade, and most of his capital was tied up in these ventures. He was quite willing to commit himself for 100,000 guilders in a United Company, provided he were given time to pay his share after some of his ships had safely returned. In the meantime, he demanded that he be accepted by the Middelburg chamber as a full-fledged director. He also insisted that all trade on the east coast of Africa, from Sofala to the Red Sea, should be his private monopoly.

For the sake of harmony and to avoid further delay, most of Moucheron's demands were met, but the problem was far from solved. Following Veere's example, other towns in Zealand were anxious to be included: Flushing, Goes, and Zierikzee. The whole month of February went by, and the possibility of an agreement seemed more remote than ever. Once again Oldebarnevelt stepped into the breach. On March 3, he arrived at Middelburg with a small delegation from Holland. This time he minced no words. Again referring to the need for a United Company to combat the machinations of the King of Spain, he as much as accused the Zealand merchants that there must be some among them who were enemies of the State. How otherwise could it be explained that Zealanders always tried to put a spoke between the wheels? Prince Maurice arrived at Middelburg at about the same time, but the records do not state whether this was by chance or design. Posterity must draw its own conclusions.

Confronted by the stadholder of Holland and Zealand and the republic's senior statesman, the opposing factions in Zealand reached an accord. On March 16, with the deadline rapidly approaching, Zealand agreed to the formation of a United East India Company on terms which were acceptable to Holland. Within two days the combined resolutions of Holland and Zealand were presented to the States General. In that august body, the discussions lasted another two days, and on the evening of March 20 a charter was voted by a majority of those present for a period of twenty-one years.

This is how the United East India Company came into being. The foregoing can at best give only a sketchy outline of the many problems involved. There were many more negotiations, all crowded with heated arguments, but the result had been achieved. Centuries of fishing and trade had prepared the Dutch for this moment: to go as far as they could and make money in the far corners of the world. Actually, the final negotiations had taken less than five months, and Dutch historians are almost unanimous in giving Oldebarnevelt full credit for bringing the issue to such a speedy conclusion. They are also in agreement that the charter spelled the beginning of Dutch authority over a large area of Asia.

Oldebarnevelt could not have foreseen that his creation would keep the English out of the Spice Islands, force them to be satisfied with the Indian mainland, and ultimately, establish there the greatest possession of the British Empire. All he said was: "In order not to be taken solely for an advisor, I risked 5,000 guilders in the United East India Company." [6]

The company was known officially as *De Vereenigde Oost-Indische Compagnie*, or simply the ꙮꙮ in common usage. In time, every piece of property the Company owned, from knives to forts, would carry this symbol.

The charter was the blueprint of the Company and, considering its far-ranging consequences. it ranks among the historic documents of all time, although among the English speaking peoples— with their Magna Charta and Declaration of Independence—it is hardly known. But no less can be said about a document that spelled out the beginning of a huge empire in Asia, an empire that lasted three and a half centuries!

The original charter is one of the most prized possessions of the National Archives in The Hague. It consists of sixteen pages of strong parchment tied with a yellow, red, and white cord which holds the great seal of the States General. The seal is a disc of red wax some five inches across, and it has been broken and patched many times since it was affixed on March 20, 1602, but the writing is as black and clear as it ever was.

There were 46 articles in all, and most dealt with the internal management of the organization, such as financial participation, appointments, the duties of the directors, and their responsibilities towards the shareholders.[7] Considering the fact that this was the first joint-stock company of any importance, it is remarkable how closely these resemble the articles of incorporation of modern companies, although there were of course some significant differences.[8]

The capitalization was close to six and a half million guilders, a considerable amount considering the real value of the guilder in those days.

6. J. van Oldebarnevelt, *Remonstrantie aende Staten van Hollandt ende West-Vrieslandt* (The Hague, 1618), p. 50.

7. The complete charter together with annotations is given in Van der Chijs, *Stichting*, pp. 98–115.

8. Vacancies in the directorate were filled by the mayors of the towns where the various chambers were located by selecting one name out of three supplied by the directors of that chamber. The stockholders had no chance to express their preference. See J. G. van Dillen, *Oudste aandeelhoudersregister*, pp. 27–28.

Besides Amsterdam and Middelburg, there were chambers in Rotterdam, Delft, Hoorn, and Enkhuizen. Each of these chambers was responsible for supplying its allotted share of the capital; each also retained a certain amount of autonomy by being allowed to ready its own ships and have the return cargo brought to its town. All the profits, however, were to go into a single account. Each chamber, moreover, had its own set of directors. These were the merchants who had actively participated in the fore-companies; by simple addition, their total was 73 directors for all the chambers together.[9] It was logical that only men of experience should be entrusted with the management of such an important enterprise. The States General was not represented in this group because it was intended that the United Company should be a private organization in which the government was not directly involved.

One of the requirements for a director was that he subscribe for a minimum of 6,000 guilders (with the exception of those of Hoorn and Enkhuizen who were allowed to put up only half this amount). Although some directors subscribed for considerable sums, the fact remained that their total share did not have to be more than six or seven per cent of the whole capitalization. The bulk of the capital was to be supplied by outsiders, on the principle that the opportunity to profit from the East India trade should be extended to as many people as possible.[10] The charter specifically stated that every person had the right to participate for as much or as little as he was willing to risk. In case the issue was oversubscribed, those with more than 30,000 guilders would have to reduce their share proportionally in order to make room for the small investors. The ordinary stockholders had no voice in the management; all they could demand was their share in the profits, which were to be distributed as soon as they amounted to more than five per cent of the capital.

Besides their financial interest, the directors had other advantages. As a body they received a commission of one per cent of the cost of all vessels, and one per cent of the return cargoes as well. This was certainly preferential treatment, because the direc-

9. Each of the original directors is mentioned by name in the charter.
10. The Amsterdam chamber had 1,143 subscribers who paid in some 3,675,000 guilders. Of these there were 301 refugees from the southern Netherlands, who accounted for about 1,400,000 guilders. This clearly shows the importance of these refugees in the Dutch economy. For a more detailed breakdown and a list of the principal subscribers (10,000 guilders and over) see Van Dillen, *Oudste aandeelhoudersregister*, pp. 55, 61.

tors' risks were covered whether or not the Company made a profit. This was not their only additional source of revenue at the expense of the ordinary stockholders. The clause which prescribed that profits should be distributed almost as fast as they were made overlooked the important fact that during certain periods, outlay might exceed income. To meet such an eventuality, provisions should have been made to create a reserve fund, but this matter was either overlooked or it was regarded as being incompatible with the interest of the common shareholders who wanted their dividends as soon as a profit was made.

On the principle of limited liability, no one, directors included, was responsible for more than he had paid in. This meant that the need for additional funds could be met only by borrowing. Since the directors were the only ones among the shareholders who had a clear picture of the financial situation, they were quick to avail themselves of the opportunity. They and their friends bought these short-term obligations, which paid a handsome interest and were practically devoid of any risk, since they were secured by large stocks of spices, either safely stored in warehouses or still en route. The stockholders would complain that the directors were lining their pockets at the expense of themselves, and they demanded to know why the directors did not convert the stocks of spices into cash, instead of borrowing against them. To this, the directors had a ready answer: to sell them at one fell swoop would so depress the market that there would be no profits at all. But none of these problems had been anticipated at the time the charter was written. It was to be a trading company only, and little thought was given to the fact that, in order to protect this trade and extend it, vast sums were needed to maintain armed forts and, in addition, to support a fleet to keep out envious competitors.

It soon became evident that the original board of directors was a bit unwieldy, and it was agreed that in case of death no vacancies were to be filled until the total number had been reduced to sixty. The smaller towns were again favored, and Amsterdam had only twenty members although it supplied over fifty per cent of the capital. There is no ready explanation for this discrepancy except, perhaps, that Amsterdam felt it could afford to be magnanimous because it was represented in full strength on the highest level—the committee of the Lords Seventeen, where it commanded eight votes.

These 17 men were chosen from among the directors, and it was this small group which actually ran the Company during the whole of its long existence. From the beginning, it was a secretive institution, and there are almost no details available as to what occurred during its frequent deliberations. Only the final results became known, but nothing about the stand taken by individual members on certain issues. The administrative duties were handled by the advocate (solicitor) of the Company.[11]

The Seventeen determined everything that concerned the Company, often to the smallest details, and their decisions were mandatory. All were men of considerable wealth, but the Charter nevertheless provided a member with compensation if a meeting was held in a town other than his own. In such cases they were allowed a per diem allowance of four guilders for food and lodging, but this was all, and each had to defray his own travel expenses.

Article 34 of the Charter contained the important monopoly clause. It gave the United Company the sole right for twenty-one years to sail east of the Cape of Good Hope and west through the Strait of Magellan. All other citizens of the republic, regardless of "what condition or quality" were specifically excluded from these waters on the penalty of forfeiting their ships and cargoes.

Not everyone in the Lowlands agreed that such a stringent monopoly should have been granted to a single company for the exploitation of the East India trade. But the main object in forming a United Company had been to serve the commonwealth as a whole by bringing greater prosperity, and at the same time to deprive the enemy of valuable trade. Logically, this could only be accomplished if this trade were profitable. The rivalry between the fore-companies had come close to ruining trade before it had even been properly developed. Consequently, competition had to be eliminated. A monopoly seemed to offer the only solution. In this respect, the States General had taken a much more liberal attitude than either Spain or Portugal.

In those countries, the whole India trade, as well as the means

11. Pieter van Dam served in this capacity from 1652 to 1689. He was charged by the directors to write the Company's official history, not for publication but only for their own records. His *Beschryvinge van de Oostindische Compagnie* remained in manuscript in the National Archives in The Hague until it was finally published in six volumes, edited by F. W. Stapel (The Hague, 1927–43).

of transportation, were the prerogatives of the king. Not only did he see fit to exclude his own subjects but also, on the basis of a Papal Bull, all other nations as well. The Dutch government, on the other hand, made it easy for many individuals to participate as stockholders, and it tacitly acknowledged the fact that other countries were equally free to trade in the Indies if they had a mind to do so.

Although the Charter dealt almost exclusively with the aspects of trade and management of the company, there was one article that veered away from this subject. Ostensibly designed to cover the protection of trade, it would soon prove to have more far-reaching effects. It was the article which authorized the Company to make treaties with princes and potentates in the name of the States General. The Company was also allowed to establish forts and garrisons at strategic points and to appoint governors and officers of justice to preserve law and order. These officials had to take an oath of allegiance to the States General, to Prince Maurice, and to the Company itself.

The original purpose of giving the Company such broad powers was to safeguard its property in the Indies against attacks by the Spanish and Portuguese. They also implemented the government's desire to extend the war into that theater and thus weaken the enemy indirectly at home. But these same powers also helped to create a merchant republic, rather than a simple mercantile enterprise. This, in turn, soon opened the door to territorial acquisitions, something that had never been contemplated. Without being aware of it, Oldebarnevelt had been instrumental in promoting a Dutch empire in Asia.[12]

12. In his *Remonstrantie* Oldebarnevelt stated his primary motive: "The great East India Company, with four years of hard work, public and private, I have helped establish in order to inflict damage on the Spaniards and Portuguese."

5

By Trial
and Error

As a statesman, Oldebarnevelt had good reasons to be pleased with what had been accomplished. In the first place, there was the prospect of a profitable trade which could only benefit the country and aid the treasury. Secondly, and just as important, the war against Spain was to be extended to Asia at no expense to the government, because the United Company would bear the full brunt.

In other respects, the government's direct interest was minor. For granting the charter, the States General had received a share in the United Company amounting to 25,000 Flemish pounds— little more than a token, considering the capital involved. The States General also had the right to settle a specific issue in case the Seventeen were unable to agree among themselves. In practice, this never happened. These men had no intention of letting the government meddle in the internal affairs of the company; it was only when problems with outsiders arose that they asked the States General to act in behalf of the company.

From the start, the Seventeen were obliged to make some important decisions. During the period of the fore-companies, individual commanders had been ordered by their principals to avoid hostilities as much as possible, because trade was the prime objective and fighting the enemy was liable to result in damage or loss. Such a defensive attitude was no longer valid, and the Seventeen acted accordingly. Trade was still the prime objective, but the prospect of taking valuable prizes was equally alluring. Word soon spread that the Company intended to pursue a policy of fighting *and* trading. The Dutch were a nation of individualists, and they were by no means bashful in voicing their opinions. It was therefore understandable that the issue became one of the main topics whenever the newly established East India Company was discussed.

Those who were in favor stressed the benefits that would accrue from aggressive action combined with trade: profits *and* prizes

151

promised high dividends to the stockholders, and it would weaken the enemy as well. What could be better? Others were not so sanguine. They pointed out that Dutch trade had flourished because war and trade had been kept separate. Unlike their neighbors, they had built two types of ships, one designed for convoy duty and the other for the sole purpose of fostering trade. The latter ships, light and practically unarmed, had been able to compete successfully with all comers. From now on, all vessels sailing to the Indies would have to be heavily armed and manned accordingly, and there were quite a few, even among the directors, who thoroughly disapproved.

This new policy might have been more generally accepted if the Dutch had had an inkling that this was the beginning of a colonial empire and a tight monopoly of practically the whole spice trade. At that time, however, there was not a single person in the whole republic who gave the slightest thought to such a possibility. The Dutch were still fighting for their independence, and, as individuals, they were pursuing the time-honored profession of trying to make a profit. To consider the possibility of depriving the enemy of a large slice of its empire under these conditions would have been as incongruous as if, at a later date, the American colonists would have had a similar objective in mind when they were fighting the English for their independence.

The problems that could be anticipated from this dual function of the United Company were thus fully recognized, but there was no easy solution. The Spanish and Portuguese, after having recovered from the surprise of seeing the Dutch invade their domain, would certainly strengthen their fleets in the Indies and try to evict the interlopers by force. Peaceful trading would thus be out of the question in any case.

The Seventeen decided to meet the situation head-on. Granting that trading *and* fighting was a costly procedure, they realized that there was no alternative. There was also a good chance that some valuable caracks might be captured in the process and this would help to defray the cost of war. The instructions they issued to the commanders were brief and to the point: "Attack the Spanish and Portuguese wherever you find them." [1] The main purpose was to chase the enemy out of the Indies, so that Company ships could go wherever they pleased without being molested. In time, this aim would be achieved, but it took much

1. Instructions to Admiral Steven van der Hagen in 1603.

longer than had been expected. The combined forces of the Spanish and Portuguese proved to be formidable opponents, and when
they were defeated at one end of the archipelago they often
gained a victory elsewhere. When at last they began to weaken,
another strong rival would cause almost as much trouble: the
English rightfully felt that they had as much right to trade in the
Indies as the Dutch.

The Seventeen had no misgivings so far as the prospects of trade
were concerned. The advantages to be derived from having consolidated all the individual companies into one were obvious.
Monopoly prevented competition in buying, and thus the purchase price could be kept within reason, and, by the same token,
selling on the European market could proceed in a more orderly
fashion because there was now no possibility of dumping goods
on the market. Factories were to be established in the Indies so
that buying could continue in anticipation of following vessels,
which could then be loaded with a minimum of delay and thus
assure a quicker and less costly round trip.

Because the prime objective was trade, no thought as yet had
been given to the need for a central point where orders from the
Seventeen could be processed. There was, moreover, no single
authority in the Indies to act upon them, although theoretically
the admiral of the fleet arriving in Indian waters was the supreme
commander. Bringing the latest instructions, he superseded his
predecessor even if the latter had not yet departed for home.
There were, of course, reasons why these two important matters
had not been settled immediately.

The Indies covered a vast area, and most of it was still almost
entirely unknown to the Dutch. Nowhere did they have a firm
footing, and trading was actually at the sufferance of local potentates. The admirals had to protect this trade from the time the
ships rounded the Cape of Good Hope, where they were likely
to run into Portuguese men-of-war. The danger area stretched
as far east as the Moluccas, within easy reach of the Spanish stronghold in the Philippines. In this arena, covering some 120° longitude, or one third the circumference of the globe, a number of
Dutch ships had to keep the enemy at bay while others were
trying to obtain a cargo of spices. How to implement this ambitious program could only be learned from experience.

The Seventeen wasted no time before sending out the first fleet
for the account of the United Company. A squadron of three

ships sailed on March 31, 1602 under Sebald de Weert, and the main body, numbering twelve ships, left on June 17 with Admiral Wybrand van Warwyck in command. Their instructions indicated that the Seventeen had much more in mind than confining the Company's activities to the Spice Islands. De Weert was to sail to Ceylon and from there to Achin in North Sumatra. Van Warwyck was ordered to send three ships directly to Achin and the rest to Bantam, where three vessels were to pick up a cargo and return forthwith to the Lowlands. A few ships should continue to the Moluccas, and the remainder were to head north to China and open up that country for trade. These instructions covered a huge territory, and made it clear that the United Company intended to play for high stakes.

De Weert reached his destination according to plan, landing at Batticalao on the east coast of Ceylon. Finding no cargo there, he was about to leave for Achin when the local rajah induced him to pay a visit to the Maharajah in Kandy who, he said, was a great friend of the Dutch.[2] De Weert did not want to lose an opportunity to establish a foothold in Ceylon, where the Portuguese obtained their cinnamon. Not knowing how much time he would have to spend in Kandy, De Weert decided to let two of his ships proceed to Achin according to his instructions. He also realized that it might be quite a while before anything concrete could be accomplished, because the Portuguese had a firm hold over the west coast of the island where most of the cinnamon was produced.

Having been educated by the Portuguese, the Maharajah of Kandy had become a Christian and had taken the name Dom João. This close relationship, however, had long since turned into bitter enmity. The vice-admiral was received with many protestations of friendship and for a good reason: Dom João counted on the Dutch to help him get rid of the Portuguese.[3] He painted a rosy picture. If the Dutch blockaded Galle and thus prevented the Portuguese from bringing up reinforcements from Goa, Dom João would attack the town by land. After Galle had been taken,

2. Joris van Spilbergen was the first Dutchman to visit Ceylon. In the service of Moucheron, he visited Kandy in 1602, on which occasion he presented the Maharajah with a portrait of Prince Maurice on horseback and in full armor.

3. Dom João had been forced to withdraw to the interior of Ceylon after the Portuguese established their authority over the productive coastal areas.

the same could be done at Colombo. For this help the Dutch would receive a yearly tribute of 2,000 quintals of cinnamon "to last forever." Dom João also agreed to turn the Portuguese forts over to the Dutch as well as the whole of Ceylon's cinnamon trade.

De Weert had every reason to be pleased with his visit to Kandy. "I do not know how we can justify ourselves if we should ignore this opportunity," he wrote Admiral Van Warwyck. For the present, however, there was nothing he could do about it. He had only one ship at his disposal, and he was thus forced to leave matters as they were for the time being and sail to Achin.

In Achin he found not only his own two ships but also three which had been sent there by Van Warwyck. North Sumatra was presumed to be an important source of pepper, but it turned out that its reputation was greatly overrated: there was barely enough pepper available for one ship.[4] Nor did the king of Achin prove to be very cordial. Of all the people the Dutch had to deal with in the Indies, the Achinese were the most independent. Other local potentates were usually anxious to enlist Dutch support against the Portuguese, but the Sultan of Achin reasoned adroitly that in the end the one would be as bad as the other.[5] And now, with no less than six Dutch ships in his waters, he and his people became more suspicious than ever. De Weert did manage to obtain a house near the beach for future use but, when he wanted to protect it with a palisade, he was clearly forbidden to do so. The vice-admiral did not feel too badly about these reverses, and actually regarded them as a good omen. He now had six vessels under his command and with these he could return to Ceylon and reap the rewards Dom João had dangled before his eyes.

His squadron left Achin in April 1603, and such were the expectations that De Weert proclaimed a day of prayer: "in being thankful for all the bounty already bestowed, and that the voyage may add to the glory of God's name and to the prosperity of the

4. The Dutch themselves precipitated this situation by buying pepper directly at Patane on the Malay peninsula which had formerly shipped considerable quantities to Achin via Queda.

5. The title *sultan* should be regarded as a holy sanction of his position as Moslem ruler, accorded him by Moslem authority presumed to have the right to do so (the *sherifs* of Mecca). See B. Schrieke, *Indonesian Sociological Studies*, 2, 327.

fatherland and the Lords Seventeen, and bring about the destruction of all the Portuguese." [6]

Three weeks later De Weert was back at Batticalao where he
was received with open arms. A courier was sent to Dom João,
and while they waited for a reply the crews disported themselves
ashore. Everyone was convinced that the lucrative cinnamon trade
of Ceylon was to be presented to them on a silver platter,
and there was enough arrack [7] around to color their imagination.
During their stay at Batticalao, the Dutch had only one complaint. Fruit and vegetables were readily obtainable, but the men
were thoroughly tired of the salted beef that had been their fare
ever since leaving home. Their craving for a juicy steak or a joint
of beef was whetted even more by the cows they saw grazing in
the countryside. Several times De Weert tried to buy some cattle
but without success. The Singalese threw up their hands in horror,
because the beasts were not only holy but also harbored the souls
of departed relatives. De Weert refused to take the Singalese
seriously, and he finally allowed his men to slaughter a few animals, relying on his offer of payment to overcome their scruples.
Once before the Dutch had fallen into disrepute when they handed
the sultan of Achin a letter of salutation from Prince Maurice
which had been written on parchment made from pigskin.

The Dutch were discovering by stages that there were other
things besides silver reals which made for a harmonious intercourse with the peoples of Asia and their baffling customs. The
rajah of Batticalao was furious. "The Hollanders had professed
to come as friends," he raved, "but they were worse than enemies.
The Portuguese, at least, never committed such a dastardly deed.
He would sooner give his own life than allow the killing of cattle
to continue."

"From that time on," Jacob Rycx wrote in his journal, "we
were on a bad footing with the king and his subjects. But we did
not worry too much about this as the King of Kandy is on our
side, and he is feared by all the other kings in Ceylon who have
to obey him." [8]

In this uneasy atmosphere the awaited letters from Kandy arrived in which the Maharajah repeated the promises he had made
earlier. In accordance with the original plan, the Dutch ships

6. The data on this voyage of De Weert and Van Warwyck is derived
from several documents in the National Archives in The Hague. See also
De Jonge, *Opkomst, 3,* 3–26, 145.
7. Arrack is a spirit distilled from palm toddy.
8. See n. 6.

would sail to Galle, but, before they were ready to leave, four Portuguese ships appeared off the coast. With his superior force, De Weert captured them all. He could spare only enough men for two of these prizes, and, feeling chivalrous after this easy victory, he allowed the Portuguese to sail for Goa on the others, not knowing that a son of Dom João was among them as a prisoner.

After the news of this victory reached Kandy, Dom João sent word that he was coming to Batticalao in person to show his gratitude. He also requested that all the Portuguese prisoners should be delivered to him. It takes little imagination to picture Dom João's reaction when he learned that the Portuguese had been allowed to escape carrying his son with them. This event, added to the incident of the cows, was soon to have a bloody ending.

At first the inscrutable potentate acted as if nothing had happened to mar his friendship with the Dutch. To celebrate the victory and to discuss the next move, Dom João invited De Weert and twenty-five others to an elaborate feast at the house of the Rajah of Batticalao. What happened then was similar to an incident in the history of the feuds between the clans of Scotland, when the Gordons exterminated the Forbes at the banquet table. In simple words, Jacob Rycx wrote about the event in his journal:

> While the Vice-Admiral and the King discussed various matters, there was quite a bit of drinking. Suddenly the King berated the Vice-Admiral for having allowed the Portuguese to escape. By then Van Weert was pretty drunk. He denied the accusation heatedly and insisted that the King and his retinue pay him a courtesy visit on his ship, adding: 'The Dutch are not accustomed to bend their knee without receiving some respect in return.' This added fuel to the fire and the King apparently convinced himself that the Dutch were not to be trusted, and that the invitation was for the sole purpose of taking him prisoner. At a signal the King's followers drew their swords, slaughtering the Vice-Admiral and all those who were with him. There were three hundred Singalese hidden in the woods near the beach, and when they learned what was happening in the palace they attacked those of us who were ashore. In all we lost forty-seven men and six wounded . . . And so it was all enmity and we not knowing what had caused this because we thought we were all friends. This happened on June 1 1603.

De Weert's death spelled the end of his grandiose plans to take Galle and make it into a second Goa, to acquire the cinnamon trade, and, from this stronghold, eventually to drive the Portuguese out of the Indies. The Dutch would eventually accomplish all this, but not until many years had passed.

After the deed was done and his fury had cooled, Dom João tried once more to ingratiate himself with the Dutch. Not only did he want them as allies against the Portuguese, but he was also afraid that the Dutch might some day return and take their revenge. His overtures and promises, however, no longer impressed the Dutch. The newly chosen commander, Cornelis Pietersz. from Enkhuizen, and the plenary council minced no words; they refused to listen—"we are sailing for other lands where we shall be treated less treacherously." If Dom João meant what he said he should gather enough cinnamon and pepper for two ships, ready to be loaded at once in case the Dutch returned. They also warned him of the consequences should he ever dare raise his hand against the Dutch again.

The ships headed for Patane in the Gulf of Siam which was an important mainland trading center for pepper and goods from China and Japan. In the Strait of Malacca, Cornelis Pietersz. learned that the Sultan of Johore was at war with the Portuguese who were blockading the town. The Dutch managed to chase away the Portuguese but without any profit to themselves. The Sultan, however, professed his eternal gratitude, and this later inspired the thought that with his help the Dutch might be able to take neighboring Malacca from the Portuguese. This, too, was eventually accomplished, but by then this age-old trading center had lost much of its former importance.

Admiral Van Warwyck had in the meantime arrived at Bantam after a long and difficult voyage. Trying to obtain a cargo quickly for a few ships, he was immediately confronted with the vexing problem of harbor dues and other tributes demanded by the king of Bantam. With each successive arrival of ships in his port, these levies had been increased, and now the Dutch felt that they were exorbitant. In the long and tedious negotiations that followed, the *shahbandar* (harbor master) proved that he could outsit any commander who hated to see his vessels remain idle on the roadstead. In another respect, Van Warwyck was more successful. He gained possession of a stone house, conveniently located and apparently safe from fire or sneak attack. It was the first establishment of the United Company in the Indies, and might have become a general headquarters if constant trouble with the Bantamese had not forced the Dutch to go further east along the north coast of Java, to a small village called Djakarta.

From Bantam Van Warwyck sailed to Grise near the town of Surabaya in east Java, where he also obtained permission from the local king to establish a factory.[9] From there he sailed to Sukadana on the south coast of Borneo. This place had little to offer except some diamonds which the natives washed out of the river gravel in the interior. These few diamonds lent more glamor to the town than it deserved and led to several useless ventures in that direction.

Time had not been on Van Warwyck's side, and it was June 1604 before he finally sailed to the China coast in accordance with his instructions from the Seventeen. The prospects for trade there were not very promising. From Bantam he had dispatched two ships to China, but they had been unable to do any trading and, in an encounter with the Portuguese, 18 men had been taken prisoner and subsequently hanged at Macao.[10] Van Warwyck found the Chinese equally adamant in refusing him a foothold for trading. All he accomplished was a promise from some merchants to ship their silk and porcelain to Patane or Bantam where the Dutch could buy it from them. After a few more time-consuming side trips, he finally sailed home from Bantam in February 1606. En route his vessel sprang a bad leak, and he had to spend a long time on Mauritius for repairs. It was June 1607 before he finally returned to Holland, five long years since he had departed.

One can be certain that the Seventeen listened carefully to all he had to report. It was mainly a saga of delays and frustrations, some good opportunities missed through bad judgment or the lack of a sufficient force at the proper time and place. There were nevertheless a few valuable cargoes and the establishment of a more or less permanent office at Bantam. By trial and error the directors at home were learning the ways of the East.

9. On Grise, see Meilink-Roelofsz, *Asian Trade*, pp. 107–10, 269–84.

10. In the annals of the Company the Seventeen refer to this incident in a manner calculated to rouse the Dutch: "the manner in which they (the Portuguese) deliberately strangled and hanged fifteen to sixteen of our people in number, for no other reason than that they had asked them for victuals in all friendship" (De Jonge, *Opkomst*, 3, 146–47).

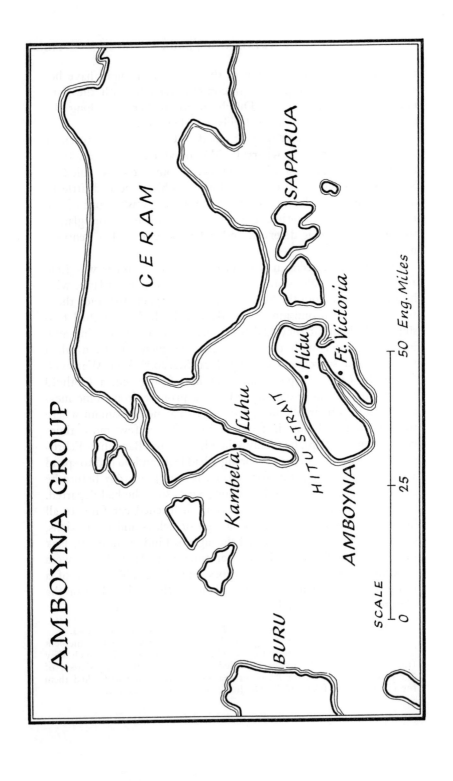

AMBOYNA GROUP

CERAM

SAPARUA

BURU

Luhu

Kambela

HITU STRAIT

Hitu

Ft. Victoria

AMBOYNA

SCALE

0   25   50   Eng. Miles

6

War
and Trade
Do Not Mix

The second fleet sponsored by the United Company left the Low-lands in December 1603. It numbered thirteen vessels including two pinnaces, carrying a total of about twelve hundred men. The commander was Steven van der Hagen, a man of experience who had made one previous voyage to the Indies in the employ of the Old Company of Amsterdam. Previous to that he had sailed with Liorne of Hoorn on the first Dutch venture into the Mediter-ranean. His instructions from the Seventeen complemented the ones Van Warwyck had received, and called for intensified action against the enemy.[1]

After rounding the Cape of Good Hope, he was to first cruise in the Strait of Mozambique and intercept the Portuguese caracks which used this passage on the journey homeward from Goa. From there he was to sail to the west coast of India and show the flag before Goa. If possible, he should take the town, but in any case he should capture and destroy all Portuguese ships en-countered in those waters. Treaties of friendship were to be con-cluded with the native kings along the coast. After this had been accomplished, he was to sail for the East Indies and, with the help of the Sultan of Johore, try to seize the town of Malacca. Finally he should sail for the Moluccas at the far eastern end of the archipelago and destroy the Spanish, who were causing con-siderable trouble from their stronghold in the Philippines.

1. These instructions, preserved in the Dutch National Archives, indicate Oldebarnevelt's motive for promoting the United East-India Company. After enumerating a series of abuses suffered at the hands of the Spanish and Portuguese, the Seventeen state that "we are now obligated to protect our people and the natives of the islands and our other friends . . . against all offense of the Spaniards, the Portuguese and their adherents." The Seventeen, however, did not overlook their own interest: they added "also to the advantage and assurance of the East India trade."

It was a large order, but the Seventeen reasoned that these war-like ventures were entirely feasible in view of the earlier victories over the Portuguese. None of these men, however, knew the situation in the Far East at first hand. Not one had ever been there, and, as the records prove, they never showed a great desire to leave the safe and comfortable firesides in their countinghouses for a dubious chance of returning in good health, if they managed to survive the ordeal at all. The accounts they had received from returning commanders and merchants were undoubtedly reliable, but they did not always agree in assessing enemy strength. So far, the Dutch had been quite successful in their encounters with the enemy, but this was mainly due to the fact that their ships had appeared in the Indies in greater numbers than the Portuguese had anticipated. Now that the enemy realized what the Dutch had in mind, it could be assumed that the Portuguese and the Spanish were preparing to defend their domain in force. This, however, could not deter a people who had for centuries been guided by the principle *Die waagt die wint* (nothing ventured, nothing gained). The stakes were certainly high enough: if these instructions were carried out successfully, the United Company would have acquired, within the span of a few years, that vast Asiatic domain which the Spanish and Portuguese had been building for a hundred years.

The dual function of the Company was once more emphasized in the instructions to the Admiral because, while aggressive action against the enemy was stressed, the commercial aspect of the voyage was by no means neglected. Trade goods amounted to less than 100,000 guilders, experience having taught that the home country had little to offer that proved salable in the Indies. On the other hand, the ships carried 740,000 guilders in silver reals which were in great demand. The directors had provided Van der Hagen with a letter of information, which was a detailed and elaborate compilation of all the knowledge in their possession about almost every port in the Indies. It described the towns, the people, and their customs; it enumerated the products that could be obtained as well as prices and methods of trading. No merchant could have wished for a more comprehensive handbook to guide him in his dealings with natives and local traders. The information was based on personal observations by many skippers and merchants who had been charged with recording everything they saw and heard in the smallest details. It was a far cry from Linschoten's *Itinerary*, which had appeared less than ten years earlier. The man responsible for collating this vast amount of material was Stalpaert van der Wiele, who had spent several years in the Banda group as a member of the small contingent placed there by Heemskerck in 1599.[2]

The results of the second voyage proved that the Seventeen had expected too much too soon. It took Van der Hagen more than six months before he reached the waters of Mozambique, where he cruised in vain for two months without ever sighting a Portuguese carack. At Goa he exchanged shots with the fort, but the admiral wisely refrained from trying to take this strong-hold with his small force. At sea he was prepared to tackle a fleet twice his size, but he was not strong enough to lay siege to a fortified town. Further south, however, he entered into a treaty of friendship with the Samorin[3] of Calicut, which in time gave the Dutch an important foothold on the Malabar Coast. This ruler, like Dom João in Ceylon, was anxious to enlist support against the Portuguese, and he offered the Dutch a suitable loca-tion to build a fort. Not wishing to deplete his forces, this matter had to be postponed and the maharajah had to be satisfied with the admiral's promise that additional ships and soldiers would be sent from the Lowlands to implement the treaty.[4] By now Van der Hagen no longer had the original thirteen ships at his immedi-ate disposal; three had been left behind at Mozambique to inter-cept any Portuguese carack that might still appear, and two others had been dispatched north to Gujerat to investigate the situation there.

Following the customary route along the west coast of Sumatra, Van der Hagen arrived at Bantam in December 1604, after a voyage of more than a year, and with little to show for his trouble. At Bantam he learned the bad news about the situation in the Moluccas. The Portuguese had taken a bloody revenge on the people of Amboyna for the friendship they had shown Van der Hagen when he had been there in 1600. The admiral decided to sail on without delay, as it was of the greatest importance that the enemy should be dislodged from this valuable source of cloves.

Before leaving, he appointed Jan Willemsz. Verschoor, the

2. This important document has been reproduced, almost in its entirety, in De Jonge, *Opkomst, 3*, 149–63.

3. This title is derived from the Sanskrit *samudri*, "son of the sea."

4. M. A. P. Roelofsz, *De Vestiging der Nederlanders ter kuste Malabar* (The Hague, 1943), pp. 32–36.

chief merchant on his fleet, as president of the office at Bantam, in accordance with instructions issued by the Seventeen. While most of these instructions covered warfare and trade, there were two which showed that the directors were also concerned with other matters. Under no conditions should the president of a factory give any assistance or advice to the English, French, or any other nation on penalty of forfeiting all his wages and being held responsible for any loss or damage this might cause the Company. This was the earliest mention, in any official document, of the English as rivals in the East India trade. Before long it became apparent that this fear of competition was by no means unfounded, and the ensuing troubles between these two emerging maritime powers had far-reaching consequences. The second item dealt with the possibility of colonization, Verschoor having been instructed to approach the king of Bantam and obtain his permission to settle a few Dutch families and skilled workers in the town.[5] Nothing ever came of this, but colonization on a modest scale was begun before long in other parts of the archipelago.

At Amboyna, Van der Hagen managed to execute one of his directives in full. The small Portuguese force there surrendered without a blow, and he closed a treaty of mutual assistance against the Portuguese, with the Amboynese taking an oath of allegiance to the States General of the Netherlands. The important factor in this treaty was the solemn promise by the *Orang Kayas* (headmen—literally "rich men") to sell their cloves only to the Dutch Company.[6] Frederic Houtman was appointed governor of this first important foothold the Company attained in the Indies.

From Amboyna the admiral dispatched a squadron of five ships under Cornelis Bastiansz. to Tidore, which was held by the Spanish. After heavy fighting, Bastiansz. took the fort, but he did not have the foresight to leave an adequate garrison behind. The Dutch still had to learn the hard way that local victories did not mean total defeat of the enemy. In the meantime, Van der Hagen had gone to the Banda group, where he arranged a treaty similar to the one with Amboyna.

5. "Ordinances and instructions for the merchants and others who remain at Bantam," issued at Amsterdam, December 1603. For a complete copy, see De Jonge, *Opkomst, 3,* 206–08.

6. As noted earlier (p. 114), the northern part of this island was called Hitu, where one of four headmen had managed to gain supremacy and became known as capitan Hitu. In the southern part of Amboyna, called Ley-Timor, a quasi-independent status of the *Orang Kayas* was maintained.

On paper at least, it looked as if the Dutch had achieved one of their major ambitions. The treaty with Amboyna and their close relationship with the king of Ternate gave them a monopoly of the world's supply of cloves, and the same held true of nutmegs and mace as far as Banda was concerned. If the United Company could make those contracts permanent, the profits from this trade would more than meet the expectations which had induced the people at home to invest their money in the company. But the Spanish soon took advantage of Bastiansz.' miscalculation of their strength with the result that, for a number of years, it looked as if all of the Moluccas might be lost; and while Van der Hagen was congratulating himself on the monopoly he had acquired at Banda, English ships under John Saris were en route to these same islands to purchase spices for the English East India Company.[7] It was a foregone conclusion that this would lead to trouble, because the English could hardly be expected to abide by the terms on an alien piece of parchment, especially when the Bandanese proved only too willing to accept the higher prices they offered.

From the Moluccas, Bastiansz. sailed to the Malacca Strait where he met Van Warwyck. They discussed the possibility of taking the town and decided to chance it only if the Sultan of Johore provided a strong force for a simultaneous attack by land. The sultan, however, was unwilling to commit himself to such an extent. Like most rulers of small principalities in the Indies, he was impressed by the number of Dutch ships appearing in his waters, but he was also aware that the Dutch were unwilling to risk them in an all out battle with the Portuguese. To show their good will, the Dutch gave the sultan a few cannon and munitions, and promised that some day they would return in greater force.

Admiral Van der Hagen returned to Holland by the end of July 1606, almost a year ahead of Van Warwyck, who was still sailing in the Indian Ocean. Although the tactical exploits of the second United Company voyage had fallen short of expectations, the venture had been successful in other respects. A number of ships had returned with full cargoes, and additional avenues of trade had been opened as well. The two pinnaces in the fleet had been used to explore the area more fully and to gather economic

7. These two ships had sailed from England in March 1604, two of four representing the second venture of the English company under Henry Middleton.

intelligence which could be exploited by larger vessels if the prospects were sufficiently promising. One, the *Delft*, had sailed to Coromandel on the east coast of the Indian peninsula, where large quantities of cotton textiles were produced. Achin in North Sumatra, halfway between Coromandel and Bantam, was a logical center for this trade, and the Dutch had already tried to obtain a foothold there. The Sultan of Achin, however, preferred his independence to possible economic gain. The Achinese had seen the Portuguese entrench themselves at Malacca on the opposite coast of the Strait, and they were loath to see the same happen to them at the hands of the Dutch. Only a small part of the pepper which came to the Achin market was produced locally, and the textiles shipped from it in the past had all originated in India. The Dutch were quick to exploit Achin's original sources of supply when they saw that their motives were not appreciated. Direct trade had already deprived Achin of much of its former pepper business, and now it was about to be bypassed in the textile field as well.[8]

The results of this first contact with the coast of Coromandel were quite successful. A merchant with a few assistants remained at Mazulipatnam while the *Delft* made several trips between there and Bantam, her holds bulging with bales of cottons. This trade eventually became of the utmost importance, as it provided the Company with an additional commodity for the purchase of spices which, until then, had to be paid for with silver.

The other pinnace, the *Duifke* (*Little Dove*), was in a class by herself, although her voyage on this occasion did not lead to such profitable returns as those of the *Delft*. The successes of the *Duifke*, more than those of any other single vessel during the early period of the Dutch in Asia, deserve to be placed high on the list of accomplishments. This little yacht had already two round trips to the Indies to her credit: first with Cornelis Houtman on his history-making voyage and again with the fleet of the Old Amsterdam Company in 1601. She had acquitted herself well in the battle with the Portuguese before Bantam when, under Willem Cornelisz. Schouten, she inflicted considerable punishment on the enemy by helping to take a large galley. Now she was back in the Indies for the third time, about to place her name next to

8. On the decline of Achin see Schrieke, *Indonesian Sociological Studies,* 1, 53-54.

those of *Nina* and *Pinta* as the discoverer of a whole new continent.

The *Duifke* sailed from Bantam in November 1605 under skipper Willem Jansen, with instructions to explore the south coast of New Guinea. Reaching the shallow waters of what is now known as the Torres Strait, the ship headed south, rather than sail into what was believed to be a cul-de-sac. On this southern tack, Australia was discovered, although the Dutch did not recognize it as a new continent—having failed to pass through the Torres Strait, they considered it part of New Guinea.[9]

Now there occurred one of those coincidences rare in the annals of the Age of Discovery. A few months after the *Duifke* had been in these waters, the Spaniard Diego de Prado y Tovar, with Luis Vaez de Torres as second in command, sailed across the Pacific bound for the Philippines. At the eastern tip of New Guinea, adverse winds prevented him from keeping to the north, and he sailed along the south coast of New Guinea instead. The Spaniards were unaware of land on their port bow, although they had actually traversed a strait. It was not until many years later that a letter from Torres to the King of Spain was recovered in the archives at Manila which put these two almost simultaneous discoveries in their proper perspective. Jansen on the *Duifke* had discovered Australia, and the Spanish, the Strait, the one mistaking his find for that of the other.

As a result of the disclosure of Torres' letter, the Strait was named after him. This was an injustice to Prado y Tovar, who had been in command of the voyage. His journal, however, did not come to light until the twentieth century. By then every map and chart showed the passage as Torres Strait, and it was too late to give Prado y Tovar the credit due him.[10] The *Duifke* continued for years to serve the Company until in the end her timbers were left to rot in some forgotten port.

The United Company sent a third fleet to the Indies in May 1605. It consisted of eleven ships and was headed by Cornelis Matelief. As a former director of the Company for the Rotterdam chamber, he was unique among the commanders; his desire for

9. For the exploits of the *Duifke* on this voyage, see J. E. Heeres, *The Part Borne by the Dutch in the Discovery of Australia* (London and Leiden, 1899).

10. Stefansson, *Great Adventures*, pp. 630–32.

action must have outweighed the security he had at home. On the outward journey he touched at Mauritius, which was gradually becoming an important stopover for Dutch ships sailing to and from the Indies. Here he encountered Admiral Van der Hagen who was repairing his ship. This gave Matelief an opportunity to learn the latest news about the situation in the Indies, and, as a result, he modified his instructions from the Seventeen. He had been ordered to split his fleet in squadrons of two and three vessels each, and send them on various missions while he himself sailed with four ships to Malacca. When he heard that the Portuguese had greatly strengthened their position in Malacca under Furtado de Mendoza, he decided to keep his fleet together for a strenuous effort to eliminate this threat.

Matelief blockaded the town for four months, and during this period he defeated a strong Portuguese fleet which had arrived from Goa to assist the garrison. Although successful to this extent, he was unable to take Malacca, and moreover lost two of his own ships in the battle. He had tried in vain to enlist the support of the Sultan of Johore. As on the previous occasion, this cautious potentate preferred to watch the struggle from the side lines. All he did was to allow the Dutch to erect an unfortified factory at nearby Batu Sawer.[11] As a result of these inconclusive engagements, the Strait of Malacca, the logical route between Bantam and Coromandel, was still not safe for Dutch ships, and for the time being they all had to sail the long way around the west coast of Sumatra.

While the Portuguese had proved that they were able to hold their own in the western part of the Indies, the Spaniards had an even greater success in the Moluccas. Arriving at Bantam, Matelief learned the bad news that the Spanish had retaken the fort at Tidore, which Bastiansz. had left with too small a garrison to withstand the siege. Neighboring Ternate had also been overrun and King Said Barkat, a staunch friend of the Dutch, had been captured and carried off to Manila. This meant that the whole of the Moluccas was threatened, as were the important spice islands, Banda and Amboyna. Matelief wasted no time in going to the rescue. At Amboyna he augmented the garrison with a number of soldiers who had originally been destined for Malacca. With this contingent, the first attempt was made at establishing

11. De Jonge, *Opkomst*, 3, app. 9, pp. 217–18.

a Dutch settlement in the Indies, in that these men were allowed to marry native women. This experiment was only partly successful—the women of Amboyna showed little inclination to prefer these redheaded bearded roughnecks above their own men.[12]

Matelief had eight ships under his command, but the Spanish were too strongly entrenched on Tidore and Ternate for an outright attempt to dislodge them. As a temporary measure, the admiral built a fort at Malayo, in the hope that it would be able to fight off the Spanish until additional reinforcements could be brought in. It was expected that the Ternatans would gladly help in building the fort, but the Dutch soon found that the natives, here as well as elsewhere in the Indies, had no enthusiasm for such menial tasks. The Dutch crews likewise rebelled; they had no objection to doing the heaviest work on board a ship, but digging under "that brass bastard," as they nicknamed the sun, was something else. Matelief and his council had a near mutiny on their hands before the fort was half finished.[13]

Matelief reasoned that he should remain in the Moluccas and defend them against the enemy, but the Seventeen had decided on a policy of war *and* trade. According to his instructions, he should sail as quickly as possible to China, to try to open that legendary country to Dutch trade with better luck than his predecessors. Ironically enough, he was even less successful than those who had been there before him.

As anticipated, the Spanish soon attacked the half-finished fort at Malayo. It was only the knowledge that they were fighting for their lives that made the small garrison hold out until other Dutch ships came to the rescue. Matelief learned the news when he returned to Bantam after his fruitless journey to the China coast. Being a man of good judgment, he realized that this was only a temporary relief, and that the situation in the Moluccas remained precarious. To make matters worse, he also learned that the English were beginning to cause trouble for the Dutch at Banda and Amboyna. The *Orang Kayas* ignored the treaties with the Dutch Company and gladly accepted the higher prices offered by the English, who paid for the spices with cannon and munitions, which might some day be used against the Dutch themselves.

12. Ibid., p. 53.
13. Ibid., pp. 55–56.

Matelief sent Willem Jansen, the discoverer of Australia, on a secret mission to Banda and Amboyna in order to restrain the English in this nefarious practice by every possible means.[14]

The situation at Bantam also left much to be desired. It had become a rendezvous for the fleets, but the difficulties with the ruler and his avaricious retinue were growing. Matelief appointed a new president of the factory, Jacques l'Hermite, whom he considered the best man available for this important function. It turned out that he was not mistaken in his judgment. L'Hermite pointed out the advantages of Djakarta, fifty miles east of Bantam, as a central point from which the Company's activities could best be controlled. It took time before the Seventeen agreed, but when they finally did so, a new and important chapter was opened in the history of the Dutch empire in Asia.

While Matelief was getting ready to sail for home, the fourth fleet of the United Company arrived at Bantam. Commanded by Paulus van Caerden, it had left in April 1606; it was now January 1608. It had taken almost two years to make the outward journey. Some of the contributing factors causing this delay were the same instructions that the Seventeen had issued before: Mozambique had to be captured, if it had not yet been taken by a previous fleet, and richly laden caracks, homeward bound from Goa, had to be intercepted in those waters. After a long and costly siege, and aimless cruising in the Strait, Van Caerden finally sailed for Goa, his next objective. On the west coast of India he was equally frustrated, and, after much loss of time and without having accomplished anything of profit to the Company, he finally arrived at Bantam.

Their meeting gave Matelief an opportunity to apprise Van Caerden of the dire situation in the Great East, as the Moluccas were usually called. He may well have wished that Van Caerden had not wasted so much time because his help there was sorely needed. Matelief tried to convince his successor that nothing was more important than to sail at once for the threatened Spice Islands before they became a total loss. Van Caerden, however, had other plans. The directors had instructed him to try to wrest Malacca from the Portuguese or, if this proved impossible, to take some valuable prizes en route from Macao to Goa. Matelief not only stressed the greater importance of the Moluccas, but pointed out the impossibility of sailing into the Strait of Malacca

14. Ibid., p. 59.

against the prevailing west monsoon. Van Caerden refused to listen. Earlier in his career he had made a name for himself by capturing a number of Portuguese caracks on the coast of Brazil; it was more in his nature to pursue the role of privateer than to bother about ordinary trade. Twice before on this voyage he had been thwarted in his attempts to gain booty and glory; the third time, he believed, his luck was bound to change.

It is not surprising that Matelief had little confidence in Van Caerden. "Heart and courage he does possess," he wrote in his report, "but one could wish that he were endowed with better judgement." [15] This estimate of the man proved to be correct. After Van Caerden had tried in vain to enter the Malacca Strait against the prevailing winds, he finally turned eastward toward the Moluccas. In an engagement with the Spanish, he foolishly allowed himself to be taken prisoner, and his shipmates were chained to the galley oars.

Before starting the homeward voyage, Matelief had given Van Caerden a final bit of advice: "This I found out," he wrote him, "that when a soldier and merchant is united in one person, all labor is lost. Therefore, my dear Admiral, if you think you can accomplish something by war, then forget about trade, as otherwise you will have neither one nor the other." [16] This, in a nutshell, was the main problem that confronted the Company during the early years of its existence.

15. Ibid., p. 61.
16. Advice of Admiral Matelief to Admiral van Caerden, dated January 4, 1608.

7

The
Seventeen
Under Attack

The establishment of the United Company in 1602 had caused feverish excitement throughout all the Netherlands, especially in the towns where the Chambers were located. The charter stipulated that everyone be permitted to participate, and it actually favored the small investor, by putting restrictions on the amount a wealthy person could subscribe. In this manner, Oldebarnevelt had envisioned a company of wide national scope, which would make it a powerful instrument in the war against Spain. There were few who could resist the temptation to become a shareholder and thus share in profits which were said to be fabulous. Small tradesmen, artisans, and men of all walks of life contacted someone who knew a director, no matter how tenuous the connection might be. An Amsterdam merchant is recorded as having acted for his wife's seamstress and laundry woman. As a result, the issue was soon oversubscribed. The many who had been disappointed tried to buy shares at a premium from those who had been more fortunate, among whom there were some who preferred a small, sure profit over a long-term gamble. Before a single penny had been paid in, the shares were selling on the Amsterdam Exchange at a premium of fifteen per cent. After the first ships returned with their cargoes of spices, the shares rose to 125, and, when it became known that Van der Hagen had captured Amboyna and Tidore, they were quoted at 140, and in 1606 they rose to over 200. It was the first large-scale speculation the world had ever seen, and it set the style for all subsequent ventures in capitalist society. It fed on favorable news but reacted just as quickly when subsequent events demanded a more sober view of potentialities.

When the news trickled back that Tidore had been recaptured by the Spanish, and that the whole situation in the Moluccas was deteriorating, the shares began to drop, and before long could be bought below par. The repeated failures at Mozambique, Goa, and Malacca brought the unhappy realization that the Portuguese were stronger than expected, and it turned the erstwhile boom into a panicky rush to unload shares in what was already a buyer's market. It did not help matters when the Company's ships continued to arrive with their holds bulging with pepper. There was more pepper in Europe than ever before. In Amsterdam, according to Buzanval (the French ambassador, and a shareholder), warehouses were filled to the roofs with pepper, worth more than a million guilders, which could not be sold for lack of buyers. In a short time, the formerly so eagerly sought shares could be bought at 60 per cent of their face value.[1]

For the Seventeen, these were difficult years, and not only because of the setbacks suffered in the Indies and the glut of pepper on the market. A dissident element had arisen among the directors, flatly opposed to the policies advocated by the majority, and there had been serious squabbles. The leader of this group was Isaac Lemaire, a merchant refugee from the Spanish south like Moucheron, who had established himself in Amsterdam.[2] Together with a few other refugee merchants, he had formed the Brabant Company, which had since become part of the United Company. Lemaire was a man of restless energy and his grandiose plans went far beyond even the heavy load the Company had to shoulder in pursuing the dual function of warfare and trade in the Indian Ocean and the East Indies. Lemaire, himself a member of the executive board, complained vociferously that, instead of too much, far too little was being done. Among other ventures, he wanted to fortify the Strait of Magellan and blockade this passage against the Spanish caracks sailing to and from Chile and the west coast of New Spain (Mexico). This was on the order of what Moucheron had planned to do in the Nassau Strait, if a northeast passage had proved feasible. Next he would conquer these gold and silver producing lands and clear the whole Pacific Ocean of enemy ships, thereby isolating the Philippine Islands and Macao.[3] The other members of the Seventeen rejected his

1. Remonstrance by a group of dissident stockholders to the States General against the directors of the Company: see De Jonge, *Opkomst, 3,* 120, and app. 46.

2. See R. C. Bakhuizen van den Brink, "Isaac Lemaire," *De Gids, 29* (1865), 1–56.

3. See Lemaire's elaborate remonstrance against the practices of the

ambitious schemes as being entirely beyond the capacity of the Company. Each fleet of ten to twelve ships, including cargo and silver, cost about 2 million florins and at this rate the capital of 6.5 millon florins would be expended before any real profits were made. The Seventeen would have to enlist the support of the States General and would be obliged to borrow large sums of money.

By 1605, the rift had become so great that Lemaire withdrew from the company and sold his shares just at a time when the market reflected the early good news from the Indies. Although he made a good profit on this transaction, it did not soften his antagonism, and from that time on he was an outspoken enemy of the Company, vowing that he would do everything in his power to obstruct it. He did not have to wait long for an opportunity. When less favorable news reached the Lowlands and the shares began to sag, Lemaire and his allies abetted the decline by selling large blocks of stocks they did not own but hoped to purchase later at a much lower price. Lemaire wanted to get even with the Company and make a profit for himself as well. To further this scheme, he spread false rumors, which were much worse than the situation justified, and, as a result, the shares of the once so promising Company fell to an unprecedented low of about 48 per cent. Lemaire thus earned himself the dubious reputation of being the first to instigate a bear raid in a capital market and to use the tricks which were to become a part of such manipulations for all time to come.[4] The Company's future looked black indeed, and there was talk that it might be forced to liquidate. As a last resort, the Seventeen appealed to the government for help. The States General did what it could; short sales were prohibited and delivery had to be made within 30 days of all stocks that had been sold.

This was by no means the end of Lemaire's machinations against the Company. Knowing that Oldebarnevelt and the Amsterdam merchants were not on the best of terms, he approached the Advocate with a detailed account of where, in his opinion, the

Seventeen, presented to Oldebarnevelt, to show "how prejudicial it would be to the interest of the fatherland to amplify the charter of the United Company to include the northern route" in De Jonge, *Opkomst*, 3, app. 47.

4. See J. G. van Dillen, "Isaac Lemaire en de handel in actien der Oost-Indische Compagnie," *Economisch-Historisch Jaarboek*, *16* (1930), 1–165.

Company had fallen short in its responsibilities as laid down in the charter. He argued correctly that, although the Company had the sole franchise to sail westward through the Strait of Magellan, it had yet to send its first ship into those waters. If the westward franchise were to be turned over to him, he would quickly show, he pleaded, how profitable it would prove to be for the country.[5] When this remonstration did not have the expected results, Lemaire decided to try something else.

The charter said nothing about either a northeast or a northwest passage to the Indies for the reason that all previous attempts to find a northern route had been failures. Since this was the only way to get around the charter, Lemaire decided to give that route another try. With the secret support of Henry IV, who had ambitions for a French East India Company, he made plans to fit out a ship for this purpose. His choice of commander was Henry Hudson, an English navigator who, like John Davis before him, was not appreciated in his own country and who was in Holland looking for backing. The Seventeen learned of these preparations, and succeeded in binding Hudson to themselves, mainly for the purpose of thwarting Lemaire and the King of France. Hudson's voyage led to the rediscovery of the Hudson River, and eventually to the settlement of New Amsterdam. If it had not been for Lemaire, the United Company would never have launched this voyage of the *Half Moon*, and he is therefore entitled to his share of the credit.[6]

Some years after this event, the relentless Lemaire tried once more to find a loophole in the charter. The Strait of Magellan was thought to be the only passage between the Atlantic and Pacific Oceans: the land sighted south of the Strait was presumed to be a vast continent, the legendary Southland. Lemaire was not convinced: if he could find a passage further south, he could literally sail around one of the clauses in the charter and thus find his own route to the Indies. His ships sailed from the town of Hoorn, and they proved that his surmise was correct; they found the passage and called it Strait Lemaire. They also discovered the southernmost tip of South America, which they

5. See above, note 3.
6. See H. C. Murphy, *Henry Hudson in Holland, An Inquiry into the Origin and Objects of the Voyage Which Led to the Discovery of the Hudson River* (The Hague, 1909).

named Cape Horn, and which was to be the nemesis of sailing men for hundreds of years to come.[7] Isaac Lemaire was not allowed to reap the benefits from this remarkable discovery. After the ships had arrived safely in the East Indies, they were ordered confiscated by a young governor, Jan Pietersz. Coen, who had the interest of the Company at heart to the same fanatic degree as Lemaire had its undoing. He refused to believe that the commander had actually discovered such a passage; and even if it were true, Lemaire was guilty of having violated the clear intent of the monopoly clause in the charter.[8]

Isaac Lemaire died not many years later, keeping up his feud with the United Company until the end. He was without doubt a prolific man, not only in his numerous attempts to best the Company but in his private life as well—he sired no fewer than 22 children.

Lemaire was not the only one who made it difficult for the Company during the early years of its existence. Another was Pieter Lyntgens, a wealthy Amsterdam merchant who had originally subscribed for a large amount.[9] Unlike Lemaire, who demanded a more aggressive attitude against the enemy, he wanted none of that. He belonged to the Mennonite sect who, like their offshoot the Amish, were conscientious objectors and abjured warlike action in any form. When the intentions of the Seventeen became clear, Lyntgens sold his shares and withdrew from the Company. He claimed that he would not accept gain from privateering or any other activities which resulted in spilling blood. It was noticed that the wily old merchant had not suffered because of his pious belief, as he sold his shares at the peak of the market.

Turning his back to the United Company did not mean that Lyntgens had given up his desire to profit from trade with the Indies, provided hostilities could be avoided. He devised a clever scheme both to salve his conscience and to circumvent the obnoxious charter which effectively barred any but the United Company

7. See W. A. Engelbrecht and P. J. van Herwerden, eds., *De Ontdekkingsreis van Jacob Le Maire en Willem Cornelisz. Schouten in de jaren 1615–1617* (2 vols. The Hague, 1945).

8. See Book III, Chapter 11.

9. Lyntgens was one of the refugees from the Southern Netherlands. He was born ca. 1540 and settled in Amsterdam 40 years later, after having lived some years in Lisbon. See A. J. van der AA, *Biographisch woordenboek der Nederlanden*, 7 (Haarlem, 1851–78), col. 819. See also Van Dillen, *Oudste aandeelhoudersregister*, pp. 62–63.

from trade with the Spice Islands. He, too, turned to France. At first, Henry IV was keenly interested in obtaining a share in that lucrative trade. Lyntgens promised him ships and some experienced men to direct the first voyage; his own son, who had been in the Indies with Cornelis Houtman, was to be in command. The peace-loving merchant counted on the fact that the States General would not dare to affront the powerful king of France by trying to prevent him from establishing his own East India Company.

Henry was impressed. Since he was now at peace with Spain, he agreed with Lyntgens that ships under the French flag could trade without engaging in costly warfare, and thus return greater profits than the Dutch Company. It sounded like a good proposition, and plans were made to put the venture into effect.

As soon as the Seventeen learned of these plans, they demanded protection from the States General. In their petition they likewise pointed out that the French "can do as much with one guilder as the Company could do with four," because they did not have to fight Spain. For a while the government was unwilling to take a firm stand, but the directors kept up the pressure. To emphasize their contention that a French Company directed by Lyntgens would be ruinous to the Dutch, they made veiled threats of withdrawing from the field rather than continue their operations against such heavy odds. Prodded by Oldebarnevelt, who did not want his creation to die in infancy, the States General finally took action.

In July 1606, the Dutch government issued a strong edict to the effect that no one in the Lowlands, either directly or indirectly, was allowed to sail to the East Indies, or to fit out ships for this purpose, except under, or for the account of, the United East India Company. Even this might not have deterred the aging merchant but, fortuitously for the Seventeen, Pieter Lyntgens soon afterwards died.[10] It is indicative of the economic situation in western Europe at that time that King Henry abandoned his plans to launch a French East India Company. Without experienced Dutch merchants and skippers, the French did not feel ready for the task.

Although the directors undoubtedly had the interest of the Company at heart, they were selfish enough to look out for themselves as well. They were the first to receive news of what

10. De Jonge, *Opkomst*, 3, 116–19.

was happening in the Indies, and when the news was bad they unloaded their shares on unsuspecting buyers who had no access to such advance information.

The small stockholders began to realize that their investment might not pay off as well as they had expected. To be sure, the Company promised to pay dividends, but at the same time they saw their shares drop to almost half of what they had paid for them. It is natural that they blamed the directors for their plight. The clause in the charter which gave the directors a steady commission of one per cent on the cost of all ships and cargoes provided the small investors with still another grievance. When large profits were confidently expected, such a nominal fee had not seemed exorbitant, but, now that prospects had changed, it became a sore point.[11] The Seventeen, formerly so highly respected, were now being abused from many directions, and the Company's reputation suffered both at home and abroad.

There were some who predicted that the days of the Company were numbered and that it lacked viability to surmount the serious problems which had not been anticipated at the start. They were wrong. The Seventeen, that autonomous and secretive body of men, would never admit defeat, not even when still greater difficulties had to be overcome.

As soon as the Seventeen realized that the enemy was far stronger in the Indies than had been expected, they petitioned the States General for some much needed support. Since all enemy reinforcements had to come from Spain and Portugal, they argued, much would be gained if enemy ships were destroyed before they sailed to the Indies. It was sound reasoning, and the States General agreed, especially since this was clearly a matter for the admiralties to deal with rather than the United Company.

Twice during 1606 a fleet of about twenty warships sailed into Spanish waters under Admiral Haultain, who had the reputation of being an able and ruthless commander. During the previous year while cruising up and down the Channel, he had intercepted some Spanish transports and, rather than take prisoners, had thrown them overboard tied back to back. He was considered to be just the man for the task at hand.

11. The directors' commission on all outgoing equipment was abolished in 1623, but retained on the return cargoes. Not until 1647 was the whole system abolished and replaced by a flat payment, which amounted to 3,000 guilders yearly for the Amsterdam Chamber (Van Dillen, *Oudste Aandeelhoudersregister*, p. 30).

Aside from destroying enemy ships wherever he could, Haultain had orders to intercept the silver fleet which was reportedly on the way home from the Spanish Main. On his first attempt, Haultain captured a few small vessels, but of the silver fleet there was no sign. When the enemy ships stayed in port rather than risk an encounter with the Dutch fleet, Haultain was forced to return to the Lowlands practically empty-handed.

In September he sailed forth for the second time, but now the enemy had been alerted. Instead of meeting the silver fleet, Haultain found a far superior Spanish armada, which had been sent out to escort the treasure ships into port. There was a bloody but inconclusive battle, and Haultain decided that he had better disengage himself while there still was a chance. One of his ships made history in that battle. Surrounded by Spanish galleons and with the main mast shot away, the captain, Regnier Klaasz., ordered his vessel to be blown up rather than let it fall into the hands of the enemy.

While Haultain was withdrawing and heading for home, the silver fleet was just beyond the horizon. A few days later it arrived safely at San Lucar, carrying the greatest hoard of silver and gold that had ever arrived in Spain. It amounted to about 8,000,000 reals and represented a two years' output of the mines in the Spanish Americas. Had Haultain been unlucky, or had he run away from a fight? There were many at home who accused him of the latter, especially after the news reached the Lowlands of how great a fortune had slipped through his fingers.[12]

The Seventeen renewed their pressure on the States General for another expedition to Spanish waters in the following year, and stated their willingness to provide a sizable amount of money for this venture, as well as some of the Company's most experienced commanders. They also planned to send out another fleet of their own to the Indies in order to take advantage of the damage the admiralty might inflict upon the enemy off its own coast. Although harassed by adversities, both at home and abroad, the Seventeen were plainly of no mind to abandon their ambitious objectives.

12. For Haultain's exploits during 1606, see Motley, *United Netherlands*, 4, 251–55.

8

1607:

The Burgeoning Year

Some years attain a lasting historic significance almost at once, while others reach such status only through the alchemy of time, when events can be seen in their proper perspective. Among the former is 1957, the year when man put his first satellite into orbit and quickly proved that he could do so at will. What this will mean to the world at large is an open question, although one is reminded of Cecil Rhodes, the last of the great empire builders, who lamented the fact that in the world of his day, there was nothing left to conquer. "To think of these stars that you see overhead," he told his friends, "these vast worlds which we can never reach. I would annex the planets if I could." [1] Perhaps Rhodes died too soon.

In most cases, however, historically important years have not achieved such immediate recognition. Events which seemed important when they occurred fade with time—great battles, won or lost, are superseded by greater battles; treaties often become mere scraps of paper. On the other hand, some events of tremendous importance pass almost unnoticed: often it is only by looking backward, from the vantage point of the present, that one can assess the true value of what has occurred.

Such a year was 1607, exactly 350 years before man started to explore the heavens. The significant events of this year were also linked with explorations—those which had been made during a previous century, but which still remained to be exploited.

Under Captain John Smith, the English founded Jamestown in Virginia, the first such settlement in the New World that proved to be lasting. At about the same time, a number of English Puritans, to escape the religious persecution of James I came to Holland. Oddly enough their leader carried the same name as the hero of the Virginia plantation—spelling it John Smyth.

1. W. T. Stead, ed., *The Last Will and Testament of Cecil John Rhodes* (London, 1902), p. 190.

By the end of the year, members of the Scrooby group of dis-
senters, led by Brewster and Bradford, were ready to follow
their example. On the banks of the Wash near Boston, England,
they waited for a Dutch vessel to cross the North Sea. They
stayed in Holland for twelve years—at least those among them
who eventually sailed in the Mayflower, the vanguard of the
Pilgrims who established the first English colony of importance
in New England. According to at least one American historian,
the things they saw and learned in the Lowlands had an everlasting effect upon the future development of the United States.
"There is scarcely a fact in American history of more signficance,
as there is scarcely one whose significance has been more neglected," Bradford Smith wrote about his remote ancestor, Governor Bradford of Plymouth Plantation, and his followers.[2]

Two men called John Smith, the simplest of names among the
English-speaking people, planted the seeds in the year 1607 from
which grew our great country. It is only in retrospect that one
can begin to appreciate the importance of their efforts.

The Dutch, too, record a number of events during this same
year which, in their cumulative effect, had far-reaching consequences. After almost forty years of war, Spain, the most powerful nation on earth, made overtures for peace with the young
rebel republic. A lost sea battle made Spain all the more anxious
to sign at least a truce, and negotiations began to succeed. By
the end of the year, a Company fleet sailed for the Indies with
secret instructions from the Seventeen to extend the sphere of
operations as far as possible, and thus put the United Company
in a favorable position in case a peace or truce with Spain should
establish a status quo in Asia. With this fleet, a young man made
his first voyage to the Indies, never dreaming that he was destined
to put his stamp on a future empire that would last hundreds of
years. His name was Jan Coen, as simple a name as John Smith.

In the early stages, the Spanish peace overtures had all the
characteristics of political intrigue and secret diplomacy so dear
to the hearts of historical novelists. They began on February 6
with an unexpected visit to the house of Cornelis Aerssens in
The Hague. Aerssens was the registrar of the States General, and
in that capacity he had signed the charter of the United East
India Company to certify its authenticity. His son, Francis, was

2. Bradford Smith, *Bradford of Plymouth* (Philadelphia and New York,
Lippincott, 1951), pp. 72 ff.

the republic's ambassador in Paris, who had dissuaded Henry IV from trying to establish a French East India Company.

The visitor was a relative of the registrar, Werner Cruwel of Brussels, a small merchant and more or less in disrepute because of his recent bankruptcy. After some awkward pleasantries, he stated his mission. He brought a letter from Father Neyen, a Franciscan monk high in the favor of the Archduke Albert and Isabella, the titular heads of the Spanish provinces. Cornelis Aerssens felt ill at ease. In those uneasy days, even to talk of peace was a crime little short of treason. He refused to accept the letter, but offered to discuss the matter with someone higher up. The hour was late and Oldebarnevelt would have to be awakened, but the registrar saw the need for haste. "He appears shy and boorish," Aerssens is recorded to have cautioned the Advocate, "but I know him to be cunning. I think you better question him in the presence of witnesses." [3]

The secret interview took place two days later, and Oldebarnevelt chose the best possible witness: Prince Maurice. It was no secret that the Stadholder was against peace; he had never known any other state of affairs but war, and it had given luster to his name. As Lieutenant-General of the United Provinces, he wielded great power, but the supreme authority he craved had been denied him by the States General, where Oldebarnevelt was in control. Maurice was known to brood over the role he would play if ever there were peace. Such personal considerations played no part in Oldebarnevelt's thinking. His own province, Holland, had borne half the cost of waging war and, notwithstanding the ever mounting taxes and levies on all economic activity, its debt had risen to an astronomical figure.[4] He also knew that after forty years of war, the people were becoming tired, and that many longed for peace on honorable terms. By calling in Maurice as a witness, Oldebarnevelt was protecting himself against the possibility that he might be accused of having engineered the negotiations.

The communication conveyed by Cruwel was brief and to the point. The Archdukes were willing to grant a truce for ten or twelve years, provided the Dutch refrained from any further

3. M. L. van Deventer, *Gedenkstukken van Johan van Oldebarnevelt* (The Hague, 1860–65), 3, 104–09.
4. For the province of Holland alone, which carried more than half the burden, the debt had risen to 26 million guilders. See Blok, *Geschiedenis Nederlandsche Volk, 3,* 505.

activities in the Indies. Father Neyen requested permission to come secretly to The Hague and discuss the matter in greater detail. Thus it was a truce the Spanish offered, no final peace, and the price they demanded was steep. Oldebarnevelt was too keen a statesman not to realize that this was only a first offer and therefore subject to improvement. The best terms obtainable could only be learned by diplomatic maneuvering, and in this field he was willing to match his wits against anyone.

Towards the end of February, Father Neyen arrived in The Hague, dressed as an ordinary burgher. The Archdukes could hardly have chosen a better man to act as their emissary. He had been born in Antwerp, and his father had been confidential agent of William of Orange. Father Neyen was equally at home in the courts of Brussels and Madrid, and was at ease in dealing with Dutch Protestants. Hugo Grotius, a keen judge of men, noted that the worthy friar had an open face which inspired confidence but actually disguised a "most wily and unscrupulous disposition." He was as impervious to insults as he was incapable of acknowledging any rebuff. Invariably he would revert to his original purpose "when less subtle negotiators would have been crushed." [5] Gallucci, also in the service of the Archdukes and a friend of Father Neyen, stated that he "combined the wisdom of a serpent with the guilelessness of a dove." [6] It would thus appear that both sides were in agreement as to what type of man he was. For Oldebarnevelt, however, he was just another in the long line of adversaries whom he had faced in the past, in the Lowlands, London, and Paris.

Their first meeting is described by Gallucci who, as historian at the court in Brussels, had access to Father Neyen's own journals and letters. John Motley used this material in his *History of the Netherlands* and part of it is worth repeating:

> The monk arrived at the village of Ryswyck, a short distance from The Hague. He was accompanied by Cruwel and they settled at the hostelry, announcing themselves as traveling merchants. After nightfall a carriage called for them. The friar, driving through these hostile regions, was startled to find himself accompanied by four mounted musketeers, but they were there only for his protection. The first stop was

5. Motley, *United Netherlands*, 4, 281.
6. Ibid., 4, 281.

Aerssen's house and then, after a short delay, he was driven to the palace. Here he was received by a silent attendant who led him through empty corridors and finally to the door of an inner apartment. Entering, Father Neyen found himself in the presence of two men seated at a table covered with books and papers. One was in military undress, a rather stout man of middle age and inclined to baldness; he had regular features, large blue eyes and a pointed beard. The other wore a velvet cloak and severe habiliments of a civil functionary. He was about sixty years old, with a massive forehead, heavy features and a long shaggy beard. The soldier was Maurice of Nassau, the civilian was Oldebarnevelt. Both rose as the friar entered.

"How did you dare come here," said the Prince, "with only the word of a *Beggar* to rely on?"

"Who would not trust the word of so exalted a *Beggar* as you, most excellent prince?" Father Neyen replied smoothly.[7]

With this opening gambit the talks began, the first of a series of discussions in which a delegation of the States General soon participated. As each side was feeling out the other, it became apparent that the southern provinces were badly hurt by the continued blockade of the Channel ports, and that Spain was equally disturbed about the Dutch fleets which periodically preyed on its shipping off the coast. On the part of Spain it appeared to be a minimum condition for armistice that both these harassments should cease. In return, the Spanish were willing to grant the republic its independence. The matter of trade with the Indies was to be explored during the armistice.

From the outset there was no unity among the Dutch representatives as to whether these terms were acceptable or not. Prince Maurice was all for turning them down, but Oldebarnevelt wanted to explore the possibilities to the fullest. Although these deliberations were supposed to be held in the greatest secrecy, it was inevitable that the terms under consideration should leak out. Maurice wanted to gain as much support as possible for his point of view, and the Advocate, on his part, had no desire to fight an intramural battle alone.[8]

7. Ibid., *4*, 281–83. For 'beggar' see p. 28.
8. For the opposition to Oldebarnevelt with respect to the negotiations for a truce, also see Geyl, *Nederlandse stam, 1*, 523–27.

Amsterdam was vehemently opposed to any talk of peace. Truce was equally odious, because a cessation of hostilities in the Channel meant the reopening of the Scheldt, with Antwerp regaining much of the trade it had lost to Amsterdam. Middelburg was also bound to suffer from this. And what of the East Indies? Were the Company's activities to be curtailed, or perhaps suspended? Either prospect was unthinkable.[9]

It would be difficult to overestimate the power of the Seventeen. Officially they comprised nothing more than the board of governors of the United East India Company, but the caliber and influence of the individual members made it much more than that. The United Provinces was a republic of merchants, and the Seventeen, backed by some sixty directors of the individual chambers, were the mightiest of them all. They had the dominant voice in their respective town councils which appointed delegates to the provincial government that decided who should represent it in the States General. The more important the town, the greater its voice in the central government.

With eight votes in the Seventeen, Amsterdam theoretically needed only one outside vote to have a majority; in practice, Amsterdam controlled the affairs of the United Company. The deliberations of the Seventeen were secret and there is no written evidence as to which individuals wielded the greater influence. We can, however, apply a criterion which, in our day, has proved useful in evaluating the power of persons in the hierarchy of the Soviet Union whose Politbureau is equally noncommittal about its internal affairs. We look at the order in which his name appears on official pronouncements—the higher on the list, the more important he probably is.

Applying this rule to the United Company during its early years, we find one name constantly at or near the top: Reynier Pauw, the same who, some fifteen years earlier, had instigated the first Dutch attempts to sail to the East Indies. Since 1590 he had been a member of the Board of Regents of Amsterdam, and in 1605 he had been elected by this body for his first term as mayor. During the next fifteen years he was re-elected eight times to this high office, but even during the off years he retained his

9. Van Ravesteyn, *Economische ontwikkeling van Amsterdam*, pp. 231–34. The United Company also found it convenient to use the name of Prince Maurice as a foil in dealing with Asiatic rulers, who knew the meaning of kingship but to whom "republic" meant nothing.

power. He had a broad face and unflinching eyes under a pair of heavy eyebrows; his full head of hair was kept short, and he had a beak of a nose. Like many others, he had a formidable moustache which stuck straight out on either side, but his beard was kept narrower than most, a large bushy tuft jutting out, which added to his bellicose appearance.

His contemporaries described him as fearless, and in the councils he was a dangerous opponent who usually got his way. He believed that only in aggressiveness could an issue be joined, and he therefore rarely allowed himself to be put in a defensive position. He had an uncanny insight in spotting the weak point in the opposition's arguments, and he hammered at it with full force. He was a man of simple tastes. To be sure, he wanted power and wealth, but he disdained the trappings. Although knighted by the kings of France and England, he never used the titles. His sons had no such qualms—they acquired domains, a coat of arms, and proudly flaunted their brand-new aristocracy. After becoming a widower, Reynier Pauw married a woman "of plebeian background." This, and the fact that he was an ardent Calvinist, assured him the loyalty of the lower classes who, as a rule, were violently opposed to the aristocratic regents.[10]

Comparing the character traits of Pauw and Oldebarnevelt, we find a close similarity. Both were ambitious, unequalled in debate, and neither hesitated to use rough tactics to subdue opposition. But when we look at the things for which each man stood, we find them at opposite poles, and it is not surprising that the feud between two such strong personalities should have ended as it did.

Pauw was a staunch supporter of Prince Maurice, and of his endeavors to become absolute ruler of the Lowlands. The Advocate, as already noted, opposed this ambition, believing that the young country would best be served by a federation of the seven independent provinces, governed by the States General in which all were represented. Pauw was a merchant who used politics to serve his own interest, while Oldebarnevelt, although not eschewing personal gain, had the interest of the whole country in mind.[11]

The issue of war or peace also found the two men in opposite camps. As soon as the news leaked out that the Archdukes had sent an emissary to The Hague, the town fathers of Amsterdam

10. Elias, *Vroedschap*, pp. lix–lx.
11. Oldebarnevelt had accepted a gift of 20,000 guilders which was somewhat difficult to explain. See Motley, *United Netherlands*, 4, 443–45.

EFFIGIES DOM. REGNERI PAVW EQVITIS.
CIVITATIS AMSTELODAMENSIS CONSVLIS ET SENATORIS.
IN CONCILIO DELEGATORVM ORDINVM HOLLANDIÆ WEST
FRISIÆQVE ET DEINDE IN CONSESSV ORDINVM GENERALIVM
FŒDERATI BELGII DEPVTATI AD MAGNÆ BRITANNIÆ ET DANIÆ REGES NEC NON
AD DVCEM IVLIACENSEM ABLEGATI AC MAGNÆ SOCIETATIS INDIÆ ORIENTALIS INTER
Ioan Ravesteyn pinxit. PRIMOS AVCTORIS ET PROMOTORIS. *Theod. Matham sculpsit.*

4. *Reynier Pauw, age 61.*

made it clear where they stood. On March 22, 1607, they drew up a resolution stating that "peace can only lead to an irreparable damage and eventual demise of these lands and its people." When they said this, the venal merchants were thinking not only of the East Indies trade, and the prizes which could be taken in those waters while a state of war existed between Spain and the Republic. They had been casting their eyes toward the West Indies, and the fabulous hoards of gold and silver which the enemy collected there year after year. Since the Dutch republic was now the only country openly at war with Spain, they saw no reason why such a promising field should not be exploited.

The merchants wanted to organize a West India Company. Its field of operations was to comprise the entire east coast of the American continent, from the French settlements in Newfoundland to the Strait of Magellan, the Pacific coast, and the rich mines of Chile and New Spain. For good measure they added the west coast of Africa, from the Tropic of Cancer to the Cape of Good Hope. Such a West India Company was to have a monopoly of all trade and privateering, and thus prevent any other enterprising Dutchman from venturing into this hemisphere. One must admire the audacity of these merchants: between the East and West India companies, they intended to cover the world.

Enthusiasm ran high, and it was freely predicted that this new enterprise would transfer the wealth of Spain to the Dutch. Only the year before, a great silver fleet had slipped through their fingers. Such a misfortune, it was argued, would never happen again, once privateering was organized on a large scale under the proposed West India Company. A charter was drawn up, similar to the one that had been granted to the East India Company, with the Amsterdam chamber having the same prominent voice in its management. Money was readily available to fit out a strong fleet. All that remained to be done was to have the charter approved by the States General.[12]

The Amsterdam merchants were greatly chagrined when the States General, at the direction of Oldebarnevelt, refused them. The Advocate was firmly convinced that, after 40 years of war, the country needed peace. The Spanish had made overtures, and were willing to grant the republic its independence, something which a few years earlier had been unthinkable. With the pros-

12. Elias, *Vroedschap*, pp. xlviii–li. See also Ravesteyn, *Economische ontwikkeling*, pp. 234–36.

pect of peace in the offing, Oldebarnevelt was determined that nothing drastic should be done to jeopardize its chances. He also knew that the opportunities for lucrative trade in the western hemisphere were not promising, and that the prime incentive of a West India Company was the capture of Spanish galleons. This could only be done if the state of war were to continue.

There were other sound reasons why the Dutch should not extend their field of operation to the American coast at this time. The year before, James I had proclaimed the east coast of North America, between latitudes of 34° and 45°, to be the property of the English crown. Henry IV was now urging the States General to desist from operations in the area of the St. Lawrence River, which had been explored by Champlain in 1603 and which was thus considered to be French territory. A West India Company, operating in American waters, could easily run afoul of these two powerful neighbors.

Still rankling from this setback, the Amsterdam merchants and their friends in other towns were dealt a second blow. The States General announced that an armistice had been concluded for a period of eight months beginning on May 4. Hostilities were to be suspended both on land and in the Channel. The Dutch fleet which had already sailed to the coast of Spain and Portugal would be recalled. The matter of trade in the East Indies was left in abeyance until terms for a longer truce, if not a formal peace, could be more fully discussed.

The courts of Europe could hardly believe the dispatches they received about the events at The Hague. It seemed incredible that an absolute monarch would sue for peace with a rebellious faction in his realm.[13] But while this feat astounded Europe, it also widened the rift within the republic. Little did Oldebarnevelt realize that each time he bested Amsterdam and Prince Maurice, he took one step nearer the scaffold.

Considering the slow means of communication in those days, the armistice had been arranged in a very short time, but it had not come soon enough to save Spain from a decisive drubbing. The Dutch admiralty fleet had sailed early in April. Consisting of twenty-six warships and a few smaller pinnaces, it was stronger than the two previous ones. After his poor performance on the earlier expeditions, Haultain was not given the chance to vindicate himself. Sponsored by the Seventeen, the dependable Jacob

13. Motley, *United Netherlands*, 4, 293-94.

van Heemskerck was put in command. The fact that he had brought back more booty than anyone else was another reason why he was chosen. Calvinists like Pauw firmly believed that everything was foreordained, and they also considered it reasonable that the Lord should continue to smile upon a man he had favored in the past. On this venture, Heemskerck's personal remuneration was to be 13 per cent of the booty over and above half a million guilders.

Heemskerck had some good men under his command. The viceadmiral was Laurensz. Alteras of Zealand; among the captains were Hendrik Jansz. of Amsterdam, commonly known as 'Lange Hendrik' because of his height, and Lambert Hendriksz. of Rotterdam, a tough sailor with a craggy face who was nicknamed 'Mooie (Pretty) Lambert.' [14]

By the tenth of April the fleet was at the mouth of the Tagus River. From spies he had sent ashore, Heemskerck learned that no Portuguese ships were ready to sail, but that practically the whole Spanish home fleet was at Gibraltar. This was good news; Heemskerck headed for the Strait. Encountering strong head winds, he did not arrive until the morning of April 25, and he saw at once that his informants had been correct. There were 21 ships, including ten of the largest galleons that ever carried the Spanish flag. The admiral, after signaling his captains to come aboard the flagship, announced the strategy they were to follow. The ships were to go in pairs, each pair to attack one of the galleons on both sides at the same time. "Hold your fire until you hear the hulls crack," Heemskerck told them. [15]

The Spanish fleet was commanded by Don Juan Alvarez d'Avila. When he saw the approaching vessels he called a certain Gevaerts on deck, the skipper of a Dutch merchantman he had captured earlier. He wanted to know whether the sails were Dutch, and the skipper affirmed that they were. "What do you think they want?" the admiral asked. "It looks to me as if they want to fight," Gevaerts replied. This amused Don Juan, and he said with a laugh that his flagship alone could easily take care of the whole lot. [16]

The battle began early in the afternoon, and within the narrow confines of the bay it soon became a bloody slaughter. The fort

14. Ibid., *4*, 296–305.
15. Ibid., *4*, 301.
16. Idem.

on the Rock of Gibraltar could do little to help, because the com-
batants were locked together in tight clusters. Heemskerck had
taken on d'Avila's galleon and the battle had barely started when
his luck ran out. A salvo from the *St. Augustine* severed his leg
at the groin. Just before he bled to death, Heemskerck ordered
his captain, Pieter Verhoef, to continue the battle as planned and
to withhold the news that he had been mortally wounded.

Verhoef, suddenly raised to command from a relatively minor
rank, acquitted himself well and so did the other captains. By dusk
the battle was over. Not a single Spanish vessel remained afloat,
and some two or three thousand Spaniards had either drowned or
been burned to death, Admiral d'Avila among them.[17] The Dutch
had not lost a single ship and only about 100 men, but they included, besides Heemskerck, 'Lange Hendrik' of Amsterdam.

The battle at Gibraltar proved to be one of the turning points
in history: it spelled the end of Spain as a first-rate sea power, and
the Dutch were ready to step into her place.

17. See also Blok, *Geschiedenis*, 3, 504–05.

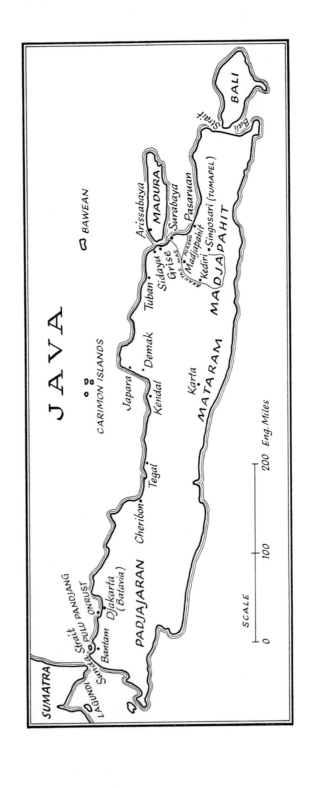

JAVA

SUMATRA

CARIMON ISLANDS

BAWEAN

Strait Pandjang
PULU PANDJANG
ONRUST
Bantam
LAGUNDI
Sunda Strait
Djakarta
(Batavia)

PADJAJARAN

Cheribon

Tegal

Japara

Kendal

Demak

Karta

MATARAM

Tuban

Sidayu
Grise

Arissabaya

MADURA

Surabaya

Pasaruan

Madjapahit
BRANTAS R. PORONG MAS
Kediri
Singosari (TUMAPEL)

MADJAPAHIT

BALI

Bali Strait

SCALE

0   100   200 Eng.Miles

9

Early
Asiatic Trade:
the Hindu Period

The Asia with which western Europe had come into contact was
by no means a backward continent in the sense that Africa or
Australia was. Civilization had had its origin in the lands border-
ing the eastern Mediterranean, the fertile crescent, but China had
not been far behind. In time, these two cultures mingled, benefit-
ing not only each other but other Asiatic peoples as well. Long
before the tribes of northwestern Europe exchanged their animal
skins for the coarsest of homespun, the people of most of Asia
knew silk and fine cotton textiles. It is a well-documented fact
that, at least until the end of the Middle Ages, most Asiatic countries had reached a higher level of cultural development than
those of northwestern Europe—in science, in civil administration,
and in many other respects.[1] By the same token, the peoples of
Asia enjoyed a higher standard of living than those of western
Europe; in fact, it was higher than in modern times of tremendous
population pressure against a limited amount of arable land and
other natural resources.

Cultural development, then as now, was primarily an economic
process, motivated by an urge for the better things of life. As this
process developed, it became evident that no single country had
all the prerequisites to meet the demand. The Indian peninsula
had cotton textiles, China had silk and porcelain, Japan had copper, the Indonesian archipelago had spices. It was inevitable that
these disparities should engender an intercourse between the countries of ancient Asia. This trade must have begun many centuries
before Christ, but recorded history gives us only a fragment of

1. Even in pre-Christian centuries these countries must be considered
to be on a par with the old Mediterranean and Hellenistic states. See J. C.
van Leur, *Indonesian Trade and Society* (The Hague, van Hoeve, 1955),
p. 21.

what we would like to know about it. It is known, however, that every Asiatic country fronting on the Pacific and Indian oceans, participated in the slow but irresistible process of economic development.

Archeological finds confirm the existence of this trade in ancient times. Porcelain beads from Japan have been found in the kitchen middens of the Malay Peninsula, and fragments of early Chinese pottery in Sumatra and Java. Chinese records show that the list of trade goods had become much more extensive by the beginning of the Christian era. From this period we also find ivory, pearls, gold, silver, and precious stones, as well as silk fabrics, rhinoceros horn, and tortoise shell. There were also less exotic goods, such as cottons, base metals and, of course, spices. But even in the latter category there was never any question of a trade in massive quantities. Although international in scope, this Asiatic trade bore no resemblance to modern commerce. It was, in fact, an international peddlers' trade, in which even the most ordinary goods became extremely costly once they had reached their destination. It could hardly have been otherwise, considering the distance and the length of time involved in moving from one place to another, while at every transit port, rulers exacted their tribute and merchants added their profits.[2]

The periodic monsoons dictated the flow of this early trade, as they would for centuries to come. From about April to September the prevailing winds in the Indian Ocean and the China Sea blew from the southwest, thus facilitating voyages from west to east and north to China and Japan. During this same period, winds in the Java and Banda seas, being located south of the equator, blew from the southeast, thus favoring a passage from east to west. A look at the map will show that these three routes converged in the Strait of Malacca. In the early stage, when vessels were small, the Isthmus of Kra was a favored transfer point, the goods being carried overland.[3] In due course, however, it proved cheaper to sail around the Malay Peninsula, thus enhancing the importance of the Strait of Malacca as the artery through which all east-west trade must flow.

Most merchants accompanied their own goods which, more

2. Compare B. Schrieke, *Indonesian Sociological Studies*, *1* (The Hague, 1955), 11.
3. R. A. Kern, "De Verbreiding van den Islam," in F. W. Stapel, ed., *Geschiedenis van nederlandsch Indië*, *1* (3 vols. Amsterdam, 1938), 320.

often than not, consisted of only a few bales or bundles. At times the merchants actually outweighed the cargo, giving the decks the appearance of a crowded market place. The captain and the crew likewise carried goods for their own account. The wealthier classes had little desire to risk their lives on such long and dangerous journeys. They preferred to entrust their goods and money to others against a prearranged share in the profits. Van Leur points out the clear distinction between the "passive" role in this trade, played by nobles and patricians, and the traveling merchants who were the "active" element, both for their own account and by means of commenda-money and commenda-goods furnished by others.[4]

The idea one receives of this trade is that of a large number of vessels of varying types and sizes converging on their destination during one monsoon, and returning with the next. A single round trip might last as long as a year. The objects of this ancient trade were both "splendid and trifling," as Gibbon wrote, in the *Decline and Fall of the Roman Empire*.[5] It was indeed a fragile, golden thread which, like a spider's web, gathered the precious products of Asia and thus made them available to Europe.

The passage of time did little to change the general pattern. The number of traders arriving at any of the many ports might vary from year to year; ships could fail to arrive because of war, piracy, or other causes; volume might increase or decrease. Basically, however, business was transacted in the same manner: the merchant standing next to his goods in the market place and bargaining for the best possible price. Van Leur views this Asiatic trade as an "historical constant" because "no qualitative transformations can be indicated in the course of history." [6] The arrival of Islam in Southeast Asia caused considerable political change, but left untouched the old established pattern of trade.[7] The Portuguese likewise did not alter it; they added only an additional thread to the existing web. As Van Leur states flatly, "the Portuguese regime was of little significance commercially or economically." [8]

The Indonesians may have participated in this trade since pre-

4. Van Leur, *Indonesian Trade*, p. 67.
5. W. H. Moreland, *From Akbar to Aurangzeb, A Study in Indian Economic History* (London, 1923), p. 196.
6. Van Leur, *Indonesian Trade*, pp. 87–88.
7. Ibid., p. 112.
8. Ibid., p. 164. Compare Meilink-Roelofsz, *Asian Trade*, pp. 119–35.

historic times; there are indications that Indonesia was part of an extensive area with similar cultures that comprised India, the mainland of Southeast Asia, and the Archipelago, all connected by a kind of maritime culture. It is quite likely that, in view of this intercourse, each part had small colonies of traders in the others and that this was established long before the introduction of any marked Hindu influence in Indonesia. Hall stresses this point, because it has long been assumed that Indonesian trade had developed as a result of Hinduization, rather than the reverse.[9]

The arrival of Hinduism in Indonesia is generally considered to have taken place at the beginning of the Christian era because it was during the first few centuries A.D. that kingdoms emerged which, in organization and in the principle of kingship, closely resembled those of earlier realms in India. Although the exact process by which this developed has not yet been established, it is likely that native chiefs were attracted by the culture of the Hindu merchants who frequented their shores. The possibility cannot be excluded that sons of Indian potentates, either voluntarily or having been banished for political reasons, settled in Indonesia, and through marriage with daughters of native rulers succeeded in establishing kingdoms of their own below the equator.[10]

Whatever the process may have been, the Hindu states first came into being at the sites which had been the ports of call of traders from India since earliest times. With the arrival of priests and *gurus* (men of learning), there gradually developed a culture with strong Hindu overtones, comprising the conception of royalty, the acceptance of the sacred laws of Hinduism, and the use of Sanskrit for religious ceremonies, as the native language was inadequate for this purpose. Hinduism deeply affected the culture of the aristocracy, but it made little impression on the large peasant class. It introduced a caste system which admirably reflected the feudal form of government that developed. The priests were at the top, followed by the warrior class, to which the king and his followers belonged; the merchants came next, and the *sudras* (peasants) were the lowest.

The lines between the castes, although less stringent than in India, were sharply drawn, even to the extent that they created

9. D. G. E. Hall, *A History of South-East Asia* (London, Macmillan, 1958), pp. 12–13. See also W. F. Stutterheim, *Het Hinduïsme in de archipel* (Djakarta and Groningen, Wolters, 1952), p. 10.
10. Stutterheim, *Hinduïsme*, pp. 19–20.

different languages to be used when one addressed an equal, a superior, or an inferior caste person. In no other culture does one find a social structure in which separate languages are used to identify different social levels.[11] The Indonesians, before the arrival of the Hindus, had already developed a culture of their own: the complicated cultivation of wet rice fields, international trade, and, on Java at least, a well organized political structure. The Hindus brought their religion, and they introduced batik, money, and a metric system. They also influenced government administration and jurisprudence, but in both, the rudiments of the old Indonesian institutions were retained. Architecture was at first strongly influenced by that of India, primarily because large buildings and sanctuaries were unknown prior to the arrival of the Hindus. Gradually, however, there developed a distinct Hindu-Javanese style, which differed greatly from the Hindu architecture of India. The result was a cultural process in which Hindu ideas and innovations became accepted but from which the old Indonesian culture was never eradicated.[12]

Southeast Asia was divided into a large number of petty principalities, among which one would rise, from time to time, able to extend dominion over a wider area, sometimes a very extensive one. Funan was the first such great power known. It was situated on the mainland in what is now Cambodia. It probably originated in the first century A.D., but the earliest Chinese reference to it dates from the third century. Funan's rule extended to the Malay Peninsula, and its fleet is said to have dominated the seas. The fall of Funan at about the middle of the sixth century opened the way for a new power to rise in Sumatra.

In the year 644, there appears for the first time the name Malayu, from which the word Malay is derived. It was situated at the site which later became known as Djambi. A half century later, according to I-tsing, the Chinese-Buddhist scholar, it had been conquered by another rising power. This was Srivijaya, which had its seat at Palembang. I-tsing reveals that the Srivijaya king had designs on other areas as well, and that he was about to launch an attack on Java. The origin of this kingdom is not recorded, but some ascribe it to an influx of people from either Java or the

11. H. J. de Graaf, *Geschiedenis van Indonesië* (The Hague and Bandung, 1949), pp. 24–29. For a detailed account of the various languages, see the *Encyclopaedie van Nederlandsch-Indië*, s.v. *Javaansch*.

12. F. W. Stapel, *Geschiedenis van Nederlandsch-Indië* (Amsterdam, Meulenhoff, 1943), p. 24.

Malay Peninsula.[13] Van Leur presents the hypothesis that Srivijaya was established by an aristocratic group from elsewhere, who amassed wealth from direct trade, levies on goods in transit, and plunder.[14] This exercise of power is confirmed by Chinese writers, who refer to the predatory expeditions sent out by Srivijaya and its enforcement of compulsory stapling at Palembang. "If some foreign ship, passing this place, should not enter here, an armed party would certainly come out and kill them to the last." [15] At the zenith of its power, Srivijaya dominated all traffic through the Strait of Malacca and Sunda Strait, thus maintaining a commercial hegemony over Indonesia as well as the India-China trade. Its power extended as far as the coast of Coromandel, and several times it attacked Ceylon.

Srivijaya had a long history, but eventually it succumbed. This was brought about by the rise of new kingdoms in Java, but the decisive blow is said to have been struck by the Thai kingdom, which was expanding to the Malay peninsula during the latter part of the thirteenth century. Marco Polo does not mention it, and thus perhaps Srivijaya had ceased to exist by the end of the thirteenth century.

In Java, too, dynasties had risen and fallen. In 1222, the kingdom of Kediri in East Java was subjugated by its neighbor Singosari. This kingdom lasted only some seventy years. It had its beginning with an unscrupulous individual of low origin, King Angrok, whose story is related in all its unsavory details in the Javanese Chronicle, the Pararaton, or Book of Kings.[16] He was the illegitimate son of a peasant woman who abandoned him on a dung heap, where he was found by a thief who adopted him. After he had grown up, Angrok ("he who upsets everything") stole his foster father's belongings and launched a career of crime of his own. He murdered the regent of Tumapel, who had orders from Kediri to take him into custody. By marrying the regent's widow, Angrok usurped his place, and by various ruthless means, rose to power. His reign lasted only five years, and he was murdered at the instigation of his own stepson, who thus revenged

13. Hall, History of South-East Asia, pp. 38–39.
14. Van Leur, Indonesian Trade, pp. 105–06.
15. Schrieke, Indonesian Sociological Studies, 1, 15–16. See also Meilink-Roelofsz, Asian Trade, pp. 14–17.
16. For further details on the Pararaton, see B. H. M. Vlekke, Nusantara: A History of the East Indian Archipelago (Cambridge, Mass., Harvard, 1943), p. 40, n. 19.

the murder of his father. This apparently set the pattern for a series of murders by which one king was replaced by another during the early period of Singosari.

Kertanagara was the last king of Singosari, and certainly the most illustrious, according to the history of his reign in the *Nagarakertagama*, an epic poem written in 1365 by the Buddhist priest Prabanca. He came to the throne in 1268, and in 1275 he inaugurated a plan to create an Indonesian confederacy against a possible threat from China. In 1280 he established his sovereignty over East Java, and four years later he had subdued both Madura and Bali. With the conquest of the kingdom of Sunda around 1289, Kertanagara had all of Java under his control. He next prepared himself for an attack on Malayu which, after the demise of Srivijaya, had once more become the leading power in Sumatra.[17]

Kublai Khan, the Mogul conqueror of China, was then trying to extend his power into Southeast Asia by sending ambassadors to the various rulers, with demands that they travel to Peking to pay him homage. Kertanagara openly defied the Khan's ambassadors; when they arrived at Singosari, he arrested them all and sent them back to China, according to Chinese records, with "mutilated faces." The Dutch Sinologist Duyvendak suggests that this statement should not be taken literally but figuratively, signifying that the Khan was deeply insulted by this rude reception of his mission.[18] In 1292, Kertanagara launched his so-called Pamalayu expedition to Sumatra, which is said to have extended to the west coast of Borneo and the Malay Peninsula as well. Preoccupied with building an empire, Kertanagara had apparently not prepared himself for internal difficulties. While his forces were employed elsewhere, Kediri launched a surprise attack on Singosari in the same year. The capital was taken and the king and his entourage, according to the *Pararaton*, were slain while drinking palm wine. For a while it appeared that this was the end of Kertanagara's grandiose designs, but he had planted the seeds well, and, fortuitously, support came from an unexpected quarter.

Kertanagara's son-in-law and nephew, Vijaya, managed to ingratiate himself with his uncle's murderer. In due course he was given a district to administer on the river Brantas. He settled at a site located near the present town of Modjokerto, and named it

17. See C. C. Berg, "Kertanagara de miskende empirebuilder," *Orientatie*, 34 (1950), 3–32. See also Meilink-Roelofsz, *Asian Trade*, pp. 17–18.
18. Hall, *History of South-East Asia*, p. 70.

Madjapahit ("bitter fruit"). The year was 1294, the beginning of
the one era in old Indonesian history, according to the *Nagarakertagama*, in which most of the archipelago was dominated by
a central power. Berg disputes this; it is his belief that the state of
Madjapahit was limited to East Java, Madura, and Bali.[19] In the
absence of a fully documented history of Madjapahit, we have
only the evidence of a contemporary chronicler, whose reliability
is, of course, an open question.

The support for Kertanagara's scheme of empire came when
Kublai Khan sent a strong force to avenge the "mutilated faces"
of the Chinese ambassadors. Kertanagara by then was dead, and
Vijaya appeased the warlords by offering to accept Kublai Khan
as his sovereign, provided the Chinese would help him to regain
his kingdom. The warlords agreed, and thoroughly defeated the
king of Kediri, not without serious losses to themselves. Vijaya
saw his chance and turned his own forces against the Chinese,
who retreated to their fleet at Tuban. From there the warlords
sailed home, consoling themselves that they had at least executed
their orders to the extent of punishing *one* Javanese king. Vijaya
was clever enough not to press his luck too far. He sent ambassadors to Peking to pay homage to Kublai Khan who, in turn,
dropped his demand that Vijaya come in person.[20]

In this manner, Vijaya not only revenged the death of Kertanagara but gained control over the former kingdom of Singosari as well, now to be revived in that of Madjapahit. Shortly
after the departure of the Chinese fleet, Kertanagara's Pamalayu
expedition returned from Sumatra, bringing back a few princesses,
one of whom Vijaya married. Vijaya was the founder of Madjapahit, but the real empire builder was a commoner, Gajah Mada,
who had started his career in the service of Jayanagara, Vijaya's
son by the Sumatran princess. As an officer in the royal body-
guard, he had quelled a rebellion in the army, for which he was
rewarded with the high office of *patih*, or chief administrator, of
Madjapahit. He held this office for 31 years until his death in
1364. He considered himself destined to make Kertanagara's ambitions a reality, and he swore that he would not rest until all the

19. C. C. Berg, "De Sadeng-oorlog en de mythe van Groot-Majapahit,"
Indonesië, 5 (1951), 385–422.

20. De Graaf, *Geschiedenis van Indonesië*, pp. 62–63. See also Stutterheim,
Hindüisme, pp. 71–73, and Meilink-Roelofsz, *Asian Trade*, pp. 25–26.

islands of Indonesia were brought under the rule of Madjapahit.

According to Prabanca, Gajah Mada was eminently successful: the *Nagarakertagama* records that the empire stretched from Sumatra to the Moluccas. But Berg and Stutterheim recommend that this not be taken literally, in the sense that the empire consisted of a series of dependencies ruled by a central government. At best it could have been little more than a loose confederation in which individual rulers, while retaining power in their own states, could be forced to pay tribute to Madjapahit. It is conceded that Gajah Mada's powerful fleet, and a strong government at home, enforced payment of these obligations.[21]

Gajah Mada was undoubtedly a great man, and his administration became a model of sound statecraft. A kind of cabinet was formed with members of the royal family in charge of its various departments, such as taxation, public and military affairs, justice, and others. The *Wadanas,* the district heads, were ordered "to attend to the dikes around the ricefields, so that drainage can be controlled . . . roads and bridges have to be kept in constant repair . . . for the good of all people." [22] Almost the same words were used by the early Frisian-Dutch when they proclaimed their laws for diking to protect themselves against the sea and keep their land intact. The Javanese and the Dutch, separated by half the world and centuries in time . . . little could either have guessed that some day their paths would cross.

Gajah Mada died in 1364, but the forces of empire building he had set in motion were not to die with him. His sovereign Hayam Waruk reigned for another twenty-five years, and under his rule the empire, such as it was, remained more or less intact, although it does not appear that he paid much attention to affairs of state. "King Hayam Waruk is truly a great potentate," Prabanca wrote. "He has no cares or worries and indulges in all sorts of pleasures. Many beautiful maidens are collected for him, as many as can be found." Madjapahit witnessed the oriental counterpart of the spectacles of ancient Rome, except that they were less sophisticated. "The King gave great feasts for thousands of his subjects. Hayam Waruk himself gave song and it was admired by all. It was as lovely as the call of a peacock in a tree, sweet as

21. Stutterheim, *Hinduïsme,* pp. 83–84. Compare Meilink-Roelofsz, *Asian Trade,* pp. 22–23.
22. Vlekke, *Nusantara,* p. 65.

honey." There was more of the same—the King masquerading with the young men of his court, and his queen sporting a funny wig.[23] Such a man could hardly be called a forceful ruler, but, since there were no serious threats to his authority, the empire retained some of the glitter acquired by the power of Gajah Mada.

With the death of Hayam Waruk in 1389 the decline of Madjapahit began, and it was the king himself who gave it impetus. His legal successor was his son-in-law, but, unwilling to leave a son by a lesser wife unprovided for, he had divided his East Java kingdom. This soon led to great rivalry, and by 1401 civil war broke out. This struggle lasted five years and, although finally won by Madjapahit, the kingdom was left so enfeebled that it could no longer maintain authority abroad. The vassal states in West Borneo, the Malay Peninsula, and eventually, Sumatra, began to look to China for protection against a resurgence of piracy in their waters after the dissappearance of Madjapahit's fleet.[24]

This crumbling at the edges was only a prelude to the consequences in Java, which followed the pattern of the rise and fall of earlier Javanese kingdoms: when the glory of a maharajah waned, his vassals turned their backs to him, refusing to pay homage and tribute. A strong ruler, another Gajah Mada, might have prevented this, but there were none. One after the other the vassals broke away, first Kediri in 1437; around the middle of the fifteenth century a kingdom in Central Java began to assert itself. In 1478 the *kraton* (palace) of Madjapahit itself was taken by a ruler of Kediri, and this, according to the annals, is presumed to spell the end: "disappeared and lost is the glory of the empire." [25]

But Madjapahit was a long time in dying, and it was still alive in the early part of the sixteenth century. According to Portuguese records, a king of Madjapahit named "Pateudra" (presumably Pati Udara, last recorded king of Madjapahit) sent a mission in 1512 to Albuquerque, after his conquest of Malacca, to enlist support against his Moslem enemies on the north coast of Java. In 1514 the Portuguese governor of Malacca, de Brito, reported that there were two heathen (Hindu) kings in Java, one in Sunda and the other in East Java, but that the coasts were ruled by the

23. Ibid., pp. 62, 67.
24. Stutterheim, *Hinduïsme*, pp. 87–89.
25. De Graaf, *Geschiedenis van Indonesië*, pp. 77–78.

Moors.[26] This suggests that it was primarily the rise of Islam in the archipelago which at last brought about the end of Madjapahit, by cutting it off from the outside world. It also ended the long Hindu period in the history of Java.

26. N. J. Krom, "De Hindoe-Javaansche tijd," in Stapel, ed., *Geschiedenis van Nederlandsch Indië, 1,* 296–97.

10

Background
in Asia

The political situation in Asia during the fifteenth and sixteenth centuries largely determined the pattern of European conquests on that continent. A strong power in Asia Minor had impelled the Portuguese to discover a direct sea route to the Indies. Political weakness in India and Southeast Asia facilitated European encroachments; in China and Japan, however, they were kept at bay by relatively strong central governments.

Since ancient times, the goods of Asia had reached Europe via three main routes. The legendary silk route across central Asia reached the Black Sea at Trebizond, and from there the goods went mainly to Constantinople, but also found their way into Europe up the Danube River. Spices from Southeast Asia mainly followed a route through the Persian Gulf and, via Baghdad, to the Syrian coastal towns on the eastern shore of the Mediterranean. For a long time, this was the main artery, until it was disrupted as a result of the Crusades and, especially, after Mogul hordes invaded Mesopotamia and destroyed Baghdad in 1258. From then on the third route, across the Indian Ocean and through the Red Sea to Egypt, became the most prominent. It has been estimated that during the fourteenth and fifteenth centuries the annual flow of goods through Cairo alone amounted to about five million guilders in absolute gold value.[1] In this trade the merchants of Gujerat, with headquarters at Cambay, became the most important link between east and west.

Venice and Genoa had profited greatly from this trade, and they were the first to feel the pinch when the expansion of the Ottoman empire threatened to interfere with their supply line. A joint effort on the part of these powerful city-states might have kept the Turks in check, but the intense rivalry between them precluded any kind of coalition. The Genoese, in fact, actively supported the enemies of Christendom, both for their

1. Schrieke, *Indonesian Sociological Studies, 1,* 10.

own gain and to hurt Venice. In 1444, their ships ferried a large Turkish army across the Bosporus at one ducat a head.[2] The fall of Constantinople in 1453 effectively closed the Black Sea route. During the remainder of the fifteenth century the Turks intensified their activities against Venice both by land and by sea. Not only Genoa but the Pope in Rome openly encouraged the Turks to crush Venice. The Turks gained a decisive victory over Venice in the sea battle at Lepanto in 1499. Selim I ("the Grim") gained control over the remaining routes to Asia by capturing Damascus in 1516 and Egypt in the year following.

This occupation of the land bridge to Asia by a non-Christian power did not necessarily block the supply of spices and other Asiatic goods, but trade no longer flowed as freely as it had before. The word "freely" should not be taken literally in this connection, because every ruler who successfully straddled an important trade route always managed to demand his tribute. With respect to the Red Sea supply line, the Venetian Marino Sanudo wrote in 1306, "Earlier the largest share of Indian merchandise used to make its way over Baghdad to ports in Syria . . . in those days spices and other products were cheaper than nowadays. Now they come mostly via Alexandria, and in that way a third of their value flows into the treasury of the sultan of Egypt." [3] The point is that the Turks, for political reasons as well as for gain, tried to extort all they could out of this trade. This was one of the main reasons why the leading countries of Europe, Spain and Portugal, were anxious to gain access to the goods of Asia, mainly spices, behind the back of the Ottoman empire.

The need to thwart the enemy became the more pressing when the momentum of empire-building carried the Turks westward along the north coast of Africa. Haired-Din, known as Barbarossa to the Europeans, captured Algiers and created the Barbary states which, for centuries to come, were the scourge of shipping in the Mediterranean. In 1538, the Christian powers made a belated attempt to combat the Turks by joining their forces. Spain, Rome, Genoa, and Venice combined their fleets under the command of the celebrated Genoese admiral Andrea Doria, but they were soundly defeated by a Turkish fleet under Barbarossa. Three

2. W. W. Hunter, *A History of British India*, 1 (London, Longmans, Green, 1919), 36–37. The value of a golden ducat was about 2 reals, equal to about 5 guilders.

3. Schrieke, *Indonesian Sociological Studies*, 1, 11–12.

years later, Charles V of Spain tried to dislodge the Turks from
Algiers, but the attempt was a failure. On this occasion a Dutch
painter and etcher, Cornelis Antoniszoon, had been taken along
to record the anticipated victory over the infidels. His name,
however, is better known for the fact that he produced the first
detailed map of Amsterdam in the year 1536.[4]

In the meantime, a new factor had been introduced in the
Indies which would have far-reaching consequences. It was the
spread of Islam, and for this the Moslem traders of Gujerat
had been largely responsible. It is said that, while Hinduism
brought a culture to Indonesia, Islam gave it a new religion.[5] In
broad historical perspective this may be true, but the arrival of
Islam, although essentially a peaceful penetration, also produced
political changes which, for one thing, accelerated the decline
of Madjapahit.

It was logical that the new faith should attain its first foothold
at the northern tip of Sumatra, the first point of contact for
Moslem traders on their journeys to Southeast Asia. Marco Polo
reported evidence of this when he visited Perlak in 1292 on his
homeward voyage from China. "The people are for the most
part idolaters," he wrote, "but many of those who dwell in the
seaport towns have been converted to the religion of Mahomet
by the Saracen merchants who constantly frequent them." [6]
Islam must have arrived shortly before, because the neighboring
principality of Samudra, where the Polos spent five months await-
ing a favorable monsoon, had not yet been converted. But
Samudra, which became Sumatra in Arabic and thus gave its name
to the whole island, followed shortly afterwards. Sultan Malik al
Saleh was its first Moslem ruler and, when he died in 1297, his
grave was adorned with a tombstone imported from Cambay.

The next stepping stone, and of far greater importance for the
spread of Islam, was Malacca, on the west coast of the Malay
Peninsula. Malacca apparently had its origin during the middle
of the fourteenth century as a fishing village and a pirate's nest.
Because of its favorable location on the east-west trade route, it

4. F. J. Dubiez, "Cornelis Antoniszoon," Ons Amsterdam, 12 (1959),
354–66.
5. W. F. Stutterheim, De Islam en zijn komst in de archipel (Djakarta and
Groningen, Wolters, 1952), p. 150.
6. M. Komroff, ed., The Travels of Marco Polo in Marsden's Translation
(New York, Boni & Liveright, 1926), pp. 274–75. See also Meilink-Roelofsz,
Asian Trade, pp. 20–21.

gained prominence in the early years of the fifteenth century, after a Javanese prince named Paramesvara settled there.[7] Not long afterwards he adopted the Moslem faith, presumably as a result of his marriage with a daughter of the Sultan of Pasai, which had superseded Samudra. Malacca was considered to be a dependency of Madjapahit, but Paramesvara, who had now taken the name Megat Iskandar Shah as a result of his conversion, was one of the vassals anxious to break away from the empire and turn to China for protection.[8] Around the middle of the fifteenth century, Malacca was strong enough to force all passing vessels to put into its harbor, which made it the most important staple town in Southeast Asia. It became the meeting place for east and west. The Gujerati had a permanent settlement there of about a thousand merchants, and three or four times that number traveled constantly between Cambay and Malacca.

These Gujerati were keen merchants. For their trade with the east they depended mostly on cotton textiles and silver coins; oriental trade had long since been based on a money economy, and silver was the accepted medium of exchange. They also added another salable product: wherever converts were made for the "true faith," there developed a demand for authentic Islamic tombstones, which were regarded as a necessary key to the everlasting pleasures of the Moslem heaven. The Gujerat merchants were only too willing to supply the demand. They obtained material cheaply enough by tearing down the old Hindu temples at home—a good many still had Hindu relief carvings on their backs. The stones were dressed a bit and inscribed with a quotation from the Koran. It is not unlikely that this profitable sideline, which also made good ballast on the outward journey, enhanced their zeal to spread the Moslem faith as widely as possible. After the Portuguese captured Malacca, these same stones were made to serve still another useful purpose; they were taken from the graveyards and used as building material for the Portuguese fort.[9]

During the second half of the fifteenth century, Malacca was not only the most important commercial center in Southeast Asia but also the strongest political power as well. Practically the

7. G. P. Rouffaer, "Was Malakka emperium voor 1400 A.D., genaamd Malajoer?" *BKI*, 77 (1921), 1–172, 359–600.
8. See p. 202.
9. Vlekke, *Nusantara*, pp. 70–71.

whole of the east coast of the Malay Peninsula had been brought within its orbit. At the expense of Madjapahit it also controlled Djambi, Kampar, Bengalis on Sumatra, and the offshore Carimon Islands and Bintang.[10] If these conquests could have been consolidated and war with Siam avoided, it is possible that this Moslem state would not have surrendered so quickly to the Portuguese in 1511.

The spread of Islam in Southeast Asia was by no means a spontaneous movement. It had taken about one hundred years to move from North Sumatra to the Malay Peninsula, and at the end of the fifteenth century it was still largely confined to the western half of the archipelago. The conventional explanation of this conversion is that Moslem traders, especially the Gujerati, married native women, usually of the upper classes of the native society, and thus managed to become part of ruling circles which gradually adopted the new faith.[11] There is no doubt that Islam followed the long established trade routes, and that the Gujerati were mainly responsible for its propagation, but the manner in which it was accomplished may not have been quite so simple. Since ancient times, foreign merchants were at the mercy of local rulers whose permission had to be obtained, usually by means of gifts, before any trading could take place. The link between the ruler and the foreign merchants was the *shahbandar* (harbor master), whose duty it was to collect port fees as well as levies on imports and exports. Because of the language problem, it was usually a foreigner who held this important office, and when trade came into the hands of the Gujerati, it can be assumed that the *shahbandar* also belonged to this group and was thus Moslem.[12] It is Schrieke's theory that these Moslem *shahbandars* were the channels through which Islam gained acceptance by the royal courts. They also introduced Moslem scholars, who gave the spiritual impetus to local rulers to extend their power. This began at an early stage; Ibn Batuta mentions the presence of several Persian scholars at the court in Pasai in 1345–46. They were the real missionaries, highly regarded both at court and among the people.[13]

10. See Hall, *History of South-East Asia*, p. 182. On the rise of Malacca, see Meilink-Roelofsz, *Asian Trade*, pp. 27–35.
11. Kern, in Stapel, ed., *Geschiedenis van nederlandsch Indië*, 1, 309–10. See also Schrieke, *Indonesian Sociological Studies*, 2, 230–31.
12. See Meilink-Roelofsz, *Asian Trade*, pp. 67, 240, 244.
13. See Schrieke, *Indonesian Sociological Studies*, 2, 237–44.

There are good reasons why Java was the last to feel the full impact of Islam. It was farther east, and the Hindu empire of Madjapahit did not encourage the introduction of an alien religion. During the fifteenth century, Madjapahit had lost most of its overseas dependencies, but in East Java, the most important part of the island as far as trade was concerned, it could still make its power felt. Colonies of Moslem traders, however, were tolerated, and there is evidence that they existed in various coastal towns prominent in the trade with the Moluccas. The earliest known Moslem grave in Java is that of Malik Ibrahim, who died in 1419. Prior to this perhaps the influx had not been great. According to the inscription on his tomb, he was a merchant in spices who had been born in Persia. He was buried at Grise, now a sleepy little town a few miles north of Surabaya.

As we have seen, the waning power of Madjapahit on Java itself encouraged former vassals to cut themselves loose.[14] A number of coastal towns, which had prospered through their trade with Malacca in rice and spices, had similar restless ambitions.[15] Thus there appeared about a dozen coastal principalities which, because their affluence depended almost entirely on trade, had colonies of Moslem merchants. This in itself was not enough reason to embrace Islam—the Hindu tradition was still strong. Not until 1498 is there mention of "some ports" which had accepted the new faith.[16] The tempo quickened in reaction to the arrival of the Portuguese, who considered themselves blessed by God "to rid the earth of as many Moslems as possible." [17] Before long all the coastal rulers of any importance had converted to Islam while, at the same time, severing their last ties with what was left of Madjapahit. In this campaign the Moslem scholars or scribes, who were called *wali's* in Java, had been extremely active. As a result they were held in high esteem and it was generally believed that they were endowed with magic powers.[18]

Among these principalities there soon was one that attempted supremacy, just as had happened repeatedly during the Hindu period. This was Demak, whose ruler claimed that he had come

14. See above, p. 202.
15. For a detailed account of the trade at Malacca, see Meilink-Roelofsz, *Asian Trade*, pp. 36–88.
16. Kern, in Stapel, ed., *Geschiedenis, 1*, 329–30.
17. Schrieke, *Indonesian Sociological Studies, 2*, 234.
18. For an account of the Moslem scholars in Java, see De Graaf, *Geschiedenis van Indonesië*, pp. 80–90.

into possession of the regalia of Madjapahit, which were to entitle him to become ruler over all Java if he were able to establish his authority. Through marriages and conquests, Demak not only extended its hegemony over a large part of the coast but, by subduing Mataram and the former Singosari, also penetrated the interior of Java. Of special significance for the later history of Indonesia is the fact that Demak added Bantam to its other conquests. Falatehan, a Malay from North Sumatra who had married a sister of the ruler of Demak, became its first regent. In the past, Bantam had been bypassed on the route which led from Malacca to the ports of East Java. After the fall of Malacca to the Portuguese, however, Bantam gained rapidly in importance and eventually became the great emporium the Dutch found when they first came to the Indies. In 1568 Bantam freed itself from Demak and became an independent sultanate, politically important because it included the whole of West Java and a part of South Sumatra as well.[19]

Bantam's secession must have been the result of a political upheaval in Demak. It appears that the ruler of Padjang, a former vassal state of Madjapahit, had succeeded in overthrowing Demak's dynasty. In 1568 he had himself proclaimed Sultan of Padjang and proceeded to annex most of Demak's dependencies as well as some other areas in Central Java. The supremacy of Padjang was short-lived, mainly due to a successful rebellion by the ambitious young regent of Mataram. His name was Suta Vijaya, but he became better known as Senapati Ingalaga (leader in war) or just Senapati.

The name Mataram goes back to the eighth and ninth centuries, when it was the core of a powerful Hindu empire which signified its grandeur by erecting magnificent Buddhist monuments (*chandis*) of which the Borobudur is the most famous. But when Senapati's father had settled there, the area was little more than a jungle, and the glory of Hindu Mataram had long since been forgotten. Only the overgrown ruins of the temples were mute reminders of the past. But now, in 1586, the golden *payong*, the ceremonial umbrella signifying supreme kingship, moved from Padjang to Mataram.[20] Thus began the rise of a new Mataram, destined to become the last great realm in Java.

19. On the early history of Bantam, see Kern, in Stapel, ed., *Geschiedenis*, 1, 335–40.
20. Stutterheim, *De Islam*, p. 44.

At the death of Senapati in 1601, Mataram's power was firmly established in the interior. It was an inland state, its prosperity based mainly on agriculture; it never developed any great interest in trade, except in the export of rice. As a result, the coastal principalities in East Java, while paying their yearly homage at the *kraton*, largely retained their independence. This was noted by the Dutch, who were now arriving in increasing numbers. Of Mataram they noticed next to nothing, and all their dealings were with the petty rulers on the coast, whom they referred to as "kings." [21]

On Sumatra, Borneo, Celebes, the Moluccas, and elsewhere, this fragmented picture was not much different. The state of political disunity prevailed when the Dutch arrived in Indonesia, a promising situation for a young Dutchman who knew enough about statecraft to apply the principle of "divide and rule." Among the large number of independent principalities, there were only three that had more than a minor significance, Achin in North Sumatra, Bantam in West Java, and Ternate in the Moluccas. These three caused the Dutch the most trouble but they were not strong enough to stop them.

Ever since Marco Polo had told Europe about the wonders of Cathay and Cipango, these two countries had fired the imagination of people in western Europe whose horizon had been widened during the Age of Discovery. The exploitation of this promising field, however, was effectively hampered by an all-consuming fear of foreign encroachment on the part of China and Japan. Neither country was powerful, but both proved to be strong enough to keep the Europeans in check if for no other reason than that each had a centralized administration.

The political situation in China during the sixteenth century was somewhat analogous to that of India, in that it was threatened from across its borders. The Moguls had renewed their attacks from the northwest, the Mongolia that was their home base. The Ming emperors tried to avert this threat by fortifying China's border towns and by repairing the ancient Great Wall. At about the same time, the Japanese were harassing China's coast. They plundered Ningpo in 1523, and they besieged Nanking some thirty years later. Pirate fleets from Formosa disturbed the shores of the Celestial Kingdom, and the southern border proved to be

21. On the rule of Senapati, see H. J. de Graaf, *De Regering van Panembahan Senapati Ingalaga* (The Hague, 1954).

vulnerable as well, when Burmese and Siamese forces moved into
the province of Yunnan.

Confronted by these sporadic attacks all along its borders,
China had quickly abandoned imperial plans for Southeast Asia.
It was more important now to preserve the Middle Kingdom, the
eighteen original provinces of ancient China. Guided by this
policy of self-preservation, the Ming dynasty did not approve
the arrival of the Europeans—first the Portuguese, later the Dutch.
It was only through subterfuge and the reluctance of Peking to
take positive action that the Portuguese succeeded in gaining a
foothold at Macao, a small and practically uninhabited peninsula
at the mouth of the Canton River. The Chinese allowed them to
stay there but stiffened their determination to bar the Europeans
from any other points along the coast. This policy was effectively
sustained for almost three hundred years, and during this period
no European country succeeded in gaining more than a highly
restricted contact.

The political situation in Japan at first seemed to favor the
Portuguese, because the country was riven by internal conflict.
There was a bitter struggle between, on one side, the Shogun and
his powerful liege lords, the Daimyos, and, on the other, the
militant Buddhist priesthood. This conflict raged during the greater
part of the sixteenth century with neither side being able to gain
a decisive victory over the other. The Shogun was persuaded to
admit a Jesuit mission to Japan in 1549, soon to be followed by
others. The Shogun and the Daimyos actually encouraged the
Jesuits in their campaign to spread the Catholic faith, hoping that
this would turn the people against the Buddhist hierarchy. Many
thousands of Japanese were converted, but this also brought a
third factor into the already unstable political situation. Flushed
with their early success, the Jesuits had visions of converting the
whole of Japan, and this led to their downfall. Those Japanese
who had already been converted were incited by the Jesuits to
take aggressive action, which took the form of conspiracies and
uprisings in various parts of Japan. Unfortunately for the Portuguese priests, central power in Japan had been restored under
the Tokugawa Shogunate, essentially a military dictatorship
which firmly ruled the country with the emperor as a mere figure-
head. The Christian insurrections were ruthlessly suppressed,
and in 1614 all Portuguese priests were ordered to leave the country. For a while a distinction was made between priests and mer-

chants, but gradually the notion grew that all foreigners were a threat to the country. During the 1630's, Japan proceeded to seal itself off from the world, and in 1637 an edict was passed which forbade any Japanese to leave the country, on penalty of death.

All foreigners were henceforth barred from Japan, with one exception. The Dutch had never tried to make any converts to their Protestant religion. All they had come for was trade, and they had never tried to meddle in the internal affairs of the country. They were allowed to maintain a factory on Decima, a small island in the harbor of Nagasaki. This remained Japan's only window to the western world for three centuries, until the Americans, under Admiral Perry, arrived in Japan in 1852.

Obstruction of trade by a strong power, Turkey, had sent Europeans to Asia in the first place. A suspicious China had largely succeeded in keeping them at bay, and they were expelled from Japan after a relatively short stay. It was in Southeast Asia, the source of spices which had been the magnet from the start, that the political situation was most propitious. Weak and divided, the area was no match for the newcomers. The door to empire-building was indeed ajar.

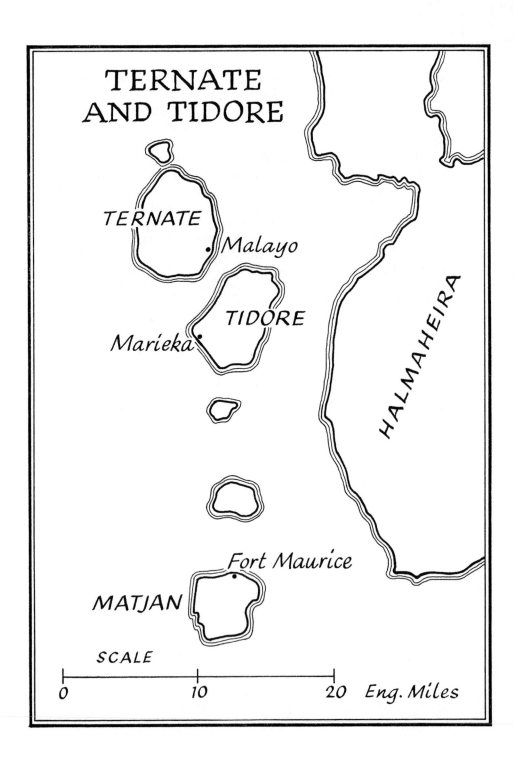

TERNATE
AND TIDORE

TERNATE

• Malayo

TIDORE

Marieka •

HALMAHEIRA

Fort Maurice

MATJAN

SCALE

0   10   20   Eng. Miles

The
Portuguese
Age

The Portuguese were the first Europeans to make territorial conquests in Asia, but their tenure was based on feudal principles,
and had none of the characteristics by which modern colonialism
is identified. Since this view is not generally accepted, the Portuguese period in Asia, lasting about a century, deserves more
than passing mention.

In 1488, four years before Columbus discovered America in
search of a direct route to the Spice Islands, the Portuguese reached
the southernmost tip of Africa. This feat was accomplished by
Bartolomeu Dias, and should be rated as one of the most important discoveries of all time. It had taken the Portuguese about
a hundred years of intermittent probing along the west coast of
Africa to get this far, mostly under the able guidance of Prince
Henry the Navigator. Now the need for original explorations on
the part of the Portuguese was over, because from this point on
the further route to the Indies had already been thoroughly
charted by others. The Atlantic Ocean had been the problem,
not the Indian Ocean, nor the Pacific—these seas had long since
been explored by others.

From the ninth century on, information about this part of the
world had reached Europe, gathered by such men as Abu Hassan,
Marco Polo, and Ibn Batuta of Tangier, the latter spending some
thirty years, from 1325 to 1355, in constant travels throughout
Asia and North Africa. It was no virgin territory that was about
to be invaded by the West.

The first Portuguese expedition to reach India left Lisbon in
1497 under Vasco da Gama. At Malindi on the east coast of
Africa, he engaged two pilots from Gujerat to guide him across
the Indian Ocean. With pride he showed them his astrolabes and
other nautical instruments, but the Moslem navigators did not

seem to be impressed. They, and others before them, had been using such instruments for a long time.[1]

It was clear from the beginning that the Portuguese looked upon their venture into the Indian Ocean as some kind of a crusade. Da Gama had been instructed to look for the land of the fabled Prester John in East Africa, the object being to find a Christian ally who could help the Portuguese in their fight against the Moors. This quest, based upon a myth, proved fruitless, but it reveals one of the underlying motives for going to the Indies. After Da Gama had returned from his voyage, the enthusiasm at home knew no bounds, and a larger fleet was soon brought together to exploit to the full that half of the world which had been allotted to Portugal by the Treaty of Tordesillas in 1494. This treaty was based on a papal bull issued by Alexander VI the year before, in which all of the unknown world was divided between Portugal and Spain.

King Manuel of Portugal assumed the title "Lord of the Conquest and Commerce" of India and all adjacent lands. In assuming this title it was clear that the Portuguese had no peaceful trading in mind. It was meant to be trade by conquest, and this same conquest was also designed to convert the indigenous population to the Christian faith. The fleet that sailed in the year 1500 under Pedro Alvarez Cabral included eight friars and eight chaplains led by a chaplain-major. No mention is made of any merchants.[2]

Although the Portuguese never realized their ambitious project in all its phases, they were, nevertheless, able to gain important footholds at strategic points. In this they were favored by the current political situation. India was divided among a number of Moslem and Hindu rulers over whom the decaying Afghan dynasty in Delhi no longer had any control. In addition, there was the imminent threat of an invasion from the north. This threat became a reality when, in 1526, the Mogul hordes swept across the Hindu Kush into the plains of northern India. During the first half of the sixteenth century, India remained a conglomeration of petty kingdoms, all jealous of their neighbors and seething internally with discordant elements. During the second half of the century, Akbar the Great managed to subdue the inde-

1. Van Leur, *Indonesian Trade*, p. 159.
2. Hunter, *History of British India*, *1*, 105–06. On this voyage Cabral discovered Brazil, thus strengthening Portugal's claim to this part of the American continent.

pendent states in northern and central India, but he was unable
to extend Mogul rule in the south.

The Samorin of Calicut on the Malabar Coast had at first welcomed the Portuguese with open arms, counting on the presence
of their heavily armed ships to protect him from his neighbors
and to deter the Moguls if they ever came this far south. Another important consideration was the prospect of increased trade,
from which he hoped to derive great benefit. The Moslem merchants, who were a powerful faction in his domain, quickly realized that these newcomers from Europe threatened their long
established monopoly. They might not have been quite so militant in their objections if they had been able to anticipate the
somewhat indifferent approach of the Portuguese towards matters of trade. Serious trouble broke out at Calicut, and this convinced the Portuguese that they needed a settlement of their
own, free from the interference of a local ruler. They found it
at Goa, which was captured by Albuquerque in 1510. From this
safe and fortified stronghold, they were able to control the whole
west coast of India.

The political situation in Ceylon was no less conducive to conquest. This relatively small island was divided in no less than seven
kingdoms, each ruler living in constant fear of being attacked by
his neighbors. The Maharajah of Kandy was as anxious to enlist
the support of the Portuguese as the Samorin of Calicut had been.
In 1506 he agreed to pay them a yearly tribute in cinnamon and
ivory in exchange for protection against his enemies. This was
only the beginning, for some ten years later the Portuguese managed to obtain his permission to build a fort at Colombo on the
pretext that this would put them in a better position to fulfill
their part of the bargain.

The Malabar Coast produced a certain amount of pepper, and
Ceylon was the source of cinnamon, but the bulk of the pepper,
and all the nutmegs, mace, and cloves originated in the Indonesian
archipelago farther east. This area had been the primary target
for every navigator who had searched for a sea route to the Indies.
Now that this feat had finally been accomplished, the Portuguese
lost no time in reaching their goal. The conquest of Malacca by
Albuquerque in 1511 seemingly opened the door to the Spice Islands. Malacca was indeed a key point and the Portuguese derived great benefit from it, but they were unable to develop it
into a power center such as the Dutch developed at Batavia in

the following century. To have done so, the Portuguese would have needed a powerful fleet and a tight organization, both of which they lacked. Their Moslem enemies, the rulers of Achin, Djambi, Bantam, and Johore, harassed them periodically throughout the sixteenth century, usually in turn. If these Indonesian rulers had recognized the danger threatening them in the intrusion of the Europeans, by joining forces, they might well have been able to dislodge the Portuguese from Malacca.[3]

The arrival of the Portuguese in India, once their intentions became known, caused great consternation among the Moslem traders. Since they looked upon their venture as a holy mission, the Portuguese attacked the Moors wherever they found them, plundering their settlements and capturing their vessels at sea. The Moslems fought back as well as they could, but they lacked the strength and unity to drive the enemy away. There was another faction in India that did not welcome the arrival of the Portuguese—the Jews, who had settled in India after having been driven out of Portugal and Spain. Most of them were successful merchants, and the Spanish and Portuguese were their sworn enemies. Albuquerque, the second Viceroy, anticipated that the Jews might cause trouble, and in 1513 he asked permission from his king to "exterminate them one by one as I come across them."[4]

The Portuguese committed a number of atrocities during the early years of their conquest. Gaspar Correa, a Portuguese and a long-time resident at Goa during the sixteenth century, reported some of them in his *Lendas da India*. On his second voyage in 1502, Vasco da Gama destroyed a Moslem fleet before Calicut. On this occasion he cut off the ears, noses, and hands of some eight hundred Moors, and sent them ashore to the Samorin of Calicut with the suggestion that he make curry of them. One of Da Gama's captains, Vincente Sodre, flogged the chief Moslem merchant at Cannanore until he fainted, then stuffed his mouth with filth and covered it with a slab of pork. There were many more examples of this kind, all part of a deliberate policy of intimidation to gain control over India.[5]

From Malacca, the Portuguese quickly reached the Moluccas—

3. Compare Hall, *History of South-East Asia*, pp. 198–99.
4. F. C. Danvers, *Report on the Portuguese Records relating to the East Indies at Lisbon and Evora, 1* (London, 1892), 287. See also, Meilink-Roelofsz, *Asian Trade*, p. 131.
5. Hunter, *History, 1,* 109. Compare Schrieke, *Indonesian Sociological Studies, 2,* 234.

the legendary Spice Islands. Here they were able to exploit the ancient rivalry between Ternate and Tidore, both rulers appealing to the Portuguese for assistance against their rival neighbors. The Portuguese sided with Ternate, which thus became the first state in Indonesia to enlist the support of a European power against a belligerent neighbor. In exchange for this the Portuguese were promised a monopoly of the purchase of cloves and given permission to build a fort. In the beginning the relationship was most amicable, but it deteriorated when the Portuguese meddled in internal affairs, which led to open hostility. The situation improved again under the able Antonio Galvao, but after his departure in 1540, Portuguese prestige steadily declined. Matters reached a climax when in 1570 the Portuguese instigated the assassination of Sultan Hairun. This deed caused Ternate and Tidore to forget their troubles temporarily and together they drove out the Portuguese, who were now forced to retreat, mainly to Amboyna, where they had been established since 1525. When Sir Francis Drake arrived at Ternate in 1579, he was royally entertained in the former Portuguese fort.[6]

In 1522 Enrique Leme had concluded a treaty of friendship with the regent of Sunda Kalapa, the port of the realm Padjajaran, the last remnant of Hindu rule in West Java, which welcomed the Portuguese as an ally against their common enemy, the Moslems. It was to no avail because, before the Portuguese could marshal a large enough force, the town was captured by Moslem Bantam, which changed the name to Djakarta.

In exploiting their conquests, the Portuguese counted on four major sources of income: the capture and looting of Moslem ships and property, the levy of customs and taxes, profits from trade between Asiatic ports, and profits on the return cargoes to Lisbon. According to Fonseca, these were expected to provide a gross revenue to the royal exchequer of some two million reals yearly, half to be derived from loot and imposts, the other half from trade.[7] This, however, was gross income, and the net gain to the crown fell far short of the estimate. The king had to bear the cost of protecting his far-flung empire, and his revenue was still further reduced by corruption among his servants.

6. De Graaf, *Geschiedenis van Indonesië*, pp. 130–36. For the Portuguese in the Moluccas, see also Meilink-Roelofsz, *Asian Trade*, pp. 153–62.
7. J. N. da Fonseca, *Historical and Archaeological Sketch of the City of Goa, with A Statistical Account of the Territory of Goa* (Bombay, 1878), p. 24.

In the early stages of the conquest, King Manuel had opened the trade to private merchants, provided they were Portuguese and that their ships measured at least 200 tons. Charters were granted for a single voyage, and the crown was to receive a flat thirty per cent of the value of the cargo. It was a steep royalty considering that the merchants had to carry the full burden of an extremely hazardous voyage. In addition, they had to allow their crews free cargo space for a certain amount of private merchandise to induce them to sign up at all. The Lisbon merchants were not up to the task. When the king's share fell below expectations, private trade was abandoned and replaced by a royal monopoly. Under this system, crews were still allowed to bring back a stipulated quantity of goods on their own account provided they paid their royalty upon arrival at Lisbon. It proved almost impossible to control the size of this private traffic. The crews were large, and it was not difficult to overstep the allotment, and to evade paying the king his due share. Before 1580, when Portugal came under Spanish domination, Lisbon was an open port, frequented by a large number of ships from northwestern Europe. This made it fairly easy to sell goods to Dutch and English merchants before they had gone through the customs.

A similar type of corruption prevailed in the trade between Asiatic ports which had also been turned into a royal monopoly. In theory, the king's ships had priority to buy all goods available at the various ports. Only after the royal merchants had obtained a full cargo were private merchants allowed to buy what was left. In the absence of Portuguese vessels, the native suppliers still had to offer their goods first to the royal factor, who would store them until their arrival. With such stringent measures, the royal monopoly was, theoretically, adequately protected; in practice, the protection failed.

The king had some loyal servants in the Indies, but the majority were self-seeking adventurers. Almost all land in Portugal was held by a small number of wealthy grandees, who employed a large number of slaves imported from Africa. The landless members of the gentry would never consider working with their hands, and they were also unwilling to turn to so demeaning an activity as trade. They held what jobs were available in government, but, since these were limited, there were many who had no visible means of support. For them the Indies became the promised land. Through connections at court and in the Church, many succeeded in obtaining an appointment to one of the administrative positions that had suddenly become available in the Indies. For Portuguese grandees and court officials, the opening empire provided a welcome opportunity to rid themselves of indigent relatives, and, after the available positions had been filled, others were created. But even this failed to meet the demand, and large numbers of Portuguese set sail for the Indies on their own, expecting to make their fortunes one way or another. In a single year, no less than 240 such penniless adventurers left Lisbon for Goa.[8]

The records of this period are filled with accounts of their activities. Some engaged outright in piracy and pillage all along the extended life-line of the empire. Less intrepid individuals hired themselves out to the tax collectors, the royal factors, and the private merchants who operated under grants issued by the higher officials. In such an atmosphere, where almost everyone, from the highest to the lowest, was out to make a fortune, the opportunities for graft and corruption were practically limitless. A few conscientious officials, including the High Judge at Goa, complained to the king in 1552, "In India there is no justice, either in your Viceroy or those who are to mete it out. The one object is 'the gathering of money by every means.' There is no Moor who will trust a Portuguese. Help us Senor, for we are sinking." [9]

His complaint was fully justified. Taxes and other levies were high, but only a fraction of this revenue found its way into the royal treasury; the rest went into the pockets of the tax collectors and their henchmen. When taxed unlawfully, the victims found little or no redress at the courts of law, as the High Judge himself complained. The abuses in trade were equally pernicious. On the pretext that there were not enough royal ships available fully to exploit the inter-Asiatic trade, high officials at Goa were granting permits to private individuals, who thus cut deeply into the royal monopoly. Quite a few officials participated openly in this traffic, as a means to line their own pockets, to reward someone for past favors, or to take care of poor relatives. With the vast amount of intermarriage that began soon after the Portuguese had arrived, there was no dearth of the latter. According to a

8. Letter of Affonso Mexia, January 15, 1530, India Office MSS, London.
9. Letter of the Judge and Aldermen of Goa, November 25, 1552, India Office MSS, London.

letter from Manuel Coutinho to the king, dated November 26, 1541, a certain governor had rewarded some 40 relatives in this manner. It is not surprising that under such conditions private trade soon surpassed the royal monopoly, which itself was ridden with corruption.

The king's own captains participated in this illegal traffic by using his ships for personal gain. On a single voyage between the Malabar Coast and Bengal in 1530, the captain realized some 12,-000 reals against the king's share of less than 400. On another occasion, as reported by Affonso Mexia, a captain in charge of two ships on the king's mission crowded the official cargo into one of them, which capsized because it had been overloaded. The other, carrying his personal cargo, came through safely. The archives at Lisbon are full of similar examples of malfeasance. They were the rule, not the exception.[10]

At various times attempts were made to counteract such flagrant corruption. Tenure in office was limited to three years, which was presumed to be short enough to keep a man from becoming established firmly in thieving on a grand scale. This measure failed to solve the problem. At one point the crown decided to exclude all officials from participating in trade. A similar restriction had been in force in the empire of Madjapahit, when every captain and ambassador was prohibited from trade under penalty of death. The Dutch, too, were to adhere to this same principle.

In a final effort to make all trade a royal prerogative, all native trade was prohibited as well. Such a stringent policy could be enforced temporarily, at points where the Portuguese had their strongholds, but it was impossible to police all coasts. The native traders, already adept at circumventing Portuguese customs, proved able to cope with this latest problem as well. In one way or another they managed to push their wares along. The king heard about this too. "The native merchants lose their interest in trade," Pedro de Faria wrote him. "Allow the ports to be opened to native vessels. There are none now because Your Majesty ordered the ports closed, except to your own trade." [11] But it seemed as if nothing could effectively remedy the situation. Only a fraction of what had been expected from the riches of the Indies

10. Hunter, *History*, *1*, 176–78. On corruption among the Portuguese, see also, Meilink-Roelofsz, *Asian Trade*, pp. 125–28.
11. Letter of Pedro de Faria, January 18, 1522, India Office MSS, London.

reached the king, but even this small share was enough to make Lisbon for a while the richest town in Europe.

Finally, in 1587, after Portugal had become part of Spain, all trade with the Indies was farmed out to the Fuggers and Welsers of Augsburg and the new monopoly operated under the name *Companhia Portugueza das Indias Orientaes*.[12] Before these powerful merchant bankers could put their talents to work the Portuguese empire in Asia faced a new and determined enemy. Before the century was out, the Dutch had found their own direct route to the Indies and had begun to exploit it.

What was the net effect on Asia and its trade of the one hundred years of Portuguese domination? Marked on a map, their strategic strongholds would indicate that they controlled a huge empire, especially after the administrative divisions are sketched in. The viceroy had his seat at Goa, and under him were the governors of seven large provinces. The first stretched from the Cape of Good Hope to the Red Sea, thus comprising the whole east coast of Africa; the second covered southern Arabia and the entrance to the Persian Gulf; the third ran from the Persian Gulf to the mouth of the Indus River; the fourth covered the west coast of India to Cape Comorin; the fifth included the east coast as far as Bengal; the sixth took in the west coast of southeast Asia and the western half of the Indonesian archipelago; everything eastward belonged to the seventh, including the Spice Islands (the Moluccas) and the sandalwood-producing islands, Flores and Timor. Macao was part of this province, as was Ceylon. For a while the inclusion of the Moluccas caused trouble with the King of Spain, who laid claim to this area on the strength of the Treaty of Tordesillas of 1494. The matter was settled amicably when Charles V sold his claim to Portugal in 1529 for 350,000 golden ducats.[13]

Impressive as it might appear, the contemplated Afro-Asian empire never developed beyond the limited boundaries of the isolated Portuguese strongholds, mainly because the king lacked the force to control so vast an area. The Portuguese, moreover, were largely motivated by a desire for loot and tribute. Such an attitude hardly favored the development of peaceful trading, which might have produced great revenue for the crown, had it

12. Compare Schrieke, *Indonesian Sociological Studies*, *1*, 45.
13. Convention of Saragossa between João III and Charles V, April 22, 1529. Compare Hall, *History of South-East Asia*, p. 201.

been a primary goal. Nor did the Portuguese succeed in eradicating the Moslem traders. On the contrary, this old established trade flourished as never before. According to their own figures, during the 1530s the Portuguese shipped an average of 80 tons of spices yearly, against 1300 tons which the Moslem traders shipped to the Red Sea. In later years, when there was a much greater demand for spices in Europe, the Portuguese share of the clove production in the Moluccas was only about fifteen per cent. Since these were the most important export products from Southeast Asia, we may conclude that the volume of Portuguese trade was exceeded many times over by the trade carried on by the peoples of Asia.[14] A striking example of the inability of the Portuguese to gain control over a significant share of Asiatic trade is provided by their experience in the Spice Islands which had been their goal from the outset. By the middle of the sixteenth century, the Portuguese began to realize that they were unable to enforce a monopoly in the Moluccas, and some years later they freely allowed the shipping on the Spice Islands to be resumed by the Javanese. Their earlier attempts to gain control had been a stimulus for increasing clove production over a larger area. It had also led to the intensification of the pan-Islamic movement in the Moluccas, which created an opposition the Portuguese were unable to combat.[15]

In other areas the Portuguese were equally unsuccessful, because their position was militantly held in check or rebuffed by native rulers. Van Leur blames this on the fact that their power was typically medieval in character, based on a "conglomeration of nobles and *condottieri*, each with his own retinue of henchmen bound to him by a vassal's loyalty or a lust for gain." [16] Thus the Portuguese, notwithstanding their strongholds, never succeeded in establishing even a rudimentary type of colonial administration, in the sense of a European power gaining significant control over large areas. The long-established pattern of Asiatic trade remained the same, and the political independence of native states was barely touched. It is for these reasons that the age of imperialism in Asia did not begin with the Portuguese. Another Euro-

14. Van Leur, *Indonesian Trade*, pp. 162, 165. Compare Meilink-Roelofsz, *Asian Trade*, p. 134.

15. Schrieke, *Indonesian Sociological Studies*, *1*, 47–48.

16. Van Leur, *Indonesian Trade*, p. 170. Compare Meilink-Roelofsz, *Asian Trade*, pp. 178–81.

pean nation, arriving with an entirely different concept, laid the foundation for capitalistic colonialism in Asia.

In one area, the Portuguese were slightly more successful. This was in religion, one of their avowed motives for going to the Indies. In Japan, the conversion to Catholicism proceeded so rapidly that the government uprooted the movement by the most drastic means and expelled the Portuguese priests from the country. In other parts of Asia, however, the results were more permanent. This was not only the case in the Portuguese key points but also at Manila, where Lopez de Legaspi established a Spanish settlement in 1571. Strongholds such as Mozambique, Goa, Galle, Malacca, Macao, and Manila put up such a stiff resistance, with the aid of converted natives, that the Dutch, and to a lesser degree the English, were rebuffed time and again in their attempts to capture these towns.[17]

The Dutch motives for going to the Indies were almost the reverse of the Portuguese. Their prime incentive was profit from trade as is clearly indicated by the considerable number of merchants who sailed with the fleets from the start. Territorial conquest had not been contemplated, and, when it did occur, it was only to be a means for protecting trade after treaties with local potentates had been broken repeatedly. The propagation of Protestantism was of no concern to the United East India Company; nothing in the charter even alluded to it. For years the fleets carried not a single clergyman. A member of the crew would serve as a lay reader to say the daily prayers and to read passages from the Bible, but this was intended only to supply the spiritual needs of the men in the company's service.

17. On the solidarity of native and half-blood converts, see Meilink-Roelofsz, *Asian Trade*, pp. 117–18, 121–22, 129–30.

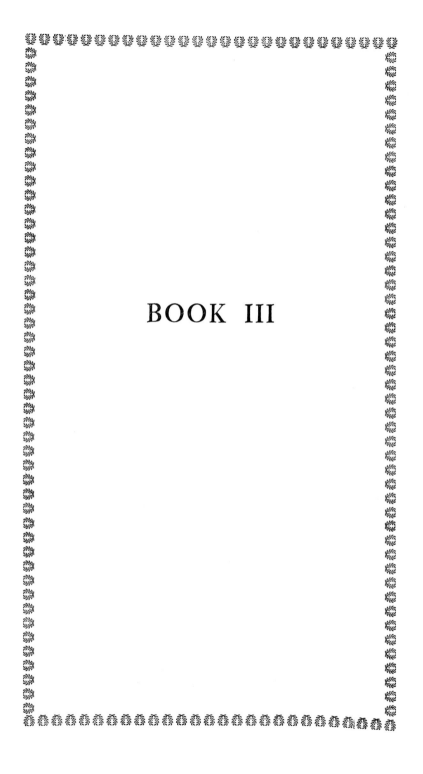

BOOK III

I

Jan
Pieterszoon
Coen

Jan Pieterszoon Coen was baptized on January 11, 1587, in the Reformed Church in Hoorn, the Zuiderzee town north of Amsterdam. Considering the custom that a child should be baptized as soon as possible, he must have been born on a day early in January of that same year.

His father was Pieter Willemszoon van Twisk. The name van Twisk simply meant that he came from a village of that name in the vicinity of Hoorn. Like many others, he may have decided that the thriving seaport offered better opportunities for a young man than the pastoral village where he was born. There are no records showing that he ever occupied an important office in the town government, but there are a number of documents extant which indicate that he became a fairly well-to-do merchant. One states that Pieter Willemsz. van Twisk, "now a burgher of Hoorn and about twenty-four years old," was in San Lucar as a merchant during March 1585.[1] San Lucar in Portugal produced the salt needed for the herring fisheries, and it can thus be assumed that Pieter Willemsz. was engaged in the salt trade, possibly trading it against butter and cheese. Another affidavit gives his address as being "in Mallegum." There still exists a street by that name, now a short alley, in the oldest part of Hoorn. At one time there may have been a house there called Mallegum, indicating perhaps that its occupant was trading with Malaga in Spain, but there is no evidence that it was Pieter Willemsz.', or that his son was born there.

In order to distinguish himself from the many other van Twisks in Hoorn, Pieter Willemsz. adopted the name Coen. The chang-

---

1. Protocol of the notary W. D. Codde, dated August 24, 1585, in the Notarial Archives of Hoorn. See J. C. Kerkmeyer, *De Historische Schoonheid van Hoorn* (Amsterdam, De Lange, 1946), p. 58.

ing of names was quite common but, considering the stature this name was to attain, there has been some speculation as to why Jan Coen's father selected it. The most logical explanation is that he had an ancestor by that name; the court records in Hoorn actually mention a Pieter Coenesz. in the year 1574. It has also been suggested that he took this name because the word means "bold" and "daring." In his capacity as an independent and seafaring trader, Pieter Willemsz. might have felt that the epithet was fitting. Still another speculation is so farfetched that it would hardly deserve mention had it not been suggested by so eminent a historian as Werner Sombart. This keen student of modern capitalism was greatly impressed by the role the Jews had played in its development. Enthusiastic in his admiration for Jan Coen's talents, he suggested that these might be attributed to a Jewish background, and pointed out the close similarity between Coen and Cohen. There is, however, no evidence of any kind which substantiates his conjecture.[2] Whatever may have been the origin of the name, genealogically it is one of the least lasting. Pieter Willemsz. adopted it during the 1590s. Jan was his only son, and he died in 1629, leaving no one to carry on the name.

Pieter Willemsz. was married to Geert Jansdr. (Jan's daughter) Mol, and he named his first-born son after his wife's father, a custom which still prevails in Holland. On September 1, 1599, the parents made their will and from its wording it would appear that they were a devoted couple, even if one makes allowances for convention and the somewhat lofty style of such documents. In this will, the usufruct of their property was left entirely to the surviving spouse "out of consideration for the singular love, regard, and affection they have shown each other as man and wife."[3] That the family ties must have been close was proved once more when the son, as governor-general in the Indies, bequeathed one half of his estate to his only sister, the other half to his wife. Subject to records that might still turn up, this is about all that is known about the ancestry of the man who laid the foundation of the Dutch empire in Asia. To the English, his bitter enemies, he was known as John Peter Sacone.

Jan Coen's boyhood is unfortunately a largely unrecorded chapter in his life. It is only by inference that something can be

2. C. Gerretson, *Coen's eerherstel* (Amsterdam, 1944), p. 99.
3. Date of will, September 1, 1599; in the Notarial Archives of Hoorn, 2041, f. 61.

gleaned about Jan Coen's early years—from what he must have been taught at school, and from certain events that took place at Hoorn during his boyhood.

During the last quarter of the sixteenth century, the desire for knowledge, as distinguished from manual dexterity, noticeably increased in the Lowlands. After the Dutch had cut themselves loose from Spain, the Protestants were anxious to prove that learning was not the prerogative of the Catholic clergy alone, and that Protestants could teach and write as brilliantly. The towns were the first to benefit from this enlightened point of view, and before long some form of elementary education was available to practically every burgher's son.[4] It can be assumed that young Coen learned something about the history of his town. The formation of the United Provinces was of too recent a date to have created a spirit of national pride and solidarity—a man's allegiance was still primarily to the town where he was born. Jan Coen retained this loyalty to a marked degree. After having taken Djakarta, he renamed it New Hoorn, but he was overruled by the Seventeen who insisted on the name Batavia.

The earliest mention of Hoorn goes back to the eighth century. The Frisian chronicler Winsemius relates that it was established by a certain Hornus in the year 719.[5] Another venerable historian, Ockam Scharlensem, is a little more specific. In his *Chronicle and truthful Description of Friesland after the Creation of the World* he writes, "In the year 726 a certain Hornus, that bastard son of King Radbode, built himself a homestead in a corner of West Friesland, which he surrounded with some small earthworks and a canal, and which he named *Horne* after himself." This settlement, however, was only short-lived because, as Ockam relates further, "the place burned to the ground in the year 727, and it took a long time before it was rebuilt." Almost five centuries passed before Hoorn appears once more in the annals, but the fact that the name remained throughout this long period would indicate that the place slowly developed into a small market place.

The great floods of the thirteenth century which created the Zuiderzee gave Hoorn its real start because, like Amsterdam, it

4. From 1396 on, Hoorn had a schoolmaster. The pupils paid tuition and the town provided books, robes, and other necessities. See Pieter Koster, *Hoorn in de Middeleeuwen* (Amsterdam, 1929), p. 49.

5. P. Winsemius, *Chronique ofte historische geschiedenisse van Vrieslant* (Franeker, 1622).

then automatically became a seaport. Mention of the place became more frequent; for example, in the year 1316 three brothers
from Hamburg, who had been shipping beer there, decided to
settle in Hoorn. "These men," according to Velius, "seeing the
favorable location of the place, and the many people who came
there, each built a house." Between themselves they established
an inn which appropriately carried the sign of a horn.[6] Hoorn
gradually acquired the characteristics of a town. The first church
was erected in 1323; it was built of wood with a thatched roof,
and five years later, burned down. By 1338 Hoorn counted some
seventy adult males, which would indicate a total population of
between three and four hundred.

From the beginning these townspeople engaged in trade, and
by the middle of the fourteenth century, they maintained a regular traffic with such English towns as Lynn and Newcastle. The
goods they shipped included linen, flax, rope, canvas, lumber,
pitch, and tiles. Iron, presumably coming from Sweden, was another export item. Of foodstuffs there were smoked eels, dried
flounders, apples, and onions. In return for these, the merchants
of Hoorn obtained wool, woolen cloth, lead, millstones, grind-
stones, and coal. The latter had become indispensable for iron
forging, but for ordinary heating, the people continued to use
peat, which was locally available and therefore cheaper. As more
land was being created in the surrounding area by intensive diking, butter and cheese were added to the list of export products.
During the fifteenth century, when the power of the Hansa was
waning, Hoorn's trade increased in size and variety, adding Baltic grains of all kinds, lumber in larger quantities, and other goods.
Before long, ships from Hoorn plied the southern seas as well.
As we have seen, Hoorn tried in vain to become a member of the
College of Great Fishery which controlled the lucrative herring
trade, but its refusal did not prevent Hoorn from entering the
trade in salt which was so essential to this rising industry.[7] In their
quest for salt, ships from Hoorn ventured ever further south, first
to the coast of France and later to Portugal. Other and more
exotic products were produced in those countries, and Hoorn
became a market place for wine, olive oil, honey, figs, and raisins.

Among the citizens, there was little to distinguish one burgher

6. Th. Velius, *Chronyk van Hoorn* (Hoorn, 1740).
7. Large quantities of salt were also required for preserving butter and
curing cheese.

from another. Hoorn was still too young and too small to have developed a preferred class, and every man considered himself the equal of all the others, irrespective of what he earned or how he made his living.[8] Such independent people did not defer gladly to any kind of authority, even when it were necessary for the proper functioning of the town. The levying of taxes, in particular, often led to serious trouble, and Hoorn became known for its riots. At such times the word quickly spread that "the cats are dancing," as these fights were called, and mothers herded their broods inside and kept them behind locked doors. But authority gradually asserted itself, and the Red Stone became its symbol.

This stone was exactly what the name implied: it was a relic of the glacier period, a large boulder of reddish color on the bank of the River Gouw. For many years it had marked the place where the farmers brought their produce and bartered it for the things they needed. The one road leading into town from the hinderland ended there, and when the first sea dike was built it crossed the river at this same spot. As the town expanded, additional land was reclaimed beyond the dike and the Red Stone became the center of Hoorn.[9] It was also the spot where the executioner beheaded the "cats (who) had danced" with too much exuberance. Young Jan Coen must have crossed the market place almost daily, and it is not unlikely that he looked at the Red Stone in awe, knowing that it was here that men lost their heads for their revolt against law and order. But no matter how vivid his imagination might have been, he could not have anticipated that some 300 years later a monument would be erected in his honor on the exact same spot.

When Jan Coen was eight years old, the first *fluit* (flute) ship was built in Hoorn. It was designed by Pieter Jansz. Liorne, a well-to-do ship builder and merchant who had been among the first to open Dutch trade in the Mediterranean. He had adopted the name Liorne because of his interests in that Italian port, now called Livorno.[10] These ships were also called *Vlie-boot*, a name

8. This was the situation when Hoorn became a town in 1357. During the next hundred years, with the rise of a merchant class, different social strata gradually developed, but the average burghers stubbornly adhered to their spirit of independence. See Koster, p. 45.

9. Kerkmeyer, *Historische schoonheid*, pp. 11–12.

10. See Book I, chapter 6, for additional data on the flute ships. Liorne is also credited with having established a school at Hoorn for the "great navigation." See also J. E. Elias, *De Vlootbouw in Nederland, 1596–1655* (Amsterdam, 1933).

derived from the channel *Vlie*, which was an important water-way for sailing from the Zuiderzee into the North Sea. To the English, this type of ship became known as a fly-boat. The Span-ish called them *filibote*, a phonetic adaptation of the original name. Before long the Spanish had reason to fear these ships, which preyed on their shipping on the Main. They coined a word for the sailors who manned them and named them *fili-busteros*.[11] Thus, originating in Hoorn and via the Spanish Main, the word filibuster became part of the American political ver-nacular.

Jan Coen and his friends may have enjoyed going to the water-front after school to watch the first flute ships take shape, from the keel up. The tools used in building the ships were not very different from those that are still used by conservative carpen-ters: hammers, mallets, planes, chisels, augers, axes. One of the most important tools was the adze, which was indispensable for shaping ribs and elbows. It is still fascinating to watch a man swing the heavy head, with its razor sharp edge, in a great arc directly toward his feet and bite into the wood a mere inch or two from his toes. In pace with his strokes, he shuffles forward on the work, leaving a perfectly smooth surface, either straight or curved, as the plans requires.

The boys would have learned about the kinds of wood that went into building a ship. Oak for the hull, ribs, and elbows came from the German forests and were known as "Rhine straights" and "Westphalian elbows." Pine and fir planking were best for the decks: these came from the forests around the Baltic Sea. Tall, straight firs from Norway were used for masts and spars. Important, too, were the wooden pegs, to fasten the pieces of wood together and make them into a sound ship. These pegs were turned from iron-hard knots cut out of gnarled oaks, the best of which came from Ireland. There was also a lore about wood. Lumber was considered to be at its best when cut in winter, and it was deemed advisable to bore several holes criss-cross through the base of a tree before it was felled. "Never cut a tree when it bears fruit," the carpenters warned, "because, like women, they are weakest when they carry." To indicate that something was utterly worthless a man was apt to remark, "It is like a ship built of fig wood." [12]

11. J. T. Shipley, *Dictionary of Word Origins* (New York, 1945), p. 152.
12. N. Witsen, *Aeloude en hedendaegse Scheepsbouw en Bestier* (Amster-dam, 1671), pp. 178–84.

It would be interesting to know who some of the boys were with whom young Coen might have shared such experiences. One of them may well have been Willem Ysbrandtsz. Bontekoe, who was born the same year as Coen. Years later their paths crossed in Djakarta, after Coen had become Governor-General, and Bontekoe had to explain to him just how it had happened that his ship had blown up in the Indian Ocean. Coen's reaction can easily be imagined when he learned that a butler had dropped a burning candle into a keg of brandy and that the ship had been the *New Hoorn*, commissioned by the Chamber in their own town.[13]

The beginning of a new century also opened a new chapter in Jan Coen's life, one which may well have been decisive in preparing him for his later career. "In 1600 Jan Coen went to Italy to serve his apprenticeship with the house of Pescatore in Rome." Early historians were content to relate this turning point in Coen's life in words such as these. No specific reasons are given for sending a thirteen year-old boy so far from home, but the archives of Hoorn offer a plausible explanation. Jan Coen's father was about thirty-eight years old when he made his will in 1599. Shortly thereafter, during the early part of the year 1600, the elder Coen was no longer able to attend to his business in person. The evidence for this conjecture is a notarial document, at the signing of which his wife had to be assisted by someone other than her husband because the latter was unable to be present. Two years later he is referred to in another document as "the deceased." [14] While the exact date of his death cannot be established, it is clear that during the year 1600, if he were not already dead, he must have known that the end was near. It may have been the father's hope that his son would some day take over the business, but in such circumstances this would now be impossible. Besides, a 13-year-old boy still had much to learn.

Elementary education was about all a town could offer in those days. For higher learning, a young man had to go to the university, at Leiden or abroad. There is no reason to assume that there was enough money in the Coen family to pay for such an education, and it is also unlikely that Jan Coen was the type to choose the law or theology as a career. He had been raised in a merchant environment, and it would seem logical for him to want to fol-

13. Willem Bontekoe, *Memorable Description of the East Indian Voyage, 1618-25* (London, Routledge, 1929), pp. 37-42, 73-74.
14. March 9, 1602; in the Notarial Archives of Hoorn, 2043, f. 80.

low in his father's footsteps. Elsewhere in the Lowlands there was feverish interest in the newly opened East Indies trade, but the merchants of Hoorn were still largely preoccupied with the Mediterranean trade of which they had been the instigators. Thus, when the question of Jan Coen's future arose, perhaps it was deemed advisable that he should prepare himself for a career in this field.

The decision to send him to Italy suggests circumstantial evidence that two men in particular may have been instrumental in opening this chapter in Coen's life. One was the Reynier Pietersz. van Twisk who had initiated the trade between Hoorn and the west coast of Italy in 1586. He had prospered in this trade, especially after crop failures in Italy had caused a greatly increased demand for Baltic grains, which he and other Hoorn merchants were only too willing to fill. This Reynier van Twisk, if not directly related, was at least a clansman of the elder Coen because they both came originally from the same village.

The other was Jan Martensz. Visser, a merchant from Oudenaerde in the southern Netherlands who, with many others, had fled north to escape the Spanish Inquisition. Another member of this same family, Joris Visser, had established himself as a merchant in Rome, translating his name into Italian as Giorgio Pescatore.[15] Jan Martensz. Visser and Reynier van Twisk knew each other well; both occupied important positions in the magistracy of Hoorn. They may have together decided that Jan Coen should go to Rome, with recommendations from Jan Martensz. Visser to his namesake Giorgio Pescatore. By learning the business from that end and studying the art of Italian bookkeeping, Jan Coen's future would be assured, after he had served his apprenticeship and returned to Hoorn.

It is unlikely that young Coen had ever been far away from home. Possibly he had been to Kampen, across the Zuiderzee, with one of the vessels that went there regularly for a cargo of bricks, or perhaps to Amsterdam, but these must have been the full extent of his travels. For a thirteen year-old boy it must have been the height of adventure to go to a foreign country, especially at a time when all eyes were looking beyond a horizon immeasurably widened by the recent exploits of Dutch navigators.

According to Velius, Jan Coen returned to Hoorn as a full-

15. Gerretson, *Coen's eerherstel*, p. 21.

grown man, thoroughly grounded in all the wisdom of a merchant.[16] No details are given about his life or experiences during the six or seven years he stayed in Italy. It is possible, however, to illuminate this obscurity somewhat by considering the prevailing situation in Rome and how this may have affected Coen's later development as a statesman.

The Joris Visser from Oudenaerde, now known as the "magnificus et perillustris" Giorgio Pescatore, may well have wondered about the consequences of the arrival of the Calvinist boy from Hoorn on his doorstep. Whatever may have been the innermost belief of this Flemish expatriate, there can be no question that in all outward appearances he had to live as a Catholic. The fact that Jan Coen stayed in Rome for more than six years suggests that Giorgio Pescatore was able to cope with this problem. The Pescatores had no children of their own, and this may have been a further reason for taking the boy under their wing.[17] Whatever the personal relationship may have been, it was the expatriate Fleming who became Coen's mentor and the guiding influence during his formative years.

In Rome, Jan Coen learned all the intricacies of Italian bookkeeping, and he became so adept in this field that he later was able to put the books of the East India Company in order and to become its first bookkeeper-general. He must also have been taught the principle of "good faith" as the basis of all agreements. Throughout his whole life, Jan Coen adhered to the precept that a man's word was his bond, regardless of the color of his skin. When in later years the king of Djakarta and the headmen of Banda broke their word to him, it was a foregone conclusion that they must be punished severely.

There were other things a young man could learn in the Rome of those years, where important events were taking place which had political implications for the whole of Europe. Shortly before Coen's arrival in Rome, Pope Clement VIII had brought about the Treaty of Vervins, ending the hostilities between Spain and France. Henry IV had found it increasingly difficult to subdue the powerful league of Catholic noblemen who greatly resented the fact that he had become a Protestant. Rather than allow this internal strife to destroy both himself and his country, the king

16. Idem.
17. Ibid., p. 24. See also K. Heeringa, *Bronnen tot de geschiedenis van den Levantschen handel, 1* (The Hague, 1910), 99, 109.

decided that "Paris was worth a Mass," submitted, and returned to the Catholic fold. Prior to this, the political influence of the Holy See had been deteriorating for a long time. For almost half a century Philip II of Spain had been fighting to undo the Reformation and he had, in fact, become the temporal leader of the Church. The Popes had been unable to assert authority over Philip but now, shortly after his death and with two great Catholic powers vying for supremacy, Rome saw an opportunity to regain much of its former prestige by becoming an active third party in the fight against Protestantism—its weapon, the Counter Reformation. Not only had the Dutch lost an ally in France, but Spain now was free to pursue a more aggressive policy against the Republic.

In domestic matters as well, Pope Clement proved to be an astute statesman. He rectified the dissolute morality that had prevailed in Rome for many years by vigorously suppressing banditry and corruption. By curbing the powers of the College of Cardinals and those of the nobility, he succeeded in establishing more effective civil administration.[18]

It was in this political atmosphere that Jan Coen grew up. He witnessed at firsthand that a strong leader is needed to maintain law and order, and he must have absorbed other rules of statecraft as well, judging by his later accomplishments. In this citadel of the Counter Reformation, the young Protestant learned to keep his personal beliefs to himself, both for his own sake and that of his benefactor. The habits of caution he had to maintain while in Rome apparently had a permanent effect on his character—there is no record that he ever disclosed his innermost feelings, religious or otherwise. He was, of course, Protestant but, being away from Holland during his formative years, he had not been exposed to the narrow dogmas of Calvinism. This may account for the fact that Jan Coen acquired a more liberal view of religion than was characteristic of this period. As Governor-General in the Indies, Coen would approve thoroughly his ministers' censorship of the morals of the unruly under his command, but when they tried to assume power in governmental and judicial matters he quickly subdued them. In this he followed the policy of the town fathers of Amsterdam who were confronted with a similar problem, but it was in Italy that Jan Coen first witnessed

18. Gerretson, *Coen's eerherstel*, pp. 25-26.

strong opposition to the dictates of the Church in non-ecclesiastical matters.

Pope Paul V, even more than his predecessor, was ambitious to restore Rome's historical jurisdiction over Christendom and even to extend it throughout the world. Among the measures he undertook to achieve his goal, Pope Paul prohibited all trade by those under his jurisdiction with non-Catholic countries. This quickly led to conflict with Venice: this powerful city did not intend to permit any interference with its far-flung trade. Venice commissioned its counselor, Paolo Sarpi, to draw up his now famous treatise, *Rispota di un Dottore in Teologia*, which argued that the Pope had no right to interfere in secular matters. Since the Pope's interdict would also affect the Lowlands, the Dutch offered to assist Venice in its quarrel with Rome. Doge Donato accepted this offer in June 1606, and as the year progressed the relationship between Rome and the Dutch republic became more and more strained.

It was around this time that Jan Coen left Italy and returned to Hoorn. It is quite likely that Giorgio Pescatore had been training young Coen for a permanent place in his organization, just as he had trained his nephew Pietro, who eventually became the head of the house of Pescatore. The current political situation, with its possibility of open conflict, may well have changed such plans and made it seem best to send Coen back to Holland. The decision may also have been Coen's own. He knew, of course, that during his absence the United East India Company had been organized and that several fleets had already returned from the Indies with rich cargoes. Having been in Rome for some six years, he may have felt that his opportunities there were more limited than in the East Indies.

Whatever the reasons were, Jan Coen returned to Hoorn either late in the year 1606 or early in 1607. He had left as a boy and now, returning at the age of twenty, he was thoroughly schooled in bookkeeping as well as in all other aspects of commerce. With this commercial background, he could expect to find some promising employment, and whatever he had learned in addition, in statecraft for example, would be useful in rising to higher levels.

Hoorn had been growing during Coen's absence. At the time of his departure, most of its foreign trade had been confined to the Baltic and the Mediterranean, but now the East Indies had been added. Hoorn was represented in the United Company, and its chamber had contributed several ships. The first of these had returned shortly before Coen's return, carrying goods worth more than a million guilders which gave the shareholders a profit of 75 per cent on their investment. Subsequent ventures were expected to be equally profitable. Some of the most important men in Hoorn were directors in the United Company, including Pieter Jansz. Liorne whose first flute ship Jan Coen may have seen being built. Hoorn had now also caught the Indies fever, and the town fathers voted the necessary appropriations for improvements in keeping with its growing prosperity. Streets were being paved, the town hall was renovated, and extensive alterations were made on another building to house the College of the Admiralty.[19]

If there were still doubts in Jan Coen's mind as to what direction his future should take, they were soon dispelled. With his training and through connections in Hoorn, it was not long before he was considered for a position with the United East India Company. He had to start at the bottom, as a sub-merchant on a ship fitted out by the Chamber of Hoorn, and at the prevailing salary of about 35 guilders per month plus keep, to go into effect when the next fleet of the United Company set sail for the Indies. The departure of this venture was set for December, which meant that Jan Coen undoubtedly was witness to the important events that took place during the year 1607.

Long before he was born his country had fought for its independence; it was almost incredible that Spain should now begin to sue for peace, but this was nevertheless the case. In this same year the Dutch annihilated the Spanish fleet at Gibraltar, bringing to an end the great sea power of Spain. This victory was of greater importance than that gained over the Armada twenty years earlier by the combined forces of the Dutch and the English. The importance of both events was recognized almost as soon as they happened, unlike that of the unheralded arrival of English Puritans in Holland during that same year, the prelude to the establishment of the United States in North America—or Coen's own unsung departure for the Indies during the last month of the year, the beginning of modern colonialism.

19. Ibid., pp. 27–28.

2

The
Bottom
of the
Ladder

Nothing has been recorded about Jan Coen's early years with the company, and thus his first contact with the Indies can only be reconstructed in the light of the general events that took place during this period. Since the truce with Spain had been concluded in May 1607, the directors of the United Company had been discussing plans for forestalling any ill effects of the truce on their position in Asia. To be sure, the armistice was for only eight months, and it pertained only to the war in Europe, but it was impossible to predict what concessions Oldebarnevelt might grant when the matter were considered anew. Whatever the terms would be, there was little doubt that a status quo in Asia would result, barring the Company from making any further encroachments upon Spanish and Portuguese possessions. It was finally decided to send a strong fleet into Asian waters for the purpose of occupying as much enemy territory as possible, thus placing the Company in a favorable bargaining position.

Jacob Heemskerck had been chosen to command this fleet, but his death at the battle of Gibraltar forced the Seventeen to select someone else. Their choice was Pieter Verhoef, the captain to whom Heemskerck had delegated command of the fleet just before he died. None of the other captains were aware of this until after the battle had been won, but his name was thereafter identified with this great victory. In October, the Seventeen, convening in Amsterdam, drew up two sets of instructions for the important new venture. The contents of one set became generally known; they indicated that nothing more than the pursuit of normal trade was contemplated. The second set were sealed orders, to be opened in plenary council after the fleet was well past the Spanish coast.

The fleet was to consist of thirteen vessels, eleven of which were commissioned by the various Chambers and two contributed by the States General, who thus gave their approval to the real purpose of the expedition.[1]

The officer personnel, after careful screening, had been engaged well in advance of the sailing date, set for the latter part of December. Skippers and navigators were ordered to attend the school of Dominie Plancius to learn about the latest developments in geography and celestial navigation. The merchants assigned to the fleet spent a good deal of time studying the voluminous reports of previous voyages which were kept under lock and key at the East India House. It was their duty to acquaint themselves not only with all the aspects of trade but also with the political situation in Asia. It was from these merchants that the Company expected most, both in gaining profits and in providing future administrators for the various affairs of the vast area which had become its field of operations. This cadre, having the usual high death rate, had to be constantly augmented by young men of promise, usually recommended by directors of the Company. Many of these men failed to rise to prominence, but continued to serve the Company in minor capacities. For those who could prove their courage and skill, there was opportunity for rapid promotion, irrespective of social background or connections at home. The Seventeen wanted results; nothing else mattered.

In the fleet under Verhoef, the fifth to be sent out by the United Company, there were two young men who rose to the highest office, the Governor-Generalship of the Indies. One was Jan Coen and the other Jacques Specx. Both were about twenty years old when they began their service and received a first glimpse of the alien lands over which they were some day to rule. Beyond this, they had little in common. Jan Coen was a dour Frisian from the north, inflexible in the pursuit of his duties to the Company as he interpreted them.[2] Specx came from Dordrecht and, judging by his name, he may have had French blood in his veins; he was vivacious, easy to live with, and, in his later dealings with the Japanese, he proved himself an able diplomat. Coen possessed none of these traits. Hewing straight to the mark and favored by circumstances, Jan Coen reached the high office

1. De Jonge, *Opkomst*, 3 (1865), 71.
2. This character trait of Coen was recognized by his contemporaries. See Velius, *Chronyk van Hoorn*, p. 962.

sooner than Specx. It took Coen a mere ten years, while Specx had to wait ten years more until his fleet-mate had died. However, Specx in the meantime made a name for himself in Japan, opening that country to Dutch trade. Coen became the founder of Batavia, the former Djakarta; it was Specx who later laid out the town, with its stately canals on the pattern of Amsterdam.

Mustering of the crews took place early in December. This fleet, like others before it and many more to follow, needed a large number of sailors to handle the intricate gear, and soldiers to do the fighting. Where did the manpower come from, and how was it enticed to sail on the Company's ships? Wages were extremely low, life on the ships was hard, and the chances of coming back alive were slim indeed. Experienced sailors found ready employment elsewhere, in the ever expanding European trade, especially in the Baltic; the fisheries also welcomed them. Both alternatives were more attractive, especially to men with families, than the Indies trade. The answer is that crews were recruited from the hinterland, where life was harder still; at least men believed so who labored twelve to sixteen hours a day, digging peat and moving earth for dikes, often for little more than food and lodging. Such peasants were easily impressed by stories of the glamor in the sea ports, and of fabulous treasure in the lands beyond the sea, stories which became more and more miraculous the farther they reached into the hinterland. For these people, as for the merchants, the Indies became the lodestone. From all directions they converged upon the sea ports, especially Amsterdam—dissatisfied men, misfits, adventurers, all of them poor.

What happened after they arrived, by foot, by boat, by whatever means? They had no money, knew no trade, belonged to no guild. All they had was a pair of hands. This was enough for some clever townsmen, living on the fringes of an emerging capitalistic society, quick to see an opportunity to make some money. As soon as news spread that the Company was planning to send out another fleet, these rising entrepreneurs scoured the waterfront, the squares, or any other place where penniless and hungry men might congregate. They enticed them into their lodging houses, to stay until mustered on one of the Company's ships. No payment was required; that would come out of future earnings. Those who proved reluctant were regaled with stories about the fabulous Indies: a warm sun all the year round, beau-

tiful maidens galore, and jewels for the taking. In their eagerness
to make recruits, these lodging-house keepers, or shipping masters
as they preferred to call themselves, showed no lack of talent in
describing the wonders of life at sea and in the Orient. Some even
promised a little hammer as a bonus, to make it easier for a man
to separate the precious stones from the rock in which they were
embedded.

Once they had accepted, the men were herded into dank cellars or drafty attics and given the scantiest of rations, sometimes
no better than offal. The good things of life were not to be theirs
just yet. They were also closely guarded because they were an
asset only if they could be produced at mustering time. That
the burghers did not have a high regard for these employment
agents is illustrated by the fact that they called them "traffickers
in souls" and "cats and dogs." Nevertheless, they served a useful
purpose in supplying the Company with much needed manpower. In earlier times, ships were largely manned with slaves
and prisoners of war, a system still followed by the Moslems of
the Barbary Coast and to some extent by the Spanish as well. In
the Lowlands, however, men were theoretically free agents who
had to be persuaded to serve, and in this the "cats and dogs" acted
as middlemen. When the English later made their bid for world
trade and naval supremacy, they found it difficult to obtain the
required manpower in a similar manner. They resorted to the
use of press gangs to forcibly abduct their countrymen and drag
them to the ships.

It was a day during the early part of December when rich and
poor alike in Amsterdam were awakened by the sound of trumpets, the trills of pipes, and the beating of drums. It was the
Company's announcement that the day of mustering had arrived.
At a time when public spectacles were rare, this was a day to be
remembered. From all parts of town the burghers converged
upon the East India House, to get a glimpse of the activity. The
lodging-house keepers had a far greater stake in this performance
than the onlookers, and they herded their charges into the narrow
High Street long before daybreak.

Hundreds of men milled around, urged and prodded by their
keepers, who had plied them with brandy to put them in the
proper mood to fight their way to the head of the line, as near the
gate as possible. Since most were of the same eager belligerence,

the High Street became the scene of bloody fighting, the more ferocious as the time neared for the gate to be opened. Then the men spewed into the courtyard.[3]

Jan Coen must have witnessed this turmoil—his first glimpse of the men who were the workhorses of the Company, at sea and on land. The sight of these men, clawing their way through the gate like animals, underfed and gray with the pallor of confinement in stinking cellars or attics for weeks on end, created an impression which became intensified as time went on. He would have many opportunities to refer to it in his reports, when he had reason enough to complain about the low caliber of men hired by the directors.

Having been mustered, a crew-man signed a note, known as a Letter of Transport. The amount was well in excess of what he owed his keeper. It was computed at the rate of about five guilders per week, a high price for the kind of food he had been given. In addition there was an amount of some thirty guilders for his outfit: a hat, a pillow, a horse blanket, a knife—not much more. It also included a few guilders for drinking money, which was enough to keep a man drunk for days. The note was made out to the bearer; this was what the keeper had been waiting for. In proportion to the number of men he had been able to get signed on, the lodging-house keeper acquired for himself a sizable amount of money, at least on paper. The Company paid off these notes in installments at the rate at which the men earned their wages. At a monthly wage of about ten guilders, it might take a man a year or more before he was in the clear. The Company took no chances. Wages stopped when a ship went down or if a man died, and the paymaster at the East India House made doubly sure that nothing was paid until records came back from the Indies showing that a man had actually earned his money.

Few keepers could afford to wait that long. In need of ready cash, many were forced to sell their notes to wealthy merchants who made a practice of buying them up at a discount, sometimes as high as 70 per cent. Spreading the risk over many ships and men and having a clearer picture of the odds, the note buyers made the profits, while the "cats and dogs" barely made enough

3. For an account of the mustering process and the boarding-house keepers, see J. de Hullu, "Sailors and Soldiers on the Ships of the East India Company," *BKI, 69* (1914), 318–23.

to support themselves. There were some who, in desperation, came to believe their own tall stories about the Indies and ended in mustering themselves.

A few days after mustering, the men returned to the East India House to sign the Articles and take an oath of loyalty to the Company. After a few more days they were summoned once more, this time with great fanfare. This was the day! Carrying their gear, they boarded lighters, and off they went to the road-stead in the Y.

Many had never been on a seagoing ship in their lives. With a hundred men or more assigned to a single ship, the decks were in utter confusion before each man found his place and stowed away his gear in the sea-chest provided by the Company. The more experienced were not averse to appropriating someone else's dunnage (gear), or whatever else they could lay their hands on. The skipper and his mates observed the mob, not bothering as yet to evaluate individual capabilities; there would be enough time for that later. It took time to sober the men and achieve some semblance of order. In the presence of one or more of the directors, the skipper then called all hands on deck and spoke to them: once more the Articles were read, someone read a sermon, and a psalm was sung. The pilots came on board and, with cannon shots from all the ships in port, the fleet sallied forth into the Zuiderzee on its way to Texel where, at the first favorable wind, the voyage would begin.[4] Another Company fleet was ready to go forth, for the glory of the Republic and for the profit of the stockholders.

It was a bitter winter that year of 1607, but fortunately the Zuiderzee did not freeze over until after the ships had reached Texel. It sometimes happened that a fleet had to wait there for weeks on end before a northwester had blown itself out. Still weak from undernourishment and without proper clothing against the wintry gusts, many of the crew suffered greatly, especially those who had gorged themselves on the heavy naval food for which their stomachs were unprepared. But Admiral Verhoef's luck held, and on December 22 he sailed into the North Sea.

Thus started the voyage proper; no time was lost in shaping the ill-assorted lot of men into a smoothly functioning whole. With the exception of the merchants, provost, constable, surgeon, steward, cook, chief-carpenter, and a few others, all hands were

4. Ibid., pp. 323–24.

assigned to "quarters" (watches). The officer in charge of the watch was called the quartermaster; it was his responsibility to whip the crew into shape—no easy task.

Normally there were three watches, giving the crew four hours on duty and eight off. In heavy weather and in uncharted waters, there were only two watches, all hands alternating every four hours. A half hour before the end of each watch, as many men as were needed took turns at the pumps, in order to leave a "dry ship" for the next watch. Each watch, moreover, had to clean the ship and attend to the sick. At eight o'clock in the evening, the provost gave the signal for "all lights out" by beating three times against the main mast with a stout piece of wood, accompanied by bell ringing. After this hour, there was to be no smoking or drinking, either on deck or below; those who were off duty had to stay in their bunks. A new watch was awakened by the time honored chant of "Ri-se, Ri-se, Ri-se!" When all hands were needed on deck for a maneuver, they were summoned with repeated shouts of "Overal! Overal!"

Sailors had to obey and perform at the slightest command and without complaining, even if they were presumably off duty. The skipper and his mates firmly believed that "idleness was the devil's own pillow," for they had learned by experience that only hard work would keep the men out of trouble. The Articles prescribed punishments for all kinds of infractions, but it was preferred to try to forestall crime by keeping men out of mischief. Among men so closely confined, homosexuality was a serious problem. The Dutch called it the "stupid sin" and it was severely punished, sometimes by death.[5] Saltpeter in the food was supposed to cool a man's flesh, and the cooks used it liberally, but nothing was more effective than to have a man fall exhausted into his bunk. The officers were ingenious at finding work for their charges: up and down the rigging, bending new sails just to see if the old needed mending; splicing lines at the end of a yardarm because it looked as if there were a ravel; a deck was never so bright that it did not need another scouring with holystones—large blocks of sandstone which a man, on his knees, had to push back and forth for as long as he was told. The mates knew their business well and saw to it that the work never ended.

5. English sea law was equally severe in this respect. Articles issued to the *Clovetree* included one (number 32) which demanded the death penalty for an act of sodomy "on man or beast." See Witsen, *Scheepsbouw*, p. 216.

Admiral Verhoef arrived at Isla de Mayo in the Cape Verde group with his main squadron at the beginning of February 1608. Here he made rendezvous with the few ships commissioned by the Chambers of Zealand and the Meuse. All thirteen bottoms were now together and the plenary council was summoned to the flagship, the *United Provinces*. The secret orders were opened, and they declared that the Seventeen had great expectations.[6]

As on previous occasions, the enemy was to be attacked in the Mozambique Channel and at Goa. While on the west coast of India, Verhoef was to make arrangements to establish a new line of communications, either overland via Ormuz, Aleppo, and Tripoli, or through the Red Sea to Cairo and thence to Venice, so that news from the Indies would reach the Seventeen more quickly than by the long route around the Cape of Good Hope. The coast of Malabar and Coromandel was to be visited anew to strengthen connections with the local princes and develop more trade. Depending upon the monsoon, the Admiral should either sail directly into the Malacca Strait, or go first to Bantam. A strong effort should then be made to capture the town of Malacca and to make treaties with the sultans of Johore and Achin, thus depriving the Portuguese of an opportunity to ally themselves with these "kings."

At this point the directors anticipated that Malacca might be too strong to be captured without a long siege. "If this cannot be done within a reasonable time," they admonished, "the fleet should proceed after destroying as many enemy ships as were encountered . . . because we are vitally interested in the silk trade with China, and especially the spice trade with the Moluccas." [7] Armed with these instructions, which promised some heavy fighting, the fleet continued the voyage.

Before long the ships entered the dreaded doldrums, where ships could wallow in a leaden sea for weeks and weeks on end with not a breath of wind to carry them along. But this time was not wasted. The crew having mastered the art of handling the ship, close attention was now given to training in naval warfare. Simulated battles began with the command *"Overal!"* With all hands rushing on deck, the ship was alive in minutes, each man

---

6. Instructions for the admiral, vice-admiral, and plenary council drawn up by the Seventeen at Amsterdam on October 13, 1607, in the National Archives, The Hague.

7. De Jonge, *Opkomst*, 3, 72.

going to his assigned place. The gun deck was cleared of all impediments. Lashings were taken off the cannon and replaced by block and tackle which acted as snubbers to brake the recoil and which hauled the pieces back into place. The axles were greased. Powder and shot—round, long, and sharp shrapnel—was hauled on deck, where it was put into boxes or belayed with iron hoops. Tubs of water were placed at strategic points and swabs put near the cannon; they were needed for cooling the pieces and for dousing fires. Smoldering rope punk was kept in readiness, and salt was strewn on the decks to provide firmer footing. The constable's mates issued muskets, bandoleers, storm hats, sabers, and other side arms. Stays were reinforced with heavy chains to prevent a lucky shot through the rigging from knocking down one or more of the masts, a hit that would make a ship immobile, helpless.

The sailors went through repeated maneuvers to learn how to turn a ship around in minimum time when real battle was joined. The main purpose of these maneuvers was to keep the vessel above the wind from the enemy; cannon smoke would then act as a screen, and this strategic position, besides making it easier to close with the enemy, would also make it possible to send off fire boats. In actual battle, boys would lie with an ear to the deck, listening for hits below the waterline, which the carpenters would try to close promptly with wooden plugs and leaden sheets. Most engagements in actual battle would culminate in the grappling of another ship, especially if booty were expected. For this purpose, vicious iron hooks were attached to the end of the yardarms to catch and hold the enemy's rigging, and grappling irons were held in readiness to lock the ships together.[8]

This arduous drilling was not resented so much as the drudgery of the regular labors the crew was made to perform. It made the men eager for real battle, not indeed for the glory of the Republic or for love of the Company but because all would share in the prize money. It was a chance of getting something more out of the voyage than their miserable wages, four to six guilders monthly for boys and young sailors and from ten to 12 for able seamen and cannoneers. The crew's share amounted to one sixteenth of the prize, to be divided in proportion to a man's wages.[9]

8. De Hullu, "Sailors and Soldiers," 337–40.
9. The division of prize money was an intricate affair, subject to many revisions. Basically, the States General received one fifth and the Stadholder,

Even such a modest share was enough to arouse their imaginations to speculate how to spend it once they had returned home. Some would think of buying a farm, others of owning a little grog shop; as for going back to sea—Never!

The officers could have predicted how they would really spend their money. It would all be gone within a short time, and in most cases even before they had a chance to leave the waterfront. These men, with few exceptions, did not know the value of money and how it might best be used. In Holland they became known as "Lords for six weeks" and, more ironically, as *Sapitans*, a word derived from the Malay language, meaning "who cares" or "what the hell." De Hullu tells of one sailor who, refusing to spend his money on the waterfront, hired three coaches—one for his hat, another for his pipe and tobacco box, and a third for himself. In this opulent procession he drove around the streets and canals of Amsterdam until his money was gone and another keeper took him under his wing.

Besides prize money there were other ways of adding to one's wages, but for the crew they were few and far between. The first man to sight land or to volunteer for something dangerous was marked down for a bonus of one month's wages. Reporting a smoldering mutiny was more lucrative. If a man were involved himself the reward was fifty guilders, and a hundred or more if he were not a party to the conspiracy. Such an opportunity, however, rarely presented itself.

The fleet dropped anchor at St. Helena on May 15, almost five months after leaving the Lowlands. There was the usual high rate of sickness among the crews—the Atlantic was the real travail of a voyage to the Indies. It was one of the reasons why the Portuguese needed almost a hundred years to get as far as the Cape of Good Hope. First there had been the cold winter climate at time of departure, to be followed by the heat of the equator when the ships were in the doldrums, sometimes for months. Having survived this ordeal, the crews were once again confronted by wintry gales in the South Atlantic.

All this had to be endured on a most unsuitable diet. Fresh meat and vegetables had been consumed within a few weeks after

---

as admiral-general of the fleet, one thirtieth. Of the remainder, after all repair costs to the ships had been deducted and the ordinary crew had been allotted its one sixteenth, the balance was divided in three equal shares between the skipper, the chief officers, and the owners (the Company).

departure. Beer, an important item to keep a man content, had not lasted much longer; it had been served at the rate of a quart or two a day before it, too, had spoiled. From then on it was salt beef, salt pork, stockfish, and beans. Breakfast usually consisted of barley and a salt herring; for their digestive properties, prunes were often cooked with the barley. The other victuals were served in rotation, on meat days and fish days. Butter, vinegar, and olive oil were served in small quantities to make the food more palatable. When supplies ran short, the food was of course strictly rationed.

On such a salty diet a man could drink enormous quantities of water. A sufficient quantity was usually carried, but in the torrid zone it quickly spoiled. Like stagnant pools, the casks soon swarmed with a variety of flora and fauna, most of it in an advanced state of decay. It was said that a man, trying to drink this soupy mixture, had to hold his nose to keep out the stench, and clench his teeth to strain out the scum. A red-hot poker stuck into a water cask was supposed to purify the water, but this made it no less repulsive to drink. The main source of the problem was the wooden casks, but it was a long time before it was realized that water should be carried in metal containers. Periodic squalls were a mixed blessing. Sails caught a certain amount of rain water, but the tar in them made it taste bitter as gall. Some men, trying to quench their thirst, chewed on lead bullets, which poisoned them.[10] The water was not the only thing that stank. Everyone could tell when another meat barrel had been opened, by the stench that filled the ship. Personal cleanliness was a matter of small concern, but the lack of fresh water made it impossible to provide even a minimum of sanitation and clean clothing. The whole ship was infested with lice, which might eat a hole in a man's flesh while he slept. There were articles specifying scrubbing and airing, with penalties listed for failure to comply, but the air on the decks below where the crew slept was sometimes so bad that a candle would not burn. As a last resort, vinegar was sprinkled below decks and every week or so the ship was smoked out with sulphur fumes.

The inevitable result of all this was a great deal of sickness, for which there was no other cure than to take the patients ashore at a proper refreshing place, of which St. Helena was one, and

10. Bontekoe, *East Indian Voyage*, p. 51. He added, "I drank my own urine as long as it was good, but it became later unsuitable for drinking."

give them a few weeks to recuperate. Someone wrote in 1640, "This ship is like a plague house. Scurvy, red runs, dropsy, burning fever, insanity, and delirium are most common." [11] There was also a disease called "rot fever" from which a man rarely recovered. This may have been typhoid but considering the primitive level of medical science, few diseases could be diagnosed properly, let alone treated.[12]

The most prevalent disease was scurvy. It manifested itself in progressive stages, first by a great lethargy and an unusual paleness, as if the blood were being drained from the body; bluish spots appeared, and the limbs became swollen and finally paralyzed. The gums became swollen, inflamed, and bleeding, causing teeth to loosen. Decaying blood between the teeth and open sores in the mouth produced a stinking breath. In due course, the skin burst, causing sores on the body that did not heal. The patient had bloody stools, bad vision, and an insatiable thirst caused by high fever. Finally there were convulsions. Not all of these symptoms had to be present to cause death. The remedy for scurvy, if the disease had not advanced too far, was well enough known, but on a ship at sea it was unavailable: fresh greens and citrus fruit were all that were required. Even in those early days, lemon juice was carried on the ships, but this, too, was quick to spoil and thus lose its effectiveness.

The standard preventive medicine for any and all diseases was alcohol in any form whatever, the stronger the better. Rations of French and Spanish wine were issued daily, and brandy on suitable occasions. These rations were doled out in the morning because alcohol was presumed to be especially beneficial taken on an empty stomach. Boatswains, cooks, and carpenters received a double ration and the "boys" a half. It had to be swallowed on the spot because, for fear of drunken brawls, hoarding was prohibited. On the return voyage, arrack, distilled from palm wine and a favorite liquor of the Indies, would take the place of brandy.

To take care of the sick, the ships carried a surgeon and a surgeon's mate. The title in those days simply meant barber, and the practitioner's knowledge of healing, and his pay, were in

11. A report by the surgeon Nicolaes de Graaff, cited in M. A. van Andel, *Chirurgijns, Vrije Meesters, Beunhazen en Kwakzalvers* (Amsterdam, Van Kampen, 1947), pp. 121–22.

12. About "Food on the ships of the East India Company" and "Sickness and Doctors on the ships of the East India Company," see the two informative essays by J. de Hullu in *BKI*, 67 (1913), 541–62 and 245–72.

keeping with his low status—only 22 guilders per month and 16 for his mate. Twice a day there was sick call at the main mast for those who could still walk, and the others were attended to below. In the case of scurvy, the blackened gums were cut back and washed with water, sores were dressed as best they could be, and blood was let, supposedly to reduce swellings. Leeks, onions, and a certain "scurvy grass," crushed and salted, were given as medicine. Being clever with the razor, the surgeons might perform successful amputations, necessitated by a cannonball hit or by splintered wood. The surgeon would neatly trim the flesh, fold it back, saw off part of the splintered bone, and cauterize the stump in hot tar. After that, the patient was in God's hands.

As a sub-merchant with a monthly salary of about 35 guilders, Jan Coen was part of the higher echelon, and did not have to take part in the routine drillings, although it was his first trip out. In his position he also had the advantage of quarters in the cabin, aft below the poop deck. Conditions there were more sanitary and, although the victuals were much the same everywhere on the ship, the cooks would serve the officers the best available. In the cabin, moreover, there was no restriction on wine and brandy consumption, and this tended to make life at sea a little more bearable.

Watching the men at their daily tasks and observing the conditions under which they had to work, Jan Coen learned to recognize a man's capabilities. In later years he was to prove that he had learned this lesson well.

3

Coen's
First Contact
with the Indies

Early in August 1608, Admiral Verhoef reached the Channel of Mozambique, ready to execute the first of his instructions from the Seventeen. Now the men could put into practice what they had been taught about naval warfare. An enemy carack was sighted, and two yachts were detailed to capture her. They managed to do so after some heavy hand-to-hand fighting while the ships were board-to-board. Shortly afterwards, the Dutch landed cannon, soldiers, and armed sailors in an attempt to capture the fort. Under Don Estaban de Tayda, the Portuguese defended themselves valiantly, and Verhoef soon realized, as his predecessors had, that Mozambique was not to be so easily taken. Unwilling to rearrange the time schedule set for him by the Seventeen, Verhoef broke off the siege after a few weeks. He had lost thirty men in the attempt, and many more had been wounded. Piqued by the stiff resistance, he ordered the houses outside the fort to be burned down before continuing his voyage.[1]

One month later, the fleet was before Goa where Verhoef was to execute his next set of instructions. They were threefold: to intercept the Portuguese caracks which had escaped from the Tagus River the previous year, shortly before Heemskerck appeared on the scene; to establish a line of communication with the homeland, either through the Red Sea or by overland route to Aleppo or some other port in the Mediterranean; finally, to renew contact with the Samorin of Calicut and make any other connections that seemed feasible.

The Admiral deployed his forces to cover the coast in the shortest possible time. Only one carack was encountered, which the Portuguese themselves destroyed rather than surrender it. No arrangements were made for the much desired new line of com-

1. De Jonge, *Opkomst*, 3, 74.

munications. Such an enterprise required a well-established starting point in the north, at or near Surate, which the Company
did not acquire until some eight years later. De Jonge, in his exhaustive study of the Dutch East Indies, makes a cryptic reference to a certain David van Deynsen who, with his companions,
was murdered at Gujerat in 1608, the same year Verhoef was off
the coast. These men may have been left there by the Admiral
for the express purpose of establishing an office although no
specific information has come to light on this point. The overland
route did not materialize until the Dutch had gained a firm foothold in Persia in 1622.[2]

Pressed for time, Verhoef turned south and by October 9 he
had rejoined his other squadron before Calicut. The treaty Van
der Hagen had earlier concluded with the Samorin was reaffirmed,
with protestations of mutual assistance against the common enemy,
the Portuguese.[3] To implement this agreement, a fast sloop sailed
to Bantam with instructions for the president of the office to send
a few ships to Calicut. Jacques l'Hermite's reply, dated November 19, 1608, reached Verhoef while he was at Johore in the
Malacca Strait. It was short and to the point. "The ships we have
in the Indies," he wrote, "are badly needed in these quarters.
Moreover, they are all in the Moluccas and not expected to return
from there until August of next year." He added a sound observation to the effect that he did not consider trade with Malabar
important enough to employ ships and merchandise which could
be used elsewhere to better advantage. "There is to be had only
pepper at that place," he reasoned, "and this we can obtain abun-
dantly here, as it is the mainstay of business in these quarters."[4]

The Malabar Coast was unattractive for still another reason.
It was close to Goa, the nucleus of Portuguese strength in Asia.
Goa presented a constant threat to the Company's agents during
the long periods when ships were engaged elsewhere and thus
unable to provide the necessary protection. In the year 1603, two
merchants from the Zealand Company, Hans de Wolff and Lafer,
had been taken prisoner by the Portuguese and hanged at Goa.
The emphasis the Seventeen placed on the capture or harassment

2. See H. Dunlop, *Bronnen tot de geschiedenis der Oostindische Compagnie in Perzie, 1* (The Hague, 1930), lx. See also P. A. Leupe, "Brieven-
vervoer over land naar Indie," *BVGO,* new series, 6 (1870), 54–76.
3. For this treaty, dated October 13, 1608, see De Jonge, *Opkomst, 3,*
278–79.
4. De Jonge, *Opkomst, 3,* 76.

of Portuguese strongholds at this early stage was ill advised in that they underestimated the power of the enemy. This was proved time and again: at Mozambique, Goa, Malacca, and Macao.

Before Verhoef left Calicut, he attended to another matter in his list of instructions. It called for a survey of the conditions on the coast of Coromandel, on the east coast of the Indian peninsula. For this purpose the Admiral sent off two yachts under the chief merchant, Jacob de Bitter, assisted by a few other merchants, one of whom was Pieter Bourgonje. The latter, as merchant on the *Hoorn*, was Jan Coen's superior, and his new assignment may well have given Coen the opportunity to step into his place, perhaps giving him his first promotion.

The coast of Coromandel offered greater possibilities for trade than Malabar. It produced large quantities of cotton goods (calicoes) for which there was a ready market throughout all of Southeast Asia. The Dutch had established themselves early on that coast, and had factories at Mazulipatnam and Patapouly, the result of a treaty made by Paulus van Soldt with the ruler of Golconda. As elsewhere throughout Asia, the Dutch discovered that the search for profitable trade was never without problems. At Coromandel they were created by the method with which the king administered his realm. The office of governor in the coastal towns was let out to the highest bidder. The king insisted on receiving his full rental promptly, and there were to be no excuses. As a result, the governors used all means at their disposal to exact as much as possible from the population and from foreign traders. The arrival of the Dutch was considered a gift from heaven because it afforded the local governors an opportunity to acquire a substantial amount over and above their obligation to their king. It was a *zemindar's* (tax collector) paradise of arbitrary taxes and levies, to which the Dutch soon objected. When the pressure became too great, the Dutch retaliated by applying economic sanctions—slowing down trade—and continued to operate as well as they could under these uneasy conditions.

Jacob de Bitter was successful in his mission to establish a third office on the coast farther to the south and beyond the sphere of influence of Golconda. He was well received and the prospects of trade in calicoes was extremely promising. In time it would be used as a lever to bring the governors in the north to reason. Bourgonje was appointed head of this new factory.[5]

5. Ibid., 3, 76–78, 280–82. For an account of the early Indian textile in-

Meanwhile, Verhoef had continued his voyage eastward. In the Strait of Malacca he took a few Portuguese ships but dared not attack the heavily fortified town of Malacca without help, and the Sultan of Johore was in no mood to accommodate him. Shortly after the previous Dutch fleet under Matelief had left the Strait, the Portuguese had returned in force. The population of Johore had fled, and the Portuguese sacked the town. An important faction at the Sultan's court was for making peace with the Portuguese because the Dutch seemed unwilling or unable to provide the promised protection. When l'Hermite at Bantam learned of this unfortunate state of affairs, he sent a ship to carry away the Company's funds from the factory at nearby Batu Sawer before it fell into enemy hands. Verhoef, apprised of the situation, did his best to placate the Sultan. He was received with great ceremony, but it was plain that the Sultan was in constant fear of the Portuguese. He had serious misgivings about a siege of Malacca, and Verhoef, on his part, was unwilling to make the attempt alone. His orders from the Seventeen did not give him much time to waste. There were other items on his agenda.

As a sign of good will the Dutch left two ships at Johore, the *Red Lion* and the *Griffin*. They were to give the Sultan protection, and would also be on hand to intercept some Portuguese caracks that were expected in the ensuing months. The capture of these caracks might pay for the costly delay in having two ships tied up for what was no more than a grandiose gesture.[6]

At this point the two young men, Jacques Specx and Jan Coen, parted company. The first stayed behind at Johore for the time being, while Jan Coen sailed with the fleet to Bantam, arriving there in February 1609. Near the Sunda Strait they encountered the *Good Hope*, a yacht some ten months out of Holland. It had been sent to inform the admiral of the latest developments at home and to transmit the latest orders from the Seventeen. The news was important. A long truce with Spain appeared imminent. Consequently, the directors ordered Verhoef to take steps to secure as many points and treaties as possible for a favorable status quo. As could be expected, the Seventeen were specific about the Spice Islands, the only source in the world for cloves, nutmegs, and mace. "The Islands of Banda and the Moluccas are our main target," they wrote. "We recommend most strongly that you tie

dustry, see N. W. Posthumus, *Documenten betreffende de buitenlandsche handelspolitiek* (The Hague, 1921), pp. 54 ff.
    6. De Jonge, *Opkomst, 3,* 79–82.

these islands to the Company, if not by treaty then by force!" [7] They set a deadline of September 1, 1609, which was the date that the States General had in mind for the beginning of the truce period. After this date, each nation would be free to trade wherever the other had no treaties or territorial possessions.

Immediately upon his arrival in Bantam, Verhoef convened his plenary council to plan for the execution of these latest orders. There was also another matter which demanded attention. When Admiral Matelief sailed for home on January 28, 1608, he had left with l'Hermite an encouraging report about trade with Japan. During his travel through the Indies, Matelief had unexpectedly discovered his nephew, Jacob Quackernaeck, who had been presumed lost on the ill-fated voyage of Mahu and Cordes, of which only a few survivors had managed to reach Japan. Jacob had told his uncle how well they had been received and that the possibility for trade seemed excellent. Lack of ships had so far prevented further investigation of this encouraging news. Now that a truce was in the offing, it became urgent that firm relations with Japan should be established before Spain could claim this territory as her own.

The situation at Malacca being what it was, the council decided that the two ships left at Johore could serve the Company better by going to Japan, and orders to this effect were dispatched at once. After the usual vicissitudes, the *Red Lion* and the *Griffin* arrived in Japan on July 1, 1609, well ahead of the deadline set by the Seventeen. Jacques Specx, serving as sub-merchant on the *Griffin*, was instructed to contact the provincial governor. He acquitted himself so well in this assignment that a larger delegation, headed by the chief-merchants Puyck and Van den Broek, were allowed audience with the Shogun himself. A liberal treaty for trading privileges was concluded, and permission given to establish a factory at the town of Firando. Jacques Specx was put in charge of this office when the two ships returned to southern waters. [8]

At Bantam, Jan Coen made his first contact with that part of the Asian world where, in the not too distant future, he would have his headquarters. The Sultanate of Bantam comprised not

7. Letter from the Seventeen to Verhoef, dated March 29, 1608.
8. About the exploits of Specx in Japan, see O. Nachod, *Die Beziehungen der Niederländisch-Ostindischen Kompagnie zu Japan im 17en Jahrhundert* (Leipzig, 1897). See also E. M. Thompson, ed., *Diary of Richard Cocks, Cape Merchant in the English Factory in Japan, 1615-22* (2 vols. London, 1883).

only the western part of Java but also a good slice of South Sumatra, where large quantities of pepper were produced. This alone would have made it an important link in the Company's scheme, but its location at the crossroads of important trade routes made it even more desirable.

Among the many tasks which Verhoef had been given was the renewal of an earlier treaty, but he could achieve very little. For some time the Sultanate had been in the throes of palace revolution, between the court circle headed by *Pangeran* [9] Aria Rana Mangala, uncle and guardian of the Sultan who was still a minor, and the *Pangawas*, the provincial governors. Verhoef wrote in his journal, "I find the king's affairs very confused. Each party has fortified itself in separate parts of the town and they are openly at war with each other." Because of this situation, there was no central authority with whom a firm agreement could be concluded. Rana Mangala (referred to by the Dutch as the *Pangeran*) and his court circle won the battle, and, indirectly, this proved to be a boon to the Company, but not because the *Pangeran* was a friend of the Dutch: on the contrary, because one of the rebellious governors, Widjaja Krama, was the local governor of Djakarta.[10] Widjaja Krama, being on the losing side, was more than willing to allow the Dutch to build a warehouse at the mouth of the river at Djakarta. This seemed like a good proposition to him not only because it meant added revenue but also because the presence of the Dutch would shield him from his enemy, the *Pangeran* of Bantam.

Verhoef did not stay at Bantam long enough to initiate these overtures to Djakarta. He had to leave it to l'Hermite, for there were other important matters demanding his personal attention. The Spice Islands were the Company's main objective, and Verhoef lost no time in accomplishing this task before the deadline set by the Seventeen. Jacob de Bitter had rejoined the main fleet at Bantam after his successful sojourn on the Coromandel coast, and he was sent ahead as a vanguard. The vice-admiral, Francois Wittert, sailed to Macassar with four ships to buy rice and other victuals, and to try and make a compact with this Sultanate for future trade. After that he, too, was to continue to the Spice Islands.

9. *Pangeran* was the highest title of Bantamese nobility.

10. M. L. van Deventer, *Geschiedenis der Nederlanders op Java*, 1 (Haarlem, 1886), 74–77.

Anxious to accomplish his mission, Verhoef, with the main squadron, sailed directly for Banda. Had he known what was in store for him, he might not have been quite so eager to get there. One of his ships was the *Hoorn* with Jan Coen on board, a witness to what was about to happen. Another witness at Banda was Captain Keeling of the English ship *Hector*, a competitor intent on obtaining a cargo of spices.

The Banda group consisted of ten islands of volcanic origin which covered no more than about twenty square miles of total land area. The largest, Lonthor, also called Great-Banda, is shaped like a boomerang, and only a little over seven miles long. The importance of this island group far surpassed its size because it was the only known source of nutmegs, covered by the still more valuable fleece, mace. The most important island from the Dutch point of view was Neyra, where they had built a warehouse. As noted earlier, the Dutch had concluded a treaty with the headmen, *Orang Kayas*, for exclusive purchasing rights. To assure delivery, the merchants of the Company often paid in advance, a practice which seemed safe enough in view of the agreement. Aside from the usual squabbles about quality and weights, about which Heemskerck had so vehemently complained, trade proceeded satisfactorily enough as long as there were no other buyers on the scene. But the picture changed drastically after the English arrived. The wily *Orang Kayas* saw an opportunity to sell the same lot twice, pocketing the advance received from the Dutch and selling the lot again to the English. The English, by offering higher prices than the Dutch, were annoying competitors. The Dutch had trouble enforcing their contracts under these conditions and the former amicable relationship quickly deteriorated.

When Verhoef appeared at Banda and requested permission to erect a small fort on Neyra, the Bandanese became greatly aroused. The primary purpose for such a fortified warehouse was as proof of settlement, as specified by the Seventeen, and to protect the stocks of spices from attack by enemy forces. The Bandanese realized, not without reason, that this would also put an end to their devious practices, and prevent them from dealing with any but the Dutch—and on Dutch terms. The Bandanese opposition was strengthened by the presence of Captain Keeling, who offered to put Neyra under the protection of King James who, he argued, was far more powerful than the upstart Prince Maurice. The Bandanese were clearly preparing for action when they moved their women and children into the mountains and sur-rounded the Dutch factory with some two thousand men.

Verhoef did his best to arrive at a peaceful solution, but after three days of fruitless consultations with the *Orang Kayas,* who were obviously delaying, his patience was exhausted. Time was running short and, because so much more remained to accom-plish before the deadline set by the Seventeen, the admiral insisted on an immediate reply. Unwilling to resort to open warfare, the headmen finally agreed, and on May 5 the Dutch began to re-pair the old Portuguese fort. On May 22, while this work was in progress, the *Orang Kayas* entreated Verhoef to discuss the terms of a new agreement on prices to be paid for nutmegs and mace. Verhoef agreed willingly, hoping to conclude a firm understand-ing, thus accomplishing his task quickly and peacefully.[11]

It was agreed that the meeting take place on the east coast of Neyra. The Bandanese demanded hostages and the admiral, in good faith, sent two of his merchants, Jan de Molre and Nicolas de Visser, who had been stationed at the Banda office for some time. Accompanied by his full council and a detachment of mus-keteers, Verhoef went to the designated place but found no one there with whom he could deal. Sending one of his men who spoke the Malay language, he learned that the *Orang Kayas* were some distance away, and claimed to be afraid of the soldiers. Would the Admiral please come into the woods a short distance, ac-companied only by his council? Verhoef, the guileless sailor, agreed.

No sooner had he arrived at the designated spot than he found himself and his council completely surrounded by a large number of armed men. The last words he ever heard were shouted by a certain Jan de Bruin, "Admiral, we are betrayed!" The Dutch were defenseless and taken by surprise, the melee was bloody. Verhoef's head was severed from his body and others in his en-tourage suffered a similar fate. More than thirty Dutchmen were massacred, including the two hostages.[12] Most of the leaders of the Company were wiped out. It was a black day for the Com-pany, but the consequences would prove to be even more terrible for the Bandanese, and for the English.

A hastily convened council appointed Skipper Simon Hoen as commander of the fleet. The blood flag was hoisted and the Dutch

11. De Jonge, *Opkomst, 3,* 96–97.
12. F. Valentyn, *Oud en Nieuw Oost-Indien, 3* (Amsterdam, 1862), 72–74.

declared war on the people of Neyra.[13] Their villages and vessels were destroyed; the Dutch showed no mercy. Native resistance continued on Lonthor, where more Dutchmen, including Jacob de Bitter, lost their lives. On this occasion the Dutch accused Captain Keeling of having sided with the Bandanese by warning the Bandanese of Lonthor with signals that the Dutch were coming, thus giving them an opportunity to prepare themselves. Whatever may have been the role that Captain Keeling had played in this affair, there is nothing in his own journal that refers to the massacre; perhaps his conscience was not quite clear in the matter. The Dutch had their own opinion of his participation, and the council issued a written order for him to leave Banda.

On August 10, 1609, a peace treaty was signed on the ship *Hollandia*. By this treaty, the island of Neyra was considered to have been taken by armed conquest forced on the Dutch by the massacre of Admiral Verhoef and his council. The island, in fact, was annexed in the name of the States General, Prince Maurice, and the United Company, "to be kept by us forever." [14] This was the first territorial acquisition by the Dutch in their quest for trade in the Indies, but the Bandanese had not yet relinquished their independence.

It is difficult, in retrospect, to understand the reasons which could have moved the Bandanese to such a precipitous step, one which was bound to cause them great misery. Heemskerck, having experienced the non-European business morality of the Bandanese, might not have fallen so easily into the trap set for the unsuspecting Verhoef who took his place. Granting that the Bandanese wanted to trade on their own terms, and resented the ground rules laid down by the Dutch, these are hardly sufficient reasons for jeopardizing their independence. It may well be that Captain Keeling gave them the impression that the English, in time, would make short shrift of the Dutch.

There was at least one man who proved by his subsequent actions that he believed these three factors had played a part in the affair: the gullibility of Admiral Verhoef, the treachery of the Bandanese, and the machinations of the English. Jan Coen had been at Banda throughout these events, and his inquisitive mind

13. The blood flag showed a raised arm holding a sword against a red field.

14. In this treaty the Dutch granted the Bandanese freedom of trade, except in spices. See De Jonge, *Opkomst, 3,* 313–14.

must have considered the reasons why such things could have happened. He may also have begun to think of means by which they might be prevented in the future.[15]

As soon as the treaty was signed, the Bandanese arrived at the Dutch factory from all directions, freely offering their spices. It soon was business as usual. The ships *Rotterdam* and *Hoorn* were quickly loaded and ordered to return to Holland via Bantam.

With peace at Banda at least outwardly restored, the vice-admiral, Simon Hoen, set sail for Amboyna, the important clove island. Here he found everything serene under the durable governor Frederic Houtman, who had served the various Dutch companies since 1595. After renewing the old treaty of 1605, Simon Hoen continued to Ternate where he arrived on September 23, just one day after Vice-Admiral Francois Wittert had departed for the Philippine Islands for the purpose of harassing Spanish shipping in those waters. Wittert had already renewed the contract of 1607 with Ternate, and Simon Hoen decided to solidify the Dutch position there by blockading the Spanish stronghold on nearby Tidore, hoping to force its surrender as the garrison was reportedly short of food. His main objective was to effect the release of Van Caerden, the reckless admiral of the previous voyage, who was held prisoner on Tidore. While thus engaged, Simon Hoen suddenly died on January 12, 1610. There was a strong suspicion that he had been poisoned, but no one could tell why and by whom.[16]

His sudden death created utter confusion among the remaining skippers. With Hoen gone, the last vestige of leadership, already undermined by the massacre at Banda, evaporated. Adrian Corssen, factor on one of the less important islands, reported: "Having no leader, there is no unity whatever among the skippers. Each wants to be president of the council whether or not he is qualified." Every skipper tried to promote his own project, with the result that little was accomplished and the morale of the crews deteriorated rapidly.[17]

15. Another witness to these events was Piet Heyn, who then served on *Hollandia* in a minor capacity. He became a great popular hero when, as admiral of a fleet of the West India Company, he captured a rich Spanish silver convoy in 1628 off the coast of Cuba. This feat earned the Company a net profit of about 7 million guilders. See S. P. L'Honoré Naber and Irene Wright, *Piet Heyn en de Zilvervloot* (Utrecht, 1928).

16. De Jonge, *Opkomst*, 3, 102–05.

17. It did not help matters that the skipper who presided over the Council was named "Crackeel," which means "squabble." In due course this skipper's

One thing, however, was accomplished. The Spanish had sent a squadron of six frigates from Manila to relieve their garrison at Tidore, and the Dutch managed to capture two of them. They were able to exchange the prisoners they had taken for Admiral Van Caerden, and this temporarily restored order and confidence in the fleet. On June 6, Van Caerden was unanimously chosen as commander of all the forces in the Moluccas, and the period of indecision and bickering had apparently come to an end. But this composure proved to be short-lived. On July 15 Van Caerden once more fell into enemy hands while sailing from Ternate to Matjan on a poorly armed yacht. This time the Spanish took no chances with their high-ranking prisoner, and they carried him to Manila.

The skippers, once more deprived of leadership, anxiously awaited the return of Francois Wittert. They waited in vain. His expedition to the Philippines had started favorably enough. He had taken valuable booty from the Spanish, and disrupted their trade between Manila and the mainland, thereby influencing Chinese merchants that they would do better to trade with the Dutch. Flushed with this success, Wittert had stretched his venture too far, and he had also become reckless. While some of his ships were making much needed repairs and others were engaged in relieving some Chinese junks of their cargo, he was attacked by Spanish warships. Although they put up a stiff fight, two of his ships, with all the loot, were lost to the enemy, and in the battle Francois Wittert and many of his shipmates lost their lives. Only a yacht and a sloop escaped to carry the bad news back to Ternate.

The news was as bad at Banda. The arrival of the English *Expedition* under Captain Middleton had brought an end to the uneasy peace. Encouraged by the presence of the English, and with no Dutch ship in sight, the Bandanese rose up in arms to rid themselves of their oppressors. Every Dutchman who happened to be outside the fort was slaughtered, and the garrison itself was nearly overrun. Middleton promptly took advantage of the situation by trading a quantity of weapons and munitions for a full cargo of nutmegs and mace. He left the Bandanese with advice as to how much better they would fare under the protection of the English Company.[18]

---

council was widely ridiculed and was referred to as the Lords States of Banda.

18. De Jonge, *Opkomst*, 3, 106–08.

Thus, most of the high hopes with which the Verhoef voyage had started had come to naught. Valuable ships had been lost, no new significant treaties had been concluded, the Spanish fleet was as strong as ever, and no enemy strongholds had been taken. In addition, the admiral, two vice-admirals, and most of the higher personnel had lost their lives. On the credit side were only the cargoes in the *Rotterdam* and the *Hoorn*, and the fact that relations had been opened with Japan.

While these two ships were at Bantam preparing for the long voyage home, the president of the office, Jacques l'Hermite, had ample opportunity to learn from Jan Coen and others about the events at Banda and the role the English had played in this affair. The news, although worse than expected, could not have been too much of a surprise to him. For some time he had been fully aware of the difficulties facing the Company in those islands. His views on this problem had already been expressed in his message to the Seventeen, dated January 28, 1608. "With those of Banda," he had written, "a different stand shall have to be taken [from in Ternate] else the situation will go from bad to worse. They are deliberate scoundrels and other nations see their profit in this. It is sad that *we* have to fight [to keep the Spanish and Portuguese at bay] and look on while the English fill their holds under our protection. It will be necessary to teach the Bandanese a lesson as otherwise it will be impossible to keep the English from fishing in troubled waters. There is much at stake for the Company." [19]

Considering Coen's later activities—his preoccupation with Banda and the English—there can be no doubt that he shared l'Hermite's views. It was too early in Coen's career for him to have issued any reports under his own name—he was still serving in a minor rank—but it can be assumed that he made a good impression on the president of the Bantam office, who had turned out to be one of the more capable servants of the Company in the Indies. [20]

19. In this same letter appears the first mention about a possible monopoly of the spice trade. "How much greater would the profits be," L'Hermite wrote, "if Your Lordships had the Moluccas products exclusively in your hands."

20. L'Hermite's record was not without blemish. In July 1612, Pieter Both, the first governor general, complained about his clandestine trade. See W. P. Coolhaas, ed., *Generale Missiven*, p. 16.

4

The English
versus
the Dutch

Jan Coen returned to Holland in 1610, after an absence of about three years. The Verhoef voyage had been lucky as well as instructive: he might have lost his life at Mozambique, or Banda, or have succumbed from natural causes, as had so many of his shipmates. Best of all for his future career was the fact that he had been sent home with the *Hoorn*, instead of having been assigned to some outpost in Asia. He had come in contact with some of the major problems confronting the Company in the Indies— the stubborn strength of the Portuguese and the Spanish, the cupidity of the Bantamese rulers, the unreliability of the Moslem headmen of Banda who considered it a virtue to break agreements with Christians, and above all, the irksome rivalry with the English. Jan Coen could not have anticipated that he was to play a major role in the attack on these problems, and that one day King James would single him out as England's greatest enemy in the Indies.

Friction between the English and the Dutch was by no means confined to Asia. There were other areas of conflict: the trade in woolen cloth, the herring fishery, whaling in Arctic waters, and conflict of interest in the Baltic and Russian trade. These differences did not arise all at once. Some had been brewing since the beginning of the Dutch rebellion against Spain, and they grew in intensity as Holland prospered in the new economic age. They reached their peak during the first few decades of the seventeenth century; when a peaceful solution seemed impossible, the two countries went to war.

For a better understanding of the origin of these frictions, it is necessary to review the relationship which had existed between the two countries since the Middle Ages. During the thirteenth and early fourteenth centuries, wool was the single most important item England had for export. This trade flourished because of increased demand from Flanders, whose weavers turned it into cloth. King Edward I realized the advantages of unrestricted intercourse with his neighbors across the sea, and in 1303 he proclaimed the famous Carta Mercatoria which offered free trading privileges to any foreign merchant coming to his shores.[1] The sale of wool to foreign merchants was conducted by Merchants of the Staple under a royal patent. The guild had offices in the so-called staple towns which were situated within reach of the sea and close to the sheep-grazing lands belonging to the king and the great landholders. The members of this guild gradually took over their own export trade, and during the first half of the fourteenth century their staple on the continent was located at Bruges.

It was under his grandson, Edward III, that the first Flemish weavers settled in England, mainly in Norwich, Suffolk, and Essex, and taught the English how to weave the coarser fabrics. This soon led to an export trade in unbleached woolen cloth, such as baize and kersey. The Merchants of the Staple had no patent to deal in anything but raw wool, and thus this cloth trade came into the hands of another English Guild, the Merchant Adventurers. As the cloth trade grew in importance, so did the Merchant Adventurers, and they soon overshadowed the Merchants of the Staple, whose business declined and passed into oblivion during the middle of the sixteenth century.[2]

The Merchant Adventurers might have become an influential and aggressive body of traders, as did their Dutch counterparts, had they been able to operate in a political and social climate more favorable to such enterprise than England was at that time. The guild system, with its many restrictions and regulations, did not allow the individual merchant to exercise his ability to the full. In a society whose economy and prestige were based on land ownership, a merchant class had little standing and thus did not attract many people of stature and ability. In addition, the unsettled political conditions in England during the fourteenth and fifteenth centuries interfered with whatever normal expansion might have taken place. The Hundred Years' War with France

1. Colin Clark, *The Economics of 1960* (London, Macmillan, 1944), pp. 115-18.
2. G. Edmundson, *Anglo-Dutch Rivalry During the First Half of the Seventeenth Century* (Oxford, 1911), pp. 163-66.

gave glory to some but brought an end to English aspirations on the continent of Europe. At home it had actually resulted in an economic regression, compounded with the ravages of the Black Death, which took its fearful toll. The Wars of the Roses during the latter part of the fifteenth century caused still greater derangement of the English economy.

The sixteenth century dawned on an impoverished England, in many respects less prosperous than it had been under the Norman kings. Agriculture and industry were in dire straits, and most of the overseas trade and shipping was in the hands of foreigners. The cultural level was equally low, as illustrated by the small number of books published in England. Printing had been introduced from the Netherlands in 1476, but in the subsequent thirty years only 141 books were published there against some 15,000 on the continent. There were peers of England who could neither read nor write, and the father of Shakespeare, holding the important function of high bailiff of Stratford, could not write his own name. Not until the second half of the sixteenth century under Elizabeth, who realized the need for education, was any serious attempt made to establish grammar schools.[3] By this time elementary schooling was already well established in the Netherlands.

The Reformation, which had brought a solid middle class into being in the Netherlands, had the opposite effect in England. Henry VIII had not cut himself loose from the Catholic Church for ideological reasons; it was an act of vengeance that prompted him to introduce the Reformation in 1531. The Pope had refused to agree to the annulment of his marriage with Catherine of Aragon and to sanction a proposed union with Anne Boleyn. After having himself proclaimed head of the new Church of England, Henry promptly confiscated the vast land holdings and numerous cloisters of the Catholic orders. He kept some of these for himself and the rest were parcelled out to his noble vassals.

The fisheries were also hard hit. With more than one hundred fast days on the calendar of the old Church year, fishing had been one of the main sources of revenue for many coastal towns and villages. After the Reformation, and in spite of the lenten fasts proclaimed by the Tudors, many people were afraid to eat fish,

3. F. Dekker, *Voortrekkers van Oud-Nederland* (The Hague, Boucher, 1947), pp. 7–9.

for fear of being accused of favoring the old religion. The fisheries declined.

The byproducts of the Reformation in the Netherlands had a far greater effect on England than the advent of Protestantism by royal decree. After the outbreak of the rebellion against Spain, refugees from the southern Netherlands brought knowledge and new techniques to the northern provinces. A considerable number also crossed over to England. These immigrants brought their knowledge of weaving the finer cloth for which Flanders and Brabant had become known throughout all Europe. This influx primarily benefited England's cloth industry. But many other new arts were introduced as many refugees were skilled artisans in different fields.

Some of the new industries they developed were the manufacturing of linen, yarn, and lace. Lace required starch, and a Dutch woman, a certain Mrs. Dinghem van der Plasse, is said to have made a fortune by teaching the art of starching at her school in London. Complementary to this field was the making of needles and pins which brought improvements in the metal industry. At the beginning of Elizabeth's reign, window panes were almost nonexistent, even in the most imposing homes. Once again the artisans from the Lowlands put their knowledge to work. According to Louis B. Wright in his *Middle-Class Culture of Elizabethan England*, those who could afford to do so tore down their homes and built new ones to provide space for window panes. By 1589 there were 14 glass works in London.

The first public water supply in London was installed by the Dutch who used their knowledge of hydraulics for pumping water out of the Thames. They also introduced the first coaches, which were greatly admired. Elizabeth drove around in one with a Dutch coachman holding the reins.

The Dutch made equally important contributions to the English economy in the field of agriculture. They showed the farmer how to cultivate his land better and introduced the growing of root crops which, by their far greater yield of nutriment per acre, had made it possible to sustain the growing population of western Europe. Improved types of grass and clover aided husbandry, as did the Dutch knowledge of selective breeding and the introduction of the famed Flemish draft horses. They introduced the growing of hops and established the first breweries, thus providing the English with another favorite beverage.[4]

During the early part of Elizabeth's reign, this influx was mainly confined to Netherlanders of modest means, but after the fall of Antwerp a number of its prosperous merchants fled to England, perhaps more than had escaped to Holland, where they would have had to compete against a well entrenched merchant class. Many of these merchants went to London at the instigation of Thomas Gresham, the famous English economist who had for a long time been the queen's fiscal agent in the Netherlands. It was he who established the Royal Exchange at London, copying the system developed at the Antwerp exchange over many years. The building itself was designed by a Flemish architect and most of the workmen were Flemish. Before long many Dutch merchants were active on this exchange.

This influx of new ideas and techniques brought by energetic men who were determined to establish a new life in their adopted country aided the rapid rise of a middle class in England. The immediate results of this immigration were sufficiently apparent to win it permission to take its course rather than suffer suppression. It cannot be said that Elizabeth always received the immigrants with open arms. All of these refugees had escaped from the tyranny of the Catholic Church and were prompted by their ardent Calvinist beliefs, which they were not inclined to abandon in their new environment. Thus their settlements became the breeding grounds for the Puritan sects that preached the purification of the Anglican Church by ridding it of the remaining trappings and dogmas which they hated with all their hearts.

Elizabeth could hardly condone this, and at various times she established quotas for the number of immigrants that were to be allowed to settle in her realm. By and large, however, she must have felt that the advantages outweighed the disadvantages, and it is one of the wise and tolerant policies of her reign that she allowed this immigration to continue.

It is also understandable that this influx of Dutch people was not generally welcomed by the English with whom they came in contact. The yeomen of the shires, set in their ways, did not like these dour Calvinists and even resented the fact that they were able to show them a better life in a material way. They complained that these aliens worked too hard, that they took their religion too seriously, and that they generally refused to sub-

4. Ibid., pp. 10–12.

scribe to the customs of their adopted country. When the big landowners brought over Dutch dikemasters and "polder boys" to reclaim the marshes of East Anglia and the mouth of the Thames, this friction rose to new heights. The local fishermen and fowlers resented being deprived of their ancient livelihood.

In the towns, the lower classes resented the prosperity of the immigrants who, by hard work and ability, were soon able to improve their economic status and who preferred to hire their own countrymen rather than English labor. They also envied them their education because most could read and write.

The English merchants, especially those of London, were equally incensed by the inroads made in their established trade by this new element. Those who were engaged in foreign trade felt this competition most keenly and had no qualms about feeding the fires of dissension by exhorting the lower classes to stand up for their rights as Englishmen. In this they received full support from the Spanish agents at the court of Elizabeth and James I. The Italian Campanella put it plainly enough. "There is no better way," he wrote, "to weaken the power of the English than to foment dissention and rivalries." He suggested that the heretics of the Netherlands, especially those versed in trade, should be encouraged to go to England where they would soon create a climate of discord from which the Spanish could profit.[5]

With the development of a textile industry, the English entered a field that had been virtually a monopoly of the Netherlands. They were now making cloth up to the finest grades, which was highly profitable, but the finishing and dyeing was still done mainly on the continent. By withholding the unfinished cloth, the English could seriously hamper this Dutch industry. Threats to do so had been made from time to time, but they became a reality about 1615 when James I granted a patent to a man named Cockayne for the dyeing of cloth. The Dutch refused to accept dyed cloth, and for a while this trade came to a standstill. Cockayne was unable to carry out his ambitious project and his company failed after a few years. It is not known whether this was because of the Dutch boycott or because he was not able to hire experienced dyers and finishers.[6] It is almost certain that the Dutch boycott on dyed cloth proved a serious obstacle to

5. Ibid., pp. 12–13.
6. A. Friis, *The Alderman Cockayne Project and the Cloth Trade* (Copenhagen and London, 1927).

the development of this industry in England. James I heatedly referred to it when a Dutch mission came to London to discuss the various conflicts between the two countries. "In the dyed cloths you are playing at *Passe-passe*. You refuse to buy them, causing a mutiny, wellnigh a rebellion in my Realm." [7]

The Dutch herring fishery created a more serious area of friction. Over the centuries it had provided the Dutch not only with a much needed foodstuff but it had grown to such proportions that it also supplied an important export product. The best fishing grounds were off the Scottish and English coasts, and when the English began to object to having a large Dutch fishing fleet on their coasts for the greater part of the year, there was bound to be trouble. Dutch rights to fish in those waters had been established by ancient treaties. Edward I had granted them as early as 1295. Another treaty in 1496 between Henry VII and Philip the Fair, the Duke of Burgundy who counted the Netherlands among his territorial possessions, reaffirmed these rights in explicit terms. The Treaty of Binche in 1550 specifically allowed the Dutch "free trade and navigation in Scottish waters." James I confirmed this treaty in 1594 while still King James VI of Scotland.

Spurred by the economic development at home and pressed by a rising middle class of merchants, James I took a second view of these treaties. An island kingdom, England had for centuries relied upon the principle of *Dominium Maris*, implying that they owned the adjacent seas. Envy of Dutch enterprise in waters which he considered his own made James decide that *Dominium Maris* was actually divine right although there was no legal basis for such an assumption. In a number of steps he tried to force his theory upon the Dutch. In 1604, James yet again proclaimed the annual edict to enforce the eating of fish on fast days, "for the better increase of Seamen, to be readie at all times to serve in the Kings Majesties Navie, of which the fishermen of England have ever been the chiefest Seminarie and Nurserie." [8] Having been declining for the greater part of a century, such a fishing industry, requiring ships and trained men, could not be reestablished merely by royal decree. There appeared at this time a number of pamphlets lamenting the sorry state of fishing, shipping, and trade. English resentment against the Dutch is best summed up by the words of Nicolo Molin, the Venetian ambas-

7. Edmundson, *Anglo-Dutch Rivalry*, p. 78.
8. Ibid., pp. 21–25.

sador in London. In 1607 he reported to his government, "Just as this profession of the Sea is on the wane in England, so more and more is it increasing and acquiring force and vigour among the Dutch."

In May 1609, James issued an edict stating that "from beginning of August next, no person of whatever nation shall be permitted to fish on our coasts unless a license has been requested and obtained from us." This may well have been an answer to the famous treatise by Hugo Grotius, *Mare Liberum*, in which the Dutch jurist expounded the legal aspect of freedom of the seas. This treatise had been published in March 1609; it was a part of *De Jure Praedae* which had been written at the request of the Dutch East India Company for the express purpose of denying the Portuguese claim to Asiatic waters.[9] It served just as well to dispute the English claim of *Dominium Maris:* "Can the vast, boundless sea be the appanage of one country alone?" Grotius argued his case. "Can any one Nation have the right to prevent other nations which so desire from selling to one another, from bartering with one another?" And on the fisheries: "The right of fishing ought everywhere to be exempt from tolls, lest a servitude be imposed upon the Sea, which is not susceptible to a servitude." [10] It is interesting to note that Great Britain today employs somewhat the same argument in its dispute about fishing rights off the Icelandic coast. With Iceland arbitrarily extending her territorial waters, the British appeal to the same kind of established rights which James I denied the Dutch.

As soon as this edict was delivered to the Dutch, the doughty Oldebarnevelt reminded the English ambassador, Winwood, of the ancient treaty of 1295 and those subsequent which had reaffirmed the same rights. But James was obdurate, especially since he was constantly needled at home on this subject. In 1610 Sir Walter Raleigh, still in favor at court, admonished the king: "This great sea business of fishing should be kept in our hands . . . the Hollanders already have as many ships as eleven kingdoms, including England . . . they want the whole trade and shipping of Christendom in their hands." [11] The fires of dissension were aroused still more by the constant flow of pamphlets on this subject which were circulated in England. One such pamphlet was meant to be

9. See p. 131.

10. C. Wilson, *Profit and Power* (London, Longmans, Green, 1957), pp. 35–36.

11. W. Oldys and T. Birch, eds., *Raleigh's Works*, 8 (Oxford, 1829), 351–76.

a direct refutation of Grotius' *Mare Liberum*. It was published by William Wellwood, probably at King James' direction, and entitled *De Dominio Maris*. This attempted to prove that the sea may be privately possessed, and stated that England possessed the dominion of the sea over a zone extending one hundred miles from the shore. According to Barker, Wellwood's tract is a very poor exposition of international law, and it reveals with childlike simplicity the practical object of the treatise, declaring that "a nation which had become rich and haughty with the spoils of all peoples had claimed that the sea was free to all" and lamenting that "the British are robbed in their own seas by foreign fishers who, like an inundation, have overwhelmed their shores." [12] Another pamphlet made a similar impression upon the English, supporting their conviction that the seas should be theirs. Entitled *England's Way to Win Wealth* by Tobias, Gentleman, Fisherman, and Mariner, it appeared in 1614 and presented statistics on the herring fisheries and the profits of the Dutch. He admonished his countrymen to take a lesson from the Dutch and made them bridle under the alleged taunt of a Dutch fisherman: "Just be patient you English, we will let you wear our old shoes!" [13]

There were endless discussions on this subject between the two nations, and they led nowhere. The herring fisheries were too important to their economy for the Dutch to relinquish them. In 1611, the Venetian Marcantonio Correr related, "in the herring fisheries alone, the Dutch yearly send to the east coast of England 1,700 vessels, employing 30,000 men." Around 1619 the Dutch claimed it gave employment to 50,000, and as Charles Wilson points out, in *Profit and Power*, "The English were only too aware that the Dutch Gold Mine [the Great Fishery] was a shaft sunk, without permission and tribute, in what the new national consciousness chose to regard as British territory."

In 1617, the fisheries problem came to a head. James was determined to make the Dutch pay for the privilege of fishing in his waters and announced that every fishing boat would be taxed in money one angelot, worth about six guilders, or in kind, one barrel of herring and twelve codfish.[14] The king's collector of

12. See J.E. Barker, *The Rise and Decline of the Netherlands* (London, 1906), p. 262.
13. T.W. Fulton, *The Sovereignty of the Sea* (Edinburgh and London, 1911), p. 145.
14. Kranenburg, *De Zeevisscherij van Holland*, p. 144. A barrel contained about 100 Dutch pounds of herring, averaging 200 fish.

these fishing tolls, a certain John Browne, tried to execute his master's orders by force when the Dutch refused to pay. Jan Albertsz. the captain of the Dutch convoy ship guarding the Enkhuizen fleet, decided that the simplest way to solve the difficulty was to take John Browne prisoner. When this news reached London, James retaliated by imprisoning the captains of two Dutch merchantmen in the Thames. More deliberations followed, but the Dutch stood firm.[15] They referred to the old treaties, bolstered by the legal treatise of Grotius. Neither side wanted to go to war over this matter so long as there was a chance to solve it through diplomatic channels. Prince Maurice and the States General made it clear a few years later that the Dutch would go to war rather than give up their fishing rights.

Whaling in Arctic waters added to the Anglo-Dutch conflict. The only tangible result of the Dutch ventures to find a northern route to the Indies had been the discovery of large schools of whales in the waters near Spitsbergen. Keen to turn to advantage these otherwise profitless ventures of the final years of the sixteenth century, the Dutch began to develop a thriving whaling industry. The English navigators, Chancellor and Willoughby, had been the first to penetrate the Arctic seas; James believed this gave him claim to the waters by right of discovery. In 1613, he granted a charter to the Muscovy Company for sole fishing rights in the north. On their first venture, the English encountered a few Dutch whaling ships, which they boarded and plundered. The Dutch, with Plancius as their spokesman, argued vehemently that there was no foundation for the English claim, because it was on one of the voyages Plancius had planned that the Dutch had discovered Spitsbergen, when Barentsz. had tried in vain to reach Asia by setting a course across the North Pole.[16] The States General countered the English claim by issuing a charter in January 1614 to the Greenland Company. A few years later the Dutch retaliated and dispersed ships of the Muscovy Company.

These economic rivalries—the cloth trade, the herring fishery, and whaling—were vexing enough, but worse was to come when the English tried to reap benefits from what the Dutch had accomplished in the Indies.

15. Edmundson, *Anglo-Dutch Rivalry*, pp. 52-54.
16. Ibid., pp. 43-45.

5

The English
East India Company

The search for spices had taken the Dutch to the Indies, and
their proficiency in both shipping and overseas commerce made
it possible for them to develop a profitable trade soon after the
route had been established. Considering that the English had only
recently emerged from an agrarian and largely self-sufficient
economy, it is not surprising that they moved more slowly. Much
of what the English knew about shipping had been learned from
the Dutch, as had been the case in the weaving and other industries. Wilson also emphasizes this point: "Dutch sailors, ship-
wrights and merchants introduced many new words in our
nautical vocabulary—yacht, sloop, boom, skipper—and a hundred
others." [1]

There was nothing wrong, however, with English seamanship
once the skill had been mastered. It was put to good advantage
in the pursuit of piracy which, until the end of Elizabeth's reign,
was one of the favored exploits of English sailors. They actually
developed a greater daring on the high seas than the Dutch, who
preferred to stick to trading. This urge for adventure produced
men like Frobisher, Chancellor, Drake, and a host of others, who
blazed a trail to the far corners of the world while the Dutch
waited until they were certain such ventures would yield profits.
This English drive, according to Hunter, led to explorations, and
ended in a gold mania: "they developed into voyages, partly of
discovery though chiefly for plunder, of whose corsair-command-
ers Drake forms the heroic figure-head." [2]

The Dutch merchants recognized the spirit and ability of English sailors and did not hesitate to employ them when the occasion arose—Adams, Davis, Hudson, and others. It was mainly the
belated awareness of the importance of overseas trade, and the
relatively low esteem for the merchant class that made the English

1. C. Wilson, *Holland and Britain* (London, Collins, 1946), p. 12.
2. Hunter, *History of British India, 1,* 252–53.

fall behind the Dutch in the new economic age. This was true in the European trade where the Dutch had been dominant for a century or more, and it was now being repeated in the Asiatic trade as well.

These were the facts, and, for a nation that prided itself on a long history under a succession of illustrious monarchs, difficult to accept. London had been a thriving town a thousand years or more before Amsterdam even existed. English frustration was heightened even more by the recollections of the exploits of Francis Drake, the first Englishman to reach the Spice Islands on his famous voyage round the world, from which he returned with great treasure looted from the Spanish. But these and other feats had not been sufficiently supported. Pietro Contarini, the Venetian envoy, reported ca. 1617, "loud praises of past times and the worthy deeds of forefathers form the topic of conversation . . . Great Lords lament the present state." [3]

The first Englishman known to have visited India was Thomas Stephens. He had studied in Oxford, and in 1579 was rector at the Jesuits' college in Goa. The letters he wrote home were apparently circulated, thus creating an interest about this part of the world in England. As a result, an expedition, headed by the merchant Ralph Fitch, was organized to reach India by land through the Euphrates valley and to make contact with the rulers of Cambay and Cathay. At Ormuz, at the mouth of the Persian Gulf, Fitch and his companions were taken prisoner by the Portuguese and brought to Goa. After being released in 1584 the party broke up. Unconfirmed reports state that one of them married an Indian woman, another entered the service of Emperor Akbar, while a third became a monk at Goa. Ralph Fitch himself traveled further east, visiting Burma, Malaya, and other countries before he returned to England in 1591.[4] The account of his adventures roused the interest of London merchants. A company for trading with Turkey had already been established in 1581, and it now applied for a charter to extend its sphere of operations overland to the East Indies. The request was granted, but this Turkey (or Levant) Company never gained its objective, primarily because it suffered heavy losses in the Mediterranean from the Barbary pirates and the fleets of Philip of Spain.

The first English voyage to sail around the Cape of Good Hope

3. Edmundson, *Anglo-Dutch Rivalry*, p. 38.
4. Hunter, *British India*, *I*, 231–32.

(both Drake and Cavendish had followed Magellan's route) left in 1591. It was an unfortunate voyage, and of the three ships, only one returned in 1594 under Captain James Lancaster. Of the original complement of some two hundred men, all but 25 had perished. Nevertheless, Lancaster had reached Ceylon and the Malay Peninsula, and his one ship brought back a valuable cargo.[5] If this voyage had been followed up vigorously, the English might have been able to gain a firm foothold in the Spice Islands: the Amsterdam merchants were still in the planning stage. The merchants of London, however, were more preoccupied with either the Muscovy or the Levant Companies, each of which had a charter for overland travel to Asia. Neither company was anxious to have a third enter the field.

In 1596 another sea venture was launched, under the patronage of Sir Robert Dudley, son of the late Earl of Leicester. The three vessels, commanded by Benjamin Wood, were heard from only vaguely, then vanished completely; not a single man returned to tell what had happened. This still further dampened English enthusiasm for a direct route to the Indies.[6] At the same time the Dutch had raised the necessary capital and the fore-companies were sending out their first fleets.

The London merchants blew hot and cold on the subject, but national pride became aroused when the word spread that the Dutch were buying English ships, and there was a great deal of interest among the English people about the achievements of their own navigators. Richard Hakluyt, Preacher, as he signed himself, had published in 1589 *The Principal Navigations, Voyages and Discoveries of the English Nation*. The book was an immediate success, sufficient proof of public interest in this subject. A still greater interest was created when the first English edition of Linschoten's *Itinerary* appeared in 1598. His detailed account of the wealth of the Indies had already inspired the Dutch, and it now made the London merchants realize that something concrete should be done. The *Itinerary* was translated by William Phillip, and he prefaced the edition with an admonition which gave food for thought. "I doo not doubt," he wrote, "but yet I doo most heartily pray and wish that this poore Translation

5. C. R. Markham, *Voyages of Sir James Lancaster to the East Indies* (London, 1877).

6. Noel Sainsbury, ed., *Calendar of State Papers, East Indies, 1513–1616, 1* (London, 1870), par. 250.

may worke in our English nation a further desire and increase of honour over all Countreys of the Worlde by means of our Woodden Walles." [7]

Need for action on a direct route to the Indies had also become more pressing because of the failure to open an overland route by the Muscovy and the Levant Companies. European trade had also deteriorated, as is shown by Sir Walter Raleigh's bitter complaint: "Foermerly we sent store of goodly ships to trade in those parts, and three years past we sent out but four, and this last year two or three." He added, "The Dutch have gained all the foreign freight whilst our ships lie still and decay, or go to Newcastle for coals." [8]

In September 1599, two months after four Dutch ships had returned with unprecedented cargoes of spices, a number of London merchants, with the Lord Mayor presiding, met in Founders' Hall. They represented some one hundred citizens who had signified their willingness to subscribe over £30,000. They petitioned the queen for the privilege of establishing a joint stock company for the "Trade of the Indias." This time Elizabeth and her Privy Council were the stumbling block, the reason for their opposition being that to grant the petition would "forego the opportunity of the concluding of peace." France had already made peace with Spain, and similar negotiations were being conducted to end the state of war between England and Spain. With peace in the balance, Elizabeth did not want to antagonize Spain by granting a charter to a company that would prey on Spanish ships and trade.[9]

There followed a year of legal protestations to the court aiming to prove that Spain had no exclusive rights in the Indies. Two men, Thomas Smythe and Richard Staper, were particularly active in pressing the company's suit. Both had been among the founders of the Levant Company and, since its fortunes had ebbed, they were all the more anxious to establish a new company which would use a direct sea route. After a second Dutch fleet returned to Holland in May 1600 with a cargo as fabulous as the first, Elizabeth began to realize that the potentials of the Indies trade outweighed any ill effects it might have on her relations with Spain.

7. A. C. Burnell and P. A. Tiele, eds., *The Voyage of John Huyghen van Linschoten to the East Indies, 1* (London, 1885), p. 52.

8. Oldys and Birch, eds., *Raleigh's Works, 8* (Oxford, 1829), 351-76.

9. Henry Stevens, *The Dawn of British Trade to the East Indies* (London, 1886), p. 10.

On December 31, 1600, Elizabeth granted the charter, "For the Honour of our Nation, the Wealth of our People, the Increase of our Navigation, and the advancement of Lawful Traffick to the benefit of our Commonwealth." [10] The charter was for a period of fifteen years, but the operation was only continuous as far as the membership was concerned. Each voyage was considered to be a separate venture for which money had to be raised, and which had to be liquidated upon its completion. This was similar to the pattern of the first Dutch companies before they amalgamated into the United East India Company in 1602. The capital the English subscribed this time was some £68,000, more than twice what had been available the year before but still no larger than the average of the seven or eight fore-companies operating out of the Lowlands. After these Dutch companies were consolidated, the United East India Company had a capital of about 6,500,000 florins (£540,000) or eight times as much as the English company could command. It follows that its accomplishments would be in somewhat the same proportion.

Alderman Thomas Smythe became the first Governor of the "Honourable Company of Merchants of London Trading into the East Indies," as it was originally called. The address was listed "At Mr. Smythe's house in Philpot Lane," where it was to occupy a few rooms for the first twenty years of its existence.[11] The English Company was equally frugal in other respects, using a book of the Levant Company to record its early proceedings. Elizabeth intended to maintain a strict control over the Company; a separate commission had to be obtained for each subsequent voyage. The sale of pepper at London had to be delayed until after the royal share had been sold, thus giving the crown the benefit of a non-competitive market. In other respects, such as the emphasis on participation by individuals rather than anonymous capital, the English Company retained many of the characteristics of the earlier trade guilds. Hunter concludes that it was "an intermediate link between the medieval guilds and a modern commercial association." By eliminating this transitional phase, the Dutch Company was more nearly the forerunner of the stock companies as we know them today.

10. G. Birdwood and W. Foster, eds., *The First Letter Book of the East India Company, 1600–1619* (London, 1893), pp. 163–89. The original charter is missing.

11. For Thomas Smythe and details of the Company's housekeeping in London, see W. Foster, *John Company* (London, John Lane, 1926), pp. 1–30.

In its management, the English Company also differed from the Dutch Company, in which the Seventeen had complete authority. The governing board of the English Company consisted of the governor, his deputy, a treasurer, and 24 committeemen. They had to submit all decisions to the "General Courts" which included all the "freemen" of the Company and which could (although it rarely did so), overrule the board. Since each voyage was a separate financial enterprise, the Board of Governors was actually no more than a connecting link between various groups of investors.[12] As the Dutch had already learned, such a system would cause great conflict of interest in the Indies, with different commanders, each responsible to their own group of investors, competing against each other for the purchase of spices.

A slight improvement was made in 1612 when money was raised not for a single voyage but for several, to last over a certain number of years. This, however, proved to be only a halfway measure and did little to solve the basic problem of coordinating the activities of the Company for the benefit of all its stockholders, as the Dutch had done in 1602. Not until sixty years later, in 1661, did the English finally abandon their adherence to the remnants of a guild system.

James Lancaster, a man of proven ability, commanded the four ships of the first voyage which left England in April 1601. Lancaster was eminently successful because, aside from obtaining full cargoes of spices, he also captured a Portuguese carack, "richly laden." One of his ships had preceded him home, and when the news reached London that his *Ascension* was at the mouth of the Thames, the Board of Governors ordered "six suits of canvas doublet *without* pockets" for the dockers who had to unload the precious cargo.[13] The profit on this initial venture would have been enormous had all the cargoes been sold promptly. Pepper bought at Bantam for less than sixpence per pound was worth that many shillings or more at London. Unfortunately, the plague of 1603 had brought all business to a standstill, making the governors lament that "Trade hath utterly ceased within the City for almost half a year." [14]

After local conditions had somewhat improved, difficulty arose

12. Real authority, however, was in the hands of the governor, the deputy governor, and the treasurer, who "thus exercised a unifying influence in the midst of conflicting and overlapping interests." See Hunter, *British India*, 1, 270–71.

13. Sainsbury, ed., *Calendar of State Papers, East Indies*, par. 321.

14. Birdwood and Foster, eds., *First Letter Book*, p. 39.

about the disposal of the spices. For a company which lacked experience in the intricate facets of foreign trade, selling its goods to best advantage was a problem. Participants had to accept their share in kind, thus each had to sell his pepper as best he could. It was 1609 before this first venture was finally liquidated. It showed a profit of 95 per cent, but, with the money tied up for a period of about eight years, this was hardly a suitable return.

At the time the charter was granted, it had been contemplated that the Company should send out "six good ships and six pinnaces at all times." Elizabeth understood this to mean on a yearly basis. By the end of 1601, she became displeased with the tardiness of the Company in making preparations for a subsequent voyage, and admonished the governors "to heed the example of the Dutch, who do prosecute their voyages with a more honourable resolution." [15]

The Governors found it extremely difficult to raise the necessary capital, and it took three years after the first voyage before a second set sail. This was only made possible by using the same four ships of the first voyage, and by putting their profits in escrow for the second voyage. The combined value of trade goods and silver amounted to only £12,000, less than half of what was carried on the first venture.

There was a good reason why the English Company found it difficult to compete with the Dutch at this stage. English merchandise, consisting mainly of woolen textiles, had virtually no market in the Indies. Silver was the favorite medium of exchange for buying spices and other Asiatic goods. The Dutch, with their near monopoly of European trade, had little difficulty tapping the vast store of silver that Spain gathered yearly in the Americas. The English had no such ready source of bullion. The store of precious metals was considered the yardstick of a country's national wealth, and every English court, backed by its Privy Council, jealously guarded the supply of silver in England.[16] As a result the English East India Company had great difficulties in obtaining royal permission for the export of a commodity which was indispensable in the pursuit of Asiatic trade. It is under-

15. Hunter, *British India, 1,* 280–81.
16. Gerard de Malynes, *A Treatise of the Canker of England's Commonwealth* (London, 1601). For a more enlightened view of this problem, see Adam Smith, *The Wealth of Nations, 2* (4th ed. London, 1786), 139–75.

standable that, under these circumstances, investors expected more from privateering than from normal trade.

The second voyage was commanded by Henry Middleton. At Bantam he loaded two ships with pepper and sent the other two to Amboyna for cloves. Although one ship foundered on the homeward journey, this venture also showed a modest profit. The subscribers, however, were far from satisfied, primarily because of disappointing yields and the tardy disbursement by the governors. It was reported that "most of the Members were inclined to wind up their affairs and drop the business." [17] Another factor cooled the ardor of the London merchants. After James I had ascended the throne, one of his first acts was to make peace with Spain. This eliminated any possible windfalls through the capture of Spanish and Portuguese prizes. Nor did James fully respect the rights granted the Company by Elizabeth.

In 1604, James granted a license to one of his favorites, Sir Edward Michelborne, a soldier-adventurer of the Elizabethan school, "for discovery and trade from India to China." It turned out to be nothing more than a pirating expedition. There could be no pretense that it was based on lawful privateering because England, at that time, was not at war with any nation. Michelborne's activities blackened the name of the English in Asiatic waters, and at Bantam he made the mistake of plundering a Dutch vessel. "If there should any more such as he be permitted by His Majesty to come into these parts," the English factor at Bantam wrote to London, "our estate here would be very dangerous." [18]

It was mainly because of the exhortations of James, including a veiled threat that the charter might be revoked, that made the governors send out its third fleet of three ships in the year 1607, the captains being Keeling, Hawkins, and David Middleton. Then came the fourth voyage in 1608—two ships both of which were lost. In 1609 there was a fifth voyage, comprising just one ship and involving a capital of about £14,000, a fraction of what had been subscribed for the first English voyage. Thus, over a period of nine years, the English had managed to fit out fourteen ships in all.[19] This was about the strength of a single fleet which the Dutch Company was able to dispatch almost every other year.

17. Hunter, *British India*, *1*, 284–85.
18. Idem.
19. For this early phase of the English Company, see also Hall, *History of South-East Asia*, pp. 235–39.

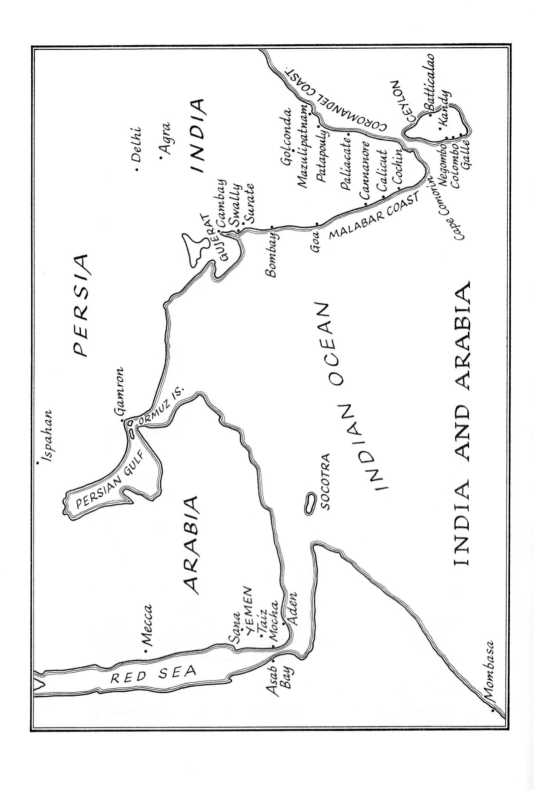

INDIA AND ARABIA

6

A Servant
of the
English Company

It was as a result of their third voyage on behalf of the London Company that the English made their first contact with the Mogul Empire in North India. It occurred in 1607, thus adding another important event to that burgeoning year, and it paved the way for the English to develop a foothold in India proper after they had withdrawn from Southeast Asia and Japan. Personnel of the fourth voyage participated in making this contact after their ships had foundered. One of the men on this voyage was a merchant named John Jourdain who, more than any other servant of the English Company, can be called the counterpart of Jan Coen.[1] Their occasional meetings signify the conflict between the two companies, and Jourdain's experiences reveal the somewhat different approach the English used in their dealings in Asia. Both companies were, of course, interested in spices, but the Dutch made the producing areas in the East Indies their primary goal. The English, perhaps intrigued by the early adventures of their own countrymen, Stephens and Fitch, devoted part of their endeavors to Northern India, Persia, and Arabia. This division of interest, considering the limited resources of the English Company, weakened their position in the Spice Islands and in other parts of East Asia. Jourdain's death preceded by only a few years the complete withdrawal of the English from this area.

John Jourdain was engaged by the English Company on December 7, 1607, as "General and Chiefe Factor" as a salary of £3 per month. He received an additional £10 for his outfit. This

1. W. Foster, ed., *The Journal of John Jourdain, 1608–1617* (Hakluyt Society, 2d series, *16*, Cambridge, 1905). Most of the material in this chapter has been derived from this source.

date was within weeks of the time that Jan Coen had entered the service of the Dutch Company, at an almost identically small salary.[2] Here the comparison ends because, while Jan Coen was a young man starting his career, Jourdain was a mature man of about thirty-five years with a great deal of experience. He was born in 1572 or 1573, at Lyme Regis in Dorsetshire. His father was a man of some importance, eventually becoming mayor of the town and at his death leaving £400 to his widow and "lands and houses to each of his four sons." According to available records, John Jourdain was trading with the Azores and other Portuguese possessions on his own account as early as 1595, and he remained in this trade until the year he joined the English Company.

By that time he was, if not affluent, a man with an established business. He was married to a woman of his own town by whom he had two children, a daughter, and a son named John. It has been a matter of speculation as to what could have prompted Jourdain to give up this more or less settled way of life for an uncertain future in Asia, at a salary which must have been considerably less than his income as an independent merchant. It could hardly have been the sole urge for adventure; for this he was too old and he must have had adventure enough during the twelve years he had sailed hither and yon. Although Jourdain kept a voluminous journal covering his experiences with the Company, he never referred to his private life, but there is at least one record which might throw some light on his reasons for leaving home and hearth.

Shortly before sailing on his second voyage to the Indies, in February 1618, Jourdain made a will appointing his sister, Mrs. Susan Viney, executrix and leaving to her and her children a large part of his estate. To his wife he left nothing directly and only made provision that a sum of £550 be invested and the interest of it be paid to her for the support of his son, John, who was then still a minor. If John married, the whole amount should be paid to him. Since John died that same year, Jourdain's wife was, for some reason or other, completely excluded from his will. It is dangerous to draw conclusions from this meager evidence,

---

2. The dates in this chapter follow the Julian or Old Style calendar, to which the English adhered long after the continent of Europe had adopted the Gregorian calendar, which advanced the date by ten days. Thus December 7 in England was December 17 in Holland.

but perhaps it is suggestive that Jourdain's journal records that he hated bickering, of which there was a great deal among the servants of the English Company. Whether he simply tried to get away from a nagging wife or whether there was a more profound reason must remain unanswered questions.

John Jourdain sailed from Woolwich on March 14, 1608. He had been assigned to the *Ascension*, a ship of 260 tons which was commanded by Alexander Sharpeigh and had already made one voyage for the Company. The other vessel was the *Union*, an old ship of 400 tons which had been bought for a mere £1,250. By the end of April, the two ships reached Ilha de Mayo in the Cape Verde group and learned that "Thirteen sayle of Flemings" had been there two months earlier. As their journey continued, the English were constantly reminded that they were sailing in the wake of Verhoef's fleet.

On July 4 the *Ascension* was overtaken by the Dutch pinnace *Good Hope* which had been dispatched by the Seventeen to inform Verhoef of the impending truce with Spain. Ten days later, the two English ships reached the Cape of Good Hope where it was decided to build a pinnace for easier reconnoitering of the coastal areas they were to visit. At the Cape they found the Dutch had left some sheep and a pewter plate nailed to a stake, with Verhoef's name scratched on it. This was a favorite method of the Dutch to let it be known that they had passed certain points.

Jourdain made an astute observation about the Cape itself. It appeared to him that it was an excellent place for refreshment and that a fort should be built there.[3] It is indicative of the relative strength of the rival nations that it was the Dutch who first settled this strategic spot. The two English ships and the newly built pinnace left the Cape on September 19, only to be driven apart the following day by a storm. The *Union* disappeared completely and was never heard from again.

After a great deal of trouble at various places along the African coast, especially with "treacherous merchants" near Mombassa, the *Ascension* reached the island of Socotra near the mouth of the Red Sea on March 30, 1609. This rather inhospitable place was known to produce aloes, a product widely in demand as a purgative. The English also hoped to gather there some information about Aden and Mocha, the two ports which served as transit points for the ancient trade between the Indies and the Mediter-

3. Foster, *Journal*, pp. 18–19.

ranean. The *Ascension* arrived at Aden on April 7, the first English ship to reach this key point of the future British empire.

All the Arabian coastal areas were in Turkish hands, and the English had to deal with the local governor, a young renegade Greek named Rajab. He was the favorite of the highest Turkish official in Yemen (the legendary realm of the Queen of Sheba), a Hungarian who had his seat in the interior and who was known as the Pasha of Sana. Rajab played cat and mouse with the English, demanding the usual gifts and high levies, but claiming to have no authority to allow them trading facilities. On May 15 the boredom was relieved by the arrival of the pinnace, from which the *Ascension* had been separated for eight months. It brought no happy tidings. The crew had mutinied en route and had murdered the captain by "bashing his brains out with a mallet while he was leaning over the rail." A jury of seamen condemned the two main culprits to hanging.[4]

Since nothing could be accomplished at Aden, it was decided to send Jourdain overland about 300 miles to the north to Sana. There, while the *Ascension* would continue to Mocha, he would plead with the Pasha in person. Jourdain left on May 26 and covered the distance in about fifteen days, traveling by camel and mostly at night to escape the heat of the day. He was the first European to penetrate into the interior of Arabia. The main purpose of Jourdain's mission was to obtain permission to establish an English factory, but the Pasha was unwilling to allow this without explicit orders from the Grand Turk at Damascus. Jourdain noticed how thoroughly the traders from Gujerat were entrenched at Sana, whence they controlled most of the Red Sea traffic through their agents along the coast. He also remarked on the large number of Arab hostages—more than a thousand—that the Turks were holding at the capital to keep the Arab population in check.

After a week, Jourdain retraced his steps, with nothing more to show for his arduous journey than a pass for trading privileges for the duration of the *Ascension*'s stay in Yemen waters. At Taiz, the second largest town in the interior, Jourdain turned west towards Mocha.[5] As the small Banda group was the only source for nutmegs and mace, so was the hinterland of Mocha the only place in the world where coffee was produced in com-

4. Ibid., pp. 78–80.
5. Ibid., pp. 81–98.

mercial quantities; an average of 16,000 bags were shipped yearly to Suez. In 1609 Jourdain was the first European to visit this important area, not to be followed until 1616 by the Dutchman Van den Broek, who repeated the performance. The English Company might have benefited from this early contact, but, while spices had been used in Europe for centuries past, the taste of coffee was still unknown.[6] The first coffee reached Europe around 1616, imported at Venice via the Levant, but it was not until 1652 that the first coffeehouse was opened in London to be followed by many others.

Arriving at Mocha on June 30, Jourdain learned that his commander, Sharpeigh, had allowed the local governor to deceive him, which caused Jourdain to note: "Butt is a general rule with the English that if they have but a parcell of faire words given, that there neede noe more feare." [7] By a rare coincidence, Jan Coen had come to the same conclusion about the gullibility of his own countrymen when he witnessed the massacre of the trusting Admiral Verhoef and his council at Banda at almost the same time. Other entries in Jourdain's journal show that the English and the Dutch were of one mind in realizing what they were up against in their dealings with the Moslems. "I wish all Christians to beware of them," he put down, "for they are full of treachery, and never hold their words except it be for their own profits." [8]

By the end of July the *Ascension* left Mocha for Surate to contact some of their countrymen of the previous voyage, hoping to find a more congenial reception. But worse was in store for them. On September 2, the *Ascension* ran aground on the shoals at the mouth of the Gulf of Cambay. The crew had to abandon ship, but they managed to reach land by open boat with part of their trade goods. Jourdain blamed the skipper (chief navigator) for this misfortune, calling him "drunken, headstrong, and reckless." This skipper was a Dutchman, actually a Fleming, named Philip de Grave, a man of proven ability and experience in the service of the English Company by whom he had been

6. Van den Broek had this to say about coffee: "It is a kind of black beans . . . of which they make a black water and drink warm." See Glamann, *Dutch Asiatic Trade* (Copenhagen and The Hague), p. 183.

7. Foster, *Journal*, p. 99. To this Jourdain adds, "the Turks themselves saye: 'If thou wilt have anie thinge of an Englishman, give him good words and thou shalt bee sure to wynne him.'"

8. Ibid., pp. 102–03.

employed from the start. He had been a second pilot on the first voyage and master of the *Dragon* on the second, but on the third, his luck ran out as it did with so many others who tempted fate during those early years. The next year he lost his life, dying on an overland voyage from Surate to Mazulipatnam. It was said he had been murdered.

Both vessels having foundered, the fourth voyage of the English had to be written off as a total loss. There were only a few survivors left, among them Sharpeigh and Jourdain, who might still serve the Company to some advantage. In the beginning, this meager dividend did not seem to be promising because Jourdain's experiences in northern India were as fruitless as those in Yemen, and a great deal more time was wasted.

Captain William Hawkins had arrived at Surate in 1607, carrying a royal missive from James I to the Emperor Akbar, who had died in 1605. His son, Jehangir, had ascended the throne and Hawkins traveled to Agra to present his credentials. At first he was received well enough, although the emperor was not greatly impressed by a letter from an unknown king delivered to him by a simple ship's captain. As elsewhere in Asia, the Portuguese did all they could to blacken the name of their competitors, in this case the English.

In this they had the willing cooperation of the queen mother, Akbar's widow. She was an important merchant, with ships sailing to Mocha for her own account, and did not welcome newcomers who were anxious to trade in the same commodities as she. Hawkins married an Indian woman and tried hard to remain in favor at the court, his main object being permission for the English Company to establish a factory at Surate.

Soon after the crew of the foundered *Ascension* had reached Surate, Sharpeigh joined Hawkins at Agra while Jourdain stayed behind to manage the affairs of the Company as best he could. This turned out to be a difficult problem because of the cupidity of the chief merchant in the town, a certain Hoghanazan, onetime governor of the province. After more than a year of enforced idleness and frustration, Jourdain was summoned by Sharpeigh and Hawkins to sell the company goods at any price and join them in Agra.

Once more Jourdain set out on an overland journey. He left Surate on December 15, 1610 and arrived at Agra two months later. He found little to encourage him, and it was obvious that Hawkins had made the English position almost untenable at court. Jourdain noted that Hawkins had pressed hard for payment for goods he had sold in Surate, had bought indigo which had been set aside for the queen mother, and had appeared at court while he was drunk. After months of idleness at Agra, Jourdain and Sharpeigh decided to return to the coast, hoping to contact ships of a subsequent voyage. The conditions under which they left appear from the following entry in Jourdain's journal: "Hawkins, out of his liberalitye, gave me 100 mahmudis [equal to £4] for my expense down, which I would have refused but I thought it better to depart in peace than otherwise." [9]

Their expectations of contacting English ships proved correct for when they arrived at the coast in October 1611, they learned that Henry Middleton had recently arrived "before the barre with three ships and a pinnace." Unfortunately there was a Portuguese fleet of twenty sails on hand to prevent them from landing. Through natives, Jourdain established contact with Middleton, but when the latter asked the Portuguese for a safe conduct to allow the English merchants to board his ship, the Portuguese admiral haughtily replied that he would "take them to Goa and show them as much courtesy as as he would do to Turks, Moors, and other nations that use these seas." [10]

Eventually, on October 14, Jourdain managed to board the *Peppercorn*. He was able to tell Middleton of a safer anchorage further north where the larger Portuguese ships would have trouble following him. This was a town called Swally, which later was the famed Swally Hole in the annals of the English Company. The *Peppercorn* and the *Darling* safely crossed the bar at Swally but Middleton's flagship, the *Trades Increase*, had to stay outside because of its size.

The *Trades Increase* was the most ambitious undertaking of the English Company to date. It had been launched in 1609 and measured no less than 1,100 tons. As related in the *Marine Records of the East India Company*, James I named the ship and witnessed the launching with his queen, the prince, and most of his court. The governors regaled him with "a great banquet, all served on dishes and plates of China-ware. The King put a chain of gold

9. Ibid., pp. 154–67: Jourdain's observations about the situation in Agra.
10. Ibid., p. 176, n. 3.

and a medal around the neck of Sir Thomas Smythe." It is further noted that "for beauty, burthen, strength, and sufficiency, the ship surpasses all merchants ships whatsoever." [11]

With this powerful vessel, attempts were renewed to open trade relations with the merchants of Gujerat and Cambay. Negotiations started off well enough, and Jehangir's governor was greatly impressed during his visit on the *Trades Increase*. With this heightened prestige, there was talk that the English might be allowed to establish a factory at Surate, but this expectation was short-lived. Trouble arose with the wily Hoghanazan about weights, and the arguments rose to such bitterness that Middleton laid hands on the merchant while he was on board the *Peppercorn*. Although more serious consequences were avoided, this incident did little to promote a harmonious relationship. The Portuguese saw their opportunity to try to evict their rivals. Late in November and again in December, they attacked while the English were ashore guarding their goods. Both times the Portuguese were beaten off, but the people were not at all pleased with this armed conflict between two foreign powers on their soil. The Portuguese had been in India for close to a century and so far appeared to be more powerful than the English. It was not difficult for Jehangir to decide between the two.

English prestige deteriorated rapidly. They were blamed for delaying the departure of the *Rahimi*, a large vessel of 1,200 tons belonging to the queen mother and bound for Mocha with a valuable cargo. With the Portuguese and English fighting each other off the coast, there was fear that the *Rahimi* might become involved. Jehangir complained that he had lost one million mahmudis in customs because the presence of the English fleet was interfering with normal trade. In January 1612, the Emperor revoked his tentative offer to allow the English trading privileges at or near Surate, and ordered them to leave forthwith.

Middleton summoned his general council to decide upon the next step. His own instructions were to proceed to Bantam for a cargo of pepper, but this prospect did not seem enticing. Bantam was far away, and the plan was rejected for the time being because, according to Jourdain, "for want of provisions, and that ships of another voyage had already been there, not leaving enough pepper to lade our vessels." It was suggested that they

11. Hunter, *British India, 1*, 288–89.

sail to Goa and demand satisfaction from the viceroy for the losses he had caused the English at Surate. But another plan met with the best response: to sail to the Red Sea and intercept the native vessels heading for Mocha. The distance was short and promised immediate returns. Although it was piracy pure and simple, Middleton and his council took the stand that such action was justified by the wrongs they had suffered at Surate, and at the hands of the Turks in Yemen.[12] It would be a simple matter to blockade the entrance to the Red Sea and take booty to their hearts' content.

Arriving in the strait at the beginning of April 1612, Middleton unexpectedly found himself forestalled by his own countrymen, the three ships sent out by the London Company in April 1611 under Captain John Saris. Saris must have read Middleton's mind: he had already taken some vessels before Mocha. From the start there was bitter rivalry between the two commanders. Each voyage was a separate undertaking, backed by different subscribers, and there thus arose a dispute about the division of the spoils. On April 15 the two men were on the verge of coming to blows. Saris vowed that he would sail to windward and intercept the Indian vessels sailing to the Red Sea. Middleton countered by threatening to fire on Saris' ships and sink them if he carried out his plan. After three days, the two buccaneers arrived at a provisional agreement. Saris would hold on to what he had already taken, but future booty was to be divided on the basis of two thirds to Middleton's company and one third to Saris'. By the end of the month, the English had taken twelve Indian vessels, including the queen mother's *Rahimi*. The prizes were taken to Asab Bay on the African coast opposite Mocha, where arrangements were to be made for the disposal of the cargo on the best possible terms for the English, and with at least a semblance of legality.

The system the English evolved was a kind of bartering arrangement enforced upon the Indian merchants, which they tried to justify in a letter Middleton wrote to the Great Mogul, Jehangir. This letter was translated into Portuguese by John Jourdain, and contained a number of half-truths and exaggerations of the 'bad treatment' the English had suffered at Surate, such as the slighting remarks made in Agra about King James, when Hawkins asked for a reply to his king's message to the Mogul

12. Foster, *Journal*, pp. 196–97.

emperor. Abdul Hazan, Jehangir's chief minister, had then stated: "It was not the custome of so great a monarch to write in the kind of letter unto a pettie prince." [13]

The terms of the English barter were apparently quite profitable: the division of the proceeds caused a renewed outbreak of vituperation between Middleton and Saris. There were other differences, some of them rather childish. Jourdain wrote that there were "very gross speeches, not fitting for men of their rank." Middleton threatened to put a dagger in Saris' throat, claiming for all to hear that "he was a more important man—the King knew him, but not Saris." [14]

When Jourdain heard that Middleton intended to send the *Darling* to Sumatra, to pre-empt the pepper market, he asked to go along, "myself being weary to see and heare daily such controversies between the two Generalls." After supper on the *Trades Increase* on May 18, "Wee took our leaves of him, leaving them with their dissention and their prizes together." The *Darling* arrived at Tiku on July 7, only to be met by one of Saris' ships. Saris was no fool, and when he had correctly guessed his rival's plan, he had sent the *Thomas* to beat Middleton at his own game. The chief merchant on the *Thomas* had been given a sealed letter from Middleton for the master of the *Darling* but "he had opened it," Jourdain reports, "and made a copye and cunningly sealed it again. But the heads not being there, we proceeded like loving friends."

The merchants of the two competing ships got along well together. They agreed to trade at different ports and to keep in touch with each other in order not to spoil the market by overbidding. This harmony was quickly dispelled when another of Saris' ships arrived at Tiku, the *Hector* under Captain Towerson. "Having had his Generall's lesson," Jourdain wrote in his journal, "he told us that our General Middleton was returning to England and, seeing that the *Darling* was so leaky, we should put our pepper on his ship." Jourdain, being a sound merchant, refused to part with any of his cargo without written instructions from Middleton, which Towerson of course could not produce. So great was the rivalry between personnel of the separate voyages that, when the *Darling* requested Towerson for some much needed

13. For a copy of this letter, see Foster, *Journal*, pp. 218–24.
14. Ibid., p. 216, n. 1.

victuals and supplies, "he would not spare us anything." [15]

Eventually all ships of both voyages arrived on the coast of Sumatra, competing against each other for the limited supply of pepper available. As a result, none obtained a full cargo. One by one the ships sailed on to Bantam, and John Jourdain arrived there in the *Darling* on December 22, 1612. His former chief, Sharpeigh, had preceded him by a few weeks and had already departed on a native vessel for Sukadana on Borneo where he expected to buy diamonds. On this trip he died.

At Bantam arose again the ever recurring quarrels between Middleton and Saris, this time over the appointment of a chief factor. Eventually Saris sailed to Japan, making a name for himself by opening this trade for the English Company, although its activities there lasted only ten years. The *Trades Increase*, that proud ship, came to an inglorious end. She had sprung a bad leak on the coast of Sumatra and had been careened at Pulu Pandjang in the Bay of Bantam for repairs. Here she caught fire, and her timbers were left rotting in the mud. Henry Middleton died at Bantam shortly afterwards.

John Jourdain was not present when it happened. In February, he had sailed with the *Darling* to the Moluccas at Middleton's request. Jourdain had told him that he "was not wedded to Bantam and would go at his pleasure to do the Worshipful Company any service." [16] Jourdain had been traveling now for five years; it was not his fault that he had accomplished so little during this long period. He was now about to meet Jan Coen, who had started his first voyage to the Indies at about the same time as Jourdain, and who was now also headed for the Moluccas, where the two would meet face to face.

15. Ibid., pp. 232–34.
16. Ibid., p. 243.

7

Up
the
Ladder

Jan Coen had returned to Holland in the latter part of 1610. He had been away for about three years and during his absence the Seventeen had made an important decision. The system of having the last arriving admiral supersede his predecessor had proved unsatisfactory, making for divided authority in the Indies which, in turn, led to mismanagement and negligence on the part of the Company's servants. Above all, it did not provide continuity of sustained effort for the United Company. The directors had only to look at the returns on the capital invested to realize that a change had to be made. The profits had dropped from 75 per cent in 1606 and before to 40 per cent in 1607, 20 per cent in 1608, and 25 per cent in 1609.[1] The telling fact was that they were steadily declining, and to a level hardly commensurate with the risk of enterprise.

In consultation with the States General, it was decided to appoint a governor general who would hold office for an unspecified number of years and who would be assisted by a Council of the Indies consisting of five members in which the governor general would have a deciding voice.[2] In principle it was the same system followed on the various fleets where important decisions had to be made by a plenary council presided over by the admiral. The Seventeen had no intention of putting their affairs into the hands of a single man, and all decisions had to be made in council. This was parallel to the national Republic as well, which had rebelled

1. H. P. Geerke, *Jan Pieterszoon Coen* (Utrecht, W. de Haan, 1929), pp. 41–42. Compare Mansvelt, *Rechtsvorm en geldelijk beheer bij de Oost-Indische Compagnie* (Amsterdam, 1922), pp. 80–81. The first dividend was declared in 1610, a total of 132.5 per cent covering eight years of operation.
2. De Jonge, *Opkomst*, 3, 129–34. For a detailed account of this important resolution by the Seventeen, dated September 1, 1609, see P. Mijer, *Verzameling van instructien, ordonnantien en regelementen voor de regering van N.I., 1609–1836* (Batavia, 1848).

against putting too much power into the hands of one man. The system, of course, had its disadvantages, but occasionally there appeared a man who by ability and sheer strength of character managed to gather the reins into his own hands. Such a man was Jan Coen, the fourth to hold the important office of governor general.

Jan Coen spent over a year in Holland before he sailed again in 1612. Very little is known about this interval, but there can be little doubt that he made a good impression on the Seventeen, because when he did sail he had the title of Chief Merchant and was put in command of two ships though he was only twenty-five years old. It is known that he submitted a report on conditions in the Indies and on what, in his opinion, should be done to improve matters. The report itself is lost, but Coen referred to it in a subsequent document, of which mention will be made later.

It is also possible that Jacques l'Hermite, the former president at Bantam and a member of the first Council of the Indies, may have recommended the young man for a higher post. He had returned to Holland late in 1611, and thus had opportunity to continue discussions he may have had with Coen at Bantam. L'Hermite himself presented an elaborate report about the state of affairs in the Indies at a meeting of the Seventeen on August 20, 1612, some two months after Coen's departure on his second voyage. In this report l'Hermite suggested that a director general be appointed with a permanent residence, at Bantam for the time being, so that all the commercial activities of the Company could be coordinated and continued without interruption even when conditions demanded the presence of the governor general in the Moluccas or elsewhere. Jan Coen was the first to be appointed to this office. The report also mentioned the need for a general rendezvous where the Company could establish its headquarters.

There was also mention of the need for "planting colonies" of Dutch families, especially in the Spice Islands, where they could become a welcome balance for the troublesome native traders. Nor did l'Hermite overlook the English who, by taking advantage of the cupidity of the natives, were trying hard to undermine the Dutch wherever they could.[3] There is no direct proof

3. "Short Remonstration of the present state of certain places in the Indies and what remedies should be taken about them," reprinted from the original in the Dutch National Archives in De Jonge, *Opkomst, 3,* 380–94.

that Jan Coen had a hand in l'Hermite's report, but such problems as a rendezvous, colonization, the Spice Islands, and the English, were to be among Coen's major preoccupations during the whole of his subsequent career.

It is also quite possible that it was merely the impression he made on the Seventeen when he reported to them about the train of events on the unfortunate Verhoef voyage that led to his appointment. No minutes of such a meeting are left, but it can safely be assumed that it took place. The Seventeen were not in the habit of appointing someone to a responsible position without subjecting him to a penetrating cross-examination. Whatever young Coen had to tell about himself must have impressed Reynier Pauw who, twenty years earlier, had launched the first attempts to enter the Indies trade. Now close to fifty, already three times Mayor of Amsterdam and on the verge of taking over the Magnificat, he may have remembered his own ambition when he was the same age as the young man standing before them.

There are in existence two paintings of Jan Coen.[4] They show a long, narrow face with deep-set brown eyes. The nose is well proportioned but large and long; there are deep grooves on either side running down the cheeks. Coen has a strong mouth with thin lips, and his lower jaw juts out; his short beard and long moustache, curved up at the ends, are reddish. His dark brown hair is kept short and comes down his high forehead in something of a widow's peak. The cheekbones are pronounced and the cheeks are hollow. The whole face is drawn in sharp lines and planes, giving him a dour expression. Old Dutch historians, such as Velius and Valentyn, describe Coen as being taller than average, the more pronouncedly so because he was a slender man with large bony hands and pointed fingers. He was nicknamed *De Schraale*, literally meaning "spare and lanky" but which also alludes to his gaunt and grim appearance.

This much can be discerned from his portraits, but what were his other characteristics? Very little material is available about them from Coen's own contemporaries. One of these, Aert Gysels, called him a man "full of Italian tricks." This was not meant as a compliment, for it must be remembered that Gysels bore a

4. One, a somewhat primitive portrait on a wood panel, is at the Rijks Museum in Amsterdam. Presumably it was painted in Batavia during Coen's first tenure as governor general. The other, in the heroic tradition of the time, is at the West-Frisian Museum in Hoorn.

5. *Jan Pieterszoon Coen, ca. 1626.*

grudge against Coen, who had once fined him heavily for being delinquent in his duties to the Company. With such a paucity of eyewitness reports, an evaluation of Coen's character and mentality can be made only by a psychographic analysis based on his writings and actions. Such a study was made in 1933 by Bergman, who consulted more than 1,200 items, and produced the following evaluation: [5]

> He was a reserved man, always preoccupied with what he considered to be his duty. He was cool and businesslike, often critical of others and not likely to forgive easily. He was persevering to a degree of stubbornness. He was a good judge of people and constant in his affections. He had a great practical ability and was a wizard at figures. He was self-centered, hard to talk to, and minced no words. He could be extremely sarcastic but it is interesting to note that he was more inclined to be so towards his superiors, the Seventeen, than to his subordinates. He was highly religious, as most men of his time, but as a Calvinist he was void of any frivolities and one must look in vain for evidence that he had a sense of humor. Coen was obviously not a man with whom to spend a pleasant evening or with whom one would feel at home, but he was just the man the Seventeen needed.[6]

In the words of the Dutch historian Romein, Coen was a hardbitten authoritarian, a man without friends and without a smile, a realist who accepted every responsibility because things *had* to be done.[7] An evaluation of the man Coen is not quite so simple, as will readily appear from the following chapters.

Jan Coen was twenty-five years old when he sailed on May 12, 1612 as Chief Merchant in command of two ships. At Ilha Bravo, in the Cape Verde Islands, 13 of his men were ambushed after he had specifically warned them to be on the alert, remembering all too vividly what had happened to Admiral Verhoef on Banda.[8]

5. R. A. M. Bergman, "Jan Pieterszoon Coen, een psychographie," *TBG*, 73 (1934), 1–56.

6. Bergman types him as a schizothyme, a complete introvert.

7. J. and A. Romein, *Erflaters van onze beschaving*, 2 (Amsterdam, E. M. Querido, 1938), 73. A more objective analysis of Coen's character and deeds can be found in W. P. Coolhaas, "Over Karakter en daden van Jan Pieterszoon Coen," *BVGO*, 8th series, 4 (1943), 201–37 and 5 (1944), 60–74.

8. *Jan Pieterszoon Coen, Bescheiden omtrent zijn bedrijf in Indië*, 1 (The Hague, Martinus Nijhoff, 1919), 1–2. This is the first item in the 7-volume series of documents dealing with Coen's administration in the Indies, of

Such recklessness was characteristic of the Dutch but completely lacking in his own nature, and he fought it in others as best he could during his whole career.[9]

Arriving at Bantam during February 1613, Coen learned that the warehouses with all the goods in them had burned down and that several Dutchmen had been murdered. He attributed part of this trouble to the mismanagement by Coteels, who had succeeded l'Hermite as president of the office, but it also strengthened his opinion that Bantam was not the right place for a headquarters. Following his instructions from the Seventeen, Coen sailed for the Moluccas via Djakarta where the first governor general, Pieter Both, a year earlier had obtained permission from Widjaja Krama, the vassal of Bantam, to establish a factory at a suitable place on the right bank of the river. On this occasion, Coen already visualized that Djakarta would be a good spot to establish a "rendezvous and headquarters, provided we build a stronghold there to guard our merchandise and where [Dutch] colonies should be planted to be no longer at the mercy of the perfidious Moors." [10]

With the appointment of a governor general, the Seventeen had also decided to make a start in settling Dutch families in the Moluccas, the only place where the Company had so far attained a firm footing. A number of such families, including artisans of various skills, sailed along with Both's fleet and landed at Amboyna, where the Dutch maintained a garrison whose soldiers had been permitted in 1607 to marry native women—a plan that had not worked out well, because the native women objected to this dubious honor. To these first settlers, Both granted freedom of trade with the neighboring islands in foodstuffs and calicoes.

Jan Coen arrived at Amboyna on March 19, and soon became disgusted with the licentious behavior of these first colonists. They

which volumes 1–6 have been edited by H. T. Colenbrander (The Hague, Martinus Nijhoff, 1919–34) and volume 7, in 2 parts, edited by W. P. Coolhaas (The Hague, Martinus Nijhoff, 1952–53). These works, hereafter referred to as "Documents," were compiled from material in the National Archives at The Hague.

9. About this outward voyage Coen reported that there had been many inexperienced men among the crew and that they were quickly whipped into shape (see Book III, Chapter 2). Aside from the 13 men lost at Ilha Bravo, only one died during the voyage, and this one was already sick when the ships left Texel. Coen attributed this "good convalescence" to the fact that the men were served "prunes and lemon juice" (Documents, 1, 3).

10. Documents, 1, 6–7.

had apparently been chosen from the lowest classes in Amsterdam, as few respectable persons would want to engage in such a precarious and dangerous undertaking. Coen recommended that preachers should be sent "to spread God's word among them." [11]

Amboyna is about 35 miles long and 12 miles across at the widest point. It is separated from the much larger island Ceram to the north by the Strait of Hitu, named after that town on the north coast of Amboyna. The town of Amboyna is on the south coast of the island. There were then two other towns, Luhu and Kambela, situated on either side of a narrow peninsula jutting south from Ceram across the strait. It was on these four towns that most of the world's supply of cloves was based and thus, as in the case of Banda, the importance of the area was far in excess of its size. This whole area belonged to the Sultan of Ternate, with whom the Dutch had a long-standing treaty as his defenders against the Spanish who were entrenched on the nearby island of Tidore. In exchange the Sultan had given the Dutch exclusive rights to purchase cloves. The Dutch established a price of 50 reals per *bahar* [12] and instituted a system of giving advances on future deliveries, mainly in the form of cotton goods on which, of course, they made a profit.

Two days after Jan Coen had reached the town of Amboyna, John Jourdain arrived at Hitu on the opposite side of the island. The Dutch factor at Hitu was Steven Coteels, presumably a younger brother of the Mateo Coteels who was then drinking himself to death in Bantam. Coteels asked Jourdain to refrain from buying until he had received word from his chief at the town of Amboyna, Jasper Jansz., about this matter. The reply came promptly and was as could have been expected: the English were not to be allowed to buy in the open market. "We built and maintain castles," Jasper Jansz. said, probably prompted by Jan Coen, "and you come to reap the fruits of our labor." There was undoubtedly some justification for this remark, and the English historian Furnival admitted as much when he wrote that the English were "pursuing the Dutch in the Indies like gadflies." [13]

After five years of frustration, finally in a position to do some

11. "From such bad plants there is little hope to reap good fruit" (*Documents, 1,* 9–10). See below, p. 337.

12. The weight of a *bahar* differed considerably throughout Southeast Asia. For cloves at Amboyna, the *bahar* was established at 550 Dutch pounds (ca. 600 English pounds).

13. J. S. Furnivall, *Netherlands India* (New York, 1944), pp. 26–27.

real trading, Jourdain refused to lay down his hand. "The country is free for all men," he told Coteels, "these people not being in any subjugation to the Dutch." He offered the native merchants another 10 reals per *bahar*, but still they were reluctant to sell. A Gujerat trader told Jourdain that "the people were very desirous to deal with the English, but the Hollanders had threatened to burn their houses if they did." Trying to solve the problem as amicably as possible, Coteels told Jourdain that the governor was willing to sell him cloves if he did not deal directly with the natives. To this Jourdain replied, according to his own journal, "I told him I had been once deceived and I would believe no more, showing him he had not learned his lying tongue at London, but among the Portugalls, for he had spent most of his youth at London and Portugal and could speak both languages perfectlie. So I bid him to keep his cloves for I would have none of him. I would sail in the morning."

The Orang Kayas at Hitu suggested to Jourdain that he cross the strait to Luhu, where they would secretly supply him with cloves. Jourdain makes it clear that he suspected this to be a ruse to get rid of him, but he secretly hoped that his higher offer might tempt them to take a chance. Besides, he had no alternative. Coteels knew full well what Jourdain intended to do, and asked him to wait until Coen arrived at Hitu. "He would follow me to Luhu," Jourdain wrote in his journal, "and prevent us trade. I bade them do their worst." [14]

It was at Luhu that Jourdain met his adversary for the first time. According to Jourdain, "Coen upbraided me in a chollericke manner, saying that buying cloves without Dutch consent was like stealing it from them, and they would prevent it by any means they might." To this the Englishman replied that "The Dutch were following him like the Jews did Christ, doing us many injuries for which one day they might answer for betwixt Dover and Calais." It was a prophetic statement, although it took some forty years more before the commercial rivalry between the English and the Dutch culminated in declared sea war.

On April 2, the two men confronted each other again. Coen had not been idle. He had told the Orang Kayas at Luhu that the English were not strong enough to protect them against their enemies, "being unable to set out but six ships to the Moluccas in more than twelve years." The native merchants told Jourdain

14. Foster, *Journal*, pp. 247–57.

that they would be willing to deal with the English but that the Dutch threatened them daily. Jourdain told Coen to his face that the Dutch were the cause of his dilemma. Coen countered by telling Jourdain that he was acting contrary to his orders from Middleton. Jourdain's reply appears from the following entry in his journal: "I wonder you know so much about my commission. Your long beard (for he had none at all) cannot teach me to follow my commission—advise you to look after your own business!" [15] This was a scathing reference of a mature man in his forties to a mere youth of twenty-six who exercised more power than Jourdain thought Coen able to handle.

Jourdain refused to pull up stakes without doing all he could to obtain a cargo for the *Darling*. On April 5, the Orang Kayas offered him thirty *bahar* of cloves at 100 reals each, twice the sum they could get from the Dutch. Jourdain offered to pay seventy, which the natives accepted although they insisted on proving the English weights to see how they compared with the Dutch. On April 6 Coen sent an ultimatum to Jourdain, telling him to desist from trying to buy cloves. The message was written in Dutch, and Jourdain refused to accept it on that ground, telling Coen to put it in Portuguese, French, Italian, or English. Jourdain was clever enough to elude Coen, and the actual weighing took place at night from April 6 to 9 at the house of a certain Tikus, who was willing to take his chances with the Dutch for the increase in price of 20 reals per *bahar*. Tikus, impressed by this windfall, told Jourdain to return the following year with more ships because then the Dutch would certainly not dare to interfere. Plainly, Tikus was aware of neither the weakness of the English Company nor the strength of the Dutch.

In the meantime, Coen had translated his ultimatum into Portuguese. It was to the effect that the English should leave the area or take the consequences. From Luhu, Jourdain sailed to Kambela, but Coen had preceded him there also, warning the natives not to sell to the English. Nevertheless, Jourdain managed to buy another fifteen *bahar* of cloves, but that was all he could get.

On May 3, Jourdain left the Amboyna area with only a small part of what he had expected to buy. He returned to Bantam via Macassar where the Dutch had so far neglected to make any definite contacts, because it had little to offer on which the

15. Ibid., pp. 265–69.

Company could make a profit. As a result Jourdain was able to make arrangements to establish a factory there, leaving George Cokayne as factor, with instructions to entice the Macassar merchants to attempt to smuggle cloves out of the Moluccas under the noses of the Dutch.[16]

During the middle of August, Jourdain was back at Bantam, only to find the affairs of the English Company in a terrible state. Middleton had died a few weeks earlier and the *Trades Increase* was reduced to a mass of burned timbers on the shores of Pulu Pandjang. No less than 140 Englishmen were lost, and those still alive were divided into two opposing camps, each representing a different voyage. They lived in separate houses, and there was great dissension between them. Both parties refused to accept John Jourdain as their chief, something that Middleton had instructed them to do before he died. Jourdain was anxious to leave this hornets' nest, and sailed from Bantam for Mazulipatnam, hoping to barter his cloves for a quantity of calicoes. Putting in at Tiku for water, he found General Best there with two ships of the tenth English voyage. Best insisted that Jourdain return with him to Bantam: "The cloves in the *Darling* smellinge soe sweete that wee must return in his compagnie." [17]

At Bantam, Best succeeded in bringing the opposing factions to a provisional agreement, accepting John Jourdain as their chief. On November 14, 1613, Jourdain reluctantly accepted the post of Chief Factor. He proved himself a capable administrator, although during the next few years he tried in vain to obtain a firm footing in the Spice Islands, which were, after all, the real target for both the English and Dutch. The main reasons for his failure were that the English Company suffered from a restricted and often divided authority in the Indies and that its factors had to operate with utterly inadequate means, the result of weak policy in London and inadequate financial support.

Jan Coen was much less explicit in relating the incidents at Amboyna than Jourdain. It appears, however, that he respected his opponent. "He gave us much trouble," Coen wrote, "and I had many disputes with him, for he is a clever fellow and left no means untried to serve his design, which was to establish a factory [at Amboyna] and start trade." [18]

16. Ibid., pp. 292–95. See also Hall, *History of South-East Asia*, p. 241.
17. Foster, *Journal*, pp. 309–11.
18. Ibid., p. 366. See also Hall, *History of South-East Asia*, p. 240.

Shortly after John Jourdain had left the area, Pieter Both arrived at Amboyna with his large fleet of ten or eleven ships. He had been at Banda, where he had renewed a treaty with the Orang Kayas for five years. He was fully aware that it was hardly worth the parchment on which it was written and that the Bandanese would break their contract by selling to the English and others whenever they had an opportunity to do so. Jan Coen now joined the governor general for an attack on Tidore, whose Spanish governor had refused to abide by the terms of the twelve-year truce concluded in Europe. The old Portuguese fort was successfully stormed by a force of 690 men, including 40 Japanese soldiers. "They prove as brave as ours," it was reported. "Their banner was the first on the wall." This was the first time the Company had made use of the Japanese soldiers recruited by Jacques Specx who had cautioned, however, to keep them under close control because they were difficult to deal with.[19]

A newer Spanish fort on Tidore proved harder to win and the siege had to be abandoned. It was suggested that the fleet sail north to Manila, but this plan was defeated in the plenary council as too ambitious an undertaking.

Early in 1613 news reached the Moluccas that the situation in Bantam was far from satisfactory. Before leaving for Bantam the governor general appointed Doctor Laurens Reael, and educated jurist with important connections in Holland, as Governor of the Moluccas, Banda, and Amboyna. On the return voyage Pieter Both, accompanied by Jan Coen, touched at the island of Buton, off the south coast of Celebes. Here they learned that Commander Schotte had taken the Portuguese fort on Solor, thus opening the island of Timor to the Dutch. This was welcome news, and Coen realized that it meant the Company now had access to the sandalwood which grew only on that island and which was highly valued in China. "No one should be allowed to trade on Timor except at the fort on Solor," Coen reported to the Seventeen. "It will need a few ships to police the area, but it is worth all of that. With [this] sandalwood we can force the Chinese to trade us their silk." [20] Pieter Both and Coen arrived at Bantam on October 6, 1613, and they learned at once that the news had not been exaggerated. Mateo Coteels had died—no

19. *Documents*, *6*, 45, 47.
20. "But Your Lordships should provide us with the means to promote this" (*Documents*, *1*, 22).

great loss to the Company except that it had left the factory without a chief. The Pangeran Rana Mangala, pushing the king aside,
had taken complete charge in the town and, at his instigation, the
Company's factory had been burned down a second time. Natives
had dug up Coteel's body, decapitated and dragged it through the
streets.

Conditions at Djakarta were equally bad. Theunemans, a member of the Council of the Indies, had been placed there as a factor,
but his conduct had been such that Widjaja Krama, who had
originally been well disposed towards the Dutch, now heartily
resented their presence. Theunemans had been insulting, high-
handed, and rude. He was a thorough ruffian, ordering natives
to be beaten, and he had shown extremely poor judgment in ac-
costing the wives of high-ranking Javanese. Such incidents caused
the governor general to complain to the Seventeen in bitter words:
"Indeed, my Lords, it is not only scandalous, but also horrible and
abominable what is being committed by your servants in these
various places."

The five or six months they had been together had given Pieter
Both ample opportunity to recognize in Coen a man of entirely
different caliber. Within a week of their return to Bantam, the
council appointed Coen to succeed Mateo Coteels as president
of the Bantam office as well as Djakarta. At the same time he was
made bookkeeper-general and his salary was raised to 150 guilders
per month. In confirming this to the Seventeen, Both wrote: "This
Coen is a person with a thorough grasp of commerce as well as
statecraft. He is honest, well-balanced, and does not waste any
time. I am certain that there has never been anyone here, nor will
there be, who surpasses him in efficiency, as Your Lordships will
be able to judge from his letters." [21] It was a bold prophecy, but
history would prove that it was justified.

21. De Jonge, *Opkomst*, *4*, ix–x.

8

Blueprint
for Empire

Jan Pieterszoon Coen, in his new position as bookkeeper-general, had the responsibility of presenting a comprehensive financial report of all the activities of the United Company. This involved a detailed knowledge of the state of affairs at each of the many factories established by the Company since its inception: stocks of goods and silver on hand; contracts made for future delivery and advances paid against them; the number of personnel employed, salaries and wages both paid and held in escrow. A similar knowledge was required of each ship of the Company, whether temporarily assigned to a certain area or sailing hither and yon. The area involved was vast, stretching from the west coast of India to the Moluccas in the eastern corner of the archipelago and north as far as Japan.

To visit all these factories in person would have been too time-consuming. Coen had promised to finish his task within a year and it would have taken him twice that long just to sail from place to place. A more expedient method was to demand detailed financial statements from each office, and Coen relied on his own perspicacity and knowledge of bookkeeping to interpret them correctly. Waiting for these reports gave him time to devote to a task even more important, as far as he was concerned: an analysis of the whole state of affairs in Asia as it applied to the fortunes of the Company, and recommendations on how they should be managed to assure the Company of success in its operations, so that it could expand beyond its original conception. The result was Coen's famous *Discourse to the Honorable Directors touching the Netherlands Indies state.*[1] He sent it off to the Seventeen on January 1, 1614, only a few months after he had returned to take up residence at Bantam with Governor General Pieter Both.

1. *Discoers aen de E. Heeren Bewinthebberen touscherende den neder-lantsche Indischen staet,* National Archives, The Hague, 4464 T. See also *Documents, 6,* 451–74.

It was not the first time that he had presented his ideas to the Seventeen. In the *Discourse* Coen referred to an earlier report which he had submitted upon returning to Holland after his first voyage in 1610. Since the first report has been lost, one can only guess to what extent his thoughts on the subject had then been formulated. But even at the later date, he was barely twenty-seven years old when he disclosed his ambitious blueprint to reconstruct the "trading imperium," as the United Company had until then been intended to be, into an Asiatic empire with Indonesia as its nucleus. The Seventeen were greatly impressed by Coen's report, which was perhaps the lengthiest (some 10,000 words) and certainly the most elaborate they had so far received from any of their servants. On October 14, 1614 the *Discourse* was submitted in full to the States General.

Coen began by pointing out the importance of the United Company, not solely for the return of profit to its stockholders but for the Dutch Republic as a whole. The power and presence of the Company could prevent the enemy, Spain and Portugal united under one crown, from access to the spices of Southeast Asia. But even more important, Coen argued, was the need to exclude the enemy from inter-Asiatic trade, which was "more profitable than the entire spice trade with Europe." [2]

Coen further related how it had been the original intention of the Company to trade only at such places where the enemy had no territorial possessions. This policy had been partly successful, and many alliances had been made with the local 'kings' of the Malabar and Coromandel coasts, in Sumatra, Borneo, the Moluccas, Siam, Japan, and other places. At these places "the kings have given us equal privileges as other nations and with courage and perseverance we should win out over our rivals." But the Spanish, refusing to abide by the terms of the armistice, were by no means inclined to see their erstwhile sphere of operations invaded by the Dutch.

"It is as clear as crystal," Coen wrote, "that the Spanish will try to force us out of the Indies, and their power is indeed still great!" Rumors had persisted in the Indies for three years that the Spanish were fitting out a large fleet for this purpose. "This year for certain, it is said, they plan to attack us in the Moluccas with twenty-four great ships, five galleys and a large number of frigates and other vessels." Against such a large force the Com-

2. *Documents*, 6, 451–52.

pany could muster no more than twelve ships, which on the average were far smaller and carried many fewer soldiers than the Spanish caracks. In addition, the Spanish strongholds at Manila, Macao, and elsewhere had stronger garrisons than the Dutch, who in all their forts together could count on only 500 men. The enemy, Coen explained, was able to maintain this power because of their colonial policy in which "they show us a good example. They can rely on the help of their Christian subjects."

Referring to the axiom that "evil has to be attacked at the root," he proposed that the Dutch move from the defensive to the offensive. It would require a "grand resolution in our fatherland that for several years in succession a powerful fleet should be sent here, and that Dutch colonies should be planted—this being the only means by which the enemy could be subdued." If the Company were unable to finance such an operation privately, then the Republic should come to its assistance.

Even more than the Spanish, Coen feared the competition of the "English and other European nations that may be expected." The English were already bragging, "You do the fighting in the Moluccas and we will reap the benefits!" Having a well-grounded opinion of the people of Amboyna and Banda, Coen realized that something of the sort was quite likely to happen unless counter-measures were taken. These islands belonged nominally to the Sultan of Ternate, with whom the Dutch had a longstanding treaty for defense against the Spanish. In return, he had given the Company a monopoly of the spice trade. In reality, however, the Sultan's jurisdiction over these islands was extremely limited. For centuries, the lure of the spices of the islands had attracted large numbers of small traders, not only from all parts of the archipelago but also from Arabia, India, and China as well. The indigenous population had long since been absolved by intermarriage with the immigrants. The result was a heterogeneous population which was known throughout the whole of Asia for its unreliable character. 'To act in good faith' had no meaning for these people, and there was no central authority from whom the Dutch could find redress for their grievances.

Coen reviewed the situation in plain words. The Dutch would have preferred to deal with a strong ruler who could guarantee them delivery of large quantities of spices and whose interest would lie in making certain such contracts were honored, but the absence of a central government made such a procedure im-

possible. Coen realized that the situation had evolved into a condominium, in which the Sultan of Ternate had absolute jurisdiction over his people and the Dutch had jurisdiction over the
forts and ships—"A body with two heads." "Each has its own
kind of jurisdiction," Coen proceeded, "but there is also a common interest, because the King of Ternate is obliged to us and
we to him. He is bound to sell his spices to no one but us, and
we are bound to defend him. Who, I ask, is the supreme head of
these two? If there arises a difference of opinion with what authority can it be settled? Where could one find a mediator or
judge?" And on a broader scale he posed the question: "Who
shall exclude the Portuguese, Spaniards, English, French, Germans and those from India if we, who have the sole right to be
there, have no authority?"

Such a condominium, Coen maintained, could never be successful, especially since the two parties were essentially enemies.
"They are Moslems and we are Christians. They hate us and do
not allow their women to marry Christians. They kill their children or abort them so that the mother won't bear heathens." Nor
were they to be trusted in matters of trade. "We are not obliged,
they say, to keep our word to a Christian." Considering the fact
that whatever authority the Sultan of Ternate had in his far-flung
territory was maintained solely by the Dutch, Coen called it
absurd that the Dutch themselves should not enforce the terms
of the treaty. This should be done "with vigor but not tyrani-
cally," as the King of Spain and the Sultan of Ternate himself
had dealt with these people. Coen wanted to combine force with
justice because, he avowed, "there is nothing in the world that
provides greater justice than to have it vigorously enforced." [3]
Coen wanted to establish law and order, the aim of all honorable
administrators. In this manner he hoped to establish a political
climate conducive to peaceful trade. This approach, in effect, led
eventually to a *Pax Neerlandica* which, by and large, kept Indonesia free from invaders for some three and a half centuries.

Amboyna and Banda were the island groups to which Coen
specifically referred in his report. These two names meant cloves
and nutmegs, the most valuable of all spices, and to gain direct
access to them had been the reason for nearly all the searching
voyages of the Age of Discovery that opened the world to western Europe. The exploits of Columbus, Magellan, Dias, Cabot,

3. Ibid., 6, 462–64.

Hudson, and a host of others would not have occurred had it not been for these small island groups in the Indies archipelago. Situated in close proximity to each other, they were in fact a true El Dorado.

Like others before him, Jan Coen was fully aware of their importance. He disapproved of the haphazard manner in which the Company's servants had thus far tried to exploit them. Referring to his earlier report, Coen once more pointed out the "evil treason and great murder" committed by the Bandanese. A peace had been concluded and a new contract signed but it was plain that the Orang Kayas had no intentions of adhering to its terms, although the Dutch had built a fort. "You keep your fort, they say, and we will keep our mace and nuts. It is well known in Europe," Coen continued, "that in spite of our great expenditures (to protect our contract) the English are still able to obtain nuts and mace and that the Portuguese buy them from the Javanese." Such clandestine trade made in bad faith could not be permitted, and Coen suggested that it might be prevented by patrolling the islands with a few small vessels, and that, in addition, the importing of rice, which had to come from Java, should be controlled by the Company. But even with these measures, Coen had misgivings about the Bandanese being brought to terms, and he foresaw the possibility that a "more vehement remedy" might have to be applied. Subsequent events proved that his surmise was correct. It had also been suggested that the Dutch should try to convert the Moors, as the Portuguese had done, but to this Coen gave a firm rejection.[4]

In order to create a balance against the native population, Coen emphasized the need for the presence of Dutch colonists who could develop into a burgher class, but he repeated that a much better class of settlers should be sent than those who had arrived in the fleet of Pieter Both. Those were a sad lot, given to much "drinking and whoring." What was needed was a group of dependable people, men skilled in various trades: "Even if they come naked as a jaybird we can still use them." The Seventeen should also send orphans, male and female, whether Dutch or foreign. This would be a great boon to the Company, to the waifs themselves, and to the crowded orphanages as well. This was perhaps the first time that the subject of "company maidens" was ever

4. "For the time being religion in the Moluccas should in no way be touched" (Documents, 6, 463).

mentioned. It was to develop into a more or less continuous flow of future brides for Dutch soldiers, sailors, and higher personnel, who found the native women reluctant to share their lives.

Coen also asked the Seventeen to send a number of "solid Protestant clergymen, not such stupid, uncouth idiots as you have sent heretofore." They were needed not to proselytize the Moors but to police the morals of the Dutch element. "It is human beings Your Honors have here, not angels!" By this time Coen had also become aware of the mediocre caliber of administrators with which the Company had to cope. A higher type was badly needed, particularly in the upper ranks, men with experience in trade, legal matters, and especially in statesmanship. The Council of the Indies should consist of eminent men of proven ability. Its members should remain in one place rather than travel on individual missions throughout the Indies, and all orders to "skippers, merchants and captains should emanate from this body alone."

Coen did not confine his program to the Indies archipelago. After the truce with Spain had ended and open hostilities were resumed, he foresaw the possibility that such strongholds as Macao, Manila, and Malacca could be successfully attacked. "With money we can get all the Japanese soldiers we need." He was also optimistic that the Company would be able to dislodge the Portuguese from Ceylon. Nor should trade with China and Japan be neglected, once the Dutch had sufficiently secured their position in these waters.

It was an ambitious program, truly a blueprint for empire. Coen had little doubt that the Seventeen would approve his plan in principle, but would they implement it by sending the required ships, men, and especially, money?

During 1614 the Dutch made their first official contact with Mataram in Central Java.[5] This principality was becoming the most important single power on Java, anxious to subdue the coastal areas and practically the sole source of rice to feed Djakarta, the Moluccas, and other trading areas. On the return voyage from the Moluccas, the fleet of Pieter Both had touched at some of the Javanese ports, and an office had been established at Japara which was favorably situated for the rice trade.[6] On that occasion it was learned that the *Penembahan*, Sultan of Mataram, was inclined to favor the Dutch because they might help him in

5. See p. 210 for the origin of Mataram.
6. On Japara, see Meilink-Roelofsz, *Asian Trade*, pp. 286–94.

his conquest of the coastal states, especially those in East Java. As a result, Commander Gasper van Zurck was sent to Mataram in April 1614, as an emissary of the United Company.

Sultan Agung, a forceful young man in his early twenties who had illegally usurped the throne a year before, received Van Zurck cordially on this first occasion. He was willing to enter into an alliance with the Dutch, to allow them trading privileges free of tolls, and to grant permission to build a small house at Japara. "I am a prince and a soldier," he said proudly, "not a merchant like the other princes of Java. I also know that you did not come here to conquer Java. I am not now at war with Bantam, but if they cause you trouble I shall gladly come to your assistance." [7] On the face of it this first contact with Sultan Agung was a complete success. But it did not end so happily for Van Zurck. On his return to the coast he died of dysentery, another in the ever growing list of high officials who had given their lives for the Company without reaping some personal benefit for services rendered.

Coen, meanwhile, applied himself to his dual task of organizing the Bantam and Djakarta offices, and setting up a comprehensive system of bookkeeping. This required a great amount of paper work—reports going back and forth between the many offices throughout the archipelago and other parts of Asia, minutes kept of the frequent meetings of the Council of the Indies, and records of court proceedings and the many activities associated with an organization as large and with as many ramifications as the United Company. Extracts had to be made of all these documents for the Seventeen, and, in the case of resolutions taken in Council, they had to be verbatim. In many instances several copies were required, to guard against possible loss at a time when the means of communication were slow and hazardous. All of this had to be written by hand, in coal-black india ink applied with quills on almost indestructible Dutch paper of folio size. The quantity of this paper work can best be visualized by the fact that the ships returning to Holland around the first of the year became known as "book ships."

Such voluminous paper work required clerks, whose numbers grew with the ever-expanding activities of the Company under the stewardship of Jan Coen. During the Middle Ages, being a member of the unofficial brotherhood of clerks implied at least

7. De Jonge, *Opkomst*, 4, xi–xii.

a knowledge of Latin and the ability to read and write. Clerks were then respected, as they were responsible for the dissemination of knowledge throughout medieval Europe. In the seventeenth century, however, all that was required of the copyist was a trained hand; others would do the thinking for them. It is from this time that the word clerk acquired a rather derisive sense, indicating an inferior and manual profession. The earlier and more exalted meaning of a clerk is now largely restricted to courts of law.

In the Indies the clerks were known as *pennists* (penpushers), and they were just that but with a skill in penmanship which has become almost a lost art. Their labors strike one as works of art, with their elaborate capitals and graceful loops, the letters as black and clear as when they were first put down on paper which has barely yellowed. The *pennists* comprised an essential, but unsung, corps in the emerging economic age of the United East India Company. They were usually housed in the attic of a warehouse, a kind of dormitory, partitioned by bamboo screens from the rest of the floor. Their salaries were in proportion to their low standing; after ten years of service they might earn no more than thirty guilders a month. The hours were long, from six to six, with a half hour off for breakfast, eaten standing up, and two hours for the noon meal. If the day's stint were not finished, writing continued in the evening by candlelight. Discipline was strict, and only on Wednesday and Sunday afternoons were the scriveners allowed to leave their quarters, and they had to be back by seven for the evening prayer. Infractions meant corporal punishment: being chained to the writing table and beaten on their bare backs by their own colleagues, or standing guard in the torrid heat with an iron storm hat on their heads to which a cannonball might be attached.[8]

Coen was a prolific writer, producing an average of 100 documents a year himself, most of them quite long. There is, however, not a single document extant which is known to be in his own handwriting; we have only his signature.[9] From this the conclusion must be drawn that either he dictated his letters, or prepared a rough draft which was later destroyed. There can be little doubt that he kept his *pennists* busy.

8. See F. de Haan, *Oud Batavia* (Bandung, 1935).
9. On the authority of Miss Ch. van der Plas, curator of the Tropical (formerly Colonial) museum at Amsterdam (June, 1957).

Upon his appointment as bookkeeper-general, Coen had stated that it would take him about one year to prepare a complete set of books, and he proved to be as good as his word. On November 10, 1614, a detailed financial statement was dispatched to the Seventeen comprising everything necessary to evaluate the financial position of the Company in Asia. For this work, as well as for his other accomplishments, he was promptly rewarded. The new governor general, Gerard Reynst, arrived at Bantam on November 5 to replace Pieter Both who for some time had been anxious to return home, but had been forced to postpone his departure until his replacement arrived. On November 14, 1614, a new Council of the Indies was sworn in, and Jan Coen was elected a member. In addition, he was appointed director general of all the offices, charged with their administration and the pursuit of trade. This made Coen, while still in his twenties, second in command of the Company's far-flung activities.

9

The Rendezvous

Nutmegs, mace, and cloves! These were, with pepper, the main products upon which the early fortunes of the Dutch East India Company were based. To reap the full benefit from this trade, a monopoly was essential, both to control the purchase price and to prevent the market in Europe from being glutted by unwanted competitors. With this goal in mind, the Seventeen had always instructed their successive admirals, and even the governor general, to proceed to the Moluccas in order to organize the buying, to protect these islands against the enemy, and to keep out interlopers.

There was a good reason why the new governor general, Gerard Reynst, should not tarry too long at Bantam. The English had received reinforcements, and under the instigation of John Jourdain (now the chief factor at Bantam and the counterpart of Jan Coen) they decided to renew their efforts to acquire a good share of the lucrative trade in nutmegs, mace, and cloves. Gerard Reynst and his squadron got away first, but he was closely followed by English ships under George Ball and George Cokayne, who had instructions not only to buy spices but also to establish factories. Coen anticipated what would happen, and, in March 1615, he wrote the Seventeen that the English were intent on trading in the Spice Islands, disregarding the exclusive contracts the Dutch had with the Orang Kayas. "They want to reap what we have sowed, and they brag that they are free to do so because their king has authority over the Netherlands nation." [1]

Reynst indeed encountered the English in the Moluccas. He had chased them away wherever he found them, but two ships, fully laden, had safely returned to Bantam. They also carried an important Bandanese who had been persuaded by Sophony Cozucke, a Russian in the service of the English Company, to come to Bantam and confer with John Jourdain about a mutual alli-

1. *Documents*, 6, 65.

ance to get rid of the Dutch. Coen was not unduly alarmed about these developments, but they afforded him an opportunity to prod the Seventeen for more active support. "You can be assured," he wrote, "that if you do not send a large capital at the earliest opportunity . . . the whole Indies trade is liable to come to nothing."[2]

The Seventeen soon realized that Coen was a man who, young as he was, did not hesitate to speak his mind.[3] In submitting his detailed financial statement, Coen had suggested that the directors make available a capital of 700,000 reals for inter-Asiatic trade and 1,200,000 reals yearly to purchase return cargoes for the Netherlands. It was clear that he wanted to conduct the affairs of the Company on a sufficiently large scale to support the monopoly which the Seventeen so greatly desired. In reporting the arrival of Gerard Reynst, he added: "It is a pleasure to see the ships and their crews, but I am distressed that three such beautiful ships carried no more than six chests of silver (in all 48,000 reals). It almost seems as if Your Lordships, deliberately or inadvertently, want to diminish your status and progress, because rarely some ships arrive or something is lacking, be it skilled workmen, soldiers, ammunition, victuals, ships gear, or money!"[4]

Money, or rather the lack of it, was Coen's constant theme during his tenure as director general. His request for substantial working capital was brushed off by the Seventeen as excessive. It was Coen's intention to use the profits from inter-Asiatic trade to defray the cost of waging war against the Spanish and Portuguese, who were still far from beaten. "We cannot do business without war, nor make war without business," he had written in December 1614. The Spanish Governor of the Philippines, Juan da Silva, planned to attack Bantam with a large force and had sailed to the Strait of Malacca to join a Portuguese squadron. The Dutch had more than suspected the enemy's intentions, and tried to forestall the attack before it could be executed.[5] Governor General Reynst, who had returned to Bantam from his cruise in the Moluccas, detailed as many ships as he could safely

2. Ibid., 6, 116.
3. See Romein, *Erflaters*, pp. 75–76.
4. *Documents, 1,* 91.
5. The information had reached Bantam in January 1614 through a Dutchman, Joost Pietersz., who had been in the service of the Spanish for no less than 23 years. See *Documents, 1,* 49.

spare to reinforce Admiral Van der Hagen, who was cruising before Malacca and Johore. The admiral attacked in early December and destroyed the enemy fleet in the port of Malacca, but not without sustaining severe losses himself.

It would be several years before Jan Coen became governor general, but his appointment as director general had made him, in fact, the chief administrative officer of the United Company in Asia. All he lacked was the title and the salary. Since he coordinated all economic activities, his place of residence became the nerve center of the Dutch Company. For the time being, this was Bantam.

Bantam had many advantages. It was centrally located in the archipelago, easily accessible from the Indian Ocean and the China Sea, and was thus at the crossroads of the main arteries of Asiatic trade. It had a safe anchorage and was a convenient source of the pepper from south Sumatra. Coen was loath to give up these advantages, and for a number of years did his best to come to terms with the *Pangeran* of Bantam about the establishment of a general rendezvous. The need for such a rendezvous had long been felt by the Seventeen, and they had stipulated its prerequisites: aside from convenient geographical location, it should not be subject to exorbitant tolls and other levies, and the Company should be allowed to trade freely and build a sound warehouse, safe against fire and strong enough to repel an attack. The Seventeen had no territorial ambitions in Java or elsewhere, and such an establishment would therefore depend entirely on an agreement with the local ruler.

Excepting the first, none of these conditions could readily be found at Bantam. *Pangeran* Rana Mangala, guardian of the 'king,' was as anxious as any other ruler to attract Dutch trade, which gave Bantam a considerable revenue, directly through tolls and other levies and indirectly by taxing the local merchants. In addition he managed to extract additional revenue in the form of costly presents, expected whenever the Dutch approached him with a specific request. In the beginning Bantam had been quite anxious to enlist Dutch support against the Portuguese, but now that this danger was waning the *Pangeran* had second thoughts about these newcomers, who anchored their heavily armed ships before the town. Above all he wanted to remain master in his own house, and he had justifiable misgivings about permitting the Dutch to build a warehouse of stone that, in reality, would be a fort. The

Dutch could hardly agree to less. Fires had been all too frequent, and there were strong suspicions that not all of them had been accidental. The goods held in warehouse were of great value— spices, calicoes, and silk, not to speak of the Company's books and store of silver. Jan Coen would have been remiss in his responsibility if he had not wanted to protect them to the fullest possible extent.

After intimations that the Company might be forced to leave Bantam if it were not allowed to build a stone warehouse, the *Pangeran* finally relented, but he specified that it should be no higher than any other house, including his own. This meant that only a one-story warehouse could be built, not at all to Coen's liking, because at ground floor level the goods would be liable to serious damage from dampness, worms, and other vermin. However, the *Pangeran* was adamant.

It gradually became apparent that, considering such difficulties, Bantam did not offer much hope as a permanent rendezvous, but where to go? There was a considerable difference of opinion, both in the Indies and in the Netherlands. Malacca had been suggested, if it could be taken from the Portuguese, or neighboring Johore, with whose Sultan the Dutch were on friendly terms. The main deterrent here was the problem of sailing through the Strait of Malacca during the adverse monsoon. The Seventeen preferred an island off the southeast coast of Sumatra or one in the Sunda Strait. If it should be uninhabited, so much the better, because this would eliminate irksome tolls and other interference. Japara was considered for a while because Sultan Agung of Mataram had been cooperative, even to the extent of extending freedom from tolls to the Dutch.

Before significant progress had been made at Japara with the building of a substantial warehouse—still only of wood and bamboo—it became plain that little could be expected and that the proffered cooperation would not be forthcoming. Mataram was engaged in a war with the princes of East Java, and as long as the outcome of this conflict was in doubt the political situation was too delicate for the Dutch to press Agung for a definite contract.

From the very beginning of his stewardship, Jan Coen had made clear his feeling on the matter. On November 10, 1614, he wrote the Seventeen: "Our rendezvous should be near Strait Sunda. If we would threaten to leave, he [the *Pangeran* of Bantam] would be more tractable. There is great jealousy between Jacatra and Bantam about ourselves." [6] This briefly divulged his plan. He intended to play Djakarta against Bantam, still hoping that this would force Bantam to come to terms. He realized that this would not be an easy task. The Seventeen favored a continued relationship with Djakarta provided it did not impair the relationship with Bantam. Not mincing words, Coen replied that such an attitude was unrealistic. "To refuse Bantam its high tolls, to seek free trade at Jacatra and still remain friendly with Bantam are contrasting maxims." [7] In time it would have to be one thing or the other, friendship or enmity, and Coen prepared himself for either eventuality.

When it became known in Bantam that the Spanish planned to attack, the *Pangeran* seemed inclined temporarily toward a more amenable attitude. But no sooner had the news of the Dutch victory been received and the Spanish danger alleviated than he reverted to earlier tactics; he arbitrarily demanded higher tolls. Coen tried once more to come to a lasting agreement with the *Pangeran*, indicating that he might meet these new demands, provided that Bantam close its port to all other European nations. Coen had the English especially in mind. The *Pangeran* refused to accede, well aware that only by playing the English against the Dutch could he hope to maintain his position. This firm attitude on the part of the *Pangeran* presented Coen with a dilemma; he knew that Bantam would not provide the much needed rendezvous, but he did not want to relinquish it to the English. Coen soon proved that he, too, could play a double game.

The political situation in Java at this time reflected that of the whole of Southeast Asia after the dissolution of the empire of Madjapahit which, even on Java itself, had broken up into splinter principalities. Mataram was the strongest and the most prosperous. It was well populated and its plains grew enough rice to supply not only its own needs but also those of other areas.[8] On these same plains were the great temples of the Hindu era— Borobudur, those of Prambanan, and others—constant reminders to Sultan Agung of the glorious past. It was his ambition to unite the whole of Java under his sovereignty.

6. *Documents*, 6, 58.
7. Van Deventer, *Nederlanders op Java*, p. 91.
8. The total population of Java could not have been more than 2 million. See Schrieke, *Indonesian Sociological Studies*, 2, 139.

The coastal kings were well aware of his plans, and Bantam in particular was afraid of what might happen once Mataram had managed to get control over East Java. This was one of the main reasons why the *Pangeran* played his uneasy duel with the Dutch, extracting from them all he could but also counting on their support if Mataram should move against him. Coen referred to Bantam's dilemma in his letter to the Seventeen, dated October 22, 1615: "The *Pangeran* fears not, they say, the Portuguese, the Spaniards, the Hollanders or the English, but only the Mataram. From them, he says, no one can flee, but for the others we have the whole mountains behind us; they can not follow us there with ships." [9] Coen kept this in mind and tried his best to maintain good relations with Mataram, whose ruler had told the Dutch that he was "no merchant and not interested in trade," and therefore might be easier to deal with than the *Pangeran* should he succeed in subduing Bantam.

Bantam had internal problems as well, especially with Djakarta. Although in name a vassal of Bantam, Widjaja Krama, the governor, acted as if he were an independent ruler and had welcomed the Dutch. Again it was for the double purpose of both gaining revenue from Dutch trade and having protection when he found himself squeezed between Bantam and Mataram should that conflict break out. By 1615 the friction between Bantam and Djakarta was such that war seemed imminent.[10] Thus the whole political situation in Java was in a turmoil—Mataram fighting the coastal princes in the east and Bantam and Djakarta at each other's throats in the west.

Coen correctly saw that it could do the Company no harm, and might possibly be profitable, for him to heighten the tensions between Bantam and Djakarta. In order to pursue this policy, all that was necessary was for him to divide his patronage between the two towns, which in this case meant giving Djakarta a larger share than it had received before. By the end of 1614, most ship-repairing was therefore transferred to Djakarta, where there were a few small islands off the coast suitable for the purpose, the most important of which the Dutch had named Onrust. In time workshops and a hospital were added.

Against a payment of only 200 reals, the king of Djakarta allowed the Dutch to build a two-story stone warehouse sur-

9. *Documents, 1,* 119.
10. Van Deventer, *Nederlanders,* p. 93.

rounded with a stockade, such as Coen had wanted to erect in Bantam. It is perhaps worth noting that ten years later a servant of the Dutch West India Company, Peter Minuit, made a similar bargain when he bought Manhattan Island from the American Indians for an even smaller amount.

While Djakarta was becoming more attractive as a possible rendezvous, Bantam could not yet be disregarded. Bantam's importance was also based on the fact that it was a main source of pepper, by virtue of its sovereignty over South Sumatra. This gave the *Pangeran* a powerful weapon with which to make the Dutch bow to his terms. He could raise the pepper price or even withhold supplies entirely, regardless of contracts that might be outstanding. Coen decided to free himself from this stranglehold by going directly to the source of supply. He chartered a large junk from a Chinese trader named Simsuan and sent it to Djambi for a cargo of pepper. As soon as the *Pangeran* learned of this, he had Simsuan incarcerated.[11]

Coen countered this indirect affront by taking a more positive stand than before. He removed most of the Company's goods from the Bantam warehouse and loaded them on the ships in the roadstead, with the announced intention of shipping them to Djakarta. He also told the merchants from China, then at Bantam, to sail to Djakarta in the coming year, where he would buy from them all the goods they carried. This move was not yet meant as an ultimatum, but Coen hoped that it might make the *Pangeran* more tractable. Having no desire to leave Bantam entirely to the English, he intended to use both places and await further developments before deciding which of the two would be the better rendezvous. In this policy of wait and see, Coen was prompted by the fact that the English had also obtained a concession from the king of Djakarta for the building of a warehouse on the west bank of the River Tjiliwung, opposite the Dutch establishment. Widjaja Krama, although anxious to draw trade away from Bantam, was no less concerned about the advisability of putting it into the hands of a single foreign power. He, too, realized the importance of having more than one party bid for what he had to offer. Such a policy had become the accepted practice throughout most of the Indies, and from the standpoint of the coastal rulers it was undoubtedly a reasonable one.

The unstable political situation in Java was not conducive to

11. *Documents, 1,* 116–17.

peaceful trading, but it presaged something far more important than what the Amsterdam merchants had originally anticipated when they launched their first venture to the Indies. In East Java there was an active state of war between the petty princes and Mataram. In West Java there was not only rivalry between Djakarta and Bantam, but within Bantam itself there was also great dissension. On one side stood the *Pangeran*, Rana Mangala, who had usurped the power, but the young king also had his followers. Aside from hostility against each other, each faction favored a different policy towards the Europeans, the court being the more lenient but also the weaker of the two.

In such an unstable situation, it would not be difficult for a man like Coen, whose vision went far beyond the concept of the Seventeen, to see his opportunity. For the present, he could not visualize what all this might lead to, but behaved as if he could. By keeping both Djakarta and Bantam on tenterhooks and playing one against the other, Coen remained in control of the situation. In the meantime, he also exploited the fear Djakarta and Bantam shared of Mataram [12] by doing everything possible to promote good Dutch relations with Sultan Agung. A rumor was spread that the Dutch had entered into an alliance with Mataram, which led Jourdain to report to London that "The Flemmings will, with their whole force, come to take Bantam and to place the King of Mataram in the government." [13]

Such an alliance never came into being, but one can speculate what might have been the result had Mataram, with or without Dutch support, succeeded in extending its hegemony over the whole of Java. It might well have changed the whole course of capitalistic colonialism in Asia: the Dutch would probably not have attempted to gain territory in the realm of such a powerful ruler. Their reluctance to do so is evident from the comment of the next governor general, Laurens Reael, about Japara, the only port in Mataram's territory where the Dutch had an office. "This is certain," he wrote, "that we could never establish a rendezvous there without hostilities." [14]

Whether by design or not, the rumors about a Dutch-Mataram alliance spread, but Jan Coen was not content to rely on this

12. See Coolhaas, *Generale Missiven*, p. 80.
13. This rumor had reached Jourdain from his factor at Macassar. See Van Deventer, *Nederlanders*, p. 98.
14. Letter from Reael to the Seventeen, dated November 10, 1617, in Dutch National Archives. See Van Deventer, *Nederlanders*, p. 97, n. 2.

alone. Palembang was all that was left of the ancient Empire of Srivijaya, and there was no love lost between its ruler and Bantam. It was known that the *Pangeran* of Bantam was ambitious to take over Djambi, the most important pepper port in Sumatra, especially since he already controlled the southern part of this large island. Following his decision to circumvent Bantam and buy pepper in Djambi, Coen had sent Andries Soury on a mission to Palembang, to establish a factory there and to explore the possibility of entering into an alliance with the king against "his and our enemies." Soury was to give the king a suitable present, but Coen's underlying purpose is clearly revealed by what he added to his instructions: "And if you happen to meet one of the king's people, ask him if their king would like to become King of Bantam." [15]

It was inevitable that the news of these dealings should find its way back to Java. Widjaja Krama of Djakarta was particularly worried about this chain of events, feeling himself hemmed in on all sides. Because of his ambition to make himself independent of Bantam, he had repeatedly refused the *Pangeran*'s invitation to go there and pay homage. What should he do? If Mataram moved against Bantam, Djakarta would become the first line of defense, and he would have to carry the brunt of the attack.

Widjaja Krama expressed his premonition to Coen, "I have seen at Bantam that what the Pangeran orders is done because he is feared. From the young king I cannot expect any help. Mataram has already taken Pasaruan. What is to happen? War is in the offing." Perplexed by the difficulties facing him, Widjaja Krama decided to throw in his lot with the *Pangeran* of Bantam. As Coen wrote the Seventeen: "We did our best to talk him out of going to Bantam, but apparently he wants to stand in well with all the world." [16] It was Coen's way of saying that the king of Djakarta trusted no one, least of all the Dutch.

In due course, Widjaja Krama of Djakarta turned not only to Bantam but also to the English and Mataram as well. When that time came, there were three forces against the Dutch, and war had come to West Java.

This was still a few years away, and, in the meantime, Jan Coen played a Machiavellian game. When the moment arrived

15. *Documents*, 2, 153.
16. Van Deventer, *Nederlanders*, p. 99.

he grasped it, turning a near fiasco into a resplendent success. In dealing with this problem he proved that he had learned more in Italy than the art of bookkeeping and the fundamentals of trade.

10

The Price of Monopoly

Vexing as the Bantam situation was, it was only one facet of a greater problem, which also involved Banda and the British. In solving it, Jan Coen laid the foundation for a Dutch empire in Asia, a feat made all the more remarkable by the fact that the directors at home were reluctant to carry the financial burden, while at the same time pressing him for profitable results.

The news that Governor General Reynst had brought back from his sojourn in the Moluccas was that the situation was anything but serene, and that, aside from the activities of the interloping English, existing contracts were being violated right and left. Short of taking the Spice Islands by force and subjugating their inhabitants, it was obvious to Coen that, once and for all, a drastic step had to be taken to secure monopoly over the trade in cloves and nutmegs. He still had no intention of accomplishing this in any other way than by the legal means at hand: the existing treaties. The Spanish and Portuguese, although still strongly entrenched at Manila, Macao, and Malacca, were no longer a serious threat. It would be expedient if those strongholds could be taken, but the Seventeen were unwilling to provide the necessary support, financial and otherwise, to accomplish it. However, the Dutch Company, with the limited military force at its command, had succeeded in keeping them away from the Moluccas. The real threat was the diversion of trade by the natives and by the English. The latter would carry their spices to London and flood the European market. The natives could do the same by selling them to the Portuguese at Malacca. All this ancillary trade had to be stopped to prevent the price of spices from falling on the European market.

Coen suggested that all non-Dutch trade be halted, and Reynst readily agreed. The Council of the Indies issued a decree to this effect, especially in regard to native trade. From then on, all such trade was to stop, on penalty of confiscation of goods carried. The places specifically mentioned were Malacca, the Moluccas (Amboyna and Banda), and Solor, the latter island being the chief source of sandalwood. Notice in the form of an ultimatum was given to all the coastal princes involved. Coen was firmly convinced that he was within his rights. For centuries the Dutch had sworn by the adage that a "man's word was his bond." The Dutch may have distrusted the "good intentions" of the native princes with whom they concluded agreements, but this was no reason to abrogate contracts. If a contract were made to be broken, then the offending party would have to bear the consequences.

The decision to interfere with alien trade was made during the latter part of 1615. Realizing that there might be repercussions against the employees of the Company, the factories at East Java, Buton, and Macassar were closed.[1] Thus, from a territorial point of view, the Company was entrenching, but by doing so it actually consolidated its position in Southeast Asia. According to available records, the Sultan of Macassar was most vocal in expressing his resentment. He refused to honor certain contracts he had made with the Dutch Company. The skipper of the *Enkhuyzen*, with orders to close the factory and to insist upon the completion of deliveries against contracts, took two important Macassarese as hostages to insure the terms earlier agreed upon. The ruler of Macassar complained to the Dutch at Bantam in touching terms: "Allah created the earth and sea. The earth he divided among the people and the sea became common to all. It has never been heard that anyone prohibited navigation. We need the trade; I am only a poor king."[2] He thus echoed the words Grotius had used in his plea for "freedom of the seas," but now such argument was mere pathos and sophistry, as far as the Dutch were concerned. It should be pointed out, however, that the Macassarese had only recently entered the spice trade, and this mainly through foreigners—Malays, Chinese, and others. At the beginning of the seventeenth century, the indigenous population was still entirely dependent upon farming. Macassar's rise as a trading center actually began after the Dutch had tightened

1. The 'kings' of Surabaya, Buton, and Macassar were individually apprised of this resolution. See *Documents*, *1*, 120–21.
2. *Documents*, *1*, 122.

their hold over the Moluccas,[3] and it gained momentum after John Jourdain established an English factory there [4] to encourage smuggling from the Spice Islands.

The tightening of the spice monopoly in the Moluccas was one of Reynst's final acts as governor general. In early December 1615, the *White Bear* arrived at Bantam with letters from the Seventeen which were none too encouraging, but for Reynst the arrival also brought a great personal grief. He was then at Djakarta suffering from dysentery. He now learned that his son had been on the *White Bear* and had died in the Sunda Strait a few days earlier. "The death of his son," Coen reported, "as well as the bad news from the home land, affected him so much that the Honorable General Reynst joined the Lord on December 7." [5] It is typical of Coen that he blamed the Seventeen in part for Reynst's demise.

The bad news Coen alluded to was actually the reply to his letter of two years before, of January 1, 1614 in which he had presented his comprehensive program for the future of the Company. The directors agreed on minor points such as the need for better preachers instead of the "uncouth idiots" Coen had complained of, and they promised to send them. But on the main issue, the provision of an adequate working capital, they replied scornfully that they were of a different opinion. Coen minced no words and in reply promptly took them to task. "How can you seriously demand large cargoes without sending us the required capital? Is it perhaps your intention that we should capture them only from the enemy? . . . Obviously you want large profits but without digging into your Pockets!" He lectured the Seventeen on the functions of capital: "Money, not used, is nothing but a dead metal. To profit from it, it has to be used, like a workman uses his tools!" [6] Boldly he repeated his earlier demands for a sufficiently large working capital for inter-Asiatic trade, and at least a million reals yearly for adequate return cargoes. He pointed out that "the Chinese deliver much more silk than we are able to buy, all because of lack of money. Although we have been here now for twenty years, the big Chinese merchants do not believe that we are honest traders, but that we are mainly

3. Schrieke, *Indonesian Sociological Studies*, 1, 65–70.
4. See p. 303 f.
5. *Documents*, 1, 153.
6. Ibid., *1*, 164.

interested in booty—These same people tell us: 'You Dutch have all the nutmegs, mace and cloves, and since you have an office at Djambi, also the pepper. You can also get hold of the whole China trade. If you blockade Manila for six months or a year, you will not be lacking in China goods." In relating this to the Seventeen, Coen mockingly added: "Little did these Chinese know that you allow the English so many privileges." [7] Coen was referring to the fact that while the directors wanted to keep the English out of the Moluccas, this should be done "without resorting to force." This was an obviously impossible request. At the very moment Coen was dictating his reply, four English ships and one yacht were preparing to sail from Bantam to the Moluccas under Captain Castleton.

Coen ignored the Seventeen's admonition to refrain from using force, and Commander Jan Dirckz. Lam was dispatched after the English. Lam succeeded in dispersing the English ships in the Banda group, and afterwards made another meaningless treaty with the Bandanese, in which a higher price for their spices was agreed upon. Castleton proceeded on his journey as far as Tidore, where he bartered arms and munitions for spices with the Spanish and the natives. Coen enumerated his grievances against the English, imploring the Seventeen to come to an understanding with the Company in London, "otherwise there will be trouble—they are too audacious. In the Moluccas they side with our enemies and try to corrupt Ternate. In Amboyna they incite the people against us and they arm those of Kambela. We are sending you two big English cannon and other arms which we collected at Banda. They have a place at Jacatra, across the river from us and just as big. They followed us to Djambi, Patane, Siam and Japan —in fact, everywhere! Unless you come to an agreement with them we will have to oppose them by force." [8]

A major grievance, one to which Coen kept returning, was the fact that the Dutch, regardless of the truce in Europe, were in a state of war with the Spanish in Asia. This meant that warships and forts had to be maintained at great expense while the English sailed in peace. The English Company at times actually delivered more spices to the European market than the Dutch,

7. Ibid., *1*, 158.
8. Ibid., *1*, 130–33. On January 11, 1616, Coen served notice to John Jourdain that the Dutch would use force if the English continued their machinations in the Moluccas. See *Documents*, *2*, 74–75.

as the Seventeen remarked when they asked for greater return cargoes. At the same time, the English Company had become more enterprising. The meager results of the early voyages, mainly due to insufficient financial backing, had taught the English that something more had to be done about the Indies trade if they ever wanted to catch up with the Dutch. In 1609 James had granted a new charter, much broader than the one granted in 1600 by Elizabeth. It was given in perpetuity and, by excluding other Englishmen from the Indies trade, it offered what was in fact a monopoly. This attracted more capital from the merchant class, and the nobility also became interested in the venture. Salisbury, Nottingham, Worcester, and other courtiers were proud to participate, now that James had taken an active part in the rejuvenation of the Company.[9] More capital meant more ships, and the governors ordered new ones to be built instead of buying old ones.

This effort, while an improvement, fell short of what the Dutch Company was able to accomplish. But, as Coen's letters show clearly, it was enough to cause the Dutch distress, leading to awkward entanglements and recriminations. When the governors of the London Company learned how their captains and factors were being harassed by the Dutch, they appealed to the Earl of Salisbury, Lord High Treasurer of England. "Being enforced at last to break silence and complain our griefs . . . (having) long and patiently endured sundry notorious wrongs and injurious courses at the hands of the Hollanders, and being now reduced to extremities . . . (we) do humbly implore your Lordship's honorable assistance and mediation to the States (General)."[10] The governors referred to the English claim of free trade by virtue of the prior discoveries made by the Elizabethan navigators who had been in the Indies long before the Dutch. The argument was not very convincing because it ignored the Portuguese and Spanish, whose claims had a far stronger legal basis. Nevertheless, it opened a period of diplomatic negotiations which were carried on almost without interruption for many years.

Grotius had joined the first Dutch mission to London in 1613, and, after lengthy and acrimonious discussions, an agreement was

9. Hunter, British India, 1, 287–88.
10. Petition dated November 1611. See G. Birdwood and W. Foster, eds., The First Letter Book of the East India Company, 1600–1619 (London, 1893), pp. 429–32.

reached whereby each nation should "enjoy such places as it had conquered or discovered, and pay customs duties to the other at those ports." [11] The English interpreted this to mean that if they allowed the Dutch to come to the coast of Cambay then the English, in turn, should be allowed free access to the Spice Islands. This would have given the English by far the best of the bargain. The Seventeen, unwilling to fight the States General head-on, sent guarded instructions to the Indies to the effect that the English should be kept out of the Spice Islands. This was, of course, wishful thinking and, consequently, the agreement was of little value.

In the meantime, the London Company was bombarded with complaints from its people in the Indies about the obstructionist attitude of the Dutch. In 1614, another futile attempt was made to smooth over the difficulties, and this time the diplomatic maneuvering took place in The Hague. Oldebarnevelt took an active part in the discussions, and he made it clear that he would like to come to a peaceful solution. Much to the chagrin of the Amsterdam members of the Seventeen, the Advocate proposed that the two companies join forces and divide the trade on some equitable basis scaled according to past performances. He was hoping that, if the English and the Dutch were united, they could quickly eliminate the Spanish from Asiatic waters. James proved to be unwilling, and forbade the English Company to engage in any open warfare with Spain, but at the same time continued to insist on "free trade by the law of nations." [12] The Dutch countered with the familiar argument that trade would hardly be possible unless the Spanish were kept at bay at the great expense of ships, forts, and garrisons. How could the English expect to profit from this trade if they refused to pay their share?

Under these circumstances it was highly improbable that an amicable settlement could be arranged in Europe. Diplomatic negotiations did not cease, but, though they dragged on for years, they never produced any tangible results. Each company instructed its own administrators, and though they eschewed open hostilities, the London governors intended to gain a foothold in the Spice Islands and the Seventeen equally intended to keep them from doing so. This could only lead to serious friction between

11. Noel Sainsbury, ed., *Calendar of State Papers, East Indies, 1513–1616* (London, 1870), par. 678 and par. 691.
12. De Jonge, *Opkomst, 4,* lxxv-lxxvi.

the two companies, but it was not anticipated that within a few years commercial rivalry would result in open warfare.

Whom did the English have in the Indies to put their policy into effect? They had John Jourdain, their president at Bantam and the coordinator of all their activities. It was at his instigation that Castelton's expedition to the Spice Islands had been organized. His position, however, was not so strong as that of the Dutch governor general who, in conjunction with the Council of the Indies, had complete authority. Jourdain was little more than a mediator between the often opposing interests of the various undertakings which were still organized on the basis of separate joint stock companies for a limited number of years, each with its own capital and shareholders. Men like Saris and Castleton, commanders of fleets, were not enthusiastic about taking orders from a mere merchant at Bantam. Nevertheless, it was through Jourdain's efforts that repeated attempts to gain access to the Spice Islands had been made during the three years since his appointment as chief factor. He deserved to see his efforts crowned with greater success, but he failed largely because he had only restricted authority and the means at his disposal were utterly inadequate to the task. In spite of these difficulties, Jourdain managed to send home rich cargoes during his tenure in office. He managed to do this by using all the tricks of the trade —buying in the open market, outbidding the Dutch, bartering armaments for spices, using smugglers. But the main reason for his limited success was that he had no war to fight. As a result of Jourdain's stewardship, the shares of the first joint stock company, in operation from 1613 to 1616, rose 207 per cent.

It was hardly surprising that money should flow in from all directions when the governors opened a new subscription for a second joint stock company. The Annals of the Honorable East India Company show that the subscribers numbered 954, among them 15 dukes and earls, 82 knights, judges, and privy councillors, and 13 countesses and other ladies of nobility. There were over 300 merchants and some 22 tradesmen. They raised the unprecedented capital of more than £1,600,000, far greater than the original capital of the Dutch East India Company.[13] All of this capital, to be appropriated over three voyages, could be applied to trade, and none of it had to be allocated to fight Spain.

It looked as if the English Company might attain its objective

13. Hunter, *British India*, 1, 363–64.

at last. Why did it fail? Sir William Hunter blames it in part on the fact that the organization of the English Company was inferior to that of the Dutch, both in London and in the East. The system of separate ventures which the Dutch had found impractical as early as 1602 was not abandoned by the English until ten years later. Even then they did not form a company which carried within itself the spirit of continuity, but only changed the commercial framework to the slightly less temporary expedient of a joint stock company, comprising no more than three or four voyages within a limited number of years. During this short period each group of stockholders looked towards the greatest possible return on its investment, which meant that no allocations were made to assure future operations. Why go to that expense, the stockholders argued, when such capital expenditures had to be left behind, or at best be turned over to the next joint stock company at a fraction of the cost? Thus, while there was a permanent board of governors that administered the affairs of the Company, its hands were tied by the constantly changing group of investors, looking for quick returns without regard to a long-range objective. It was not until 1661 that the English finally adopted the pattern established by the Dutch. Sir William Hunter, in his *History of British India*, concludes that the English were a hundred years behind the Dutch.

The position of the Dutch Company was anything but favorable. The original capital had long since been expended, and the profits had far from met the high expectations. Large amounts had been spent on warships and the many fortifications and garrisons throughout the Indies. In order to raise more money, the return cargoes of spices and other goods had to be pledged against loans, which carried interest. This was the striking difference between the Dutch and English companies during the first decades of the seventeenth century. The Dutch directors continued to invest capital (by borrowing) in spite of the protests from the shareholders and their claims for closing out the general account when profits were declining. In this they had the support of the States General. The concept of "reserve capital" was still unknown in the accounting system, but the Dutch Company nevertheless managed to build up an invisible trading capital in the East, and the results of it would eventually become apparent. In England, on the other hand, the shareholders could demand their money back. The second joint stock company is a case in point. Its capital was two and a half times greater than that of the Dutch Company, but when it was dissolved in 1628 there had been no investment in Asia similar to that of the Dutch.[14]

On whom did the Dutch Company rely in the Indies to improve its position and to ward off the increased efforts of the English? The Seventeen had counted heavily on Gerard Reynst, in whom they had implicit trust. He was a man like themselves and a director of the Amsterdam chamber. They had enticed him to accept the high but hazardous office of governor general by honoring him with a gold medal and chain, and by promising him a seat on their board after his return to Holland. But Reynst died after little more than a year in the Indies. His place was taken, unofficially to be sure, by a young man about whom the Seventeen as yet knew little. When the Seventeen learned of Coen's appointment as bookkeeper-general, they replied that his increase in salary was quite steep, and they expressed the hope that he would earn it.[15]

14. See Glamann, *Dutch Asiatic Trade*, pp. 245-47.
15. *Documents, 4*, 287.

II

Second
in Command

It is quite possible that Coen expected to succeed Gerard Reynst as governor general when the latter finished his tenure in the Indies. It is certain that Reynst was greatly impressed by this young man, whose appointment as director general had been one of his earliest official acts. Reynst, before his death, told Coen that he deserved as high a salary as anyone in the Indies,[1] opening the possibility that he might have singled Coen out as his successor and might, in time, have recommended his appointment to the Seventeen.

In a situation of this kind, when a governor general died prematurely, the Council of the Indies was empowered to appoint a replacement subject to confirmation by the directors in the Netherlands. At the time of Reynst's death the various members of the council were spread far and wide, and it was not until July 1616 that a quorum could be convened to choose a successor. Coen, although himself a member, was not present because he was unwilling to leave his strategic post in West Java. But even if he had been present, there was practically no chance that he would have been appointed. He was the youngest member of the council and it could hardly be said that he had any friends among its members. By then he had often enough made it clear in his letters to the Seventeen that he had a low opinion of the men sent out from Holland, including those in high office. He was short-tempered and outspoken, and it can safely be assumed that his colleagues were aware of how he felt about some of them. If and when the time came for him to receive the appointment of governor general, it could only come from the Seventeen. As it turned out, the council elected Laurens Reael, who had previously been appointed by Reynst as governor of the Moluccas. Reael came from a patrician Amsterdam family and had studied law at the University of Leiden. His sister was married to

1. *Documents*, 6, 114.

Arminius, the foremost theologian in the Netherlands, who had begun the liberal Remonstrant movement against the Calvinists.[2] Reael was of the class of men like Grotius and Oldebarnevelt. He was known as a sober, peaceful man with no strong opinions as to what should be the policy in the Indies. He was vain, and paid a great deal of attention to his dress, for which he ordered expensive cloth from Holland. In almost every respect, he was the complete opposite of Jan Coen, and it is therefore not surprising that the two did not get along.

Coen might not be the Company's highest officer in the Indies, but he soon began to behave as if this lack of title were a mere formality. He did so because Reael preferred to stay in the eastern part of the archipelago, leaving Coen to deal with all the rest of the huge trading area, which now stretched from Japan to the coast of Malabar, and to cope with the vast amount of bookkeeping and the voluminous correspondence with the board of directors. Coen used his authority to full advantage, and the Seventeen soon became aware that they were dealing with an extraordinary, if difficult, young man who not only appeared to be aware of all the major problems which confronted the Company but who also was consistent in pointing out means, often distasteful to the tightfisted merchants, by which they should be solved.

When the Seventeen had made a chiding remark about his increased salary as bookkeeper-general, Coen replied testily: "the reason for my coming here was to serve the Company and my country, not the small salary your Lordships pay me!" [3] This comment was not directed solely to himself. The men who worked for the Company could be roughly divided into three groups. A small number, coming from good families and with connections among the directors, were considered good material for the higher positions. Among these were some eminent men, but their number was few compared with those who had joined the Company in a spirit of adventure and who had little to lose by leaving their homeland. Those who had ability took some second thought about their future after the first flush of excitement had worn off, and they came face to face with the harsh facts of life in the Indies. Those who survived their tour of duty, usually three years, returned to Holland fully convinced that they could earn a better

2. On Arminius, see Geyl, *Netherlands Divided*, pp. 44–48.
3. *Documents, 1*, 157.

LAURENS REAAL.
GOUV^R:GENER^D: VAN INDIA.

6. *Laurens Reael, painted ca. 1618 in the East Indies.*

salary at home than the meager one paid them by the Company. An added consideration were the living conditions. There was no chance for normal European family life in the Indies in those days.

At the other extreme were the sailors and soldiers recruited from the lowest classes of the towns. Most of them were the outcasts of society, derelicts from the waterfront, poor drifters from the countryside. Their main inducement for signing up was the assurance of three meals a day and a daily ration of beer and wine. Few among them had either ability or ambition to aspire to anything more. Their wages were a pittance. They were expected to supply the raw animal energy needed to keep the wheels turning and to do all the menial tasks that were required. Only by maintaining the strictest control could they be whipped into a working force, and even then discipline often broke down.

It was the third group, the one in the middle, which should have provided the vitality and cohesion so necessary for a progressive development of the Company's affairs. They were the men of the middle class, properly schooled and, at the outset, imbued with the necessary ambition to make the Company their career. From among them would have to come the important class of merchants, a term which also implied that they should also be bookkeepers and administrators.

The directors should have paid particular attention to the hiring of this middle group and to offering a sufficiently high salary to attract the best men obtainable. But the Seventeen felt otherwise. Payment of thirty-five guilders per month for a beginner and sixty to seventy guilders for a full-fledged merchant with years of experience was hardly an inducement. And such salaries were paid, moreover, only in part in the Indies—the rest was held back to be paid after an employee had returned from his tour of duty. Aside from parsimony, a trait they shared with the governors of the English Company, the Seventeen had a definite purpose in mind in keeping their servants from possession of an appreciable amount of money. They were afraid that it might be used for private trade to the detriment of the Company. This suspicious attitude also contributed to their reluctance in making a large capital available for the inter-Asiatic trade, such as Coen had proposed. Having little confidence in human nature, they could see all the possible opportunities a canny employee could devise to divert a part of the proceeds into his own pockets.

As far as Coen was concerned, it all amounted to the same thing. If the Company wanted honest and capable personnel, then it should pay adequate salaries, but the niggardly merchants at home were of a different mind. Coen repeatedly complained about this, and he epitomized the situation when he wrote: "Capable and good men will not come here under these circumstances because a forceful, clever, and honest person does not have to go to the Indies; he can do better almost anywhere else in the world." [4] It became part of Coen's credo repeated in almost every letter: "More money . . . better personnel!"

The Seventeen were not at all pleased with the tone of Coen's letters and they reprimanded him severely for his hotheadedness. It is interesting, however, that they did not reject his complaints without going to the trouble of explaining their reasons: Governor General Both had arrived in the Indies without sufficient arms and munitions because a truce with Spain had just been agreed upon at the time of his departure; Reynst had arrived without money because of reports the Seventeen had received that there was a sufficient amount of cash on hand in the Indies and that a large shipment of silver was expected from Japan. "You people want to do everything on too large a scale," they wrote. "If you had sent us the large return cargoes referred to we might not have been able to sell them profitably." In regard to the inter-Asiatic trade, they cautioned, "Do not overreach yourself. Goods might spoil in the warehouse and a quick turnover is essential." [5]

Caution was their watchword, guided as they were by their maxim, "costs come before profits." Since the stockholders had already put up their money, it was time that profits should result. They pointed out that in all the fourteen years since the Company had been established, no more than the original capital had been paid out in dividends, an average of a mere seven per cent yearly, and most of this had been borrowed back at a high interest rate.[6]

In these same letters, the Seventeen also reported that a French East India Company had been established at St. Malo. Some of the Company's enemies in Holland had participated financially, among them Isaac Lemaire, who was making one of his final bids for revenge on the United Company. He had launched a venture under the joint command of his son Jacob Lemaire and Willem

4. H. P. Geerke, *Jan Pieterszoon Coen* (Utrecht, 1929), p. 61.
5. *Documents, 6,* 81–82.
6. Ibid., *4,* 328–29.

Schouten, to try to find a passage south of the Strait of Magellan, thus circumventing the charter. By participating in the French enterprise as well, the aging Lemaire aimed to have two strings to his bow. The Seventeen informed their governor general and council that the States General had authorized the Company to arrest the Dutchmen on these French ships immediately upon arrival. (This order was based on ordinances which prohibited Dutchmen from serving on foreign bottoms.) They named seven men in key positions, but, instead of giving them corporal punishment, the Seventeen magnanimously added, they should be given minor jobs at distant forts where they could do no harm.

The French ships were not to arrive until the year following, but Lemaire's ship, the *Harmony*, reached Djakarta during the latter part of 1616. Jacob Lemaire and Schouten had been cordially received by Laurens Reael at Ternate, their first port of call in the East Indies. But Coen was not impressed by their magnificent exploit, the discovery of a more southern passage into the Pacific Ocean (which they had named Strait Lemaire) and around a cape which had been called Cape Hoorn after the town from which they had sailed. Explorations as such had no place in Coen's scheme of things, and he had harsh things to say about captains who deliberately went out of their way for the glory of discovering new lands. Such attempts lengthened voyages unnecessarily and endangered ships, he pointed out, and there was more than enough work to be done in the Indies than to waste time on such foolishness.[7] Lacking every vestige of sentimentality, he was not impressed by the fact that this ship came from his own home town or that important burghers of Hoorn were financially interested, nor did he listen to Lemaire's and Schouten's protestations that they had not sailed through the Strait of Magellan and thus had not violated the charter. Coen informed the Seventeen that he had attached the *Harmony* because Isaac Lemaire was an "opponent to the common good."[8] Complete inventory had been taken and those who were willing had been taken into the employ of the Company; the others were being returned to Holland, including Jacob Lemaire, who died en route. The father, Isaac Lemaire, eventually won his case in the Supreme Court of Holland and Zealand, but the Seventeen ignored the verdict.

7. "The months go by, the skippers say. At sea we are the lords and masters, but in the Indies we are only servants" (*Documents, 6, 108*).
8. *Documents, 1, 235.*

The year 1616 also saw a widening rift between Coen and Reael. Both men reported directly to the Seventeen, who thus heard both sides, which in turn helped them to decide whether or not they should confirm Reael's election. The main source of friction was the question of the action to be taken against the English, in view of the ambiguous instructions from the Seventeen. Coen had been for strong action all along, and he correctly read between the lines of the instructions from Holland that the directors were of like mind, but that they paid lip service to the States General who wanted to avoid an open conflict with the English at almost any cost. He was also tempted to interpret those instructions as meaning that the Seventeen wanted their people in the Indies to take the initiative, trusting that they would be able to appease the States General once this body was confronted with a fait accompli.

On January 5, 1616, a letter arrived at Bantam with the important instruction that "the subjugation of the Amboyna and Banda Islands was of prime importance and all foreign nations should be barred from this trade." [9] The word *all* was enough to convince Coen that he had the Seventeen on his side. Six days later, on January 11, he served notice on John Jourdain that all English ships appearing in the Spice Islands would be expelled by force.[10] By dispatching Commander Lam to intercept Castleton's ships, he proved that his was no idle threat.

How did Reael react to this Dutch-English problem and to the veiled instructions of the Seventeen? He adhered strictly to the original orders from the Seventeen, that the Dutch should not engage in open hostilities against the English. He, too, realized that this attitude emanated from the States General, but it was in his nature, as a cautious man and a jurist, to consider himself a servant of the States General as well as the United Company. As long as the States General regarded friendship with London as more important than a possible loss of trade, Reael was going to adhere to that policy, unless he had specific instructions to the contrary. This was clear when he wrote the Seventeen: "I wished Your Lordships would speak straight out so that your servants do not burn their fingers." As a result he allowed Castleton to trade freely with the Spanish and the people of Tidore, "barter-

9. Ibid., *4*, 313.
10. See Book III, Ch. 10, n. 8.

ing victuals and munitions of war against a large quantity of cloves." [11]

When shortly thereafter Reael was chosen governor general, he managed to persuade the council members present to agree with his stand. Five months after Coen had handed his ultimatum to the English at Bantam, the governor general and council decided that "no harsh measures were to be used to disperse the English by force, fearing that this might not only lead to war in these quarters but might spread to Europe as well." The argument is similar to that the English often used, in trying to intimidate their rivals—that some day the Flemings would have to account for their actions in the English Channel. Coen had ignored these threats as idle boasting, but the council resolved that "no force would be used against the English without specific orders to that effect." [12] There were thus during 1616 widely diverging points of view as how to cope with one of the most important problems facing the Company. It had also become a matter of personalities, Coen versus Reael. It was up to the Seventeen to make the decision.

It was Coen's letter of October 10, 1616, dealing with this and a host of other matters, which may well have been the deciding factor. He wrote in great detail of what had prompted him to take action against the English, even though he lacked specific orders to that effect. "If I did wrong (which I do not believe) please tell me and I will act accordingly. The English threaten to hang me in effigy on the highest gallows in England and to pickle my heart . . . Reael cannot decide to deal firmly with the English, demanding more pertinent orders. I hope that your latest orders will satisfy him and change his attitude because we should not have arguments among ourselves." [13]

The English question was not the only one on which Coen and Reael were not in accord. After his election as governor general, Reael had to determine what to do with the fleet of sixteen vessels then gathered at Ternate. After some deliberation, it was decided in council to send them against Manila for the purpose of capturing this stronghold, or at least destroying the Spanish fleet and

11. *Documents, 1,* 199.
12. L. Kiers, *Coen op Banda* (Utrecht, A. Oosthoek, 1943), p. 94.
13. *Documents, 6,* 85. Compare Meilink-Roelofsz, *Asian Trade,* pp. 197–202, 210–11.

thus finally eliminating this threat to the Moluccas. In reporting this resolution, Coen remarked: "I am of an entirely different opinion. I stated it before, and now I repeat, put the Moluccas, Amboyna, and Banda in a state of defense and use the excess ships to prevent Spanish trade between Manila and China, in the Strait of Malacca, or on the coast of Malabar." [14] It was clear that he did not underestimate the strength of the Spanish fleet, which had returned to Manila after Van der Hagen had destroyed the Portuguese squadron at Malacca, thus averting a planned attack on Bantam. Again Coen proved that he had a keen understanding of the situation, remembering in this case the futile attacks on Mozambique, in which he himself had participated, and on Malacca, Macao, and Manila. The battle took place October 28. It was bloody and inconclusive, and the Dutch were forced to withdraw. The news of this debacle did not reach the Seventeen until they had made their decision as to who should be the next governor general, but it must have strengthened their belief that they had made the proper choice. If there was anything the Seventeen regretted more than to put up money or to pay adequate salaries, it was to lose ships.

Coen did not confine himself in this letter to his differences with Reael. Important as the Spice Islands and the need for eliminating English competition were, they were only part of a greater picture which, in his eyes, embraced the whole of Asia to which the future of the United Company was tied. "The focal point of our trade in East Asia and the Indies is not to keep a large fleet in the Moluccas, but to patrol the Strait of Malacca." [15] The result would be to monopolize the pepper trade from Djambi [16] and the textile trade from the coast of Coromandel. It would also cut the life line between the Spanish in the Philippines and the Portuguese at Malacca and Goa. In line with this suggestion, he wished to reopen negotiations with the Sultan of Achin, with whom the English, so far, had a preferred position.

Coen also reported on his endeavors to come to an understanding with Bantam: further attempts should be made, and he was willing to pay higher tolls provided Bantam would exclude the English. If something on this order could be arranged, it would be better than leaving Bantam completely. The alternative was

14. *Documents, 1,* 201.
15. Ibid., *1,* 205.
16. On Djambi, see Meilink-Roelofsz, *Asian Trade,* pp. 258–61.

Djakarta. He had been considering building a fort there, not so much because one was urgently needed, but more to imply with-drawal from Bantam, and he would pay the king a reasonable amount for the privilege. "But it wouldn't be wise," he added, "to spend the money and then let the English trade under its protection." Considering the delay before he could get a reply from Holland, he visualized that it would be March 1618 before a fort could be started.

Such a project required a large labor force and, considering the tropical climate and the European temperament of Dutch sailors and soldiers, it had to be recruited elsewhere. As the natives were prohibited by their rulers to do such work for the Dutch, another solution had to be found. The Seventeen had already intimated that it would be desirable to get slaves for such menial work as well as for "manning galleys and rowing yachts." Coen replied that "slaves would indeed be advantageous. We can not exist without slaves. For three years already I have suggested this but nothing has been done about it. I suggest that you instruct someone on your next voyage to go to the north coast of Mada-gascar. According to Admiral Van der Hagen good lots are avail-able there at low prices. The Arabs do a thriving business in slaves and manage to obtain large quantities yearly." [17]

Coen was not enthusiastic about the trade in Japan. "President Specx" he wrote, "neglects his bookkeeping, therefore the results cannot be established." Although Jacques Specx had made a valua-ble contact with the Shogun, the Japanese were not easy to deal with. There was the serious problem of the large numbers of Japanese converts of the Jesuit missionaries, who had started riots which led to the expulsion of the Portuguese and a ruthless sup-pression of the Christians. It was to Specx' credit that during these difficult times he managed to enhance Dutch interest at the expense of the Portuguese; eventually Japan was closed to all foreigners except the Dutch. The English, of course, had quickly followed the Dutch in this market, as they had everywhere else in Asia.[18] Besides the English competition, Specx had to contend with the grasping *Daimyo* at Firando. Japanese governors were no different from others in Asia. They were fully aware that these

17. Reynst had planned, Coen added, to send a ship there for this purpose, but none could be made available. See *Documents, 1*, 218.

18. See E. M. Thompson, ed., *Diary of Richard Cocks, Cape Merchant in the English Factory in Japan, 1615–1622* (2 vols., London, 1883).

'foreign devils' would not have come to Japan if it were not profitable to them. This was the native point of view throughout the whole of Asia, that the foreigners were the only ones who benefited from trade. That it also brought economic advantages to the country itself, they ignored or did not understand. As a result, the *Daimyos* exacted tribute at every opportunity. Such 'gifts' were difficult to explain, especially since it infuriated the Seventeen to encounter such items in the books.

Coen, unlike Specx, never felt himself to be part of the country in which he served the Company. He distrusted and disliked the natives who, to him, were only an obstacle to his plans. At such places as Banda and Amboyna he would gladly have seen them replaced by Dutchmen and at a later date he did his best to accomplish as much. Specx, however, got along well with the Japanese, even to the extent of taking a Japanese woman into his house, who later presented him with a daughter which he duly acknowledged as his own. It is not recorded whether Coen, the Calvinist and celibate, frowned on such unorthodox behavior, but he made it clear that Specx was lacking in another important aspect: he knew little about bookkeeping.

It was in this letter, dated October 10, 1619, that Coen apologized for the irreverent tone of his letters to the Seventeen. He admitted having used too strong language in regard to money matters, and that instead of being polite he had used words more befitting "a rough soldier and unruly sailor." But almost in the same breath he turned his apology into a renewed criticism. "Your Lordships forgive me, but conditions here are such that it is often difficult to curb one's temper. . . . If your Lordships would only realize how much misery and trouble this lack of money has caused us, you would sooner be moved to compassion than object to my language."

The Seventeen had cut by more than half Coen's demand for a revolving capital for return cargoes. "There is nothing to be said," Coen commented drily, "because the arrow will reach no farther than the target for which it is intended." [19]

19. *Documents*, 6, 92–93.

12

The
Final
Rung

Coen need not have been apprehensive, if he ever was, about his standing with the Seventeen. From the time they received Coen's *Discourse* of January 1, 1614, in which he expounded his grandiose plans, the Seventeen had realized that they had a young man in their service who would bear watching. As his subsequent letters arrived, detailing the Company's manifold activities throughout the whole of Asia and supported by scrupulous balance sheets, they gradually acquired a better understanding of the problems than they ever had before. No one had provided them before with such a comprehensive picture of the state of affairs in the Indies. When they had learned of Coen's appointment as director general and president of the Bantam office, they were not yet convinced that Reynst had made the proper choice. Coen's youth was obviously against him, as well as the unabashed manner in which he called his principals to task. But as the picture became clearer with each additional report he sent in, his reputation began to grow.

By the end of 1616, the Seventeen were ready to accord him necessary recognition, but, because of the slow process of communication, it took until October of the following year before Coen received word. The directors complimented Coen for sending sufficiently large return cargoes regardless of the scarcity of capital. "We trust you will continue this and we shall be grateful." They agreed with Coen, rather than with Reael, that trade by foreigners in the Moluccas should be prevented, by force if necessary, "but with discretion as we should avoid the enmity of all the Indians." With respect to Coen's sarcastic remark about his salary they wrote: "We greatly appreciate your services. Your salary, as of this date, has been increased to 300 guilders monthly, provided you serve for three more years after your present term expires. If you stay for five more years you will receive fitting honors upon our return."

They were equally accommodating about the tone of his letters. "It is unnecessary for you to apologize for your harsh words. We can bear this from a faithful servant like you who has the interest of the Company at heart." [1]

Coen's reaction was typical. Now that the Seventeen had made it clear that they needed him, he had no qualms in insinuating, without specifically stating so, that he expected to be named governor general. "I thought my services were more valuable to you than what you offer." He referred to the fact that others received more than twice his salary, "and accomplish little, in fact they hurt the Company." Here he pointed directly at Reael, and it was clear that he expected to succeed him. To make doubly sure that the Seventeen understood, he referred to Reynst's promise that he deserved as high a salary as any in the Company's service. It could only mean one thing. He intimated that he was not eager to stay beyond his term unless he were duly compensated. Reael, following instructions from the Seventeen, had asked Coen to stay on after his term was concluded. "I told him," Coen wrote, "that I would not decide until next year. Now it grieves me that you offer me less than what others earn if I stay three years longer. Who has maintained and improved the prosperity of the Company? . . . But I won't diminish the work of others, therefore I leave things as they are and will work for the Company as hard as before. That the Lord may give us His blessing and you a more liberal heart." [2]

This emphasis on remuneration has led some Dutch historians to intimate that Coen could not have been so great a man as was generally believed. [3] Perhaps he should have been above such quibbling about his salary. This indictment is hardly fair. The size of his own salary was only part of his consistent campaign against the avaracious policy of the directors. Nor did he single himself out in demanding a higher compensation for his labors. He had repeatedly demanded higher salaries for all ranks, to attract the kind of men the Company needed so badly. What irked him personally, however, was the fact that Reael was earning twice as much as he, and he made it clear enough to the Seventeen that

1. *Documents, 6,* 109–10.
2. Ibid., *1,* 318.
3. Romein, *Erflaters,* p. 96.

he did not think Reael was worth it. Certainly 300 guilders a month was hardly a sufficient remuneration for a man who was responsible for millions. Had money been his main objective, he could easily have lined his pockets at the expense of the Company. Among later servants, both in the Dutch and English companies, there would be not a few who lacked his scruples.

Even Reael, with twice Coen's salary and with only the responsibility of keeping peace in the Moluccas, felt that he was underpaid. On September 22, 1616, three months after he had been chosen by the plenary council as governor general, he wrote the Seventeen a letter which had just about the opposite effect from what he had expected. He complained that he had served the Company under difficult circumstances and at great personal sacrifice without receiving a penny more in salary. He therefore decided to submit his resignation, adding that "there are enough people available, both in the Netherlands and the Indies, who could qualify for this high office." He mentioned five names, one of them being Jan Pietersz. Coen, whom he described as a man "with great insight, industrious and forceful . . . who directs the office at Bantam where the affairs of all the Indies have come to his attention." But the end of his letter revealed his real purpose. "It being human nature to change one's mind, and although I am now determined to return home after my term has expired, I might be induced to stay longer if the situation, and especially a good salary, would warrant it." [4]

It was not difficult for the Seventeen to decide which of the men should be in charge in the Indies. They promptly accepted Reael's resignation and completely ignored his none to subtle suggestion that he might be willing to stay on at an increased salary. At a meeting held at Middelburg on August 23, 1617, they unanimously appointed Jan Coen in his place. In due course this was confirmed by Prince Maurice and the States General. His salary was raised to 600 guilders per month. In informing Coen of his appointment, they added secret instructions concerning Reael. Under no conditions should he be allowed to serve his full term, even if he should desire to do so. He should return on the first available ship "for many pregnant reasons and considerations which we do not think advisable to mention here." [5]

4. Letter from Reael to the Seventeen from Ternate, dated September 22, 1616. See De Jonge, *Opkomst, 4,* lviii–lix.
5. *Documents, 4,* 377.

Although the Seventeen never elaborated on their cryptic remark, it might have been that they had still another reason for dismissing him in this peremptory fashion. It was a reason that might not have been shared by all the directors, but it may have been foremost in the minds of the Amsterdam members. The internal troubles in the Republic were rapidly coming to a head. On the one side stood the Remonstrants, representing the more liberal religious movement that had been founded by Arminius, a professor at the University of Leiden. This group was now led by such enlightened men as Oldebarnevelt and Grotius. Opposing them were the Contra-Remonstrants, unbending Calvinists who stubbornly adhered to their belief in predestination. The differences, however, were not confined to theological matters, and they had developed into power politics without regard to dialectics.[6] Some of the various disputants could not even explain their own religious concepts. Prince Maurice, heading the anti-Remonstrant party, once severely lectured a Remonstrant clergyman for his zeal in predestination. It had to be pointed out to him that he was arguing against himself: the facts were quite the opposite.[7]

It is more realistic to call this a struggle for power, a deepening feud between Oldebarnevelt and Prince Maurice in which the Prince had the strong support of the Amsterdam *Vroedschap*, now headed by Reynier Pauw, who had succeeded in gathering the Magnificat of the town into his hands. This had made him the most powerful man in Amsterdam, if not in the whole republic. Pauw had been one of the instigators of the earliest attempts to organize an East India company, and he had largely guided its subsequent endeavors. Although he was no longer an active director, it is certain that his influence in the United Company was still considerable.

Oldebarnevelt was a statesman who considered the interest of the whole country above that of partisan groups. The Amsterdam merchants had no such lofty ideals. They had never forgotten that it had been Oldebarnevelt who had deprived them of a monopoly of the spice trade by insisting that the Company should be organized on a national basis. They had also been

6. For a concise account of these religious disputes, see Geyl, *Netherlands Divided*, pp. 41–65.

7. R. Limburg, *Cultuurdragers in bewogen tijden* (The Hague, ca. 1943), p. 195.

against the truce with Spain because it brought an end to their lucrative privateering. Oldebarnevelt's refusal to grant a charter for a West India company had added still more fuel to the fire. It was under pressure for caution from the States General, guided by Oldebarnevelt, that the Seventeen had been obliged to advise moderation to their servants in their disputes with the English. Now that the power of the seventy year-old statesman was waning even within the body of the States General, it was no coincidence that the Seventeen were beginning to encourage a stiffer attitude against the English in Asia.

It was logical that a man like Coen, who had advocated sterner measures all along, should have been the choice of the Amsterdam directors, the more so because, like themselves, Coen was also a Calvinist. Laurens Reael on the other hand had consistently advocated a moderate policy, for both the English and the recalcitrant natives of the Spice Islands. In addition he was also a Remonstrant.[8] Thus there were sufficient reasons to recall Reael and replace him by Coen.

Jan Coen did not learn about his appointment until May 1618, barely in time to deal with the various problems which had gradually grown more serious. Even before his promotion, however, he had acted independently, because Reael preferred to stay in the Moluccas. Difficulties at this time largely centered on West Java, in his territory; thus Coen considered it justifiable that he should take charge of the situation, as director general and as president of the offices at Bantam and Djakarta.

Early in the year 1617, the first ships of the French East India Company arrived at Bantam. They were the *Montmorency* and the *Marguerite*. There were 17 Dutchmen aboard the ships, including seven who had originally been employed by the Dutch Company. All claimed that they did not know that they were headed for the Indies when they had entered French service. In accordance with his instructions from the Seventeen, Coen seized the Dutchmen from the ships and put them to work "at half the wages they were to receive from the French." Coen made no attempt to attach the ships, but he sent instructions to Banda and Amboyna that they were to be sent away if they appeared there.[9] Deprived of knowledgeable leadership, the French ships stayed at Bantam; they had much sickness on board and had

8. See above, 335 f.
9. *Documents, 6,* 100–01.

to sell their cannon and munitions to obtain the necessary victuals.

At about the same time two English ships, the *Swan* and the *Defense*, arrived in the Moluccas. Both were captured, but Reael offered to return them if the English agreed to leave Pulu Run in the Banda group, where they had a detachment of some sixty men. The English replied that they would defend themselves to the bitter end. Reael decided that the forces at his disposal were not strong enough to dislodge them. It is not difficult to imagine how Coen reacted to this attitude.

Towards the end of the year two more French ships, the *St. Michel* and *St. Louis* arrived in the Indies, and this time Coen was less lenient. He was having trouble enough with the English, and he refused to permit another European nation access to the area under his jurisdiction. As before, there were quite a few Dutchmen on the ships, mainly because Isaac Lemaire was a participant in this venture. The French commander had died en route and a Dutchman, Hans de Decker, had been put in command. These Dutchmen, too, were removed from the ships. Decker had already been put on a Dutch ship scheduled to sail for home when he managed to escape with the help of the English. He remained hidden at the house of the *Pangeran* Rana Mangala for several days before Coen found out were he was. Coen, in the meantime, had taken an audacious step. He had obtained confessions from some of the Dutch captives that the French, flying the Dutch flag, had committed piracy against ships belonging to the merchants from Surate.[10] Knowing that this would lead to still more difficulties, Coen attached one of the French ships and brought it to one of the small islands off Djakarta. When Coen learned of Decker's whereabouts, he appealed to the *Pangeran* to deliver to him this renegade Dutchman, "showing him in the most friendly manner the ordinances issued by the States General." But Decker had not wasted his time. With costly presents and tirades against the Dutch Company, he had managed to make the *Pangeran* his ally. Rana Mangala flatly refused Coen's request to deliver up Decker, and he insisted that the *St. Michel* should be released. All the talk about alleged piracy, he said, was nothing but an excuse to gain complete control of all trade. "He

10. Coen proved his point by submitting the journals of these two French ships to the Seventeen. See *Documents, 1,* 489.

told me," Coen wrote the Seventeen of this incident, "that Bantam's trade was open to all nations and that he would never submit like those of Banda and Amboyna." The *St. Michel*, the *Pangeran* added, was taken in waters under his jurisdiction and thus in violation of the law of nations; it should be released at once. Obviously Decker had instructed him well. Shortly afterwards Decker escaped on an English vessel.[11]

Coen refused to comprise, but the *Pangeran*, prodded by both the English and French with perhaps extravagant promises, remained equally adamant. Trying to force Coen's hand, he forbade the delivery of all pepper to the Dutch, even that which had already been bought and paid for.

Coen circulated among the *Pangeran's* opponents, the young king and his followers, pointing out what the consequences might be for Bantam, should the Dutch withdraw their patronage. This had little effect at first, because the *Pangeran* was strong and felt secure in his power, now that there were two other European nations on his side. After the arrival of a Dutch ship with a cargo of pepper from Djambi, Coen started to empty the Company's warehouses. Realizing that Coen was not making an idle threat, the *Pangeran*, under pressure of the local merchants and the court, was forced to capitulate. Rana Mangala was not the man to take such a defeat lightly, and he tried to gain by intrigue what he had lost in open conflict. By his intimidation of the Chinese merchants of Bantam, the flow of pepper to the Dutch was brought to a virtual standstill, most of it being held in warehouses if it were not sold to the English or native and Chinese traders. There were other harassments as well, mysterious fires near the Dutch warehouses and attempts to plunder them. The English felt they were gaining in favor at the expense of the Dutch, and stepped up their machinations.

The crew of the *St. Michel* had left their ship after it had been attached, and a few months later Coen confiscated the vessel and put it in the service of the Company. The *St. Louis* returned to St. Malo during 1628, carrying little cargo. Coen fully realized that his act against the French would have its repercussions in Europe, but this was something that the directors would have to settle with the States General. It led indeed to serious difficulties on the diplomatic level between the two governments, not to be

11. De Jonge, *Opkomst, 4,* xliii–xlv.

settled until five years later when the United Company agreed to pay the French Company an indemnity of 550,000 livres.[12] In the meantime, Coen had succeeded in keeping the French out of the Indies.

The situation at Bantam was rapidly deteriorating to such an extent that it would have to be abandoned as a possible rendezvous unless some firm action were taken. By the end of 1617, Coen wrote that if the Company were to stay at Bantam it must have a strong garrison there, or there would be disaster. "If we cannot be friends with Bantam, then let us have war!" [13] This was more than he could undertake on his own account, but he did not hesitate to take a drastic step on his own responsibility. In Bantam itself he informed the local traders that they were not to buy any pepper until after the Company's needs had been filled. They would be told when this had been accomplished. Those who refused to abide by his order would have their vessels confiscated on the high seas. These were high-handed tactics, but it was typical of Coen to abandon legalities after all attempts to come to a favorable agreement had failed. He reasoned that the Dutch had come to trade in peace, and when this proved impossible, other measures had to be applied. He put the interest of the Company before everything else. That was what he was there for.

Reael did not return to Bantam until the end of September 1617, more than a year after he had been named governor general. There is no record as to how the two men got along together now that they were face to face. Neither knew, as yet, what decision the Seventeen had made about their respective futures; this news would not reach the Indies until May of the following year. Now that the governor general was at Bantam, it was possible to pass resolutions in council to decide upon an official policy in dealing with some of the major problems. One was the insistence of the English in trading in the Moluccas in violation of what the Dutch considered to be their contractual privileges with the King of Ternate and the Orang Kayas of Banda. The capture of the two ships in those waters, the *Swan* and the *Defense,* had of course infuriated the English. "It caused a great to-do," Coen wrote.

12. Act of Accord (dated October 20, 1623), between the French ambassador and delegates of the States General.

13. Four employees of the Company had been killed in street fights, as well as three Japanese who had come to their assistance. See *Documents, 1,* 305.

"One day they threaten to sail to Banda in force and take revenge, and the next they say they will attack our ships at sea. They expect to get even by reprisals in the Channel at home and they are going to break our heads. Daily they come up with new threats which clearly shows that they are quite confused." [14] But the Dutch had something to complain about as well. Recently, 15 men of the ship *Harmony* had been murdered at Macassar, and the Dutch were convinced that the massacre had been instigated by the English factor there.

At about this time, some Spanish and Portuguese prisoners escaped from a Dutch ship in port, and the English gave them asylum. This brought all the antagonism to a crisis, and bitter fighting broke out in the streets of Bantam, English and Dutch sailors attacking each other with knives and cutlasses. Both sides counted several dead, and others were maimed for life. Witnessing these fights may well have induced Reael to agree with Coen and to sign the resolution taken in council on November 22 which, once more and in no uncertain terms, barred the English from Amboyna, the Banda group, and Pulu Run in particular. To make sure that this resolution should have the widest possible circulation, a copy was nailed to the outer gate of the Company compound. The English merchants, without taking the time to read the paper carefully, told Rana Mangala that the Dutch were also barring his subjects from those islands. The *Pangeran* demanded proof of this and wanted to see the resolution itself. The English ran back to the Dutch compound, "and when they were unable to detach the paper, they tore down the gate and brought it to him (document and all)." When he saw that Bantam was nowhere mentioned, "he berated them for their lies, saying that he was not concerned with the Moluccas, Amboyna, nor Banda." [15] It was of no interest to him what the Dutch intended to do there.

Although Coen and Reael were opposed on several issues, there was one on which they were in complete agreement: the need for a rendezvous. Coen would have preferred Bantam, but the tension there had risen to such heights that the prospect was all but hopeless. Djakarta had become more and more important during the quarrels at Bantam and now seemed to offer the only alternative. On December 18, 1617, the council resolved to re-

14. *Documents, 6,* 112.
15. Ibid., *1,* 305.

quest, in all friendliness, permission to build a fort at Djakarta and to use it as headquarters for the United Company.[16] In reporting this to the Seventeen, Coen added that he was certain that this would be granted because "All that the king and his nobles want is money." [17] It turned out to be not quite so simple.

Before the year was out, after only about three months at Bantam, Reael sailed back to the Moluccas, having more or less agreed with Coen to adopt a stronger attitude against native trade in that area and thus to tighten the monopoly for the Company. His brief visit at what was really the nerve center of the Company's activities in the whole of Asia might suggest that he did not like the tumultuous conditions there. It might also be that Reael did not care to be in too close contact with so hardheaded and forceful a character as Coen, who had taken on responsibilities which Reael, as governor general, should have assumed.

On April 30, 1618, Coen received the news that he had been appointed governor general and that Reael was to return home forthwith. As further proof of their implicit confidence in Coen, the Seventeen authorized him to appoint his own successor in case of such need. "Considering the debauchery and malfunction in office, even among the principal officers," the Seventeen added, "the election of a Governor General should not be left to a plurality of votes in the Council." [18] At 31 years of age, this ambitious son of a small merchant of the town of Hoorn had come a long way.

16. Ibid., 3, 413.
17. Ibid., 1, 329.
18. For Coen's commission, see *Documents*, 4, 385–90. This document was signed by each member of the Seventeen. Reynier Pauw's name does not appear, which seems to indicate that he had withdrawn from active participation on the board because of his great responsibilities as Magnificat of Amsterdam and all that this position entailed. During the next decade two of his sons became directors.

13

1618

Coen's letter of March 11, 1618, written less than two months
before he received word of his appointment, must have suggested
to the Seventeen that their new governor general would be a
difficult man to deal with. The letter ended on a note which must
have made them bristle: "I am almost weary, my voice weakens
and the pen falters, to have to repeat that while in some cases
you show great courage, there is always something in which
you fall short." He referred to the fact that he had sent eight
ships to Holland during the past year, all fully laden, but he intimated that he could have filled 20 if only the Seventeen had made
them available: "In great enterprises one needs courage else it
were better not to start them. It might suit a simple householder
to be parsimonious, but not Your Lordships. When you think
you save ten, the Company loses a hundred, nay—a thousand." [1]

Only a man who knew his own strength would have dared to
use such language to the board of directors that paid his salary.
Obviously Coen was above such considerations. He sensed that
something greater could be accomplished than a mere emporium.
He had in mind a strong territorial nucleus of Dutch colonists,
governed by Dutch law, from which the United Company would
dominate the whole of Asiatic trade. In this belief he never fal-
tered, and for it he was ready to fight all opposition, including
the Seventeen.

April 30, 1618, the day Jan Coen learned of his appointment
as governor general, must have been a splendid day in his life,
but his subsequent acknowledgment shows that he took it in his
stride. He reacted as if he had expected his promotion all along,
nor was he impressed by his new salary of 600 guilders a month.
"Salary never was my main consideration," he told the Seventeen,
"nevertheless, I feel that the services I expect to render deserve
a higher remuneration. Honor and shame keep me from men-
tioning my own accomplishments and the wages they deserve.

1. *Documents, 6,* 121-22.

I shall therefore serve you as I have in the past and leave the compensation to Your Lordships' gratitude." [2]

After appointing Jan Coen their governor general, the Seventeen expected him to sail forthwith to the Moluccas. On June 24, Coen replied that he intended to do so as soon as possible so that he could be back at Bantam later in the year. At this particular moment the situation in West Java had seemed secure enough not to require Coen's day by day supervision. The young king had asked the Dutch to stay at Bantam, informing Coen that the Company could buy pepper freely. But the *Pangeran* was an unwilling second to this overture and continued his intrigues against the Dutch. He caused the price of pepper to rise far above the limit the Company expected to pay. Coen countered by applying economic attrition, perhaps the first time in history that such a measure was consciously used. He withdrew entirely from the market and the price of pepper dropped from 48 to 33 reals for ten bags. With the fortuitous arrival of some junks from China intent on buying pepper, the Bantam merchants took hope and the price rebounded to 45 reals. Coen had had enough. Having already intimidated the native trade, he now extended his threats to the Chinese merchants as well. Unless Bantam were willing to sell him pepper at a reasonable price, between 30 and 35 reals, he would seize the cargoes of all Chinese vessels afloat, and force them to accept his price. [3]

With this new problem on his hands, Coen decided to postpone his trip to the Moluccas to take the administration of the Company and dismiss Reael. It must have been a difficult decision to make, because only by going to the Moluccas could he assume the title at once and receive the increased salary that went with it. But apparently he put the Company's interest above immediate personal gain and glory, which lends credence to his statement that salary was not his main consideration. He was loath to leave West Java: "In these quarters there is much to be done and the difficulties are great." [4] He did not see any particular advantage for the Company in his going to the Moluccas at this time. To avoid having two heads of government, Coen informed the Seventeen that he would not assume his title until after Reael was officially relieved of his duties.

Coen could, of course, have summoned Reael to come to Ban-

2. Ibid., *1*, 353.
3. Ibid., *6*, 128. See also Coolhaas, *Generale Missiven*, p. 80.
4. *Documents*, *1*, 401.

tam at once, but he did nothing of the sort. He waited until October 4, five months after receiving his appointment, before he even disclosed it to the members of the council. It was not until October 24 that he finally informed Reael, and then he did it with such courtesy that the other could not possibly have been offended. He said that the Seventeen had granted Reael's request for retirement, and that he could return to the fatherland at the first opportunity. There was not a word about the secret instructions he had received, ordering Reael home because his presence in the Indies was no longer desired. Coen had no personal animosity towards Reael.[5] It was in Coen's nature, although he was completely devoid of compassion, to side with an individual rather than the Seventeen, whom he regarded as obstructionists and the heaviest cross he had to bear.

The Seventeen had written Coen that they did not approve of a rendezvous on Java: the island was too heavily populated, and the opposition from local rulers, especially Mataram, might be too strong. In his reply to this letter, Coen completely ignored this advice. Now that he was governor general, the matter of the rendezvous was something he was going to settle on his own responsibility. He made it clear, however, that he intended to play Djakarta against Bantam in order to bring the latter to reason. "But we must have more ships, money, and other essentials to make it impossible for the Spanish, the Portuguese, and others to export anything to Europe. If you furnish these for a few years then, in the future, we shall be able to finance all the return cargoes you want from the profits we make here [inter-Asiatic trade] . . . Do not try to economize."[6]

Subsequent letters during 1618 outlined some of the problems Coen faced. Peace in Banda was one more disrupted. The Dutch had intercepted three native vessels because they had no pass and, in retaliation, the Bandanese had murdered a chief merchant. The English, unabashed by earlier reverses, were again offering higher prices in order to gain a foothold in the Spice Islands. "Reael suggested that we pay more money for nutmegs," Coen informed the Seventeen, "but I say NO! Do not give in or the whole business will go to the devil. It were better that all the Bandanese leave their islands; then we could plant Dutch colonies there, if only you would send us more people."[7]

5. Ibid., 2, 459.
6. Ibid., 1, 347–49.
7. Ibid., 1, 364–65.

There was trouble of a similar nature at Amboyna, where the Dutch were halting Chinese and native vessels that came there to trade. The Amboynese produced a letter from their king in Ternate which stated that although he had concluded a contract with Admiral Matelief to sell cloves only to the Dutch, nothing had been said about eliminating native trade. As a result, the Amboynese claimed that their roadsteads were "free to all the world." Here also Coen advocated economic attrition: "These people have to be brought to their senses with a little poverty and pressure or nothing will ever be accomplished here." [8]

By keeping native traders from buying spices, the Dutch had shut off the regular flow of rice and textiles and had not yet succeeded in filling this vacuum themselves. With the limited number of ships at its disposal, the Company had been neither able nor willing to enter this none too lucrative coastal trade. Coen had realized from the start that this problem would arise as soon as his edict against native traders was enforced. He had repeatedly requested the Seventeen to throw this trade open to employees of the Company who had served their term and to other burghers from the Netherlands. For a long time the directors had considered 'free trade' blasphemous words, and only after many exhortations did they finally relent to a limited degree. Burghers were allowed free trade in the Moluccas but only in victuals and "provided our trade does not suffer." [9]

Now that he carried the responsibility for all the Company's affairs in Asia, the tone of Coen's letters to the directors stiffened perceptibly as he outlined his plans. He demanded a fleet of twenty-five ships. Five should be detailed to go first to Madagascar to buy slaves. Three should carry nothing but free burghers for colonization. Eight ships would be returned immediately with full cargoes. "If you fear we cannot fill them," he wrote, "or that you won't be able to dispose of so much spice—as has been the absurd excuse before—I request that you relieve me of my duties, because I do not want to eat the Company's bread for nought." [10]

Including the ships already at hand in the Indies, Coen proposed that ten should be used to blockade Manila and cut the Spanish off from Tidore and the China trade. For the latter purpose, he

8. Ibid., *1*, 370.
9. Ibid., *4*, 381.
10. Ibid., *1*, 376.

wanted to use five ships to establish a fort on some island off the China coast. "The Chinese merchants want us to come as close as possible because they are not such good sailors themselves." This was only part of his project; it left no force to move against Malacca and Macao. In addition, a substantial number of ships was needed for the inter-Asiatic trade: with Arabia, Surate, Coromandel, Achin, Priaman, Tiku, Djambi, Andrigiri, Queda, Patane, Siam, Cambodia, Japan, Sukadana, Bima, Solor, Timor, and others. He wished to expand in one great operation rather than piecemeal over a number of years. Coen did not feel that he was asking too much. Knowing the wealth and capabilities of the Netherlands, he was convinced that the Company could easily put a hundred ships in the water if the Seventeen had vision enough to bestir themselves. Amsterdam alone could have accomplished as much. On a single day in the Y, there were several times the number of ships he demanded, ships engaged for the most part in the relatively safe trade with the Baltic. Jan Coen was not pleased at the thought of the directors sitting comfortably in their counting-houses, warming their feet at a hearth fired by peat or sea coal from England. None of them ever had the slightest inclination to go to the Indies whence their profits flowed. None of them knew what it meant to live in the tropics, dressed in layers of heavy woolens whose removal a puritanical background made sinful. None of them knew what scurvy could do to a man or what it meant to suffer *rooie loop*, the red sickness which made a man feel as if a stream of molten lead were coursing through his belly.

In the national archives at The Hague, in the yards of shelf space taken up by Coen's letters to the Seventeen, in that vast amount of correspondence, one word stands out: *Smeecoolen*. With this single word, meaning coal for iron-forging, Coen ended his letter of November 12, 1618. On previous occasions he had lectured the Seventeen on the importance of this commodity and on the fact that the latest ships from Holland had brought none. He asked the Seventeen to contemplate what such a seemingly small matter could lead to: "All works everywhere will come to a halt . . . with charcoal we cannot weld iron."[11] This time he just repeated the word *Smeecoolen* without any further elabora-

11. Ibid., 6, 144. Coen added that at Djakarta alone they were spending 25 guilders per day for charcoal alone. Undoubtedly he hoped that this information would make an impression.

tion. He used it almost as an epithet, as if to say, "Even this you deny me!"

As the year progressed, the affairs of the Company gradually reached a crucial stage—with Bantam, with Djakarta, and with the English. All three were hostile to the Dutch, now personified by Coen. If these three had united their forces, the flow of empire-building in Asia might have taken a different course. But Coen, who during his years in Italy may well have read Machiavelli's *Il Principe*, consciously or otherwise applied the maxim "divide and rule."

When Widjaja Krama, the king of that insignificant fishing village, Djakarta, and the uneasy liege of Bantam, granted permission for a stone house, he told Coen: "Why should I do evil to the Dutch? I loved them even before I saw them." This 'love' was fluctuating—when Coen asked permission to extend the palisades some two or three fathoms, Krama demanded 2,000 reals.[12] No matter how friendly Krama professed to be or how much he craved presents from the Company, he refused to allow the Dutch to fortify their house.

By August, in addition to the troubles at Bantam and with the English, Coen received more disquieting news. He had more or less counted on the friendliness of Mataram, or at least its neutrality, but now it seemed that this was a lost hope. The lodge at Japara, Mataram's main seaport, which had been considered for a possible rendezvous, had been plundered. Twenty thousand reals had been stolen, three Dutchmen killed, another three badly wounded, and seventeen had been taken into the interior.[13] This was all the more distressing in that it deprived the Dutch of rice, much needed for themselves and the natives in the Spice Islands. Coen sent ships far and wide to find other sources. On a subsequent punitive expedition, several merchants and skippers allowed themselves to be hoodwinked by an English merchant, William Bennet, who told them that Mataram and the Dutch were again at peace. This erroneous information led the Dutch ships to leave Japara without executing their orders to punish Mataram. Aert Gysels, in command of this squadron, was fined 100 reals for his gullibility.[14] Gysels never forgave Coen for what he considered

12. *Documents, 1,* 386, 389.

13. Ibid., *6,* 143. See also H. J. de Graaf, *De Regering van Sultan Agung, Vorst van Mataram, 1613–1645* (The Hague, Martinus Nijhoff, 1958), pp. 58–60, and Meilink-Roelofsz, *Asian Trade,* pp. 290–91.

14. Sentence of October 23, 1620. See *Documents, 4,* 225–26. See also De Graaf, *Sultan Agung,* pp. 68–69.

an insult to his integrity. After returning to Holland, Gysels wrote a pamphlet attacking Coen, saying among other things that he was a master of "Italian tricks" and that lawyers were needed in the Indies to protect the common man against his despotism: "Coen wants every trader to come to Jacatra—yea, kings, princes, and potentates, and bend them to his will." [15]

Coen must have had a premonition that armed conflict was soon to break out. "What good does it do," he wrote the Seventeen, "if we appease Jacatra and Bantam by giving them arms? They might well, today or tomorrow, be used against us." [16] Conditions being what they were, with a strong possibility that Sultan Agung of Mataram might move westward after his victories in East Java, the time had come to take decisive action.

On August 31 Coen convened his council at the house in Djakarta, and it was decided unanimously that the stone house should be fortified, whether Krama liked it or not. In justifying this move, which was the first act of open aggression the Dutch committed in the Indies—in contrast with police action in the Moluccas to enforce existing contracts—Coen wrote: "We have here the whole world on our necks, but we still have courage." He was referring to the fact that English ships were also on the way.

Thus, at last, the decision was made to establish the rendezvous at Djakarta. Coen reported this on September 29, 1618 and he might well have confined his letter to this important subject, but he was never one to pass up an opportunity to call the Seventeen to task. The letter also contained a host of requests, most of them being repetitions of what he had constantly demanded. "We need slaves. Send ships to Madagascar or let us have the ships and we will do it ourselves. We have only seventy at Jacatra and the work is too much for them, and some have run away. Speult reports from Amboyna that our own men, between thirty and forty, have to do all the heavy work and as a consequence we are ridiculed by the natives who refuse to work for us. A few slaves there, too, could solve the problem." [17] "We need small coins in large quantities, neat and round and without any numbers or lettering." These coins were badly needed, in a growing

15. See *Documents, 6,* 4, n. 4.

16. Coen proposed that the States General should issue a general order that henceforth no arms or powder should be given or sold to any Indians. See *Documents, 1,* 391.

17. *Documents, 1,* 393–94. It is indicative of Coen's future plans that he adds that it will be a long time before there will be a sufficiently large Chinese population.

money economy, to drive out the Chinese "cassies." Cassies were coins made in China of a poor alloy of antimony and tin with a little copper.[18] They were crude and had a hole in the center so that they could be gathered on a string, as well they might because their individual value was negligible. With one silver real, one could sometimes buy as many as 30,000 cassies. The native producers, many of whom would never see a silver real in their whole lives, counted their returns in cassies only. When the turnover in produce increased, the supply of coins from China could not keep up with the demand and, as a result, cassies became more scarce and more expensive. When Coen wrote, the real had dropped to 8,000 cassies and shortly afterwards to about 6,000. This was naturally reflected in the price of pepper: the price might remain the same in cassies, but in terms of reals it went up. Coen, the financier, wanted to remedy this situation by a liberal flow of small coins into the native economy. Knowing that some of the wealthy Dutch merchants had got their start through counterfeiting, he had no doubt that Holland could devise a handsomer coin, and therefore one more acceptable to the natives. Not unreasonably, Coen reported that pepper prices had been rising, but he had to follow the market to keep pepper out of the hands of competitors.

He also mentioned such a simple product as barrels. They were badly needed as casks for the ships and forts. In order to save cargo space, the Seventeen should send staves, provided they also sent coopers. The casks would be primarily for water, but there also was a need for arrack casks. He wrote that it was important that "our people should have arrack with their dry rice." [19]

Coen's letters during those final months of 1618 seem to indicate that he had a foreboding that something drastic was about to happen. Beside the 25 ships he had requested earlier, he wanted ten yachts of between 50 and 160 tons for the coastal trade, to punish the "murders at Macassar and Japara, but especially to keep the kings of Java in check. This cannot be done with large ships because the coast of Java is too shallow." [20]

Coen realized that he had been painting a dark picture and that a word of encouragement to the Seventeen might be in order.

18. *Cassies* or *caxiens* is said to be derived from the Portuguese *caixa*, a coin made of tin or lead. The Tamil *kasu* and the Sanskrit *karsa* (a weight of gold or silver) are also given as a possible origin.
19. *Documents, 1,* 395.
20. Ibid., *1,* 396.

"We have been warned that we shall be attacked, murdered, and robbed and that no profession of friendship (on our part) will deter them. Therefore we plead humbly that the Lordships send us soonest a considerable number of people, many ships, a large quantity of money, together with other necessities. If you do this everything will go well—if not, Your Lordships will regret it. Do not despair . . . there is nothing in the world that can stop us . . . Something great can be accomplished in the Indies." [21]

21. Ibid., *1*, 399. Considering the results of his own stewardship, and that of others to follow, this was indeed a prophetic statement.

14

The Crisis

In the events that were about to occur John Jourdain played an important role. He had sailed for England in December 1616. He had been away longer than most and, in his middle forties, was beginning to feel his years. Three years before he had written in his journal that he was "beginninge to growe ould." With the exception of the last three years, he had always served in a minor capacity, being ordered to go here and there at the wishes of successive English admirals. He had spent the later years at Bantam as chief agent, correlating the activities of the various and largely autonomous fleets which were operating for the English Company. Trying to keep peace between the different factions had not been easy, and he had also borne the brunt of increasing friction with the Dutch, whose young president at Bantam had been a thorn in his side from the first moment he had met him in the Moluccas. In spite of all, he had managed to send some lucrative cargoes of spices to the governors in London. Being an honest man, he had gained nothing for himself except some accumulated salary which did not amount to much. He had no plans for the future.

He arrived in England after a speedy voyage of six months. After delivering his report (he had kept a meticulous diary) to the governors, presumably he went to his home at Lyme Regis in Dorsetshire. But apparently the same conditions which originally had induced him to joint the East India Company still prevailed. Within a few months he was back in London, once more seeking employment with the Company. At a meeting of the governors held in the house of Sir Thomas Smythe in Philpot Lane, the matter of Dutch rivalry was one of the main points under discussion. Jourdain stated, "The Flemmings either dare not or will not sett upon the English." This was the beginning of the four-year period of the second joint stock venture, and the English Company had never been in better financial condition.

With over £1,600,000 subscribed, the governors set their sights accordingly. There were some London merchants who urged caution and suggested that it would be safer to come to some agreement with the Dutch Company, but Jourdain, with his many years of experience in dealing with the Dutch, carried the day. The majority decided in favor of standing firm at any cost to safeguard the business at Bantam and the trade in Banda and the Moluccas.

Early in November Jourdain signed a contract to serve the company for five years in the Indies as its principal agent. In this capacity, he would have authority over all the factories in Asia with the exception of Surate (including all territory to the west and north of it, such as Arabia and Persia) which came under the jurisdiction of Sir Thomas Roe. Jourdain's position was practically the same as that of Coen before the latter became governor general. Jourdain's pay, however, was better. Besides his salary of £350 yearly, the governors agreed to pay him a bonus of £1,600 after his five-year term was over, and in case he died they were to pay his heirs £1,200. The Dutch never stipulated what bonus they might pay; at best they made some vague comment about a "suitable reward," and if one of their employees died he was simply taken off the payroll. Jourdain also had to give bond "to forbeare all private trade." [1]

The fleet sailed in the early part of 1618, the strongest the English had yet sent out. It numbered six stout ships, each of them larger and more heavily armed than any the Dutch used in their trade. The governors had chosen Sir Thomas Dale as admiral of the fleet, and they could hardly have picked a better man. He had been with Leicester in the Netherlands, and, after the latter had returned to England, Dale had stayed on as captain of the English garrison at one of the pledged towns now about to be redeemed by Oldebarnevelt. He had been knighted by James I in 1606. From 1611 to 1616 he was High Marshall in the Virginia Colony, where he had proved himself an able, although severe, administrator. Now he was ready to seek further glory on the other side of the world. The instructions were "to seek trade in the Moluccas and not be put by with threats or attempts of the Dutch." [2] Dale and Jourdain fully intended to discharge themselves of this duty.

1. Foster, ed., *Journal of John Jourdain*, pp. 65–68.
2. Ibid., pp. 68–69.

The fleet arrived at Bantam on November 19, but not in the happiest frame of mind. Four days earlier, the *Sun* had been wrecked on the coast of Engano, but the English spirits revived when they found some eight ships on the roadstead left from previous voyages.

In almost every historical conflict between nations, the opposing parties are symbolized by individual protagonists, and this conflict between the Dutch and English companies was no exception. On the Dutch side there was no question as to the man. On the English side, Coen himself singled out John Jourdain, not Sir Thomas Dale, as the main cause of "all these calamities."[3]

During the final months of 1618, Coen considered that his chief enemies were the Javanese: Bantam in the first place and, after Japara had been overrun, Mataram. Now Djakarta itself was added to the list. Widjaja Krama had not taken it lightly when the Dutch strengthened their house, first by a small garrison and then by additional construction of a solid complex of warehouses. He invited Coen to visit him at his *dalem* (court), across the river and a little further inland, to discuss the situation. Coen declined the invitation because, aside from being inherently distrustful of all natives, he had been warned that there was a plot to assassinate him. Instead, he invited Widjaja Krama to inspect the Dutch warehouses, and the king did not like what he saw. He complained that the fort dominated his *dalem*.[4] This was something that he could not tolerate, not so much because his own sovereignty was involved (actually he was only a recalcitrant liege of Bantam) but because he was afraid of being squeezed between Bantam and Mataram. Without ever having been explicitly expressed, there had been some sort of a Monroe Doctrine for Java ever since the era of the empire of Madjapahit, which excluded any foreign domination of this prosperous island. Uncomfortably situated between powerful Bantam and the still more powerful Mataram, Widjaja Krama decided to make a show of force against the Dutch to demonstrate that he was not the one to violate this principle. To prove to Bantam and Mataram that he was in good faith, he fortified and surrounded the *dalem* with stone walls. He also announced an edict stating that neither his Javanese nor

3. Ibid., App. F, pp. 372–73. See Coen's letter to the Seventeen, dated January 22, 1620, in *Documents, 1,* 511.
4. *Documents, 1,* 408, 6, 150.

Chinese subjects were to work for the Dutch in fortifying the Dutch warehouses.

This was not the only action that he took to protect his precarious and illegal domain. He seems to have understood the adage that "the enemies of one's enemies are one's friends" and, because the English appeared the most persevering enemies of the Dutch, he allowed them to fortify their factory. It was situated on a piece of land known as Pope John's, and he permitted the English to throw up a battery there, in exchange for gifts of some much desired cannon and munitions. He actually assisted the English in building their battery, which would cover the Dutch houses across the river should a time come for an attack by land.

Viewing these activities with suspicion and alarm, the Dutch worked at their fortifications in feverish haste. The two houses, Nassau and Maurice, were connected by a high stone rampart (called a cat) to serve as protection against the *dalem*. The whole area was surrounded by a wooden palisade backed by an embankment of earth. The establishment was put into as good a state of defense as was possible with the limited means and manpower Coen had at his disposal. On November 12, he was able to report that "the people and the goods of the Company are now sufficiently protected against any onslaught." He expressed the hope that this would force Djakarta to remain at peace, but, if it did not deter them, he would "enlarge the place to such an extent that your Lordships would not require another Rendezvous in the Indies." [5]

It turned out that the preparations were made none too soon; two weeks later Jourdain and Dale arrived with their fleet, bringing the English strength at Bantam to no less than fifteen ships—"the bay was not large enough to harbour them all." With such a large force at their command, far outnumbering what Coen had available at the time, the momentous decision to open hostilities was made. The English began by capturing the Dutch ship *Black Lion* as it approached Bantam with a rich cargo from Patane; another, the *Old Sun*, barely escaped. When Coen learned of this at Djakarta, he immediately sent a message to Bantam demanding an explanation and the immediate release of the vessel. The messenger had difficulty even being admitted to the English house,

5. Ibid., *1*, 409, *6*, 151.

and when he finally was received, he was roundly cursed.[6] Sir Thomas Dale refused to give a written reply but stated verbally that he had taken the ship deliberately and had no intention of giving it back. Moreover, he would blockade the Sunda Strait and intercept there all Dutch vessels, coming and going. Soon he would appear with his fleet before Djakarta to defeat the "Flemmings," and he vowed to take Coen, dead or alive. After that he would go to the Moluccas. Dale's intentions were clearly revealed in a letter he wrote to Captain Courthope, who was stubbornly holding on to the small English factory on Pulu Run, one of the small islands in the Banda group. "My stay here (Bantam) is only to revenge in part the abuses received from them (the Hollanders), having now an opportunity by a difference between them and the king of Jacatra to put them from hence, if God give the blessing." [7] This was the English answer. Coen now turned to the *Pangeran* at Bantam, in whose waters this act of piracy had been committed, but his appeal was equally unsuccessful. What the English had done, Rana Mangala replied, was no different from what Coen himself had done with the French ship.

Coen threatened the English with reprisals although he knew that, for the moment, it was an idle threat. He had only five ships at his disposal and, of these, four were in various stages of disrepair at Onrust. Bantam, which claimed sovereignty over Onrust, had not objected when the Dutch established a workshop on this speck of land, but during the past few months, with tension heightened, Bantam had made demands that the Dutch evacuate the island. Coen had no intention of complying. The island served too good a purpose.[8] He ordered that these four ships be readied at once regardless of their present condition.

On land, the Dutch position was no less precarious. Day by day Widjaja Krama threw up bulwarks that came closer and closer— five to the south on both sides of the river and one directly opposite the Dutch fort, across the river and a little to the south of the English lodge whose guns covered the river. The king claimed that the bulwarks were only for defense, but Coen had his doubts, especially when he saw the great activity that went on at the English establishment, helped by a horde of Javanese. Coen asked

6. De Jonge, *Opkomst, 4*, lxxxi–lxxxii.
7. *Documents, 1*, 421.
8. The men of the Company had called the island Onrust (Unrest) because of the feverish activities there at all hours of the day and night.

the king if he would remain neutral in this trouble between the Dutch and the English. He received an evasive answer: "his own land should remain free above everything else." It is difficult to understand what had made him decide that the English would prove to be better friends. As it turned out, Widjaja Krama had made a fateful decision.

When Coen noticed that the Javanese were attempting to cut him off from the sea by placing a row of heavy piles across the mouth of the river, he realized that the time had come for action. The date was December 22. "I am sitting here as in a cage," he wrote, "surrounded by various bulwarks and batteries, the river closed with piles, and a strong battery at the place of the English." [9] There were rumors that a force of 7,000 men was about to attack.

The next day, a Sunday, dawned without the usual noises and chattering from the native huts that stood close to the fort. During the night, men, women, and children had stolen away, taking their possessions with them. Coen, as well as everyone else in the fort, knew what this meant. An attack was imminent, perhaps no later than the following night.

Coen convened his council at once and presented two alternatives: to wait until they were attacked, or to strike the first blow. He left no doubt about his own preference, and the council agreed unanimously. Coen demanded that the English surrender their battery, and when this was not immediately heeded a Dutch contingent crossed the river and attacked the English. After a fierce encounter, and with the loss of eleven dead and twelve wounded, the English lodge was taken and burned to the ground. The battery directly opposite the fort was also completely destroyed. In the confusion of the engagement, another bulwark, most strategically located on Pope John's land at the mouth of the river, remained untouched. In the meantime, another sortie had set fire to the buildings south of the fort, thus clearing a wide strip between the fort and the town. [10]

The sudden attack on the English position had apparently taken Djakarta by surprise; its batteries remained silent during that day. The next day, however, they opened heavy fire on the fort, their cannons handled by English constables. The Dutch replied in kind and managed to silence the guns, but only at the

9. *Documents, 1,* 424.
10. De Jonge, *Opkomst, 4,* lxxxiv.

expense of much precious powder, one quarter of the fort's sparse supply. Since things were not working out as he had expected, Widjaja Krama sent an urgent appeal to the English; Jourdain expressed the English policy in a letter written to Courthope on this occasion. "Now the King of Jacatra, seeing himself in a straite, sent a messenger to Bantam desiring aid of us. Calling here a councill, we concluded to send a fleet of eleven sails . . . not only to surprise their ships but also to destroy their fort." [11]

On the third day, the Dutch made an unsuccessful attack on the remaining bulwark at the mouth of the river. The supply route between the fort and the ships, which were expected any day from Onrust, thus remained closed. Fortunately the Djakarta batteries remained silent, possibly because they were short of powder or because the king wanted to save it for a combined attack when the English ships arrived on the scene.

On December 29, while Coen and his council were deliberating their next move, word arrived by messenger that the English fleet had left Bantam to destroy the Dutch fort and then to continue on to the Moluccas and destroy or disperse the Dutch forces in that area. In both Jourdain's and Dale's minds, this plan was as good as executed, now that the ships of Hatch and Martin Pring had been added to theirs. The only good news for the Dutch that day was seeing the ships from Onrust drop anchor in the roadstead.

Early the next morning, Coen summoned his council, and it was decided that with the help of the ships offshore, whose number had been increased to six by the fortuitous arrival of the *Delft* which had escaped from Bantam bay, the battery at the mouth of the river should be attacked and destroyed. After this had been accomplished, the most valuable goods would be transported to the ships, which then would await the English fleet to give battle. The various commanders were notified of this plan, but even while the heavily-manned sloops were getting ready to undertake the mission, the English fleet appeared on the horizon. It was close to nightfall, and once more the council met to deliberate on this new emergency. The attack on the bulwark had to be abandoned, as well as the plan to put the Company's goods in safety on the ships. Those in the fort could hear the commands given, followed by the familiar sounds as the ships were readied for battle.

11. "Journal of Nathaniel Courthope," *Purchas his Pilgrimes*, 4 (reprinted, Glasgow, 1905–07), p. 676.

It was unanimously decided that there was little to be gained by waiting for the English to come closer and that it was better to tackle the enemy in the open sea, "it being understood that they [the Dutch ships] have the will and courage to fight them as best they could." [12] Coen himself would assume command and hoist his Admiral's flag on the *Old Sun*.

That same day, Coen had written a letter to Reael in the Moluccas which, depending on the outcome of the battle, he hoped to forward by the best possible means. He ordered him, "by virtue of commission [as governor general] from our superiors," to gather all his forces and come to Bantam as soon as possible. That same night Coen boarded his ship, and at daybreak he sallied forth to meet the enemy. Fullfledged war between the Dutch and the English had finally broken out.

Dale's fleet consisted of eleven ships which he considered more than enough for his purpose. His other four ships had been left behind to cover Bantam and to execute his announced intention, to capture any and all Dutch ships coming through the Sunda Strait. From every angle his was indeed the superior squadron. Not only did he outnumber the Dutch, 11 to seven, but most of his ships were more heavily armed and carried a larger complement of fighting men. Where the Dutch ships carried at most 45 pieces and 70 men, the English had a number of ships with more than 50 cannon and as many as 250 in crew.

Dale was apparently in no hurry to begin the attack. Counting on the fact that his superior strength would impress the Dutch, he sailed his fleet above the wind and just out of range. In the afternoon he sent off a trumpeter to the Dutch in a small boat with the demand that the Dutch fleet surrender. The man spoke in Dutch and confirmed what Coen had heard before, that the English admiral intended to destroy the whole fleet, because the Dutch had made his country suffer incalculable damage and had treated his countrymen like slaves. He added that, if the Dutch would surrender without a fight, their crews would be treated royally and paid full wages. Coen interpreted this as a sign of reluctance on the part of Dale to open the attack. He replied that the English should return the *Black Lion* or he would seek his revenge by force.[13]

The following day, January 1, 1619, gave no indication that the

12. De Jonge, *Opkomst, 4,* lxxxvi.
13. *Documents, 1,* 429.

English were anxious to open the battle. The Dutch, while trying to maneuver themselves into a more favorable position, were willing to sit it out. The appearance of a sail on the horizon, behind and above the wind from the enemy fleet, made them go into action: they saw the Dutch flag carried at the top. It was recognized as the *Bergerboot*, which had been sent to Djambi for pepper. The ship would unavoidably fall into enemy hands unless promptly warned and protected. Without heeding the consequences, Coen ordered his squadron to sail straight through the English fleet before the English could capture the ship. The English obviously had not been prepared for this unexpected maneuver, and they split up with hardly a shot exchanged.[14] With the *Bergerboot* added to his squadron, Coen now had seven ships.

The next day battle was joined. It began at ten in the morning and lasted for three hours. "Both sides were not a little hit," Coen wrote, "but our people showed great courage." No ship, except a sloop of the *Bergerboot*, was lost on either side, but the engagement cost Coen about one third of his limited supply of powder. At no time did the English try to get alongside the Dutch ships and board for hand-to-hand engagement. In view of the superior strength of the English, it is difficult to explain this hesitancy. English sailors certainly did not lack courage, and their hatred of the Dutch had been sufficiently inflamed. The only explanation that makes any sense is that the English fleet had not one but three commanders—Dale, Hatch, and Pring. Each represented a separate venture and, by selfishly counting his individual interest above everything else, none wanted to risk his particular vessels for the common good. If unified action had been taken at this crucial moment, it might have changed the course of European imperialism in Asia.

Before dusk, Coen ordered his skippers to convene at one of the many nearby islands off the coast of Djakarta. There they gathered during the night, and the council met on the flagship to decide on what action to take. Some wanted to renew the battle, but others pointed out the scarcity of powder, sufficient for only a limited engagement. "All glumly looked at each other not being able to come up with an answer." [15]

14. Five English ships that were in the way hurriedly cut their hawsers, "leaving five anchors." See *Documents, 1,* 429.
15. De Jonge, *4,* lxxxviii.

The English provided the answer. When morning dawned, the Dutch counted 14 enemy ships, three more having arrived from Bantam during the night. Caution being the better part of valor, Coen made the difficult and, to some, distasteful decision to leave the scene. Continuing the battle would be dangerous, for the Dutch would certainly lose some ships and might even be completely defeated by the much stronger enemy fleet. In that case, the English would be able to execute the second phase of their plan by continuing to the Moluccas to pick off Reael's ships by twos and threes. It could easily turn into a disaster. Coen's decision meant leaving the fort at Djakarta to its own devices, surrounded by enemies, both from the land and sea, and this at almost the moment that he had expected it to become his cherished rendezvous.

A pinnace was sent off to the fort to apprise the garrison of all that had happened during the past few days and of the resolution which had, *faute de mieux*, been adopted. "We shall return by the first opportunity," Coen wrote to his people. "In the meantime try to hold the fort as best you can. If the time should come that you can no longer hold the place you should try to come to some understanding with either Jacatra or the English. It is our opinion that, if such an emergency should arise, you would do better by surrendering to the English." He finished with the warning that they should be on their guard and not fall into a trap by counting on the enemy's promises.[16]

The merchant Lefebre was given the delicate and dangerous task of sailing westward behind the English fleet to take up a position in the Sunda Strait, stationed there to warn all incoming ships that war had broken out. With his small but fast frigate, the *Ceylon*, it was hoped that he could outmaneuver the enemy there. This was all that could be done at the present, and the rest of the squadron headed west along the north coast of Java. Nearing the eastern end of the island, Coen detached the ship *Delft* with orders to sail for Holland through the Strait of Bali and acquaint the Seventeen with what had transpired. It was a long and bitter letter, in which Coen's one-man rebellion against the weak policies of the Seventeen rose to a new height. He put the cause of his latest troubles squarely on the shoulders of the directors. His demands for more ships, more money, and more men

16. Ibid., *4*, xc–xci, Resolutions of January 3 and 4, 1619. Compare Hall, *History of South-East Asia*, pp. 244–45.

had been persistently denied with the flimsiest excuses. "And now see what has happened!" The whole state of affairs of the Company is faced with "a thousand perils and even if the Almighty wills us his best, the return cargoes this year will be less by two or three million than what we could have expected. God give that next year will not be worse."

He complained that while the Seventeen had constantly pressed for the establishment of a general rendezvous, they had withheld the necessary means:

> Nevertheless we managed to obtain a fort at Jacatra. But to what good avail? Because of lack of sufficient powder it is most unlikely that the place can hold out until we return.
>
> With respect to your argument that we could never hold a place in case of war in a land as densely populated as Java, I reply that the Portuguese and the Spaniards have proven what a few Christians can do against hundreds of thousands of Indians. . . . Are we less than they? I admit that the beginning of such a war would bring no cash returns because no place can be secured with only a token force. But without war no good peace can ever be attained, nowhere in the whole world. Nature teaches us that war brings peace, and that those who do not sow shall no reap.
>
> I swear to you by the Almighty that the General Company has no greater enemies than the ignorance and shortsightedness, pardon my words, which seems to prevail among Your Lordships and outvotes the intelligent.[17]

Coen ended the long letter with an ultimatum. "If your Lordships have no intention to send me yearly large numbers of ships, people, and other necessities, I pray once more that you release me at the soonest, because without such means I cannot execute your wishes." [18]

With this off his mind, Coen set sail for Amboyna. He was going to deliver his orders to Reael in person.

17. *Documents, 1,* 437-39.
18. Ibid., *1,* 442.

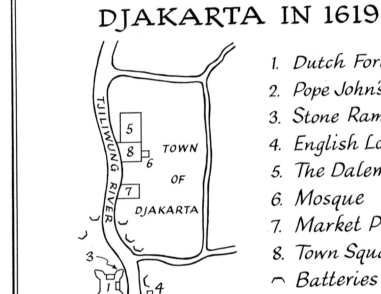

DJAKARTA IN 1619

1. Dutch Fort
2. Pope John's Land
3. Stone Rampart
4. English Lodge
5. The Dalem
6. Mosque
7. Market Place
8. Town Square
⌒ Batteries

TJILIWUNG RIVER

TOWN

OF

DJAKARTA

JAVA SEA

15

The
Siege

The feelings of the people at the fort, now left to shift for themselves, can well be imagined. At most, some 250 men could be put under arms—100 soldiers (including 25 Japanese), 15 constables, 70 blacks (slaves), and the rest workmen, clerks, *pennists*, and merchants. In addition, there were about 150 non-combatants —women, children, and Chinese.[1] All told there were 400 mouths to feed. The fort was supplied with sufficient cannon, but there were only forty kegs of powder, enough for no more than 300 rounds. For once there was no lack of money and merchandise, about 100,000 reals of each, but under the circumstances they were almost useless.

Opposing this small force were fourteen English ships, a single large one of which could muster as many fighting men as could be counted in the whole garrison. There were thousands of Javanese at their backs, if Widjaja Krama decided to put them in the field.

The man whom Coen had picked to lead the defense was Pieter van den Broek. He probably could not have chosen a better man. Van den Broek had been in the Red Sea, where he had made valuable contacts at Mocha and Aden, thus opening this trade to the Dutch. On a later occasion, after being shipwrecked on the coast of India, he had taken his crew on a perilous journey across the peninsula, leading most of them to safety. Such a trek, by sailors who were not accustomed to much marching, was a feat in itself, the more remarkable in that they had to fight their way through rough and unknown territory and hostile tribes.[2] However, it turned out that Van den Broek had the one trait that Coen had so often deplored in so many of the Dutch, and against

1. For a complete roster, see J. A. van der Chijs, *De Nederlanders te Jakatra* (Amsterdam, 1860), pp. 64–65.
2. N. MacLeod, *De Oost-Indische Compagnie als zeemogendheid in Azie*, *1* (Rijswijk, 1927), 200–01.

which he had warned the fort in his final instructions—he too was gullible.

Conflicting accounts have been written of this siege which, in its outcome, was a crucial event in the rise of European imperialism in Asia. Reputations stemming from it have been successively torn down and rebuilt by Dutch historians. It is only with the uncovering of old documents and a careful analysis of all the information now available that a comprehensive picture can be obtained of what took place. The events of the siege itself, the so-called heroic deeds and others almost the reverse, signify far less, in retrospect, than is usually expected of events that are part of a turning point in history. What happened must be reviewed in the light of three components: the roles played by Djakarta, by Bantam, and by the English.

The king of Djakarta had no desire to expel the Dutch from his territory. Only because of Dutch trade had his *kampong* (native village) grown into a prospering town. It had greatly increased his revenue. The constant flow of silver reals from duties, levies, and gifts would be sorely missed. But he wanted to remain master in his own house, and thus the Dutch fortifications had to be dismantled. This was his demand.

Bantam had its own designs. It, too, had tasted the luxuries of the new economic age introduced by the Dutch. Intensely jealous of Widjaja Krama's growing importance at the expense of Bantam, the *Pangeran* had no desire to go to his assistance, counting on the fact that Djakarta's loss would be Bantam's gain.

Only the English wanted the total elimination of the Dutch. So far this had been mainly talk, as the English were loath to risk their ships, knowing that they needed all the force they could muster to dispel the Dutch from the Moluccas. They tried in vain to enlist the support of Bantam for an attack on the fort. Coen summed it up in a subsequent letter: "While we were sailing to Amboyna, the English tried to come to an agreement with the young king of Bantam, but it was a wasted effort." [3] The English helped Djakarta, which had openly asked for support; they supplied some more cannon and powder, in exchange for the promise that they would be allowed to rebuild their lodge.

From January 4 to 13 everything was done to put the Dutch fort in the best possible state of defense. This was the time when the English could have taken decisive action, by an all out attack

3. De Jonge, *Opkomst*, 4, 215.

on the Dutch position, which was practically defenseless on the sea side. But the English could not agree among themselves as to what should be done next, a situation aggravated by a growing animosity between Jourdain, the merchant, and Dale, the admiral. The final outcome of the Dutch-English conflict might not have been different, but perhaps Dale let a golden opportunity slip by. Dale may have felt that he had already gained a sufficiently important victory by forcing the Dutch ships to flee. This is one view, at least, of Coen's departure, for which Dale is given full credit.[4] Lacking support, Widjaja was equally hesitant to attack the fort.

During this period, only a few shots were exchanged as a sign that both sides were on their guard, but when the work was completed and all cannon in place, the Dutch opened fire with all they had to prove that they were ready. Though this show of force accidentally set fire to the mosque, the king unexpectedly offered to negotiate. All he demanded was an indemnity of 6,000 reals for the damage done by the barrage, and on his side he agreed to abide by the treaties previously concluded and even to withdraw his often repeated demand that the fortifications be torn down. The fort could remain in its present state until the return of Coen, when this matter could be taken up anew. He did not want to withdraw his offer to the English to rebuild their lodge—this would have meant going back on his word—but he assured the Dutch that it would not be erected as close to the Dutch settlement as it had been before.[5]

The people in the fort were elated with this turn of events. They reasoned that all the king wanted was money, and with this the fort was well supplied. Actually the reason for his peace offer was not quite so simple. Shortly after the opening of hostilities, Bantam had sent a mission to Djakarta, not to proffer any help, but for the express purpose of inducing Widjaja Krama to make peace with the Dutch. For the time being, it best suited Bantam to retain the status quo at Djakarta rather than let the English move in and replace the Dutch.[6] It was this mission which had forced the king's hand and made him sign the treaty of peace, at the same time giving him a handsome monetary reward.

4. See "Sir Thomas Dale," *Encyclopaedia Brittanica*, 6 (14th ed., London and New York, 1929), p. 986.
5. Van Deventer, *Nederlanders*, p. 109.
6. Ibid., p. 110.

The English at Djakarta were most unhappy about this development, and no sooner had the *Pangeran*'s emissaries returned to Bantam than they renewed their efforts to woo Widjaja Krama back to their side. They had come to Djakarta at the king's bidding, they had chased away the Dutch fleet, and now they wanted their reward, which was nothing less than the destruction of the Dutch fort. The prospect of gaining much loot thereby proved too great a temptation for the greedy ruler, but rather than revoke the treaty openly, he decided to gain his end by more subtle means.

He entreated the Dutch to come to him at the *dalem* so that friendly relations could be resumed on the same basis as before. Practically the whole council at the fort was in agreement with Van den Broek that this was the wrong time to insult the king by a refusal. The only one who dissented was Dominie Hulsebos,[7] who feared that this was just the kind of gullibility of which Coen had specifically warned in his last instructions. On January 22, Van den Broek, accompanied by seven others, proceeded to the *dalem*. The Dutch had encountered treachery before; at Achin, Ceylon, Banda, and elsewhere, and now they would meet it again. No sooner had they arrived at the *dalem*, bringing a gift of a golden chain to Widjaja Krama, than they were set upon by a horde of Javanese. They were beaten to the ground, their clothes were torn off, and they were bound and dragged off to prison.

The news reached the fort late in the day. The gates were quickly barred, and once more the fort was put in a state of siege. The merchant Pieter van Raey took command, and work on the fortifications was hastily resumed. It was not long before the king announced his terms. Through his father-in-law, whom the Dutch called "the Old Count," he demanded the immediate demolition of all fortifications and a ransom of 10,000 reals for Van den Broek and the other hostages.[8] The Dutch could stay if they wished, or they could leave on a vessel which the English would make available. These unilateral negotiations did not please Thomas Dale. He had supplied the king with cannon and munitions and now he demanded that accepting the surrender of the fort and its looting be a joint venture. On January 24 Widjaja

7. *Documents, 1,* 461.
8. Ibid., *1,* 462.

Krama signed a document in which both sides agreed to attack the fort and divide the loot equally.[9]

The people in the fort were in a quandary. Lacking strong leadership, every problem had to be discussed in numerous council meetings where unanimous agreement was hard to reach. On one thing, however, they were united. Even though they were surrounded by enemies, they knew that the Seventeen took a baleful view of any free disposal of the Company's funds. Everyone would have to account some day for having voted to give the king 10,000 reals over and above the 6,000 already paid him for a treaty which had proved to be worthless. This hesitancy to agree to the ransom terms proved a boon, because it gave the garrison valuable respite in which to strengthen its position. The enemy was not idle either; the English were rebuilding their battery across the river and the king was likewise busy.

The Dutch began by asking for an explanation of this sudden change of attitude. Why had the solemn agreement of January 20 been abrogated? Widjaja, perfidious as always, replied that it was the English admiral who had put him to it. At the same time, he put pressure on Van den Broek, forcing him to plead with his countrymen to meet his demands. And plead he did. Letters from him began to arrive almost daily at the fort, and they became progressively more urgent as he described the plight of himself and his companions. Those at the fort delayed, finding excuses for not immediately acceding to the king's demands. They were dealing with the Old Count, they said, and how could they be sure that this would commit the king himself? Finally, Van Raey sent a letter to Van den Broek asking him what he personally would do if he were in his place. To this the unhappy Van den Broek replied, "Your request for advice is not reasonable. Being a prisoner I would give everything there is in the fort, but I plead with you to accept the demand for 10,000 reals and two cannons. Let him [the king] know that you people are willing to leave as soon as the President Coen returns. . . . Do not worry too much about a small loss of money, because the English are threatening to flatten the fort with forty pieces." [10]

On January 28 another letter arrived, this one signed not only

9. Van Deventer, *Nederlanders*, p. 112. From the journal of Van den Broek.

10. De Jonge, *Opkomst*, 4, xcix.

by Van den Broek but also by one of his fellow prisoners, the respected Dr. de Haen. It was a renewed plea to negotiate with the king, the more urgent in that the English were pressing him daily "with many gifts" to open an all out attack on the fort, "offering him half the loot." The letter ended with a pathetic plea to offer as high a ransom "as you people are willing to pay." [11] This was interpreted at the fort as indicating a chance to bargain over the ransom money, and it was decided to offer 2,000 reals.

By now the English and Javanese positions were in a complete state of readiness to begin the attack; they had thrown a bridge across the river, indicating only too clearly what was intended. The Dutch had not fired a single shot during these few days of diplomatic exchanges for fear of jeopardizing the lives of the hostages. Under pressure from Bantam, the king had delayed joining the English in a full attack, and he was still expecting the high ransom he had demanded. Dale felt that the time had come to negotiate directly with the Dutch.

January 29 was a critical day. In the forenoon, Dale sent a letter in which he demanded that the Dutch surrender to him, adding the pious observation that they would be better off with an honorable capitulation to fellow Christians than to fall into the hands of Javanese, Moors, and Moslems.[12] In the afternoon, while the council was deliberating Dale's proposal, Van den Broek and Dr. de Haen suddenly appeared below the ramparts of the fort, their hands tied and a rope around their necks, obviously an attempt to intimidate the Dutch to the limit. Van den Broek shouted to Van Raey and the others that the king had become incensed at the trifling counter-offer and that his patience was exhausted. Moreover he had seen the king's fortifications, and he vouched for it that they were in perfect shape with forty pieces trained on the fort. There was no use trying to hold out any longer. They should heed Coen's final recommendation to capitulate to the English rather than to Djakarta.[13] Van Raey replied that they were busy drafting a letter to the English admiral. The prisoners were taken back to the *dalem*.

The following two days were spent in anxious consultations with the English and among themselves. There were still some

11. For this letter, see De Jonge, *Opkomst*, 4, 156–57.
12. De Jonge, *Opkomst*, 4, cii.
13. Ibid., 4, civ.

who wanted to defend the fort, but the prime question was whether they could hold out for the three more months which must elapse before Coen could, at the earliest, be expected to bring relief. How about the necessary victuals to withstand such a long siege and how about powder? When the chief constable reported that at the most he had only enough powder left for two salvos daily, the desire to hold out quickly evaporated.[14] Simultaneously, Sir Thomas Dale became seemingly more generous in his terms. He guaranteed that the hostages would be released unharmed. Those who were willing to enter into the service of the English Company would not only receive their former wages but also a two-month bonus. Everyone was free to choose for himself and those who decided to stay in Dutch employment could sail away in an English ship wherever they pleased, except to the Moluccas. To keep things on a formal basis, he demanded 2,000 reals for the use of such a ship. Each man, moreover, would be allowed to carry his side arms and personal property with him, and Dale would not object if this included some bolts of silk or other costly goods.[15] The only condition he made was that each man submit an itemized statement listing his belongings. If it were found at the time of embarkation that a man's chest or dunnage bag contained more than he had indicated, all his goods would be confiscated.

Sir Thomas Dale admitted openly that he had an understanding with Widjaja Krama whereby Krama would get all of the Company's merchandise and Dale the fort, the cannon, and the money.

On the last day of January, Van Raey and his council, making much of Coen's advice, decided to accept Dale's terms. It became a signal for many to add as much as possible to their belongings before submitting their personal inventory. The argument was tempting: everything left behind would be a total loss to the Company anyway; the more they carried the less would fall into enemy hands. Discipline broke down completely, high and low participated in wholesale looting. On the pretext of looking for secret documents for the purpose of destroying them, the trunks and chests belonging to the absent officials were broken open

14. From the Journal kept during the siege. See De Jonge, *Opkomst, 4,* 143.

15. The 'king' of Djakarta was a party to this agreement. For the complete terms, see Van der Chijs, *De Nederlanders,* pp. 212–14.

and rifled. The chief steward quarreled with another man, each accusing the other of taking Coen's golden hatband. There is no record that it ever appeared again, nor of the identity of the culprit. Coen complained later that all his personal papers were destroyed or missing.

The next day, February 1, the surrender document was officially signed, but the ink was scarcely dry before it became clear that Thomas Dale was in no position to keep his part of the bargain. The reason was that the *Pangeran,* who was keeping a close watch on the affairs at Djakarta, had decided to take an active part. As a matter of precaution, he had sent a force of 4,000 men under the *Tommogong,* a trusted lieutenant. This force was in bivouac on the west side of the river and had been ordered to interfere with the evacuation of the Dutch garrison, not because Bantam had any desire to aid the Dutch but to break up the coalition between Djakarta and the English, and to prevent the latter from occupying the fort. The Bantamese themselves had designs on the fort.

The English were denied even a taste of their short-lived victory, and their position at Djakarta suddenly became precarious. The bad feeling between the Bantamese and the English rose to such heights that the latter felt themselves surrounded by an enemy. The *Tommogong* threatened to attack the English batteries, and placed his soldiers in a strong position at the mouth of the river so that the English were cut off from their ships on the roadstead. Realizing that he had lost the advantage, Dale agreed to leave, provided he could take along the 40 pieces he had landed. A heated argument broke out when the *Tommogong* refused Dale's request. The English admiral was in no position to press his demands, and he barely saved his life by escaping from Djakarta in a small boat. With his fleet, he returned to the Bay of Bantam.

At the same time, the Bantamese were putting pressure on Widjaja Krama, demanding that Van den Broek and his co-hostages be surrendered to them. With some 4,000 Bantamese ready to attack, the king dared not refuse. Before Van den Broek was carried off to Bantam, he gave the Dutch garrison some final advice: since the English, having been thwarted by the Bantam forces, were no longer a serious threat, and since Djakarta had been ordered to cease hostilities, the war council at the fort should not negotiate with any group, pending further developments, but should remain on guard lest they be betrayed. While at Bantam, Van den Broek expected to have a good *bitjara* (talk) with the *Pangeran* to discover what he had in mind.[16]

It did not take long to find out what Bantam was aiming for. The town had prospered by being the main entrepôt for the spice trade in Southeast Asia, and through the ages merchants from all of Asia had come there because it offered a ready supply of spices. The Portuguese had followed a similar pattern, in part leaving it to native traders to deliver spices to them at Malacca. All during the Portuguese period, spices remained a great luxury in Europe, and the profits could easily absorb the high levies demanded by Bantam. The Dutch merchants, however, felt that greater profits could be made by increased consumption, brought about by a lower cost to the consumer. This meant going directly to the source of supply and cutting out the middlemen, eliminating excessive tolls, and driving out competition. In short, the Dutch policy meant monopoly, and for this the Dutch needed a toll-free, fortified rendezvous in the Indies. Bantam did not realize that this was the basic issue with the Dutch merchants, and demanded tribute as usual without granting the Dutch permission to fortify their warehouse.

The king of Djakarta had hoped to benefit from this situation and had counted on the support of a foreign power to help him secede from Bantam. He might have gained his end had he accepted the Dutch wholeheartedly. The trouble was that Widjaja Krama expected too much too soon, and he was unable to gauge the relative strength of the Dutch and the English at this particular time. Now that Coen and his ships had left Djakarta, everything seemed to favor the English, who had given him armaments and who had also promised him half the loot of the Dutch fort— 100,000 reals in goods.

Bantam, although equally unable to read the situation correctly, took a more realistic view. With the Dutch fleet away in the Moluccas, and the English forced to depart, the *Pangeran* no longer hesitated to take Djakarta to task. The *Tommogon* invaded the *dalem* with his troops, and the self-styled king of Djakarta was given the choice of fleeing for his life or being cut down. Widjaja Krama choose the first, and with his family, he fled to the hinterland.[17] Thus the *Pangeran* gained his first objective: to put Dja-

16. De Jonge, *Opkomst, 4*, cvii–cviii.
17. Van Deventer, *Nederlanders*, p. 116.

karta under the hegemony of Bantam where it traditionally belonged.

It was no secret to Rana Mangala that the Dutch Company desired either Bantam or Djakarta as a rendezvous in the Indies. Now that he controlled both, it seemed a simple process to assert Bantam's supremacy. The Dutch would have to come to terms—high levies and defenseless warehouses—or else they would have nothing. All that remained to be done, now that the recalcitrant Widjaja Krama had been purged and the English had been forced to withdraw, was to make the Dutch garrison surrender its fort to the Bantamese.

Bantam offered better terms than had Widjaja Krama or the English. The *Pangeran* demanded only half the goods and cannon of the Company and, in addition, was willing to allow the Dutch garrison to go free to Bantam or elsewhere. The leaders at the fort had by now become so adjusted to the prospect of surrender —first to Widjaja Krama and then to the English—that they seriously considered this latest offer. To Van Raey and the rest of the council it looked attractive indeed. It was 50 per cent better than the offer of English-Djakartan alliance, and included a safe conduct besides. Not all were in accord. Van den Broek had suggested a surrender to Bantam, but Coen who, while not present, was still a dominant force, had said that in case of emergency it would be better to surrender to the English. The members of the council could not agree on what was best. On February 7 there were hot arguments between the opposing factions, leading to a pitched battle which actually amounted to mutiny. On that same day some fifty additional native vessels arrived from Bantam, laden with troops. They also brought emissaries from the Dutch factory, who confirmed the *Pangeran*'s terms for the surrender of the fort. This broke the resistance of those who feared the absent Coen more than the immediate threat of the Bantamese forces.

On February 9 the council decided to accept Bantam's proposal in principle but, because the train of events was moving slightly in their favor, they would first try to obtain better terms. The Dutch offered a quarter of the Company's goods instead of half and asked that the *Pangeran* arrange for a safe conduct by the English for the garrison.[18]

18. For this resolution and the terms of capitulation to the 'king' of Bantam, see Van der Chijs, *De Nederlanders*, pp. 113–16 and 215–16.

At this time there was apparently no one in the fort who did not believe that disaster had been averted. The fact that they had surrendered three times in so many weeks did not seem to weigh heavily on their consciences. They decided to have a banquet which, with heady Spanish wine, quickly developed into an orgy; during the next few weeks such became an almost daily occurrence. The National Archives in The Hague contain a journal kept during the siege; for reasons of his own the writer preferred to remain anonymous. Apparently he was not of a rank high enough to participate in these festivities, but one can gather from his observations that every appetite was gratified: [19]

> Anselien and Speranty and two other women [all Portuguese half-castes] were placed at the head of the table during the evening meal. After the sub-merchants and assistants had left, Raey, the Captain, Dominie Hermans, the Lieutenant, and the Cornet remained with the women. They were gay and happy and drank Spanish wine and dallied with those women, singing: *Tabe, tabe, Signora moeda—bawa bantal tikar—betta mau rassa!* [Greetings, young Signora—do bring your sleeping mat and pillow . . .] What the Dominie had preached during the day was already forgotten; all were too busy with those luscious women . . . the pleasures lasted until one or two in the morning when everyone went to his bunk and three women slept upstairs . . . the Cornet took Speranty home and had his fun with her in her house . . .

According to the anonymous diarist, this carousing with the women was repeated night after night and lasted until they were *heyeken* (?).

Raey was the instigator of these affairs. During the day he walked around with a golden chain around his neck, abusing

19. It has since been established that the writer of this caustic journal was a certain Melis Lants, an experienced merchant who was then 44 years old. Unfortunately for him, he had sailed on the French ship *Marguerite* as Chief Merchant and as such was among those who were re-hired by the Company at a reduced salary, in Lant's case as sub-merchant at forty guilders per month. Toward the end of 1618, Coen received a letter from the Seventeen to the effect that Lants had taken an oath, prior to his sailing, that he would not enter the service of the French or any other foreign nation. As a result he was sentenced by the Council to be returned to Holland without pay (*Documents, 4,* 164). Being under a cloud himself, he was a severe critic of all that occurred during the siege. See J. W. IJzerman, "Over de belegering van het fort Jacatra," *BKI,* 73 (1917), 558–679.

the men and treating them like dogs. The men said that they had never heard such language when the General [Coen] was around . . . On the 20th, a Wednesday, the Lieutenant with a number of others were drinking in his room, and those lissome women were with them, such as Speranty and her following. The men were gay and made those women so drunk that they laid down in their own filth and fell asleep . . . Arrack and Spanish wine flowed for carousing, but Raey refused to give it to the sick.[20]

The victory Bantam had gained over the usurper at Djakarta apparently satisfied the *Pangeran* for a while; he did not at once enforce his demand for the surrender of the fort. There may also have been other reasons that kept him from attacking. After withdrawing from Djakarta, the English fleet had returned to Bantam. The opportunity to expel the Dutch from Djakarta had slipped through Dale's fingers, as had the chance to defeat Coen's squadron. Sir Thomas Dale never followed up his avowed purpose of pursuing and chasing the Dutch out of the Moluccas. But the English fleet still controlled the waters between Djakarta and Bantam, and Dale refused to give a safe conduct to the Bantamese vessels which were to debark the Dutch garrison.

There were overriding fears that kept the various factions from bringing the Dutch to submission. The king of Djakarta, having invited the Dutch, was afraid of being squeezed between Bantam and Mataram. Bantam was afraid of losing its preferred status as entrepôt to Djakarta. And the English were afraid of tackling the Dutch in the Moluccas and the Bantamese at Djakarta. The only one who was not afraid was Jan Coen. He had run away— at least this was the impression—but it was certain that he would return.

The indecision on the part of its enemies gave the garrison a much needed respite. Javanese, who had profited from business with the Dutch, returned to the fort, and a brisk trade was resumed. The gates were thrown open, and it seemed as if nothing had happened. The situation became even more promising when four Dutch vessels arrived off Djakarta. They had been hailed by the *Ceylon* in the Sunda Strait and, apprised of the events, had avoided Bantam. These reinforcements did much to discourage the enemy and to give the garrison new heart.

20. Lant's journal, in De Jonge, *Opkomst, 4,* 149–50.

Vessels arrived from Javanese ports as they had before, bringing rice and other needed victuals, and trade was resumed as usual. Disregarding the fact that they had surrendered three times in succession, Van Raey and his colleagues began to consider themselves heroes. After the orgies of the night before, they walked around with bleary eyes overseeing the labors of those who were to do the menial tasks of strengthening the fortifications. But they were also afraid, because for them, too, there would come a day of reckoning when Coen returned.

On February 24, the leaders at the fort took a more sober view of the situation, possibly impelled by the knowledge that before long they would have to face the governor general and give an account of their actions. It may have been simply that it was a Sunday and that Dominie Hulsebos had preached a rousing sermon. It is a recorded fact that after his sermon that day, ten couples were married:

> There were six Dutchmen who married six black women, and four black couples who married. Six black women and one Dutchman were baptized and after this there was a great feast, much like a *boere kermis* (farmer's fair).[21]

One thing may have led to another—the resurgence of Calvinist morality, the absence of hostility—but two days later, the resolution was made that the fort should be held at any price, to be defended by old and young alike. On March 12 morale had been restored to such an extent that an official proclamation seemed to be in order. With trumpeting and flag-waving, the bastions of the fort were named after the four most important regions of the Lowlands: Holland, West Friesland, Zealand, and Gelderland. The fort itself was named Batavia, after the earliest tribes that had settled in the Netherlands in the dim past.[22]

All this had taken place while Coen was absent. How would he react, upon his return, to the roles played by Bantam, by the English, by Djakarta, and by the garrison itself?

21. Ibid., *4,* 151.
22. Ibid., *4,* 153.

16

The
Birth
of an Empire

Coen arrived at Amboyna early in February 1619 and immediately began to assemble as large a force as possible. It was a slow process because the Dutch ships were spread all over the eastern part of the archipelago. Reael, with the largest number under his command, was at Ternate and was slow in coming to Amboyna. It took well over a month before a sufficiently large number of ships was brought together.

On March 10, Jan Pieterszoon Coen officially assumed his duties as governor general. The council convened to discuss a plan of action. No one had any idea, of course, of what had happened at Djakarta. To the best of their knowledge, the English fleet was on its way to the Moluccas, and those rich islands should therefore not be left without protection. In February an English yacht had arrived at Pulu Run with the word that Sir Thomas Dale had taken the *Black Lion* and dispersed the Dutch fleet, that the fort at Djakarta was practically theirs, and that the English fleet was about to sail for Banda. This news was celebrated by the English factory at Pulu Run "with many cannon shots, just as if they had already conquered us," Dutch observers reported.

Leaving a minimum force behind for the defense of the Moluccas, Coen began the return voyage during the second half of March. A frigate with the newly appointed council members, De Carpentier and Soury, was sent ahead to tell those at the fort, if it were still in Dutch hands, that relief was coming. The other ships headed for Japara where a final decision would be taken, based on what could be learned there about the actual state of affairs at Djakarta.

Plagued by doldrums and adverse winds, Coen did not arrive at Japara until the middle of May. He learned to his satisfaction that the fort was still held by the Dutch and that the English fleet had withdrawn. Coen decided that the time had finally come to establish the long desired rendezvous. The town of Djakarta should be stormed and destroyed because, by their alliance with the English, the Djakartans had proved to be enemies of the Dutch.

The fleet reached Djakarta on May 28. Under the sound of cannon shots from the shore as well as from the ships, Coen entered the fort and quickly appraised the situation. Two days later, not wanting to give the enemy time to bring up reinforcements from Bantam, Coen launched the attack, putting himself at the head of 1,000 men. Most of the people of Djakarta had already fled into the interior, but there were 3,000 Bantamese in the walled town. They proved no match for the Dutch and put up little or no defense. The walls and bulwarks were flattened, and the whole town, including the *dalem* and mosque, was burned to the ground.[1]

It had never been Coen's intention to occupy Djakarta by force and depose Widjaja Krama. It was the *Pangeran* of Bantam who had done this, and after his forces had in turn been expelled, Coen was clever enough to take advantage of such an opportune turn of events. Now that the deceiver himself had been deceived, he considered it no more than just that he should fill the vacuum. At once he realized what this eventually might mean to the Company. He wrote the Seventeen,

> It is certain that this victory and the fleeing of the English will create quite a furor throughout the Indies. This will enhance the honor and the reputation of the Dutch nation. Now everyone will want to be our friend. The foundation of the Rendezvous is now established and a good part of the most fertile land is yours. This ought to show you what a bit of courage can accomplish. We implore Your Lordships to send us now a large number of people with all the necessities so that we can build a strong fort and a town . . . stop being negligent and short-sighted, thinking that we can manage here just by ourselves.[2]

It was like Coen to add to this good news his often repeated admonition. The second important item on Coen's agenda was Bantam. The day Djakarta had been taken he sent word to Rana Man-

1. De Jonge, *Opkomst, 4,* cxiii.
2. *Documents, 1,* 472.

gala that he would soon appear before the town. Fearful of having to suffer the same fate as Djakarta the people of Bantam tried, in limited time, to prepare themselves as best they could. There was really not much they could do if Coen decided to bombard the town. Rana Mangala, however, still held an important trump card. Van den Broek and his co-hostages had never been set free, and the people at the Dutch house were also virtual prisoners, surrounded by strong guards. To the original numbers of Dutch at Bantam had been added the crew of the *Black Lion* with whose capture Thomas Dale and John Jourdain had opened their campaign. The ship itself had shortly afterwards burned to the waterline when some English sailors, who were prowling through the hold with lighted candles in search of arrack, accidentally set fire to the ship. All told, there were about a hundred Dutchmen in Bantam whose lives hung in the balance.

Rana Mangala, proud and unyielding as ever, had threatened to kill every Dutchman in Bantam if Coen dared to attack the town. "We are not like those of Jacatra," he said boldly. "We shall not run away and, if we are forced to evacuate the town, every pepper vine in the land will be cut down."

Coen was aware of the *Pangeran*'s mood when he appeared before the town on June 6, and he decided against taking Bantam by storm. As an early student of economic warfare, he knew there were other means for bringing Bantam to terms. Coen did nothing for two days, but the ominous presence of his powerful fleet impressed the Bantamese. It was the *Pangeran* who made the first move. He sent an emissary to Coen with word that he would hold the hundred Dutchmen until he had the assurance that no harm would come to the town. Coen refused to bargain and replied that, unless all the Dutchmen were released within twenty-four hours, he would take stern measures. He had read Rana Mangala's mind correctly, and before the stipulated time had passed all the prisoners were freed. In reporting this Bantam incident to the Seventeen, Coen added, not without irony, "The *Pangeran* complained bitterly that we had treated him badly, and this in spite of all the great favors he had done for us!" [3]

Coen remained at Bantam until June 21, attempting to resume trade on less restrictive terms than those the *Pangeran* had imposed before. It was Bantam's last chance to retain some of its former glory, but the *Pangeran* allowed the opportunity to slip

3. Ibid., *1*, 472–73.

by. Smarting at having had to bow to Coen, he became more difficult than ever. The Dutch house was surrounded day and night
by armed Bantamese, and it was almost impossible for a merchant
to go about the town and do business. Rana Mangala was apparently willing to cut off his nose to spite his face.

Realizing that nothing could be accomplished at Bantam, Coen
returned to Djakarta. On June 30 a resolution was passed in the
council stating that henceforth all relations with Bantam would
be terminated and the town blockaded. Every bit of the Company's merchandise and money was taken from the Dutch house
and brought to Djakarta. Chinese and native traders were urged
to come to Djakarta with the none too subtle warning that their
goods would be confiscated from their vessels at sea if they persisted in sailing to Bantam. They would, however, be paid the
going price for their wares.

The blockade was to last almost continuously for forty years,
and by the end of that period little was left of the glory of that
once great market place, the consequence of the refusal of a stubborn native ruler to bow before an equally stubborn European.
Basically it was more than a clash of personalities that had brought
this about. There was a more deep-seated reason. Rana Mangala
represented an outmoded system, Jan Coen the new economic
age, and the two were incompatible.

Coen still had some unfinished business to attend to at Djakarta.
After the first flush of relief had subsided, the garrison of the
fort, especially its higher personnel, soon realized that the day of
reckoning had also come for them. In a mere few weeks, they had
capitulated no less then three times; to Djakarta, to the English,
and to Bantam. Only a freak of circumstances, the lack of unified
action among their enemies, had averted the loss of the fort and
its contents, not to speak of the incalculable loss of Dutch prestige.
The supply of gunpowder on hand at Coen's return was practically the same as when he had left, certainly not an indication
of a vigorous defense. Coen demanded a look at all the documents
and resolutions and a day-by-day account of all that had transpired. It can easily be imagined how Coen, the puritan discipli-
narian, reacted as the picture gradually evolved. The evidence of
gullibility, indecision, dissipation, and looting did not add up to
a heroic defense. The one thing which enraged Coen in particular was perhaps not the theft of his personal belongings and the
destruction of his papers, but that the fort had been named Ba-

tavia. It had been his ambition to name the rendezvous Nieuw Hoorn, after the town of his birth.

To those who tried to justify their actions by reminding the governor general that he himself had advocated a surrender to the English in case of emergency, Coen could acidly point out that they also had surrendered to Djakarta and Bantam. All those who had been involved were summarily reduced to the rank they held when they entered the service of the Company. A complete inventory was ordered to establish the exact amount the Company had lost through neglect and outright theft. Those who had participated in the looting—all too many—would be held responsible for what they had taken even if it meant working years to pay for it.[4]

The final and most important item on Coen's agenda was the complete dispersal of the English fleet from the Indies. With the arrival of additional ships from the Netherlands, the Company had gathered a formidable fleet at Djakarta, more than enough to engage the English. It was tempting to pursue the enemy in force, but Coen and his council finally decided that the financial interest of the Company had priority over the desire for revenge. Normal trade had been at almost a standstill for six months, and it was high time that it be resumed. Besides, no one had any clear idea of where the English might have gone. Six Dutch ships were sent to the pepper ports on the northwest coast of Sumatra, and three to Patane in the Gulf of Siam. Although trade was their main object, the various commanders were explicitly instructed to attack any English ships they might encounter if they felt they could "profit thereby." [5]

Unknown to the Dutch at the time, the English fleet had separated. Already dismayed by the fateful and unexpected turn of events at Djakarta, just as victory had seemed to be within his grasp, Sir Thomas Dale became still more alarmed when he learned that Coen was on his way back from the Moluccas with a strong force. Following Coen's example, the English admiral decided that discretion was the best tactic and that he had best withdraw for the time being, while he still had all of his ships. It was by no means a rout but a well thought out plan to make the retreat as profitable as possible, by picking up as much cargo as

4. For the sentences, dated July 9, 1619, see *Documents*, 4, 171–74.
5. See the Resolution, dated June 26, 1619 in *Documents*, 3, 519.

they could at various points before sailing for home, or returning to Bantam if that seemed advisable.

John Jourdain, with two ships under his command, sailed for Djambi first and then continued to Patane. Four other ships headed for Tiku and other ports on Sumatra's west coast to load as much pepper as was obtainable. The admiral loaded the goods of the factory and embarked all the English personnel from the Bantam office, fearing they might find themselves in dire straits if the Bantamese decided to join forces with the Dutch. Sir Thomas Dale had been stricken by malaria and was a very sick man. He wanted to seek asylum for the time being at Mazulipatnam, where he had recently offered to provide a safe passage for the Dutch garrison at Djakarta.

By sheer luck, or divine Providence the Dutch squadrons were headed for the same ports as the English. John Jourdain was the first to run foul of the Dutch. He was anchored in the bay of Patane on July 26 when three Dutch ships hove into view. They were under the command of Hendrik Jansz., the former skipper of the *Black Lion*, who thus had a special account to settle. According to English depositions concerning this encounter, there were conflicting opinions as to the best procedure. Some were all for raising anchor and escaping during the night, but John Jourdain preferred to stay. George Muschamp, chief merchant in Siam, who lost his right leg in the ensuing battle, stated later, "We might have escaped during the night if the President had not stood too much upon points of honour in the sight of the Countrye people . . . the Master and all of us importuned we might sett sail. Jourdain replied that 'it should never be reported that he would run away from a Fleming.' " Marmaduke Stevinton testified, "The President nott possiblie perswadable to set saile, scorning to budge an anchor in the face of the towne."

Thomas Brockedon and Augustine Spalding deposed that the president, John Jourdain, had been surprised by Henrick Jonson who came to "revenge the loss of the lion [*Black Lion*], which he could not have done if the President had weighed anchor and fought under sail . . . however, his resolution pretended the credit of our nation in the presence of the country people and deserves a favorable censure." [6]

These depositions make it clear that it was Jourdain's decision,

6. Foster, *Jourdain's Journal*, app. F, pp. 368–72.

and his alone, to stand firm and fight it out. One may speculate as to what made him make such a fateful decision when the odds were all against him. An Englishman's pride for his country? Most likely. He was not going to run away in full view of the people of Patane, and, as a servant of the English Company, he was not going to run away from a Fleming either. There had been disagreement between Dale and Jourdain about the stand to be taken with the Dutch, but the records do not state just what the argument was about. In the light of what happened one must assume that, while Dale wanted to withdraw completely (he went to Mazulipatnam) Jourdain wanted to hold out as best he could, and this must have been the reason why he did not follow Dale and the others on their westward voyage. There may have been something more personal in his decision, the idea that this was a private battle between himself and Jan Coen.

The next day the battle was joined, and Coen reported the event to the Seventeen as follows:

> As we advised you earlier, the *Angel*, the *Bergerboot*, and the *Morning Star* was dispatched to Patane with a good capital for trading purposes, and with the specific instructions to engage any English vessels they might encounter. Arriving there on July 26, they found there two English ships, the *Sampson* and the *Hound*. Our ships anchored close by and the next morning they went to the attack. Both sides fought furiously for a period of three glasses (one hour and a half) and then the English capitulated. They lost 39 men and among them was Jean Jardyn, the head of their commerce, whom we consider the author of all our recent troubles . . .
> In the *Sampson* we found original resolutions, missives, contracts, copy books, and other English papers which clearly show what they had been up to. These papers make it clear that they wanted to ruin the Company by setting both Bantam and Jacatra against us.[7]

The English version of how John Jourdain lost his life is more emotional. It is worth repeating here because it displays one of the reasons why the Dutch succeeded and the English failed in the earliest attempts to acquire the trade of the Indies. The English looked upon these conflicts in terms of personalities. If a man were killed, wounded, or insulted, the English invariably took

7. *Documents, 1,* 510–12.

great pains to attribute it to the perfidy of the enemy. The Dutch, by and large, limited themselves to recording the facts—we lost this, the enemy lost that. This different approach, small as it may seem, was in fact one of the reasons why the Dutch succeeded in driving the English from the Spice Islands, their avowed goal, and eventually forced them to seek their fortune in India proper. While the English Company was still adhering to a guild system based on personal honor, the Dutch, perhaps unwittingly, were driven by the power of anonymous capital, perpetual as long as profits were made and without conscience or emotional reaction.[8]

English history rings with the names of heroes, but one searches in vain for the name of John Jourdain. He deserves a greater recognition. He was perhaps the one man in the service of the English Company at that time who was a merchant rather than an adventurer in the style of the Elizabethan age. Perhaps no greater tribute was ever paid him than when Coen singled him out as his chief antagonist. John Jourdain failed not because he lacked capabilities but because the English governors at London refused to break with tradition. On July 29, 1619, John Jourdain, almost fifty years old, gave his life for his country and for the London Company.

Both Dutch and English records agree on the fact that John Jourdain was killed after the English had hoisted the white banner to signify their willingness to surrender. What differs is the emotional reaction. Muschamp stated, "The President had sounded a parley and in talking with Hendrike Johnson (the Dutch commander) received his death wound with a musket." Stevinton said the same thing, "Our noble minded President was slayne in parley with Henrie Johnsen." Others went further in accusing the Dutch of treachery in taking Jourdain's life. "General John Peter Sacone [Coen] gave Hendricke Janson a gold chain (worth 1,400 guilders) putting it himself about his neck. He also gave 100 Real to the man who actually shot the President." It was also reported that Coen had said on this occasion, "Dale is dead, and Jordayne's blood I have; if I had George Cockayne's life too, I were then satisfied." This deposition was signed by Cassarian David, Bartholomew Churchman, and George Pettys.[9] One must assume that

8. See J. C. Riemersma, "Government Influence on Company Organization in Holland and England (1550–1650)," *Journal of Economic History*, supplement X (1950), 31–39. See also Meilink-Roelofsz, *Asian Trade*, pp. 191–94.

9. Foster, *Journal*, app. F, p. 374. In this deposition Jan Pietersz. Coen is

the deponents actually believed that Jan Coen had spoken these words, but nowhere is there further substantiation of their story.

In the Dutch annals, there is no evidence that Jan Coen said this or that he rewarded Hendrik Jansz., the former skipper of the *Black Lion,* with anything whatever. In fact, there is no record that Jan Coen ever gave a golden chain to anyone in the Company; this was an honor bestowed only by the Seventeen. Sir Thomas Dale, however, was dead at the time the deposition was made. This former high sheriff and leader of the Virginia colony at Jamestown, had died at Mazulipatnam in August of that same year, as a result of the tropical fevers which had overcome him at Djakarta.

These various depositions became part of the English Company's complaints against the Dutch. In due course, the Dutch presented their version of Jourdain's death:

> Your President and our Commander came above the hatches and beginning to confer (while the two ships were alongside). Our other ships could not be advertised of the aforesaid parley by reason of shortness of time. The *Morning Star* coming up fired in ignorance of what before had passed between the chiefs of both fleets. A musket shot hit your President in the belly, without any special aim, but the mishap might as well have befallen our own Commander because a cannon ball (from the *Morning Star*) went through his own ship.[10]

The larger squadron which had sailed up the west coast of Sumatra under Willem Jansz., a member of the Council of the Indies, was even more successful than that of his namesake Hendrik Jansz. In the vicinity of Tiku, on October 11, they encountered four English ships and an immediate decision was taken to close in and fight board-to-board. Once more the English put up a strong fight but, as had been the case at Patane, here they were also outnumbered. In the engagement, the English ship *Dragon,* having two Dutch ships on either side, caught fire, and its crew jumped for their lives to the decks of the *Haarlem.* They were driven back to their burning ship to douse the fire before

---

referred to as John Peter Sacone. Compare Hall, *History of South-East Asia,* p. 246.

10. Letter handed by the Seventeen to Robert Barlow, the English Company's agent in Amsterdam. See Foster, *Journal,* app. F, p. 373.

being permitted to surrender. By nightfall all four ships were in the hands of the Dutch. All prisoners were put ashore at Tiku and were given back one of their ships, the *Rose*, with enough victuals to go wherever they wished, as long as it was towards the west, away from the Spice Islands.[11]

At the age of thirty-two, Jan Pieterszoon Coen had established not only a rendezvous at Djakarta but also a firm territorial foothold. He had subdued Bantam and dispersed the English—two factors which had stood in the way of Dutch supremacy in the Indies. The English would make another feeble attempt to acquire a share of the spice trade, but it was only a matter of a few more years before they completely withdrew from the whole of East Asia.[12]

11. *Documents*, *1*, 513–14.
12. For a brief but lucid account from a British point of view, see "The Anglo-Dutch Struggle for the Spice Trade," in Hall, *History of South-East Asia*, pp. 235–51.

17

Steps
Toward
Consolidation

In retrospect, the establishment of a general rendezvous at Djakarta can be seen as the keystone to the foundation of Dutch colonialism in Southeast Asia. That this involved territorial acquisition could hardly have been anticipated at the time. The Dutch had at this stage no conquests in mind, nor were they interested in the political affairs of the interior of Java.[1] All they wanted was a free-flowing trade based on contracts with local potentates, contracts which, as merchants, they considered inviolable. Only when such contracts were repeatedly broken did they resort to the establishment of territorial strongholds which would free them from the cupidity of local rulers. Djakarta was a case in point, and so was Banda.

In reporting this event to the Seventeen, Coen did not fail to point out that there had been considerable opposition to his decision to take Djakarta by force. "Against the advice of many, even within our own Council, we succeeded in dispersing three powerful enemies, namely the English, the Bantamese, and those of Jacatra."[2] The opposing council member he singled out was Laurens Reael, whom Coen had replaced as governor general and who was now on his way to Holland. Although Reael signed the resolution to attack, he added a provision that he could not approve it because it was based on events about which he had no personal knowledge. It is true that Reael had been in the Moluccas during the period preceding the event, but the main reason may well have been that he was unwilling to submit to Coen's recommendations. The feud between these two was by no means over, and ultimately affected Coen's program.

At the moment, however, it was of little importance, and Coen

1. Hall, *History of South-East Asia*, p. 252.
2. *Documents, 1,* 472.

proceeded to reiterate his program which was actually an elaboration of his famous *Discourse* which he had written almost six
years before.[3] Announcing a resounding success, he confidently
expected greater cooperation from the directors in Europe. After
reporting how the Company had obtained a foothold "in the land
of Java," he added, "It is certain that this victory and the fleeing
of the arrogant English will spread fear throughout the Indies.
Now everyone will want to be our friend." [4] It was Coen's reasoned opinion that without the rivalry and machinations of the
English, who had been following the Dutch "like gadflies," his
troubles with Banda and Bantam would soon be a thing of the
past and that orderly trade could be resumed. With victory in
his grasp, Coen could hardly have expected that, even as he was
writing, a ship was on its way with news that effectively curbed
these expectations.

Coen was convinced that the profits from the inter-Asiatic
trade would eventually enable the Company to pay its own way
in the Indies and even provide the necessary capital to send large
cargoes to Holland. Here, too, he elaborated on what he had already outlined in his *Discourse*. After some years of experience,
he had a clear view of the potentials. He wanted to trade textiles from Gujerat in Sumatra for pepper and gold. With silver
reals and cotton goods from the coast of Coromandel, he expected to obtain pepper from Bantam and South Sumatra. Sandalwood, pepper, and reals could be traded for Chinese goods and
gold; silver from Japan could be obtained with the Chinese goods.
Nor did Coen overlook Arabia, where silver reals were obtainable against spices and other goods. Before long Coen would include Persia in this vast trading empire. They were all tied in
together; such a lucrative trade was entirely possible so long as
the Company controlled the spices, the lifeblood for this inter-
play of multiple transactions.

What was lacking to accomplish all this? "Nothing but ships
and a little water [money] to prime the pump," [5] Coen stated
flatly. He pointed out that there was a multitude of ships available in the Netherlands, "more than anywhere else in the world."
And he wanted only the amount of money necessary to get this
trade under way. "Your Lordships are greatly mistaken if you

3. See Book III, Chapter 8.
4. *Documents, 1,* 473.
5. Ibid., *1,* 486.

think that it is possible to establish this most eminent trade of the world, and to hold and protect it, with 30, 40, or 50 ships and yachts." Actually there were at this time 38 ships and yachts in the Indies, and some 17 of these were practically useless, "Some of them leak so badly that they can hardly be kept afloat." [6] The power of the Dutch in Asia depended entirely on the ships available; it was a trading empire that could be developed and maintained by ships only. A number were required to patrol the Sunda Strait, others to blockade Bantam, and still another contingent to stave off the Spanish who, from Tidore, remained a constant threat to the Spice Islands. Nor could the English be ignored; their fleet had been forced to withdraw but it was still largely intact. Throughout his whole tenure in office, Coen considered the English his greatest stumbling block. He was well aware that the English, drawing on an illustrious naval history often threatened more than they were able to accomplish; nevertheless, their tenacity could not be denied. Thus there was the important problem of what measures to take at this time to prevent the English from repeating their exploit of December 1618, which had come close to evicting the Dutch from both West Java and the Spice Islands. Knowing that the English were the strongest enemy, a considerable part of Coen's inadequate fleet had to be set aside to prevent their return.

Coen had written the Seventeen that the Moluccas should have priority. This source of mace, nutmegs, and cloves was in fact the mythical El Dorado. Without a tight control of this source of wealth, not only the basic purpose of the Dutch East India Company but also his own program of inter-Asiatic trade would founder because spices were its keystone. Coen had the vision to realize that complete control of supplies and sales of these products was essential. The big question was what to do first: to secure the Spice Islands or to prevent the English from returning to resume their disruptive practices?

By this time Coen realized that letters as such were not enough to convince the directors and stockholders that there was a fortune, an empire, at their feet. His communications began to contain references to the fact that he had been in the Indies longer than anyone else and that it was about time he returned to Holland. At first he put it that simply, but if the Seventeen had read between the lines they would have realized that he had

6. Ibid., *1*, 529.

something more important in mind than returning to his homeland after a lengthy tour of duty. Anything related to his basic
program was always fully covered, but Coen had little patience
with what he considered to be trivial. When the Seventeen wrote
him that the professors of Leiden University had requested roots
and bulbs of strange flowers and herbs for their herbarium, Coen
replied drily, "We have never come across anything with bulbs
or roots. If we happen to hear of anything we will send it." [7]
He was not going to waste time looking for them. He responded
vigorously, however, to an admonition to refrain from taking
arbitrary measures against other European nations. The Seventeen
expected serious difficulties because Coen had confiscated a
French ship and stressed that "all further bellicosity between us
and neighboring kings, our allies, should be avoided in order
not to hurt the interest of the United Company." [8]

The Seventeen and the States General still labored under the
misunderstanding that disputes could be solved by invoking the
authority of local potentates. Coen knew that this was unrealistic.
If the Seventeen should insist that he turn the other cheek, "such
as the Mennonites do," he replied, "one should first find here the
kind of judges under whose protection we can live and trade.
But I say they are not to be found in the Orient." Coen made
it clear that there was no such thing as justice in the Dutch sense
of the word. "A farmer in Europe can do with his cattle what
he likes. In the same fashion the King here deals with his subjects because they belong to him, the same as the dumb cattle in
Holland belong to the farmer. He can do with them what he likes.
The law of this land is the will of the King." [9]

The Dutch in the Netherlands, in their rebellion against the
king of Spain, had stood up against arbitrary rulers, and Coen
considered it no more than just that they should do the same in
the Indies. Coen felt that the Dutch should take the responsibility for establishing law and order and seeing to it that they
were enforced. "There is nothing in the world that gives a greater
protection to human rights," he wrote, "than backing up justice
with force." [10]

While it might appear from Coen's letters that things were

7. Ibid., *1*, 492.
8. Ibid., *6*, 172.
9. Ibid., *1*, 484.
10. Gerretson, *Coen's eerherstel*, p. 32.

not going to progress well unless he received greater support from the mother country, it was evident that the establishment of the rendezvous at Djakarta was beginning to pay dividends. With the blockade of Bantam, it was inevitable that the supplies of pepper, which the *Pangeran* was determined to withhold in order to bring the Dutch to terms, soon found their way to Djakarta. The same was true of other Asiatic products, which for a century or more had been brought to this ancient emporium. Chinese merchants and artisans also found it more profitable to converge on Djakarta rather than on Bantam. Having no fleet such as had solidified an earlier Madjapahit, the *Pangeran* was powerless. Correctly blaming Coen for his misfortunes, Rana Mangala plotted to have his enemy eliminated. On October 17, 1619, three armed natives managed to enter the governor general's quarters at Djakarta. They were apprehended and after having duly "confessed," were executed. Coen made no great alarms about this incident to the Seventeen, but he intended that it should emphasize what the Company was up against.

Banda and the English were still matters of major consideration. It was finally decided in Council that it might be better to postpone an expedition to the Moluccas until the English fleet had been dealt with. It seemed a logical decision because by eliminating the English, a final solution of the Banda problem would be much easier.

This decision was reached on February 18, 1620. The forces the Dutch had at their disposal at this time were inadequate to engage in both operations at once. The English problem, moreover, had become the more pressing because, in addition to the ten English ships still in Asiatic waters, six more were reported to be under way. The Dutch plan was to hunt them down along the west coast of Sumatra, on the coast of Coromandel, and as far west as Surate and Arabia. To the Moluccas, which had been stripped of ships for the relief of Djakarta, seven ships were dispatched to protect them against the Spanish. The Sunda Strait demanded no less than 12 ships, to guard Djakarta against a surprise attack, to cut wood for strengthening the fort, and to build houses at the newly established rendezvous. Coen knew he was spreading his forces thin, but he was confident of the outcome.

Protecting the Spice Islands and barring the English from returning was a sound program, but it fell to pieces before it could be executed. While the Dutch squadron was being readied to sail westward against the English ships, the news reached Djakarta on March 27 that an agreement had been reached between the English and Dutch companies concerning trade in the Indies. It had been concluded in London on July 30, 1619, practically the same date that Coen and his council had clinched their victory over the English by deciding to build a larger fort at Djakarta and to blockade Bantam.

England was unprepared as yet to assume a dominant part in the new economic age where trade and industry spelled power. Nowhere was this more apparent than in the Indies. Unable to hold its own there, the London Company time and again invoked the help of the crown. This led to diplomatic representations at the highest level which the young and insecure Dutch republic could not ignore. As a result there had been consultations since 1611, in which both sides attempted to come to an understanding about a division of the spoils—the Spice Islands primarily. On both sides of the North Sea there were voices which objected to such an alignment. Not only did the Seventeen fear that they might lose their hard-won monopoly, but the English were equally apprehensive. Ambassador Winwood expressed it clearly when he said, "In case of Joyning, the art and industry of their people will wear out ours." [11]

In Holland, it had been Oldebarnevelt's view that friction between the Dutch and English in the Indies could best be solved by consolidating the two companies into one. It was an ambitious project but perhaps no more difficult than that accomplished by welding the various Dutch fore-companies into one united whole. Had Oldebarnevelt still been in power, such a consolidation might well have been accomplished, because neither company was primarily concerned with national prestige or territorial conquest.[12] But the aging advocate was in prison and about to be executed for having led the opposition against Prince Maurice and the Amsterdam oligarchy.

The arguments in favor of Anglo-Dutch consolidation were strong enough to survive even Oldebarnevelt's demise and the

11. J. E. Elias, *Het Voorspel van den Eersten Engelschen Oorlog*, 2 (The Hague, Martinus Nijhoff, 1920), 37.

12. The possible results of such a merger defy the imagination. Not only would it have changed the course of colonialism in Asia, but it would have affected Dutch-English relations in Europe. It might have prevented the three wars between the two countries during the seventeenth century, in one of which the Dutch lost New Amsterdam to the English.

matter was seriously considered, urged especially from the side of the emissaries of James and the States General, who kept pressing the delegates of the London and Dutch companies to come to an agreement. The main dispute was over the share to which each company should be entitled, based on its capital outlay to date, or how much either might have to contribute to arrive at a fifty-fifty basis, if such were desired. The English claimed a capital investment equal to 24.5 million guilders, while the figure the Dutch submitted was only 19.5 million.[13] Since neither side was willing to budge, the plans for a joint company at last had to be abandoned. There can be little doubt that the London company had grossly overplayed its hand, because its accomplishments over the past twenty years had been so meager that even an equal capital would hardly have been justified.

The Amsterdam merchants, the real power in the Seventeen, had never been enthusiastic about a consolidation of the two companies, and the fact that the plan had been Oldebarnevelt's made them even less so. Nevertheless, the need for some kind of agreement remained. The truce with Spain would come to an end in 1621, and it was undeniable that, with a resumption of hostilities, a friendly England would be an advantage if not a necessity to Holland. Aside from the prodding of the States General, there had also been voices within the Company calling for an accord with the English. Admiral Steven van der Hagen had suggested some sort of agreement as early as 1615, and in 1618 he again stressed the fact that "it would ruin the Company if it would have to fight both the Spanish and the English in the Indies." [14]

After a great deal of acrimonious debate, a Treaty of Defense —to last 20 years—was finally concluded during July 1619. The first point stipulated that all grievances from both sides were to be "forgiven and forgotten," prisoners were to be released, and captured ships and goods returned to their rightful owners. At this time the delegates were not aware that, because of the withdrawal of the English fleet, only the Dutch were in a position to meet this requirement. The second article expressed the pious hope that "both companies and all their employees, high and low, should henceforth live and converse as trusted friends, neighbors, and allies." [15]

13. De Jonge, *Opkomst*, 4, cxxi.
14. Elias, *Voorspel*, 2, 37.
15. De Jonge, *Opkomst*, 4, cxxiv.

The most important concession made by the Dutch was that the English were granted one third of the trade in the Moluccas. With one stroke, the Seventeen were relinquishing the hard-won monopoly which they had always considered essential to the success of the Company. In return, the English agreed, for the first time, to participate actively in the defense of the Indies against the Spanish and Portuguese. For this purpose a Council of Defense was to be established, consisting of four Dutch and four English members, who would have at their command a joint Fleet of Defense to which each company was to contribute ten ships.

It had obviously been intended that the two companies would operate in the Indies in some form of "regulated company," in which each would employ its own capital and do its own trading, subject only to certain regulations regarding prices to be paid to the native merchants, with a rather loose arrangement as to the share allotted to each. Much of this wishful thinking was based on the assumption that both companies were of equal power in the Indies, but it would soon become clear that Winwood's warning that the Dutch would run away with the spoils had been all too true. Blinded by national pride, the English had entered into a *pactus leoninus* that would prove to be ruinous.[16] The main reason for its failure arose from the fact that the English were unable to support the financial burden of their agreement. When this became apparent, Coen managed to turn the agreement into a dead letter.

One of the stipulations in the agreement was that each side should keep the areas it already possessed. It was hardly a coincidence that within two days after receiving a copy of the treaty, which had been sent with the English ship *Bull*, Coen and his council delineated the extent of the former 'kingdom' of Djakarta which the Dutch had acquired by conquest. On March 29, 1620, the boundaries were established somewhat arbitrarily as extending from Cheribon in the east to Bantam in the west, including the islands off the north coast. To the south the area was considered to extend to the south coast of Java. Coen apparently wanted to accomplish two things: to keep the English from building a fort in or near Djakarta, and to put a wedge between Mataram and Bantam. This became the first Dutch territorial acquisition of any size on Java, but it is indicative of how little

16. Elias, *Voorspel, 2,* 38.

interest there was for gaining territory per se; the Dutch did not reach the south coast of Java until the last decades of the seventeenth century.[17]

Coen's letter to the Seventeen dated May 11 made it clear how he felt about the so-called Treaty of Defense. The diplomats in Europe had hoped that it would lead to peace between the two rival companies, but they had overlooked the fact that the principle of monopoly to which both subscribed would undermine any form of harmony and cooperation. Nor had they considered the bitter hatred which had been gradually rising between the two factions in the Indies, and which could not be effaced by a document drawn up by men who had no personal knowledge of the conditions in the field.

"The English owe you a debt of gratitude," Coen wrote, "because after they have worked themselves out of the Indies, your Lordships put them right back again . . . We are afraid that you have taken a snake to your bosom . . . It is incomprehensible that the English should be allowed one third of the cloves, nutmegs, and mace [because] they cannot lay claim to a single grain of sand in the Moluccas, Amboyna, or Banda." [18] Coen was not so singleminded that he did not recognize some of the predicaments which had prompted the Dutch statesmen to enter into the agreement. "I admit that a servant should not criticize his masters' actions, and I know how important it is for the United Provinces to have the friendship and alliance of the Crown of England, but I maintain that you acted too hastily." [19]

It was in this mood that Coen met the English Admiral Martin Pring near Bantam, to inform him of the new treaty. Pring had gathered his forces and was sailing straight for Bantam to take revenge for the inglorious withdrawal of Dale. He had 11 good ships under his command against Coen's 13 of dubious worth, but his hands were tied by the treaty, as were Coen's. In addition, as Coen reported the situation, the English expected to be reinforced by three more ships from Surate and "their ships are stout, larger and in better condition than ours . . . and they came to take their advantage of us." [20]

The two leaders met on April 19, 1620. "The English an-

17. Vlekke, *Nusantara*, p. 160.
18. *Documents*, *1*, 544.
19. Idem. Compare Meilink-Roelofsz, *Asian Trade*, pp. 196–97, 202–03.
20. *Documents*, *1*, 547.

nounced publicly on all their ships to maintain peace and unity with the Dutch and to forget all that had happened in the past . . . Having heard this we did likewise." [21] Among the crews there was much rejoicing, although both sides had bitter memories of past encounters and many still carried scars. On the lower level, all this was now forgiven and forgotten, but, among the higher echelons, the seeds of discord were sprouting as before. Both Pring and Coen were contemplating ways and means of turning the terms of the treaty to advantage.

Pring demanded the immediate return of those ships of Dale's which had been captured by the Dutch. Coen, gauging the relative strength of both fleets, hedged by hiding himself behind the fact that, as yet, he had only received the treaty from an English source and had to await the ratification of the States General. In his mind, the English were as great a menace as they had ever been, and he was not going to tip the balance of power in their favor by returning the captured ships. He was sparring for time. This somewhat arbitrary action on the part of Coen greatly displeased Martin Pring, but, for the time being, short of disregarding the treaty and using force, there was nothing he could do about it.

It was only the first of a series of incidents which tended to defeat the intent of the Treaty of Defense. A Council of Defense was quickly set up, with Coen and Pring heading the group of four members from each side. Pring tried to strengthen his position by asking the *Pangeran* of Bantam for permission to establish a factory at Bantam, from which the Dutch had withdrawn and which therefore was open territory to the English. Bantam, having a clearer picture of the effect of the treaty than had the statesmen in Europe, refused to become a pawn in a struggle between the two powers which seemed sure to be revived. After having been beaten decisively by the Dutch and seeing his town blockaded by them, the *Pangeran* had no intention of siding with the weaker of the rivals.

According to the treaty (articles 23, 24, and 25), an English foothold was envisaged in the neighborhood of Bantam, as a counterpart to the Dutch stronghold at Djakarta. Thwarted at Bantam, Pring had no alternative other than settling at Djakarta. To this Coen could not object. After all, his instructions were that the two companies should work "in harmony and friendship." Pring

21. Idem.

wanted to re-establish his factory on Pope John's land at the mouth of the river, which had previously been granted the English by the former king of Djakarta. Coen demurred. All land surrounding the fort at Djakarta had become Dutch territory by virtue of the resolution of March 29. To allow the English to return to the mouth of the river, thus cutting him off from the sea if they desired, was of course out of the question. The English would be allowed to settle at a designated place and only if they subjected themselves to Dutch law, which was quickly being established.

"It is a superb nation," Coen informed the Seventeen on May 11. "They pretend much but we have no intentions to acknowledge any other authority in the land of Djakarta than that of the States General, the Prince and your Lordships." [22] One may well ponder the audacity of Coen, who invoked the highest authorities at a time when they were as yet totally unaware of what he had done in their name.

Being faced with the resolution, against which the Treaty of Defense had given no answer, the English were forced to put themselves under the jurisdiction of the Dutch. It is understandable that they did not do so willingly or with good grace. The bad feeling within the higher echelons quickly spread to the lower levels. This caused frequent street fights between Dutch and English sailors; actual and imagined insults were a ready excuse. A relatively unimportant incident brought matters to a head. Taking matters into his own hands, an English butler dragged a Chinese merchant into the English house and had him flogged. Coen refused to allow this to happen in Dutch territory and under Dutch jurisdiction. The Englishman was arrested, tried before a legally appointed court, and publicly flogged. The president and council of the English house greatly resented this sentence, claiming that "the King of England, as well as the whole English nation, has been greatly humiliated." Coen replied, "because of this misdemeanor our authority is impaired. We can not acknowledge any other law in this land than that of the States General." [23]

Among the significant attributes of the English during this period is their long memory: this small incident was duly preserved in the annals of the London company—one more com-

22. *Documents*, *1*, 553.
23. De Jonge, *Opkomst*, *4*, cxxx.

plaint recorded against the Dutch in their seemingly calculated campaign to obstruct and defame not only the English Company, but His Majesty the King and the whole English nation. There was more to come; the accumulated effect played an important part in inflaming the English temper in the years ahead until finally it seemed only war could efface the insults.

There can be no doubt that Coen had authority in the Indies, but he was keen enough to keep his own personality in the background. It was never "I did this or that" but always "It was decided in Council." In this manner ordinances and resolutions were promulgated in quick order during the months following the annexation of the land of Djakarta. To mention a few—a Court of Justice was established to relieve the council of this responsibility (August 15). Lands were to be given in leasehold on long and short term with the right of inheritance (August 18). This fitted Coen's basic plan to establish the nucleus of a Dutch contingent which eventually might grow into a prospering middle class.

At this time Coen put into practice his emerging belief that Dutch interest in the Indies could not be fostered solely by a trading company whose only concern was dividends for its shareholders and remuneration and prestige for its directors. A monopoly of the spice trade was indispensable, but Coen's vision extended a great deal further. He felt that the Company alone could never finance the great scheme he had in mind: a vast trading empire that would encompass the whole of Asia. This would require outside capital and independent merchants to pursue trade energetically, as in the Baltic, the Mediterranean, and elsewhere in Europe. From this activity, the Company would profit indirectly by levying taxes, and Coen anticipated that it should eventually pay the overhead in the Indies, both the cost of administration and the defense. "We are confident," Coen wrote in October, "that before long our monthly revenue will amount to 25,000 guilders, if not more . . . enough to maintain a garrison of 1,000 men." [24] Now that Djakarta had become a Dutch domain, it was the logical starting point, and Coen lost little time in establishing ordinances that would make the place self-sustaining. Tolls and excise taxes were established for a variety of goods on October 1. This brought over 200,000 guilders into the treasury within the next two years.

24. *Documents, 1,* 601.

By the end of 1620 the population of Djakarta, soon to be named Batavia by order of the Seventeen, had risen to more than 2,000 people, of which about half were Chinese. They too provided a source of revenue, because they were subject to a monthly head tax of three and a half guilders for the privilege of residing in Djakarta. They also had to pay 20 per cent on gambling, but the records do not show how this tax was determined. Coen liked the Chinese, and rated them a good deal higher than the average Dutchman sent out by the Seventeen. "It is a shame," Coen wrote, "to see the scum that arrives with your ships." [25] He wanted solid citizens, preferably married, so that colonies could be established. In order to attract such people the minimum wage should be raised to at least 10 guilders per month.

With such measures as these, Coen proceeded to consolidate the power of the Dutch in the Indies: a strong and impregnable rendezvous which was to be self-supporting through taxes and other levies; colonies of Dutch people to develop the surrounding land and bring it into production. The Chinese could participate in this scheme, but Dutch burghers should have the preference. Slaves would have to be imported in larger numbers to provide a labor force, and these were easily obtained in Africa and elsewhere. Djakarta should become the hub of the vast trading empire Coen envisioned, perhaps emulating in Asia the role of Amsterdam in Europe. In these plans the Javanese and the Indonesians played little or no part, and Coen had no desire to draw them into his orbit.

Based on this principle of remaining aloof from the indigenous population, Coen laid the foundation of that "dual economy" which became the outstanding characteristic of capitalistic colonialism; a capitalist economy superimposed upon a native non- or pre-capitalist one.[26]

25. Idem.
26. J. H. Boeke, *The Structure of Netherlands Indian Economy* (New York, 1942), p. 5.

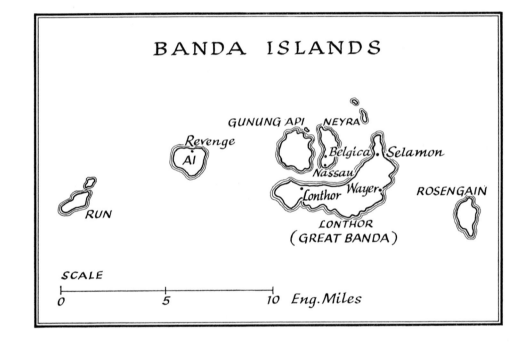

BANDA ISLANDS

GUNUNG API   NEYRA

Revenge
AI

Belgica . Selamon

Nassau

RUN

Wayer

Lonthor

ROSENGAIN

LONTHOR
(GREAT BANDA)

SCALE

0   5   10 Eng. Miles

18

The
Conquest
of Banda

If the directors of both the English and Dutch companies expected their mutual agreement to solve all problems, they were soon to learn differently. Since the Dutch forces were superior to the English, Coen set up an ambitious program for the use of the Fleet of Defense, more or less anticipating that the English would balk and thereby forfeit at least part of the advantages granted them. A joint expedition was planned to secure the China trade by isolating Manila, and another to chase the Portuguese out of the Indian Ocean, thus gaining possession of the important trade on the Malabar coast. Both expeditions involved great distances and were therefore time-consuming. In neither case was anything worthwhile accomplished, but they served Coen's purpose by taxing the English capabilities and bringing them to a point where they would refuse to participate in an expedition to the Moluccas, where Coen wanted to 'normalize' the situation once and for all. The English argued, not without some justification, that the treaty called for defensive action and not for conquest. They also felt that their one-third interest in the spices of the Moluccas was fully assured by the treaty. Coen did not share this view; if the Dutch were to solve this problem, they alone should benefit.

Coen wrote the Seventeen that he intended to go to the Moluccas and personally head the expedition. This was one more service he wanted to do the Company before leaving for Holland. He also intimated that it might well be necessary to "settle Banda with other people," [1] as this seemed to be the only way in which a tight monopoly could be attained. In this respect he was in complete accord with the Seventeen, who had repeatedly indicated that the Spice Islands should be the Company's main tar-

1. *Documents, 6,* 205.

get. For the directors it meant primarily that the Company would then control the spice market in Europe, but Coen realized that, in addition, such a monopoly would give him strong bargaining power in the inter-Asiatic trade, where spices would represent a first-rate working capital.

In these same letters Coen did not overlook his more ambitious plans. One of the terms of agreement between the English and Dutch companies had been the establishment of a joint colony at the Cape of Good Hope, which had become increasingly more important as a place of refreshment ever since it had been proved that a route to the Indies due east from the Cape, along the thirtieth parallel to the west coast of Australia and thence north, was quicker and healthier than the conventional route through the Indian Ocean. Coen observed that such a colony might not be a bad idea, but he added, "since you have neglected to establish colonies here, which are of far greater importance, how can one believe that you will execute this plan? Send your people here, even if it costs the Company, or the State, a lot of money. It will repay you a hundredfold." [2]

Coen also made it clear that the treaty had done nothing to lessen friction with the English. He neglected to say that this was mainly his doing because he was determined to regard the English as interlopers. By giving the Seventeen the necessary ammunition, he hoped the States General might be led to adopt a more antagonistic attitude towards England. The English had cut lumber around Djakarta without obtaining permission, claiming that the treaty gave them that authority. There were other incidents of a similar nature, none of them important but all adding up to the fact that the English greatly resented being in Djakarta on sufferance of the Dutch. Coen had no intention of deviating from his policy. If they did not like it, he told them, they could go back where they came from. These incidents had a cumulative effect, and the English Company took particular pains to record them in their books in London; always their whipping post was Jan Pieterszoon Coen, whom they referred to as John Peter Sacone. All their grievances seemed to be personified in him, and without a doubt he was the most militant obstruction to the English ambitions in Southeast Asia.

At this time Coen also tried to impress the directors with the benefits already accruing from the recently established rendez-

2. Ibid., 6, 203–04.

vous. Besides revenue from the Chinese taxes, tolls were levied on all incoming and outgoing goods as well as on the making of arrack; the English were also being charged tolls ranging from 5 to 10 per cent. Coen asked the Seventeen for suggestions as to what levies could be charged the French, Danes, and others, should they arrive. In other ways as well the Seventeen learned that Coen had created a bit of Dutch territory in the Indies, a place where law and order was maintained according to the Dutch code of law. Since the time he had become director general, some 400 cases had come before the council, involving major or minor infractions against ordinances declared in the name of the Company and the States General. Sixty per cent of these were crimes against the Company: dereliction in duty and treason, about fifty in each category; dishonesty, conspiracy, and subordination, about thirty each.[3] Irrespective of its original intention, the Company was gradually becoming a political power.

Coen sailed for the Moluccas on January 13, 1621, arriving at Amboyna one month later. Here he gathered his forces, which amounted to less than 1,000 men, including 80 Japanese mercenaries. His fleet of sixteen ships and yachts was augmented with 36 *tingans*, flat-bottomed boats which were to be used as landing craft. The Bandanese were understandably worried by this show of force and enlisted the aid of Capitan Hitu, a leading headman in Amboyna, and a friend of the Dutch.[4] Through him they offered the Dutch a new contract. Coen turned it down. He had learned by experience what these "treacherous agreements" amounted to, and he was not going to "let himself be abused once more."[5] Accompanied by Capitan Hitu, the fleet sailed to Banda where Coen at once contacted the English factory on Pulu Run whose commander had already been apprised of the Dutch intentions. Referring to the Treaty of Defense, Coen invited him to join forces, but the English once more declined to become involved. The brief but decisive campaign that followed can best be described in a chronological account of the events.

On February 28, Coen and his plenary council decided to start the campaign forthwith because the rainy season was approaching. But the door was still left open to the Bandanese to avoid bloodshed. On March 1, the council, at the pleading of Capitan

3. Ibid., *6*, 216–29.
4. See p. 114 f.
5. Gerretson, *Coen's eerherstel*, p. 34.

Hitu, empowered him to seek a definite understanding with the village heads of Lonthor on the island Great Banda, which had long been the hard core of opposition to the Dutch. This stubborn resistance had been stiffened by the fact that Lonthor was an almost impregnable stronghold. It was situated on the north coast of the island against the side of a steep mountain, and it boasted three lines of fortifications: at the shore, halfway up the mountain, and near the top. The English, always ready to fish in troubled waters, had provided the Lonthorese with a quantity of cannon, munitions, and other weapons, in exchange for a promise that they would accept the sovereignty of the king of England. Capitan Hitu returned the following day with a few Bandanese emissaries who offered a new contract promising to recognize the Dutch Company as the sole buyer. Coen did not reject this offer, but demanded, in view of past experiences, that the Dutch be allowed the right of fortifications on all islands of the group. This was a legitimate demand and actually no more stringent than what was agreed upon after Admiral Verhoef and his aides had been assassinated. When this condition was turned down, all hope for a peaceful settlement vanished.

On March 15, after a number of bloody engagements on the mountainside in which the Dutch were repulsed several times with considerable losses—"because one man above was worth twenty below"—the Bandanese capitulated on Coen's terms.[6] These included the surrender of all weapons, the raising of all fortifications, and, most important, a submission to Dutch sovereignty whereby the Bandanese agreed to "become trusted subjects, to live in peace under our protection."[7] By these terms the Bandanese relinquished their independence and became Dutch subjects. Any uprising from then on was no longer an act of war but one of high treason which, according to Roman law, was punishable by death, as it was throughout all Europe.

It soon became apparent that the Bandanese were not adhering to the terms of capitulation. The arms they reluctantly delivered, piecemeal, were either very old or useless, and it was estimated that more than 500 muskets were still unaccounted for. It was also reported that instead of tearing down their fortifications in the mountains, more were being added. On May 2, Coen sent a task force of about 200 men into the mountains to investigate these

6. Ibid., p. 37.
7. Kiers, *Coen op Banda*, p. 6.

rumors. The Dutch ran into an ambush where they lost nine dead and 35 wounded.[8] The 45 Orang Kayas who had been kept as hostages on a Dutch ship were immediately "interrogated," and they confessed that the Bandanese had never intended to abide by the terms of surrender. They had deliberately kept their best weapons, and planned to overrun the Dutch forts and murder the garrison a month or two after Coen and his force had left the islands.

By due process of law, torture being a recognized means of proving guilt, the council condemned all the hostages to death. Two had died under torture, and one committed suicide. The Dutch did not act as executioners and allotted this task to six of the Japanese mercenaries. The prisoners were put to death on May 8 in a bamboo stockade just outside the fort. In addition some 800 Bandanese were transported to Djakarta where they found work as best they could, either helping the burghers in the building of houses or gathering fruit in the outlying area. "They are indolent people," Coen wrote, "of whom little good can be expected. We must wait and see what can best be done with them." [9] Some 300 of the rest of the population had managed to escape, but most of the others, about 2,500, perished in the mountains.

There is no record of Coen's personal reaction to this wholesale slaughter but it is unlikely that he had any qualms. In his mind it hardly compensated for the cold-blooded murder of Admiral Verhoef with some 30 other Dutchmen, which he had witnessed 12 years before. Coen did, moreover, take full responsibility. Contrary to his usual custom of reporting actions as having been instigated in council, he singled out himself when he reported to the States General in September 1623 that "all the Bandanese Islands were finally reduced and conquered in 1621 by the General Coen, thus bringing them into the free possession of the United Company." [10]

The verdict of contemporaries was not wholly favorable to the manner in which the conquest had been accomplished. Aert Gysels, who held a grudge against Coen [11] and who rarely lost an opportunity to criticize his actions, had this to say when the

8. *Documents*, 6, 240.
9. Ibid., 1, 644.
10. Ibid., 4, 584.
11. See p. 360 f.

news reached the Lowlands: "It should be said that we have been far too ruthless in the execution of the principal heads of the county . . . we should remember that they fought for the independence of their own country, the same as we did sacrifice our lives and goods for so many years." [12] This must be interpreted as a calculated appeal to enlist sympathy for the Bandanese, affording Gysels another opportunity to cast aspersions on his former superior. No other conclusion is possible since Gysels himself had suggested, while he was chief merchant at Banda, that the situation could only be stabilized by the forceful expulsion of the whole population.[13] Nor is it likely that he would have adopted a more moderate policy had he been in charge. This appears from his own actions after he became governor of Amboyna in 1631. He then stated that there was no other way "to rid us of the over-abundance of cloves and the burden of the unreliable Moors, than to destroy their clove trees and level them to the ground." [14]

The Seventeen, while greatly appreciating what Coen had done for the Company, expressed themselves thus: "we had wished that it could have been accomplished by more moderate means." [15] If this were meant as criticism, then the Seventeen had apparently forgotten that they themselves had written to the Indies in 1615 that they considered it advisable to get rid of the principal Bandanese.[16]

It is more difficult to understand the harsh criticism levelled at Coen for the Banda affair by Dutch historians of the nineteenth and early twentieth centuries. While most acknowledge Coen's talents as a merchant, statesman, and empire builder, there is hardly one among them who refrains from showing his abhorrence of the execution of the Orang Kayas. The Dutch empire had become an historical fact, and the mother country had derived enormous wealth from it since the State had taken over

12. Kiers, *Coen*, p. 237.
13. Ibid., p. 241.
14. Ibid., p. 242.
15. Gerretson, *Coen's eerherstel*, p. 101.
16. The Seventeen minced no words in their instructions of April 30, 1615. They highly recommended that "the Bandanese should be overpowered, the chiefs exterminated and chased away, and the land be repopulated with heathens." See *Documents*, 4, 307. The Javanese felt no differently about the Bandanese. As reported by Matelief, the ruler of Tuban was understood to have said, "The people of Banda must be subdued. If the Portuguese do not do it, or the Dutch, then I shall do it myself." See De Jonge, *Opkomst*, 3, 323.

from the East India Company. In an age in which the social conscience of nations was being re-examined, this gave rise to guilt.
Unlike other European nations, the Dutch had never previously
indulged in aggression; they had found their enviable niche in
the world by peaceful trading. This had been the original intention in the East Indies as well, but the conquest of Banda
marred this record. Self-criticism was almost a national trait
and, more than many nations, the Dutch were almost devoid of
chauvinism. The Banda affair was a blot and Coen became the
scapegoat.

One of the earliest detractors of Coen was Van der Chijs, the
archivist at Batavia. "There is blood on his name," he writes,
"and if his statue had not already been erected, I doubt very
much if it would now be done." [17] De Jonge speaks of the "all
but ineradicable blood spot that sullied the name of the Netherlands." [18] Tiele mentions "Coen's cruelties" and the "cold-blooded
manner in which he eradicated a prosperous people." [19] With
these the tenor is established, and subsequent historians vie with
each other in expressing their horror. Blok calls the conquest
of Banda "a tale of murder and manslaughter, destruction and ex-
termination which, in its shocking simplicity, exceeds all others." [20] Huybers speaks of the "inhuman and bestial judicial
murder" committed with "unheard of cruelty." [21] And so it con-
tinues: Geerke,[22] Kalff,[23] MacLeod,[24] Van der Woude and
others.[25] It will be difficult to find, in the historiography of nations, a similar example of censure of a national figure by his own
countrymen.

Coen was not on hand to defend himself against these accusations which, until 1940, blackened his name. Confutation of these
criticisms coincided with the advent of the Second World War,

17. J. A. van der Chijs, *De vestiging van het Nederlandsche Gezag over
de Banda eilanden, 1599–1621* (Batavia, 1886), p. 159.
18. De Jonge, *Opkomst*, 4, lxi.
19. P. A. Tiele, *Bouwstoffen voor de Geschiedenis der Nederlanders in
den Maleischen Archipel, 1* (The Hague, 1886), xlii–xlvii.
20. Blok, *Geschiedenis van het Nederlandsche Volk*, 4, 245.
21. H. F. M. Huybers, *Jan Pieterszoon Coen* (Utrecht, Bruna, 1914), pp.
104 ff.
22. H. P. Geerke, *Jan Pieterszoon Coen* (Utrecht, 1929), p. 158.
23. S. Kalff, *De "Loffelycke Compagnie"* (Amsterdam, 1916), p. 55.
24. N. MacLeod, *De Oost-Indische Compagnie als zeemogendheid in
Azie, 1* (Ryswyk, 1927), 271.
25. J. van der Woude, *Coen. Consequent koopman* (The Hague, 1937)
p. 64.

after Rotterdam was bombed out by the Germans without provocation and without warning. Two historians, Kiers and Gerretson, reviewed the evidence in great detail and came to the conclusion that Coen's reputation had been grossly maligned. Actually Banda was only one in a long series of similar events in the age of capitalistic colonialism, when indigenous peoples found themselves in the way of the self-imposed rights of vigorous nations seeking to exploit their resources.

Denuded of its population, the Banda Islands became virgin territory which the Company could now exploit as it wished. No great experience was required to collect and cure the nutmegs and Coen introduced the so-called *perkenier* system whereby parcels of land with about 50 trees each were allotted to Dutch burghers who were to receive stipulated prices, subject to an export tax of 10 per cent to help defray the cost of the conquest. The Company agreed to supply the necessary slaves. Coen thus hoped to establish a self-sustaining colony to replace the original population. It was an ideal opportunity for Coen to impress the directors once more with the importance of sending out industrious emigrants for his colonization plan. He complained that the soldiers and sailors who had served their time "were wholly unsuitable for the planting of colonies . . . some are worse than animals." Their abominable behavior cost the Dutch the respect of the native people, "causing them to believe that our whole nation is just as godless and depraved." As burghers little good could be expected of them, and Coen once more implored the Seventeen to send him responsible people. In Holland, he averred, "the population pressure is so great that new land has to be created out of water with great expense." Here he alluded to the reclamation projects then being undertaken in many parts of Holland. He remarked that it would be much cheaper to settle Dutch people in Batavia, Amboyna, and Banda. "If this is done the State of the United Netherlands will find no better nor more loyal ally than the State of the United Company." [26] His use of the word "State" in connection with the East Indies is quite suggestive. It was the first time he had used it with this particular connotation, and it disclosed his ambition to achieve something that went far beyond the trade imperium visualized by the directors at home.

From Banda, Coen sailed to Amboyna, which was equally im-

26. *Documents*, 6, 245.

portant to the Company's policy of acquiring an absolute monopoly of the spice trade in the Moluccas. The situation here was more complex than that in Banda, because the area where the cloves grew was much more extensive and consequently more difficult to bring under control. Before returning to Batavia, Coen instructed the governor, Herman van Speult, to take all measures necessary to force the natives of Ceram to abide by their contracts and to prevent them from selling their cloves to the English, Portuguese, and traders of Macassar.[27] All native traffic in the Moluccas was thus to be strictly controlled, if not entirely prohibited. It was obvious that this would prove the end of the formerly thriving native trade, but this was the price the natives were to pay. In Dutch eyes the monopoly was essential, and if it were less than complete it was no monopoly at all.

27. F. W. Stapel, *Geschiedenis van Nederlandsch-Indië* (Amsterdam, 1943), p. 71.

19

The
English
Withdrawal

By now the Seventeen were fully aware that in Coen they had a formidable administrator, who had safely carried the Company through its formative years. He had, in fact, accomplished just about everything the directors had desired: the monopoly of the Spice Islands, the establishment of a general rendezvous, an almost complete dispersal of the Spanish and Portuguese from the archipelago, favorable treaties with local rulers, the curbing of English competition, the opening of trade with Persia, solidification of the Company's hold on the valuable trade in calico on the coasts of Malabar and Coromandel, and the extension of trade with China and Japan. Coen's requests, on the other hand, had been only partially met when not completely ignored.

At various times Coen had signified his desire to return to Holland if the directors did not provide the means which he deemed necessary to further his plans for a Dutch imperium in Asia. To accomplish this, he had demanded more money, more ships, and better men for administrative personnel than the frequently incompetent and unreliable friends and relatives of the directors of the various chambers for whom no suitable employment could be found at home. He also wanted the directors to revise their wage scale upwards rather than to adhere to the absurdly low standard which could attract none but misfits and riffraff.[1] Nor had the directors paid much attention to his often repeated requests for Dutch colonists of a sufficiently high caliber to create the nucleus of a middle class of burghers, which he considered so essential to his plans, and the further request that the Seven-

1. Stipulated monthly wages for certain catagories were: "boys," 14 to 19 years old, 4 guilders; sailors and soldiers, 7 to 10; coopers, 13 to 16; sailmakers, 14 to 18; chief boatswains, 26; mates, 34; assistant merchants, 18 to 24. For a complete list see P. van Dam, in F. W. Stapel, ed. *Beschryvinge van de Oostindische Compagnie, 1* (The Hague, 1927), 557–58.

teen ease their attitude on monopoly so that these people would be
able to make a decent living. They had also dismissed Coen's complaint about the "completely unwarranted surrender" to the English Company by the treaty of 1619 with the blunt statement
that "the States General found it necessary that this should be
done and they know best what is the country's interest." [2] At the
same time, however, the Seventeen confirmed the relative weakness of the English Company by reporting that a delegation had
arrived in The Hague requesting the Dutch Company to reduce
the size of the Fleet of Defense because the English were unable
to maintain their share of ten fully equipped ships. It was indeed
a fact that the London governors, after a temporary flurry of
enthusiasm during the years 1617 and 1618, had again been plagued
by a shortage of capital. This was no news to Coen, who had
already anticipated this weakness by taxing the activities of the
Fleet of Defense to the limit, and thus had more or less forced
the English to renege on the terms of the treaty. In March 1622,
Coen could report that the English had withdrawn six ships from
the Fleet of Defense, leaving only three ships and a frigate.[3]

At home Coen's request for repatriation was interpreted as a
veiled insinuation that he wanted an increase in salary. In replying
to Coen's announcement that he wanted to return early in 1622,
the Seventeen hastily informed him that if he were willing to
serve for another three or four years, his salary as director general would be raised retroactively by 100 guilders monthly and
his salary as governor general would be increased from 600 to 800
guilders per month. In the unlikely event that Coen declined this
offer and insisted on returning, he and the council were commissioned to appoint his successor. They also informed him that they
had complied with his wishes to pay some 14,000 guilders out of
his accumulated earnings to Abraham Lamberts, whom Coen had
designated as his agent for the purchase of stock in the Company.[4]
Undoubtedly Coen expected to profit from this transaction, but
there may well also have been the contributing factor that this
stock purchase would lift him above the status of a mere employee, thus strengthening his position and inducing the directors
to pay more attention to his suggestions. In contrast with his usual
verbosity when dealing with Company matters, Coen simply

2. *Documents*, 4, 492.
3. Ibid., 1, 701.
4. Ibid., 4, 510.

thanked the Seventeen for their "honest offer" but he refused to commit himself about staying much longer, stating that the matter of appointing his successor had been postponed until word had been received from the governors of Amboyna and Banda.[5]

It is difficult for us to visualize the communication problem of the seventeenth century. Would the States General have insisted on a treaty with the English, had it been known that the English fleet had scattered far and wide and could no longer pose a threat in the East Indies? It was not until January 1623 that Coen received a reply to his letter of May 6, 1621, in which he had reported the conquest of Banda and reiterated his suggestions for improving and consolidating the Dutch hold on the trade of Asia.

The Seventeen accused him of flying too high, stating that it was clear that "you people have a far greater concept of what should be done than our present means allow." [6] The directors had been forced to borrow 8 million guilders and the Company's credit could stand no more. Coen may have wondered whether his plunge in Company stock had been a sound investment, but he need not have worried. The directors voted regular dividends even if they had to borrow money to do so. By present standards this was an unsound financial policy but the directors expected better times and in the meantime it satisfied the stockholders. Among the latter, the Seventeen admitted freely, were many who criticized their management.

It was obvious that the Seventeen were also worried that their twenty-year charter might not be renewed, and they knew that there was pressure on the States General from foreign countries to this effect. They referred to the protestations of the English and French, who had not taken lightly Coen's obstructions of their efforts in the East Indies. "It would have been better," they wrote, "if you had been more accommodating to the English . . . it would have made a great difference in our situation at this end." [7] They repeated their admonition that force should be avoided and that Coen should do everything possible to promote peaceful relations which, after all, were the only means by which profitable trade could be obtained. Now that Banda had been secured, the people of the Moluccas should be treated kindly but should not be allowed to resume their former lawless practices.

5. Ibid., 1, 679.
6. Ibid., 6, 282–83.
7. Ibid., 4, 537.

The directors did not say how this could be accomplished without resorting to force. For more than twenty years, successive administrators had tried unsuccessfully to gain the Company's objective by means of treaties and agreements. It was only as a final resort that Coen had put the islands under Dutch sovereignty, the only means by which the English and other European nations could be effectively barred from sharing in this trade, which could be profitable only if it were in the hands of one party as a true monopoly. Instead, the Seventeen wanted Coen to resume friendly relations with the English and allow them a substantial share.

This latest missive from the Seventeen, the tone of which was different from any he had ever received, made Coen decide not to postpone his departure any longer. In the past, the Seventeen had cautioned him to go slowly in developing his ambitious plans, but this time he was told flatly that his policies did not meet with the approval of the directors. This was something that could not be argued by letters that would require eighteen months for an answer; he must present his case in person. On January 23 he announced his decision to the Council, and Pieter de Carpentier, the director general, was appointed as his successor. The instructions Coen left behind dealt with every phase of the Company's affairs and indicated that he expected his successor to pursue his broader program as well, regardless of the advice of the Seventeen. It is indicative of the high regard his colleagues had for his judgment that De Carpentier endeavored to follow these instructions as far as he could.[8]

Coen began by pointing out that the financial condition of the Company at home was such that little or no support could be expected from that quarter, both because of the considerable debt which had been incurred and the fact that the market for spices in Europe appeared to be overloaded for the time being. It was therefore necessary to manage with the means at hand, and the following broad categories deserved the closest attention: the need to economize; levying of tolls and taxes; the creation of a slave labor force; the development of trade with China. Coen proposed the following plans. Average expenses during the past three years had amounted to more than 1,600,000 guilders yearly. Of this amount roughly 400,000 was for victuals, 540,000 for salaries and wages, 450,000 for ships and repairs, 200,000 for fortifications, and 65,000 for presents to local rulers. To reduce these expenses,

8. For the complete instructions, see *Documents*, 3, 288–307.

Coen proposed that henceforth the Company's employees pay for their own food; wages should be paid as much as possible in cloths and other necessities; better control should be exercised over the Company's ships; the building of additional fortifications should be halted and those already in existence should be maintained by slaves. The burghers should help pay for the building and maintenance of the walls and canals at Batavia. The giving of presents should be restricted.

In order to increase revenue, tolls and taxes should be levied at Banda and Amboyna at a rate of 10 per cent on imports and exports as was done at Batavia, which already produced enough revenue to maintain a garrison of 600 men. To build up a working force, slaves should be bought at the usual markets: on the east coast of Africa, the Indian peninsula, and Ceylon. The China coast should not be neglected, because "there is no people in the world who can serve us better than the Chinese." [9] Such long-range recruiting involved considerable expense, which might have been avoided if native Indonesians could have been pressed into service.[10] The Dutch, however, did not consider this possibility. The chances that trouble might break out with the Javanese rulers were always present, and it would have been highly imprudent to have a considerable number of their subjects either within, or in close proximity to, the town.

For the trade with China, as much money and as many ships and men should be used as possible, and no effort should be spared to establish a permanent settlement on either the Pescadores or Formosa.[11] With control of the China trade, an important link in the inter-Asiatic network, Coen was confident that Batavia could become self-sufficient and would no longer have to depend on capital from Holland. It was his firm belief, however, that this trade could never be developed properly if it were kept in the hands of the Company. Private traders could operate more economically, and their taxes and tolls would outweigh any profits the Company might make by trying to monopolize it. Until the

9. *Documents*, 3, 293.

10. The word "Indonesia" was coined by Adolf Bastian, a German ethnologist, in the latter part of the nineteenth century.

11. The Chinese government would not allow a Dutch settlement in the Pescadores, which they considered Chinese territory. On Formosa the Dutch could do what they liked, the Chinese said, because they laid no claim to it.

burghers could afford to do this with their own vessels, Company ships should carry their goods at legitimate freight rates.

These were the main points of the instructions Coen left behind when he set sail on February 2, 1623. During his ten years in the Indies he had accomplished a great deal, but he felt that his achievements could not be adequately exploited unless he could convince the directors of the need for establishing colonies of industrious Dutch who could prosper by free trade in almost any commodity except spices destined for Europe. Knowing the predilection of the directors and shareholders for complete monopoly, he knew that only by pleading for his program in person could he hope to meet with success.

At the time of his departure, Coen had reason to believe that the English problem had practically solved itself. Only a week or so earlier, the heads of the English Company at Batavia had appealed to him to lift their goods and personnel in the Moluccas and transport them to Batavia in Dutch ships. They gave as their reason that lack of adequate support from London made it no longer possible for them to live up to their part of the obligations stipulated in the Treaty of Defense. For the same reason the English Council at Batavia decided shortly afterwards to close the office in Japan, leaving the liquidation of its affairs in the hands of the Dutch factory.[12] With this drastic retrenchment, the English proved that they were unable to compete with the Dutch, and were forced to withdraw from practically the whole of East Asia. At the time it seemed as if this withdrawal would be a peaceful one, but a nasty incident was in the making in the eastern corner of the archipelago, which would inflame anti-Dutch feelings in England as never before. The Dutch would refer to it as the Amboyna incident, but the English bluntly called it the Amboyna massacre. Here again the slow line of communications, even between points that were relatively close, was a significant factor. There can be little doubt that if the English at Amboyna, where they had been allowed to establish a factory, had been quickly informed of the English Council's decision at Batavia to withdraw from the Moluccas, this regrettable affair might well have been avoided.

The first signs of an English conspiracy at Amboyna came to

12. E. M. Thompson, ed., *Diary of Richard Cocks*, 1 (London, 1883), 39–41.

light some three weeks after Coen had departed for Europe, and thus technically he had no part in what followed. In the preceding year, Coen had warned all the Company's factors to be on their guard against any suspicious activities on the part of the English that might undermine Dutch authority. The governor at Amboyna, Herman van Speult, had acknowledged this admonition in June: "we hope to direct things according to your orders that our sovereignty shall not be diminished or injured in any way by their activities. And if we may hear of any conspiracies of theirs against the sovereignty, we shall with your sanction do justice to them without delay." [13]

On February 23, 1623, Van Speult felt that there were indications of just such a conspiracy. On this date, while the Dutch garrison was holding evening prayers, a Japanese soldier in English service had been caught inspecting the fortifications at a spot where the English were prohibited. A preliminary examination disclosed that such spying had been going on for some time. As a result, others were interrogated and confirmed the fact that an attack on the Dutch fort was contemplated. Now all the English personnel were examined individually. A few confessed freely, but others had to be tortured, as was the accepted procedure. The instigator of the plot had been the head of the English factory, Gabriel Towerson; he was an impetuous and disagreeable person, disliked by some of his own countrymen.[14] His plan was to overrun the Dutch fort and kill off its garrison as soon as an English ship had arrived to give the required support. Towerson had planned this entirely on his own responsibility and without the knowledge of the Batavia office. The plan was of course foolhardy in the extreme; even if the Dutch fort could have been taken by surprise, the English would not have been able to hold it for any length of time, and the consequences would have been worse.

On March 8, Van Speult convened his council and submitted the question, whether the defendants should be sent to Batavia or be executed on the spot. He favored the latter because it would have a salutary effect on others who might have a similar conspiracy in mind. The council agreed with his view, and on the following day, ten English merchants and nine Japanese soldiers were beheaded. Two Englishmen were spared and sent to Batavia. One of them, John Beaumont, admitted without compulsion that

13. Stapel, *Geschiedenis van Nederlandsch-Indië*, p. 74.
14. See p. 294 f.

he knew of the conspiracy but had been sworn to secrecy by Towerson.[15] De Carpentier pardonned them both, and thus they lived to relate their harassing experience in London. A review of this unfortunate affair indicates that Van Speult and the members of his council had taken far too serious a view of a plot that had been hatched on the spur of the moment during a New Year's celebration.[16] In any event, they had greatly exceeded their authority by carrying out death sentences on the spot. The accused should have been sent to Batavia, where the case could have been reviewed by a higher court. This would have avoided serious consequences.

English reaction when the news reached London can easily be imagined. The Amboyna 'massacre' was the greatest ignominy the English had yet suffered at the hands of the brazen little republic across the North Sea. Through his ambassador, Dudley Carlton, King James protested vehemently to the States General, claiming that the 'conspiracy' was a figment of imagination, because the confessions had been obtained under unendurable torture: the whole procedure had been for no other purpose than to dislodge the English Company from Amboyna. It made little difference that the directors of the Dutch Company denied these allegations, claiming that the proceedings had been conducted legally and that they could have expelled the English by quite different means if they had wished to.

The English retaliated by apprehending Dutch vessels in their waters, and they demanded that the men responsible for the executions be sent home to stand trial for their crimes. Prodded by the States General, the directors recalled their key men at Amboyna, but the special court which investigated their actions could find no sound reason to punish them for something they might have done too hastily but, nevertheless, in the full belief that they acted in the interest of their country. Van Speult, one of Coen's faithful disciples, was unable to answer the summons; he had died in the meantime. The English had long memories, and the 'massacre' was a collateral cause for the outbreak of the first English-Dutch war. At its conclusion in 1654, the Dutch Company paid the heirs of those who had been executed an indemnity of

15. De Jonge, *Opkomst*, 5, xxi.
16. See W. P. Coolhaas, "Aanteekeningen en opmerkingen over den zoogenaamden Ambonschen moord," *BKI*, *101* (1942), 49–93. Compare Hall, *History of South-East Asia*, pp. 249–50.

more than 43,000 guilders. In 1665 the massacre was brought up as one of the reasons for England's going to war with the Dutch a second time. In 1673 the poet John Dryden used the subject as a means to inflame public opinion against the Dutch with his tragedy, *Amboyna, or, The Cruelties of the Dutch to the English Merchants*.[17]

The Amboyna affair also aggravated the uneasy relationship between the Dutch and the English at Batavia, causing the governor general to write, "we are stuck with them here as with a difficult woman." [18] In 1624 the English decided to leave Batavia and establish their own headquarters on the island Lagundi in the Sunda Strait, where they intended to build an 'anti-Batavia.' This plan failed miserably, as the climate of the island was extremely unhealthy and all water had to be brought from the mainland of Sumatra. Within a few months, several hundred Englishmen died, and the survivors asked De Carpentier to take them back to Batavia. The Dutch agreed, and for a few more years the English stayed at Batavia. In 1628 they moved their factory to Bantam, but this was only the beginning of the end. Although they managed to stay there until 1684, their resources were so meager that they practically eliminated themselves as competition in the East India trade.

This was the aftermath of an issue that had been decided when Dale's fleet was forced to flee after the debacle of 1619 at Djakarta. It had been the one period during the seventeenth century in which the English Company had managed to command a sufficiently large capital to make its bid for a substantial share of the trade of the Indies. The attempt had failed through bad judgment and divided leadership. After this, English interest at home once more lagged and there seemed no way in which they could back their demands against the Dutch with sufficient force and enterprise. The English also lacked a man like Coen who had the foresight to act quickly and decisively when the interest of the Company was at stake, even if it meant going against his instructions from the directors at home. It was not until the English began to adapt themselves to the new economic age and produced men like Robert Clive and Warren Hastings that they could make their bid for empire in Asia. But that was more than a century later.

17. Stapel, *Geschiedenis*, p. 76.
18. De Jonge, *Opkomst*, 5, xli.

20

Monopoly

or

Free Trade?

Ignorant of what had occurred at Amboyna, Coen arrived at the Cape of Good Hope on May 11, 1623, where he received the latest missives from the Seventeen carried by the outbound fleet. In one of them Coen was severely criticized for the tone of his letters. "We note that you complain about various issues, and in some cases with such candor that it exceeds all measure of discretion . . . it is as if *you* are giving *us* the orders, instead of the other way round as it should be . . . we appreciate your zeal in pointing out some of our shortcomings, but we consider it impertinent that you insinuate that we deliberately neglect our duties by not providing you with the means for your exorbitant schemes. We warn you to curb your pen." [1] These criticisms could not have troubled Coen overmuch. He had never hesitated to speak his mind, and if he made his point the Seventeen were entitled to take umbrage at his lack of respect. He was more concerned about the thinly veiled accusations against his statesmanship.

It was primarily through his efforts that the Company had attained its main objectives: the establishment of a rendezvous, control over the Moluccas, and the curbing of French and English competition. How this could have been accomplished by any other means than those Coen had employed, the Seventeen did not say. But, while accepting the fruits of his endeavors, they objected to the manner in which they had been achieved. Coen should have cultivated friendly relations with the rulers of Bantam and Mataram, the conquest of Banda should have been less severe, and he should have maintained a cordial relationship with the English. All this made little sense to a man who in his youth

1. *Documents, 4,* 552.

in Italy must have been exposed to the doctrines of Machiavelli.[2]
The London treaty of 1619, concluded while the English fleet
had fled in all directions, had been a blow to Coen. He had
managed to cope with this setback by overtaxing the English
capabilities within the terms of the treaty until, shortly before
his departure, the English had announced their voluntary withdrawal from the Moluccas. And now, once again, the Seventeen
implied that the English Company should be given all possible
consideration and that they should be consulted in matters of
policy, such as the levying of tolls.[3]

It was clear, however, that the directors had compelling reasons for adopting such a cautious policy. The successful rebuffs
of the English and the French in the Indies were far removed
from the much closer threat of possible retaliation in Europe.
Powerful monarchies as they were, they could not gracefully accept defeat on the far side of the globe at the hands of a small
country which, only a few decades ago, had offered to relinquish
its precarious independence to either crown.[4] With the termination of the truce with Spain in 1621, the States General were
greatly concerned that either country, or both, might now also
turn against them. The English demanded an indemnity of 1.5
million guilders for having been driven out of the Banda group
and for other so-called injustices. Fearful of reprisals, the Seventeen gave orders that no ships were to touch at French or English ports, and that they should avoid the Channel and sail around
England instead. "You must realize," they wrote, "that we are
lashed to a battering ram, so to speak. Where would we be if the
States General were unable to protect us?"[5]

Coen liked neither the censure nor the meek attitude of the
Seventeen, as appears from the letter he wrote to De Carpentier
from the Cape. "It seems almost as if the Masters want to delude
themselves with the notion that we in the Indies could have prevented that they are being harassed by the English in Europe.
I must say that this is farfetched indeed. Is it possible that the
ignominies the fatherland had to endure under Leicester have
so quickly been forgotten?"[6] But Coen stuck to his guns and told
De Carpentier to proceed according to plan:

2. See Schrieke, *Indonesian Sociological Studies*, 1, 260.
3. *Documents*, 4, 556, 570.
4. See p. 36.
5. *Documents*, 4, 556.
6. Ibid., 3, 315. See also p. 37 ff.

It may well be that I shall receive no other reward for my labors than reproaches . . . I must impress upon you most strongly that, regardless of dangerous and vexing problems, you should not falter or become discouraged. The spirit should surmount all difficulties and never bow before them. Maintain the sovereignty of the States General and the rights of the Company without sparing the English, the French and other so-called friends . . . I tell you candidly: our country has to bear the burden of Spain; if England and France should also attack her, some people say, 'what will happen then?' My reply is: should the whole world attack us, a lack of courage could not save us. Even with death staring us in the face, we should not lose courage, nor should we bow to English and French demands because this, in the end, would lead to ruin and death . . . By this I mean to say that there is nothing in the world that can hurt us as long as we insist on our rights.[7]

With these brave words Coen declared once more that he was aiming for something far greater than the merchants at home had ever intended. The rights he spoke of had been obtained by treaty and conquest; thus they were inviolable. With the concept that these rights had to be defended at any cost, Coen assumed the role of an empire builder.

After an absence of more than eleven years, Coen arrived in his homeland on September 9, 1623. The Committee of the Seventeen was not in session at the time, and his first appearance was before the States General. On September 21 he gave them an oral account of his stewardship. We know in retrospect that this was the high point in Coen's life, but we will never know what his emotions were when he addressed this body of men who, now that the power of Spain was fading away and that of England had not yet matured, were the dominant power in the new economic age. There Coen stood, the son of a small merchant, none too successful in his own right in the eyes of men who considered wealth a measure of status. It remains a dubious question whether Coen was impressed by this honor. An objective analysis of his actions and statements of policy until this time gives the impression that he considered the States General only another instrument with which he could forge something bigger than a mere

7. *Documents*, 3, 315–16.

trade imperium in Asia. The States General thanked Coen for his presentation and asked him to put his report in writing.

Salutary as his address to the States General may have been, it was more important to impress the tough-minded merchants who were the Company's managing directors. In the final analysis it was the approval by the Seventeen of Coen's far-reaching program that was needed to make the States General decide on a national policy. The Seventeen convened on October 9 for the express purpose of hearing Coen's report.[8] The presentation and discussions lasted three days. It speaks for Coen's singleness of purpose that his report was actually an elaboration of his *discourse* of January 1, 1614,[9] refined only to the extent that he could now be more specific in his recommendations, based on additional years of experience. It also followed closely the instructions he had left his successor. Stripped to the bone, Coen's report dealt with two main issues: why had profits to date fallen below expectations, and how could this be remedied?

During the past ten years, the Company had expended 9,396,000 guilders in the Indies against which the books showed a return of 9,388,000 guilders.[10] Although this showed a loss, the directors had, nevertheless, paid regular dividends in anticipation of future profits. Because of this policy, based on the premise that the exploitation of the Spice Islands would by necessity be profitable, the Company had already incurred a debt of some 8,000,000 guilders. Coen did not suggest a moratorium on dividends, which might have been construed as an admission of failure on his part. Such an action, although financially sound, would also have created a furor among the stockholders that might well have precipitated the Company's bankruptcy, the last thing Coen desired, because the solvency of the Company was indispensable to his plans. The remedy, he argued, had to be found by decreasing expenses and by increasing the volume of inter-Asiatic trade. Both, he insisted, could only be accomplished by a large scale colonization by stable Dutchmen who could be induced to go to the Indies in the prospect of making a good living in free trade. Experience had shown that this principle worked well in Europe. Why not apply it in Asia as well? The Company should retain

8. For the complete report, see *Documents*, *4*, 577–601.
9. See above Book III, Chapter 8.
10. *Documents*, *1*, 792.

its monopoly of the spice trade, but most other products should be thrown open to free trade.

On October 12, the Seventeen passed a resolution that the items Coen had raised be submitted to the individual chambers for their consideration. The Seventeen's attorney, Willem Boreel, was instructed to circulate not only Coen's proposals regarding the opening of trade to the burghers but also the objections raised against them by certain members. It was obvious from the beginning that a hard core of directors had strong reservations about relinquishing even a part of their sacrosanct monopoly. On October 21, Coen wrote De Carpentier that he had proposed to the Seventeen that a number of private individuals be allowed to sail to the Indies with their own ships and settle at Batavia, Amboyna, and Banda, to start trading on their own account. "Some are favorably disposed but others disagree," he stated. "The matter is being considered." [11]

On October 23, 1623, the Seventeen decided how to reward Coen for his services. It is typical that rather than grant him a good round sum of money they itemized each of his accomplishments and put a price on it, as a merchant would do with his wares.

1. As commander of the return fleet he received 100 reals, as was customary, over and above his salary.

2. His salary as director general was made retroactive at 400 guilders, which meant an increase of 100 guilders per month. In consideration of the "good services rendered in that office," he was granted an additional sum of 3,000 guilders.

3. His salary as governor general was raised from 600 to 800 guilders from the time he had received his commission (April 30, 1618).

4. For establishing a general rendezvous, the conquest of Djakarta, and the founding of Batavia "and the new republic," [12] the sum of 7,000 guilders.

5. For the conquest of Banda, the sum of 3,000 guilders.

6. Finally, for everything else Coen had accomplished and to forestall any additional claims he might have, an additional

11. Ibid., 6, 330.
12. The use of the word "Republic" in connection with the founding of Batavia must be understood to mean that the Seventeen acknowledged the fact that the Company had become a sovereign power in Asia.

amount of 10,000 guilders, a golden chain "valued at fl. 2,000" as well as a medallion "suitably inscribed" and a sword of honor, the last two valued at 400 guilders.[13]

Eliminating salary increase and the trinkets, Coen was offered a total of 23,000 guilders for laying the foundation of a Dutch empire in Asia. Elsewhere in Europe such services as Coen had rendered his country would have been rewarded with more munificence, but not so in a money-conscious merchant republic. Coen was far from satisfied, but the Seventeen, looking at the balance sheets, may have felt that he had been overpaid. On September 25, 1624, the Seventeen, after some distasteful bickering, granted him an additional 20,000 guilders, as well as 5 per cent interest on the 23,000 guilders they had offered him the year before. This would indicate that the Seventeen had held up payment until they were sure of Coen's quitclaim against the Company.

The deliberations on free trade dragged on. It took time to get the opinions of members of the individual chambers and, as Coen had already discovered, there were quite a few who were adamant as far as the monopoly was concerned. They remembered too vividly how close to disaster the East Indies trade had come during the period of the fore-companies, when the principle of free trade had prevailed. Why then revive it? Again we are faced with a hiatus in the record of Coen's life. What did he do while this matter was being discussed? What part did he play, and to what extent was he able to influence the final decision?

The opposition had an eloquent spokesman in Laurens Reael who, since his return, had managed to ingratiate himself with the directors of the Amsterdam chamber. He and Coen had been at loggerheads in the Indies. A patrician, Reael could never forget that he had been eliminated by a commoner,[14] and he now proceeded to attack Coen's program point by point.[15] The basic difference between their opposing views was that Reael pleaded for the narrow interests of the stockholders while Coen was thinking of an empire. The deliberations, discussions, and presentations took a full year, but after the arguments from both sides had been carefully considered, the majority of the directors sided with

13. *Documents*, 6, 331.
14. See p. 335 f.
15. *Documents*, 6, 332–42. Compare Meilink-Roelofsz, *Asian Trade*, p. 385, n. 97.

Coen. They did so perhaps for the same reason that had motivated them a few years earlier to dismiss Reael as governor general. Reael had advocated moderation—towards the natives, the English, and other nations; Coen was a man of action and, considering all he had accomplished, his program should at least be tried. The directors approved it on October 17, 1624, and asked him at the same time to return to the Indies to take full charge of his program. Coen would have liked nothing better, but he told the directors that he first wanted to "make a respectable and suitable marriage" so that his wife could accompany him.[16] His choice was a young woman half his age. Eva Ment was the daughter of an outstanding Amsterdam family, related through marriage to one of the founders of the Old Company. It is certain that Coen wanted to set an example for others, people of substance who, with family and capital, could be induced to make the East Indies their new home.

The date of his wedding and departure was set for early December, but had to be postponed because Coen fell seriously ill. The many years he had spent in the tropics took their toll during the second winter he spent in Holland. Coen was sick all winter and the marriage did not take place until April, 1625. This delay gave Coen's enemies time to marshal their forces.

Although the resolution granting free trade in a number of commodities had been taken in secret, as in all cases, the news had nevertheless leaked out. A number of stockholders protested vigorously, claiming that it was their capital which had built the Company and that the advantages derived therefrom were now about to be handed over to outsiders. The fact that the resolution was passed without their consent and without the approval of the States General made them all the more suspicious that their interests were not protected. On December 17 they lodged a formal complaint with the States General, expressing their grievances against the directors and Coen. They had timed their protest well, and it was certainly no coincidence that on that same day the English ambassador, in the name of King James, objected vehemently to Coen's return to the Indies. The aftermath of the Amboyna affair had finally caught up with Coen. Although it had been none of his doing, he was nevertheless held responsible for this outrage, because in English eyes he personified all the evils that had befallen the English Company. When James I

16. *Documents, 4,* 645.

addressed a Dutch delegation that was in London to arrange a possible revision of the treaty of 1619, he singled out Coen as the main obstacle to English ambitions in Asia. "Over there you represent your Prince of Orange as a great King, and hold me up as a little kinglet, as if I stood under him, thus misleading the barbarian kings . . . You have in the Indies a man [Coen] who well deserves to be hanged." [17] Through his ambassador at The Hague, James made it clear that he would consider it an hostile act if Coen were allowed to return to the Indies.

The States General were in a difficult position. Coen's vigorous policy threatened to embroil the republic with England, and, in addition, there had now arisen a growing opposition to his colonization plan within Holland itself. Although prompted by entirely different motives, both factions were strongly opposed to Coen's departure. Hoping that the death of James I on April 6, 1625 might bring about a more favorable political atmosphere, the States General sparred for time. On April 15, they demanded a full transcript from the Seventeen of the free trade resolution, and while this was being studied, Coen's departure was postponed until further notice.[18]

For Coen this was a great disappointment. Throughout his whole career he had tried to impress the directors with the soundness of his plan, and now, after they were finally persuaded, it was the government which tried to thwart him. Coen's spirit was still equal to the task. In his letter to the States General dated April 22, he in effect berated them for bowing to the dictates of a foreign power. He also stated that his prompt return to the Indies was in the interests of the republic if for no other reason than that the English tried to prevent it.[19] As it turned out, this was Coen's last act of defiance against forces of circumstance he was unable to control.

Neither the English nor the committee of stockholders eased their pressure on the States General. Charles I proved to be as intractable as his father, and tension was heightened when the English apprehended Dutch vessels in their ports. The rebellious stockholders submitted a lengthy protest purporting to show the "evils of free trade." There was no way in which Coen could force the issue; all he could do was to mark time. We know some-

---

17. G. Edmundson, *Anglo-Dutch Rivalry* (Oxford, 1911), p. 78.
18. *Documents*, 6, 365.
19. Ibid., 6, 366.

thing about his state of mind during this period of uncertainty and enforced delay from a letter he wrote from Amsterdam on April 17, 1626 to Daniel van der Leck who, accompanied by his family, was outward bound for the Indies. Van der Leck, a director of the Rotterdam chamber, was just the type of man Coen wished to see in the Indies. To him he wrote: "I am buffetted back and forth by the winds of chance, and without being given the opportunity to make myself heard. In the meantime I can only hope that, with God's will, everything will come out for the best." [20]

The Seventeen, too, were in a quandary. De Carpentier had asked to be relieved of his office, and Coen seemed the logical person to resume the governor generalship and take charge of his own program. But the States General were vascillating. They had intimated they wanted Coen's departure postponed, but they had not set a time limit. The decisive fact was that Coen himself wanted to go back. He felt that he was best qualified to execute his own program, and his conviction was shared by a number of the directors who had learned from experience that the choice of a governor general was the most important decision they were called upon to make. Realizing that there was no one better qualified than Coen, the Seventeen decided to force the issue. Ignoring the demands of the English and an important segment of the stockholders, and against the implied wishes of the States General, a minority of the Seventeen decided to let Coen set sail for the Indies. This time he had no imposing document, but only a letter signed by six members to the effect that he was authorized to take over the governor generalship from De Carpentier.[21] Even before his departure, Coen must have known that his colonization project was in serious jeopardy, although the Seventeen had not as yet countermanded their free trade resolution. On the other hand, they had submitted the transcript of this resolution to the States General with the undersanding that it should be kept in strictest confidence, which meant that they were unwilling to bring the issue into the open and face the disgruntled stockholders.

Thus Coen was without a mandate. In order to attract people of substance and induce them to go to the Indies, his plan should have received the greatest possible publicity. No one would have been better qualified to launch such a campaign than Coen him-

20. Ibid., *4*, 689.
21. Ibid., *4*, 711.

self. Instead he was forced to remain silent while waiting for the States General to make its decision. As the months dragged on without word one way or the other, it became apparent that this august body was refusing to take action, and it never did.

The circumstances of Coen's actual departure were an anticlimax to his whole previous career. To avoid embarrassing questions, his name was nowhere mentioned in the resolutions passed by the Seventeen around this time, much less the fact that he was to resume his former post. He departed in great secrecy with a squadron that sailed from Texel on March 19, 1627, accompanied by his young wife and her sister Lysbeth. None of the other ships knew that Governor General Coen was in their midst, and it came as a great surprise when about one month later, while approaching the Cape Verde Islands, he ordered that his flag be displayed.

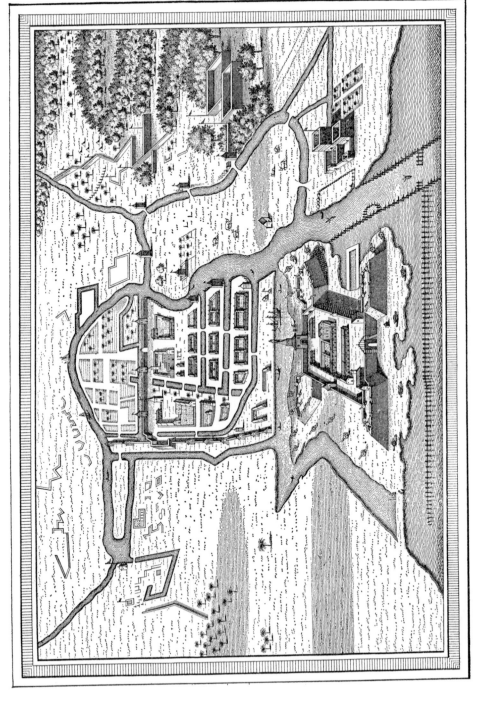

Batavia in 1629.

21

Mission Accomplished

Coen arrived in Batavia on September 28, 1627 after an uneventful voyage of a little over six months. From Ilha de Mayo, he reported his safe passage through the Channel under the nose of the English. He had taken this shorter route against the instructions of the directors, who wanted him to sail around Scotland and Ireland. The only incidents were caused by the presence in the squadron of the Persian ambassador, Musa Beg, who was sailing home with his retinue on board the *Utrecht*. He demanded special privileges, and when these were denied, he threatened to kill the officers and himself as well. When he saw that no one took him seriously, he began to sulk and swore an oath that, for three months, he would not touch any wine. At the Cape of Good Hope he demanded that a ship be put at his disposal so that he could sail directly to Surate. Coen refused to disrupt his schedule and took Musa Beg with him to Batavia. "The man is so arrogant," Coen reported to the Seventeen, "that he demanded the respect due him as admiral of the fleet . . . when I hoisted [my flag] he became sick with envy." [1] Before long Coen would brush off a similar kind of arrogance on the part of Sultan Agung of Mataram, but that incident would have more serious consequences.

Coen had no reason to complain about what had been accomplished at Batavia during his absence. The history of the Dutch Company contains many examples of governors who tried to prove their own mettle and originality by changing, or even reversing, the policies of their predecessors. De Carpentier was not one of those, and he had seen no reason to deviate from the broad patterns which had been established during Coen's first tenure in office. He had also proved himself to be an able administrator. The town government, at the time of Coen's departure little more than a blueprint, had developed into an organization which compared favorably with any town in the Netherlands. Nor had he

1. *Documents, 6*, 388–89.

neglected the physical aspects of Batavia. The fort was enclosed by four strong walls surrounded by a moat 300 feet wide. The town was properly laid out with canals and streets south from the fort. It stretched for more than a mile, with an average width of about one quarter of a mile. On the west and south the town was protected by the river, and on the east, the land side, an earthwork had been thrown up to a height of 36 feet, interspersed with a number of redoubts.

Such a sight must have pleased Coen because Batavia, which had risen on the ruins of Djakarta, was now a thriving town and already more important than Bantam or Malacca had ever been. On such a strong foundation Coen planned to establish the nucleus of a future Dutch empire, and the town seemed large enough to accommodate the colonists he needed for this purpose. To this task he wanted to devote his remaining years. As it turned out, Coen was too far ahead of his time; he found himself colliding with the ambitions of a powerful England unwilling to admit that she was not yet qualified to stake her claim in the new economic age, and opposed as well by the parochial views of the stockholders in the republic.

Coen was soon to learn that, from mere apathy towards his colonization plan, the Seventeen as a body had been aroused to strong opposition to it. In no small measure, this was brought about by a change of government in Amsterdam during the year 1627. The Calvinist majority had been unseated and replaced by the Arminians.[2] This also changed the composition of the Amsterdam chamber and one of the newly elected directors was Coen's predecessor Laurens Reael, the brother-in-law of Arminius.[3] On August 10, 1627, the Seventeen wrote to Governor General Coen and the council, "rigorously" forbidding them to permit any kind of free trade whatsoever.[4] With this the earlier resolution was completely revoked. Laurens Reael was one of those who signed the letter. Thus for the time being Coen's farsighted plan was doomed, and although some of his successors did their best to have it revived, the Seventeen never budged. It was not until two centuries later, after the Dutch government had taken over the defunct East India Company, that Coen's principle of free

2. Compare Geyl, *Netherlands Divided*, pp. 75–76.
3. See p. 438 f.
4. *Documents, 4,* 709.

enterprise finally received the recognition it deserved.[5] It had, of course, never been Coen's idea to include the European trade in his plan but only the inter-Asiatic trade, and even this with certain restrictions.

The Seventeen's letter did not reach Batavia until June 22, 1628, and by this time Coen had more immediate problems to contend with: a train of events had been set in motion which seriously threatened Batavia itself. His long range plan would have had to be postponed in any case until this danger had been averted, and he replied briefly: "As per your orders, nothing shall be done to open up free trade." [6]

The threat to Batavia came from Mataram. This possibility had been recognized ever since Sultan Agung had begun to subdue the coastal states in East Java. In 1614, Surabaya had allied itself with Kediri, Tuban, and Pasaruan, hoping to gain a decisive victory and thus kill Mataram's designs upon their territory. In a battle which lasted three days Mataram was the victor, and the coalition fell apart. From then on, Agung proceeded to subdue them one by one. Pasaruan fell in 1616 and Tuban three years later.[7] Surabaya and Madura presented a greater problem which Agung tried to solve by calling on the Dutch. In June 1622, he sent his envoys to Batavia proposing an alliance against Bantam, expecting that the Dutch would assist him in turn against Surabaya. Coen rejected this offer as diplomatically as possible, knowing full well that it would be Batavia's turn once Bantam had fallen into the hands of Mataram. It had become his expressed policy not to let Mataram become too big or Bantam too small. He had emphasized this in 1620 when the council claimed Dutch sovereignty over the hinterlands of Djakarta stretching to the south coast of the island.[8]

Coen's last instructions to De Carpentier prior to his departure had also touched on this matter. No attack on Bantam should be made. If Mataram should request a free passage to attack Bantam alone then "I advise that no definite answer be given and that they should be brushed off with vague promises. If he (Agung) persists in moving against Bantam by land or by sea, you can be

5. Ibid., 6, 444.
6. Ibid., 5, 132.
7. See De Graaf, *Sultan Agung*, pp. 30–52.
8. See p. 407.

certain that his attentions are directed more to Batavia than to Bantam. Therefore be prepared." [9] At the same time Coen had cautioned that if at all possible, a friendly relationship with Mataram should be maintained.

De Carpentier had acquitted himself well in this respect. In 1623 and 1624, he had sent missions to Karta, Mataram's capital, primarily for the purpose of obtaining sufficient quantities of rice which the growing population of Batavia needed badly. The second mission under Jan Vos arrived just when Sultan Agung was celebrating his latest victory over Madura. Flushed with success, Agung demanded that the preamble of the letter from the governor general be rephrased in more respectful terms. It should read: "The slave of His Majesty sends this present with his slaves, etc." Vos protested that the governor general "was not the Sultan's slave nor his servant, and that he was subservient to no one but God and the King of Holland." This byplay was settled by the simple procedure of holding back the original letter and by presenting instead a transcript of the text. Agung must have felt that he was fully entitled to demand such homage because, as a result of his conquest of Madura, he had taken the title of "Susuhunan" (to whom all are subject).[10]

Through Vos the Sunan, as the Dutch began to call him now, transmitted his request for a few Dutch ships to aid him in his contemplated attack on Surabaya, the last of the coastal principalities still independent. De Carpentier's refusal enraged Agung, and when the Dutch sent another mission in 1626, he refused to receive it. His disdain for the Dutch was heightened by the fact that he had in the meantime conquered Surabaya unaided.

Since 1620, Agung's attacks on Surabaya had been a yearly occurrence, but each time he had been driven off. It was not until 1625 that, after cutting off Surabaya's water supply, he was finally successful. This was done at Terusan, where the *kali* (river) Brantas splits itself into the *kali* (river) Mas, leading to Surabaya, and the *kali* Porong which empties into the Strait of Madura. At that point the river is usually shallow; during the dry monsoon, when the river flow was at its lowest, a dam constructed from palm trees, bamboo, and stones was thrown across the *kali* Mas. The fact that such a dam was subject to a certain amount of seepage was used to advantage by contaminating the

9. *Documents, 6*, 291.
10. De Graaf, *Sultan Agung*, pp. 127–29.

water with cadavers and the fruit of the *aren* palm. The effect of the first requires no explanation, and the rind of the *aren* fruit is highly toxic.[11]

This was the situation that confronted Coen upon his return to the Indies. Bantam tried to retaliate for the continued blockade of the town by sending bands of marauders into the land around Batavia, pillaging and burning the new plantations. An attempt to take Batavia by surprise on Christmas night, 1627 had been fore-stalled in the nick of time. Coen ordered doubling of the guards and strengthening of the town walls. It became apparent that Mataram had something in mind when the regent of Kendal, Baureksa, closed all ports in the beginning of 1628. The old rumor that Agung was going to attack Batavia with a force of from 50,000 to 100,000 men persisted. Coen had only about 500 good soldiers at his disposal. He dared not count on the 3,000 Chinese in the town because "their way of fighting is usually in fleeing." [12] There were, of course, ships in the roadstead, but their crews would not be called in until a state of emergency existed.

Mataram's intentions became even more clear when, on April 13, Agung's envoy appeared at Batavia demanding that the Dutch assist him in subduing Bantam, and that they send a mission to Karta to pay their proper respects to the 'supreme king' of Java. Coen turned down both demands on the ground that they were unreasonable as long as Mataram's ports were closed to Dutch trade. In the face of this, the arrival of a large number of native vessels on August 22 laden with quantities of cattle, rice, and other foodstuffs raised suspicion. Part of the cargo was unloaded, but most of the vessels were kept outside the boom (a floating barrier across the mouth of the river), to the obvious displeasure of the Javanese. Two days later still more *tingans* arrived, os-tensibly only for the purpose of obtaining permission to sail to Malacca. They were kept separate from the first flotilla, but, notwithstanding these precautions, the Javanese succeeded in making a surprise attack during the middle of the night. The bitter fighting lasted five hours before the enemy withdrew with heavy losses, whereupon the whole flotilla took shelter in a little river east of Batavia.

The whole campaign had been well planned. On August 26, Baureksa approached the town from the south with a large army.

11. Ibid., pp. 95–96.
12. Stapel, *Geschiedenis van Nederlandsch-Indië*, p. 81.

Knowing that he could not defend the entire town against such a force, Coen ordered the southern part evacuated and burned to the ground. By September 11, Baureksa had advanced his lines to within a pistol shot of the town, and Coen ordered a sortie, which temporarily relieved the situation. On September 21 the Javanese renewed the attack, this time aiming at the redoubt Hollandia which was built of stone and coral and could only be entered by means of a tall ladder. Located at the southeast corner of the town, it was a key point. The 24 men under Sergeant Hans Madelyn acquitted themselves well, but the situation became awkward after they had used up all their powder. It was then that Madelyn had the inspiration to empty the latrine buckets over the heads of the Javanese. This turned the tide and the attackers fled in horror.

The Dutch followed with another sortie which drove the Javanese from their advanced positions. From prisoners it was learned that the total remaining force was less than 4,000 men and that many of them were tramping through the woods looking for food. For a month everything was quiet, and on October 21 Coen decided to counterattack with his whole force. In this battle the enemy lost 200 men, including Baureksa and his son. This relief, however, was of short duration; two days later a second Mataram army appeared on the scene under Sura Agul Agul. Under him stood two brothers, Mandura Redja and Upa Santa; they were direct descendants of the famous Senapati, the founder of Moslem Mataram. They had fully expected that Batavia had already been taken and that they would only have to gather the loot and then quickly subdue Bantam. When Mandura Redja saw what the situation really was, he is said to have beaten his breast crying, "What shall I tell my Lord, the Mataram!" [13]

Profiting from the experience of Baureksa, Sura Agul Agul realized that Batavia could not be stormed; he decided to employ the same tactics which had been so successful at Surabaya. He started to dam the river about a mile above the town. Three thousand Javanese labored at this for a month but without success. Here there was no convenient runoff such as at Surabaya, and when the rainy season set in, the job had to be abandoned. In one final attempt, the only active engagement in this later stage of the siege, the redoubt Hollandia was again stormed, on the night of November 27. This time the Dutch were prepared,

13. De Graaf, *Sultan Agung*, p. 148.

and the attackers were driven off. Mandura Redja and Upa Santa, the two brothers, had been charged with this operation. On Agung's orders, Sura Agul Agul had them both executed together with the men under their command because "they had failed to take Batavia and had not fought to the death." On December 3, 1628, the Javanese broke camp, leaving dead bodies strewn around "as a spectacle to his cruel execution. If we had not seen it with our own eyes," Coen reported to the Seventeen, "we would not have believed it. We counted 744 bodies." [14] If Sura Agul Agul had thought that this would appease Agung, he was apparently mistaken. Upon his return to Karta with his defeated army, he and many nobles were said to have paid with their lives for the dismal failure of their mission.[15]

Agung, the supreme king, refused to accept this defeat as final. He had only to look at the ruins around Karta to remind himself of the great glory of the old Hindu Mataram.[16] He was determined to emulate or even surpass it. On Java, only Batavia stood in his way, and he could not believe that Djangkung (Jan Coen) was a more formidable opponent than any of the other petty rulers he had already brought to their knees. It had taken five attempts before he had finally captured Surabaya and now he did not hesitate to attack Batavia a second time.

Artillery and munitions were sent from Karta at the end of May 1629, followed three weeks later by the rest of the army. Vast quantities of rice were collected and stored along the coast, ready to feed his army. All this was good logistics. Knowing that it might look suspicious, Agung applied a little psychological warfare by sending a certain Warga to Batavia. This man was instructed to tell Coen that the king of Mataram pleaded forgiveness and that henceforth his subjects were free to trade with Batavia. This would have been an excellent cover to supply Mataram's forces by sea, but Coen was not fooled so easily. Through his own sources he was fully aware of Mataram's real intentions. Two Dutch yachts patrolling the coast had spotted large numbers of native vessels heading for Tegal, all laden with paddy (unmilled rice). When Agung's regent at Tegal was asked what this meant, he

14. Ibid., p. 149.

15. De Jonge, *Opkomst*, 5, lxxx. Other sources seem to indicate that Sura Agul Agul was killed before Batavia in 1638, having been sent there by Agung with a small force, and with orders to fight to the death. See De Graaf, *Sultan Agung*, pp. 251–52.

16. See p. 210.

replied that the paddy was brought to Tegal to be milled and that all of it was destined for the Dutch at Batavia. Warga made a second visit to Batavia on June 20, this time bringing 13 vessels laden with victuals to show good faith. He was taken into custody on suspicion of deceit. After being interrogated in the customary fashion, he confessed that Tegal was indeed the supply depot for the army.

Coen decided to retaliate with economic warfare. He sent three ships to Tegal with orders to destroy everything in sight. On July 4 this mission was accomplished. Some 300 native vessels, 400 houses, and a mountain of paddy, 12 rods long and 4 wide, were destroyed. A few weeks later another paddy mountain at Cheribon suffered the same fate. This, for all practical purposes, decided the issue.

The vanguard of Agung's army reached the outskirts of Batavia toward the end of August after a long and difficult trek across the mountainous interior. The enemy made its usual preparations, positioned its cannon, dug zigzag trenches, and built parapets, but the fighting never gained major significance and business went on as usual all during the siege. Among the Javanese the shortage of rice was beginning to have its effect.

On September 17, Coen inspected the enemy's positions from the ramparts, and it was decided to make sorties against the approaches which had come close to two redoubts. This resolution was taken on the 18th. It was the last resolution Coen signed. On the 20th, word reached Batavia that there were famine conditions in Mataram's army. On October 2, the starving army abandoned its positions to wend its way home as best it could. Dead and dying fell by the wayside, their numbers increasing with every mile. De Graaf, the able historiographer of Sultan Agung's reign, calls it "a turning point in the history of Batavia, of Java, and of the whole of Indonesia." [17] Coen did not live to witness the actual retreat.

One of Coen's last letters was written to Prince Frederick Henry, who had succeeded his half-brother, Maurice, as stadholder in 1625. In this letter Coen described the fortifications of Batavia, but he also included a seemingly irrelevant bit of news: "As I write this a large snake, some twenty feet long, was brought into the fort—it had swallowed a whole deer." [18] Could this have

17. De Graaf, *Sultan Agung*, p. 151.
18. *Documents*, 5, 169.

been a subconscious reflection that he, too, had bitten off more than he could chew?

During the siege Coen suffered from dysentery, but he continued to perform his duties until September 20. By nightfall it was apparent to everyone that the governor general would not live much longer. His wife, who three days earlier had given birth to a daughter, came to his bedside.[19] Afterward he summoned members of the council to give them some last instructions. At one o'clock in the morning of September 21, 1629, Jan Pieterszoon Coen died. The following day he was buried with great honors. The Seventeen were incensed when they learned that the cost of the funeral had been charged against the Company.

The exact location of Coen's grave has been lost with the passage of time, except for the knowledge that it is somewhere under the foundations of a large warehouse. It is perhaps a fitting tribute to his memory that this warehouse belonged to one of the independent Dutch trading companies that prospered after Coen's free enterprise policy had belatedly been adopted.

19. Apparently the child died within a year.

Epilogue

In contrast with the Spanish and Portuguese whose avowed purposes were conquest and crusade, the Dutch had gone to the
East Indies for the sole purpose of buying spices. At the outset,
the policy of free enterprise, which had been highly beneficial
in the development of Dutch trade in Europe, prevailed. That
trade, however, had been based on bulk goods of a low unit value,
carried out over relatively short distances and largely without
danger of enemy interference. One or more voyages could be
made within a year with vessels that were economical to handle.

The trade with the Indies presented an entirely different picture: the ships had to be larger, heavily armed, and a voyage
might last two years or more. It also became quickly apparent
that the available supply of spices was by no means sufficient to
meet the demands of the individual companies that had been
organized to exploit the direct route to the Indies. The Dutch
were confronted with a virtual sellers' monopoly because native
rulers, owning the spice-producing areas, controlled both prices
and quantities. As a result the cost of spices quadrupled within a
few years.[1] Nor was this the only problem that prevented peaceful trading. The Dutch had always been guided by the principle
of "good faith." It had become a national trait, and, if a contract
was made, both parties were expected to live up to its terms.
Should differences arise, as could be expected, the Dutch were
willing to submit their case to the local authorities. In this appeal
to justice, the Dutch were quickly disillusioned. Moslem traders
and petty rulers regarded it a virture to deceive the unbelievers,
and they knew all the tricks: inferior quality, loading spices with
water, short weights, and similar unsavory tactics. They did not
hesitate to sell the same lot twice if a higher price were offered,
even in cases where they had already been paid in advance. In
the absence of a court of law, there was no redress to be obtained against such malpractices. Although the independent companies were bitterly competing against each other,[2] they were

1. J. A. van der Chijs, *Stichting van de Vereenigde O. I. Compagnie* (Leiden, 1856), p. 130. Compare Schrieke, *Indonesian Sociological Studies, 1,*
50–51.
2. See p. 130 ff.

unanimous in their complaints about this state of affairs in the Indies.

It was for this reason that a clause was inserted in the charter of the United East India Company which empowered its servants in the Indies to "take suitable measures" in case they were "deceived or treated badly." [3] By this clause, the Company was authorized to make treaties with foreign potentates in the name of the States General, to establish forts, and to appoint governors and judges to maintain law and order. Although this was for the express purpose of creating stable conditions for trading, it actually authorized the Company to take the law into its own hands. When contracts were repeatedly broken, it was inevitable that such authority would establish a basis for territorial conquest.

The monopoly clause in the charter could safeguard the Company only against competition from other Dutch nationals. It had no effect on other European countries or on the extensive native trade. In order to make the Dutch monopoly effective, such loopholes had to be closed and for this the Dutch relied heavily, in the beginning, on their treaties with native rulers. During a century-long tenure in South and Southeast Asia, the Portuguese by their ruthlessness had made themselves thoroughly hated. The arrival of the Dutch had been welcomed everywhere, and almost every potentate invoked the help of the newcomers against the common enemy. The demands made upon the Dutch were so great that they had to limit their active support to those areas in which they were particularly interested. From the Sultan of Ternate, who nominally controlled the Moluccas, the Company obtained exclusive contracts for the purchase of all cloves, nutmegs, and mace produced in his domain. In exchange, the Dutch guaranteed him protection against the Spanish and Portuguese. This burdened the Company with a considerable outlay for forts as well as an armed fleet to patrol the large area constantly, but the price was well worth it. On the strength of these exclusive contracts the Dutch based their right to bar all interlopers, European or Asiatic.

It soon appeared that these contracts or treaties did not have the expected results. The English refused to recognize them, and the native traders, who bartered rice for spices, likewise ignored them. After the English had withdrawn from the Moluccas, there still remained the native trade to be eliminated. Both the directors

3. Van der Chijs, pp. 111–12.

at home and their administrators in the East Indies were in complete agreement that only an absolute monopoly of the spice trade could produce sufficient profits. As far as Europe was concerned, it was obvious that sales had to be controlled by a single seller to prevent glutting a market which, although expanding, was by no means unsaturable. The control of the sources of spices was equally essential not only to keep the cost down, but also because spices were the working capital needed to develop the inter-Asiatic trade. A complete monopoly was eventually established, but the means used to acquire it were different in each case.

A monopoly of nutmegs and mace was effectively secured with the conquest of the Banda group in 1621. With cloves, a different policy had to be applied. Unlike nutmegs, cloves grew in a much larger area, a number of large and small islands stretching more than 400 miles from Ternate in the north to Buru and Ceram in the south. The island of Amboyna, just to the south of this area, had been the staple of cloves since ancient days; it had fallen into Portuguese hands shortly after their arrival in the Indies. Since 1605, when the Portuguese had surrendered, the island had been under Dutch sovereignty. For cloves, too, the contract system had not been successful. The long, indented coast lines were almost impossible to police, and substantial amounts found their way to Macassar, which had become the center of a thriving smuggling trade.[4] English, Portuguese, and a medley of Asian merchants situated in this independent sultanate offered twice as much as the contract price established by the Dutch Company. The native suppliers naturally took advantage of this price difference, and as a result they gradually fell behind in their contractual deliveries to the Company, ignoring the fact that in many cases they had already been paid in advance, usually in the form of calicoes and rice. By 1628 their debt had risen to almost half a million guilders. There was no possibility that any significant part of this amount could ever be recovered, and the loss would have been difficult to explain to the money-conscious directors at home. Whether by design or otherwise, the Company's servants in the Indies used this debt as the vehicle by which to acquire a complete monopoly of the production of cloves. As they had done at Djakarta, the Dutch proved that they were able to turn a temporary setback into a long-range advantage.

4. See Schrieke, *Indonesian Sociological Studies, 1,* 65–72.

At an earlier date, the Dutch had started to plant more clove trees on Amboyna. When these plantings proved successful, it was decided to confine the cultivation of cloves to that island and a few others nearby which were also under Dutch jurisdiction. This could only be feasible if production in the original clove-producing areas were abolished completely. In order to accomplish this, the Dutch felt legally justified in applying a wholesale foreclosure against their debtors' property by cutting down their clove trees.[5] Such a drastic measure required the consent of the Sultan of Ternate, but this was easily enough obtained when the Company offered him a yearly compensation in lieu of the revenue he had previously obtained from the clove trade. Like all other rulers in Southeast Asia, he was not much concerned with the well-being of his subjects. These annual payments appeared in the Company's books under the unabashed heading of "extirpation moneys." From 1625 on, when some 65,-000 clove trees were cut down, the islands were visited regularly by Dutch contingents who enforced this policy and who had to report the additional number of trees which had been cut down. For the Company, this curtailment of production had become the more pressing because the stocks of cloves in Europe were reported to be enough to meet a ten years' demand. This ruthless policy gradually tightened the clove monopoly, but it was not complete until some decades later, when the Dutch subdued Macassar and thus closed the final loophole.[6]

In unit value, pepper was the least costly of the spices, but because of the large quantities involved it was the most important of all.[7] It was cultivated in the interior of Sumatra, the northern part of which was controlled by Achin and the southern

5. The Dutch were not the first to apply this method to eliminate competition. The Achinese had done the same on the Malay peninsula, the Portuguese during their rule in the Moluccas, and the rulers of Ternate and Tidore had applied it against each other. See Schrieke, *Indonesian Sociological Studies, 1*, 73.

6. In the course of time the English promoted the cultivation of nutmegs in the West Indies, and they acquired a virtual clove monopoly when they assumed the protectorate over Zanzibar and Pemba in 1890. By then, however, cloves as well as all other spices had long since lost their significance in world trade.

7. The market in Europe fluctuated considerably, but the following prices, quoted in florins (guilders), can be taken as a rough average, all per Amsterdam pound (1.1 English lbs.): Pepper fl. 0.50, Cloves fl. 3.75, Nutmegs fl. 2.75, Mace fl. 6.00 and Cinnamon fl. 2.50. For yearly prices from 1649 to 1738, see Glamann, *Dutch Asiatic Trade*, app. C.

part by Bantam. The rulers of both were adamant in their refusal to allow the Dutch to gain a foothold.[8] Pepper was also produced in the hinterland of Patane on the Malay Peninsula. To eliminate this competition, Iskandar Muda, the Sultan of Achin, had sent his people across the Strait of Malacca to destroy the pepper vines there. Iskandar Muda boasted that in time he would have the monopoly of all the pepper and that then the Dutch would have to come to him. In this connection Coen had written the Seventeen: "The Achinese may bluster and blow a little, (but) in due time he will also be taken care of."[9] Coen felt quite sure of this because he had already formulated a plan to deprive both Achin and Bantam of an important source of their pepper. This source was Djambi on the east coast of Sumatra, which was able to deliver between 40,000 and 50,000 bags yearly.[10] The rivers in Sumatra flowed east toward the Strait of Malacca, providing easy transportation to Djambi at the expense of the west coast ports, including Bencoolen where the English had a factory.

At an earlier stage, Coen had established relations with Djambi, and he gradually built it up as a main source of supply, cutting out both Achin and Bantam. The sustained blockade of Portuguese Malacca which culminated in its surrender in 1641 practically secured a pepper monopoly. The fall of this important entrepôt not only spelled the end of Portuguese trade in the East Indies but also breached the life-line between the Portuguese-Spanish possessions in East Asia and Goa. It also precipitated the decline of Mataram, which had maintained a lively trade with Malacca, now doomed to fade into insignificance. Many Portuguese families moved to Batavia, and when Javanese merchants began to frequent the town more and more, Sultan Agung had to revoke his prohibition of the export of rice to the Dutch.[11] He died in February 1646, and later that same year a peace treaty was finally concluded between the Dutch and Mataram.

By the middle of the seventeenth century, the Dutch Company had thus attained its goal, a strong monopoly over the legendary spice trade. It now also included cinnamon since the Portuguese had been forced to cede Galle and Negombo on Ceylon in 1644.

8. Compare Schrieke, *Indonesian Sociological Studies*, *1*, 49–65.
9. *Documents*, *6*, 206.
10. Bags weighed 60 pounds each. Total estimated pepper consumption in Europe was somewhat over 100,000 bags. See Glamann, *Dutch Asiatic Trade*, pp. 74–75.
11. See Hall, *History of South-East Asia*, pp. 257–58.

The treaty with Mataram, moreover, made the Dutch the sole buyers of rice, and by controlling its flow throughout the archipelago, the Company was able to enforce the monopoly on its own terms.

The Company's policy was to buy at the lowest possible price and sell at the highest, both in the areas under Dutch sovereignty (Banda, Amboyna, and Ceylon) and where exclusive contracts were in force (Sumatra and Mataram). The prices the Company paid native growers had no relation to what might be called a fair market price. The Amboynese received less than fl. 0.25 per pound for their cloves, whereas the sale price in Europe averaged about fl. 4.00, a gross profit of more than 1,500 per cent.[12] For other spices, the ratio was about the same. This, however, gives an erroneous impression because, after shipping costs were taken into account, the gross profit ranged between 250 and 300 per cent.

The Company also maintained an import monopoly for calicoes and opium. Coen, like some of his successors, had tried in vain to open this inter-island and, on a broader scale, inter-Asiatic trade, to private individuals. During the first few decades, the directors, after looking askance at the practice, had more or less closed their eyes to it, and a growing number of the Company's personnel had engaged in it after having completed their tours of duty. The same applied to the colonists who had come out in a small but steady flow during the same period. In 1632, the Seventeen laid down restrictions, implementing their letter to Coen of five years earlier in a strict resolution.[13] From then on, private trade was to be sharply curtailed, limited to a few places outside the archipelago, only where the Company itself had been unable to operate profitably. Even more deadly to private trade was the provision that burghers were allowed to settle only at Batavia, Amboyna, and Banda where their activities were under constant surveillance.

Jacques Specx, who succeeded Coen as governor general, had delayed putting the ordinances into effect and appealed to the Seventeen to be more lenient because of the hardships it would cause the burghers, who by then represented a significant part of the population at Batavia. The Seventeen replied by relieving Specx of his office because he had been less than diligent in

12. Calculated at the established price of about 50 reals per *bahar*. See p. 301. See also Stapel, ed., *Geschiedenis*, *3* (1939), 513.
13. See p. 446 f.

carrying out his orders. He was replaced by Hendrik Brouwer, who had been sent out with emphatic instructions to root out private trade. The Seventeen left no doubt as to their feelings on this matter. "Our orders must be your laws," they wrote in an accompanying letter. "Your communications can only serve to advise while you await our orders." [14] Thus they had written, shortly after having learned of Coen's demise; it is not likely that they would have used such strong language had he been still alive. About the burghers they also expressed themselves in no uncertain terms: "If you tell us that the burghers cannot exist without trade, then it would be better that none were at Batavia . . . if one or the other has to suffer, the Company or they, it is far better that the burghers do the suffering . . . Do not be led by a misplaced compassion because first and foremost comes the wellbeing and profit of the Company." [15] From that time until the Company finally collapsed towards the end of the eighteenth century, the directors never retracted their firm stand on monopoly and private trade. Periodic appeals for a more enlightened policy fell on deaf ears. The shortsighted carried the day, and before too long it became apparent that the Company would suffer for it.

The results of this policy can best be assayed by a brief analysis of how it affected the various groups that were involved in this massive undertaking: the Indonesians, the burghers, the Company's servants in Asia, the stockholders, the Company itself, and the homeland.

For the population in the Moluccas the consequences were drastic. The people of Banda had been banished from their islands, thus losing everything which had been their age-old heritage. In the clove-producing islands, the natives did not fare much better after the cultivation was restricted to the island of Amboyna. The Moluccas had always been dependent on Java for rice. Having eliminated native trade, the Company proceeded to supply this need but only to the small areas where spice production had been localized. It was indifferent to the needs of the people in the islands where the clove trees had been extirpated. By paying the rulers their annual indemnity, the Company felt that it had discharged its obligations. To avoid starvation, these people turned

14. De Jonge, *Opkomst*, 5, xcvi.
15. Ibid., 5, xcviii–cii.

to harvesting the wild sago palm, a poor substitute for their customary rice.

Without their normal export product, the islands' native trade also withered away. The Company's ships patrolled the waters constantly. Native vessels were obliged to carry passes; if they lacked one or carried even the smallest quantity of cloves, they were quickly sent to the bottom.[16] Deprived of the two main sources of their former prosperity, the cultivation of spices and free shipping, the renowned principalities of the Middle Ages, Ternate, Tidore, Matjan, and Batjan, were reduced to little more than subsistence level. Such was the penalty for having a valuable product that was coveted by a determined group of European entrepreneurs.

Elsewhere in the archipelago, the situation was not much better. Because of the stringent blockade, Bantam, formerly the great emporium of Southeast Asia, saw its trade diverted to Batavia. By the end of the seventeenth century, it had lost all of its earlier glory. The main pepper towns in Sumatra, Djambi and Palembang, tried a few times to throw off the intolerable yoke of forced deliveries, but they were helpless against the Company's power. With the fall of Malacca, the last link with free markets was severed, simultaneously ending Mataram's thriving trade with that important transit port. The price the Indonesians had to pay for the Company's long desired monopoly was impoverishment.

It does not speak for the perspicacity of the directors at home that they refused to recognize that their policy would eventually kill the profitable trade in calicoes.[17] Towards the end of the seventeenth century, the natives had become so poor that they could no longer afford to buy them and turned to weaving their own.

Among the administrators in the Indies, there were some who openly disagreed with the cynical attitude prescribed by the Seventeen for their dealings with the native population. In 1618 Laurens Reael pointed out that a strict enforcement of the monopoly could only lead to a wholesale impoverishment of the natives. "We are so much concerned with profits," he wrote, "that we do

16. Abel Tasman, the discoverer of New Zealand and the first to circumnavigate Australia, was at one time engaged in this patrol duty.
17. The profits on this trade ranged from 50 to 75 per cent.

not allow anyone else to make a penny." [18] In this same year Admiral Van der Hagen complained that the exclusion of native traders had so increased the cost of foodstuffs that the people of the Moluccas were close to despair. In replying to an order to prevent native trade he said: "It can be done, but with what right?" Jacobus Bontius wrote: "I am often surprised at the stupidity of our people who call these natives barbarians, while they excel us not only in the knowledge of plants and herbs but in economic management as well." [19] There were others who spoke in favor of the natives, including Pieter van Dam, the Company's advocate in Amsterdam for most of the latter half of the seventeenth century. But not even he could convince the directors that anything but a strictly enforced monopoly was feasible.

The Dutch burghers were even worse off than the natives. A very few had been able to take up the leaseholds of lands surrounding Batavia which could be brought into cultivation with slaves. These leaseholds were only made available to the higher ranking ex-personnel, and the lower ranks, sailors and soldiers, lacked influence with the authorities as well as capital to exploit such lands. Being restricted to Batavia, they tried to make a living by small-scale usury and in the building trade in the rapidly expanding town. In these fields they soon felt the competition of the more industrious Chinese who were actually favored by the Company above the burghers. The latter repeatedly petitioned the government, both in the Indies and in Europe, to find redress for their plight. It was all in vain; the directors, as they clearly indicated, considered them no better than fungus that might better wither away. This is exactly what happened to the large majority. Had there not been such a wide schism between the Dutch and the Javanese, these burghers would soon have been assimilated by the native population, but under the circumstances they became entwined with liberated slaves who were known as *Mardykers*.[20] The result was a "progressive physiological and psychological bastardization" in which the *Mardykers* proved to be the stronger

18. Stapel, ed., *Geschiedenis, 3* (1938), 516.
19. Idem. Bontius was one of the earliest highly educated men to serve in the Indies. Being a medical doctor, he attended Coen at the time of his death.
20. Derived from the Malay word *merdeka*, meaning "freedom from slavery."

strain.[21] Most of them had come from the Portuguese possessions on the west coast of the India peninsula, and in the process of assimilation with them the Dutch burghers lost even their mother tongue, speaking a mixture of Malay, Dutch, and Portuguese in which the latter was predominant. Thus, in addition to being impoverished, the Dutch burghers lost their identity. As a result, all hope of creating a viable Dutch middle class, as had been visualized by Coen, was completely destroyed. The Chinese gradually began to weld the essential bond between the Dutch and the Indonesians. After the East Indies had become a Dutch colony in the nineteenth century and the principle of free enterprise was finally accepted, it was too late to create a Dutch middle class. The Chinese were thoroughly entrenched, and the new era of private trading companies and plantations drew a different type of Dutchman to the Indies—the organization man.

The Company's servants, as distinct from its soldiers and sailors, were in a way a new breed of men. Unlike the Spanish and Portuguese, they were not serving a sovereign but were in the employ of anonymous capital. We might consider them the forerunners of a managerial class. Throughout the Company's existence, the caliber of the average personnel left much to be desired. Governor General Antonio van Diemen, who brought the Company to the peak of its prosperity, pointed out in 1631 that the Company suffered from two cancers: superfluous employees, and incompetent and dishonest ones.[22] The blame for this was largely due to a system which allowed each chamber to send out as many people as it liked, usually on the recommendation of the friends and relatives of its many directors, without regard for character or ability.

The directors were also indirectly responsible for the graft and corruption that was to rise to alarming proportions. A man might have been expected to show some loyalty to his king's interest (although the Portuguese period had its own share of corruption), but this could hardly be expected when he served a mere trading company, personified by a board of directors who were known to look out for themselves. In the merchant's republic, money had become one way by which a man's loyalty might be obtained, but the directors were too shortsighted to realize this. It was their

21. Gerretson, *Coen's Eerherstel*, p. 105.
22. De Jonge, *Opkomst*, 5, xcviii.

stubborn belief that any form of private trade was detrimental to the Company, and they meant to enforce it by putting as little money as possible into circulation in the Indies. Thus they not only adhered to an abominably low wage scale, of which a good part was moreover held in escrow, but they insisted that only a portion be paid in cash and the rest in cloth and other necessities.

It turned out that the directors greatly underestimated the ingenuity of the men in their employ. From the far-flung offices in Asia, the Company's factors had little difficulty in developing a lucrative private trade; they could even count on the connivance of the Company's skippers, who were only too willing to transport goods free of charge for a share in the profits. This so-called "spoil-trade" embraced the whole range of Asian commodities, but opium seems to have been one of the most profitable. There are cases on record of employees who within a few years managed to put aside a tidy fortune on a salary of less than 100 guilders per month.[23] Nor was this illicit trade confined to Asia; accommodating skippers could also be found on the European route. It happened at times that quantities of such goods reaching the Netherlands were so great that they actually depressed the price the Company was asking for its legitimate merchandise. This was especially true in silk, tea, and Chinese porcelain, all goods of a very high unit value and which in the aggregate gradually surpassed the spice trade. During the greater part of the seventeenth century, illicit trade remained a minor issue, mainly because men in the highest echelon, like Coen, Van Diemen, and Maetsuycker, were incorruptible. During the last two decades and throughout the following century, graft and corruption had free rein, and all who found opportunity participated quite openly. In certain areas, such as Surate, Malabar, Coromandel, and Bengal, the Company's officials pooled the spoils and redistributed them in proportion to the salary each received to make sure that everyone received his 'legitimate' share. One such combine, because of its widespread activities, was commonly referred to as the "Small Company." [24] The Council of the Indies tried to curb this evil by repeatedly sending inspectors to the outlying factories to unearth any malpractices. It was of no avail; even the execution of 26 Company employees on a single day in 1722 had only a passing

23. Stapel, *Geschiedenis*, p. 133.
24. Ibid., pp. 135–36.

effect. A sanctioned private trade could have prevented such wholesale corruption, but since the directors persisted in their monopoly policy it was inevitable that it should continue to spread. The Seventeen tried to combat the problem by sending out their own inspectors-general, but virtually admitted that little could be done about it. Pieter van Dam in his great history of the United Company lamented: "If the servants disregard their oath of loyalty, then the Company is powerless." [25] During the eighteenth century, the directors actually participated in this corruption by selling posts in the Indies to the highest bidder, following the example of the oligarchic town governments in the Republic.

The United East India Company was the first joint stock company in history, and thus it was the forerunner of the modern corporation. The stockholders were liable for no more than they had paid for shares, and, although no stock certificates were ever issued, all transfers were recorded in the Company's books. In other respects, however, it was only the rudimentary beginning of a properly functioning corporate structure. For the scope of its operations, the Company was grossly under-capitalized. The 6.5 million guilders paid in were exhausted almost before the first return cargoes arrived in Europe. In 1610, the directors distributed their first dividend, amounting to 132½ per cent covering 8 years of operation. The Company's cash position is clearly revealed by the fact that all but 7½ per cent of this was paid in spices, at prices set by the directors. Since the Company had been unable to sell these spices on the open market because supplies greatly exceeded the demand, it is natural to imagine that the stockholders were not at all pleased with this disbursement. During the ten-year period from 1635 to 1644, a shortage of cash once more forced the directors to resort to this same expedient, but it created such a furor among the stockholders that it was never repeated. Henceforth dividends were paid in cash except during the bad years of 1673–82 and 1696–98, when they were paid in debentures.

The principle of limited liability was so ingrained that no thought was ever given to increasing the capitalization by selling more stock; thus the capital remained fixed at the original subscription of about 6.5 million guilders throughout the almost 200 years the Company was in existence. Pressed for more capital in 1613, the directors initiated an "insurance contract" which offered subscribers a return, actually a premium, of 5 per cent, covered

25. Ibid., p. 140.

by the expectation that the fleet then being outfitted would return intact with a full cargo.[26] This was in effect a separate undertaking which provided a temporary relief to the extent of some 8
million guilders. This cumbersome type of financing was dropped
after the directors found that it was easier to borrow money
against debentures.

Although profits did not measure up to expectations, the Company, during the first 90 years of its existence, was a successful
concern. During this period it paid an average cash dividend of
13.6 per cent with an additional 3.7 per cent in spices and 1.4 per
cent in debentures, making a total of 18.7 per cent yearly.[27] The
stockholders were generally of the opinion that far greater profits
were made because the directors were under no obligation to open
their books to them. The directors, moreover, were known to
profit from the wide fluctuations in the shares, a market situation
which they often engineered themselves by making use of favorable or unfavorable conditions in the Indies of which they had,
of course, advance knowledge. Since all private letters were subject to a strict censorship at Batavia only the directors knew the
true state of affairs, and they took full advantage of this knowledge to manipulate the market.[28]

Considering that the spices were sold in Europe at about $2\frac{1}{2}$
to 3 times their cost, a far greater profit margin seemed indicated which would also have enabled the Company to create
substantial reserves. By the end of this generally prosperous 90-
year period however, the Company was actually some 4 million
guilders in debt. This was not a very large amount considering the
length of the period, but it points up the fact that the cost of
maintaining the monopoly absorbed all but a fraction of the gross
profits. Every year an average of 18 ships and 3,700 men had to
be sent to the Indies, and by the end of the seventeenth century
there was a permanent force of about 12,000 men there.[29] Coen
had clearly anticipated this problem when he repeatedly pointed
out to the Seventeen that a burgher class would greatly reduce
the cost of maintaining substantial garrisons. As a civil guard, they
would be anxious to serve in time of need because they would be

26. Van Dillen, *Oudste aandeelhoudersregister*, pp. 73–78.
27. For the yearly dividend figures see Van Dam, *Beschryvinge*, *1*,
appendix II.
28. Compare "Profit and Loss" in Glamann, *Dutch Asiatic Trade*, pp.
244–65.
29. Stapel, *Geschiedenis*, p. 138.

protecting their own interests as well. As private traders using their own vessels, they would largely have eliminated the uneconomical warships the Company was using in the inter-Asiatic trade, and the revenues from this private trade in tolls, taxes, and convoy duties might well have been greater than the Company's earnings under its monopoly. This argument seems to be borne out by the results of the 40-year period after Coen had promoted the inter-Asiatic trade and when it reached its greatest expansion. Out of a gross profit of 101 million guilders, only 10 million could be remitted to Holland, the rest going for operating and administrative expenses.[30] And this was at a time when corruption had not yet become an issue. Since Coen's program was effectively scotched, it is unfortunately impossible to determine to what extent it could have improved the Company's position.

Judging by the balance sheets, the Company went into a sharp decline after 1692. The expenses remained as high as ever, but the gross profits declined due to the ever spreading "spoil trade" and other types of corruption which reached into the highest levels. When Governor General Van Hoorn resigned in 1709, his fortune was estimated at 10 million guilders.[31] Annual losses mounted from 2 million to 4 and even 6 million guilders. Before long the Company was theoretically bankrupt, but the general public was unaware of its shaky condition. In the face of this reversal, the directors managed to maintain credit by continuing to pay dividends even if the money for it had to be borrowed. Money was abundant because, although the republic had entered a period of economic decline, it had become the capital market of Europe. With its chambers housed in imposing buildings, its warehouses filled with costly merchandise, its heavily-laden ships and wealthy ex-servants returning from the Indies regularly, the Company was still able to present an appearance of great power and wealth. This prolonged the process of disintegration, but it could not prevent the final outcome. In this denouement, the United States indirectly played a part. Because of the open support given by the Dutch to the American colonies during their revolution, England declared war on the Republic in 1780. This war lasted four years, and for the Company it was the beginning of the end. While the Dutch Company had gradually deteriorated during the eighteenth century, the English Company had strength-

30. Vlekke, *Nusantara*, p. 144.
31. Stapel, *Geschiedenis*, p. 133.

ened its position enormously, and it was now able to inflict heavy losses on the Dutch in ships, merchandise, and territories. As a last resort, a reorganization was suggested which embraced three main points: the States General, in whose name the Company had acquired an empire, would assume responsibility for its defense; the trade in the Indies would be opened to private enterprise under certain conditions (this was a belated recognition of the soundness of Coen's program); the Company's debt, which by then had risen to 134 million guilders, should be redeemed by taxation. In the opinion of the Company's advocate, S. C. Nederburgh, these measures would keep the Company alive.[32] The Republic was willing to assume these heavy financial burdens provided the Company relinquished all its possessions in the Indies. Thereafter, the Company ceased to exist as a corporate body. In this manner, the Dutch Republic, later the Kingdom of the Netherlands, acquired in 1798 a colonial empire in Asia for about 140 million guilders which included the original capital. It turned out to be a sterling investment, including as it did all the Company's hidden assets in the Indies which had never appeared in the books.

These hidden assets were in fact the total of the territorial acquisitions during the Company's existence and which towards the end comprised practically the whole archipelago. The exploitation of this empire during the nineteenth and twentieth centuries brought great wealth to the Netherlands. During the preceding two centuries, however, the share of the East India trade in the total Dutch economy had actually been minor. The annual fitting-out of a few ships in each of the various towns where the chambers were located had produced a certain amount of economic activity, as had the more or less regular dividend payments which became available for investment in other enterprises. Available statistics indicate that the capital employed in the East India trade during much of the eighteenth century was only about 7 per cent of the total amount invested in Dutch overseas trade, which was estimated at close to 500 million guilders.[33] The trade with the Baltic stood, as it had since the beginning of Dutch economic development, at the top, but trade with England and France also accounted for a large share, while that with Spain

32. Ibid., pp. 182–83.
33. A. Kluit, *Historie der Hollandsche staatsregering tot 1795*, 2 (2 vols. Amsterdam, 1805), 255.

did not fall far behind. It was not until the hidden assets the Company had amassed during the two centuries of its existence were brought into use that the East India trade gained a predominant place in the Dutch economy—a vast empire in Asia created by one of the smallest countries in Europe.

Afterword:
Three Men

Jan Pieterszoon Coen laid the foundation for a Dutch empire in Asia, but the preliminary work had been done by a number of energetic men in the Netherlands. Among them three were outstanding: Johan van Oldebarnevelt, Hugo Grotius, and Reynier Pauw.

JOHAN VAN OLDEBARNEVELT. By 1618, time was running out for the venerable statesman who had rendered the young republic such invaluable service. He might have lived years longer, but fate decreed otherwise. Oldebarnevelt had made many enemies who, joining forces, brought about his downfall. The Calvinist dominies, repeatedly thwarted by the advocate in their attempts to usurp political power, had long been his enemies. Prince Maurice came to regard Oldebarnevelt as the main stumbling block in his ambition to gain greater personal power, and allied himself with the Calvinists. The magistrates of Amsterdam, now headed by Reynier Pauw, had their own reasons for opposing the advocate.

The friction between Liberals and Calvinists had reached a point of such intensity that a peaceful solution could no longer be reached. Intolerant leaders aroused the passions of the Calvinists, who mostly belonged to that level of society which, through ignorance and poverty, was most susceptible to propaganda. Houses of prosperous Liberals in Amsterdam were looted and burned. The disturbances spread to other towns and became increasingly more difficult to control. Oldebarnevelt asked Prince Maurice to make his troops available to suppress these riots, but the stadholder refused. This caused the advocate to proclaim his so-called "Sharp Resolution" which, among other things, empowered the town magistrates to hire their own soldiers. At the same time the troops were ordered to obey the States and not the stadholder.

Oldebarnevelt had gone too far. With this order, countermanding the army's oath of loyalty, he had touched Prince Maurice in a most tender spot. Maurice felt that his honor was at stake; he must revenge himself for this offense. Openly siding with the advocate's enemies, the stadholder increased his power rapidly. In the States General there were fewer and fewer who dared to support their former leader, and before long this body extended virtual dictatorial powers to Maurice. Flushed by this victory and prompted by the conviction that there was not room for both in the United Provinces, Maurice struck the final blow.

Some of Oldebarnevelt's friends, having been forewarned, pleaded with him to flee the country while there was still a chance. A man like Oldebarnevelt could only ignore his well-wishers, and he went about his business as usual. On the way to his chambers at the *Binnenhof* (Inner Court) in The Hague on August 29, 1618, he was accosted by one of Maurice's chamberlains, who asked him to come to the prince's apartment. Here the advocate was put under arrest. He was kept in the closest confinement for several months while the Calvinists took control of the country. The Liberal clergy were chased from their pulpits, and their adherents were banished from their offices in town and state governments.

As in most cases dealing with alleged offenses against the state in a highly charged emotional atmosphere, the procedure against Oldebarnevelt was a judicial farce. From November on he was examined more than sixty times by a special commission appointed by the States General. At no time was he allowed to consult notes or put his defense in writing. These 'examinations' occurred almost daily and had no other purpose than to make the old statesman confess his alleged misdeeds. Oldebarnevelt refused to accommodate his prosecutors. On February 20, 1619, the case against him was finally brought into court. There were twenty-four judges, every one of them either a fierce opponent or a personal enemy. The presiding judge was Reynier Pauw.[1] The composition of such a court foretold its verdict. Nevertheless, the spectacle was needlessly prolonged, seemingly to torture the old man to the limit and to portray him as a traitor to the country which he had guided through its darkest days.

On the evening of May 12, a Sunday, the judges at last brought in their verdict: death by beheading and confiscation of all his property. Johan van Oldebarnevelt refused to enter a plea for pardon, knowing that it would be construed as an admission of guilt. Conversely, it was to Prince Maurice's discredit that he lacked the moral courage to grant a pardon voluntarily. The sentence was quickly executed. The advocate was to be beheaded the following morning. A scaffold was hastily erected in the *Binnenhof*, directly in front of the Knight's Hall. During the night, from his nearby cell, he heard the sound of hammering.

Willem de Groot, a brother of Hugo Grotius, wrote of Olde-

1. See Geyl, *Netherlands Divided*, pp. 62–65.

barnevelt's final hours. "During the reading of the sentence the Advocate alternately nodded and shook his head, and he was heard to say, 'That goes too far.'" After the sentence had been read, he asked that, in view of his many years of service to the country, his *Confessie* (rebuttal) be published together with the sentence "'I had not expected that the Lordships would draw such a conclusion from my *Confessie* . . . I had hoped that the Lordships would have been content with my blood and that, considering my faithful services, they would have left my house-wife and my children in possession of my property.'"

"Undaunted," De Groot continued, "he went to his slaughter. The scaffold was filthy . . . the sand was blackish, mixed with straw . . . the coffin was made of rough planks. He turned to the crowd and said: 'Men, do not believe that I die as a traitor. I have always been a good Patriot and a faithful servant of the fatherland. If anyone tells you differently, do not believe it.'" Before putting his head on the block he looked at the sand and the coffin, saying, "'Is this for my faithful service of forty years?'" Then he knelt down, facing the chamber of the States General where he had so often led the deliberations. His last words were: "'Christ is my leader. Lord! have mercy upon those of mine. In your hands I deliver my spirit.'"

His head was at once cut off. The crowd surged upon the scaffold and dipped their kerchiefs in the blood, continuing until there was neither blood nor sand left . . . "Yea, they cut the bloody splinters out of the scaffold . . . Yea, the kerchief with which the sword had been wiped was sold for a double pistolet." [2]

Thus died the architect of the United East India Company. It is a fatal irony that his death occurred within a few weeks of the day Jan Coen established the rendezvous at Djakarta.

HUGO GROTIUS. The universally acknowledged 'father of inter-national law' was among the important Liberals who were ar-rested along with Oldebarnevelt. Grotius was sentenced to life imprisonment and all his worldly possessions were confiscated. He was imprisoned at Castle Loevesteyn, where his wife and chil-dren were allowed to share his confinement. Much of his time was spent in tutoring his children and in continuing his studies of theology and law. For the latter purpose he was permitted to re-ceive books, which were transported back and forth at periodic intervals in a large chest.

This chest was at first carefully inspected, but in time this formality was gradually dispensed with. This laxity gave Grotius' wife, Maria van Reygersberg, the idea that the chest might be

2. Limburg, *Cultuurdragers*, pp. 202–03.

used to spirit her husband out of the castle. Having freedom of movement herself, she made arrangements with friends in a neighboring town to receive the chest, with Grotius inside, and to assist him in crossing the border. The plan worked, and in April 1621, Hugo Grotius arrived in Paris, where he had influential friends and a brilliant reputation. The Dutch ambassador demanded his extradition but to no avail. Through the good offices of his friend Jeannin, president of the High Court of Justice of Paris, King Louis XIII gave Grotius asylum, considering the "extraordinary capabilities of Mr. De Groot" and an annuity 3,600 guilders.

Grotius was joined by his family and was soon engrossed in his monumental work on international law, *De jure belli et pacis*, which was published in 1625. Life in Paris had its drawbacks, and Grotius anxiously waited for a reprieve. In 1631, nostalgia made him return to Holland, hoping that the lapse of ten years had mellowed his enemies. He misjudged the implacable attitude of the Calvinist element and, threatened with imminent arrest, he fled to Hamburg. Here he continued his studies and at the same time made repeated efforts to be reinstated persona grata in his own country. His efforts were in vain.

In 1635, Grotius accepted an offer from Sweden to become its ambassador to Paris. The ten years he spent there in that capacity, while relieving him of financial worries, were not so smooth as might have been expected.[3] His whole character rebelled against the hollow atmosphere of the court, with its intrigues and conspiracies; he felt most at home in his study, surrounded by his books. He submitted his resignation, but the Swedish Chancellor Oxenstjerna refused to accept it, with the remark that it was for him "a duty and an honor to protect an ambassador of whom one could only say that he took the interest of Sweden too much to heart."

Grotius traveled to Sweden in order to submit his resignation in person. The scholarly young Queen Christina tried hard to keep him in her service but the 62-year-old jurist had only one remaining desire—to go back to the land of his forefathers and live out his declining years there, no matter under what conditions. On the voyage home, his ship foundered on the coast of Pomerania. Grotius continued his journey by land but only as far as Rostock; he was a very sick man, and died there on August 29, 1645. His was one of the greatest legal minds of all time, but

3. Grotius was a great jurist, but "a failure as a diplomat and politician." See J. and A. Romein, *Erflaters*, pp. 65–66.

in his own country he found no respect, not even in death. His coffin was stoned by his enemies as it was carried through the streets.[4]

REYNIER PAUW. Since 1591 this forceful merchant had been a member of the Amsterdam magistracy, but it was not until 1615 before his chance came to assume the Magnificat. His predecessors, Frans Oetgens and Barthold Cromhout, had become involved in a real estate scandal at the expense of the town, which caused their downfall. From that time on, the Calvinist Pauw became the undisputed head of Amsterdam, and his power increased as the tide turned against the Liberals.

He was now perhaps the most powerful man in Holland and one of Oldebarnevelt's most bitter enemies. This enmity was of long standing, having begun with Oldebarnevelt's successful maneuvering to deprive the Amsterdam merchants of monopoly in the East India trade. Pauw's tenure as Magnificat lasted about five years. Many of Amsterdam's magistrates had not been happy under his Calvinist regime, which leaned heavily on the raucous support of the plebeian element. When, after the execution of Oldebarnevelt, emotions cooled somewhat, opposition to Pauw increased. Gradually his support in the *Vroedschap* dwindled, and on February 1, 1621, he was relieved of the office of mayor. He was accused of nepotism, but this was only an excuse, for nepotism had been the prerogative and practice of every mayor since the office had been established.

The subsequent election brought Oetgens and Cromhout back, and this pair immediately replaced Pauw's relatives and friends with their own clique. Nor did they have any scruples about profiting on their land speculations. During their earlier tenure, they had bought tracts of land outside the walls of Amsterdam, knowing that the land would eventually be needed for contemplated expansions of the town. Abusing their high office, they made the town pay them 15 times the price to them ten years earlier.

Unwilling to be satisfied with a minor office, Pauw gradually withdrew from politics and concentrated on his business enterprises, in which he continued to prosper. In 1625 the rumor spread that he was selling butter and cheese to the enemy. Pauw offered a reward of 200 guilders for the names of those who were responsible for this slander. No one ever came forward to claim the reward. With the aid of his Calvinist followers, Pauw tried

4. Limburg, *Cultuurdragers*, 282–83.

twice to regain power, but failed both times. After the last set-back, he withdrew completely from the political scene. He died in February 1636, at the age of seventy-two.[5]

5. Elias, *Vroedschap, 1,* lx–lxxix.

Bibliography

1. *History of the Netherlands* 478
    General
    Early Dutch History
    Zuiderzee Towns
    Amsterdam
    The Reformation
    The Eighty Years' War
    The Armada
    Political Organization
    Social Conditions
    Jurisprudence

2. *Economic History of the Netherlands* 485
    General
    Fisheries
    Dutch European Trade
    Hanseatic League
    Maritime History

3. *Voyages of Trade and Discovery* 490
    Cartography
    Voyages-General
    Voyages to the North
    Voyages to the South
    Jan Huyghen van Linschoten

4. *Early History of Asia* 495
    Early Asiatic Trade
    India
    Indonesia

5. *The Portuguese Age* 497
    Spain and Portugal—General History
    The Portuguese in Africa
    The Portuguese in Asia
    The Portuguese in Japan

6. *The Dutch East India Company* 500
    General History
    Basic Reference Works
    Activities in specific areas
    The Dutch in Siam and Indo-China

The Dutch in India, Arabia and Persia
Dutch Relations with Japan and China
Jan Pieterszoon Coen
Aspects in the Netherlands
Johan van Oldebarnevelt

7. *History of England* 506
   General
   Economic History
   Anglo-Dutch Relations in Europe

8. *The English East India Company* 509
   Basic References
   Anglo-Dutch Friction in the East Indies

9. *The Mediterranean* 510

ABBREVIATIONS

BKI	Bijdragen tot de Taal-, Land- en Volkenkunde van Nederlandsch-Indië uitgegeven door het Koninklijk Instituut voor Taal-, Land- en Volkenkunde.
BMHG	Bijdragen en Mededeelingen van het Historisch Genootschap gevestigd te Utrecht.
BVGO	Bijdragen voor Vaderlandsche Geschiedenis en Oudheidkunde.
KHG	Kronijk van het Historisch Genootschap gevestigd te Utrecht.
RGP	Rijks Geschiedkundige Publicatiën.
TBG	Tijdschrift voor Indische Taal-, Land-, en Volkenkunde uitgegeven door het Koninklijk Bataviaasch Genootschap van Kunsten en Wetenschappen.
VBG	Verhandelingen van het Koninklijk Genootschap van Kunsten en Wetenschappen.
VMKA	Verslagen en Mededeelingen der Koninklijke Akademie van Wetenschappen, Afdeeling Letterkunde.
WHG	Werken van het Historisch Genootschap gevestigd te Utrecht.

1. HISTORY OF THE NETHERLANDS

GENERAL

Edmundson, George, *History of Holland*, Cambridge, Eng., 1922.
Fruin, Robert, *Verspreide Geschriften*, 10 vols. The Hague, 1900–05.

Geyl, Pieter, *Geschiedenis van de Nederlandse stam*, 3 vols., Amsterdam, Wereldbibliotheek, 1930–37.

Grimestone, Edward, *A Generall Historie of the Netherlands: with genealogie and Memorable Acts of the Earls of Holland, Zeeland and West-Friesland . . . Continued unto 1608*, London, 1608.

Hooft, Pieter C., *Nederlandsche historien*, Amsterdam, 1656.

Huizinga, Johan, *Tien studien*, Haarlem, 1926.

Wagenaar, Jan, *Vaderlandsche historie*, 21 vols. Amsterdam, 1749–59.

EARLY DUTCH HISTORY TO THE SIXTEENTH CENTURY

Boeles, P., *Friesland tot de elfde eeuw*, The Hague, 1951.

Eeckhoff, Wopke, *Beknopte geschiedenis van Friesland*, Leeuwarden, 1851.

Eikelenberg, Simon, *Gedaante en gesteldheid van Westvriesland voor 1300*, Alkmaar, 1714.

Emo en Menko, Kronijken van, H. O. Feith and G. Acker Stratingh, eds., Utrecht, 1866.

Epkema, Ecco, ed., *Die Olde Freesche Cronike*, Workum, 1853.

Giffen, Albert E. van, *De Hunnebedden in Nederland*, 2 vols. Utrecht, 1925–27.

Holwerda, Jan H., *Dorestad en onze vroegste middeleeuwen*, Leiden, 1929.

———, *Nederland's vroegste geschiedenis*, Amsterdam, 1925.

Loos, J. C. D. van der, *Geschiedenis van Amstelland tot 1300*, Amsterdam, 1907.

Obreen, Henri, *Floris V, Graaf van Holland en Zeeland, Heer van Friesland, 1256–96*, Ghent, 1907.

Paludanus, Ruthgerus, *Oudheid en natuurkundige verhandelingen, betreffende Westvriesland en het Noorderkwartier*, Leiden, 1776.

Reygersbergh, J. van, *De Oude Chronycke ende historien van Zeelandt*, Middelburg, 1634.

Scharlensis, Ockam, *Croniicke en warachtige beschryvinghe van Vrieslant: Beginnende nae des werelts scheppinghe tot 1565*, Leeuwarden, 1742.

Unger, Willem S., ed., *Bronnen tot de geschiedenis van Middelburg, 1294–1574*, 3 vols. The Hague, 1923–31.

Veen, Johan van, *Dredge, Drain, Reclaim: the Art of a Nation*, The Hague, Martinus Nijhoff, 1948.

Winsemius, P., *Chronique ofte historische geschiedenisse van Vrieslant, beginnende van den jaere nae des werelts scheppinghe tot 1622*, Franeker, 1622.

Witkamp, Pieter H., *Geschiedenis der Zeventien Nederlanden*, 3 vols. Arnhem and Nijmegen, 1885.

ZUIDERZEE TOWNS

Abbing, Cornelis A., *Geschiedenis van Hoorn of Vervolg van Velius' Chronyck, 1630–1773*, 2 vols. Hoorn, 1841–42.
Allan, Francis, *De Stad Enkhuizen en hare geschiedenis*, Schager-burg, 1856.
Brandt, Geraert, *Historie van Enkhuizen*, Enkhuizen, 1666.
Heeringa, K., *Het oude Staveren*, Groningen, 1893.
Kerkmeijer, Johan C., *De Historische schoonheid van Hoorn*, Amsterdam, Allert de Lange, 1946.
Koster, Pieter, *Hoorn in de Middeleeuwen*, Amsterdam, H. J. Paris, 1929.
Kroon, H. Dz., and F. Kapteyn, *Nieuwe Kroniek van Hoorn*, Hoorn, 1891.
Rijp, Fryken, *Chronijk van de vermaarde zee en koopstad Hoorn, tot 1706*, Hoorn, 1706.
Soet, Hendrik, *Op en nedergank van de oude anzeestadt Stavoren. Outs tijds hoofd en moederstad der friesen*, Haarlem, 1647.
Velius, Theodorus, *Chronyck van Hoorn*, (*augumented by S. Centen*), Hoorn, 1740.

AMSTERDAM

Barbour, Violet, *Capitalism in Amsterdam in the Seventeenth Century*, Baltimore, Johns Hopkins Press, 1950.
Bloom, Herbert I., *The Economic Activities of the Jews of Amsterdam in the Seventeenth and Eighteenth Centuries*, Williamsport, Pa., 1937.
Breedvelt-van Veen, F., *Louis de Geer, 1587–1652*, Amsterdam, 1935.
Brugmans, Hajo, *Amsterdam in de gouden eeuw*, 2 vols. Amsterdam, 1938.
———, *Geschiedenis van Amsterdam van den oorsprong af tot heden*, 8 vols. Amsterdam, 1930–33.
———, *Handel en Nijverheid van Amsterdam in de 17e eeuw*, The Hague, 1904.
———, *Opkomst en bloei van Amsterdam*, Amsterdam, J. M. Meulenhoff, 1944.
Bunk, W., *Staathuishoudkundige geschiedenis van den Amster-damschen Graanhandel*, Amsterdam, 1856.
D'Ailly, Antoine, ed., *Zeven eeuwen Amsterdam*, 6 vols. Amsterdam, 1942–50.
Dessing, Ch. S., "De Amsterdamsche schoolkeuren uit de 15e eeuw," *Amstelodanum, 36* (1939), 23–38.

Dillen, Johan G. van, *Amsterdam in 1585, het kohier der capitale impositie van 1585*, Amsterdam, 1941.
————, *Bronnen tot de geschiedenis van het bedrijfsleven en het gildewezen van Amsterdam, 1512–1611*, The Hague, 1929.
Dubiez, F. J., "Cornelis Antoniszoon," *Ons Amsterdam, 12* (1959), 354–66.
Elias, Johan E., *De Vroedschap van Amsterdam, 1578–1695*, 2 vols. Haarlem, V. Loosjes, 1903–05.
————, *Geschiedenis van het Amsterdamsche regenten patriciaat*, The Hague, 1923.
Gouw, Johannes ter, *Geschiedenis van Amsterdam tot 1578*, 8 vols. Amsterdam, 1879–93.
Hofdijk, Willem J., *Amsterdams opstanding, 26 Mei, 1578*, Amsterdam, 1878.
'tHooft, C. G., "De Stelle of Reede in het Y, als verklaring van den naamsoorsprong van 'Ame Stelle Damme,'" *Amstelodanum, 32* (1935), 1–34.
Ketner, F., *Handel en scheepvaart van Amsterdam in de zeventiende eeuw*, Leiden, 1946.
Kok, A. A., *De Historische schoonheid van Amsterdam*, Amsterdam, Allert de Lange, 1947.
le Long, Isaak, *De Koophandel van Amsterdam en andere Nederlandsche steden*, 4 vols. Amsterdam, 1801–02.
Mens, Jan, *Amsterdam, paradijs der herinnering*, Amsterdam, Kosmos, 1947.
Oldewelt, Willem F. H., "De Oorsprong van het College van Burgemeesteren te Amsterdam," *Amstelodanum, 36* (1939), 15–21.
————, "Topographische bijzonderheden betreffende Amstelland en Amsterdam in de Middeleeuwen," *Amstelodanum, 36* (1939), 1–14.
Posthumus, Nicolaas W., *Het Oudst bewaarde Amsterdamsche koopmans boek*, Amsterdam, 1947.
Ravesteyn, Willem van, *Economische en Sociale ontwikkeling van Amsterdam gedurende de 16de en het eerste kwart der 17de eeuw*, Amsterdam, 1906.
Roever, N. de, *Uit onze Amstelstad*, 4 vols. Amsterdam, 1890–93.
Smit, Homme J., *De Opkomst van den handel van Amsterdam, tot 1441*, Amsterdam, 1914.
Wagenaar, Jan, *Amsterdam, in zyne opkomst, aanwas, geschiedenissen, voorrechten, koophandel, enz.*, 4 vols. Amsterdam, 1760–88.
Westermann, J. C., "Statistische gegevens over den handel van Amsterdam in de zeventiende eeuw," *Tijdschrift voor Geschiedenis 61* (1948), 3–15.

Wolf, M., *De eerste vestiging der joden te Amsterdam, hun politieke en economische toestand, BVGO,* 4th series, *10* (1912), 134–82; 5th series, *1* (1913), 88–101.

THE REFORMATION

Fanfani, A., *Catholicism, Protestantism, and Capitalism,* New York, 1936.

Hyma, Albert, "Calvinism and Capitalism in the Netherlands, 1555–1700," *The Journal of Modern History, 10,* no. 3 (1938), 321–43.

Naber, Jean C., *Calvinist of Libertijnsch? 1572–1631,* Utrecht, 1884.

Rachfahl, F., "Kalvinismus und Kapitalismus," *Internationale Wochenschrift, 3* (1909), 1217–1366.

Schelven, Aart A., *Het Calvinisme gedurende zijn bloeitijd,* Amsterdam, 1943.

Smith, Preserved, *The Age of Reformation,* New York, 1920.

Tawney, Richard H., *Religion and the Rise of Capitalism,* New York, Harcourt Brace, 1937.

Weber, Max, *The Protestant Ethic and the Spirit of Capitalism,* trans. Talcott Parsons, New York, Scribner's, 1958.

Winkelman, Petrus H., *Remonstranten en katholieken in de eeuw van Hugo de Groot,* Nijmegen, 1945.

THE EIGHTY YEARS' WAR

Aitzema, Liewe, *Saken van Staet en Oorlogh in en omtrent de Vereenigde Nederlanden,* 7 vols. The Hague, 1669–72.

Bax, J., *Prins Maurits in de volksmeening der 16de en 17de eeuw,* Amsterdam, 1940.

Beeloo, Adrianus, *Noord-Holland en de Noord-Hollanders in de vrijheidsoorlog tegen Spanje,* Haarlem, 1852.

Bets, Petrus V., *De Pacificatie of bevrediging van Gent, in hare wording, wezen, voorstanders en verdrukkers,* Thienen, 1876.

Blok, Petrus J., *Frederik Hendrik, Prins van Oranje,* Amsterdam, 1924.

——, *Geschiedenis van het Nederlandsche volk, 3, 4,* 8 vols. Groningen, 1896, 1899.

——, *History of the People of the Netherlands, 3,* trans. R. Putnam, 5 vols. New York and London, 1900.

——, *Willem I, Prins van Oranje,* 2 vols. Amsterdam, 1919–20.

Bor, Pieter, *Oorsprongk, begin en vervolgh der Nederlandsche oorlogen, 1555–1600,* 4 vols. Amsterdam, 1679–84.

Brouwer, Johan, *Kronieken van Spaansche soldaten uit het begin van den tachtigjarigen oorlog,* Zutphen, 1933.

Brünner, E. C. G., "Die dänische Verkehrsperre und der Bildersturm in den Niederlanden im Jahre 1566," *Hansische Geschichtsblätter, 53* (1928), 97–109.

Commelin, Izaak, *Wilhelm en Maurits van Nassauw, Prince van Orangien,* Amsterdam, 1651.

Delfos, L., *Die Anfänge der Utrechter Union, 1577–1587,* Berlin, 1941.

Essen, Leon van der, *Alexandre Farnese,* 5 vols. Brussels, 1937.

Fruin, Robert, *De Tachtigjarige oorlog,* 6 vols. The Hague, 1909.

———, *Het Voorspel van den tachtigjarigen oorlog,* The Hague, 1939.

———, *The Siege and Relief of Leyden in 1574,* trans. E. Trevelyan, The Hague, 1927.

———, *Tien jaren uit den tachtigjarigen oorlog, 1588–1598,* The Hague, 1899.

Gelder, H. A. Enno van, "De Scheiding van de noordelijke en zuidelijke Nederlanden in de 16de eeuw," *BVGO,* 7th series, *10* (1939), 145–58.

Geyl, Pieter, *The Netherlands Divided, 1609–48,* trans. S. T. Bindoff, London, Williams & Norgate, 1936.

Harrison, Frederic, *William the Silent,* London, 1897.

Heijnsbergen, P. van, *De Pijnbank in de Nederlanden,* Groningen, 1925.

Lohman, B. C. de Savornin, ed., *Prins Willem van Oranje,* Haarlem, 1933.

Meteren, Emanuel van, *Historie der Nederlanden en haerder nabueren oorlogen . . . tot 1612,* The Hague, 1623.

Motley, John L., *History of the United Netherlands, from the Death of William the Silent to the Twelve Years' Truce, 1609,* 4 vols. London, 1876.

———, *The Rise of the Dutch Republic,* 3 vols. London, 1856.

Reyd, Everhard van, *Oorspronk ende voortganck vande Nederlandsche oorloghen . . . 1566–1601,* Arnhem, 1633.

Schaper, P. W., et al., *De Tagtigjarige oorlog,* Amsterdam, 1941.

Stirling-Maxwell, William, *Antwerp Delivered in 1576,* Edinburgh, 1878.

Romein, Jan, et al., eds., *De Tachtigjarige oorlog,* Amsterdam, 1942.

Vloten, Johannes van, *Nederlands opstand tegen Spanje in zijn eerste ontwikkeling en voortgang, 1557–77,* 4 vols. Haarlem, 1856–60.

Vrankrijker, Adrianus C. J. de, *De Motiveering van onzen opstand, 1565–81,* Nijmegen, 1933.

Wijn, J. W., *Het beleg van Haarlem,* Amsterdam, 1942.

————, *Het krijgswezen in den tijd van Prins Maurits*, Utrecht, 1934.

THE ARMADA

Brouwer, J., *De Onoverwinnelijke vloot, naar berichten van opvarende en tijdgenoten*, Amsterdam, Van Kampen, 1944.
Laughton, John K., *The Defeat of the Spanish Armada*, 2 vols. London, Navy Records Society, 1894.
Mattingly, Garrett, *The Armada*, Boston, Houghton Mifflin, 1959.
Oria, E. H., *La Armada Invencible*, Valladolid, 1929.
Overeem, J. B. van, "Justinus van Nassau en de Armada, 1588," *Marineblad*, 53 (1938), 821–31.
Tideman, Jan, *De Ondergang van de onoverwinnelijke vloot in 1588*, The Hague, 1888.
Williamson, James A., *Hawkins of Plymouth*, New York, 1949.
————, *The Age of Drake*, London, 1938.

DUTCH POLITICAL ORGANIZATION

Fouw, A. de, *Onbekende Raadspensionarissen*, The Hague, Daamen, 1946.
Fruin, Robert, *Geschiedenis der Staatsinstellingen in Nederland, tot den val der Republiek*, The Hague, 1901.
Groot Placcaetboek van de Staten-Generaal en van de Staten van Holland en Zeeland, 1576–1795, 10 vols. Amsterdam and The Hague, 1638–1801.
Japikse, N., et al., eds., *Resolutien der Staten-Generaal van 1576–1609*, 12 vols. The Hague, 1915–50.
Rees, Otto van, *Geschiedenis der staathuishoudkunde in Nederland tot het einde der 18de eeuw*, 2 vols. Utrecht, 1865–68.

SOCIAL CONDITIONS

Francken, A. W., *Het Leven onzer voorouders in de Gouden Eeuw*, The Hague, Stols, 1942.
Huet, C. Busken, *Het Land van Rembrand, Studien over de Noord-Nederlandsche beschaving in de 17de eeuw*, 2 vols. Haarlem, 1886.
Huizinga, Johan, *Nederlands beschaving in de 17de eeuw*, Haarlem, 1941.
Schotel, Gilles D. J., *Het Maatschappelijk leven onzer vaderen in de 17de eeuw*, Haarlem, 1869.
Vrankrijker, Andrianus C. J. de, *Het Maatschappelijk leven in Nederland in de Gouden Eeuw*, Amsterdam, Van Kampen, 1937.

JURISPRUDENCE

(Anon.), "Verhooren en andere bescheiden betreffende het rechtsgeding van Hugo de Groot," *WHG*, new series, *14* (1871), 1–368.

Böhm, A. H., *Het Recht van kolonisatie*, Utrecht, 1936.

Brandt, Gaspar and A. van Cattenburgh, *Historie van het leven des Heeren Huig de Groot*, 2 vols. Dordrecht, 1727.

Duval, J. J. Th., *Het Recht verstand der Unie van Utrecht, met betrekking tot de stadhouders van Holland en Zeeland*, Utrecht, 1790.

Goudsmit, M. Th., *Geschiedenis van het Nederlandsche Zeerecht*, The Hague, 1882.

Groot, Willem de, *Broeders gevangnisse: Dagboek betreffende het verblijf van Hugo de Groot op Loevensteyn*, (*augmented by H. Vollenhoven*), The Hague, 1842.

Grotius, Hugo, *Mare Liberum: Of the Freedom of the Seas*, ed. J. B. Scott, Washington, 1916.

Hallema, A., *Hugo de Groot, het Delftsch orakel, 1583–1645*, The Hague, 1946.

Higgins, Alexander P., "International Law and the Outer World (1450–1648)," in J. Holland Rose, et al., eds., *The Cambridge History of the British Empire*, *1*, 8 vols. Cambridge, Cambridge University Press, 1929, 183–206.

Holdsworth, William S., *A History of English Law*, 12 vols. London, Methuen, 1922–38.

Hoogenberk, Hendrik, *De Rechtsvoorschriften voor de vaart op Oost-Indië, 1599–1620*, Utrecht, 1940.

Kan, Joseph van, *De Rechtstitels der Compagnie*, Amsterdam, 1942.

Kist, J. G., *Beginselen van het handelsrecht volgens de Nederlandsche wet*, The Hague, 1907.

Oordt, Johannes van, *De Privaatrechtelijke toestand van den Nederlandschen koopman in de landen van den Islam*, Leiden, 1899.

Stapel, Frederik W., "Bijdragen tot de geschiedenis der rechtspraak bij de Vereenigde Oost-Indische Compagnie," *BKI*, *89* (1932), 297–313; *90* (1933), 89–139.

2. ECONOMIC HISTORY OF THE NETHERLANDS

GENERAL

Baasch, Ernest, *Holländische Wirtschaftsgeschichte*, Jena, 1927.

Barker, J. Ellis, *The Rise and Decline of the Netherlands: A*

Political and Economic History and a Study in Practical States-manship, London, 1906.

Berg, Willem E. J., *De Refugies in de Nederlanden na de herroe-ping van het Edict van Nantes*, Amsterdam, 1845.

Boorsma, P., *Duizend Zaanse molens*, Wormerveer, 1950.

Brakel, Simon van, *De Hollandsche Handels–compagnieen der Zeventiende Eeuw*, The Hague, Martinus Nijhoff, 1908.

Court, Pieter de la, *Interest van Holland ofte Gronden van Hollands Welvaren*, Amsterdam, 1662.

Davies, D. W., *A Primer of Dutch Seventeenth Century Overseas Trade*, The Hague, Martinus Nijhoff, 1961.

Diferee, Hendrik C., *De Geschiedenis van den Nederlandschen Handel*, 3 vols. Amsterdam, 1905–08.

Dillen, Johan G. van, *Bronnen tot de Geschiedenis der Wissel-banken*, The Hague, RGP, 1925.

——, "De Economische Ontwikkeling van Nederland," in J. S. Barstra and W. Banning, eds., *Nederland tusschen de Na-tien*, Amsterdam, Ploegsma, 1948.

——, "Honderd Jaar Economische Ontwikkeling van het Noor-den," in J. A. van Houtte et al., eds., *Algemeene Geschiedenis der Nederlanden*, 7, 8 vols. Utrecht, De Haan, 1954.

Gelder, Hendrik E. van, "Zestiende-eeuwsche koopmansbrieven," *Economisch-Historisch Jaarboek*, 5 (1919), 136–191.

Huet, Pierre D., *Mémoires sur le commerce des Hollandais dans tous les états et empires du monde*, Amsterdam, 1717.

Jameson, J. F., "Willem Usselinx," *Papers of the American Histori-cal Association*, 2, no. 3, New York, 1887.

Kooy, Tjalling P. van der, *Hollands Stapelmarkt en haar verval*, Amsterdam, 1931.

Laspeyres, E., *Geschichte der volkswirtschaftlichen Anschauungen der Niederländer zur Zeit der Republik*, Leipzig, 1863.

Luzac, Elie, *Hollands rijkdom*, 4 vols. Leiden, 1780–83.

Niermyer, Jan F., *De Wording van onze volkshuishouding: hoofd-lijnen uit de economische geschiedenis der Noordelijke Neder-landen in de middeleeuwen*, The Hague, 1946.

Posthumus, Nicolaas W., *Documenten betreffende de Buiten-landsche handelspolitiek*, 6 vols. The Hague, Martinus Nijhoff, 1919–31.

Pringsheim, Otto, "Beiträge zur wirtschaftlichen Entwickelungs-geschichte der Vereinigten Niederlande im 17en Jahrhundert," *Staats und Sozialwissenschaftliche Forschungen*, 10, book 3 (1890), 1–126.

Schelven, Aart A. van, *Omvang en invloed der zuid-nederland-sche emigratie van het laatste kwart der 16de eeuw*, The Hague, 1919.

Sérionne, Joseph, A. de, *The Wealth of Holland*, London, 1778.

Smit, Homme J., *Bronnen tot de geschiedenis van den handel met Engeland, Schotland, en Ierland, 1150–1485*, 2 vols. The Hague, RGP, 1928.

——, "Handel en scheepvaart in het Noordzeegebied gedurende de 13de eeuw," *BVGO*, 6th series, 7 (1928), 161–204.

Soeteboom, Hendrik, *Zaanlants Arcadia*, Amsterdam, 1658.

Stoppelaar, Johannes H. de, *Balthasar de Moucheron: Een bladzijde uit de nederlandsche handelsgeschiedenis tijdens den tachtigjarigen oorlog*, The Hague, 1901.

Verkade, Margaretha A., *De Opkomst van de Zaanstreek*, Utrecht, De Vroede, 1952.

Vliegen, W. H., *Het Kapitalisme in Nederland*, Rotterdam, 1906.

FISHERIES

Beaujon, Anthony A., *Overzicht der geschiedenis van de Nederlandsche zeevisscherijen*, Leiden, 1885.

Elder, J. R., *The Royal Fishery Companies of the Seventeenth Century*, Glasgow, 1912.

Gelder, Hendrik E. van, "Gegevens betreffende de Haringvisscherij op het einde der 16de eeuw," *BMHG*, 32 (1911), 1–62.

Hoogendijk, A. Jzn., *De Grootvisscherij op de Noordzee*, Haarlem, 1895.

Jenkins, J. T., *The Herring and the Herring Fisheries*, London, 1927.

Jong, D. de, et al., *Nieuwe Beschrijving der Walvischvangst en Haringvisscherij*, Amsterdam, 1791.

Kranenburg, H. A. H., *De Zeevisscherij van Holland in den tijd der republiek*, Amsterdam, H. J. Paris, 1946.

Semeyns, M., *Een korte beschryving van de haringvisscherye in Hollandt*, Amsterdam, 1640.

Tillema, Johan E., "Ontwikkeling van de Nederlandsche haringvisscherij in den loop der eeuwen," *Nederlandsche Zeewezen*, 15 (1916), 330–76; 16 (1917), 3–88.

DUTCH EUROPEAN TRADE

Bang, Nina E. and Knud Korst, eds., *Tabeller over skipsfart og varetransport gennem Oresund, 1497–1660*, 2 vols. Copenhagen, 1906–1933.

Barbour, Violet, "Dutch and English Merchant Shipping in the Seventeenth Century," *Economic History Review*, 1st series, 2 (1929–30), 261–90.

Becht, Harold E., *Statistische gegevens betreffende den handelsomzet van de republiek der Vereenigde Nederlanden gedurende de 17de eeuw, 1579–1715*, The Hague, 1908.

Blok, Petrus J., "De Handel op Spanje en het begin der groote vaart," *BVGO*, 5th series, *1* (1913), 102–20.

Bijlsma, R., "De Opkomst van de Rotterdamsche koopvaardij," *BVGO*, 5th series, *1* (1913), 56–87.

———, *Rotterdams welvaren, 1550–1650*, The Hague, 1918.

Cate, I. B. ten, *Geschiedenis van Nederlands Zeevaart en Handel*, Amsterdam, 1836.

Christensen, Aksel E., *Dutch Trade to the Baltic about 1600: Studies in the Sound Toll Register and Dutch Shipping Records*, The Hague, 1941.

Gelder, Hendrik E. van, "Zestiende-eeuwsche vracht-vaart-bescheiden," *Economisch Historisch Jaarboek, 3* (1917), 124–290.

Hoeven, F. P. van der, *Bijdrage tot de geschiedenis van den Sonttol*, Leiden, 1855.

Jansma, Taeke S., "Olivier Brunel te Dordrecht: De Noord-Oostelijke doorvaart en het West-Europeesch-Russische contact in de 16de eeuw," *Tijdschrift voor Geschiedenis, 59* (1946), 337–62.

Kernkamp, Johannes H., *De Handel op den vijand, 1572–1609*, 2 vols. Utrecht, Kemink, 1931.

Rooij, Evert W. de, *Geschiedenis van den Nederlandschen handel*, Amsterdam, 1856.

Snapper, F., *Oorlogsinvloeden op de overzeese handel van Holland, 1551–1719*, Amsterdam, Ellerman Harms, 1959.

Sneller, Z. W., "De Drie cargasoenen rogge van Daniel van der Meulen, anno 1592, en hunne verzekering," *Amstelodanum, 32* (1935), 89–118.

——— and Willem S. Unger, *Bronnen tot de geschiedenis van den handel met Frankrijk, 753–1585*, The Hague, RGP, 1930.

Unger, Willem S., "De Hollandsche graanhandel en graanhandelpolitiek in de Middeleeuwen," *De Economist* (1916), 243–69, 337–86, 461–86.

———, "De Publikatie der Sonttoltabellen voltooid," *Tijdschrift voor Geschiedenis, 71* (1958), 147–205.

Verviers, Emile, *De Nederlandsche Handelspolitiek, tot aan de toepassing der vrijhandelsbeginselen*, Leiden, Futura, 1914.

Vrankrijker, Adrianus C. J. de, "De Nederlanders in Oostzee en Middellandsche Zee," in C. W. Wormser, ed. *Nederland in de vijf werelddeelen*, Leiden, Burgersdijk & Niermans, 1947.

IJzerman, J. W., "Amsterdamsche bevrachtingscontracten, 1591–1602: De vaart op Spanje en Portugal," *Economisch Historisch Jaarboek, 17* (1931), 163–291.

Zuiden, D. S. van, *De Hollandsch-Russische relaties in de 16de–18de eeuw*, Amsterdam, 1911.

HANSEATIC LEAGUE

Berg, F. E., *De Nederlanden en het Hanseverbond, 1241–1587*, Utrecht, 1833.

Häpke, Rudolf, "Der Untergang der Hansischen Vormachtstellung in der Ostsee, 1531–1544," *Hansische Geschichtsblätter*, *18* (1912), 85–119.

———, *Niederländische Akten und Urkunden zur Geschichte der Hanse und zur deutschen Seegeschichte*, 2 vols. 1913–23.

Hülshof, A., "Rostock und die nordlichen Niederlande vom 15. bis zum 17. Jahrhundert," *Hansische Geschichtsblätter*, *16* (1910), 531–53.

Vogel, W., "Handelskonjunkturen und Wirtschaftskrisen in ihrer Auswirkung auf den Seehandel der Hansestädte, 1560–1806," *Hansische Geschichtsblätter*, 74 (1956), 50–64.

Vollbehr, Friedel, *Die Holländer und die deutsche Hanse*, Lübeck, 1930.

Warnsinck, J. C. M., *De Zeeoorlog van Holland en Zeeland tegen de Wendische steden der Duitsche Hanze, 1438–1441*, The Hague, 1939.

MARITIME HISTORY

Andel M. A. van, *Chirurgijns, vrije meesters, beunhazen, en kwakzalvers, 1400–1800*, Amsterdam, Van Kampen, 1947.

Bijl, A. Mz., *De Nederlandsche convooidienst*, The Hague, 1951.

Crone, G. C. E., *Onze Schepen in de Gouden Eeuw*, Amsterdam, 1943.

Elias, Johan E., *De Vlootbouw in Nederland in de eerste helft der 17de eeuw*, Amsterdam, 1933.

———, *Schetsen uit de Geschiedenis van ons Zeewezen*, 6 vols. The Hague, 1916–30.

Hullu, J. de, "Voeding op de schepen der Oost-Indische Compagnie," *BKI*, 67 (1913), 541–62.

———, "Zeelieden en soldaten op de schepen der Oost-Indische Compagnie," *BKI*, 69 (1914), 318–65.

———, "Ziekte en doctors op de schepen der Oost-Indische Compagnie," *BKI*, 67 (1913), 245–72.

Jonge, Johannes C. de, *De Geschiedenis van het Nederlandsche zeewezen*, 6 vols. Haarlem, 1858–62.

Kampen, S. C. van, *De Rotterdamsche particuliere scheepsbouw in de tijd van de Republiek*, Assen, Born, 1953.

Mollema, J. C., *Geschiedenis van Nederland ter zee*, 4 vols. Amsterdam, 1939–42.

Witsen, N., *Aeloude en hedendaegse scheepsbouw en bestier*, Amsterdam, 1671.

3. VOYAGES OF TRADE AND DISCOVERY

CARTOGRAPHY

Keuning, Johannes, *Petrus Plancius: Theoloog en Geograaf, 1552–1622*, Amsterdam, Van Kampen, 1946.
Ravenstein, E. G. and C. F. Close, "History of Cartography," in *The Encyclopaedia Brittannica*, 14th. ed., *14*, 836–45.
Stevenson, Edward L., *Portolan Charts*, New York, 1911.
Wauwermans, Henri E., *Histoire de l'École cartographique belge et anversoise du 16ième Siècle*, 2 vols. Brussels, 1895.

VOYAGES: GENERAL

Balen, Willem J. van, *Nederlands Voorhoede*, Amsterdam, Amsterdamsche Boek en Courant Mij., 1941.
Boer, M. G. de, *Van oude voyagien*, Amsterdam, 1923.
Bonaparte, Prince Roland, *Premiers Voyages des Néerlandais*, Versailles, 1884.
Davis, J., *Voyages and Works of John Davis, the Navigator*, Albert H. Markham, ed., London, 1880.
Hakluyt, Richard, *Principal Navigations, Voyages, Traffiques and Discoveries of the English Nation*, M. Michon and E. Carmont, eds., 12 vols. Glasgow, 1903–05.
Hart, Henry R., *Sea Road to the Indies*, New York, 1950.
Loon, Hendrik van, *Dutch Navigators*, New York, 1916.
Payne, Edward J., *Voyages of Elizabethan Seamen to America*, C. R. Beazley, ed., Oxford, 1907.
Penrose, Boies, *Travel and Discovery in the Renaissance*, Cambridge, Mass., 1952.
Purchas, Samuel, *Hakluytus Posthumus, or Purchas his Pilgrimes, contayning a history of the world in Sea-Voyages and Lande Travels by Englishmen and others*, M. Michon, ed., 20 vols. Glasgow, 1905–07.
Saint-Martin, Vivien de, *Histoire de la Géographie et des Découvertes Géographiques*, Paris, 1873.
Southey, Robert, *English Seamen: Howard, Clifford, Hawkins, Drake, Cavendish*, London, 1895.
Stefansson, Vilhjalmur, *Great Adventures and Explorations*, New York, Dial Press, 1947.
Tiele, Pieter A., *Mémoire Bibliographique sur les Journaux des Navigateurs Neerlandais*, Amsterdam, 1867.
———, *Nederlandsche Bibliographie van Land- en Volkenkunde*, Amsterdam, 1884.

Tresoor der zee– en landreizen: Beredeneerd register op de werken der Linschoten Vereeniging, D. Sepp, C.G.M. van Romburgh, and C. E. Warnsinck-Delprat, eds., 2 vols. The Hague, 1939–57.

VOYAGES TO THE NORTH

Asher, G. M., ed., *Henry Hudson, the Navigator*, Hakluyt Society, 1st series, *27*, London, 1860.

Bacon, Edgar M., *Henry Hudson: His Times and His Voyages*, New York, 1907.

Bezemer, K. W. L., "Ter zee en te land in het hooge Noorden," in C. W. Wormser, ed., *Nederland in de vijf werelddeelen*, Leiden, Burgersdijk & Niermans, 1947.

Burger, C. P., *De Poolzee-reizen van 1595–96*, The Hague, 1921.

Conway, M. W., ed., *Early Dutch and Spanish Voyages to Spitzbergen in the Seventeenth Century*, Hakluyt Society, 2d series, *11*, London, 1904.

Dubiez, F. J., "De Ontdekkingsreis van Henri Hudson," *Ons Amsterdam, 4* (1959), 98–108.

Harrissé, Henry, *John and Sebastian Cabot*, London, 1896.

Muller, Fzn. S., *De Reis van Jan Cornelisz. May*, Linschoten Vereeniging, *1*, The Hague, 1909.

Murphy, Henry C., *Henry Hudson in Holland: An inquiry into the origin and objects of the voyage which led to the discovery of the Hudson River*, Linschoten Vereeniging, *1a*, The Hague, 1909.

Naber, S. P. L'Honoré, ed., *Henry Hudson's Reize: Onder Nederlandsche vlag van Amsterdam naar Nova Zembla, Amerika en terug naar Dartmouth in Engeland*, Linschoten Vereeniging, vol. *19*, The Hague, 1921.

Nunn, George E., *The La Cosa Map and the Cabot Voyages*, Jenkintown, Pa., 1946.

———, *The Origin of the Strait Anian Concept*, Philadelphia, 1929.

Quinn, D. B., ed., *The Voyages and Colonising Enterprises of Sir Humphrey Gilbert*, 2 vols. Hakluyt Society, 2d series, *83, 84*, 1940.

Rundall, T., *Narratives of Voyages towards the North-West in search of a Passage to Cathay and India from 1496–1631*, Hakluyt Society, 1st series, *5*, London, 1849.

Veer, Gerrit de, *Reizen van Willem Barents, Jacob van Heemskerck, Jan Cornelisz. Rijp en anderen naar het Noorden*, S. P. L'Honoré Naber, ed., Linschoten Vereeniging, *14, 15*, 2 vols. The Hague, 1917.

——, *Willem Barents: Three Voyages to the Arctic Regions, 1594–96.* Hakluyt Society, 1st series, *54*, London, 1876.

Wieder, F. C., *The Dutch Discovery and Mapping of Spitsbergen, 1596–1829*, The Hague, 1919.

VOYAGES TO THE SOUTH

Castro e Almeida, Virginia de, *Discoveries of Henry the Navigator*, London, 1906.

De Eerste Schipvaart der Nederlanders naar Oost-Indië onder Cornelis de Houtman (1595–97), G. P. Rouffaer and J. W. IJzerman, eds., 3 vols. The Hague, 1915–29.

Dijk, L. C. D. van, *Twee Tochten naar de Golf van Carpentaria*, Amsterdam, 1859.

Engelbrecht, Willem A. and Pieter J. Herwerden, eds., *De Ontdekkingsreis van Jacob Le Maire en Willem Cornelisz. Schouten in de jaren 1615–1617*, 2 vols. The Hague, 1945.

Foster, William, ed., *Nicholas Downton: Voyage to the East Indies, 1614–15*, Hakluyt Society, 2d series, *82*, London, 1939.

——, *Sir Henry Middleton: Voyage to the Moluccas, 1604–06*, Hakluyt Society, 2d series, *88*, London, 1943.

——, *Sir James Lancaster: Voyages to Brazil and the East Indies, 1591–1603*, Hakluyt Society, 2d series, *85*, London, 1940.

——, *Thomas Best: Voyage to the East Indies, 1612–14*, Hakluyt Society, 2d series, *75*, London, 1934.

Geyl, Pieter, ed., *Willem Ysbrantsz. Bontekoe: Memorable Description of the East Indian Voyage, 1618–25*, London, Routledge, 1929.

Gottfried, Johan L., *De Aanmerkenswaardigste en alomberoemde Zee- en Landreizen der Portugeezen*, Leiden, 1727.

Greenlee, W. B., ed., *P. A. Cabral: Voyage to Brazil and India*, Hakluyt Society, 2d series, *81*, London, 1938.

Guibon, A., *Sur les traces des Dieppois à Sumatra, 1529–34*, Dieppe, 1936.

Guillemard, F. H. H., *Life of Ferdinand Magellan*, New York, 1890.

Heeres, Jan E., *The Part Borne by the Dutch in the Discovery of Australia, 1606–1765*, Leiden and London, 1899.

Hildebrand, Arthur S., *Ferdinand Magellan*, New York, 1924.

Hoogewerff, G. J., ed., *Journalen van de gedenckwaerdige reijsen van Willem Ysbrantsz. Bontekoe, 1618–1625*, Linschoten Vereeniging, *54*, The Hague, 1952.

Keeling, William, "Voyage of William Keeling, 1607," in *Purchas his Pilgrimes*, 2, Glasgow, 1905, 502–49.

Keuning, Johannes, ed., *De Tweede Schipvaart der Nederlanders naar Oost-Indië onder Jacob Cornelisz. van Neck en Wybrant Warwijck, 1598–1600,* 5 vols. The Hague, 1938–51.

Kuiper, E. T., "Schouten en le Maire," *Tijdschrift voor Geschiedenis,* 35 (1920), 151–79.

Markham, Clements R., *Early Spanish Voyages to the Straits of Magellan,* London, 1911.

———, *Voyages of Sir James Lancaster to the East Indies,* London, 1877.

Middleton, David, "Voyage of David Middleton, 1609," in R. Kerr, ed., *A General History and Collection of Voyages and Travels, 8,* Edinburgh, 1813.

Moll, Gerrit, *Over Eenige vroegere zeetochten der Nederlanders,* Amsterdam, 1825.

Mollema, J. C., *De Eerste Schipvaart der Hollanders naar Oost-Indië,* The Hague, 1935.

———, *De Reis om de wereld van Olivier van Noort, 1598–1601,* Amsterdam, 1937.

Moreland, William H., ed., *Peter Floris: Voyage to the East Indies in the 'Globe,' 1611–15,* Hakluyt Society, 2d series, 74, London, 1934.

Morison, Samuel E., *Admiral of the Ocean Sea,* Boston, 1942.

———, *Portuguese Voyages to America in the Fifteenth Century,* Cambridge, Mass., 1940.

Nunn, George E., *The Columbus and Magellan Concepts of South America,* Glenside, 1932.

Nuttall, Zelia, ed., *New Light on Drake: A Collection of Documents relating to his Voyage of Circumnavigation, 1577–80,* Hakluyt Society, 2d series, 34, London, 1914.

Parr, Charles M., *Magellan: So Noble a Captain: The Life and Voyages of Ferdinand Magellan,* London, 1955.

Ravenstein, Ernest G., ed. and trans., *A Journal of the First Voyage of Vasco da Gama,* London, 1898.

Satow, E. M., *The Voyage of Captain John Saris to Japan, 1613,* Hakluyt Society, 2d series, 5, London, 1900.

Spilbergen, Joris van, *De Reis van Joris van Spilbergen naar Ceylon, Atjeh en Bantam, 1601–04,* The Hague, 1933.

Stanley, Henry E. J., *Three Voyages of Vasco da Gama,* Hakluyt Society, 1st series, 42, London, 1869.

Stevens, H. N., ed., *New Light on the Discovery of Australia: As Revealed by the Journal of Captain Don Diego de Prado y Tovar,* Hakluyt Society, 2d series, 64, London, 1930.

Tiele, Pieter A., "Steven van der Hagen: Avonturen van 1575–97," *BMHG,* 6 (1883), 377–421.

Unger, Willem S., ed., *De Oudste reizen van de Zeeuwen naar*

Oost-Indië, 1598–1604, Linschoten Vereeniging, *51,* The Hague, 1948.

Villiers, J. A. H. de, ed., *East and West Indian Mirror: The Voyage of Joris van Spilbergen, 1614–17,* Hakluyt Society, 2d series, *18,* London, 1906.

Warnsinck, J. C. M., ed., *De Reis om de wereld van Joris van Spilbergen, 1614–17,* The Hague, 1943.

Wichmann, A., *Dirck Gerritsz.: Ein Betrag zur Entdeckungsgeschichte des 16ten und 17ten Jahrhunderts,* Groningen, 1899.

Wieder, F. C., ed., *De Reis van Mahu en de Cordes door de Straat van Magelhaes naar Zuid-Amerika en Japan, 1598–1600,* 3 vols. Linschoten Vereeniging, *21, 22, 24,* The Hague, 1923–25.

Wright, Irene A., *English Voyages to the Caribbean, 1527,* London, 1929.

IJzerman, J. W., "Aanteekeningen betreffende Steven van der Hagen," *BKI, 83* (1927), 473–78.

———, ed., *Dirck Gerritsz. Pomp, alias Dirck Gerritsz. China: De eerste Nederlander die Chind en Japan bezocht,* The Hague, 1915.

———, ed., *Reis om de wereld door Olivier van Noort, 1598–1601.* 2 vols. Linschoten Vereeniging, *27, 28,* The Hague, 1926.

Zweig, Stefan, *Magellan: Pioneer of the Pacific,* trans. E. and C. Paul, London, 1948.

JAN HUYGHEN VAN LINSCHOTEN

Balen, Willem J. van, *Naar de Indische wonderwereld met Jan Huyghen van Linschoten,* Amsterdam, Amsterdamsche Boek en Courant Mij., 1942.

Burnell, Arthur C. and Pieter A. Tiele, eds., *The Voyage of John Huyghen van Linschoten to the East Indies,* 2 vols. Hakluyt Society, 1st series, *70, 71,* London, 1885.

Itinerario: Voyage ofte schipvaert van Jan Huyghen van Linschoten naer Oost ofte Portugaels Indien, 1579–92, 8 vols., H. Kern, et al., eds., Linschoten Vereeniging, *2* (in two parts) (1910); *39* (1934); *43* (in two parts) (1939); *57; 58; 60* (1955–57).

Naber, S. P. L'Honoré, ed., *Reizen van Jan Huyghen van Linschoten naar het Noorden, 1594–95,* Linschoten Vereeniging, *8,* The Hague, 1914.

4. EARLY HISTORY OF ASIA

EARLY ASIATIC TRADE

Boelen, H. J., "Iets over Malacca," *Nederlandsch Indië, Oud en Nieuw*, 5 (1920–21), 366–79.

Edkins, Joseph, "Ancient Navigation in the Indian Ocean," *Journal of the Royal Asiatic Society*, new series, *18* (1886), 1–27.

Ferrand, Gabriel, *Instructions nautique et routiers arabes, XV siècle*, Paris, 1921.

——, *Relations de voyages et textes géographiques arabes, persanes, et turques relatifs a l'Extrême Orient du 7me au 18me siècles*, 2 vols. Paris, 1913–14.

Gibb, Hamilton A. R., ed. and trans., *Ibn Battuta: Travels in Asia and Africa, 1325–54*, London, Routledge, 1953.

Groenevelt, W. P., *Notes on the Malay Archipelago and Malacca Compiled from Chinese sources, VBG, 39* (1880), i–x, 1–144.

Hasan, Hadi, *A History of Persian Navigation*, London, 1928.

Hirth, F., *China and the Roman Orient*, Shanghai, 1885.

Hourani, G. F., *Arab Seafaring in the Indian Ocean*, Princeton, 1951.

Hyde, W. W., *Ancient Greek Mariners*, New York, 1947.

Komroff, Manuel, ed., *The Travels of Marco Polo*, New York, Boni & Liveright, 1926.

Leur, Jacob C. van, "De Wereld van Zuid-Oost Azië," in J. C. de Haan and P. J. van Winter, eds., *Nederlanders over de Zeeën*, Utrecht, De Haan, 1940.

——, *Eenige beschouwingen betreffende den ouden Aziatischen handel*, Middelburg, Den Boer, 1934.

——, *Indonesian Trade and Society*, The Hague, Van Hoeve, 1955.

Major, Richard H., ed., *India in the fifteenth Century: A Collection of Narratives of Voyages to India . . . from Latin, Persian, Russian, and Italian Sources*, Hakluyt Society, 1st series, *22*, London, 1857.

Meilink-Roelofsz, Antoinette P., *Asian Trade and European Influence, in the Indonesian Archipelago between 1500 and about 1630*, The Hague, Martinus Nijhoff, 1962.

Oppert, Gustav, *Ancient Commerce of India*, Madras, 1879.

Orta, Garcia da, *Simples and Drugs of India (1563)*, London, 1913.

Pires, Tome, *Suma Oriental: An Account of the East from the Red Sea to Japan*, ed. and trans. A. Cortesao, 2 vols., London, 1944.

Rockhill, W. W., "Notes on the Relations and Trade of China

and the Eastern Archipelago and the Coast of the Indian Ocean during the Fourteenth Century," *T'oung Pao*, *15* (1914), 419–47; *16* (1915), 61–159, 237–71, 374–92, 435–67, 604–26.

Yule, Henry, ed. and trans., *The Book of Ser Marco Polo, the Venetian, Concerning the Kingdoms and Marvels of the East*, 3d ed. revised by Henri Cordier, 2 vols., London, 1903.

INDIA

Haig, W. and R. Burn, "The Mughul Period," in *The Cambridge History of India*, *4*, Cambridge, 1937.

Havell, E. B., *The History of Aryan Rule in India from the Earliest Time to the Death of Akbar*, London, 1918.

Hunter, William W., *A Brief History of the Indian Peoples*, Oxford, 1893.

Jackson, Abraham V. W., ed., *The History of India*, 9 vols. London, 1906–07.

Logan, William, *Malabar*, 3 vols. Madras, 1887–91.

Macpherson, David, *History of the European Commerce with India*, London, 1812.

Moreland, William H., *From Akbar to Aurangzeb: A Study of Indian Economic History*, London, Macmillan, 1923.

———, *India at the Death of Akbar: An Economic Study*, London, 1920.

Panikkar, Kavalam M., *India and the Indian Ocean*, London, 1945.

INDONESIA

Berg, Cornelis C., "De Arjunawiwaha: Erlangga's levensloop en bruiloftslied," *BKI*, *99* (1938), 19 ff.

———, "De Sadeng oorlog en de Mythe van Groot-Majapahit," *Indonesië*, *5* (1951), 385–422.

———, "Javaansche Geschiedschrijving," in F. W. Stapel, ed., *Geschiedenis van Nederlandsch Indië*, *2*, 5 vols., Amsterdam, 1938.

———, "Kertanagara, de miskende empire-builder," *Oriëntatie*, *34* (1950), 3–32.

Casparis, J. G. de, "Twintig jaar studie van de oudere geschiedenis van Indonesië (1931–1951)," *Oriëntatie*, *46* (1954), 626–64.

Coedès, George, "Le Royaume de Çrivijaya," *Bulletin de l'École Francaise de l'Extrême Orient*, *18* (1918), Part 6, 1–36.

Djajadiningrat, Hoesein, "Critisch overzicht van de in Maleische werken vervatte gegevens over de geschiedenis van het soeltanaat van Atjeh," *BKI*, *65* (1911), 135–265.

Drewes, Gerardus W., *Drie Javaansche Goeroe's*, Leiden, 1925.

Graaf, H. J. de, *De Regering van Panembahan Senapati Ingalaga*, The Hague, Martinus Nijhoff, 1954.

———, *De Regering van Sultan Agung, vorst van Mataram*, The Hague, Martinus Nijhoff, 1958.

Haan, F. de, *Priangan: De Preanger-regentschappen onder het Nederlandsch bestuur tot 1811*, 4 vols., Batavia, 1910–12.

Hall, Donald G. E., *A History of South-East Asia*, London, Macmillan, 1958.

Kern, J. H. C., *Verspreide Geschriften*, 15 vols., The Hague, 1913–28.

Krom, Nicolaas J., *Hindoe-Javaansche geschiedenis*, The Hague, Martinus Nijhoff, 1931.

Leur, Jacob C. van, "Enkele aanteekeningen met betrekking tot de beoefening der Indische Geschiedenis," *Koloniale Studiën*, *21* (1937), 651–61.

Meinsma, J. J., *Babad Tabah Djawi in Proza: Javaansche Geschiedenis tot 1647 der Javaansche jaartelling*, The Hague, 1874.

Pleyte, C. M., "Bijdrage tot de kennis van het Mahayana op Java," *BKI*, *52* (1901), 362–80; *54* (1902), 195–202.

Poerbatjaraka, Raden, "Aanteekeningen op de Nagarakertagama," *BKI*, *80* (1924), 219–86.

———, *De Dood van Raden Wijaya, den eersten koning en stichter van Madjapahit*, Leiden, 1926.

Rouffaer, G. P., "Wanneer is Madjapahit gevallen?" *BKI*, *50* (1899), 111–99.

———, "Was Malakka emporium voor 1400 A.D., genaamd Malajoer?" *BKI*, *77* (1921), 1–172, 359–600.

Schnitger, F. M., *Forgotten Kingdoms of Sumatra*, Leiden, 1939.

Schrieke, B., *Indonesian Sociological Studies*, 2 vols., The Hague and Bandung, Van Hoeve, 1955–57.

Stutterheim, W. F., *De Hindu's*, Groningen and Batavia, Wolters, 1932.

———, *De Islam en zijn komst in den Archipel*, Groningen and Batavia, Wolters, 1935.

———, *De Kraton van Madjapahit*, The Hague, 1948.

———, *Hinduisme in den Archipel*, Groningen and Batavia, Wolters, 1932.

Vogel, Jean P., "Het Koninkrijk Çrivijaya," *BKI*, *75* (1919), 626–37.

5. THE PORTUGUESE AGE

Spain and Portugal: General History

Brandi, K., *The Emperor Charles V*, London, 1939.

Carvalho, Antonio P. de, *Das Origens da Escravidao Moderna em Portugal*, Lisbon, 1877.

Chudoba, Bohdan, *Spain and the Empire, 1519–1643*, Chicago, 1952.

Fontoura da Costa, A., *La Science nautique des Portugais, 1500*, Lisbon, 1941.

Herculano, Alexandre, *Inquisition in Portugal*, San Francisco, 1926.

Lea, Henry C., *History of the Inquisition of Spain*, 4 vols., London, 1922.

Livermore, H. V., *History of Portugal*, Cambridge, 1947.

Merriman, R. B., *Philip the Prudent*, New York, 1934.

Nowell, C. B., *History of Portugal*, New York, 1952.

Prescott, W. H., *History of Philip II*, Philadelphia, 1875.

Prestage, Edgar, *Portuguese Pioneers*, London, 1933.

Wyndham Lewis, D. B., *Charles of Europe*, New York, 1931.

THE PORTUGUESE IN AFRICA

Alvarez, Fr. Francisco, *Narrative of the Portuguese Embassy to Abyssinia during the years 1520–27*, Hakluyt Society, 1st series, 64, London, 1881.

Axelson, Eric, *South-East Africa, 1488–1530*, Aberdeen, 1940.

Beazley, C. R., *Prince Henry the Navigator*, New York, 1894.

Glas, George, *Discovery of the Canary Islands*, London, 1794.

Kammerer, A., *La Découverte de Madagascar par les Portugais*, Lisbon, 1950.

Major, Richard H., *Discoveries of Prince Henry the Navigator*, London, 1877.

———, ed., *J. de Bethencourt, the Canarian, or Book of the Conquest and Conversion of the Canarians, 1402*, Hakluyt Society, 1st series, 46, London, 1872.

———, *Life of Prince Henry of Portugal, Surnamed the Navigator*, London, 1868.

Sanceau, Elaine, *Henry the Navigator*, New York, 1947.

Wauwermans, Henri E., *Henri le Navigateur et l'Académie Portugaise de Sagres*, Antwerp, 1890.

Welch, Sidney R., *South Africa under John III, 1521*, Capetown, 1948.

———, *South Africa under King Manuel, 1495–1521*, Capetown, 1946.

Whiteway, Richard S., *Portuguese Expedition to Abyssinia, 1541*, London, 1902.

THE PORTUGUESE IN ASIA

Barbosa, Duarte, *A Description of the Coasts of East Africa and Malabar in the beginning of the Sixteenth Century*, ed. and trans. H. E. J. Stanley, Hakluyt Society, 1st series, *35*, London, 1866.

Birch, Walter de Gray, ed., *Commentaries of the Great Afonso d'Albuquerque*, Hakluyt Society, 1st series, *53, 55, 62, 69*, London, 1875–84.

Boxer, Charles R., *Fidalgos in the Far East, 1550–1770: Facts and Fancy in the History of Macao*, The Hague, 1948.

———, ed., *South China in the Sixteenth Century: Being the Narratives of Galeote Pereira, Fr. Gaspar da Cruz and Fr. Martin de Rada, 1550–1575*, Hakluyt Society, 2d series, *106*, London, 1953.

———, "The Portuguese in the East, 1500–1800," in H. V. Livermore, ed., *Portugal and Brazil: an Introduction*, Oxford, 1953, pp. 185–247.

———, "Three Historians of Portuguese Asia: Barros, Couto, and Bocarro," *Boletim do Instituto Portugues de Hongkong, 1* (1948), 18–25.

Bulhoes, M. E. Lobo de, *Les Colonies Portugaises*, Lisbon, 1878.

Burton, Richard F., trans., *Camoens: His Life and Lusiads*, ed. Isabel Burton, 2 vols., London, 1880.

Chang, Tien-Tse, *Sino-Portuguese Trade from 1514–1614*, Leiden, 1933.

Correa, Gaspar, *Lendas da India*, ed. and trans. H. E. J. Stanley, Hakluyt Society, 1st series, *42*, London, 1869.

Danvers, Fred. C., *Report to the Secretary of State for India in Council on the Portuguese Records relating to the East Indies at Lisbon and Evora*, London, 1892.

———, *The Portuguese in India*, 2 vols., London, 1894.

Empoli, Giovanni da, "Lettera mandata a Lionardo suo padre del viaggio di Malacca," *Archivio storico Italiano, 3* (1846), 19–91.

Faria y Sousa, Manuel da, *Portuguese Asia*, trans. J. Stevens, 3 vols. London, 1695.

Fonseca, Jose N. da, *Historical and Archaeological Sketch of the City of Goa, with a Statistical Account of the Territory of Goa*, Bombay, 1878.

Haring, C. H., *Trade and Navigation between Spain and the Indies*, London, 1918.

Lefitau, Joseph F., *Histoire des découvertes et conquestes des Portugais*, 2 vols. Paris, 1733.

Meilink-Roelofsz, M. A. P., *Asian Trade and European Influence*, The Hague, Martinus Nijhoff, 1962.

Montalto de Jesus, C. A., *Historic Macao*, Hongkong, 1902.

Panikkar, Kavalam M., *Malabar and the Portuguese, 1500–1663*, Bombay, 1929.

Pieris, P. E., *Portugal in Ceylon, 1505–1658*, Cambridge, 1937.

Stanley, H. E. J., ed., *The Three Voyages of Vasco da Gama and his Viceroyalty*, Hakluyt Society, 1st series, *42*, London, 1869.
Stephens, H. Morse, *Albuquerque*, Oxford, 1897.
Tiele, Pieter A., "De Europeërs in den Maleischen Archipel," *BKI*, *25–29* (1877–81).
Wessels, Fr. Cornelius, *De Geschiedenis der Roomsch Katholieke Missie in Amboina, 1546–1605*, Nijmegen-Utrecht, 1926.
Whiteway, Richard S., *The Rise of Portuguese Power in India*, Westminster, 1899.

THE PORTUGUESE IN JAPAN

Boxer, Charles R., *The Christian Century in Japan, 1549–1650*, Berkeley, 1951.
Murdock, J. and Shozo Yamagata, *History of Japan during the Century of early Foreign Intercourse, 1542–1651*, Kobe, 1903.
Pagès, L., *Histoire de la religion Chrétienne en Japon, 1598–1651*, Paris, 1869.
Rundall, T., ed., *Memorials for the Empire of Japan in the Sixteenth and Seventeenth Centuries*, London, 1850.

6. THE DUTCH EAST INDIA COMPANY

GENERAL HISTORY

Colenbrander, H. T., *Koloniale Geschiedenis*, 3 vols. The Hague, 1925–26.
Coolhaas, Willem, P., *A Critical Survey of Studies on Dutch Colonial History*, The Hague, 1960.
Crawfurd, John, *History of the Indian Archipelago*, 3 vols. Edinburgh, 1820.
Du Bois, J. P. I., *Vies des Gouverneurs-Généraux*, The Hague, 1763.
Fruin–Mees, W., *Geschiedenis van Java*, 2 vols. Weltevreden, 1919–20.
Furnivall, J. S., *Introduction to the History of Netherlands India*, Rangoon, 1934.
———, *Netherlands India*, Cambridge, Eng. and New York, Macmillan, 1944.
Graaf, H. J. de, *Geschiedenis van Indonesië*, The Hague, Van Hoeve, 1949.
Hyma, Albert, *A History of the Dutch in the Far East*, Ann Arbor, George Wahr, 1953.
Kalff, S., *De Loffelycke Compagnie*, Amsterdam, 1916.

Kielstra, Egbert B., *De Vestiging van het Nederlandsch gezag in den Indischen Archipel*, Haarlem, 1920.

Klerck, Eduard S. de, *History of the Netherlands Indies*, 2 vols. Rotterdam, 1938.

Meilink-Roelofsz, M. A. P., *Asian Trade and European Influence*, The Hague, Martinus Nijhoff, 1962.

Meinsma, Johannes J., *Geschiedenis van de Nederlandsche Oost-Indische Bezittingen*, 2 vols. Delft, 1872–75.

Raffles, Thomas S., *The History of Java*, 2 vols. London, 1817.

Rhede van der Kloot, M. A., *De Gouverneurs-Generaal en Commissarissen-Generaal van Nederlandsch Indië*, The Hague, 1891.

Spaan, Gerrit van, *Opkomst der Oost-Indische Compagnie, 1595–1700*, Rotterdam, 1711.

Stapel, Frederik W., *De Gouverneurs-Generaal van Nederlandsch Indië in beeld en woord*, The Hague, 1941.

——, *Geschiedenis van Nederlandsch Indië*, Amsterdam, Meulenhoff, 1943.

Terpstra, Heert, Insulinde, *Nederland's verleden in het Verre Oosten*, The Hague, 1949.

Vlekke, Bernard H. M., *Nusantara: A History of the East Indian Archipelago*, Cambridge, Mass., Harvard, 1945.

Wijnands van Resandt, W., *De Gezaghebbers der Oost-Indische Compagnie op hare Buiten-Comptoiren in Azië*, Amsterdam, 1944.

BASIC REFERENCE WORKS

Chijs, Jacobus A. van der, ed., *Nederlandsch-Indisch Plakaatboek, 1602–1811, 1*, 17 vols. The Hague and Batavia, 1885.

Commelin, Izaak, *Begin ende Voortgangh van de Vereenighde Nederlantsche geoctroyeerde Oost-Indische Compagnie*, 2 vols. Amsterdam, 1646.

Colenbrander, H. T., ed., *Jan Pietersz. Coen: Bescheiden omtrent zijn bedrijf in Indië*, 6 vols. The Hague, Martinus Nijhoff, 1919–34.

Coolhaas, Willem P., ed., *Generale missiven van de gouverneurs-generaal en raden aan de heren XVII der Vereenigde Oostindische compagnie, 1610–38*, The Hague, RGP, 1960.

——, ed., *Jan Pietersz. Coen: Bescheiden omtrent zijn bedrijf in Indië*, The Hague, Martinus Nijhoff, 1952–53.

Dam, Pieter van, *Beschryvinge van de Oostindische Compagnie*, ed. F. W. Stapel, 3 vols. The Hague, RGP, 1927–43.

Glamann, Kristof, *Dutch Asiatic Trade, 1620–1740*, The Hague, Martinus Nijhoff and Copenhagen, Danish Science Press, 1958.

Heeres, Jan E. and Frederik W. Stapel, eds., *Corpus Diplomaticum*

Neerlando Indicum, 5 vols. *BKI, 57, 87, 91, 93, 96* (1907–38).

Heeres, Jan E. et al., eds., *Daghregister gehouden int casteel Batavia, 1624–1682*, 31 vols. The Hague, 1888–1931.

Jonge, Johan K. J. de, *De Opkomst van het Nederlandsche gezag in Oost Indië*, 13 vols. The Hague and Amsterdam, 1862–88.

MacLeod, N., *De Oost-Indische Compagnie als Zeemogendheid in Azië, 1602–1650*, 2 vols. Rijswijk, 1927.

Stapel, Frederik W., ed., *Geschiedenis van Nederlandsch Indië*, 5 vols. Amsterdam, Joost van den Vondel, 1938–40.

Tiele, Pieter A., "De Europeërs in den Maleischen Archipel," *BKI, 25* (1877), 321–420; *27* (1879), 1–69; *28* (1880), 261–340, 395–482; *29* (1881), 153–214; *30* (1882), 141–242; *32* (1884), 49–118; *35* (1886), 257–355; *36* (1887), 199–307.

—— and Jan E. Heeres, eds., *Bouwstoffen voor de Geschiedenis der Nederlanders in den Maleischen Archipel*, 2 vols. The Hague, 1886–90.

Valentijn, Francois, *Oud en Nieuw Oost-Indien*, 5 vols. Dordrecht and Amsterdam, 1724–26.

DUTCH ACTIVITIES IN SPECIFIC AREAS

Bokemeyer, Heinrich, *Die Molukken-Geschichte und quellenmässige Darstellung der Eroberung und der Verwaltung des Ost-Indischen Gewürzinseln durch die Niederländer*, Leipzig, 1888.

Broecke, Pieter van der, *Korte historiael ende journaelsche Aenteykeninghe*, Haarlem and Amsterdam, 1634.

Chijs, Jacobus A. van der, *De Nederlanders te Jakatra*, Amsterdam, 1860.

——, *De Vestiging van het Nederlandsche Gezag over de Banda Eilanden, 1599–1621*, Batavia and The Hague, 1886.

Deventer, Marinus L. van, *Geschiedenis der Nederlanders op Java*, 2 vols. *1*, Haarlem, 1886.

(Gysels, Aert,) "Grondig Verhaal van Amboina," *KHG, 27* (1872), 348–494.

——, "Verhaal van eenige oorlogen in Indie," *KHG, 27* (1872), 497–658.

Heeres, Jan E., "Pieter van den Broecke en zijne journalen," in *Geschiedkundige Opstellen*, Leiden, 1902.

Netscher, Eliza, *De Nederlanders in Djohore en Siak, 1602–1865*, Batavia, 1870.

Tiele, Pieter A., "Frederik de Houtman in Atjeh," *Indische Gids, 1* (1881), 146–52.

Wellan, J. W. J., "Onze eerste vestiging te Djambi," *BKI, 82* (1926), 339–83.

IJzerman, J. W., *Cornelis Buysero te Bantam, 1616–18*, The Hague, 1923.

——, "Het schip 'De Eendracht' voor Makassar in December 1616," *BKI*, *78* (1922), 343–72.
——, "Over de belegering van het fort Jacatra, December 22, 1618–February 1, 1619," *BKI*, *73* (1917), 558–679.

The Dutch in Siam and Indo-China

Buch, Wilhelm J. M., *De Oost-Indische Compagnie en Quinam*, Amsterdam, 1929.
——, "La Compagnie des Indes Neerlandaises et l'Indochine," *Bulletin de l'École Française d'Extrême Orient*, *36* (1936), 97–196; *37* (1937), 121–237.
Dijk, L. C. D. van, *Neerlands vroegste betrekkingen met Borneo, den Solo-Archipel, Cambodja, Siam, en Cochin-China*, Amsterdam, 1862.
Maybon, C. B., *Les Marchands Européens en Cochinchine et au Tonkin, 1600–1775*, Hanoi, 1916.
Muller, H. P. N., *De Oost-Indische Compagnie in Cambodja en Laos*, Linschoten Vereeniging, *13*, The Hague, 1917.
Terpstra, Heert, *De Factorij der Oostindische Compagnie te Patani*, The Hague, 1938.

The Dutch in India, Arabia, and Persia

Dunlop, H., *Bronnen tot de Geschiedenis der Oostindische Compagnie in Perzie*, The Hague, RGP, 1930.
Galletti, A., *The Dutch in Malabar*, Madras, 1911.
Havart, Daniel, *Op– en Ondergang van Cormandel*, Amsterdam, 1693.
Leupe, Pieter A., "Brieven–vervoer over land naar Indië door the Oost-Indische Compagnie in de 17de eeuw," *BVGO*, *6* (1870), 54–76.
Panikkar, Kavalam M., *Malabar and the Dutch: History of the fall of Nayar power in Malabar*, Bombay, 1931.
Roelofsz, M. A. P., *De Vestiging der Nederlanders ter kuste Malabar*, The Hague, Martinus Nijhoff, 1943.
Terpstra, Heert, *De Opkomst der Westerkwartieren van de Oostindische Compagnie*, The Hague, 1918.
——, *De Vestiging der Nederlanders aan de kust van Koromandel*, Groningen, 1911.

Dutch Relations with Japan and China

Boxer, Charles R., *Jan Compagnie in Japan, 1600–1850*, The Hague, Martinus Nijhoff, 1950.
Chijs, Jacobus A. van der, *Neerlands streven tot openstelling van Japan voor den wereldhandel*, Amsterdam, 1867.

Dijk, L. C. D. van, *Zes Jaren uit het leven van Wemmer van Berchem*, Amsterdam, 1858.

Groeneveld, W. P., "De Nederlanders in China," *BKI*, *48* (1898), 1–598.

Nachod, Oskar, *Die Beziehungen der Niederländischen Ostindischen Kompagnie zu Japan im 17ten Jahrhundert*, Leipzig, 1897.

Schlegel, G., "De Betrekkingen tusschen Nederland en China volgens Chineesche bronnen," *BKI*, *42* (1893), 1–28.

JAN PIETERSZOON COEN

(Anon.), "Rapport gedaen bij verscheyden persoonen comende uyt de Oost-Indien, 1622," *KHG*, *27* (1871), 321–39.

Berg, N. P. van den, "Coen en de vrije vaart en handel in Indië," *VMKA*, 4th series, *4* (1901), 300–57.

———, *Uit de dagen der Compagnie: Geschiedkundige Schetsen*, Haarlem, 1904.

Bergman, Rudolf A. M., "Jan Pieterszoon Coen: Een psychographie," *TBG*, *73* (1933), 1–56.

Colenbrander, H. T., "Coen in patria," *De Gids*, *97* (1933), 24–62, 144–72.

——— and Willem P. Coolhaas, eds., *Jan Pietersz. Coen: Bescheiden omtrent zijn bedrijf in Indië*, 7 vols. The Hague, Martinus Nijhoff, 1919–53.

Coolhaas, Willem P., "Over karakter en daden van Jan Pietersz. Coen," *BVGO*, 8th series, *4* (1943), 201–37; *5* (1944), 60–74.

Faubel, Th., "J. Pzn. Coen verongelijkt," *Weekblad voor Indië*, *8* (1911–12), 1226 ff.

Gabriël, "J. P. Coen en de Chronyk van Hoorn," *Weekblad voor Indië*, *8* (1911–12), 914 ff., 939 ff., 962 ff.

Geerke, H. P., *Jan Pieterszoon Coen: de baanbreker in ons Indië*, Utrecht, De Haan, 1929.

Gerretson, C., *Coen's Eerherstel*, Amsterdam, Van Kampen, 1944.

Huybers, H. F. M., *Jan Pieterszoon Coen*, Utrecht, Bruna, 1914.

Kiers, Luc., *Coen op Banda: De conqueste getoetst aan het recht van den tijd*, Utrecht, Oosthoek, 1943.

Lauts, G., "Jan Pietersz. Coen," *BKI*, *6* (1859), 282–302.

Leupe, Pieter A., "Jan Pieterszoon Coen, 1623–27," *BKI*, *6* (1859), 1–22.

———, "Vertoogh van de staet der Vereenigde Nederlanden in de quartieren van Oost Indien," *BKI*, *6* (1859), 129 ff.

Opperdoes Alewyn, P., "Mededeelingen over Jan Pieterszoon Koen," *Notulen van het Bataviaasch Genootschap*, *7* (1869), cxi ff.

Rochemont, J. E. de, *Pieter van Raey en Jan Pietersz. Coen*, Semarang and Surabaya, 1905.

Romein, Jan M. and Annie H. M. Romein, "Jan Pietersz. Coen, Couste Que Couste," in *Erflaters van onze Beschaving, 2*, 4 vols. Amsterdam, Querido, 1938.

Slauerhoff, J., *Jan Pietersz. Coen*, Maastricht, 1931.

Soeka Tipoe, "Een Oostersche legende over Jan Pietersz. Coen," *De Reflector, 4* (1919), 429 ff.

Woude, Johan van der, *Coen: Consequent koopman van de XVII*, Amsterdam, De Boer, 1948.

ASPECTS OF THE NETHERLANDS

Bakhuizen-van den Brink, Reinier C., "Isaac Lemaire," *De Gids, 29*, part 4 (1865), 1–56.

Brugmans, Izaak J., "De Oost-Indische Compagnie en de welvaart in de Republiek," *Tijdschrift voor Geschiedenis, 61* (1948), 225–31.

Chijs, Jacobus A. van der, *Geschiedenis der Stichting van de Vereenigde O. I. Compagnie*, Leiden, 1856.

Dillen, Johannes G. van, *Het Oudste aandeelhoudersregister van de Kamer Amsterdam der Oost-Indische Compagnie*, The Hague, Martinus Nijhoff, 1958.

———, "Isaac le Maire en de handel in actien der Oost-Indische Compagnie," *Economisch-Historisch Jaarboek, 16* (1930), 1–165.

Heer, Cornelis de, *Bijdrage tot de financiëele geschiedenis der Oost-Indische Compagnie*, The Hague, 1929.

Klerk de Reus, G. C., *Geschichtlicher Uberblick der administrativen, rechtlichen und finanziellen Entwicklung der Niederländisch–Ostindischen Compagnie*, Batavia, 1894.

Mansvelt, W. M. F., *Rectsvorm en geldelijk beheer bij de Oost-Indische Compagnie*, Amsterdam, Swets & Zeitlinger, 1922.

Stapel, Frederik W., "Het Aantal Bewindhebbers der Oostindische Compagnie in 1602," *BVGO*, 6th series, *6* (1928), 146–48.

JOHAN VAN OLDEBARNEVELT

Brandt, G., *Historie van de rechtspleging in 1618 en 1619 omtrent J. van Oldebarnevelt, Hoogerbeets en H. de Groot*, Rotterdam, 1708.

Bullen, A. H., ed., *The Tragedy of Sir John van Olden Barnavelt*, The Hague, 1884.

Deventer, Marinus L. van, *Gedenkstukken van Oldenbarnevelt en zijn tijd*, 3 vols. The Hague, 1860–65.

Groen van Prinsterer, Guillaume, *Maurice et Barnevelt*, Utrecht, 1875.

Haak, S. P., "De Wording van het conflict tussen Maurits en Oldebarnevelt," *BVGO*, 5th series, 6 (1919), 97–207; *10* (1923), 177–226.

———, ed., *J. van Oldenbarnevelt: Bescheiden betreffende zijn staatkundig beleid en zijn familie*, The Hague, 1934.

Limburg, R., "Joan van Oldenbarneveldt," in his *Cultuurdragers in bewogen tijden*, The Hague, 1943.

Motley, John L., *Life and Death of John of Barneveld*, 2 vols. London, 1903–04.

Pater, Jan C. H. de, *Maurits en Oldebarnevelt in den strijd om het Twaalfjarig Bestand*, Amsterdam, 1940.

7. HISTORY OF ENGLAND

GENERAL

Bowen, Catherine D., *The Lion and the Throne: The Life and Times of Sir Edward Coke, 1552–1634*, Boston, 1956.

Davies, G., *Bibliography of British History: Stuart Period 1603–1714*, Oxford, 1928.

Neale, John E., *Queen Elizabeth*, 3 vols. London, 1934.

Prothero, George W., *Select Statutes and other Constitutional Documents Illustrative of the Reigns of Elizabeth and James I*, Oxford, 1934.

Read, C., *Bibliography of British History: Tudor Period 1485–1603*, Oxford, 1933.

Rowse, A. L., *The Expansion of Elizabethan England*, London and New York, 1955.

Wright, Louis B., *Middle-class Culture in Elizabethan England*, Chapel Hill, N.C., 1935.

ECONOMIC HISTORY

Brodnitz, George, *Englische Wirtschaftsgeschichte*, Jena, 1918.

Burgon, J. M., *Life and Times of Sir Thomas Gresham*, 2 vols. London, 1839.

Burn, J. S., *The History of the French, Walloon, Dutch, and other Foreign Protestant Refugees, Settled in England*, London, 1846.

Clapham, John H., *A History of the Bank of England*, 2 vols. Cambridge, Eng., 1944.

Clark, George N., *Science and Social Welfare in the Age of Newton*, Oxford, 1949.

———, *The Seventeenth Century*, Oxford, 1947.

———, *The Wealth of England, 1496–1760*, New York and London, 1954.

Dekker, F., "Nederlandsche invloed in Engeland," in his *Voortrekkers van Oud-Nederland*, The Hague, Boucher, 1947.

Feaveryear, A. E., *The Pound Sterling*, Oxford, 1931.

Friis, Astrid, *The Alderman Cockayne Project and the Cloth Trade*, Copenhagen and London, 1927.

Innes, A. D., *The Maritime and Colonial Expansion of England under the Stuarts*, London, 1931.

J. R., "The Trades Increase," in William Oldys et al., eds., *Harleian Miscellany, 4*, 10 vols. London, 1808.

Lingelbach, William E., *The Merchant Adventurers of England, Their Laws and Ordinances*, Philadelphia, 1902.

Lintum, C. E., *De Merchant Adventurers in de Nederlanden*, The Hague, 1905.

Lipson, Ephraim, *Economic History of England*, 3 vols. London, 1948–49.

Macpherson, David, *Annals of Commerce, Manufactures, Fisheries, and Navigation*, 4 vols. London, 1805.

Malynes, Gerard de, *A Treatise on the Canker of England's Commonwealth*, London, 1601.

———, *Lex Mercatoria, or The Ancient Law-Merchant*, London, 1622.

Misselden, Edward, *Free Trade, or the Meanes to Make Trade Florish*, London, 1622.

———, *The Circle of Commerce, or Balance of Trade*, London, 1623.

Mun, Thomas, *Englands Treasure by Forraign Trade* (ca. 1628–32), ed. J. R. McCulloch, Oxford, 1933.

Murray, K. M. E., *Constitutional History of the Cinque Ports*, Manchester, 1935.

Power, Eileen, *The Wool Trade in English Medieval History*, Oxford, 1941.

Schanz, G., *Englische Handelspolitik gegen Ende des Mittelalters*, 2 vols. Leipzig, 1881.

Scott, W. R., *Constitution and Finance of English, Scottish, and Irish Joint-Stock Companies to 1720*, 3 vols. Cambridge, Eng., 1911–12.

Smedt, O. de, *De Engelsche natie te Antwerpen in de 16de eeuw*, Antwerp, 1950.

Violet, Thomas, *A True Discovery to the Commons of England, how They have been Cheated of almost all the Gold and Silver Coin of the Realm*, London, 1651.

Willan, Thomas S., *English Coasting Trade, 1600–1750*, Manchester, 1938.

ANGLO-DUTCH RELATIONS IN EUROPE

(Anon.), *The Case Stated between England and the United Provinces*, London, 1652.

Bense, J. F., *The Anglo-Dutch Relations from the Earliest Times to the Death of William the Third, Being an Historical Introduction to a Dictionary of the Low-Dutch Element in the English Vocabulary*, The Hague, 1925.

Borough, J., *The Soveraigntie of the British Seas (1651)*, ed. T. C. Wade, Edinburgh, 1920.

Brugmans, H., *Engeland en de Nederlanden in de eerste jaren van Elizabeth's regeering*, Groningen, 1892.

Carleton, Dudley, *Letters during his Embassy in Holland, 1616–21*, ed. P. Yorke, London, 1757.

Child, Josiah, *A New Discourse of Trade*, London, 1694.

Clark, George N., "Grotius's East India mission to England," *Transactions of the Grotius Society*, 20 (1935), 45–84.

Diferee, Hendrik C., "Die ökonomischen Verwicklungen zwischen England und den Niederlanden im 17. Jahrhundert," *Vierteljahrschrift für Sozial und Wirtschaftsgeschichte*, 9 (1911), 134–90.

Digges, Dudley, *The Defence of Trade: Letter to Sir Thomas Smith*, London, 1615.

Edmundson, George, *Anglo-Dutch Rivalry*, Oxford, Clarendon Press, 1911.

Elias, Johan E., *Het Voorspel van den Eersten Engelschen Oorlog*, 2 vols. The Hague, Martinus Nijhoff, 1920.

Fulton, T. W., *The Sovereignty of the Sea*, Edinburgh, 1911.

Gentleman, Tobias, "Englands Way to Win Wealth," in William Oldys, et al., eds., *Harleian Miscellany, 3*, 10 vols. London, 1808.

Muller Fz., Samuel, *Mare Clausem: Geschiedenis der rivaliteit van Engeland en Nederland in de 17de eeuw, –1639*, Amsterdam, 1872

Raleigh, Sir Walter, "Observations touching trade and commerce with the Hollanders," in William Oldys and Thomas Birch, eds., *The Works of Sir Walter Raleigh, 8*, 8 vols. Oxford, 1829.

Riemersma, Jelle C., "Government Influence on Company Organization in Holland and England," *Journal of Economic History*, supplement X (1950), 31–39.

Rooseboom, M. P., *The Scottish Staple in the Netherlands, 1292–1676*, The Hague, 1910.

Selden, John, *Mare clausem seu de dominio maris*, London, 1635.

Tideman, M. C., *De Zee betwist*, Dordrecht, 1876.

Wilson, Charles H., *Holland and Britain*, London, Collins, 1946.

——, *Profit and Power: A Study of England and the Dutch Wars*, London, Longmans Green, 1957.

8. THE ENGLISH EAST INDIA COMPANY

BASIC REFERENCES

Anderson, Philip, *The English in Western India*, London, 1854.

Birdwood, George, *Report on the Old Records of the India Office*, London and Calcutta, 1891.

—— and William Foster, eds., *The First Letterbook of the East India Company, 1600–19*, London, 1893.

Bruce, John, *Annals of the Honorable East India Company*, 3 vols. London, 1810.

Danvers, Fred. C. and William Foster, eds., *Letters Received by the East India Company from its Servants in the East, 1602–17*, 6 vols. London, 1896–1901.

Dodwell, H. H., ed., *The Cambridge History of the British Empire*, 4, Cambridge, 1929.

Foster, William, *John Company*, London, John Lane, 1926.

——, *The Embassy of Sir Thomas Roe to India, 1615–19*, Oxford, 1926.

——, ed., *The English Factories in India, 1618–33*, 13 vols. Oxford, 1906–27.

——, ed., *The Journal of John Jourdain*, Cambridge, 1905.

Grey, Charles, *The Merchant Venturers of London*, London, 1932.

Hunter, William W., *History of British India*, 2 vols. London, Longmans Green, 1912–19.

Khan, Shafaat A., *The East India Trade in the Seventeenth Century in its Political and Economic Aspects*, London, H. Milford, 1923.

Macpherson, James, *History and Management of the East India Company from its origin in 1600*, London, 1779.

Morse, H. B., *Chronicles of the East India Company*, 4 vols. Cambridge, Eng., 1926.

Mun, Thomas, "A Discourse of Trade from England into the East Indies, 1621," in J. R. McCulloch, ed., *A Select Collection of Early English Tracts on Commerce*, London, 1856.

Rawlinson, Hugh G., *British Beginnings in Western India, 1579–1657*, Oxford, 1920.

Reid, C. Lestock, *Commerce and Conquest–the Honorable East India Company*, London, 1947.

Russell, Francis, *A Short History of the East India Company*, London, 1793.

Sainsbury, Noel, ed., *Calendar of State Papers, East Indies, 1513–1629*, 4 vols. London, 1870.

Thompson, E. M., ed., *Diary of Richard Cocks*, 2 vols. London, 1883.

Thornton, Edward, *Summary of the History of the East India Company*, London, 1833.

ANGLO-DUTCH FRICTION IN THE EAST INDIES

Coolhaas, Willem P., "Aanteekeningen en opmerkingen over de zoogenaamde Ambonsche moord," *BKI*, *101* (1942), 49–93.

Graviere, J. de la, *Les Anglais et les Hollandais dans les mers polaires et dans la mer des Indes*, Paris, 1890.

Scott, Edmund, "Discourse of Java," in *Purchas his Pilgrimes, 2*, Glasgow, 1905–07.

Stapel, Frederik W., "De Ambonsche 'moord,'" *TBG, 62* (1923), 209–26.

9. THE MEDITERRANEAN

Bent, J. T., *Early Voyages and Travels in the Levant*, Hakluyt Society, 1st series, *87*, London, 1893.

Corbett, J. S., *England in the Mediterranean, 1603–1713*, London, 1917.

Hazlitt, W. Carew, *The Venetian Republic*, 2 vols. London, 1900.

Heeringa, Klaas, *Bronnen tot de geschiedenis van den Levantschen handel*, 3 vols. The Hague, RGP, 1910–17.

Heyd, W., *Histoire du Commerce du Levant au Moyen Age*, Leipzig and Paris, 2 vols. 1885–86.

Jonge, Johannes C. de, *Nederland en Venetie, 1596–1636*, The Hague, 1852.

McClellan, George B., *The Oligarchy of Venice*, Boston, 1904.

Sottas, Jules, *Messageries maritimes de Venise*, Paris, 1938.

Wätjen, Hermann J. E., *Die Niederländer im Mittelmeergebiet zur Zeit ihrer höchsten Machtstellung*, Berlin, 1909.

Weber, Richard E. J., *De Beveiliging van de zee tegen Europeesche en Barbarijsche zeerovers, 1609–1621*, Amsterdam, 1936.

Wiel, Alethea, *The Navy of Venice*, London, 1910.

Index

Abdul Hazan, 294
Abrolhos Islands, 72, 92
Abu Hassan, 215
Achin, Achinese, 74, 123, 155–56, 211, 342, 359, 380; Dutch at, 122 f., 248; pepper, 155, 166, 457 f.; Portuguese at, 122, 218; war against Johore, 122 f.
Adams, William, in Japan, 127, 276
Aden, 287 f.; Dutch at, 377
Admiralties: Dutch, 12, 83, 178 f., 240; functions of, 51, 55; western European, 55 f.
Advocate-General, functions of, 137 f.
Aerssens, Cornelis, 181 f.
Aerssens, Francis, 45, 181 f.
Afghan dynasty, 216
Afhuysen, Gerrit van, 73
Africa, 47, 72
Age of Discovery, 53, 167, 211; Amboyna and Banda as objects of, 310 f.
Aggression, Dutch, 361
Agra, English at, 290 f.
Agriculture, English, 269
Agung, Sultan, 313, 319, 448; campaigns of, 361, 447–52; traits of, 448 f., 451
Aitzema, L. van, describes Dutch ships, 49
Akbar, the Great, 216 f., 277, 290; widow of, 290 ff.
Albertsz., Jan, 275
Albuquerque, Alfonso d', 202, 217 f.
Alcohol, as shipboard remedy for disease, 252
Aleppo, 248
Alexander VI, Pope, 216
Alexandria, 205
Algiers, 205
Aloes, purgative, 287
Alteras, Laurensz., 189
Alteration of *1578* as victory of Amsterdam merchants, 30, 87
Alva, Duke of, 28 f.
Amboyna, Amboynese, 169, 301, 309–11; cloves, 114, 301, 456 f.;

Dutch at, 120, 164 f., 168 f., 263, 340, 358, 428, 459; English conspiracy at, 429–32; native trade, 358; Portuguese at, 163, 219
Americas, 21, 152
Amish, 176
Amstel, river, 23 f., 32
Amsterdam, 12, 16, 23 f., 27, 30, 32 f., 87, 206, 277, 359, 471, 475; Alteration effected in, 30; Anabaptists, 26 f.; Arminians, 446; Calvinism, 238, 446; economic importance of, 21, 29, 33, 45 ff., 87, 91, 172; expansion of, 32, 475; government, 25, 28–31, 348, 446, 475; granary, 29, 46 f.; loyalty to Spain, 26–30; merchants, 25, 27 f., 87, 109, 187, 278, 348 f.; northeast passage, 83 f., 86 f., 98, 103; Oldebarnevelt relations with, 139 f., 348 f., 471; opposes truce, 185 ff.; population, 32; *vroedschap*, 25, 348, 475. *See also* Dutch East India Company
Amsterdam (ship), 88, 94 f.; abandoned, 96
Amsterdam Company, 128
Anabaptists, in Amsterdam, 26 f.
Andrigiri, 359
Angel (ship), 396
Anglican Church, 270
Angrok, King, 198
Anselien, half caste, 387
Antonisz., Cornelis, 206
Antwerp, 25; blockade of, 39, 185; decline of, 21, 33, 45; importance of, 19 f., 270; Spanish in, 29, 35, 37
Arabia, Arabs, 359; Dutch in, 289; English in, 288; Gujerati in, 288; slave trade, 343; traders in, 74; Turks in, 288. *See also* Islam; Mocha
Archangel, 81 f.
Archdukes of Spain, Albert and Isabella, 182 f., 186
Arctic Seas, 266, 275. *See also* Northeast passage; Polar Sea; White Sea
Aren, fruit, 449
Arissabaya, Madura, 114

511

Aristocracy, Dutch, 60 f., 136
Armada, Spanish, 40 f., 64, 240; Dutch role in, 40 f.; Parma's advice to, 40 f.
Arminians, in Amsterdam, 446
Arminius, 336, 348, 446
Armistice, of *1607*, Dutch-Spanish, 188. *See also* Spain
Arrack (alcoholic beverage), 156, 252, 362, 388, 392
Articles, ships'. *See* Letter of Articles
Asab Bay, 293
Ascension (ship), 281, 287–90
Asia: colonialism, 405 n.; competition in, 309; cultural development, 193; customs, 156; English in, 277 f., 429; Europeans to, 213; imperialism in, 372, 378; land bridge, 205; native justice, 403; political situation, 204 f.; Portuguese in, 215, 219 f., 273 (*see also* Portuguese); standard of living in, 193; trade routes, 204 f. *See also* Netherlands; Trade
Asia Minor, 204
Astrakhan, 81
Astrolabe, 91, 215 f.
Astronomy, 123
Atlantic Monthly, 127
Atlantic Ocean, 86, 110 f., 215; doldrums, 250
Atrocities, Portuguese, 218
Augsburg, 20, 33
Australia, 416; discovery of, 89, 167
Avila, Juan Alvarez d', 189 f.
Azores, 69

Baduro, Venetian describing Antwerp commerce, 19
Baghdad, 204 f.
Bahar, weight, 301 n.
Bali, 96, 199
Bali Strait, 129
Ball, George, 316
Baltic: Dutch settlers, 10 f., 17; grains, 236; herring, 17. *See also* Trade
Banda, Bandanese, 115, 260, 309–11, 329, 401, 417; burghers in, 357, 422, 428, 459; conquest of, 418–22, 437; contracts, 260, 311; Dutch at, 117, 120, 237, 260–63, 340, 357, 380; English at, 165, 260, 262 ff., 329, 350, 357, 418; Javanese at, 119 f.; "main target," 257 f.; massacre, 261 f.;

Orang Kayas, 260 f., 419 f.; Sea of, 194; taxes, 422, 428; trade practices in, 260, 305, 311; traits of, 115 f., 265 f., 311, 357, 380. *See also* Monopoly; Treaties
Bantam, Bantamese, 210 f., 248, 258 f., 266, 324, 351, 401, 449, 461; Djakarta, subjugation of, 219, 320 f., 324, 357, 378, 385 f.; English at, 320, 351, 353, 367, 409, 432; French at, 349 f.; importance of, 210, 258 f., 318, 322, 385, 404; internal affairs, 259, 321 ff.; Mataram, war against, 321; merchants of, 124, 322, 351; pepper, 259, 322, 356, 457 f.; Portuguese at, 112, 218; tolls, 112, 158, 318, 320, 342, 385
  and Dutch, 93 f., 96, 112, 159, 164, 259, 300, 306, 319 ff., 323, 351 f., 360, 366, 368, 384 ff., 391 f., 404, 449; blockade, 393, 402, 404, 449, 461; economic attrition, 322, 351, 356, 392 f.; rendezvous, 170, 318 f., 352. *See also* Coen, Jan Pietersz.; Rana Mangala
Barbarossa (Haired-Din), 205
Barbary: pirates, 244, 277; states, 205
Barbers (surgeons), 252 f.
Barentsz., Willem, 84 f., 101, 103 f.
Barker, J. E., 274
Barlow, Robert, 398 n.
Bartjens, authority on bookkeeping, 60
Bastian, Adolf, coiner of word "Indonesia," 428 n.
Bastiansz., Cornelis, 164 f., 168
Batavia, 217, 231, 389, 393 f., 445 f.; burghers, 412, 428, 446, 459; censorship, 466; Chinese at, 449, 462; discipline, 314; English at, 432; Javanese merchants at, 458; leaseholds, 462; marauders at, 449; Portuguese at, 458; "republic," 437 n.; siege of, 449–52. *See also* Djakarta
Batik, 197
Batjan, island in the Moluccas, 461
Batticalao, Ceylon, Dutch at, 154, 156 ff.
Batu Sawer, 168, 257
Baudartius, describes preaching of Plancius, 66
Baureksa, 449 f.
Bawean, 95 f., 113
Beaumont, John, 430 f.

Beer: production of introduced by Dutch into England, 269 f.; as stimulant of trade, 11
"Beggars," Sea Beggars, 28 ff., 44
Bencoolen, Sumatra, English factory, 458
Bengal: Dutch corruption in, 464; Portuguese at, 222
Bengalis, Sumatra, 208
Bennet, William, 360
Berg, C. C., on history of Madjapahit, 200 f.
Bergen, Norway, 56
Bergerboot (ship), 372, 396
Bergman, R. A. M., analyzes personality of Jan Pietersz. Coen, 299
Bering Strait, 80
Best, Thomas, 304
Beukelsz., Willem, devises herring curing, 12, 48
Beuningen, Gerrit van, 93
Bicker, Gerrit, 110
Bima, 359
Binche, Treaty of, 272
Binnenhof, Inner Court of The Hague, 472
Bintang Island, 208
Bitter, Jacob de, 256, 259, 262
Black Death, in England, 265
Black Lion (ship), 367, 371, 390, 392
Black Sea, 204 f.
Blackbook of the Admiralty, 99
Blockades: of Channel ports, 33, 45, 184; of Magellan Strait, 173; of Malacca Strait, 168, 342, 458; at Manila, 329, 358; of Nassau (Vaigach) Strait, 173. *See also* Bantam
Blok, P. J., criticizes Jan Pietersz. Coen, 421
Bodemerij, 57. *See also* Bottomry
Bontekoe, Willem Ysbrantsz., 235
Bontius, Jacobus, describes Indonesians, 462
Book of Kings, Java, 198
Book ships, 313
Bookkeeper-general, Coen, first in East India Company, 237, 306 f.
Bookkeeping, 19, 59 f., 237
Boreel, Willem, advocate, 437
Borneo, Dutch trade treaties with, 308
Borobudur, Java, 210, 320
Bosporus, 205
Boston, England, 181

Both, Pieter, first governor general, 142, 265 n., 300, 305 f., 312, 315, 338
Bottomry, 57 f.
Bourges, France, 135
Bourgneuf, salt, Dutch need of in fish curing, 14
Bourgonje, P., 256
Brabant, 19, 44; woolen industry, 269
Brabant Company, 173
Bradford, William, 181
Brantas River, 199, 448
Brazil, 216 n.
Brewster, William, 181
Briel, 37
British Empire, 146. *See also* England
Brito, de, governor of Malacca, 202 f.
Brockedon, Thomas, 395
Broecke, Berent ten, 71. *See also* Paludanus
Broek, Abraham van den, 258
Broek, Pieter van den, at Djakarta, 377, 380 ff., 384 f., 389, 392
Brotherhood of English merchants, 54 f.
Brouwer, Hendrik, governor general of Dutch Company, 460
Browne, John, 275
Bruges, 19, 45; English at, 55; wool staple, 55, 267
Bruin, Jan de, 261
Brunel, Oliver, 81
Brussels, 66
Buccaneers, 130. *See also* Piracy, pirates
Buddhists, 212
Buick, Hendrik, 87
Bull (ship), 407
Buonvisi, House of, 19
Burghers, 136; in Amboyna, 459; at Banda, 422; in Batavia, 412, 428, 459, 462; free trade, 300, 358, 428 f., 436 f., 459; in Indonesia, 466 f.; in the Moluccas, 300, 311, 358; plight of, 460, 462 f. *See also* Trade
Burgundian-Austrian empire, 55
Burma, invasion of China by, 212
Burrough, Stephen, 80
Buru, island as source of cloves, 456
Business organization, new concept of, 54
Buton, Dutch at, 305, 327
Butter, 11, 232
Buyck, Joost, 28 ff.

Buzanval, Paul C. de, 173
Byzantine empire, 99

Cabot, John, 79
Cabot, Sebastian, instructions of, 99 f.
Cabral, Pedro Alvarez, 216
Caerden, Paulus van, 142, 170 f., 263 f.
Cairo, 204, 248
Calais, 40
Calendar, Julian and Gregorian, 286 n.
Calicoes. See Cotton goods
Calicut, 163, 217, 254 f.; Dutch at, 163, 255; Portuguese at, 217 f.
Calvin, Calvinism, 21–22, 26, 35, 44 f., 135 f., 270, 471, 474; in Amsterdam, 238, 446, 472; clergy of, 137, 471; on predestination, 66, 348
Cambay, 204, 206; English at, 292
Cambodia, 197, 359
Campanella, Tommaso, 271
Canals, in Amsterdam, 32 f.
Canary Islands, 72, 92
Cannanore, 218
Cape of Good Hope, 63, 87, 111, 248, 416; described by Jourdain, 287; joint colony with England at, 416
Cape of Storms, 63
Cape Verde Islands (Salt Islands), 92, 128, 248, 442; salt, 47
Capital, capitalism, 21, 31, 54 ff., 57 f., 87, 280, 333; in colonialism, 33, 225, 323, 412, 422; of Dutch East India Company, 146, 333 f., 397, 406, 463, 465; of English East India Company, 280, 332, 365, 406; of Jews, 230; speculation with, 172 f., 177 f.
Capitan Hitu, 114 f., 120, 164 n., 417 f.
Cardinals, curbing of powers of by Pope Clement, 238
Carel, Jan Jansz., 64
Carimon Islands, 208
Carlsen, Elling, 104 n.
Caron, Noel de, 45, 64
Carlton, Dudley, 431
Carpentier, Pieter de, 390, 427, 445, 447 f.
Carta Mercatoria, offer of free trade by Edward I, 267
Cartography: first globe, 82; Lasso, Bartolomeo de, 68; Mercator, 67, 81 f.; Plancius, 67
Cassies (Chinese coins), 362
Caste system in Indonesia, 196 f.

Castleton, Captain, 329, 332, 340
Catharina (ship), 130 f.
Cathay. See China
Catherine of Aragon, 268
Catholicism, 44, 66, 137; League of Catholic Noblemen, 36, 41, 237; orders in England, 268
Catulliacum, 8
Cautionary towns in Lowlands, 37, 365
Cavendish, Thomas, 13, 43, 62
Censorship, in Batavia, 466
Ceram, Moluccas, 301, 423, 456
Ceylon, 312; Dom João, Maharajah of Kandy in, 154 f., 157 f.; Dutch at, 154 n., 155–58; English at, 279; Portuguese at, 154, 217
Ceylon (ship), 373, 388
Chambers, organizational divisions of Dutch East India Company, 147
Champlain, Samuel de, 188
Chancellor, Richard, 80, 99, 275 f.
Chandis (Buddhist temples), 210
Charcoal, importance of to Dutch colonists, 359 n.
Charlemagne, 9
Charles I of England, 440
Charles V of Spain, 21 f.; in Algiers, 206; bottomry prohibited by, 58; sells claim in the Moluccas, 223
Charter, of Dutch East India Company, 146–50, 175 f., 455
Cheese, as Dutch export, 11, 232
Chelyuskin, Cape, 80
Cheribon, Java, 407, 452
Chijs, J. A. van der, detractor of Coen, 421
Chile, 173
China, Chinese, 80, 85, 98, 193, 204, 211, 359; in Bantam, 322, 328 f., 351; in Batavia, 449, 462; Coen describes use of, 428; in Djakarta, 404, 412; Europeans in, 211 ff.; in Indonesia, 199 f., 202, 207, 212, 361 n., 463; Japan harasses, 211; Ming dynasty, 211 f.; porcelain, 193; silk, 131, 159, 193, 248, 305, 328. See also Trade
China (Pomp), Dirck Gerritsz., 69, 79, 126
China Sea, monsoons, 194
Christians, Christianity, 205; in Japan, 212, 225; in Macao and Manila, 300; Portuguese, 216, 225
Christina of Sweden, 474

Church of England, 268

Churchman, Bartholomew, 397

Cinnamon, 155; as medicine, 74; monopoly on, 458; Portuguese control of, 154, 156, 158, 217

Cipango. *See* Japan

Citrus fruit, as preventive of scurvy, 252

Claesz., Cornelis, 67 f.

Claesz., Jacob, 96 n.

Claesz., Pieter, 129

Cleavage, of north and south Netherlands, 44 f.

Clement VIII, Pope, 237 n.

Clergy, 312, 328; Calvinist, 137, 471; liberal, 472

Clerks, of Dutch East India Company, 313 f. *See also* Pennists

Clive, Robert, 432

Cloves: from Amboyna, 164, 457; contracts for, 164; cost price, 301, 303, 459; Europe, prices for and stock of, 457, 459; extirpation of, 420, 457, 460; Linschoten, description of, 74; Macassar as smuggling center for, 456; monopoly of, 165, 456 f.; origin of, 113 n.; Pemba and Zanzibar as centers of later English monopoly of, 457 n.; Portuguese monopoly of, 219, 224; profits in, 459; in Ternate, 456

Coal, Dutch colonists' need of, 359; as import from England, 232

Cockayne, Alderman, 271

Coen, Jan Pietersz., 181, 257, 434, 464; at Banda, 262 f., 265, 417 ff., 421; and Bantam, 319 ff., 323, 350 f., 391 ff. (*see also* Bantam, Dutch at); biography, 229 ff., 235–39, 439, 453, 462 n.; on capital, 328; career, 240, 242, 297, 299, 306–07, 315, 318, 335, 347, 354, 442–53; and Pieter de Carpentier, 427 ff., 434 f.; on Chinese, 412; on colonization, 358, 416; *Discourse* of, 307–12, 401, 436; Djakarta, retreat from, 373; documents on, 299 n.; and Dutch Company directors, 425; economic attrition applied by, 356, 392 f., 452; empire builder, 306, 355, 358 f., 363, 399, 424, 433, 437–38, 446 f., 471; and the English, 301–04, 329 n., 340, 364, 366–68, 394, 396 f., 408–09, 434 (*see also* England, rivalry with Dutch); and explorations, 339;

and French East India Company, 349–52; in Holland, 240, 266, 296, 435–42; on law and order, 310, 403, 417; opposes Isaac Lemaire, 176; and Lords Seventeen, 317, 328, 336, 344, 355, 357, 359, 373 f., 391, 402 f., 408, 436 f.; in the Moluccas, 300–03, 390; personality of, 229 f., 233, 298 f., 345, 352, 360, 393 f., 410, 419 ff., 433, 451; policy of, 357, 447; opponents of, 366; and *Orang Kayas*, 302; opposes Reael, 336, 340 ff., 400, 438; religion of, 238, 349; rendezvous for Dutch ships established by, 319 f., 399, 437, 473; salary of, 306, 334, 336, 345 ff., 355 f., 425, 437 f.; and States General, 435 f., 440; and Treaty of Defense with English, 408, 434. *See also* Djankung; Jourdain, John; Sacone, John Peter; and Trade

Coenesz., Pieter, 230

Coffee, from Mocha, 288 f.

Coins, cassies, 361 f.

Cokayne, George, 304, 316

College of Great Fisheries. *See* Fisheries

Cologne, 135

Colombo, 155; Portuguese at, 217

Colonialism, Colonists, 297, 300 f., 309, 311, 459; in Asia, 400, 405 n.; at Banda, 357; at Bantam, 164; in Batavia, 446; capitalistic, 225, 442; Coen on, 358, 416; in East Indies, 412, 436, 441; modern, 215, 240; in the Moluccas, 300 f.; opposition to, 440, 446. *See also* Burghers

Columbus, 20, 53, 79, 215

Commenda (goods and money), 195

Communications, Dutch line of with colony, 248, 254 f., 426, 429

Compagnie van Verre, 87–89, 97, 109 f.; Plancius, 90. *See also* Fore-companies

Companhia Portugueza das Indias Orientaes, 223

Companies, Lowlands, 109 f. *See also* Fore-companies

"Company maidens," 311 f.

Condominium, in the Moluccas, 310

Confessie (Oldebarnevelt's rebuttal to his prosecution), 473

Constantinople, 204 f.

Consulato del Mar (Spanish sea law), 99

Contarini, Pietro, 277
Contra-Remonstrants, 348. *See also* Calvinists
Contracts: Banda, 260, 311; cloves (Amboyna), 164; Dutch East India Company, 455; Indonesia, 454; Macassar, 327; Moluccas, 309, 316, 326, 361, 423; natives, 164 f., 260; spices, 327, 400. *See also* Treaties
Convoy duties, 13, 55, 98, 109
Coolhaas, W. P., analyzes character of Coen, 299 n.
Copenhagen: Peace of, 17; tolls, 81
Copper, in Japan, 131, 193
Cordes, Simon de, 126
Coromandel, 248, 359; corruption, 464; cotton goods, 166, 256, 342; taxes, 256; treaties, 308
Corporations, origin of, 58
Correa, Gaspar, 218
Correr, Marcantonio, 274
Corssen, Adrian, 263
Cortereal brothers, 79
Coteels, Mateo, 300 f., 305 f.
Coteels, Steven, 301 f.
Cotton goods: Coromandel, 166, 256, 342; India, 193; monopoly of, 342, 459; trade, 461
Council of Defense, English-Dutch, 407, 409
Council of the Indies, 296; and Coen, 315, 335; functions of, 312, 335, 464
Counter Reformation, 27 f., 238
Courthope, Nathaniel, 368, 370
Coutinho, Manuel, 222
Cozucke, Sophony, 316
Crackeel, presides over captains' council, 263 n.
Cromhout, Barthold, 475
Crusades, 204
Cruwel, Werner, 182
Culture, spread of by sea, 196
Cunaeus, attacks Petrus Plancius, 67

da Gama, Vasco. *See* Gama, Vasco da
Daimyos, Japan, 212, 343 f.
Dairy industry, 14
Dale, Sir Thomas, 365, 368, 370, 372, 380, 382 ff., 388, 390, 394 f., 398; opposed to John Jourdain, 379, 396
Dalem (court), Djakarta, 366 f., 382, 385

Dam, Amsterdam, 33
Dam, Pieter van, 149 n.; on corruption, 465; on monopoly, 462
Damascus, 205, 288
Danser, Simon de, 127 f.
Danube River, 204
Darling (ship), 291, 294 f.
David, Cassarian, 397
Davis, John, 122, 124, 175, 276; Davis Strait, 122
Debentures. *See* Dutch East India Company
Decima, Japan, 213
Decker, Hans de, 350 f.
Declaration of Independence, U.S.A., 146
De Dominio Maris (statement of English maritime dominion), 274
Defense (ship), 350, 352
Defense, Treaty of. *See* Treaty of Defense
De jure belli et pacis, Grotius, 131, 474
De Jure Praedae, Grotius, 131, 273
Delft, 25; chamber of United Company, 147
Delft (ship), 166, 370, 373
Delhi, 216
Demak, Java, 209 f.
Denmark, Danish, 9; King of, 65, 81 ff.; tolls, 48; Vardohus, 85
Deventer, 11, 16 n.
Deynsen, David van, 255
Diamonds, 295; cutters, 98; Sukadana, 159
Dias, Bartolomeu, 20, 63, 215
Diemen, Antonio van, 463 f.
Dignumsz., Jan, 92
Dikes, Lowlands, 5; code of law, 5 f.; Hoorn, 232
Discourse. See Coen, Jan Pietersz.
Djakarta, 159, 170, 237, 259, 300; and Bantam, 219, 259, 320 f., 324, 357, 384; Chinese at, 404, 412; and the Dutch, 259, 306, 321 f., 343, 360–61, 366, 378, 391; as Dutch territory, 407, 410 ff., 417; English-Dutch conflict over, 322, 332, 361, 366–73, 377–89, 393 ff., 404, 409 ff., 416; as rendezvous, 322, 353 f., 361, 367, 391, 393 f., 399 f., 473
Djambi, 197, 208, 359; English at, 329; pepper, 322, 324, 342, 458, 461; Portuguese at, 218
Djankung (Coen), 451

Do Cerne, island of. *See* Mauritius

Does, Frank van der, 116; journal of, 94, 96

Dokkum, Friesland, 16 n.

Doldrums: African coast, 72; Atlantic Ocean, 248, 250

Dom João, 154 f., 157 f.

Dominium Maris, as principle of English sea power, 272 f.

Donato, Doge of Venice, 239

Dordrecht, 16 n.

Dorestad, 9

Doria, Andrea, 205

Double White Key Inn, 127

Dragon (ship), 398

Drake, Francis, 62, 125, 130, 276; in Spice Islands, 40, 43, 219, 277

Dranoutre, 65

Dredge, in Dutch diking, 6

Drente, as prehistoric settlement, 3 n.

Dryden, John, 432

Duc d'alves (shipping term), 33

Dudley, Sir Robert, 278

Duifke (ship), 88 f., 111 n., 166 f.

Dunkirk: campaign, 51, 139; pirates, 50 f., 139

Dutch East India Company, 147, 150–53, 162 f., 185, 266, 308 f., 313 f., 367, 411, 422, 437 n., 465; Amsterdam, 33, 144, 147 f., 185, 446; Banda, 260–63; charter, 146–50, 175 f., 455; communication, line of, 248, 254 f., 426, 429; contracts with natives, 164 f., 260, 455; corruption in, 463 ff., 467; crews, 243–53, 337; decline of, 467 f.; enemies of, 174 ff., 338 f., 366; factories, 153, 159, 166, 265; French East India Company, 352; financial aspects, 88, 146–48, 172–74, 177–78, 296, 333 f., 338, 397, 402, 406, 426–29, 436, 439–41, 463–68; Grotius, 131, 273; Maurice, 185 n.; merchants, 89, 242, 253, 260, 337; Oldebarnevelt, 150 f., 161 n., 172, 177; personnel, 249, 253, 260, 297, 306, 313–15, 335–38, 343, 346, 412, 424 n., 428, 463–67; policy, 151 f., 162, 169, 171, 173, 225, 260, 385; political power, 417; ships, 402; Spice Islands, 257 f., 285; States General, 151, 174, 177, 179, 242, 331, 339, 403, 440 f.; voyages, 88–99, 153–59, 161–71, 242–65; West Java, 360, 400 f., 407. *See also* England, and Dutch; Mata-

ram; Monopoly; Seventeen, Lords; Treaties

Dutch West India Company, 263 n., 322

Duyvendak, J. J. L., 199

Dyeing, in the Netherlands, 271 f.

Dysentery, 252, 359, 453

East Anglia, 271

East India House, Amsterdam, 33, 244, 246

East Java. *See* Java

Eastland, 10 f. *See also* Baltic

Economic attrition, 311, 452; applied in Amboyna, 358; applied in Coromandel, 256; Bantam, 322, 351, 356, 392 f.

Economic era, new, 58, 446

Economy: dual, 412; Dutch, 58 f.; medieval, 57

Edward I of England, 272; fishing rights granted Dutch by, 13; free trade advocate, 267

Edward III of England, 267

Egypt, 204 f.; tribute for shipping rights exacted by, 205

Eighty Years' War (1568–1648), 22; negotiations, 182–85

El Dorado, Spice Islands, 311, 402

Elizabeth I of England: and the Netherlands, 36 f., 51; immigrants, 270; and the East Indies, 279–80, 282

Emigration, Dutch, 10

Emo, Frisian, 10

Engano, island of, 93, 366

England, English, 46–47, 52, 64, 244, 268 ff., 271–74, 276–79, 282 f., 289, 293, 446; fisheries, 266, 268 f., 272; guilds, 54 f., 267; mercenaries, 136; merchant class, 54 f., 267, 276; refugees, Flemish, 45, 53, 267, 269 ff.; religion, 268, 270; woolen industry, 19, 45 f., 54 f., 266 ff., 269, 271 f.

and the Dutch, rivalry with, 37–41, 64, 164, 266, 278, 330 f., 340, 353, 360, 364, 368, 371, 402, 404; in Amboyna, 430 ff., in Banda, 260, 262, 264, 434, in Bantam, 353, in Batavia, 432, in Djakarta, 368, 371 f., 378 f., 410 f., 416, in Europe, 51 f., 64, 81 f., 266, 271 f., 275, 405 n., 431 f., in the Moluccas, 169 f., 297, 302 f., 329, 430 ff., in Patane, 395-

England (*cont.*)
98, in Tiku, 398 f. (*see also* Fore-companies; Treaty of Defense)
in the East Indies, 153; Amboyna, 429 ff., Banda, 165, 260, 262 ff., 329, 350, 357, 418, Bantam, 300, 306, 320, 351 f., 360, 366 ff., 378, 384 ff., 391 f., 394 f., 404, 432, 449, Batavia, 432, Bencoolen, 458, Djakarta, 322, 332, 367 f., 370 ff., 379 ff., 388, 394 f., 409 ff., 416, Lagundi, 432, Macassar, 303, 328, Moluccas, 169, 301 ff., 316 ff., 329, 340, 350, 352 f., 429 ff., Pulu Run (Banda), 350, 417, Tidore, 329. *See also* English East India Company; Jourdain, John; London; Trade

England's Way to Win Wealth (pamphlet on sea trade), 274

English Channel, 50, 139, 341

English East India Company, 143, 279–83, 288, 290, 330, 332 ff., 365, 397, 429, 432, 434, 467 f.; in Banda, 165, 264; capital, 280, 332, 365, 406, 425; management, 281, 333; and James, I, 283, 291 f.; in Spice Islands, 285; in India, 285, 290–94; internal rivalry, 293 ff., 304; in Sumatra, 294 f.; in Japan, 295, 329, 343, 429; in Macassar, 303 f., 328. *See also* England, and the Dutch; Jourdain, John

Enkhuizen, 16, 30, 70, 83, 86 f., 147; northeast passage, role in exploration of, 79, 98; and salt trade, 14

Enkhuyzen (ship), 327

Erikzen, Barent, 47

Erosion of Dutch shore lines, 6 f.

Essex, Robert, Earl of, 124

Essex (county), 267

Ethiopia, 71

Europe, 55 f.; spice market, 173, 280, 329, 416, 427, 457, 459. *See also* Trade

Exchange, Antwerp, London, 270

Exchequer, of the Netherlands, Holland's contribution to, 137

Exploration: Coen on, 339; in wooden ships, 50

Factories, Dutch East India Company, 117, 153, 159, 164, 168

Faith (ship), 126

Falatehan, Bantam, 210

Famine, in Italy, 46 f., 236

Faria, Pedro de, 222

Feudalism, Lowlands, 14

Fifth voyage. *See* Dutch East India Company

Filibote (Vlie-boot), type of Dutch ship, 234

Filibuster, origin of word, 234

Filibusteros, Spanish name for Dutch sailors, 234

Firando, Dutch at, 258, 343

Fisheries, fishermen (Dutch), 11–14, 22, 47–48, 51, 53, 232; College of Great Fisheries, 12 f., 56, 232; rivalry with England, 13, 266, 268 f., 272–75. *See also* Treaties

Fitch, Ralph, 277

Flamengos, name for Dutch crews, 19

Flanders, 19, 44; textiles, 45; woolen industry, 267, 269

Fleet of Defense, Dutch-English, 407, 415, 425

Fleets, departure of, 246

Flemish Right: to lands in Baltic, 10; to free fishing in English waters, 13

Floods, Lowlands, 5, 9 f., 231 f.

Floris V, 24

Fluit. *See* Flute

Flushing, 37, 145; Parma, 39

Flute (type of Dutch ship), 48 ff., 111 n., 233 f.

Fly-boat (Vlie-boot), type of Dutch ship, 234

Fonseca, Dom Frei Vincente da, 71, 219

Fore-companies, 133, 278, 280; competition, 110, 116, 119, 130–33, 142, 149; free trade, 141 f., 438, 454; instructions of, 111, 128, 133 f.; States General, 141 f.; unification, 133 n., 135, 141 ff.

Formosa, 428; pirates, 211

Fort Rammekens, 37

Founders' Hall, London, 279

Fourth voyage. *See* Dutch East India Company

France, French, 18, 20, 36, 350; and the Dutch, 36, 238; ships, 349 f., 368, 403

Frederic Henry, Prince, Stadholder of Holland and Zealand, 452

Free enterprise: European trade, 454; fore-companies, 110; Indonesia, 463, 468; Netherlands, 22. *See also* Trade

Freedom: of religion, Oldebarnevelt, 137; of the seas, 273, 327

French East India Company, 125, 175, 177, 182, 338 f., 349; indemnity, 352; Balthasar de Moucheron, 125; Isaac Lemaire, 175, 338 f., 350; Pieter Lyntgens, 177

Friesland, 10; Willem Lodewyk, stadholder of, 42

Frisii, Frisians, 3 f., 11, 23 f., 201; trade, 8

Frisius, Gemma, 60, 67

Frobisher, Martin, 64, 276

Fruin, Robert, on Dutch trade, 52; on Hanseatic League, 17

Fugger, House of, 19; Portuguese trade, 223

Funan, 197

Fur trade, Dutch, 80

Furnival, J. S., on English, 301

Gajah Mada, 200 f.

Galle, Ceylon, 154, 158, 225, 458

Gallucci, describes Father Neyen, 183

Galvao, Antonio, 219

Gama, Francesco da, 112

Gama, Vasco da, 20, 63, 215 f., 218

Gardiner, Charles, 104 n.

Geerke, H. P., on Coen, 421

Genoa, Genoese, 20, 204 f.

Gerretson, C., on Coen, 422

Gevaerts, Captain, 189

Geyl, Pieter: theory of political split in Netherlands, 44; on Dunkirk campaign, 139 n.

Ghent, Treaty of, 30, 35, 136

Gibraltar, battle at, 189 f., 240 f.

Globe: Langren's, 82; Plancius, conception of, 84; celestial, 92 n.

Goa, 73, 161, 163, 170, 217, 221, 225, 248, 255; Dutch at, 254; English at, 277

Goes, Zealand, 145

Golconda. *See* Treaties

Gold: Americas, 21; Sumatra, 74

Gold Coast, 47

Golden Age, Holland, 45, 61

Golden Hind (ship), 125

Golden Hoop (sea wall), 5

Goldsmiths, 98

Good Hope, Cape of. *See* Cape of Good Hope

Good Hope (ship), 257, 287

Government, Oldebarnevelt on, 138 f.

Governors general, 296, 332, 335, 354; Both, Pieter, 142, 265 n., 300, 305 f., 312, 315, 338; Brouwer, Hendrik, 460; Carpentier, Pieter de, 390, 427, 445, 447 f.; Coen, Jan Pietersz., 347; Hoorn, Johan van, 467; Maetsuycker, Johan, 464; Reael, Laurens, 335; Reynst, Gerard, 315, 328, 334–35, 338; Specx, Jacques, 459 f.

Graaf, H. J. de, 452

Grain trade, 14 f.; Baltic, 236. *See also* Trade

Granary, Amsterdam, 29, 46 f.

Grand Turk, 288

Grave, Philip de, 289 f.

Great Banda (Lonthor), 260, 418. *See also* Banda

Great East, 113 n., 170. *See also* Moluccas

Great Wall, China, 211

Greece, 20

Greenland Company, 275

Grenfell, buccaneer, 64

Gresham, Sir Thomas, 270; describes Amsterdam trade, 21

Griffin (ship), 257 f.

Grise, Java, 159, 209

Groningen, 16 n.

Groot, Willem de, 472–73

Grootenhuys, Arend ten, 88

Grotius (Hugo de Groot), 131, 183, 348, 473–75; Dutch East India Company, 131, 273; on international law, 131, 473 f.; on freedom of the seas, 273 f., 327; in London, 330 f.; evaluated, 474 n.

Gualterotti, House of, 19

Guicciardini, Francesco; describes Antwerp, 19; praises Dutch sailors, 16

Guilds, 21 f., 56; abroad, 54; English, 54 f., 267, 397

Guinea, 47

Guise, Duke of, 41

Gujerat, Gujerati, 124, 163, 204, 207–08, 255; pilots, 215 f.

Gulf Stream, effect on shipping, 81

Gurus, Hindu, 196

Gysels, Aert: on Coen, 298 f., 361, 419 f.; at Japara, 360 f.; in Moluccas, 420

Haarlem, 25, 32; linen industry, 30, 45; siege of, 70, 136
Haarlem (ship), 398
Haeff, Adriaan ten, 124
Haen, Hendrick de, 382
Hagen, Pieter van der, 125, 127
Hagen, Steven van der, 119, 161, 163, 165, 168; at Amboyna, 120, 164; at Banda, 164 f.; on English-Dutch co-operation, 406; in Malacca Strait, 318, 342; on native trade, 462
Haired-Din (Barbarossa), 205
Hairun, Sultan, Ternate, 219
Hakluyt, Richard, 98, 278
Hakluyt Society, 76 n.
Half Moon (ship), 32, 175
Hamburg, 11, 232; Grotius in, 474
Hanseatic League (Hansa), 11, 16, 55; Baltic trade, 18; decline of, 17, 232; Dutch members, 16 n.; Visby Sea Laws, 99
Harderwijk, 16 n.
Harmony (ship), 339, 353
Hasselaar, Kenau, Haarlem, 70
Hasselaer, Pieter, 87
Hastings, Warren, 432
Hatch, Captain, 370, 372
Haultain, Admiral, 178 f., 188
Hawkins, John, buccaneer, 130
Hawkins, William, 293; in Agra, 290 f., 293 f.
Hayam Waruk, 201 f.
Hector (ship), 260, 294
Heemskerck, Jacob van, 115–16, 130; describes Bandanese, 115 f., 260; at battle of Gibraltar, 188 ff., 241; in East Indies, 111, 113; on northeast passage voyage, 101, 104 f.
Heidelberg, Calvinism in, 135 f.
Helst, Bart van der, 61
Hendriksz., Lambert, 189
Henry III of France, 36, 41
Henry IV of France, 177, 182, 237; French East India Company, 125, 175
Henry VII of England, 272
Henry VIII of England, 268
Henry the Navigator, 63, 215
Herbarium, Leiden University, 403
Hermans, Dominie, 387

Hermite, Jacques l', 170, 255, 257, 259, 265, 297; on Bandanese, 265
Herring, herring fisheries, 11–14, 17, 47–48, 274; English-Dutch rivalry, 266, 272–75. *See also* Fisheries
Heyn, Piet, silver fleet, 263 n.
High Street. *See* Hoog Straat
Hindu, Hinduism: *gurus*, 196; Indonesia, 196 f., 202 f., 206, 209, 219, 320
Hindu Kush, Moguls, 216
History of British India, by Hunter, 333
Hitu, Amboyna, 114, 164 n.; Dutch fort at, 120; Jourdain at, 301 f.
Hitu, Capitan. *See* Capitan Hitu
Hitu Strait, 301
Hoen, Simon, 261, 263
Hoghanazan, Surate, 290, 292
Holland, province of, 36–39, 59, 136–37, 182 and n., 230, 422; Dutch Republic, 36 n., 137; Golden Age, 45, 61; importance of, 87; location, 24; northeast passage, 83; population, 422. *See also* Netherlands
Holland Cemetery, Madagascar, 92
Hollandia, redoubt, 450 f.
Hollandia (ship), 88 f., 93, 262
Holy See, 238
Holystones, 247
Homosexuality aboard ship, 247
Hondius, Jodocus, 92 n.
Hoog Straat (High Street), Amsterdam, 33, 244
Hook of Desire, Novaya Zemlya, 103
Hoorn, 12, 16, 30, 47 f., 231–33, 239 f.; admiralty college at, 240; Coen in, 229 f.; Dutch East India Company, 147, 240; education at, 231 n.; flute ships used in, 49; Mediterranean trade with, 236, 239; navigation school at, 233 n.; northeast passage voyage from, 98; population, 232; Red Stone, center of, 233; trade, 14, 232, 236, 239 f.
Hoorn, Johan van, 467
Hoorn (ship), 260, 263, 265
Hope (ship), 126
Horn, Cape, 176, 339
Hornus, first settler of Hoorn, 231
Hound (ship), 396
Houtman, Cornelis: at Lisbon, 68, 73, 75 f., 85 f.; voyages, 89, 93–96, 122 f.
Houtman, Frederik, 89, 92, 122 f.,

164, 263; Dutch-Malay dictionary compiled by, 123
Hudde, Hendrik, 64 f., 88
Hudson, Henry, 79, 175, 276
Hudson River, 32, 175
Huguenots, 36, 135
Hulsebos, Adriaen, Dominie, 380, 389
Hundred Years' War, 267 f.
Hunter, Sir W. W., 276; describes English East India Company, 333
Hurault de Maisse, on English-Dutch rivalry, 51 f.
Huybers, H. F. M., on Coen, 421

Ibn Batuta, 208, 215
Iceland, fishing, 273
Ilha de Bravo, 299
Ilha de Mayo, 445; English at, 287
Immigrants. *See* Refugees
Imperialism, Asia, 372, 378
Impyn, Master, 60
India, 204; English in, 277, 285, 290–294; Hindu rulers, 216; Jews, 218; Moguls, 216 f., 285; Moslem rulers, 216; political situation, 216 f.; textiles, 166, 193, 256. *See also* Portugal, Portuguese
Indian Ocean, 93, 111, 204, 215; monsoons, 194; route, 416; sailing directions, 73, 86
Indies, 71 f., 110, 243, 246, 359; routes to, 20, 62 f., 65, 68, 72 f., 79, 82, 91, 110 f., 215, 277 f., 416; West Indies, 21 n., 457 n. *See also* Dutch East India Company; England; Forecompanies; English East India Company; Indonesia; Portugal
Indigo, 291
Indonesia, Indonesians, 193, 196 f., 211
    pre-European: Angrok, 198; Asiatic trade, 195 f.; Bali, 199; China, 199 f., 202, 207, 212; East Java, 199; Gajah Mada, 200 f.; Hayam Waruk, 201 f.; Hinduism, 196 f., 202 f., 206, 209, 219, 320; Jayanagara, 200; Kediri, 198 ff., 202; Kertanagara, 199 f.; Madjapahit, 200–03; Madura, 199; money economy, 362; Moslems, 114, 202 f., 206, 208 f., 224; *Nagarakertagama* (Javanese epic), 199 ff.; Pamalayu, 199 f.; *Pararaton* (Javanese chronicle), 198 f.; Prabanca, 199, 201; Singo-sari, 198 ff.; Tuban, 200; Tumapel, 198; Vijaya, 199 f.; *Wadanas*, 201; *see also* Islam
    modern, 412, 428, 452, 461; Dutch empire, 308, 411; Chinese, 361 n., 463; Europeans arrive, 219; law and order, 310, 403; money economy, 362; native trade, 455; *Pax Neerlandica*, 310. *See also* Coen, Jan Pietersz.; Colonization; Contracts; Dutch East India Company; Free enterprise; Indies
"Indonesia," name, 428 n.
Industrial revolution, Netherlands, 47 f.
Industry, Dutch, 47 f., 53
Inn of Brille, The Hague, 142
Inquisition, 28, 45
Inspectors-General, 465
Insurance, marine, 59
Intermarriage: Dutch, 389; Portuguese, 221 f.
International law, Grotius, 131, 473 f.
Ireland, 234
Iron forging, 232
Iskandar Muda, Achin, 458
Isla de Mayo, 92, 248, 445. *See also* Ilha de Mayo
Islam, Moslems, 206; Gujerati, 208; Indonesia, 114, 202 f., 206, 208 f.; Java, 202 f., 209; Malacca, 206 f.; Moluccas, 224; and the Portuguese, 209, 218, 221, 224; *shahbandar* (harbor master), 208; Southeast Asia, 195, 208; Sumatra, 206, 208; traders, 206, 208–09, 217, 224, 454
Italy, 20; bookkeeping system of, 60; Coen in, 235–39; famine, 46 f., 236
Itinerary (early Dutch account of East): effects of, 76; in England, 278 f.; in first Dutch merchant voyage to East, 91; Paludanus, 71, 74 f.; publications, 75 f. *See also* Linschoten, Jan Huyghen van
I-tsing, 197
Ivory, tribute, 217
Ivory Coast, 47

Jacatra. *See* Djakarta
Jacobsz., Laurens, 67
James I of England, 180, 290, 440; Amboyna affair protested by, 431; and Coen, 439 f.; English-Dutch cooperation, 406; English East

James I of England (*cont.*)
  India Company, 283; and fisheries, 13, 272 f.; Neyra, 260; North America, 188; and whaling, 275
Jamestown, 180, 398
Jansen, Willem, 167, 170
Jansz., Hendrik, captain, 189 f.
Jansz., Hendrik, chief merchant, 395, 397 f.
Jansz., Jaspar, 301
Jansz., Willem, 398; Australia, 89
Japan, Japanese, 80, 98, 204, 211, 359; Buddhists, 212; and China, 211; Christianity, 212, 225, 343; copper, 131, 193; Daimyos, 212, 343 f.; Dutch in, 213, 243, 258, 265; English in, 295, 329, 343, 429; Europeans, 211, 213; Jesuits, 212, 343; Linschoten on, 79; *Love* (ship), 126 f.; mercenaries, 305, 312, 352 n., 417, 419, 430; Matthew Perry, 213; political situation, 212; Portuguese in, 212 f., 225; Shogun, 126 f., 212, 258; silver, 338; tribute exacted from Dutch by, 343 f. *See also* Trade; Treaties
Japara, Java, 390; factory plundered, 360, 362, 366; Aert Gysels, 360 f.; rendezvous, 319, 323; rice trade, 312
Java, Javanese, 75, 201, 320 f., 323, 412; Coen's policy on, 447; Dutch foothold in, 401, 407; East Java, 199, 202, 209, 211, 319, 323, 361 (*see also* Agung, Sultan); Monroe Doctrine, 366; population, 320 n.; pre-European, 194, 209 (dynasties, 198–203) (Hinduism and Islam in, 202, 209, 219); West Java, 219, 323, 356, 360, 388
Java Sea, monsoon, 95, 129, 194
Jayanagara, 200
Jeannin, Pierre, 474
Jehangir, 290, 292 ff.
Jesuits, in Japan, 212
Jewels, 98, 100
Jews: and capitalism, 230; in India, 218
John II of Portugal, 63
Johore, 158, 161, 168, 318; and Achin, 122 f.; Dutch at, 165, 257; and Portuguese, 218, 257; Sultan of, 257; treaty with Dutch, 248
Jonge, J. K. J. de, 225; on Coen, 421
Jourdain, John, 285–95, 323, 332, 365,

397; and Banda alliance, 316 f.; at Bantam, 304, 316, 370; Cape of Good Hope described by, 287; and Coen, 301 ff., 364, 366; and Sir Thomas Dale, 379, 396; in England, 364 f.; on the English, 289; at Macassar, 303 f.; in Moluccas, 301 ff.; at Patane battle, 395–98; in Yemen, 288
Jurisprudence, Djakarta (Batavia), 411
Justice, native, 403
Jutland, 9, 11

Kalff, S., 421
Kambela, Moluccas, 301, 303, 329
Kampar, Sumatra, 208
Kampen, 11, 16 n., 236
Kampong (village), 378
Kandy, Ceylon, 154–57; Portuguese at, 217
Kara Sea, 80, 84 f., 98, 102; ice barrier, 102 f.; northeast passage, 85; Plancius, 90
Kara Strait, 80; tolls, 83
Karta, Java, 449
Kasteel van Verre, Amboyna, 120
Kediri, Java, 198 ff., 202, 447
Keelhauling, 100, 102
Keeling, William, 283; at Banda, 260, 262
Kendal, Java, 449
Kertanagara, 199 f.
Keyzer, Pieter, 89, 93–94; astronomy, 91, 94, 123
Kiers, L., on Coen, 422
"King," title, 116 n.
Klaasz., Regnier, 179
Knight's Hall, The Hague, 472
Kola, 104 f.
Kola Peninsula, 81
Kra, Isthmus, 194
Kraak (carack), porcelain, 131
Kroniek van Hoorn by Velius, 17
Kublai Khan, 199 f.

Lace-making, 269
Lafer (merchant), 255
Lagundi, 432
Lam, Jan Dirckz., 329, 340
Lamberts, Abraham, 425
Lancaster, James, 278, 281
Landsadvocaat (title in Dutch republic), 138 n.
Langren, Jacob Florisz. van, 82

Lants, Melis, 387 n.
Lapland, 80
Lasso, Bartolomeo de, 68
Lauwers, River, 5
Law and order: Coen on, 310, 403; Djakarta (Batavia), 411, 417
League of Catholic noblemen, 36, 41, 237
Leaseholds: Batavia, 462; Djakarta, 411
Leck, Daniel van der, 441
Leeuwarden, 16 n.
Lefebre, Jacques, 373
Legaspi, Lopez de, 225
Leicester, Earl of, in Netherlands, 37–41, 64, 278
Leiden, 25; bars refugees, 32; siege, 136; university, 348, 403; woolen industry, 30, 45
Lemaire, Isaac, 142, 173, 176; and Dutch East India Company, 174 ff., 339; French East India Company, 175, 338 f., 350
Lemaire, Jacob, 338 f.
Lemaire Strait, 175, 339
Leme, Enrique, 219
Lendas da India (Portuguese chronicle), 218
Lepanto, Battle of, 205
Letter of Articles, ships', 99 ff., 246 f.
Letter of Bottomry, 57
Letter of information, Dutch East India Company, 162 f.
Letter of transport, crews, 245
Letters of marque, 51
Letters patent, 84, 99
Leur, J. C. van, on Asiatic trade, 195
Levant, 56; Levant Company, English, 277–80
Ley-Timor, Amboyna, 164 n.
Liability, limited, 57 f.; Dutch East India Company, 148, 465
Liberalism, and religion, 66. See also Arminians: Remonstrants
Liberals, versus Calvinists, 471; Grotius, 473
Life line, Spanish-Portuguese, 342
Lima, Peru, 129
Linen industry, Haarlem, 45; England, 269
Linschoten, Jan Huyghen van, 69 ff., 85, 91; Itinerary, 71 f., 74 ff.; on Japan, 79; on Java, 75; and northeast passage, 84, 91, 101 f.; on Plancius, 75, 90; on the Portuguese, 72

f.; on reals, 88; on spices, 74. See also Itinerary
Linschoten Vereeniging (Dutch historical society), 76 n.
Lion (ship), 123
Lioness (ship), 123
Liorne, Pieter Jansz., 48, 161, 240; flute ship designed by, 233
Lisbon, 20, 220, 222; Cornelis Houtman in, 75 f., 86
Livorno, 233
Loevesteyn, Castle, 473 f.
Logistics, of waterways, 42 f.
London, 269, 277, 405; Dutch mission, 330 f.; Frisian trade, 8; merchants, 271, 277 ff., 283; plague, 281; Royal exchange, 270
Longfellow, Henry Wadsworth, 127 f.
Longitude, compass variation, 92 n.
Lonthor (Great Banda), 260, 262, 418
Lords Seventeen. See Seventeen
Louis XIII of France, 474
Louvain, 135
Love (ship), 126 f.
Lübeck, 11, 24
Luhu, Moluccas, 301 ff.
Lumber, 49 f.
Luther, 21, 26
Lyme Regis, 286, 364
Lynn, 232
Lyntgens, Pieter, 176; French East India Company, 177

Macao, 173, 212, 225, 312; attack on, 342; Dutchmen hanged in, 130, 159
Macassar, 259; Dutch crew murdered at, 353; Dutch trading with, 259, 327; English at, 303 f., 328; smuggling, 304, 456; spice trade, 327 f.; Sultan of, 327
Mace, from Banda, 165, 260, 456
Machiavelli, 42, 360, 434
Madagascar, 73, 92, 111, 122; port on Indian route, 111 f.; slaves from, 343, 358, 361
Madelyn, Hans, 450
Madjapahit, 200–03, 207, 404; decline, 209, 320; East Java, 209; Islam, 206; Monroe Doctrine, 366; private trade, 222
Madura, 94 f., 199, 447 f.
Madura Strait, 448
Maelson, Francois, 82

Maetsuycker, Johan, 464

Magellan, Fernando, 20

Magellan, Strait of, 125 f., 128 f., 173, 175, 339; blockade, 173; Isaac Lemaire, 175

Magna Charta, 146

Magnificat, of Amsterdam, 25, 28; Reynier Pauw, 87, 298, 348, 475. See also Amsterdam, government

Mahmudis (coin), 291

Mahu, Jacques, 125 f.

Malabar Coast, 163, 248, 255, 415, 464; pepper, 217, 255; Portuguese, 222; trade, 255, 342; treaties, 308

Malacca, 75, 158, 161, 225, 248, 312, 318; blockade, 168, 342, 458; conquests, 207 f.; Dutch victory over, 458, 461; Gujerati, 207; importance of, 73, 207, 217 f.; Islam, 206 f.; origin, 206 f.; Portuguese, 168, 202 f., 207 f., 210, 217 f., 257 f., 342

Malacca Strait, 73, 158, 165, 198, 248, 257, 317 f., 342; blockade, 168, 342, 458; importance of, 168, 194; monsoon, 170 f., 319

Malaga, 229

Malay (language), 73, 86; dictionary, 123

Malay Peninsula, 73; ancient trade, 194; English in, 278; Islam, 208

Malayo, Moluccas, 169

Malayu, Sumatra, 197, 199

Malik al Saleh, 206

Malik Ibrahim, 209

Malindi, East Africa, 215

Mandura Redja, 450 f.

Manhattan, 322

Manila, 168, 225, 312; blockade, 329, 358; China trade, 264; Dutch attack, 341 f.; Spanish, 225

Mansfield, Captain, buccaneer, 64

Manuel, King of Portugal, 216, 220

Map, Mercator, 82

Marco Polo, 198, 211, 215; in Sumatra, 206

Mardykers (Liberated slaves in Indies), 462 f.

Mare Liberum (study of maritime law), 273 f.

Margaret of Parma, 27

Marguerite (ship), 349, 387 n.

Marine insurance, origin, 59

Marliani, Aloysius, 12

Mas, River, East Java, 448

Massacre: Amboyna, 431; Banda, 261 f.

Mataram (Moslem), 210, 312 f.; and Bantam, 321, 447 f.; Batavia, attack on, 449–52; Dutch relations with, 312 f., 319, 321, 323, 360, 366, 448, 459; expansion, 320 f., 324, 447 f.; Hinduism, 210, 451; rice, 312, 320, 360, 452, 458 f.; trade, 458, 461

Matelief, Cornelis, 167–71, 257, 358; on Japan trade, 258

Matjan, Moluccas, 264, 461

Maurice, Prince, 88, 99, 137, 156, 260, 452; Calvinists, 348, 471; Dunkirk campaign, 139; and Oldebarnevelt, 137, 139, 182, 184, 186, 348, 417 f.; northeast passage, 82, 85; stadholder and admiral-general, 42, 137; truce negotiations, 182 ff.

Mauritius, Island, port on route to Indies, 113, 159, 168

Mauritius (ship), 88 f., 95

Mayflower (ship), 45, 181

Mazulipatnam: Dutch at, 166, 256; Sir Thomas Dale at, 396, 398

Mecca, sherifs, 155 n.

Medemblik, 47

Medieval economy, 57

Medina Sidonia, Armada, 40

Mediterranean: Dutch trade in, 46 f., 161, 233, 236; pirates in, 205; as trade route, 18 f.; Spanish in, 277

Megat Iskandar Shah, 207

Mellema, Elcius, 60

Mendoza, Furtado de, 168

Menko, Abbot of Wittewierum, 10

Mennonites, 51, 176, 403; against privateering, 131

Ment, Eva, Coen's wife, 439, 442, 453

Ment, Lysbeth, 442

Mercator, Gerardus, 67, 81 f.

Mercenaries: English, 136; Japanese, 305, 312, 352 n., 417, 419, 430; Netherlands, 42, 136

Merchant Adventurers, England, 79 f., 100 n., 267

Merchant republic, Dutch East India Company, 150

Merchants: Amsterdam, 25, 27 f., 87, 109, 187, 278, 348 f.; Chinese, 124, 322, 328 f., 351, 359, 404; employees, Dutch East India Company, 89, 242, 253, 260, 337; Gujerati, 204, 207; guilds, 55; Hindu, 196; Lisbon,

220; Moslem, 206–09, 217, 224, 454; of the Staple, England, 267

Meridians, Mercator projection of, 82

Mesopotamia, 204

Metals, precious, 98, 100

Meulenaer, Jan, 89, 95 f.

Meuse, 248

Mexia, Affonso, 222

Michelborne, Sir Edward, 283

Middelburg, 16 n., 143, 185; Company, 124; Dutch East India Company, 144 f., 147; Moucheron, 121; northeast passage, 98

Middle class, 31; in England, 269 f., 272; in Indonesia, 411; in the Netherlands, 31, 268

Middleton, David, 283

Middleton, Sir Henry, 283, 291–95

Mierevelt, painter, 135

Ming dynasty, 211 f.

Minuit, Peter, 322

Mocha, 287 ff.; Dutch at, 377; English at, 289

Modjokerto, East Java, 199

Moguls, 204; China, 211; India, 216 f., 285

Mol, Geert Jansdr., Coen's mother, 230

Molin, Nicola, 272 f.

Molre, Jan de, 261

Moluccas, 112 f., 163, 168 f., 264, 461; burghers, 358; Coen in, 300–03; colonization, 300 f.; condominium, 310; contracts, 309, 316, 326, 361, 423; El Dorado, 402; English in, 169, 301 ff., 316 ff., 329, 340, 350, 352 f., 429 ff.; Dutch Fleet of Defense in, 415; Dutch trade monopoly in, 327 f., 354, 460 f.; Francis Drake, 40; free trade, 300; importance to Dutch, 170, 257 f., 402; Islam, 114, 224; native trade, 224, 354, 423; political situation, 310; Portuguese in, 119, 130, 218 f., 223 f.; Spanish in, 130, 165, 168, 264, 402; spices, 113 n., 248; treaties, 308, 326, 352. See also Amboyna; Banda; Spice Islands; Ternate

Mombasa, 287

Mongolia, 211

Monopoly, 132, 460–63; in Banda, 165, 415, 460; of cinnamon, 458; of cloves, 165, 456 f.; of cotton goods,

342, 459; by Dutch East India Company, 149, 151 ff., 455, 458 f.; enforcement, 326 f., 423, 455, 466; of mace, 456; in Moluccas, 327 f., 354, 460 f.; by native rulers, 454; of nutmegs, 165, 456; by Old Company, 134 f., 142; of opium, 459; of pepper, 342, 458; by Portuguese, 220, 222; by Seventeen, 405, 407, 429, 437, 460, 462; of spice trade, 152, 309, 411, 423, 436 f., 455; of spices, 75, 265 n., 317, 326, 328, 385, 401, 427, 458 f.; by States of Holland, 135

Monroe Doctrine, Java, 366

Monsoons: Asiatic trade, 194; Banda Sea, 194; China Sea, 194; Java Sea, 95, 194; Malacca Strait, 319

Montmorency (ship), 349

Moon (ship), 119 f.

Morningstar (ship), 119 f., 396, 398

Moscow: Dutch in, 80 f.; English in, 80

Moslem, Moslems. See Islam

Motely, John L., 183

Moucheron, Balthasar de, 45, 81 f., 84, 121, 125, 142, 154 n.; Dutch East India Company, 144 f.; French East India Company, 125; northeast passage, 82 ff., 91, 101, 109; States General, 98 f.; Veere, 109, 121, 125; William of Orange, 121; Zealand Company, 121–24

Mozambique, 163, 170, 225, 248, 254; attack on, 342

Mozambique Strait, 111, 161

Musa Beg, 445

Muschamp, George, 395, 397

Muscovy, 56

Muscovy Company, English, 80, 275, 278 f.

Mustering, by Dutch East India Company, 244 f.

Mutiny: among Dutch at Djakarta, 386; on Dutch ships, 102; of English crew, 288

Nagarakertagama (Buddhist epic), 199 ff.

Nagasaki, 213

"Nameless" company (the corporation), 58

Nanking, 211

Naphta, Sumatra, 74

Narwa, Baltic, 80 f.
Nassau (Vaigach) Strait, 85, 98, 102; blockade, 173
National Archives, The Hague, 299 n., 359, 387
Natives, 91, 153, 156, 361, 403, 460 f.; contracts with, 165, 260; spice monopoly by, 454. *See also* Trade
Naval warfare, 254; training, 248 f.
Navigation, Dutch: instruments, 215 f.; museum, 82; school, 84, 90 f., 233 n., 242; States General, 142
Nay, Cornelis, 84 f., 101
Neck, Jacob van, 111 ff.; Old Company's instructions to, 111; liberal policy of, 112; profitable voyage of, 114; later years of, 116
Nederburgh, S. C., 468
Negombo, Ceylon, 458
Negotiations, English-Dutch, 330 f.
Nepotism: in Amsterdam, 475; among Portuguese, 221 f.
Netherlands, 3 ff., 8–12 n., 14, 23, 31, 37, 42, 44 f., 53, 55, 60 f., 130, 139 n., 157, 159, 231 f., 239, 255, 261, 264, 339, 349 f., 353, 360, 422; capitalism, 22, 31, 47 f., 109 f., 467; cleavage, 35, 44 f., 139 n., 184; education, 230 f., 235, 268; Dutch Republic, 36 and n., 45 and n., 137, 348 (established, 35 f., 136 f.); empire, 150, 152, 307–12, 326, 402, 438, 446, 468 f., 471; England, relations with, 36 f., 45, 81, 267, 269–72, 405–10; merchant class, 22, 25, 60 f.; population, 53; refugees, 44 f., 53, 142, 147 n., 236, 269; religion, 348, 471 f. *See also* Dutch East India Company; England, and the Dutch; Fisheries; France; Portugal; Ships; Spain; Trade; Treaties
New Amsterdam, 33, 175, 405 n.
New Brabant Company, 142
New Company, 109 f.
New economic age, 58, 266, 277; Coen, 393; England, 405, 446
New Guinea, 167
New Holland (Siberia), 85
New Hoorn (Batavia), 231, 394
New Hoorn (ship), 235
New North Sea (Kara Sea), 85
New Spain (Mexico), 173
New Zealand, 461 n.
Newcastle, England, 232; coal, 279
Newport, battle of, 139

Neyen, Father, in Dutch-Spanish truce negotiations, 182 ff.
Neyra, Banda Islands, 260 ff.
Nieuw Hoorn (New Hoorn), 394
Nina (ship), 167
Ningpo, 211
Noort, Cornelis van, 128
Noort, Oliver van, 127 f.; voyage, 128 ff.
Nordenskjold, Nils, A. E., northeast passage, 102
Norsemen, 9. *See also* Vikings
North America, 79; James I, 188
North Pole, 82; Plancius, 84, 103
North Sea, 246
Northeast passage to the Indies: Amsterdam, 83 f., 103; Dutch interest, 81–85; letters patent, 84; Linschoten, 84, 91, 101 f.; Moucheron, 82 ff., 91, 101, 109; Plancius, 102 f.; States General, 83, 98, 102
Northwest passage, 79, 122
Norway: Baltic trade, 18; firs, 234
Norwich, England, 267
Note buyers, 245
Notes, Dutch East India Company, 245
Novaya Zemlya, 80; Dutch winter at, 104, 113; Plancius describes, 84; whales, 105
Novgorod, 80
Novo Cholmogory (Archangel), 81
Nutmegs: from Banda, 260; Linschoten on, 74; monopoly of, 165, 456; uses of, 74; West Indies, 457 n.

Oath of loyalty, Dutch East India Company, 246
Ob River, 81
Oetgens, Frans, 475
Old Company, Amsterdam, 110, 116, 119 f.; instructions to captains, 133 f.; monopoly, 134 f., 142
Old Count, Djakarta, 38 f.
Old Sun (ship), 367, 371
Oldebarnevelt, Johan van, 37 ff., 42, 134–39, 186 n., 471–75; and Amsterdam, 109, 139 f., 188, 348 f.; Calvinism, 136 f., 471; Dutch East India Company, 150 f., 161 n., 172, 177; Dutch-English negotiations, 36 f., 331, 405; enemies of, 137, 140, 188, 471; on fishing rights, 273; fore-companies, unification of, 135, 142–

46; freedom of religion, 137; on government, 138 f.; income, 138 n.; northeast passage, 83, 85; opposes Old Company, 134 f.; and Prince Maurice, 137, 139, 182, 184, 186, 188, 348; remonstrant, 348; "Sharp Resolution," 471; Spanish truce, 182 ff., 187 f., 241; States General, 349; States of Holland, 38 f.; William of Orange, 136 f.
Oleron, Sea Laws of, 99
Olive oil, 19 f.
Ommelands vaarders (early Dutch seamen), 11 n., 16
Onrust, 321, 368, 370
Opium, monopoly of, 459
Orang Kayas, 164 n., 169, 316; Amboyna, 164, 169, 302; Banda, 169, 260 f., 419 f.
Oresund, 83; tolls at, 18, 48, 51, 81; traffic lists of, 18
Ormuz, 248; Portuguese at, 277
Os, Dirk van, 87
Ottoman empire, 204 f. *See also* Turkey, Turks
Oudenaerde, 236
Oxenstjerna, Axel G., 474

Pacific Ocean, 80, 125 f., 173, 215
Pacification of Ghent. *See* Ghent
Pacioli, Luca, 60
Padjajaran, West Java, 219
Padjang, Java, 210
Padua, 74
Palembang, 197; and Bantam, 324; pepper, 461
Palm wine, 252
Paludanus, Bernardus, 71, 91; *Itinerary,* 74 f.
Pamalayu, Sumatra, 199 f.
Pamphlets, England, 272 ff.
Pangawas (Bantam provincial governors), 259
Pangeran (Bantam official), 259 n. *See also* Rana Mangala
Paramesvara, 207
Pararaton (Javanese chronicle), 198 f.
Paris, 474
Parma, Duke of, 37, 39–41; Antwerp, 37; Calvinists, 44 f.; Henry III of France, 41
Pasai, 207 f.
Pasaruan, 324, 447
Patane, 394 f.; battle at, 395–98; English at, 329; pepper, 130, 155 n., 158, 458; trade center, 158
Patapouly, 256
Pati Udara, 202
Patih (Madjapahit official), 200
Paul V, 239
Pauw, Reynier, 65, 68, 110, 185 f., 354 n., 471, 475 f.; Calvinists, 475 f.; enemy trade, 475; as Magnificat, 87, 298, 348, 354 n., 475; and Prince Maurice, 186; and Oldebarnevelt, 472, 475
Pax Neerlandica, Indonesia, 310
Peat, Dutch use of: for fuel, 4, 232; erosion caused by, 6 f.
Peking, 200
Pemba, East Africa, cloves, 457 n.
Penembahan (Mataram sultan), 312. *See also* Mataram
Pennists (Dutch clerks), 313 f.
Pepper, 458; from Achin, 155, 166, 457 f.; Bantam, 259, 322, 356, 457 f.; Djambi, 322, 324, 342, 458, 461; Dutch supply stopped, 351; English trade in, 280; Europe's oversupply, 173; from Malabar, 217, 255; monopoly, 342, 458; from Patane, 130, 155 n., 158, 458; prices, 356, 362; Sumatra, 294 f., 395, 457 f., 461; trade, 457. *See also* Spices; Trade
Pepper Coast, West Africa, 47
Peppercorn (ship), 291 f.
Perkeniers (Dutch colonial farmers), 422
Perlak, 206
Perry, Matthew, 213
Persia, 20; Dutch in, 255; scholars of, 208
Persian Gulf, 204
Pescadores, 428
Pescatore, Giorgio, 235 ff., 239
Pescatore, Pietro, 239
Peter the Great, 50
Pettys, George, 397
Philip the Fair, 272
Philip II of Spain, 27, 35, 44, 238; and the Dutch, 39, 50; and religion, 22, 27 f., 50
Philip William of Orange, 42
Philippine Islands, 173; Dutch in, 263 f.; Spanish in, 116, 153, 161, 342
Phillip, William, translator of *Itinerary,* 278 f.
"Pieces of eight," 72. *See also* Reals

Pietersz., Cornelis, 158
Pietersz., Joost, 317 n.
Pilgrims, New England, 181
Pinta (ship), 167
Piracy, pirates, 50 f., 62, 139, 205, 211, 277; Dutch, 264; English, 64, 276, 283, 293; French, 350; Portuguese, 219, 221, 223. *See also* Privateering
Plancius, Petrus, 45, 65–68, 75, 90, 110, 114; Cunaes on, 67; Linschoten on, 90; and navigation, 84, 89 ff., 242; and northeast passage exploration, 83–86, 102 f.; sailing directions of, 110 f.; on whaling, 275
Plasse, Mrs. Dinghem van der, 269
Platevoet, Peter, 66. *See also* Plancius, Petrus
Pliny the Elder: describes Lowlands, 3 f.; describes Polar region, 80
Plymouth Plantation, 181
Polar Sea, 80; Plancius describes, 84
Pomerania, 474
Pomp (China), Dirck Gerritsz., 69, 79, 126
"Pope John's Land," Djakarta (Batavia), 367, 369, 410
Poppen, Jan, 87 f.
Population, Amsterdam, 32; Holland, 422; Hoorn, 232; Java, 320 n.; Netherlands, 53
Porcelain, Chinese, 131, 159, 193
Porong River, East Java, 448
Portugal, Portuguese, 73, 205, 215 f., 219–25, 256, 266, 387; at Amboyna, 163, 219; in Asia, 62 f., 223 ff., 256, 326; at Bantam, 112, 218; at Batavia, 458; at Calicut, 217 f.; in Ceylon, 154, 217; Christianity, 216, 255; clove trees destroyed by, 457 n.; colonial policy, 216, 224, 309; and the Dutch, 47, 130, 159, 223, 255 f.; in East Indies, 152, 326; and the English, 291 f.; at Goa, 73, 255; in India, 218, 291; in Japan, 212 f., 225; and Jews, 218; at Johore, 158, 218, 257; at Malacca, 168, 202 f., 207 f., 210, 217 f., 257 f., 342; Malacca, Strait of, 317 f.; in Moluccas, 116, 119, 130, 218 f., 223 f., 457 n.; and Moslems, 209, 218, 221, 224; nobles and condottieri, 224; piracy, 219, 221, 223; Spain's annexation of, 38, 64, 70, 220. *See also* Macao; Trade
Prabanca, 199, 201
Prado y Tovar, Diego de, 167

Prahu (vessel), 119
Prambanan, 320
Preliminary companies. *See* Forecompanies
Press gangs, English, 244
Prester John, 17, 216
Priaman, 359
Pring, Martin, 370, 372, 408; and Coen, 409
Printing: England, 268; Netherlands, 268
Private enterprise, 54; Indonesia, 468. *See also* Trade
Privateering, 50 f., 130 f.
Privy Council, English, on Indies, 279
Prizes of war for Dutch, 187; and East India Company, 151 f.
Profit and Power, by Charles Wilson, 274
Proportional representation, Dutch Republic, 137
Protestants, Protestantism, 28, 231, 238; Dutch East India Company, 225; differences among, 348, 471 f.; Philip II, 22
Pulu Pandjang, 295, 304
Pulu Run, 350, 368, 390, 417
Puritans, English, 45, 180, 270; in Holland, 181, 240
Puyck, Nicolaes, in Japan, 258
Pythias, describes Netherlands, 3

Quackernaeck, Jacob, on Dutch trade with Japan, 258
Queda, 155 n., 359

Radbode, King of Friesland, 231
Raey, Pieter van, 380, 382 f., 386 f., 389
Rahimi (ship), 292 f.
Rajab, 288
Raleigh, Sir Walter; on Dutch, 46, 49; on English trade, 279; on fishing, 273
Rana Mangala, Aria (*Pangeran*), 259, 306, 318–24, 391 f.; Chinese merchants, 351; Dutch, 321 f., 350 f., 392 f., 404; English, 353; French, 350 f.; pepper, 351. *See also* Bantam
Ransom, demanded of Dutch by: Arissabaya, 114; Bantam, 94; Djakarta, 380 f.; Dunkirk pirates, 51
Reael, Laurens, 323, 335 f., 346 f.; at Bantam, 352; and Coen, 336, 340 f., 347, 400, 438; and English-Dutch

rivalry, 340 f.; in Holland, 438, 446; as moderate, 349; in Moluccas, 305, 339, 349 f.; as Remonstrant, 349; Seventeen recall, 354, 356 f.; at Ternate, 339; on trade, 461 f.

Reals (coins), 72, 88, 96, 156, 162

Rebeldes (Spanish name for Dutch), 62

Reclamation of land: England, 271; Friesland, 4; Holland, 422; mechanical aids, 6; Netherlands, 5

Red Lion (ship), 257 f.

Red Sea, 145, 204 f., 224, 248; Dutch in, 377; English in, 293 f.

Red Stone (Hoorn land mark), 233

Reformation: England, 268; Netherlands, 21, 268 f.; Philip II, 238. *See also* Protestants

Refreshing, of crews, 72, 92, 251; Cape of Good Hope, 287, 416; Madagascar, 111 f.; Mauritius, 113, 168; St. Helena, 250

Refugees, from southern Netherlands: as Dutch East India Company subscribers, 147 n.; to England, 45, 267, 269 ff.; industries transferred by, 53; as merchants to East, 142; to north, 44 f., 236, 269

Regents, Amsterdam, 25. See also *Vroedschap*

Religion, 348, 471 f.; Anabaptists, 26 f.; Arminians, 446; Coen, 238, 349; and Dutch East India Company, 225; on Dutch ships, 100; freedom of, 137; liberal views, 66; Remonstrants, 336, 348 f. *See also* Calvinism; Catholicism; Mennonites; Plancius, Petrus; Protestants

Rembrandt, 61

Remonstrants, 336, 348 f.

Rendezvous (for Dutch ships), 297, 300, 318 f., 353, 385, 404, 416 f.; Bantam, 170, 318 f., 352; Djakarta (Batavia), 322, 353 f., 361, 367, 391, 393 f., 399 f., 473; Japara, 319, 323; and Seventeen, 318, 357, 374. *See also* Coen

"Republic," as applied to Batavia, 437 n.

Reserve capital, concept of, 333

Revelation (yacht), 126

Reygersberg, Maria van, 473 f.

Reynst, Gerard, second governor general, 315 f., 328, 334, 338; on Coen, 335

Rhine River, 9

"Rhine straights" (wood in Dutch shipbuilding), 234

Rhodes, Cecil, 180

Rhodian Sea, 99. *See also* Sea laws

Rhone River, 8, 18

Rice, 451 f.; Banda, 311; Macassar, 259; Mataram, 312, 360, 448, 451 f., 458 f.; Moluccas, 358, 461

Rijksmuseum, Amsterdam, 104 n.

Rio de Janeiro, 128

Rispota di un Dottore, in Teologia, by Paolo Sarpi (on papal authority), 239

Roe, Sir Thomas, 365

Rome, Roman, 201, 236; corruption, 238; Counter Reformation, 238; and Dutch Republic, 239; and Frisians, 4; law, 418; political situation, 237 ff.; and Venice, 205, 239

Romein, Jan, on Coen, 299

Roodenburgh, Emanuel, 96 n.

Rose (ship), 399

Rot fever, 252

Rotterdam, 9; chamber, 147; Indian companies, 109 f., 119, 125–30; northeast passage, role in exploring; 98; Oldebarnevelt, 136

Rotterdam (ship), 263, 265

Russia, Russian, trade, 87; and English-Dutch rivalry, 81 f., 266

Rycx, Jacob, 156 f.

Ryp, Jan, 101, 103, 105

Sacone, John Peter (Jan Pietersz. Coen), 230, 397, 416

Safe House, Novaya Zemlya, 104 n.

Sago, 461

Said Barkat, 168

St. Agustin, Bay, Madagascar, 92

St. Augustine (ship), 190

St. Denis, 8, 18 f., 45

St. Helena, provisioning stop, 250

St. Lawrence River, 188

St. Louis (ship), 350 f.

St. Malo, 351

St. Michel (ship), 350 f.

Salisbury, Earl of, 330

Salt, 232; from Bourgneuf, 14 f.; from Cape Verde Islands, 47; Dutch fisheries, use of, 14, 47; refining, 14; from San Lucar, 14; from Setubal, 47; shipping developed through need of, 47

Salt Islands (Cape Verde Islands), 47
Saltpeter, 247
Samoyeds, 102
Sampson (ship), 396
Samudra (Sumatra), 206 f.
San Lucar, 179, 229; salt from, 14
Sana, 288
Sandalwood, 305; Dutch monopoly of, 327; from Flores and Timor, 223
Santvoort, Melchior van, 127
Sanudo, Marino, 205
Sao Lourenço (Madagascar), 73
Sapitans (Dutch sailors), 250
Saragossa, Convention of, 223 n.
Saris, John, 165, 293 ff., 332
Sarpi, Paolo, 239
Sawmills (in growth of Dutch commerce), 49 f.
Scharlensem, Ockam, 231
Scheldt (river), 19, 39, 185; blockade of, 33, 45
Schonen, 17
Schotte, Apollonius, 305
Schouten, Willem Cornelisz., 166, 338 f.
Scrooby, group of Puritans, 181
Scurvy, aboard ship, 72, 92, 252 f., 300 n., 359
Sea, dominion of, 53 n.
Sea laws, 99 ff.; Black Book of Admiralty, 99; Cabot, Sebastian, 99 f.; Consulato del Mar, 99; Oleron, 99; Rhodian Sea, 99; Visby, 99
Sea Wall (Golden Hoop), 5
Seine, River, 18
Selim I, 205
Sem, Syvert, 87
Senapati Ingalaga, 210 f., 450
Setubal, salt from, 47
Seventeen, Lords (directors, Dutch East India Company), 144, 146–49, 151 f., 173, 178, 185, 296, 403; and Banda conquest, 420; burghers, 460, 462; Coen, 317, 338, 345, 426 f., 433 f., 436; and colonization, 300; corruption of, 465; on free trade, 337, 358, 441, 446 f., 459 f.; Isaac Lemaire, 173 f.; monopoly by, 405, 407, 429, 437, 460, 462; parsimony of, 355, 357, 453; Laurens Reael, 347; rendezvous, ships,' 318, 357, 374; Spice Islands, 415 f.; States General, 178, 331, 333, 340, 349,
426, 441. *See also* Dutch East India Company
Shahbandar (harbor master): at Bantam, 158; Moslem, 208
"Sharp Resolution," of Oldebarnevelt, 471
Sharpeigh, Alexander, 287, 289 f., 295
Shipbuilding, Dutch, 50, 234
Shipping masters (Lodging-house keepers), 243 ff.
Ships, Dutch, 16, 48 n., 49; of Compagnie van Verre, 88 f.; crews of, 243–46, 249 f., 252 f., 337; discipline aboard, 99–102, 246–47; life aboard, 89, 93, 100–01, 243–46, 248–53; types of, 50, 111 n., 152, 362. *See also* Flute; Privateering
Shipworms, 63
Shogun, of Japan, 126 f., 212, 258
Siam, 208, 359; China invaded by, 212; Dutch treaties with, 308; English in, 329
Siam, Gulf of, 130
Siberia, 84
Sidayu, 94
Sierra Leone, 63
Silk, 20; from China, 131, 159, 193, 248, 305, 328; Dutch trade in, 131, 248
Silva, Juan da, 317
Silver, 317; Asiatic trade, 282; embargo of in England, 282; Japanese trade, 338; from Spanish America, 21, 38, 64, 72, 282; from Sumatra, 74. *See also* Reals
Silver fleet, Spanish, 179, 187, 263 n.
Simsuan, 322
Singalese, people, 156 f.
Singosari, 199 f., 210
Slave Coast, West Africa, 47
Slaves, 412; Coen on use of, 343, 361; from Madagascar, 343, 358, 361; Seventeen advocates use of, 343; sources of, 428
"Small Company," corrupt Dutch colonials, 464
Smeecoolen (coal), 359
Smith, John, 180
Smuggling: Macassar, 304; Spice Islands, 328
Smyth, John, Puritan, 180
Smythe, Sir Thomas, 279 f., 292, 364
Socotra, 287
Sodre, Vincente, 218
Sofala, 145

Soldt, Paulus van, 256
Solor, 305, 359; Dutch sandalwood monopoly in, 327
Sombart, Werner, 230
Soury, Andries, 324, 390
Southeast Asia, 204; China, 212; colonialism, 400; cotton goods, 256; Europeans, 213; Gujerati, 207 f.; Moslems, 195, 206, 208; principalities, 197
Southern hemisphere, 91 f.
Southern Netherlands: blockaded, 184; decline of, 45
Southland (Australia), 175
Soviet Union, 185
Spain, Spanish, 20, 342; in Asia, 53, 266, 308 f., 326, 342; colonial policy, 309; decline of, 41, 190, 240; and the Dutch, 28, 36, 39, 42, 50–51, 139, 178 f., 187–90, 238, 240 f. (truce, 181–85, 240 f., 257, 312, 338, 349, 406, 434); in East Indies, 149 f., 152, 326; and England, 279; in Europe, 20 f., 29, 44, 277; in Moluccas, 130, 165, 168 f., 264, 402; in Philippine Islands, 116, 153, 161, 342; Portugal annexed by, 38, 64, 70, 220; in Strait of Malacca, 317 f.
Spanish America, silver, 38, 64, 72, 179, 282
Spanish Main, 179, 234
Specx, Jacques, 242, 257; as Dutch governor general in Indies, 459 f.; in Japan, 242 f., 258, 305, 343
Speranty, 387 f.
Speult, Herman van, 361, 423, 430 f.
Spice Islands, 40, 64, 72, 74, 113 f., 217, 257, 259; Columbus, 215; El Dorado, 311; Francis Drake, 40, 43, 219, 277; native trade, 224; Portuguese, 224; Seventeen on, 415 f.; smuggling, 328. See also Moluccas
Spices, 327, 400; Antwerp, 19; Bantam, 93; cost of, 454; Dutch monopoly, 75, 152, 265 n., 309, 326, 328, 385, 401, 411, 423, 427, 436 f., 455, 458 f.; Indonesia, 193, 217; Macassar, 327 f.; Moluccas, 113 n., 248; native rulers, 454; sources of, 62, 142 n.; therapeutic qualities, 74 f. See also Monopoly; names of spices; Trade
Spiegel ships (warships), 111 n.
Spilbergen, Joris van, 154 n.

Spitsbergen, 275; discovery of, 103; whales near, 105
"Spoil-trade" (illegal trade within Dutch company), 464
Srivijaya, 197 ff., 324
Staper, Richard, 279
Staple: Amsterdam rights to, 24 n.; towns in England, 267
States (defined), 38 n.
States General, 36, 40, 142, 182, 186; Amsterdam's relation to, 30; and Coen, 435 f., 440; commercial Colleges authorized by, 56; dominion of sea sought by, 53 n.; and Dutch East India Company, 151, 174, 177, 179, 242, 331, 339, 403, 440 f.; and English-Dutch cooperation, 406; English piracy protested by, 64; fishing rights in English waters defended, 275; and free trade in Indies, 440; and Lords Seventeen, 178, 331, 333, 340, 349, 426, 441; navigation and geography, 142; northeast passage, role in exploration of, 83, 98; and Oldebarnevelt, 137, 471 ff.; Spanish truce, role in, 258; special committee as secret negotiator for, 138 n.; fore-companies' unity advocated by, 135, 141 f.
States of Holland, and Indies exploration, 89; northeast passage, role in exploration of, 102; Old Company petitions for trade monopoly, 134 f.; Oldebarnevelt as Chief Magistrate of, 38 f.
Stavoren, 16 n., 18
Stephens, Thomas, 277
Stevinton, Marmaduke, 395, 397
"Stint of trade" (sales control by medieval guilds), 54
Stock companies: Dutch, 57 f., 280; English, 333
Stroganovs (Russian merchants), 81
Sudras (Hindu peasants), 196
Suffolk, 267
Sukadana, 295, 359; diamonds from, 159
Sultan (title), 155 n.
Sumatra, 72–74, 94, 206, 394; Dutch treaties with, 308; English in, 294 f.; and Islam, 206, 208; pepper market at, 294 f., 457 f., 461; trade (pre-European) at, 194
Sun (ship), 119, 366

Sunda, 199, 202
Sunda Kalapa, 75, 219
Sunda Strait, 75, 373, 388; Dutch patrol of, 402, 404; Dutch rendezvous in, 319; English blockade of, 371; Srivijaya dominating traffic through, 198
Supercargoes, 89. See also Merchants
Sura Agul Agul, 450 f.
Surabaya, 447 f.
Surate, 255, 359; Dutch merchants at, 350; Dutch officials' corruption at, 464; English at, 290, 292 f.
Susuhunan, title of Sultan Agung, 448
Suta Vijaya, 210
Sutter's Creek, 109
Swally, 291
Swan (ship), 350, 352
Sweden, 474
Syria, 204 f.

Tabin, Cape, 80, 98, 101
Tabis, 80
Tagus, River, 189
Taiz, 288
Tasman, Abel, 461 n.
Tayda, Don Estaban de, 254
Taxes: on Amboyna and Banda imports and exports by Dutch, 422, 428; on Banda farm exports by Dutch, 422; Bantam, on Dutch for trade rights, 158, 318, 320, 342, 385; Coromandel, on Dutch for trade rights, 256; English seek from Dutch for fishing rights, 274 f.; Hoorn, cause riots in, 233; Portuguese, on Asia trade, 219, 221. See also Convoy duties; Tolls; Tribute
Tegal, 451 f.
Teredos (shipworms), 63
Ternate (Moluccas), 117, 211, 263, 309; cloves from, 456; Dutch treaties with, 301, 309, 358; extirpation (of spices) policy adopted in, 457 n.; Portuguese at, 219; Spanish at, 168; trade decline of, 461
Terusan, 448
Texel, 85, 91, 96, 101 f., 111, 246
Thailand, 198
Thames, River, 271
Theocracy, 137
Theunemans, Abraham, 306
Thing (Dutch assembly), 5 f.
Thomas (ship), 294

Tidore, 164, 219; Dutch at, 305; English at, 329; extirpation (of spices) policy adopted in, 457 n.; Portuguese at, 116; Spanish at, 116, 168, 263 f., 358, 402 (see also Spanish, in Moluccas); trade decline of, 461
Tiele, P. A., on Coen, 421
Tiku, 294, 359; English at, 304; English-Dutch battle at, 398 f.; pepper from, 294 f., 395, 457 f., 461
Tikus, 303
Timor, 359; sandalwood from, 223, 305
Tin, Willem, 70 f.
Tingan (type of boat), 417, 449
Tjiliwung River, 322
Tobias (author of English study of sea rights), 274
Tokugawa Shogunate, 212
Tolls: Amsterdam's freedom from, 24; Bantam imposes on Dutch, 112, 158, 318, 320, 342, 385; Danish on Dutch, 18, 48, 51, 81; flute ship designed to lower, 48; at Kara Strait, 83; at Oresund, 18, 48, 51. See also Taxes
Tombstones, Islamic, 207
Tommogong (Bantamese official), 384 f.
Tordesillas, Treaty of, 53, 216, 223
Torres, Luis Vaez de, 167
Torres Strait, 167
Towerson, Gabriel, 294, 430 f.
Trade, 8 f., 14 f., 22, 56, 271 f.; Amsterdam's with enemy, 37 f., 64, 475; Asiatic, 53, 166, 193–96, 205, 207, 220 f., 224, 256, 277, 282, 308, 317, 328, 337–38, 355, 358–59, 401, 411, 416, 424 f., 428 f., 436 f., 447, 453, 456, 459, 467; Baltic, 9, 11, 14 f., 17 f., 21, 38, 46, 51, 80, 232, 239, 266, 359; Chinese, 142, 154, 158–59, 169, 248, 264, 305, 312, 328 f., 342, 359, 415, 428; Dutch, 8 f., 20 f., 38, 46–47, 50, 52–53, 62, 139, 161, 232–33, 236, 402; Dutch company, clandestine, 265 n., 311; English, 19, 54 f., 266 f.; free, 14 f., 47, 141 f., 267, 300, 327, 337, 358, 411, 424 f., 428 f., 436–41, 446–47, 453–54, 459 f.; grain, 14 f.; Japanese, 158, 258, 312, 343; native, 222, 224, 260, 305, 326 f., 354, 423, 455, 460 f.; Portuguese, 18, 20 f., 53, 62, 75, 119, 149 f., 195, 219–22, 224; private, 220–22, 337,

365, 428 f., 436 f., 447, 459; Russia, 87; salt, 14 f.; Spanish, 20 f., 50, 53, 149 f., 342; spice, 8 f., 20, 64, 224, 301, 326 ff., 385, 401 f., 416, 427, 457 n.; techniques of, 19. See also Islam
Trade routes, to Asia, 204 f.; Islam spread by, 208
Trades Increase (ship), 291 f., 295, 304
Treaties: Dutch in Achin, 248; Amboyna, 164; Asia, 308; Banda, 164, 260 ff., 305; Bantam, 259; Borneo, 308; Calicut, 163, 255; Coromandel, 308; Golconda, 256; Indies, 257; Japan, 258, 308; Johore, 248; Macassar, 259; Malabar, 308; Mataram, 459; Moluccas, 308, 326, 352; Sumatra, 308; Ternate, 301, 309, 358
    Dutch East India Company, 150, 161, 163 ff., 225, 308, 427, 455, 459; English-Dutch on fisheries, 272, 275. See also Contracts
Treaty of Defense, English-Dutch, 405–10, 416 f., 425, 429, 434; Coen on, 407, 416, 434
Trebizond, 204
Tribute, on Asia sea routes, 205, 217; Dutch exacted, 385 (Bantam), 360 (Djakarta), 343 f. (Japan); Egypt exacts from shipping, 205; English demanded by Yemen, 288
Tripoli, 248
Tristan d'Acunha, 92
Trust (ship), 126
Tuban, 119 f., 200, 447
Tumapel, 198
Turkey, Turks, 20, 204 f., 213, 288, 289 n.
Turkey Company, English, 277
Twisk (Coen), Pieter Willemsz. van, 229 f.
Twisk (village), 229
Twisk, Reynier Pietersz. van, 236

Union (ship), 287
Union of Utrecht, 35 f., 39 n., 136
United East India Company, 59, 131, 143 ff., 280. See also Dutch East India Company
United Nations, 33
United Netherlands. See Netherlands, Dutch Republic
United Provinces. See Netherlands, Dutch Republic
United Provinces (ship), 248

United States of America, 181, 240, 467
United Zealand Company, 124 f. See also Zealand companies
Upa Santa, 450
Ural Mountains, 81
Usselinx, Willem, 21, 45, 133 n.
Utrecht, 16 n.; Union of, 35 f., 39 n., 136
Utrecht (ship), 445

Vaigach: Island, 80, 84; Strait, 85, 99, 173. See also Nassau Strait
Valck, Jacob, 82, 98
Valparaiso, 126
Vardohus, Norway, 85
Vasco da Gama. See Gama, Vasco da
Veen, Adriaan, 119 f.
Veer, Gerrit de, 104 f.
Veere, 83, 86 f., 145; and Moucheron, 109, 121, 124 f.
Veken, Johan van der, 125, 127
Velius, Theodorus: on Baltic trade, 17; on Coen, 236 f.; describes Hoorn, 232
Venice, 20, 33, 204 f., 248; and Rome, 239; and the Turks, 205
Ventures on parts (speculation on trade voyages), 58
Vereenigde Oost-Indische Compagnie, 146. See also Dutch East India Company
Verhoef, Pieter, 190, 241 f., 246, 248, 254–62; at Banda, 260 f., 418 f.
Verschoor, Jan Willemsz., 163 f.
Vervins, Treaty of, 237
Vijaya, 199 f.
Vikings, raid Lowlands, 5, 9, 23
Viney, Mrs. Susan, 286
Virginia Colony, 180, 365, 398
Visby Sea Laws, 99
Visser, Jan Martensz., 236
Visser, Joris, 236 f. See also Pescatore, Giorgio
Visser, Nicolas de, 261
Vlie-boot (type of ship), 48 n., 233 f. See also Flute
Vlie (waterway), 5, 234
Vos, Jan, 448
Vroedschap (Amsterdam regents), 25, 348, 475. See also Amsterdam

Wadanas (Madjapahit officials), 201
Wadden Islands, 10
Wali's (Moslem scribes), 209

Walloon provinces, 44
Walrus teeth, English trade in, 80
Warga, 451 f.
Warmoesstraat, Amsterdam, 65, 87
Wars of the Roses, 268
Warwyck, Wybrand van, 111, 113, 154, 159, 165; at Bantam, 116, 158 f.; in Moluccas, 114, 116
Wash, England, 181
Waterways, logistics, 42 f.
Water-wolf (erosion), 7
Weert, Sebald de, 154–58
Wellwood, William, 274
Welser, House of, 19, 223
"Westphalian elbows" (German oak), 234
West Friesland, 10, 231
West India Company, 187 f., 349
West Indies. See Indies
West Java. See Java
Whale oil, English trade in, 80
Whaling: English-Dutch rivalry in, 266, 275; in Polar Sea, 105
White Bear (ship), 328
White Sea, 80 f.; English-Dutch rivalry in, 81 f.
Widjaja Krama, 259, 300, 321, 324, 391; and Dutch, 356, 360, 366, 368 f., 379 ff.; and English, 380 f.; trade policy, 322, 385. See also Djakarta
Widow's Sand (shoals), Stavoren, 18
Wiele, Stalpaert van der, 163
Wijk bij Duurstede (Dorestad), 9 n.
Willem Lodewyk, Prince, Stadholder of Friesland, 42
William of Orange, 27, 35 n., 36, 121, 136 f.
Willoughby, Sir Hugh, 80, 99, 275
Wilson, George, 274
Windmills, 6, 49 f.

Window panes, Dutch-made in England, 269
Wine, Dutch trade in, 19
Winsemius, describes Hoorn, 231
Winwood, Sir Ralph, 273, 405, 407
Wittert, Francois, 259, 263 f.
Wittewierum, 10
Wolff, Hans de, 255
Wood, Benjamin, 278
Wool industry: England, 45 f., 267, 269, 271 f.; Flanders, 267; Leiden, 30, 45
Wool, trade in: Bruges, 55, 267; English, 19, 54 f., 266 f.; Veere, 121
Woolwich, 287
Woude, J. van der, on Coen, 421

Y (Amsterdam inlet), 23 n., 246
Yachts: in Dutch Indies coastal trade, 362; types of, 111 n.
Yemen, 288
York, 9
Ypres, 66
Yunnan, 212

Zaan region, Holland, 50
Zanzibar, cloves from, 457 n.
Zealand, 24, 36 f., 83; Chamber, 248; companies of, 109, 116, 119, 121, 124, 140, 145, 255
Zemindar (Coromandel tax collector), 256
Zeventien (governing-body of Dutch East India Company), 144. See also Seventeen
Zierikzee, 145
Zuiderzee, 9 f., 16, 22, 91, 231, 246; blockade of, 29
Zurck, Gaspar van, 313
Zutphen, 16 n.
Zwin, 19
Zwolle, 16 n.